W9-BRR-220

American Rhetoric:
Context and Criticism

EDITED BY THOMAS W. BENSON

WITH A FOREWORD BY LEWIS PERRY

Southern Illinois University Press

CARBONDALE AND EDWARDSVILLE

To Eugene E. White

Library of Congress Cataloging-in-Publication Data

American rhetoric : context and criticism / edited by Thomas W.
  Benson
      p.   cm.
   Bibliography: p.
    1. Rhetoric—United States—History.   2. Speeches, addresses,
etc., American—History and criticism.   3. English language—United
States—Rhetoric.   4. Oratory—United States—History.   5. American
prose literature—History and criticism.   6. Politics and
literature—United States—History.   I. Benson, Thomas W.
PE2827.A44 1989
808.5′1′0973—dc19   88-29689
ISBN 0-8093-1509-2   CIP

The paper used in this publication meets the minimum requirements of
American National Standard for Information Sciences—Permanence of Paper
for Printed Library Materials, ANSI Z39.48-1984. ⊗

Contents

Foreword

LEWIS PERRY

I MIGHT AS WELL say right off that I am not an expert in speech communication or rhetoric. In fact, I am something of a certified failure in the field. Twenty-five years ago, my initial graduate school major in theater led to my placement in a minor field in speech and hence to enrollment in an 8:00 A.M. course in persuasive speaking. In this class, undergraduate boys applied Aristotelian principles, as summarized in a few handy paragraphs of a textbook, to problems of romance, politics, and finance.

Some of my best friends are in speech communication, though. I think of Robert Gunderson, a former colleague and fine historian whose study of the election of 1840 is a standard work in two fields. I have thought of him as I read the manuscript of this book because he, like many of these authors, exemplifies the wide-ranging interdisciplinary curiosities that enliven good work in American studies. Another friend is Tom Benson, whom I have known for all those twenty-five years since my flight from persuasive speaking. Tom has always been earnest and judicious and, at the same time, intellectually playful and curious. I think these qualities are evident in this volume. To his praise of that good scholar Eugene E. White let me add my own appreciation of Tom Benson's role as the kind of searching, fair-minded person on whom intellectual life in contemporary universities depends.

This book includes a certain amount of shoptalk about how

rhetoric has been and should be defined and studied. This topic will
be of interest primarily to practitioners in the field. But there is much
else—on various kinds of institutions, utterances, and events—
that should be of broader interest to students of American culture
regardless of their disciplines. Those who browse can probably find
something to detain them.

The book brings to mind a number of recent examples of historians
turning to the literature in speech communication as a step in
interpreting some key moments of transition in American culture.
I am reminded of Gordon Wood's account of Tom Paine and the
"democratization of mind," James Stewart's analysis of the eloquence
and vision of Wendell Phillips, and Daniel Walker Howe's portrait
of the mind-set of the American Whigs.[1] My impression is that
historians prefer to focus on moments when "rhetoric" itself was
changing or challenged, while in the field of rhetoric there has been
some tendency to apply timeless principles to examples taken from
history. But in this collection of essays—with its repeated gestures
of respect to Professor White—there is a sense of the subtleties of
history and the complexities of interpretation that would satisfy a
theologian. Certainly it should be adequate for the rest of us. It seems
clear that speech communication scholars, for reasons emerging from
considerations within their own discipline, are approaching a view
of historical processes that ought to make their work increasingly
accessible and valuable to others engaged in American studies. For
this reason—as well as because it is often just plain interesting—I
wish the book good luck and a successful journey.

Note

1. Gordon S. Wood, "The Democratization of Mind in the American Revolution," in
Leadership in the American Revolution (Washington: Library of Congress, 1974), 63–88; James
B. Stewart, "Heroes, Villains, Liberty, and License: The Abolitionist Vision of Wendell
Phillips," in *Antislavery Reconsidered: New Perspectives on the Abolitionists*, ed. Lewis Perry and
Michael Fellman (Baton Rouge: Louisiana State Univ. Pr., 1979), 172; Daniel Walker Howe,
The Political Culture of the American Whigs (Chicago: Univ. of Chicago Pr., 1979), 25–28,
221–22, 303.

Preface

THIS BOOK IS designed to contribute to the long overdue revival of critical interest in American public discourse. The chapters that make up the book are addressed to students of American culture and communication and are united by the convictions that

—American public life and political culture are shaped by and reflected in symbolic actions;

—rhetorical discourse is a legitimate aspect of public policy making, and not simply a technology of influence;

—the past is continually at work in the present, actively forming the future through actions and interpretations;

—the study of a rhetorical text or communicative event is a multifaceted and open-ended affair, seeking in part for judgment but, even more importantly, for understanding;

—to understand a rhetorical text, we must see not only its form and its details, but also its relation to its context, especially as that context is perceived by the participants;

—critical analysis of public discourse contributes to historical insight and to the theory of rhetoric, by discovering or confirming the complex and only partially tractable textures of actuality;

—rhetorical action is always guided, at least implicitly, by a theory of rhetoric.

In the spring of 1979 I convened a group of colleagues (Richard Gregg, Gerard Hauser, and Lawrence Rosenfield) for lunch and put to them a proposition. I invited them to constitute an informal editorial committee to assist in developing a book about the criticism of American public discourse. The book proposed would be designed for student use in that it would display, by various strategies, the texts under study and the methods employed by the critic. The chapters would each operate as practical criticism, rather than as theoretical or methodological pieces, but would make their methods visible and, insofar as possible, usable by students. To fill a crucial gap in our literature, the essays would be somewhat longer than those usually published in our scholarly journals, permitting greater attention to context and detail and to methods of analysis. The chapters would consider early and recent American historical examples as a way of illustrating, at least implicitly, the continuities and changes in discourse. The result is intended not as a history of American public address, but rather as an exploration of some of the ways in which richly contextualized rhetorical criticism can make a contribution to that history. The informal editorial group enthusiastically agreed to my proposal, and to my suggestion that our work be dedicated to our colleague, Eugene E. White, a distinguished historian and critic of American public address.

In a recent essay in *Communication Education*, Carroll Arnold writes of the importance of uniting theory, criticism, and practice in the study of communication. These three concerns have been an abiding theme in Gene White's long and productive career as a teacher and scholar, and we hope that they are represented in the chapters that make up this tribute by his colleagues and students.

Individual chapters have been reviewed by colleagues, and editor and authors are grateful for their help. Among the reviewers were Carolyn Anderson, Carroll Arnold, Herman Cohen, Richard Gregg, Bruce Gronbeck, Gerard Hauser, Kathleen Jamieson, Lawrence Rosenfield, John Smith, and Hermann Stelzner. Gerald Phillips and Kathleen Turner reviewed the entire manuscript and made many valuable recommendations. This project has had the support of several members of the administration at the Pennsylvania State University, especially Robert Brubaker and Dennis Gouran, as Head of the Department of Speech Communication, Stanley Paulson and Hart Nelsen, as Dean of the College of Liberal Arts, and Thomas Magner and Joseph Michels, as Associate Dean for Research and Graduate Study of the College of Liberal Arts.

American Rhetoric:
Context and Criticism

ONE

History, Criticism, and Theory in the Study of American Rhetoric

THOMAS W. BENSON

> *I have attempted to demonstrate that a pervasive sense*
> *of historical configuration, or exigential Gestalt, is*
> *necessary in order to appreciate fully the rhetorical act*
> *as a becoming, an ongoing development, rather than a*
> *being or entity.*
> —EUGENE E. WHITE[1]

IN THIS BRIEF introductory chapter, I will attempt to sketch the development of twentieth-century studies in public address, to place Eugene White's work in the context of those studies, and to indicate how the essays in this volume may contribute to the revival of interest in public address that seems to be afoot.

I

Every academic field has its folklore. The folklore of the academic field now called "speech" or "speech communication" generally goes something like this: In the fifth century B.C., on the island of Sicily, two sophists named Corax and Tisias began to teach their students the rudiments of oratory as demanded by a democratic society; they based their teaching on a logic of probabilities, since in public disputes a logic of certainties was inappropriate. Their subject, called rhetoric, was taken up at Athens, where Plato first derogated it (in the *Gorgias*), and then stated what he regarded as its first principles (in the *Phaedrus*). Aristotle next took up the subject, rescuing it from Platonic idealism and seeing it as a pragmatic art founded in logic and adapted to the realities of human and circumstantial imperfection. The rise of Rome moved rhetorical studies there,

1

where the great legal advocate and senatorial speaker Cicero developed a rhetoric that reflected the actualities of public life, in which oratory was both the most important tool of public decision making and a means of personal advancement. Then rhetoric, which had flourished in Greece and Rome as a tool of free citizenship, declined, to be revived only with the rise of the English Parliament and the American Revolution.

The golden age of British and American eloquence, running roughly from the middle of the eighteenth to the middle of the nineteenth century, gradually dwindled, so the folklore continues, into the windy bombast of elocutionism and the flat acquisitiveness of an industrial age. A birth and decline of practice and theory, at Greece and Rome, were thus followed by rebirth and yet another decline. At this point, the growth of academic specialization in American universities saw the creation of speech as an academic field, with the founding of the Eastern Public Speaking Conference (now the Eastern Communication Association) in 1909–10, and the National Association of Academic Teachers of Public Speaking (now the Speech Communication Association) in 1914, largely as a breakaway movement from departments and associations of English.[2]

According to the folklore, serious academic study of rhetoric was revived in university departments of speech, and in a parallel development there was an outpouring of studies in the history and criticism of public address. Then, the folklore becomes obscure: according to one version, our journals were full of studies in public address, and within fifty years, by the mid-1960s, the history of public address was written and rhetorical criticism had learned most of what it was going to from the criticism of speeches, and so turned its attention to other media: film, television, public demonstrations, fiction, music, and so on.

There used to be a feature in the Sunday comics called "What's Wrong with This Picture?" If we were to ask what is wrong with the picture of the study of rhetoric I have just sketched, the answer would have to be that its main problem is that it is not completely and obviously wrong. There is just enough truth and convenience in the story to make it memorable and useful as a backdrop against which individual teachers and scholars, in their own specialties, can pursue their own concerns. But the picture is everywhere wrong: It is wrong as to the history of rhetorical theory. It is wrong about the history of oratory. And it is wrong about the history of the academic field called speech, speech communication, rhetoric, and communication. Most of what is wrong about the story can be traced to various omissions: for example, the leap from the end of the Roman Republic to eighteenth-century England leaves out Hellenistic rhetoric; the rhetoric of the Empire, especially as represented by Quintilian; the long rhetorical tradition of the Christian faith, beginning with Augustine; the active concern with rhetoric throughout medieval Europe; the rhetoric of the Renaissance and Reformation; the rise of preaching—the list goes on and on.

As for the twentieth-century study of public address, our folklore is equally distorted, and in a way, I shall argue, that diminishes the usefulness of speech communication as an organized academic discipline, and may even endanger it. But I shall also argue that the means are at hand for a rediscovery of public address as a subject of scholarly interest and of university instruction. Let us trace how serious academic study of public address developed within the discipline of speech communication.[3]

II

Twentieth-century scholarship in public address seems to have originated in the need of the founders of speech departments to discover materials useful in the teaching of undergraduate students in public speaking, training graduate students to teach those undergraduates, and developing a body of scholarship that would contribute both to improved teaching and to institutional respectability.

Within the emerging field of speech, a subfield called rhetoric and public address quickly claimed rhetoric as its theory and identified public address (meaning, usually, Greek, Roman, and especially British and American oratory) as the enactment of that theory. The bond between rhetoric and oratory was sealed with the famous 1925 essay by Herbert A. Wichelns of Cornell University, "The Literary Criticism of Oratory."[4] In one stroke, Wichelns established as beyond argument (for a time) that literary criticism was inappropriate to the study of oratory. Instead, argued Wichelns, since oratory was generated by the attempt to secure an immediate effect on its hearers, rhetorical criticism was the appropriate mode of inquiry into the orator's work. Studies in the criticism of oratory, which had been slow to emerge in the early years of the journals, now gradually began to appear, and the study of public address took its place in the curriculum.

Public address saw some genuine successes and flourished as a special area of study. The history of American oratory began to be pieced together from institutional and biographical perspectives. A canon of orators and speeches, considered a necessary part of the reading of every speech teacher, took shape and was reinforced by anthologies of speeches. Nearly twenty years after Wichelns's essay, the base of studies in American public address was seemingly secured with the publication in two volumes of *A History and Criticism of American Public Address,* sponsored by the Speech Association of America and edited by William Norwood Brigance. In 1955 a third volume, edited by Marie Hochmuth, was published.[5] The Brigance and Hochmuth volumes, organized chiefly as studies of important American orators, represented one of the primary modes of inquiry in public address—the career study. Other modes of public address scholarship were emerging as well, including studies of movements and genres, of single public addresses, of textual accuracy, of regional and institutional oratory.[6]

By the mid-1960s, public address was established, it seemed, as a dominant area in the field of speech. But at that point, for a variety of complicated reasons, things changed.

The primacy of public address was challenged by scholars within speech communication who charged that historical and critical work was inherently inferior, as knowledge, to "scientific" work. A struggle, not particularly edifying on either side, took place between those generally identified as "traditionalists" and those called "experimentalists." Generally speaking, the experimentalists argued that our common task was to discover the laws of communication effects, and that these laws were more likely to be discovered by controlled testing of variables than by the case-study approach of the historians and critics. Insofar as the public address critics agreed that the mission of the field was to discover the laws governing effects, they traded away much of their potential justification.

Others in the field, often those prompted by an interest in scientific investigation of communication, claimed that speech should not confine itself to the study of oratory but should instead reach out to embrace other forms of speech and communication, chiefly interpersonal, small group, and organizational.[7] To others, for whom public speeches seemed boring, hypocritical, irrelevant, and ritualistic, the turn to interpersonal, small-group, and organizational communication was at once humanistic in its concern for persons in face-to-face interaction, and pragmatic in examining the real locus of social decision making, which was, in this view, the committee room rather than the public platform.

But perhaps the most important challenge to studies in public address came from within the ranks. Younger scholars interested in rhetoric and public address began to develop in earnest the view that the domain of rhetorical activity extended beyond oratory, and that the range of rhetorical theory extended far beyond the probable "impact" of a single message. Until the early 1960s, perhaps the most influential book for students of criticism was Lester Thonssen and A. Craig Baird's *Speech Criticism*, published in 1948.[8] But in 1965, Edwin Black published his *Rhetorical Criticism: A Study in Method.*[9] Black's book, originally a dissertation directed by Herbert Wichelns at Cornell, directly attacked the methods, assumptions, and results of what he called the neo-Aristotelian critics, whose mission had been defined by Wichelns in 1925, exemplified by the Brigance and Hochmuth studies in American public address, and described as method by Thonssen and Baird. Black voiced many of the dissatisfactions that had been gathering within the field. Implicitly, his title shifted the center of studies from speech to rhetoric, and hinted at new directions. He wrote: "It should be clear by now that neo-Aristotelianism is founded upon a restricted view of human behavior, that there are discourses which function in ways not dreamed of in Aristotle's *Rhetoric,* and that there are discourses not designed for rational judges, but for men as they are. It is the task of criticism not to measure these discourses dogmatically against some parochial standard of rationality but, allowing for the immeasurably wide range of human experience, to see them as they really are."[10]

Black's call for a more wide-ranging criticism came upon the field in the midst of the 1960s, when the nation was experiencing the turmoil of the civil rights movement and the Vietnam War. For many younger academics, suspicious that neo-Aristotelian criticism had become ideologically conservative, Black's book took on a force he had perhaps not intended it to have. And in a paradox of historical timing, the younger scholars found Black's critique of effects criticism particularly appealing because of their growing conviction that effects criticism had come to mean, in the work of the 1950s, a search for ways to promote social control by the entrenched conservative establishment. What made this paradoxical, of course, was that at just this historical moment, American rhetorical practice was being reinvented in speeches, marches, sit-ins, popular music, and a variety of other means of creating social change. Effects, whisked off stage right, entered left.

And then, if I may continue the metaphor just one step further, American rhetorical critics found, waiting in the wings, a theorist who could justify the broadening of rhetorical studies demanded by Black—Kenneth Burke.[11] Burke's theories, which had been available but hardly visible to rhetorical critics, now became the chief means by which to justify a turn from Aristotelian rationality to Burkean dramatism, from probability and referentiality and effectiveness to human knowledge and action as essentially invented. The use of Burke and of other theorists to unseat neo-Aristotelian criticism did not always achieve the promised results. It had long been objected, for instance, that critics relying on Aristotle mechanically rediscovered the modes of proof (ethos, pathos, logos) and the canons of rhetoric (invention, disposition, style, memory, delivery) over and over again, and in a misdirected leap of faith vaulted from a cookie-cutter description of oratorical technique to a claim of rhetorical/historical causation. But soon other critics were to demonstrate that it was possible to achieve equally mechanical results by applying the Burkean pentad (act, agent, scene, agency, purpose).[12]

The realignments initiated in the 1960s and 1970s were not merely schisms or dichotomies, though schisms and dichotomies abounded. Some critics, for example, accepted the mantle of neo-Aristotelianism and squared off against the newcomers.[13]

Some public address historians objected that the turn toward criticism disallowed their own work. In an article published in 1977, Barnett Baskerville asked, "Must We All Be 'Rhetorical Critics?' " Baskerville argued both that history had something to teach criticism and that historical studies had merit in their own right. "A need exists for good history and biography, for meticulously researched descriptive monographs. In our field, as in most fields, there is a need for scholars who can record accurately and artistically the history of our art as it relates to more general history, to delineate its place in and contribution to the history of the nation."[14] Baskerville's call for a renewed interest in historical studies of public address was significant partly as a signal of the way an academic field was drifting. During the 1960s and 1970s, it was not uncommon for speech scholars, in conversation, to disparage public address as the study of "dead orators" and to complain that much of the history of public address was warmed-over narrative based on secondary sources. Other objections cut deeper and had a pervasive influence on the direction of the field. Very frequently, scholars submitting historical studies in public address to journals in speech communication were told that the history was all very well, but were asked, "Where is the criticism?" A sea change was occuring that led editors and their editorial boards, the central gatekeepers of the field, to discourage the publication of what was deemed merely historical. But at the same time those gatekeepers began to ask, when they received essays that presented themselves as rhetorical criticism, "Where is the theory?"

Implicitly, and sometimes explicitly, the field of speech communication adopted a scientific model of knowledge that stressed the accumulation of particulars toward the refinement of general, theoretical knowledge. Historians and critics both replied, from their sometimes combined and sometimes separate places in the hierarchy, that history and criticism were legitimate modes of knowing in their own right, with a contribution to make to theory but not legitimized only by their contribution to theory.

In the work of rhetorical criticism, it is a very different thing to pick a method or a theory first and then apply it to a text, than it is to start with the text and reconstruct or deconstruct it from a rhetorical perspective, attempting to arrive at a reading that does justice to its concreteness, its resistance to reduction. Most theories and methods can be successfully *illustrated* by using a given case as an example—that is partly why neo-Aristotelian criticism came to seem so uninformative. It was not, I think, that the Aristotelian perspective was inadequate, but that it was allowed to become hardened into a theory and method that the speech under examination must be made to fit. Paradoxically, when criticism was so stringently subordinated to theory, the theory itself was incapable of being tested or refined by the criticism: it could only be confirmed, to nobody's surprise or enlightenment.[15] Criticism, or at least some criticism, works from the event outwards and if successful will probably have some contribution to make to theory, at least in the sense that it will prevent theories from becoming simpleminded or irrelevant.

But of course the claim of the historian and the critic that they must be granted their concern with particulars may seem self-indulgent. Historical and narrative reconstructions can consume a great deal of space, and space is scarce in academic journals. Moreover, journal editors feel constrained to ask of a given manuscript whether it speaks to a broad segment of readers, and historical and critical manuscripts, which claim to be attending to particular events and texts, may seem to appeal to a very small segment of the academic community if they appeal only to readers interested in the particular event or text under discussion. Theory, on the other hand, implicitly claims to speak to the whole discipline, since it presumably accounts for large numbers of particulars.

Furthermore, because our field is speech/rhetoric/communication, we seem implicitly (and sometimes explicitly) to be a field obligated to understand general processes, to explain the process of symbolic influence—and not simply to appreciate particular instances of communication, which is assumed to be what "humanists" do, or at any rate used to do. It is not unreasonable for journal editors to ask that a manuscript describe an event not just because it happened, nor because it happened to be a spoken or symbolic event; our aim, presumably, is to understand something about the rhetorical or communicative dimensions of human actions, and that inevitably requires us to relate particular events and actions to a conceptual framework. Part of the difficulty stems from the very nature of our theories and their subjects. Presumably a theoretical account of rhetoric would try to offer among other things a general account of symbolic influence. But the best of our present theories, such as they are, specify that rhetorical effectiveness is rooted in the specific situation and is a matter not only of rhetorical effect but of audience choice. That is, the theory itself drives historical critics who take it seriously towards the particular, which makes them seem atheoretical.

Sadly, the intellectual aspiration to evaluate each scholarly manuscript as a potential contribution to a general theory of human communication is sometimes supported by a slightly less admirable ambition to achieve for the field a respectability that would presumably be granted to us if we could only discover that general theory.[16] Perhaps it is for this reason that critics and historians, who have perfectly useful contributions to make on their own terms, sometimes feel constrained—sometimes on the advice of editors—to hang their history or criticism on a theoretical hook. In this way, theory becomes a sort of piety rather than the grounds of a debate.

Resistance to the publication in our journals of detailed historical reconstruction or close critical readings of rhetorical texts would have a variety of damaging consequences. Our understanding of speech, communication, and rhetoric as processes, at the theoretical level, surely depends not only upon careful philosophical thinking but also upon a fund of particulars and a feeling for the ambiguity, concreteness, and particularity of human action. Thus, to squelch history and criticism would be to impoverish theory, which must be not only a rival but also a colleague of history and criticism. Without continued publication of historical and critical studies we will lack the crucial intellectual funding for courses in public address, to provide examples for students and teachers to draw upon. Our journals exist both to advance theory and to provide examples of what that theory makes possible in terms of increasingly sophisticated understandings of particular rhetorical texts. We cannot teach criticism from theory alone: we need examples of fully realized critical and historical readings even when those readings make no immediate and obvious contribution to contemporary theoretical debates. And although we should always be dubious and self-critical about our own claims, we do partly justify our discipline by citing its advisory function: we claim to be able to offer advice to students about public speaking skills, and to society at large about the conduct of rhetoric as a mode of public decision making. That advisory function cannot be supported without ongoing historical and critical scholarship in public address, broadly defined.

The difficulty is not confined to speech communication, of course. The study of literature in this century has undergone a series of changes, from the dominance of historical scholarship, to the rise of critical interpretation of the literary work as an end in itself, to the search for theories of literature.[17]

It is difficult to raise these issues without seeming to take sides, creating an either-or struggle between theory on the one hand and history/criticism on the other. If this account seems so dichotomized, it is unintentional. As an occasional writer and sometime editor, it seems to me that we need various forms of theoretical, critical, and historical scholarship, allowing each, if necessary, to proceed by its own urgencies and hoping that each will feel some obligation to think through its potential contributions to the other branches of our field. If I have a prejudice in the matter, it is that we need a tolerant but actively dialogic pluralism, rather than a single, legislated paradigm or grand theory. This brief commentary on the development of historical and critical work in rhetoric and public address is certainly not going to resolve the issue, nor even point out all of its dimensions. But it leads us, I think, to understand why our book is organized as it is and why we see the work of Eugene White as its starting point. White's work has been unusual in its ability to address the competing claims of history, criticism, and theory in the study of speech communication.

III

It's all there in the record and does not require detailed summary here: Gene White's more than forty years of active contributions to scholarship in rhetoric and public address span journal articles ranging from the Puritans to Harry Truman; books ranging from a highly successful introductory text on public speaking to the widely acclaimed *Puritan Rhetoric*.

When we are tempted to imagine that our journals were from the very beginning full of articles on public address, it may be well to remember that the *Southern Speech Journal*, founded in 1935, did not publish anything approaching a comprehensive study of a single speaker until 1945, when it published Gene White's "Anti-Racial Agitation as a Campaign Device: James K. Vardaman in the Mississippi Gubernatorial Campaign of 1903."[18] Later that same year the journal published Gene White's "The Great Awakener: George Whitefield," initiating his long series of studies in American preaching. These early works are admittedly the work of an apprentice critic, and from the perspective of the 1980s may seem to show some of the difficulties with the state of neo-Aristotelian criticism in the 1940s. On the other hand, they raise issues that consumed Gene White as a critic through the next decades: the relation of speech to the arousal of popular enthusiasms; the place of speaking in the context of larger historical forces; the immediacy of the past to issues of the present; the necessity of probing a communicator's expressed or implicit theories of communication; the role of religion in the continuity of the American experience; and the necessity of understanding American public communication in its larger historical and theoretical contexts—reaching back to English preaching and Greek and Roman rhetorical theory not as merely antiquarian antecedents but as living forces in the historical present.

Gene White's description of Vardaman's racist campaign against black education, which was amplified in an article in 1946 in the *Quarterly Journal of Speech,* clearly condemns Vardaman's demagoguery. That condemnation may seem mild, even indirect, compared to what might be considered possible or even necessary to say about Vardaman today, but when one considers that White was writing from and to the Deep South in 1945—when one understands, in other words, White's rhetorical context—then the criticism of Vardaman seems bold in its unambiguous judgment. In starting his career in public address by writing about racism and religion, White showed, I think, how inappropriate are the occasional dismissals of the study of American rhetoric as the exhumation of "dead orators." First, modes of talk that agitated colonial America echo from our own public platforms: the issue of emotion in religion that concerned Puritan preachers is present today in the rhetoric of television evangelists. And the twentieth-century issue of emotion in religion, or the relation of religious and civic matters, is relevant to the concerns of the Puritans not merely by analogy, but through an unbroken and immensely varied series of direct and indirect connections. The past is thus in one sense gone forever, displaced by the moving present, but is in another sense unavoidably part of the present. Second, when reading White's criticism, one feels that the "dead orator" notion is absurd. It sounds sentimental to me as I try to frame the thought, and I know that would embarrass Gene, but it seems to me to be there in his work and so I will try to state it as clearly as I can: we are all going to die soon enough; we live in a precious present, as others before us lived in their own present moments; we can share their living through the work of historians who help us to reconstruct, by scholarship and imagination, what was present to the past. Though we inevitably live in a constantly displaced present moment and cherish the immediacy of that moment, it would be arrogant to claim any special virtue for that moment. Most of what we all are is in the past or in the future. There are no dead orators.

White's control of historical sources rapidly deepened, and his critical methods became increasingly precise. His essays on Puritan preaching and the Great Awakening established him as an authority and twice won for him the highest honors of the Speech Communication Association.[19] At the same time that his scholarship was combining the highest levels of historical and critical achievement, White found time to publish several editions of a practical textbook, articles on speech teaching, and, with Clair Henderlider, essays based on interviews with Harry Truman and Norman Vincent Peale.

In 1972, Southern Illinois University Press published White's celebrated *Puritan Rhetoric: The Issue of Emotion in Religion* as part of its series on Landmarks in Rhetoric and Public Address. The volume is a lucid and informed account of what White found when he traced his early interest in the Great Awakening back to its sources, and it displays at its best the difficult business of placing rhetoric in its historical context without losing sight of the rhetoric itself. One feature of the book is curious, and points, I think, to Gene's unified understanding of his role as a rhetorician. As one of its readers, I was at first puzzled by the decision to frame much of the book as a series of guiding questions, rather than as the author's answers to the questions. A "scholarly" book, one would have thought, especially one written by an author so obviously in command of history, theory, and criticism, would sum up the author's views for his rightly awed readers. Why the questions? Some reflection on what White had accomplished, as opposed to what I had expected when I opened his book, provided at least a partial answer. First, White perceives history as a process—as becoming rather than being—and its intepretation as open: the questions with which he fills his analytical chapters suggest that critical inquiry, though it should have a focus, is fundamentally dialectical and will always remain unfinished. Second—this is especially obvious when seen against the context of his work as a teacher and author—White is constantly concerned with the role of author as teacher: a teacher whose role is not simply to fill students up with historical facts or canned critical judgments, but to aid them in the process of their own becoming. In the context of the occasional scramble for recognition that is so difficult for authors and academics to avoid, White's modesty is audacious, his methods a model of pragmatism and patient accomplishment.

The essays in this volume are unified by the authors' admiration for Eugene E. White and by their attempts, in their various ways, to come to terms with various aspects of the history and criticism of American rhetoric. No single volume, of course, could pretend to absolute unity or to completeness—nor would such an attempt produce anything but a false picture of coherence.

Gene White was a professor of rhetoric and public address for forty years, the last twenty-five of them at Penn State, from which he retired in January 1986. For four decades, this dedicated scholar and teacher honored his profession with diligent and productive service. The authors of this volume understand that we cannot repay our debt to Gene with these essays, but hope that he, and the readers of our book, will accept this work as an acknowledgment of that debt.

IV

The essays in our book are arranged chronologically. They sample moments and movements in American rhetoric with an emphasis upon fairly early and fairly recent examples—with the exception of Professor Rosenfield's essay, about which more in a moment. They hew to no single theoretical point of view or historical/critical method, nor do they pretend to demonstrate all the legitimate methods and theories.[20] The chronological arrangement is not meant to suggest that this book is a history of American rhetoric; rather, it is meant as an exploration of the rhetorical criticism of American discourse, taking admittedly a limited series of examples and trying, with each, to explore the relations of historical investigation, critical analysis of one or more rhetorical texts, and relation of our findings to matters theoretical. We have deliberately chosen a range of examples and methods of approach. In each case, authors have been invited to write something longer than the typical journal article (but shorter than a monograph!) so that they could (1) explore in some detail the historical background necessary to their analysis; (2) engage in close analysis of their rhetorical texts; and (3) without undue self-consciousness present not only their conclusions and evidence, but write fully enough so that a student, looking over their shoulder, can understand *how* they have reached their conclusions.

Stephen T. Olsen addresses the question of how to determine the disputed authorship of Patrick Henry's "Liberty or Death" speech of 23 March 1775. Did Henry actually compose and deliver the speech as it has come down to us, or is the text so often quoted the invention of Henry's biographer, William Wirt? Every rhetorical critic, especially when dealing with materials orally delivered, must deal with the question of textual authenticity. In his essay, Olsen shows how historical research and computer analysis can aid in the process— and arrives at a conclusion that will surprise American readers whose memories of Patrick Henry's speech are part of the myth of elementary-school history.

Stephen E. Lucas analyzes the Declaration of Independence not as a universal human document but as a rhetorical document, designed to do something in its own time and drawing upon a long tradition of English rhetoric. His close reading of the document is made possible by a careful placement of it in its own time.

Carroll C. Arnold examines the "communicative qualities of constitutional discourse" as they are revealed in a series of constitutional debates in Pennsylvania between 1776 and 1790. His essay, in addition to making its own substantial contribution to our understanding of the period, demonstrates analytical techniques the historical critic may usefully apply to a very extended body of written and oral documents whose aim is avowedly to construct a society.

James R. Andrews examines the early days of political pamphleteering in the new American nation, reminding us at the same time that American rhetoric is inevitably linked to the rest of the world not only through a train of historical antecedents but also through individual migrations and international conflicts.

As we designed this book, we noticed early on that we were not going to have "coverage" of all the media and genres of American rhetoric: there is no criticism here of fiction, film, television, popular music. Anyone who is acquainted with the work of the authors of this book knows that they are not traditionalists who are trying to hold the line against the expansion of rhetorical criticism. Most of the authors of our book chose as their examples discursive rhetoric because it seemed to each of them to provide a means of exemplifying the themes and methods essential to their part in the work as a whole. Partly for this reason, it is appropriate that the essay at the center of this book is Lawrence W. Rosenfield's "reading" of Central Park. The park, at the chronological midpoint of our book, is a nondiscursive scene; it is also presented as a "text," drawing on "an earlier art of rhetoric" and constituting a "celebration of civic virtue."

The final four chapters concern recent rhetorical events. Martin J. Medhurst applies Eugene White's notion of "configurational criticism" to an analysis of a unique political and religious text: inaugural prayer. Taking the inauguration of Lyndon B. Johnson as his example, Medhurst examines the generic and political exigencies that formed these instances of American civil religion.

In "Rhetoric as a Way of Being," I try to acknowledge the importance of everyday and transient rhetoric, which typically vanishes from the historical record, and to explore the ways in which rhetoric is an enactment of being and becoming not only for speakers but also for their auditors.

Gerard A. Hauser traces the Carter administration's attempt to manage public opinion during the Iranian hostage crisis and considers the whole affair as it bears on the possibility for creating rhetorical publics.

Fittingly, Richard B. Gregg concludes the book with a frankly speculative sort of rhetorical criticism, looking for "conceptual-metaphorical" patterns that may be emerging in political rhetoric in the 1980s. A volume that begins in seeking out the traces of America's rhetorical past ends with a reminder that rhetoric always, uncertainly, faces the future.

Notes

1. "Rhetoric as Historical Configuration," in *Rhetoric in Transition: Studies in the Nature and Uses of Rhetoric,* ed. Eugene E. White (University Park: Pennsylvania State Univ. Pr., 1980), 17.

2. Frank M. Rarig and Halbert S. Greaves, "National Speech Organizations and Speech Education," in *History of Speech Education in America,* ed. Karl R. Wallace (New York: Appleton-Century-Crofts, 1954), 490–517.

3. What's in a name? When the first departments were founded in the teens and twenties of this century, they were usually departments of speech or of speech and drama. Typically, they offered courses in public speaking, drama and theater, and speech pathology and audiology. In later years, drama and speech pathology (as it used to be called; it now encompasses what is called communication disorders, speech science, and audiology) often went off into their separate departments. At the same time, speech departments strengthened their offerings in rhetoric, interpersonal communication, small-group communication, organizational communication, and radio/television/film. After World War II, departments and schools of journalism became interested in mass communication, or often communications and mass communications (with an "s"), and joined forces with a newly emerging line of

empirical research based strongly on survey research, quantitative content analysis, and experimental studies of communication effects. There are now two somewhat overlapping fields both claiming to be "communication(s)": the descendants of departments of speech and the descendants of departments of journalism. At Pennsylvania State University, for example, a recent reorganization has created a professionally oriented School of Communications comprising the former School of Journalism, the film faculty formerly in the Department of Theatre and Film, and the radio and television faculty formerly in the Department of Speech Communication. Meanwhile, the Department of Speech Communication remains in the College of Liberal Arts, offering studies in rhetoric and public address, communication theory, mass media, political communication, nonverbal communication, communication education, film and television, speech science, English as a second language, and interpersonal/small-group/organizational communication. Many other departmental configurations are developing at other colleges and universities. For further discussions of the evolution of these fields, see Thomas W. Benson, ed., *Speech Communication in the Twentieth Century* (Carbondale: Southern Illinois Univ. Pr., 1985); and George Gerbner and Marsha Siefert, eds., *Ferment in the Field*, a special issue of *Journal of Communication* 33, no. 3 (Summer 1983).

4. Herbert A. Wichelns, "The Literary Criticism of Oratory," in *Studies in Rhetoric and Public Speaking in Honor of James A. Winans*, ed. A. M. Drummond (New York: Century, 1925).

5. William Norwood Brigance, ed., *A History and Criticism of American Public Address*, 2 vols. (New York: McGraw-Hill, 1943); Marie Hochmuth, ed., *A History and Criticism of American Public Address*, vol. 3 (New York: Longmans, Green, 1955).

6. Waldo Braden offers a brief and discerning guide to studies in public address in "Research: Methods, Trends, Ideas," in *The Communicative Arts and Sciences of Speech* ed. Keith Brooks (Columbus, Oh.: Merrill, 1967), 66–95. Braden's study is particularly useful since it was written when confidence and acheivement in public address studies were at their height among mature scholars in the discipline. Other guides to research in speech and communication are mixed in their treatment of history and criticism. Bormann and Auer include history and criticism; Emmert and Brooks, and Bowers and Courtright (who treat only "scientific" method) do not. J. Jeffery Auer, *An Introduction to Research in Speech* (New York: Harper, 1959); Ernest G. Bormann, *Theory and Research in the Communicative Arts* (New York: Holt, 1965); Philip Emmert and William D. Brooks, *Methods of Research in Communication* (Boston: Houghton Mifflin, 1970); John Waite Bowers and John A. Courtright, *Communication Research Methods*, (Glenview, Ill.: Scott, Foresman, 1984).

7. Of course, the study of interpersonal, small-group, and organizational communication had been pursued nearly from the beginning of the discipline. For historical accounts, see the chapters by Rawlins, Gouran, and Putnam and Cheney in Benson, *Speech Communication*.

8. Lester Thonssen and A. Craig Baird, *Speech Criticism* (New York: Ronald Pr., 1948).

9. Edwin Black, *Rhetorical Criticism: A Study in Method* (New York: Macmillan, 1965).

10. Black, *Rhetorical Criticism*, 131.

11. Black himself was not a "Burkean" critic, nor did he tie his own work to any particular theoretical or methodological star.

12. Black's book was clearly a call for change, variety, and the reinvigoration of a discipline. But so were the movements the Black accused of stultification. Wichelns's essay was an attempt to break away from unsatisfactory paradigms, not to impose unity. And in his preface to volume 1 of *A History and Criticism of American Public Address*, a volume later dismissed as speaking in a unified neo-Aristotelianism, Brigance wrote: "In the critical studies, as in the historical studies, the reader will find a wide diversity in patterns of treatment. To those who would prefer that one standardized pattern of rhetorical criticism be followed, we answer that it would have been neither possible nor, in our opinion, desirable. . . . Uniformity in so large a number of studies would inevitably have led to sterility. . . . 'Monism is the natural disease of philosophers, who hunger and thirst not (as they think) for truth, but for unity' " (x). If we are to make sensible decisions about the scholarship of our own generation, it is important that we understand both how it is that to Brigance and his authors their work seemed diverse, and how to Black, just twenty years later, that work seemed to speak from a single, narrow point of view.

13. A useful debate on neo-Aristotelianism occured in several essays commenting on Richard M. Nixon's speech on Vietnam of 3 November 1969. The contributions of Robert P. Newman, Hermann G. Stelzner, Karlyn Kohrs Campbell, and Forbes Hill are anthologized in James R. Andrews, ed., *The Practice of Rhetorical Criticism* (New York: Macmillan, 1983), 67–128. For further comments on Hill's contribution to the debate, see Richard B. Gregg,

"The Criticism of Symbolic Inducement: A Critical-Theoretical Connection," in Benson, *Speech Communication*, 41–62.

14. Barnet Baskerville, "Must We All Be "Rhetorical Critics?" *Quarterly Journal of Speech* 63 (1977): 116. Writing of another area of communication studies, Carolyn Marvin has argued that the field of journalism/communications is in need of historical writing, but that such history has often been weakened by its isolation from "mainstream historians," subordination to the professional ideologies of practical journalism, and allegiance to inadequate theories of communication. Carolyn Marvin, "Space, Time, and Captive Communications History," in *Communications in Transition*, ed. Mary S. Mander (New York: Praeger, 1983), 20–38. Baskerville's lament, coupled with Marvin's analysis, reveals something of the double bind in which historians of public address found themselves ensnared. From the point of view of mainstream history, the historian of public address is an overspecialized outsider, with a vested interest in demonstrating the importance of speech among all the other elements of the historical record. From the point of view of rhetorical and communication theory, the historian of public address may seem to suffer from antiquarianism or particularism—doing history rather than rhetoric.

15. If it took itself seriously as science, the theoretical gatekeeping would be forced to concede, I think, that in science an experiment cannot confirm a theory—it can only falsify or fail to falsify the theory. Nor does it do to reduce rhetorical history and criticism to a "case study," as a subset of social science.

On a related point, Gregg argues that it is not the theory but the critic who is to be blamed when neo-Aristotelianism becomes uninteresting. Gregg, "Criticism of Symbolic Inducement."

16. On this issue, see Arthur P. Bochner and Eric M. Eisenberg, "Legitimizing Speech Communication: An Examination of Coherence and Cohesion in the Development of the Discipline," in Benson, *Speech Communication*, 299–321. On the other hand, see Michael Leff and Margaret Organ Procario's discussion of the difficulties presented by what they call the "radical particularism" of some early Cornell rhetoricians; Michael Leff and Margaret Organ-Procario, "Rhetorical Theory in Speech Communication," in Benson, *Speech Communication*, 8–9. Roderick Hart presents a strong case against atheoretical historical and critical scholarship in "Public Address: Should It Be Disinterred? A Commentary on Scholarship in the Area" (paper presented to the Public Address Division of the Speech Communication Association, Denver, Colorado, 10 November 1985), which was published in revised form as "Contemporary Scholarship in Public Address: A Research Editorial," *Western Journal of Speech Communication* 50 (1986): 283–95. Hart has provided what is to date the most comprehensive review of the theoretical and critical implications of historical and critical studies in public address in his "The Functions of Human Communication in the Maintenance of Public Values," in *Handbook of Rhetorical and Communication Theory*, ed. Carroll C. Arnold and John Waite Bowers (Boston: Allyn and Bacon, 1984). Hart advises the critic to avoid being distracted by the details of situation, circumstance, character, or text, since this will render the derivation of generalized theory difficult or impossible. But could it not be replied that if a detailed investigation resists generalization, then the generalization that is derived from the suppression of interacting details is likely to be untrustworthy as theory? Most communication theorists seem not to draw directly upon historical and critical studies: see, for example, Stephen W. Littlejohn, *Theories of Human Communication* (Columbus, Oh.: Merrill, 1978), and W. Barnett Pearce and Vernon E. Cronen, *Communication, Action, and Meaning* (New York: Praeger, 1980). More surprisingly, even rhetorical theorists typically do not draw heavily upon historical and critical studies. It is more common for theorists to cite other theorists. My own, at least partly impressionistic, reading of the journals convinces me that historians and critics are more likely to cite theory, and attempt to contribute to theory, than theorists are likely to draw upon history and criticism. It would be absurd for these three modes of discourse to operate independently of one another, of course; but to some degree they are inevitably and legitimately three different modes of discourse, with separate agendas.

These reflections seem to underscore the need for speech communication (and presumably other disciplines) to write its own intellectual history in a way that does justice to theoretical issues and at the same time develops an ethnographically particular account of the actions of particular men and women as teachers, writers, and editors.

17. Steven Mailloux, "Rhetorical Hermeneutics," *Critical Inquiry* 11 (1985): 620–41. The debate over theory versus criticism is usefully addressed in W. J. T. Mitchell, ed., *Against Theory: Literary Studies and the New Pragmatism* (Chicago: Univ. of Chicago Pr., 1985), and Frederick Crews, "In the Big House of Theory," *New York Review of Books*, 29 May 1986, 36–42. Literary studies have become newly "rhetorical" in two senses that sharply divide

theoretical adherents and critical practice. One camp construes literature as rhetorical because it is "ideological." See, for example, Frank Lentricchia, *Criticism and Social Change* (Chicago: Univ. of Chicago Pr., 1983); Terry Eagleton, *Literary Theory: An Introduction* (Minneapolis: Univ. of Minnesota Pr., 1983). Another camp construes literature as rhetorical in the sense that it defies authoritative interpretation. See Paul de Man, *Allegories of Reading* (New Haven: Yale Univ. Pr., 1979); Jefferson Humphries, "The Sorcery of Rhetoric in French and American Letters," *Massachusetts Review* 26, nos. 2–3 (Summer-Autumn 1985): 178–97. More traditional senses of literature as rhetorical are sampled in Edward P. J. Corbett, ed., *Rhetorical Analyses of Literary Works* (New York: Oxford Univ. Pr., 1969). For an extension of the analysis to historical writing, see Hayden White, *Tropics of Discourse: Essays in Cultural Criticism* (Baltimore: Johns Hopkins Univ. Pr., 1978).

18. The first rhetorical criticism of any kind appearing in *Southern's* first decade appears to have been Mabel Morris's "Indian Oratory," which appeared in March 1944.

19. A bibliography of White's major works appears at the end of this book.

20. For anthologies and bibliographies of recent rhetorical criticism, see Andrews, *The Practice of Rhetorical Criticism*; Bernard L. Brock and Robert L. Scott, eds., *Methods of Rhetorical Criticism: A Twentieth-Century Perspective*, 2d ed. (Detroit: Wayne State Univ. Pr., 1980); Michael Leff, ed., "Rhetorical Criticism: The State of the Art" *Western Speech*, 44 (1980), a special issue; and Martin J. Medhurst and Thomas W. Benson, eds., *Rhetorical Dimensions in Media: A Critical Casebook* (Dubuque, Iowa.: Kendall/Hunt, 1984).

TWO

Patrick Henry's "Liberty or Death" Speech: A Study in Disputed Authorship

STEPHEN T. OLSEN

> *I know not what course others may take; but as for me, GIVE ME LIBERTY OR GIVE ME DEATH!*

THESE MOVING WORDS, concluding Patrick Henry's most famous speech, are an intrinsic part of our American history. They were declaimed by school children as early as 1834,[1] and the words have been printed over and over again in American histories, readers, and speech anthologies. When our nation celebrated its Bicentennial, the phrase "give me liberty or give me death" was the epigram symbolizing the spirit and dedication of the revolutionary movement that we were commemorating.

The words in Patrick Henry's "Liberty or Death" speech deserve this venerable place in our culture because, as one historian stated, they launched the Revolution.[2] Or did they? According to tradition, the speech was delivered on 23 March 1775. No stenographic notes were taken of the speech; Patrick Henry left no written account of the speech; and no text of the "Liberty or Death" speech appeared during Henry's lifetime. In 1816, seventeen years after Patrick Henry died, the text of the speech was first published as part of a biography of Henry, written by William Wirt.[3] The question that has engaged scholars ever since is whether the text reported in Wirt's book should be attributed to Patrick Henry or whether it is really the composition of some other author. One hundred and seventy-two years after the text of the "Liberty or Death" speech was published, identification of its composer is still a controversial issue.

In this study, I will provide an answer to the question, "Who authored the 'Liberty or Death' speech?" The question will be answered by examining evidence derived from using two very different methods. The question will first be answered using the traditional tools of the historian—reasoning from historical evidence, such as artifacts and writings, to explain past events. The question will then be answered using the quantitative tools of the computer scientist— statistical stylistics—to establish distinctive profiles of language use whereby authorship of doubtful texts may be determined.

In the application of both the historical and the computerized methods, I have used only materials and resources that would be available to normal students (although some students would obviously have to work harder than others to obtain some materials). For example, in the historical section, we will use only materials that are printed and in the public domain. The computer analysis that once required the resources of a major university or corporate facility can now be done on most college computers and even some high-school computers.

This study, therefore, does more than just answer its generative question. It also provides an exploratory model for students interested in doing authorship attribution studies themselves. We will discuss not only methods that worked, but also methods that did not work in this particular instance. Many author-attribution problems are waiting to be solved; the reader of this article should have a good foundation for beginning the detective work on a similar problem. The reader will also, of course, know who really wrote Patrick Henry's "Liberty or Death" speech!

The Speech

March 23, 1775, was a balmy spring day in the small market town of Richmond, Virginia.[4] The attention of many residents and visitors was focused on St. John's Church, a small parish church on the Richmond hilltop, where 122 members of the Convention of Delegates for the Counties and Corporations in the Colony of Virginia were meeting.[5] The previous three days of the convention had been devoted to predictably ordinary matters. Those members and spectators who trudged up the hill this day, however, were to hear, in the words of delegate Thomas Marshall, "one of the most bold, vehement, and animated pieces of eloquence that had ever been delivered."[6]

The Richmond Convention of 1775 was the second extralegal convention held in the colony of Virginia in less than one year.[7] The penchant of Lord Dunmore (the governor of Virginia appointed by the king of England) to avoid conflict with the House of Burgesses (the Virginia legislature elected by the colonists) by dissolving and proroguing the assembly or postponing the session resulted in Virginia's being without a legal assembly session from 26 May 1774 until 1 June 1775.[8] Thus, the legal representatives of the Virginia voters had an inadequate opportunity to respond fully to the inflammatory Coercive Acts passed by Great Britain. The legislature also had no opportunity to respond to many pressing concerns that demanded the attention of the people's representatives such as the various declarations and recommendations of the First Continental Congress and the formation of independent military companies in Virginia. The governor was unwilling to let the House of Burgesses consider these matters, but the citizens of Virginia acted anyway. On 26 January 1775, John Pinkney's *Virginia Gazette* published a notice requesting the various Virginia counties and corporations to elect representatives to the extralegal convention to be held at Richmond beginning Monday, 20 March 1775.[9]

The first day of the convention was devoted primarily to organizational matters. Peyton Randolph, Speaker of the House of Burgesses and president of the First Continental Congress, was unanimously elected president of the convention. John Tazewell, clerk of the Virginia Committee of Correspondence,[10] was elected clerk of the convention. The convention members also agreed to observe "the same rules and orders as are established in the House of Burgesses in this Colony." The only nonorganizational business occurred when Peyton Randolph laid before the convention the proceedings of the Continental Congress and a letter from Benjamin Franklin, William Bollan, and Arthur Lee advising "that the Petition to His Majesty [from the First Continental Congress] had been presented and graciously received." Consideration of the proceedings of the congress, however, was postponed until the next day.[11]

There must have been considerable activity on the second day of the convention, but the issues discussed and specific delegates' positions on those issues remain a mystery. The convention proceedings show that the only affirmative action taken that day was the seating of two newly arrived delegates from the western part of Augusta County. That should have been a perfunctory activity. By the time the convention was ready to consider the scheduled business of the day, however, the members did not have time to go through the proceedings of the Continental Congress, and, therefore, the convention "postponed the further consideration thereof till tomorrow."

The convention was more productive on 22 March. The delegates considered the proceedings of the Congress and passed two germane resolutions approving the "Proceedings and Resolutions" of the First Continental Congress and thanking the Virginia delegates to that congress for their "faithful discharge of the very important trust reposed in them."

There was no indication that the fourth session of the convention, 23 March 1775, would be a fateful day. As with Patrick Henry's two earlier oratorical triumphs—the Parson's Cause case (1 December 1763) and the Stamp Act speech in the House of Burgesses (30 May 1765)—the audience had no reason to expect extraordinary eloquence from participating speakers. St. John's Church was the biggest assembly building in Richmond, but even though the parish had enlarged the building recently, it had seats only for the delegates and perhaps a few dozen spectators.[12] The day was warm enough that the church's windows were open and the crowd that had gathered outside to listen to the proceedings heard Peyton Randolph call the convention to order at 10:00 A.M. After the Reverend Mr. Selden's prayer, a copy of a petition from the Assembly of Jamaica to the king was laid before the convention and Edmund Pendleton moved two resolutions thanking the Assembly of Jamaica for "their patriotick endeavours to fix the just claims of the Colonists upon the most permanent constitutional principles" and expressing a wish "to see a speedy return to those halcyon days when we lived a free and happy people." The Jamaica Petition was read in its entirety and "maturely considered." After probably an hour or more of debate, Pendleton's resolutions were adopted.[13]

After consideration of the Jamaica Petition was completed, the attention of the convention focused on Patrick Henry, who, after rising from his seat in pew forty-seven, handed the following series of resolutions to John Tazewell, which the clerk then read:[14]

Resolved, That a well regulated Militia, composed of Gentlemen and Yeomen, is the natural strength, and only security of a free Government; that such a Militia in this Colony would for ever render it unnecessary for the Mother Country to keep among us, for the purpose of our defence, a Standing Army of mercenary forces, always subversive of the quiet, and dangerous to the liberties of the people, and would obviate the pretext of taxing us for their support.

That the establishment of such a Militia is at this time peculiarly necessary, by the state of our laws for the protection and defence of the Country, some of which have already expired, and others will shortly do so; and that the known remissness of Government, in calling us together in a legislative capacity, renders it too insecure, in this time of danger and distress, to rely, that opportunity will be given of renewing them in General Assembly, or making any provision to secure our inestimable rights and liberties from those farther violations with which they are threatened.

Resolved therefore, That this Colony be immediately put into a posture of defence; and that ———— be a Committee to prepare a plan for the embodying, arming, and disciplining such a number of men as may be sufficient for that purpose.

As the proposer, Henry was the first person recognized by the chairman to speak for the resolutions. Therefore, Patrick Henry again rose from his seat and delivered what has come to be regarded as a classic speech in the history of American public address:

"No man," he said, "thought more highly than he did, of the patriotism, as well as abilities, of the very worthy gentlemen who had just addressed the house. But different men often saw the same subject in different lights; and therefore, he hoped it would not be thought disrespectful to those gentlemen, if, entertaining as he did, opinions of a character very opposite to theirs, he should speak forth *his* sentiments freely, and without reserve. This," he said, "was no time for ceremony. The question before the house was one of awful moment to this country. For his own part, he considered it as nothing less than a question of freedom or slavery. And in proportion to the magnitude of the subject, ought to be the freedom of the debate. It was only in this way that they could hope to arrive at truth, and fulfil the great responsibility which they held to God and their country. Should he keep back his opinions, at such a time, through fear of giving offence, he should consider himself as guilty of treason towards his country, and of an act of disloyalty toward the majesty of Heaven, which he revered above all earthly kings."

"Mr. President," said he, "it is natural to man to indulge in the illusions of hope. We are apt to shut our eyes against a painful truth—and listen to the song of that siren, till she transforms us into beasts. Is this," he asked, "the part of wise men, engaged in a great and arduous struggle for liberty? Were we disposed to be of the number of those, who having eyes, see not, and having ears, hear not, the things which so nearly concern their temporal salvation? For his part, whatever anguish of spirit it might cost, *he* was willing to know the whole truth; to know the worst, and to provide for it."

"He had," he said, "but one lamp by which his feet were guided and that was the lamp of experience. He knew of no way of judging of the future, but by the past. And judging by the past, he wished to know what there had been in the conduct of the British ministry for the last ten years, to justify those hopes with which gentlemen had been pleased to solace themselves and the house? Is it that insidious smile with which our petition has been lately received? Trust it not, sir; it will prove a snare to your feet. Suffer not yourselves to be betrayed with a kiss. Ask yourselves how this gracious reception of our petition comports with those warlike preparations which cover our waters and darken our land? Are fleets and armies necessary to work of love and reconciliation? Have we shown ourselves so unwilling to be reconciled, that force must be called in to win back our love? Let us not deceive ourselves, sir. These are the implements of war and subjugation— the last arguments to which kings resort. I ask gentlemen, sir, what means this martial array, if its purpose be not to force us to submission? Can gentlemen assign any other possible motive for it? Had Great Britain any enemy in this quarter of the world, to call for all this accumulation of navies and armies? No sir: she has none. They are sent over to bind and rivet upon us those chains, which the British ministry have been so long forging. And what have we to oppose to them? Shall we try argument? Sir, we have been trying that for the last ten years. Have we any thing new to offer upon the subject? Nothing. We have held the subject up in every light of which it is capable; but it has been all in vain. Shall we resort to entreaty and humble supplication? What terms shall we find, which have not been already exhausted? Let us not, I beseech you, sir, deceive yourselves longer. Sir, we have done every thing that could be done, to avert the storm which is now coming on. We have petitioned—we have remonstrated—we have supplicated—we have prostrated ourselves before the throne, and have implored its interposition to arrest the tyrannical hands of the ministry and parliament. Our petitions have been slighted; our remonstrances have produced additional violence and insult; our supplications have been disregarded; and we have been spurned, with contempt, from the foot of the throne. In vain, after these things, may we indulge the fond hope of peace and reconciliation. *There is no longer any room for hope.* If we wish to be free—if we mean to preserve inviolate those inestimable privileges for which we have been so long contending—if we mean not basely to abandon the noble struggle in which we have been so long engaged, and which we have pledged ourselves never to abandon, until the glorious object of our contest shall be obtained—we must fight!—I repeat it, sir, we must fight!! An appeal to arms and to the God of Hosts, is all that is left us!"

"They tell us, sir," continued Mr. Henry, "that we are weak—unable to cope with so formidable an adversary. But when shall we be stronger? Will it be the next week, or the next year? Will it be when we are totally disarmed; and when a British guard shall be stationed in every house? Shall we gather strength by irresolution in every house? Shall we acquire the means of effectual resistance, by lying supinely on our backs, and hugging the delusive phantom of hope, until our enemies shall have bound us, hand and foot? Sir, we are not weak, if we make a proper use of those means which the God of nature hath placed in our power. Three millions of people, armed in the holy cause of liberty, and in such a country as that which we possess, are invincible by any force which our enemy can send against us. Besides, sir, we shall not fight our battles alone. There is a just God who presides over the destinies of nations; and who will raise up friends to fight our battles for us. The battle, sir, is not to the strong alone; it is to the vigilant, the active, the brave. Besides, sir, we have no election. If we were base enough to desire it, it is not too late to retire from the contest. There is no retreat, but in submission and slavery! Our chains are forged. Their clanking may be heard on the plains of Boston! The war is inevitable—and let it come!! I repeat it, sir, let it come!!!"

"It is in vain, sir, to extenuate the matter. Gentlemen may cry, peace, peace—but there is no peace. The war is actually begun! The next gale that sweeps from the north, will bring to our ears the clash of resounding arms! Our brethren are already in the field! Why stand we here idle? What is it that gentlemen wish? What would they have? Is life so dear, or peace so sweet, as to be purchased at the price of chains, and slavery? Forbid it, Almighty God!—I know not what course others may take; but as for me," cried he, with both his arms extended aloft, his brows knit, every feature marked with the resolute purpose of his soul, and his voice swelled to its boldest note of exclamation —"give me liberty, or give me death!"[15]

It was more than a quarter of a century before reports of the effects of Henry's "Liberty or Death" speech were published. Although he never heard Henry speak, William Wirt reported what has become the traditional account: "He [Patrick Henry] took his seat. No murmur of applause was heard. The effect was too deep. After the trance of a moment, several members started from their seats. The cry, 'to arms,' seemed to quiver on every lip, and gleam from every eye!"[16] Edward Carrington, who later served as a distinguished colonel in the Revolution, literally was sitting in the northern window of the church while Henry spoke. He was completely over-powered by the orator and exclaimed, "Let me be buried at this spot!" That wish lasted during his life and was respected at his death in 1810.[17]

The silence that reportedly followed Henry's speech was broken by Richard Henry Lee, who seconded Henry's resolutions. Thirty-two-year-old Thomas Jefferson spoke for Henry's resolutions, as did Thomas Nelson, Jr.

It would be incorrect to assume that Henry's speech produced unanimous approval for his resolutions. Judge St. George Tucker reported that there was "an animated debate" in which Henry's resolutions were opposed by such influential members as Richard Bland, Robert Carter Nicholas, Benjamin Harrison, and Edmund Pendleton.[18]

Despite opposition by some of the most prominent and politically powerful men in the colony, Patrick Henry's resolutions were approved by the convention. The exact vote tally is unknown. We do know that the vote was not unanimous. The one contemporary report that contains a vote count declared that the resolutions were "carried by a majority of 65 to 60." While that tally is obviously incorrect, it probably does reflect the narrowness of the margin by which the resolutions passed.[19]

The Authorship Dispute

There is no doubt that Patrick Henry gave a speech on 23 March 1775; there is no doubt that according to tradition the speech had an electric effect on many auditors. There is, however, considerable doubt about just *what* he said that day. Although a Gallup poll in the 1950s reported that 48 percent of Americans identified Patrick Henry as the composer of the inspiring words, "Give me Liberty or give me Death!"[20] some historians doubt that Henry uttered that phrase or that the traditional version of the speech is authentic.

Patrick Henry left no notes and no manuscript copy of the speech.

There was no stenographic report made by John Tazewell, the clerk of the convention. Tazewell adopted a recording form typical of meetings of this period. He recorded only positive actions of the convention such as resolutions passed and appointments made. He did not record resolutions that were defeated, issues that were debated but either were never voted on or were defeated, specific delegate positions on various issues and resolutions, speeches by delegates, or the vote tally for passed resolutions. Although this form provides only scanty evidence for the historian, it did serve an important purpose for meetings of this type because the published record gave the public appearance of great unity at the meeting (even when, in reality, that may not have been the case). If any delegates summarized the convention speeches in their diaries (as John Adams was wont to do), the diaries have been either lost or destroyed. The local newspapers printed only the authorized record of the Richmond Convention proceedings. Henry's resolutions, therefore, were made public less than a week after they were passed, but no mention was made of his advocating speech.[21]

The response of Virginia's government, including both executive and legislative branches, gave testimony only about Patrick Henry's general effectiveness as a colonial leader. On 6 May 1775, Lord Dunmore issued a proclamation that stated in part "that a certain Patrick Henry, of the county of Hanover, and a number of deluded followers, have taken up arms, . . . and have written and dispatched letters to divers parts of the country, exciting the people to join in these outrageous and rebellious practices, to the great terror of all his majesty's faithful subjects, and in open defiance of law and government."[22] Dunmore did not mention Henry's "Liberty or Death" speech and alluded only indirectly to his militant resolutions. Lord Dunmore made so many charges about the extent of the organization of independent military companies and the purposes for which they had been formed that the assembly named a committee "to inquire into the Causes of the late disturbances and Commotions." Their long report showed that only four counties organized their independent companies after Henry's resolutions. No mention was made in the report of Henry's "Liberty or Death" speech as a catalytic influence.[23]

The only immediately contemporary evidence that Patrick Henry may have coined a memorable phrase on 23 March 1775 appeared later in the summer when Colonel Patrick Henry took command of the Virginia militia and called for men to join him. Featured on one side of the Culpepper Minutemen's flag was a picture of a coiled rattlesnake about to strike, and on the other side were the words

"Liberty or Death" and "Don't Tread on Me." Some of the men wore hunting shirts emblazoned with the "Liberty or Death" slogan. One humorist of the group suggested that liberty or death offered too severe an alternative; he would stay, he said, if it were cut back to liberty or be crippled.[24]

Forty-one years after the Richmond Convention, a text of Patrick Henry's "Liberty or Death" speech was first presented to the public in the December 1816 issue of the *Port Folio*. Oliver Oldschool, the journal's editor, saw the biographical manuscript that William Wirt sent to James Webster for publication and received permission to publish an excerpt before the full biography reached the market. The excerpt was faithful to Wirt's manuscript. It began with the convening of the Richmond Convention, 20 March 1775, and concluded with the formation of the convention's Militia Plan Committee. Included, of course, was the text of Henry's "Liberty or Death" speech. Although his introduction was intended as complimentary, editor Oldschool inadvertently suggested the predicament that has plagued Wirt's critics ever since: "The honourable office of embalming the memory of this fervid orator, and an intrepid statesman, who has done so much, and is known so little, has been confided to William Wirt, esq. from whose pen we have already had sufficient proof that he will treat his subject with the fidelity of the biographer, and the enthusiasm of the poet."[25]

Henry's "Liberty or Death" speech was more widely circulated in 1817 with the publication of William Wirt's *Sketches of the Life and Character of Patrick Henry*. Wirt's biography of Henry was a popular success. The book went into its fifteenth edition in 1859 and other editions have appeared since then, including one as recently as 1903.[26] Through the various editions of the book, the text of Henry's speech remained unaltered, and this text is still the only version of the speech that has come forth to this day.

In December 1824 Thomas Jefferson told Daniel Webster that Wirt's biography of Henry "is a poor book, written in bad taste, and gives an imperfect idea of Patrick Henry. It seems written less to show Mr. Henry than Mr. Wirt."[27] The book also received severe criticism from others who personally knew Patrick Henry. Patrick Henry's son, John, was "chagrined when he first read William Wirt's book." Robert Walsh consigned the book to the annals of mythology, pronouncing it "the Apotheosis of Patrick Henry & the Glorification of Virginia." John Taylor classified it as fiction, referring to it as "a splendid novel." John Randolph of Roanoke was less kind; he called the book "a wretched piece of fustian." Peter Cruse complained that "the hero . . . seemed more like the creation of a rhetorician, than a personage of history."[28] Recent historians continue the negative criticism of Wirt's biography. Norine Campbell is certain that "biographer William Wirt must have harbored a grudge against young Patrick Henry from the start." Robert Meade thought that "Wirt indulged in romanticizing the painted vivid contrasts without always considering the final effects of his efforts."[29]

Not everyone disparaged Wirt's biography. The public flocked to buy the book. The newspaper criticism "was lavish of encomiums upon the author."[30] The magazine reviews were generally favorable.[31] And later biographers of Henry, who almost inevitably deprecate Wirt's book in their texts, profusely cite him in their footnotes! Better biographies of Henry have appeared, but Wirt's was the pioneering effort, and one is thus inclined to concur with Moses Coit Tyler: "Any one who will take the trouble to ascertain the enormous disadvantages under which Wirt wrote, and which, as we now know, gave him great discouragement, will be inclined to applaud him for making so good a book, rather than to blame him for not making a better one."[32] The value of Wirt's *Sketches of the Life and Character of Patrick Henry* as historical biography or, if one prefers, fictional literature is not our immediate concern. The general criticisms of the book are relevant, however, insofar as they call into question the historical accuracy of the materials contained in the book. If the "Liberty or Death" text, too, shows more of Mr. Wirt than of Mr. Henry, then the text ought to be analyzed, interpreted, and criticized as a piece of early nationalist period rhetoric—not as American revolutionary rhetoric. If the text is authentic, then historians, rhetorical critics, and, for that matter, the general public ought to be able to deal with it confidently—despite the questionable context of its published introduction.

Although general criticisms of Wirt's book appeared shortly after it was published, Hugh Blair Grigsby was the first scholar to question seriously the accuracy of the "Liberty or Death" text. As part of a Phi Beta Kappa lecture series presented in 1855, Grigsby addressed the students and faculty of William and Mary College and said this about Henry's speech: "Some portions of his speech in their defence [Henry's resolutions] preserved in the memory of those who heard it, are still extant, and exhibit a force of argument and a beauty of expression so finely blended, that, after a lapse of eighty years, they still form the delight of the young and the admiration of the old." A footnote in the published manuscript of Grigsby's speech made this confusing comment: "Although it may well be doubted that much of the speech published by Wirt is apocryphal, some of its expressions and the outline of the argument are believed to be authentic." Did Grigsby intend to deny the charge of apocrypha or did he make the charge? Grigsby did not identify who believed some of the expressions were authentic, why they believed them to be authentic, or even which expressions were considered authentic. Nor did he supply any evidence that would support the allegation that "much of the speech published by Wirt is apocryphal."[33] Nevertheless, Grigsby did raise the issue of textual authenticity, and it has still not been satisfactorily resolved.

Virtually every historian who has dealt with the "Liberty or Death" speech has taken a strong, confident position about the source for the speech text. With few exceptions, the primary historical materials upon which these positions have been based have been available since the middle 1800s. Here is a representative catalogue of the contradictory conclusions that prominent historians have drawn from that data:

1. Hugh Blair Grigsby, *The Virginia Convention of 1775* (1855):
Although it may well be doubted that much of the speech published by Wirt is apocryphal, some of its expressions and the outline of the argument are believed to be authentic. (150)

2. Moses Coit Tyler, *Patrick Henry* (1898):
In the first place, Wirt's version certainly gives the substance of the speech as actually made by Patrick Henry on the occasion named; and, for the form of it, Wirt seems to have gathered testimony from all available living witnesses, and then, from such sentences or snatches of sentences as these witnesses could remember, as well as from his own conception of the orator's method of expression, to have constructed the version which he had handed down to us. (150–151)

3. William W. Henry, *Patrick Henry: Life, Correspondence, and Speeches* (1891):
While he [an unnamed correspondent who claimed to be a member of the convention audience] criticizes in some respects Mr. Wirt's statement of the arguments used by the opponents of Mr. Henry's motion, he has not a word to say in reference to Mr. Wirt's report of Mr. Henry's speech, and thus bears testimony to its correctness. (1:267)

4. Louis Mallory, "Patrick Henry" (1943):
The text of the speech as it has come down to us was written by William Wirt, Henry's first biographer, from the accounts of witnesses. . . . All in all, it appears that although Wirt's version of this famous speech is not apocryphal, as has been sometimes asserted, it should be regarded as incomplete. . . . There is abundant evidence to show that Henry did not soar all the time in other speeches, and there is no reason to believe that he did so in this one. (590–91)

5. Douglas Freeman, *George Washington: Planter and Patriot* (1951):
His early biographer, William Wirt, writing at intervals from 1805 to 1817, relied chiefly on accounts given him by John Tyler and by St. George Tucker, both of whom were present when Henry spoke. . . . As one or the other of these men was responsible for "we must fight" and "I know not what course," etc., those two quotations may be accepted as substantially correct. It is a

thankless duty to have to add that the other testimony concerning the content
of this famous oration is not entitled to credence. (404)

6. Bernard Mayo, *Myths and Men* (1959):

Wirt . . . proceeded to reconstruct it [the speech text] from recollections of
men who some forty years before in Richmond's Saint John's Church had
heard Henry give it. (16)

7. Daniel Boorstin, *The Americans: The National Experience* (1965):

But, in the end, Wirt, like Weems, was undaunted by his meager raw material.
Almost single-handed, he beatified Patrick Henry. . . . With no text to rely
on and only the vague recollections of contemporaries, Wirt himself concocted
what was to become the most famous utterance of the whole Revolution:
Henry's "Give me liberty, or give me death!" speech, as supposedly delivered
in the House of Burgesses. (358–59)

8. Robert T. Oliver, *History of Public Speaking in America* (1965):

Notes on Henry's speech in reply were taken carefully by Judge John Tyler,
who sent them to William Wirt. Complete authenticity is too much to expect,
but several who heard the speech testified that the version Wirt published
closely approximated what the orator said. (60)

9. Robert T. Oliver and Eugene E. White, *Selected Speeches from American
History* (1966):

More than forty years later, William Wirt—nationally known lawyer, speaker,
and author—reconstructed the language of the speech as best he could from the
accounts of witnesses. . . . The sustained, brilliant, and somewhat contrived
language of the printed speech probably reflects the style of Wirt, but it is also
suggestive of the slashing eloquence and courageous spirit of a patriot in the
process of making history. (23–24)

10. Robert Meade, *Patrick Henry: Practical Revolutionary* (1969):

It is safe to say that Wirt's text was based on a few very helpful sources plus
many bits of information. He had ample proof for certain burning phrases
especially in the last part of Henry's speech, and for its general substance.
Moreover, a close analysis proves that the speech has a remarkable resemblance
to Henry's other speeches during this period. (39–40)

11. Norine Dickson Campbell, *Patrick Henry: Patriot and Statesman* (1969):

The speech given at St. John's Church was written, published and accepted
as Patrick Henry's for 195 years. It should not be questioned now. (137)

12. Judy Hample, "The Textual and Cultural Authenticity of Patrick Henry's
'Liberty or Death' Speech" (1977):

Because the Tyler theory of authorship cannot be substantiated, and because
of the incomplete text furnished by Randolph and Tucker, it seems reasonable
to conclude that Wirt wrote the speech himself using these accounts as a basis.
As an accomplished rhetorician, Wirt was capable of writing such a speech.
(302)[34]

13. David McCants, "The Authenticity of William Wirt's Version of Patrick
Henry's 'Liberty or Death' Speech" (1979):

The extant evidence firmly supports the conclusion that Judge St. George
Tucker provided the report that constitutes Wirt's version of the "Liberty or
Death" speech. (394–95)[35]

So who really wrote the text of the "Liberty or Death" speech? In
the remainder of this study, we shall try to answer that question

using two distinct methods: the traditional historical method and computerized language analysis.

Historical Analysis

Historians have used both external and internal evidence in their attempts to prove or disprove the authenticity of the "Liberty or Death" text. The external evidence relates to three basic questions: (1) Did William Wirt invent historical data if his research failed to uncover adequate materials? (2) Was there direct confirmation of the text by contemporaries who actually heard the speech? (3) Were the potential sources for the speech text reliable? The internal evidence depends on comparisons of the content of the "Liberty or Death" speech with other Henry texts.

EXTERNAL EVIDENCE

William Wirt conceived the biographical project that ultimately became *Sketches of the Life and Character of Patrick Henry* in 1804. During September and October 1803, Wirt published a series of ten letters in the Richmond *Argus* under the adopted character of a British spy. Focusing on a wide range of topics, the essays included Wirt's opinions on eloquence; his evaluation of the personalities of Governor James Monroe and Chief Justice Marshall; theories about geology; and his impressions of the distinctive traits of Virginia society, manners, opinions, and popular institutions. The popular success of these essays surprised even Wirt. Bound in booklet form, they went through three or four editions in two years; the tenth edition appeared in 1832; and there was a London edition in 1812.[36] The success of the *Spy* (along with Wirt's desire to avoid idleness during the summer absences from his home in Norfolk which he took to avoid yellow fever) made him contemplate becoming the American Plutarch. In a letter written to Dabney Carr in June 1804 Wirt described his project:

> I have been reading Johnson's Lives of poets and famous men till I have contracted an itch for biography; do not be astonished, therefore, if you see me come out with a very *material* and splendid life of some *departed* Virginian worthy—for I meddle no more with the *living*. Virginia has lost some great men, whose names ought not to perish. If I were a Plutarch, I would collect their lives for the honour of the State and the advantage of posterity.[37]

Several men met Wirt's biographical criteria of "worthy" but "departed," including Edmund Pendleton, Richard Henry Lee, George Washington, and Peyton Randolph. Wirt decided to begin with Patrick Henry because "Mr. Henry seems to me a good text for a discourse on rhetoric, patriotism and morals. The work might be made useful to young men who are just coming forward into life: This is the highest point of my expectation; nor do I deem the object a trifling one, since on these young men the care and safety of the republic must soon devolve."[38] What was originally intended as a short biographical sketch within a work embracing several other distinguished men of Virginia developed into a full biographical work that intermittently occupied Wirt's attention for the next thirteen years.

Once his subject was selected, Wirt wrote to several men who had known and worked with Patrick Henry, including Thomas Jefferson, Charles Dabney, George Dabney, Nathaniel Pope, John Tyler, John Roane, and St. George Tucker.[39] The letters show Wirt's concern about historical accuracy in the gathering of data related to Henry's personal characteristics. Typical of Wirt's concern about acquiring accurate information is the following excerpt from a letter written to St. George Tucker in 1805:

It [an earlier letter which Wirt presumed undelivered] begged another favour of you; and that was, as you had frequently heard P.H., I had no doubt, in conversation and debate, judicial and political, to do me the kindness, at some moment of perfect ease and leisure, to sketch, as minutely as you could, even to the colour of his eyes, a portrait of his person, attitudes, gestures, manners; a description of his voice, its tone, energy, and modulations; his delivery, whether slow, grave and solemn, or rapid, sprightly and animated; his pronunciation, whether studiously plain, homely, and sometimes vulgar, or accurate, courtly and ornate,—with an analysis of his mind, the variety, order and predominance of its powers; his information as a lawyer, a politician, a scholar; the peculiar character of his eloquence, &c., &c.; for I never saw him. These minutiae, which constitute the most interesting part of biography, are not to be learnt from any archives or records, or any other source than the minute and accurate details of a very uncommon observer. [40]

By 1810 Wirt was resolved still to "treat the subject with so much candour" and was unwilling to make "a sacrifice of truth," but two years later, he began to realize the immensity of his undertaking. In a letter to Thomas Jefferson, Wirt wrote:

I despair of the subject. It has been continually sinking under me. The truth, perhaps, cannot be prudently published by me during my life. I propose, at present, to prepare it, and leave the manuscript with my family. I still think it a useful subject, and one which may be advantageously wrought, not only into lessons on eloquence, but on the superiority of solid and practical parts over the transient and gaudy show of occasion.[41]

Much of Wirt's trouble was caused by his reliance on personal reminiscence because he asked correspondents to recall instances as far back as Patrick Henry's childhood. It is not surprising that memories failed or produced conflicting accounts. Wirt summarized his woes in 1816: "But Patrick was altogether *terra incognita* to me. I had never seen him; and the portraits of him which had been furnished me were so various and contradictory as to seem to confound rather than inform me."[42]

Of all the troubles Wirt had in attempting to gather accurate historical data about Patrick Henry, the most serious was the absence of a reliable text for any of Henry's speeches. In 1813, St. George Tucker reminded Wirt that a successful biography must contain examples of Henry's eloquence, but concluded that because "the only shadow of him [Henry] that remains, is Robertson's *abridgment* of his speech in the Convention of Virginia, in 1788," a biography of the torchbearer of the Revolution would be "a hopeless undertaking."[43] The speech text problem was still with Wirt as late as 20 August 1815, when he wrote Judge Carr to detail his problems as a biographer:

The incidents of Mr. Henry's life are extremely monotonous. It is all speaking, speaking, speaking. 'Tis true he could talk: —"Gods! how he *could* talk!" but there is no acting "the while." From the bar to the legislature, and from the legislature to the bar, his peregrinations resembled, a good deal, those of some one, I forget whom,—perhaps some of our friend Tristram's characters, "from the kitchen to the parlour, and from the parlour to the kitchen." And then, to make the matter worse, from 1763 to 1789, covering all the bloom and pride of his life, not one of his speeches lives in print, writing or memory. All that is told me is, that, on such and such an occasion he made a distinguished speech. Now to keep saying this over, and over, and over again, without being able to give any account of what the speech was,—why, sir, what is it but a vast, open, sun-burnt field without one spot of shade or verdure?[44]

In the next four months, William Wirt somehow overcame the restrictive obstacles caused by the absence of "living speeches" for, by 12 January 1816, he had completed the section of the biography containing the text of Patrick Henry's "Liberty or Death" speech.[45]

How did Wirt acquire the text of the "Liberty or Death" speech, a copy he apparently did not have in August 1815? A frequently advanced answer is that William Wirt, an accomplished public speaker himself, simply wrote the text and published it as Henry's.[46] Although Wirt gave serious thought to ghostwriting several of Henry's famous but lost speeches, he rejected the idea on two grounds:

I have sometimes a notion of trying the plan of Botta, who has written an account of the American war, and made speeches himself for his prominent characters, imitating, in this, the historians of Greece and Rome; but I think with Polybius, that this is making too free with the sanctity of history. Besides, Henry's eloquence was all so completely *sui generis* as to be inimitable by any other: and to make my chance of imitating him still worse, I never saw or heard him.[47]

Of course, during the next few months, Wirt could have changed his mind, but a line of reasoning, although less direct than Wirt's letter to Carr, suggests that Wirt maintained fidelity with "the sanctity of history"—at least so far as Henry's speeches were concerned. If Wirt had decided to ghostwrite the "Liberty or Death" speech before January 1816, one might assume that he would also author copies for Henry's two earlier oratorical successes, the Parson's Cause and Stamp Act speeches. In the case of the Parson's Cause, Wirt described the setting and the effect of the speech in vivid detail, but, about the actual text, Wirt confessed: "I have tried much to procure a sketch of this celebrated speech. But those of Mr. Henry's hearers who survive, seem to have been bereft of their senses. They can only tell you in general, that they were taken captive; and so delighted with their captivity, that they followed implicitly, whithersoever he led them."[48] Although he did provide a brief sketch of the topics that Henry was thought to have discussed, Wirt did not attempt to quote Henry directly. In his treatment of the Stamp Act debate, Wirt cited Thomas Jefferson's account of the burgesses' proceedings, the statement of the Stamp Act Resolutions and the account of the debate contained in Henry's papers, and John Tyler's version (verified by Jefferson) of Henry's "treason" peroration. As with the Parson's Cause, Wirt described in detail Henry's "sublime eloquence" but he claimed as authentic only the final two sentences of the peroration.[49] In other, lesser situations Wirt could have invented words for Henry but chose not to do so. For example, concerning Henry's 2 May 1775 speech to the Hanover volunteers, Wirt wrote: "These were heads of his harangue. I presume not to give the colouring. That was Mr. Henry's own, and beyond the power of any man's imitation. The effect, however, was equal to his wishes."[50] Throughout the biography Wirt either acknowledged the absence of reliable texts or quoted a correspondent about the wording. Professor McCants summarized this position well in 1979 when he wrote: "Wirt observed sound principles of scholarship in reporting Henry's speeches. He documented his accounts and remained rigorously within the evidences supplied by his contributors, often reporting them verbatim. Only this manner of reporting Henry's speeches satisfied Wirt's requirements for veracity."[51] If Wirt wrote the "Liberty or Death" speech, it is his only ghostwriting effort in the book.

Henry's contemporaries are not helpful for determining the authenticity of the "Liberty or Death" text. William Wirt submitted the manuscript of his biography to two men who claimed to have heard Henry's 23 March 1775 speech. Neither man offered any corrections in the text. Thomas Jefferson had been asked to verify John Tyler's version of Henry's Stamp Act peroration, so Jefferson must have understood that Wirt was concerned about the accuracy of quoted texts. Yet, when he suggested revisions for the final manuscript, Jefferson had nothing to say about the "Liberty or Death" text, preferring to concentrate on details like the following: "Page 11: I think this passage had better be moderated. That Mr. Henry read Livy through once a year is a known impossibility with those who knew him. He may have read him *once,* and some general history of Greece; but certainly not twice."[52] On 23 October 1816 Wirt wrote Jefferson and asked, "Would you, as a friend, advise me to publish this book, or not?" Jefferson's response was unequivocal: "You ask if I think your work would be the better of retrenchment? By no means. I have seen nothing in it which could be retrenched but to disadvantage. And again, whether, as a friend, I would advise its publication? On that question, I have no hesitation—on your own account, as well as that of the public. To the latter, it will be valuable; and honourable to yourself."[53]

The other listener at the Richmond Convention who had an opportunity to criticize Wirt's manuscript was Judge St. George Tucker. He had only one correction related to the Richmond Convention: "P. 75. 1. 7. from the Bottom.—Qu: if the words of the Resolution be not mistaken in this line—'Some of which ARE already *expired,* and others will shortly DO SO.' I suspect 'HAVE EXPIRED' is the true reading."[54] Like Jefferson, Judge Tucker made no corrections related to the text of the "Liberty or Death" speech.

Robert Meade and Richard Beeman argue that the failure of these men to suggest changes in the text of the speech gives passive support to the accuracy of Wirt's version. Robert Meade finds the absence of suggested corrections from Thomas Jefferson to be persuasive: "Knowing Thomas Jefferson's life and writing, would one claim that he was not clear-minded in 1817? Wirt had asked him to criticize the manuscript of the Henry biography which he was about to publish. . . . Yet Jefferson did not suggest a single change in Wirt's reconstruction of the speech and called Henry the greatest orator that ever lived." A similar "passive support" argument may be found in Richard Beeman's 1974 biography of Patrick Henry.[55]

Professors Meade and Beeman may be correct, but their evidence is weak. So far as we know, Jefferson was not asked directly to verify the wording of the "Liberty or Death" speech (as he was with the Stamp Act peroration). This is also the same Jefferson who told Wirt in 1816 that publishing the book would be "honorable to yourself" and then in 1824 told Daniel Webster that it "is a poor book, written in bad taste." We shall soon examine evidence for the claim that St. George Tucker may well have been the original author of the speech text. If he was the author, it is unlikely he would suggest revisions to Wirt so long as he was quoted correctly. Both Jefferson and Tucker made their comments forty years after they heard the speech and it is extremely doubtful that either man could verify with precision the wording of an entire speech text after such a lapse of time. Finally, this argument ignores the possibility that Jefferson and/or Tucker may have offered numerous corrections to the "Liberty or Death" speech that have been lost or destroyed.

Other contemporary "verifications" are equally suspect. The secondhand account of an unnamed "old Baptist clergyman" that Henry Randall obtained described only Henry's manner of delivery and the audience effect: the report said nothing about the actual wording of the speech. Thomas Marshall's account to his son offered testimony only about the effect of Henry's address, saying nothing about the wording. Edmund Randolph's *History* described only the delivery, the audience effect, and Henry's failure to adhere to the "rules of persuasion." Randolph offered no text of the speech (or extracts), and there is no evidence that he personally heard the speech. Stories about Patrick Henry's use of a papercutter as a dramatic visual aid at the end of his speech were provided by William Fontaine and former president John Tyler. But these offer only hearsay verification of the "Give me liberty or give me death" phrase because the stories were compared, eighty-four years after Henry gave his speech, by men relying on second-, third-, and fourth-hand accounts. According to John Roane, Wirt's version of the "Liberty or Death" peroration was "often declaimed by schoolboys" as early as 1834, so Fontaine and Tyler's 1859 accounts cannot be accepted as independent authentication of the wording in Wirt's text.[56]

There is one piece of evidence, however, which is frequently cited as specific verification of the authenticity of the "Liberty or Death" speech. John Roane claimed he heard Henry deliver the speech in the Richmond Convention. In 1834, Roane (who was then more than ninety years old) supposedly "verified the correctness of the language of the speech" to Patrick Henry's great-grandson, P. H. Fontaine. Fontaine wrote the following account of the meeting:

In 1834 I visited Mr. John Roane, of King William county, Virginia, then the last surviving elector of the first President of the United States. He had represented his district in Congress more than a quarter of a century; and he was then upwards of ninety years old; but his mind was little impaired by age, and memory perfect in retaining past events. Finding that I was a descendant of Patrick Henry, he told me many anecdotes about him and interested me greatly by describing the scene in the House of Burgesses which sat in St. John's Church, Richmond, when he made his celebrated speech on his resolutions for arming the Virginia Militia. He verified the correctness of the language of the speeches, as given by Judge Tyler to Mr. Wirt. I remarked that I could not understand how that speech, eloquent as it was, could have produced the effect described by Mr. Wirt, and I supposed that the account was exaggerated. He said that it was not, and that the influence of his voice, countenance, and gestures gave force to his words; and that no description could have a proper idea of the speech, the effect of it, or of the orator to one who had never seen or heard Patrick Henry. The venerable old man, during the conversation, animated by the recollection of the sublime scene, seemed to forget his age, and in order to enable me to understand his meaning, he arose, and acted the conclusion of the speech, imitating, I have no doubt, with considerable accuracy, the voice and manner of the forest-born Demosthenes.[57]

Aside from the obvious hazards of accepting the testimony of a ninety-year-old man about the verbatim wording of a speech he had heard fifty-nine years before, Fontaine's account is unacceptable for other reasons. First, it contains substantial internal evidence that Roane did not possess a "memory perfect in retaining past events." For example, Roane was completely wrong about the body Henry addressed on 23 March 1775, and he is the only person to attribute the text to John Tyler. Second, since Roane only "acted the conclusion of the speech," one wonders if this was the only language of the speech he was expressly "verifying." Third, inasmuch as many of Roane's statements about the "Liberty or Death" speech are more compatible with the Stamp Act speech peroration, perhaps Roane had confused the two speeches. To unravel this line of reasoning, it can be observed that Roane was a member of the House of Burgesses and heard Henry's Stamp Act speech, but was not a delegate to the Richmond Convention; that the Stamp Act peroration was quite famous; that Wirt made much of the effect of Henry's Stamp Act speech; and that Judge John Tyler had written the version of the Stamp Act peroration that appeared in William Wirt's book.[58] Therefore, although at least five historians accept Roane's testimony as authenticating the wording of the "Liberty or Death" speech,[59] that testimony must be rejected as acceptable textual documentation.

Although most scholars accept either Patrick Henry or William Wirt as the originator of the "Liberty or Death" speech text, the strongest claim to authorship rests with St. George Tucker. Born in Bermuda in 1752, Tucker emigrated to Virginia as a youth and completed his education at the College of William and Mary. After a period as a practicing lawyer, he served as a professor of law at William and Mary and as a judge of the General Court before being appointed to the Court of Appeals. In 1811 he became judge of the United States District Court in Eastern Virginia, an appointment he held until his death. Two aspects of Tucker's life are particularly relevant to our purpose: (1) he claimed that he was a spectator when Patrick Henry gave his "Liberty or Death" speech; and (2) he was a close friend of William Wirt.[60]

Evidence that St. George Tucker was the source of the "Liberty or Death" speech text can be found in Wirt's book. In the preface to *Sketches of the Life and Character of Patrick Henry*, Wirt acknowledged Tucker's assistance: "The writer is indebted to judge Tucker for two or three of his best incidents; one of them will probably, be pronounced the most interesting passage of the work."[61] In making this statement, Wirt may have been referring to the "Liberty or Death" speech, which early reviewers of the book "pronounced the most interesting passage of the work." Oliver Oldschool chose it to publish in the *Port Folio*. Jared Sparks declared, "The speech he made on this occasion ["Liberty or Death"], as quoted by Mr. Wirt, is vastly the best specimen of eloquence, which we have seen among the pieces attributed to him [Henry]."[62] Since the Stamp Act peroration was already a popular "anecdote" reported by John Tyler and since Wirt secured the texts for Henry's other major speaking efforts from the transcripts of David Robertson (the Virginia Constitutional Ratification debate and the British Debt case), the "Liberty or Death" text seems to be the most likely passage for Wirt's tribute in his preface.

Turning to Wirt's presentation of the "Liberty or Death" speech, one again finds that Tucker played a guiding role. The entire text is enclosed in quotation marks—even at the beginning where it is reported in the third person. After the phrase "we must fight!! An appeal to arms and to the God of Hosts, is all that is left us!" Wirt inserted a footnote and directly identified Judge Tucker as his correspondent.[63] Unfortunately, it is unclear just what Tucker corresponded about. The placement of the acknowledgment is such that it could be construed as indicating that Tucker was responsible only for the content of the footnote that described Henry's manner of delivery. Nevertheless, Tucker is the only person acknowledged as a potential source for the speech. Some of the confusion about the citation may have been caused by publisher James Webster's decision to print the text in the way he did. Webster's format is such that it could indicate that Tucker was commenting on the text shown him by Wirt. The earlier publication of the speech in the *Port Folio* does not leave this impression. Although the *Port Folio* had footnoting capacity, it included Tucker's comments on delivery as part of the flow of the entire speech text, thus suggesting that all quoted material came from St. George Tucker.

In private correspondence dated 16 August 1815, William Wirt specifically acknowledged Tucker's influence. Wirt submitted his unpublished manuscript to Judge Tucker and wrote to the jurist: "I can tell you I have made a free use of you in this work.—Don't be startled!" In a postscript, he made clear what the use was: "I relent from my mischievous purpose of closing this letter without telling you the free use I had made of you in my biography. 1. I have drawn R. H. Lee in person and eloquence from you. 2. I have taken almost entirely, Mr Henry's speech in the convention of '75 from you, as well your description of its effect on you verbatim."[64] The "description of its effect" is the Tucker footnote. The reference to "I have taken almost entirely, Mr Henry's speech" immediately suggests that Tucker provided the text that subsequently appeared in Wirt's biography. Yet if this were the case, why did Wirt write to Judge Carr four days later, 20 August 1815, and lament that "from 1763 to 1789, covering all the bloom and pride of his life, not one of his [Henry's] speeches lives in print, writing or memory"? This apparent weakness in the argument for Tucker's authorship may be eliminated if we accept the explanation that Tucker actually gave the entire text to Wirt, but Wirt did not wish to divulge his source when he wrote to Carr. This is not an unrealistic possibility. When Wirt began collecting materials for his "famous Virginians" essays, he wrote Tucker asking for materials and essays that Tucker might make available. Along with the request for materials, Wirt made the following offer:

Nay, more; if you think proper, your name shall be kept out of the public view, and they may name me, without contradiction, as the author (for there are too many persons who have, by some means or other, got wind of my project, to suppose that it may not, at first, be imputed to me). And when their applauses become loud, general and confirmed, I will make a public disclaimer. If, by any fatality, they should not applaud, I hereby promise you that I never will disclaim. There is not much heroism in the offer,—for I know, with almost absolute certainty, that the result would be propitious. If it should, or should not, you will at least have an opportunity of seeing and hearing a fair estimate of your pen, free from the weight which it would derive from the name of the Honourable St. George Tucker, one of the Judges of the Supreme Court of Appeals of Virginia.[65]

Failing to detail Tucker's account of the Richmond Convention in the letter to Carr may have been Wirt's fulfillment of a promise made to Tucker ten years earlier.

The letter that William Wirt received from St. George Tucker detailing Henry's speech is the critical historical artifact. Unfortunately, the letter of eleven foolscap pages was lost or destroyed about 1905. Tucker's great-grandson, Henry St. George Tucker, possessed the letter at the time of the loss. Historian William Wirt Henry, however, did have access to the letter before it disappeared. He explicitly confirmed that the passage that begins " 'Mr. President,' said he, 'it is natural to man to indulge in the illusions of hope' " and concludes with " 'An appeal to arms and to the God of Hosts, is all that is left us!' " came from Tucker's letter. So at least half the speech can be directly traced to Tucker's correspondence independently from Wirt's statement to Tucker that "I have taken almost entirely, Mr Henry's speech . . . from you."[66]

Although St. George Tucker's exact contribution remains somewhat speculative, it is the primary link between Patrick Henry's 23 March 1775 speech and William Wirt's published "Liberty or Death" speech.

INTERNAL EVIDENCE

Disappointed because external data have proved inadequate, a few scholars have turned to internal kinds of data in their attempt to determine authorship of the "Liberty or Death" speech. Such efforts have consisted of a type of content analysis comparing aspects of the content of the speech with other authentic efforts by Henry. But these content analyses have also failed to produce reliable conclusions about the authenticity of the text.

Douglas Southall Freeman was one of the first scholars to use a type of content analysis in the attempt to show the speech as printed by Wirt was not authentic. As part of what he termed the "discussion of the hits and misses of some of the arguments Wirt put in the mouths of Henry and the men who opposed the resolutions," Freeman said this about the "Liberty or Death" speech: "Wirt's most serious blunder was in having Henry hint of foreign intervention to aid America if war should come. The evidence examined in this study [Freeman's seven-volume biography of George Washington] contains nothing to show that this argument was advanced in Virginia during the spring of 1775."[67] Freeman may be correct about public debate, but there is some evidence that the value of foreign aid to a colonial resistance movement was being discussed about this time. Nathaniel Pope reported to Wirt that Patrick Henry told a private gathering before the Richmond Convention: "I doubt whether we *shall* be able, *alone,* to cope with so powerful a nation [Great Britain]. But . . . where is France? Where is Spain? Where is Holland? The natural enemies of Great Britain? . . . Spain and Holland will join the confederation! Our independence will be established." Historian John Alden reports that "as early as December, 1774, Americans in London, including no doubt Arthur Lee, had hinted to a French diplomat that the colonists might be interested in French aid, in the event that their quarrel with Britain ended in military conflict.[68] Although Pope's anecdote is only hearsay evidence and private talk in London says nothing about issues discussed simultaneously in Virginia, these examples suggest that foreign intervention was a potentially relevant topic at this time. Professor Freeman may be charged with the fallacy of negative proof. He offers no affirmative evidence that Virginians were not discussing foreign intervention, and, therefore, Freeman's failure to discover evidence "that shows that this argument was advanced in Virginia during the spring of 1775" is insufficient reason to question the authenticity of the "Liberty or Death" speech.

Instead of focusing on the arguments, in his content analysis of the "Liberty or Death" speech, Louis Mallory concentrated on the general tone and style:

It is significant that the text is at first in the form of an account of the speech rather than in the form of a direct report. It is also an interesting and significant fact that this reconstructed text is rhetorically superior to that of any other of Henry's reported speeches. It has a sustained literary quality that the others do not possess. There are a conciseness, a lack of repetition, a polish, a poetic quality, beside which much of the other texts seems almost commonplace. . . .

All in all, it appears that although Wirt's version of this famous speech is not apocryphal, as has been sometimes asserted, it should be regarded as incomplete. He has taken the high points of the speech, those soaring moments when language, action, and emotion perfectly complement each other, moments that would naturally be fixed in the memory of the listener, and arranged them so as to give the impression that they alone constitute the speech. There is abundant evidence to show that Henry did not soar all the time in other speeches, and there is no reason to believe that he did so in this one.[69]

Mallory's comments are not very useful for resolving the authorship question. No speaker could ever meet the consistency requirements by which Mallory judged Henry's work. Few of Abraham Lincoln's speeches had the "sustained literary quality" of the Gettysburg Address, and Martin Luther King did not always use the poetical metaphor one finds in the "I Have a Dream" speech. If Mallory's comparative method were applied to those two speeches, we might well have to search for the William Wirt who ghosted speeches by Lincoln and King. Mallory provides no evidence to refute the possibility that perhaps the "Liberty or Death" speech was the one instance when Henry, in fact, achieved those qualities of rhetorical superiority. The history of public address is replete with instances where a person gave only one great poetic speech. Cicero's philippics at the trial of Catiline, Jesus' Sermon on the Mount, William Jennings Bryan's "Cross of Gold" speech, and Mike Mansfield's eulogy at the casket of John F. Kennedy exemplify speeches characterized by beautiful, imaginative, elevated thoughts that were never again equaled in that vein by the speaker. The method of qualitative comparisons for purposes of attributing authorship is itself suspect. Validity and reliability are both potential problems. What was Mallory measuring when he announced that a work has "polish," "poetic quality," or, worse yet, is "soaring"? Mallory's failure to define precisely his qualitative criteria leaves later critics unable to find those precise qualities either in the "Liberty or Death" text or in speeches known to be by Henry.

More recently, Norine Campbell compared specific phrases in the "Liberty or Death" text with phrasings in other Henry works in an attempt to prove textual authenticity. She found significance in the "freedom or slavery" and "chains are forged" wordings in the text: "The language and line of reasoning is certainly Henry's. One finds similar expressions in his arraignment in the Parson's Cause. His arguments against the Federal Constitution were along the same general lines: Freedom, as against 'chains and scourges.' "[70] It is difficult to think of two less discriminative variables than the occurrence or nonoccurrence of words relating to slavery and freedom in the rhetoric of a revolutionary period. These topics and terms were not unique to Henry. For example, in 1774 Thomas Jefferson described the British actions as "a deliberate and systematical plan of reducing us to slavery." The Second Continental Congress's Declaration of the Causes and Necessity of Taking Up Arms (6 July 1775) stated, "We are reduced to the alternative of Choosing an unconditional submission to the tyranny of irritated ministers or resistance by force. . . . We have counted the cost of this contest, and find nothing so dreadful as voluntary slavery."[71] The theme of "freedom" frequently occurred in such diverse works as John Dickinson's "Letters" in response to the Coercive Acts (25 May to 15 June 1774), Thomas Jefferson's *Summary View of the Rights of British America* (1774), and Joseph Galloway's *Arguments on Both Sides, &c* (1774).[72]

Although they suggest methodological alternatives to examining external, historical evidence, previous efforts at content and stylistic analysis of the "Liberty or Death" speech have produced results that are by no means definitive. A selective recourse to existing external and internal data could be used to develop a nebulous "case" for any of three persons—Patrick Henry, St. George Tucker, or William Wirt—as the actual author. Nevertheless, the preponderance of positive historical evidence strongly suggests that St. George Tucker was, in fact, the source for the text of the "Liberty or Death" speech.

Quantitative Analysis

In 1959 Bernard Mayo pronounced the "Liberty or Death" authorship dispute unsolvable when he wrote, "To the pertinent question, 'How much of it is Henry and how much is Wirt?' the historian-detective must answer that it is impossible to determine."[73] Acceptance of Mayo's conclusion is predicated on the assumptions that no new external evidence will be found and that authorship may be attributed only by historical evidence used in traditional ways. Mayo's first assumption is thus far a safe one: no primary historical artifacts have been uncovered that shed new light on the authorship. His second assumption, however, is no longer valid. Efforts of certain psychologists, linguists, statisticians, and historians, as well as researchers in communication, computer science, and political science have provided alternatives to traditional methods of establishing authorship. Working from the assumptions that every author makes use of certain distinctive stylistic features and that several of these unique stylistic features can be identified by objective means, scholars have successfully applied statistical methods in attributing authorship of doubtful texts. Such studies attempt to quantify predetermined stylistic features by methods generally referred to as "statistical stylistics" (one may also find the methods referred to as "stylistic statistics" or "linguistic stylistics").

The concept that authors incline toward unique stylistic features should not seem novel to those familiar with the literature of rhetorical theory. Aristotle thought different genres of communication had different styles. Cicero observed that "the character and tendency of eloquence in each particular age" was such that "almost every age has produced a peculiar style of speaking." Moreover, he thought individual orators develop their own distinctive styles within cultural constraints. The idea that style is individualistic does not appear only in classical writings. In his speech to the French Academy in 1753, Comte de Buffon offered this epigrammatic definition of style: "Le style est de l'homme même," or, "Style is the man himself." Thirty years later, Hugh Blair wrote, "Style is the peculiar manner in which a man expresses his conceptions by means of language." The same insistence on the individual quality of style can be found in Remy de Gourmont's 1916 definition: "Having a style means that in the midst of the language shared with others one speaks a particular, unique and inimitable dialect, which is at the same time everybody's language and the language of a single individual."[74]

Though rhetorical theorists intuitively sensed the first assumption of statistical stylistics, it was the work of mathematicians and statisticians (largely within the past hundred years) that tested and, in several instances, verified the uniqueness of authors' stylistic features. The pioneering efforts by Augustus de Morgan (1851), Thomas Mendenhall (1887, 1909), John Carroll (1938), George Yule (1939, 1944), Gustav Herdan (1955), and Frederick Mosteller and David Wallace (1964) were concerned more with developing statistical theory than with the study of language and style, but their work had important methodological implications for linguists and critics. Taking a component of language usage—"style"—which had previously been thought of in qualitative and, at times, aesthetic terms, these scholars searched for features of style that could be measured by objective, quantitative means and found that several of these measurable features could be used to discriminate one author from another.

Applying statistical methods to determine authorship requires one to adopt a limited definition of "style." The decision to count predetermined stylistic features requires that those features be unambiguously defined and that their number be predictably finite. Many definitions of "style" require quality judgments. But what we want to know about the "Liberty or Death" speech is who wrote it; we are not concerned about whether the author wrote the speech well, ill, with "propriety," force, and so on. What is important is whether an author used language in any phenomenal way that was distinctive from someone else's use of the same linguistic system. Nils Enkvist's definition of style, therefore, provides a workable focus: "The style of a text is a function of the aggregate of the ratios between the frequencies of its phonological, grammatical and lexical items, and the frequencies of the corresponding items in a contextually related norm."[75]

From the external and internal historical evidence examined

previously, we can reduce the field of possible "Liberty or Death" speech authors to three men—Patrick Henry, William Wirt, and St. George Tucker. The general method for our statistical, stylistic analysis was described by Frederick Mosteller and David Wallace as follows:

From the point of view of statistical methods, authorship problems fall into a general area called discrimination or classification problems. In these problems the task is to assign a category to an object or individual whose true category is uncertain. . . . We reduce our uncertainty about the authorship of an "unknown" essay by comparing its properties with information obtained from essays whose authorship is known.[76]

In other words, the "Liberty or Death" text will be treated as an "unknown" piece of discourse from which selected stylistic properties will be identified and compared with presumably similar properties obtained from pieces of discourse whose authors are known to be Patrick Henry, William Wirt, or St. George Tucker. To do this, we need to ask two questions. First, did one of the possible authors use language in a phenomenal manner that was distinctive from the other authors' use of the same linguistic system? And, second, how do distinctive stylistic features that are identified in texts of known authorship compare with the stylistic features of the "Liberty or Death" speech?

The first step in constructing individual linguistic behavior profiles for Henry, Wirt, and Tucker was to compile a sizable data base consisting of discourse known to have been produced by these men. The units of data were selected on the basis of three criteria: (1) the discourse must be genuine and/or authentic; (2) each unit of discourse should contain 500 words or more; and (3) the total data base for each author should approach 100,000 words or more.[77] Discourse may have been originally written or oral, but with Henry, Wirt, and Tucker we are confined to written or published artifacts of the discourse, whatever its original mode.

The total data base of words analyzed for this study was 329,450 words: 1,217 words in the "Liberty or Death" speech; 78,626 words from thirty-three texts composed by Patrick Henry; 133,890 words from twenty-nine texts composed by William Wirt; and 115,718 words from thirteen texts composed by St. George Tucker. For purposes of analysis, each author's discourse was categorized as follows: Henry—speeches, letters, all texts combined; Wirt—speeches, *Spy*, biography, all prose, all texts combined; Tucker—pamphlets, *Blackstone*, all prose, poetry, all texts combined.[78]

Details concerning the preparation of the texts for machine-readable form and a discussion of the computer programs used to convert the data into formats amenable to variable measurements may be found in appendix A. The approach to indexing the data may be of interest particularly to students who have limited storage capacity on their computer systems.

The data for this study were compiled at the Computation Center of the Pennsylvania State University using an IBM System/370 Model 165 computer. Although I wrote all the computer programs myself, there are now package programs available that could do many of the procedures used in this study. The analytical data that comes from many of the current word-processing and writing analysis programs can also provide some of this data.[79] Statistical discrimination between data groups was determined using t-tests, χ-square, and z-tests. When t-tests were used, they were two-tailed tests. Analysis of variance showed that many variables varied more when an author was compared with himself than when he was compared with another author—those kinds of variables obviously are of little value in establishing an author's stylistic "fingerprints."

Fifteen specific stylistic features were examined for each author and then compared with the same features in the "Liberty or Death" speech. Several of these variables have been used to discriminate successfully among authors in other studies.

1. Type of sentence: use of periods, exclamation marks, and question marks to achieve statement variety, express strong emotions, or raise questions. Previously used to argue that St. Paul wrote only five of the fourteen Epistles generally attributed to him.[80]

2. Mean words per sentence: average sentence length. A successful predictor of authorship in several studies, for example, authorship of works generally attributed to Plato and Aristotle.[81]

3. Mean words per verbal segment: a communicator's propensity to insert punctuation marks in writing in order to make the meaning clear or to give emphasis to particular linguistic strings.

4. Mean letters per word: average word length. Previously used to discriminate between oral and written modes of discourse by the same author.[82]

5. Rank-frequency: rank is the number of characters in a word; frequency is the number of times a word of a particular rank occurred in the text. A "characteristic curve" is established for each author. Previously used to distinguish between Shakespeare and Bacon; used to determine that Samuel Clemens was not the author of the Quintus Curtius Snodgrass letters.[83]

6. Regular type-token ratio: ratio of different words (types) to

total words (tokens). An indication of variability of vocabulary. Previously used to predict IQ level and to differentiate written and spoken language.[84]

7. Carroll type-token ratio: computes type-token ratio so as to adjust for the tendency of the ratio to vary inversely with the length of the manuscript.[85]

8. Yule's "K": A numerical value reflecting how many words were used once, twice, and so on. Another way to measure word repetitiveness. Previously used to analyze works by St. Paul and Shakespeare.[86]

9. Reading ease: Rudolph Flesch's "readability" formula.[87]

10. Preposition-token ratio: tendency to show the relation of a noun or noun equivalent to some other word in the sentence.[88]

11. Overstate-understate ratio: tendency for an author to use words that "state too strongly" versus words that "represent less strongly than truth will admit."

12. Defensive quality: (overstate words + understate words) divided by the number of tokens.

13. Qualification-token ratio: tendency to reduce statements from general to a particular or restricted form.

14. Marker words from Miller-Newman-Friedman list: unique minor-encoding habits. Words that are used frequently by one author but not another.

15. Marker words from "L-or-D": unique minor-encoding habits using words actually found in "Liberty or Death" speech.

RESULTS

Linguistic Stylistic Tests. The linguistic stylistic tests (tests 1–9) were used to examine how Patrick Henry, William Wirt, and St. George Tucker used language in its nonlexical aspect. There were only two tests that resulted in no statistical probability of Patrick Henry, William Wirt, or St. George Tucker having been the author of the "Liberty or Death" speech—type of sentence (1) and rank-frequency (5).[89] Those data groupings which were statistically significant when compared with the "Liberty or Death" speech are summarized in table 2–1 (p is the z-test probability that the data set listed is similar to the "Liberty or Death" score for that variable; p less than 0.025 was not considered to be significant).

One way to interpret the data in table 2–1 is simply to total the number of data sets for each author that were significantly close to

Table 2-1 Linguistic Stylistic Tests Indicating Potential Authorship of "Liberty
or Death" Speech:

Data Sets Significantly Close to L-or-D

Test	Henry	P	Wirt	P	Tucker	P
Words/ sentence	Speeches	.337			Poetry	.031
Words/ verbal segment	Letters	.023*	Prose	.044		
			Biography	.041		
			Spy	.038		
	All texts	.164	All texts	.063	All texts	.120
Letters/ word	Letters	.051				
RTTR	Speeches	.127	Speeches	.037	Poetry	.464
	Letters	.245	Prose	.059		
			Spy	.492		
	All texts	.326	All texts	.169	All texts	.054
CTTR	Speeches	.433	Speeches	.375	*Blackstone*	.033
	Letters	.472				
	All texts	.409	All texts	.061	All texts	.082
Yule's "K"	Speeches	.284	Speeches	.069		
	Letters	.258	Prose	.064		
			Spy	.125		
	All texts	.274	All texts	.064	All texts	.209
Readability					Poetry	.030

*This data set was included because of the weak validity of the words/verbal segment measurement relative to the
oral texts used in this study.

the "Liberty or Death" speech. The results for such a summation
are Henry, 13; Wirt, 14; Tucker, 8. Henry's total is particularly
noteworthy because this kind of summation stacks the data against
him. For each test, Henry had only three chances (speeches, letters,
and all texts) while Tucker and Wirt each had five chances.

A second way to categorize the data is to count the number
of tests in which each author had at least one data set statistically
close to the "Liberty or Death" speech. The highest score an
author could achieve by this method would be seven. The score
for each author is Henry, 6; Wirt, 4; and Tucker, 6. Both Henry
and Tucker were significantly close to the "Liberty or Death"
speech in 86 percent of the tests; Wirt was significantly close in
only 57 percent of the tests.

A third way to classify the significant data sets is to identify the number of tests in which at least one author was significantly close to the "Liberty or Death" speech, but in which at least one other author had no data sets that were significantly close (for example, the words-per-sentence variable). This kind of classification indicates only those tests that proved to discriminate among potential authors. The summation for this is Henry, 2; Wirt, 0; Tucker, 2. This result is particularly important because it shows that there were no tests in which William Wirt's discourse was significantly close to the "Liberty or Death" speech when *both* Patrick Henry and St. George Tucker were not also close to the "Liberty or Death" speech.

Although several data sets may be significantly close to the "Liberty or Death" speech when z-score significance is set at the $p >$ 0.025 level, when we examine the value of the probability scores it is obvious that some data sets are much closer to the "Liberty or Death" speech than are others. For example, using the regular type-token ratio test (RTTR), Wirt's *Spy* letters are close to the "Liberty or Death" speech at the 0.492 level, yet his speeches are close at only the 0.037 level. To compensate for this disparity, we may count the number of data sets for each author that constituted either the first or second closest set when compared to the "Liberty or Death" speech for each test. For example, in the Carroll type-token ratio test (CTTR), Henry's speeches and letters were the two data sets closest to the "Liberty or Death" speech; so Henry's total would be increased by two, and the other authors' totals would remain constant. The results for the number of data sets in the top two ranking by each author are Henry, 7; Wirt, 1; Tucker, 4.

From linguistic stylistic tests, therefore, we may draw the following three general conclusions.

First, comparing the normative linguistic stylistic features in works of known authorship with the same features in the "Liberty or Death" speech, we may rank the three author's stylistic profiles from most similar to the "Liberty or Death" speech to least similar to that speech as follows: Patrick Henry, St. George Tucker, William Wirt. No matter how we categorize the data, the significant linguistic stylistic tests show that the "Liberty or Death" speech is similar in style to Henry's other communications. The allegation by some scholars that considerable "stylistic" differences exist between the "Liberty or Death" speech and Henry's other speeches does not comport with the quantitative evidence we have examined so far.

Second, the great difference between the linguistic stylistic test scores for the "Liberty or Death" speech and Wirt's biography of Henry on almost all tests strongly suggests that the two works were not written by the same author. Claude Brinegar compares quantitative stylistic tests to "the blood test in a paternity case—a test that by itself can exonerate but cannot convict."[90] If Wirt wrote the "Liberty or Death" speech, he substantially altered most of the linguistic stylistic features of his writing that he exhibited in the rest of the biography of Henry. Even if he deliberately tried to imitate Henry's speaking style as reported by Robertson and if he completely succeeded, Wirt's ghostwritten speech would be incompatible with the "Liberty or Death" speech on three of the seven significant linguistic stylistic variables. In any event, the quantitative results reported here suggest the need for modification of the resolute conclusion by scholars such as Moses Coit Tyler, Louis Mallory, Bernard Mayo, and Daniel Boorstin that William Wirt wrote the "Liberty or Death" speech.

The third general conclusion is that the tests of these variables support the hypothesis that St. George Tucker, imitating Patrick Henry's style as he remembered it, wrote the "Liberty or Death" speech and William Wirt then published Tucker's account. Tucker's linguistic stylistic profile is a close second to that of Henry when discriminating variables are compared with the "Liberty or Death" speech; Tucker could use the same style he used in other works and produce the "Liberty or Death" speech's linguistic stylistic scores on six of the seven significant variables. It is somewhat ironic that the first publisher of the "Liberty or Death" speech, Oliver Oldschool, was correct when he wrote that Henry was treated with "the enthusiasm of the poet." It was the poetry of St. George Tucker, not Wirt's prose in the *Sketches of the Life and Character of Patrick Henry*, which comes closer to the linguistic stylistic features of the "Liberty or Death" speech.

Word-Category Tests. With the word-category tests (tests 10–13) we begin to consider tests in which the function of a word in a sentence —its meaning—does make a difference. Four linguistic categories were examined: one grammatical category—prepositions; and three semantic categories—overstate-understate words, defensive quality, and physical qualifiers.[91] Those data groupings that were statistically significant when compared with the "Liberty or Death" speech are summarized in table 2–2 (p is the z-test probability; p less than 0.025 was not considered to be significant).

The word-category tests are not particularly useful for establishing probable authorship of the "Liberty or Death" speech. One test (overstate-understate ratio) showed that Henry's speeches, Wirt's

Table 2-2 Word-Category Tests Indicating Potential Authorship of "Liberty or Death" Speech:
Data Sets Significantly Close to L-or-D

Test	Henry	P	Wirt	P	Tucker	P
Preposition/	Speeches	.386	Speeches	.397		
token	Letters	.045	Prose	.033		
	All texts	.295	All texts	.115	All texts	.152
Overstate/	Speeches	.378	Speeches	.033	Pamphlets	.053
understate	Letters	.201	Prose	.337	Poetry	.330
			Biography	.179		
			Spy	.488		
	All texts	.500	All texts	.496	All texts	.064
Defensive	Speeches	.093	Prose	.055	Pamphlets	.066
quality			Biography	.121	Blackstone	.108
					Poetry	.330
	All texts	.062	All texts	.054	All texts	.192
Qualification/	Speeches	.496	Speeches	.429	Pamphlets	.084
token	Letters	.316	Spy	.026	Poetry	.440
					Prose	.031
	All texts	.409	All texts	.171	All texts	.085

Spy, and Tucker's poetry were all close to the ratio for the "Liberty or Death" speech; therefore, this test was not a useful discriminator. From the remaining tests, two relevant conclusions should be emphasized. First, in two of the tests (preposition-token ratio and qualification-token ratio) the scores of William Wirt's biography of Patrick Henry are conspicuously different from the scores of the "Liberty or Death" speech. Second, in instances where there is clear discrimination, St. George Tucker emerges as the most likely candidate. His poetry is closest to the "Liberty or Death" speech in terms of defensive quality; considering only written modes of communication, Tucker's poetry is also closest to the "Liberty or Death" speech using the qualification-token ratio.

Marker Word Tests.   Marker word tests (tests 14 and 15) attempt to distinguish between a communicator's *potential* vocabulary and his *probable* vocabulary. A communicator encodes a message by selecting elements from a symbol system and arranging them in a pattern. When the symbol system is large (like the English language), the communicator may potentially select from an immense number of different elements (words). Yet measurements such as the type-token ratios show that communicators tend to select a relatively small number of words initially and then use them again and again. Although type-token ratios may vary among communicators, the number of unique words selected (types) is almost always small when compared with the total words (tokens) used in a particular message. This phenomenon led William Paisley to draw a useful distinction between a communicator's *potential* vocabulary and his *probable* vocabulary.

> *Encoding* is a process of selecting from what is available. Availability should be qualified in terms of the potential and the probable. Every writer has a potential vocabulary at least as large as all words found in all dictionaries plus all the neologisms his imagination can furnish. By comparison, his probabilities of use are very disparate. In extemporaneous speech, 50 most-used words make up half of all his utterances. His 500th most-used word is likely to occur only once in a string of 10,000 words.[92]

Theoretically, Patrick Henry, William Wirt, and St. George Tucker had essentially the same potential vocabulary from which to select the words they used. Ignoring neologisms,[93] we can define their potential symbol system as primarily all the words in the English language at the time they communicated and secondarily all the words in the Latin language (because all three men either quoted from the classics in Latin or used Latin phrases in their discourse). Obviously, the topic of each piece of discourse will constrain both the initial selection and frequency of occurrence of many contextual words. For example, one would expect the word *court* to occur frequently in Tucker's "Summary View of the Judicial Courts of the Commonwealth, and of the United States, in Virginia," yet *court* would be unlikely to occur in Henry's letter to his daughter discussing a wife's responsibilities in marriage.

Although some selection behaviors appear to be conscious, others are not prominent (and thus are unlikely to be imitated) and appear to be executed mechanically. Marker word tests seek to determine whether word selection is constrained not only by topic, but also by behavioral norms that may distinguish Henry, Wirt, and Tucker regardless of the topic about which they are communicating. Marker word tests have been the most productive kind of authorship measurement in recent scholarly studies, and the results of this kind of test are now accepted as evidence in the British courts for verifying confessions.[94]

Probably the best demonstration to date of the discrimination achieved by "minor encoding habits" is the study of *The Federalist* done by Frederick Mosteller and David Wallace. They looked for words in works of known authorship that distinguished Hamilton and Madison. For example, Hamilton uses *while* and Madison in a corresponding situation uses *whilst*.[95] These marker words were tested for low variance within an author's works and high variance between the works of two authors. Once a marker word profile was constructed for Hamilton and Madison from known works, the profile for each was compared with the twelve "disputed" *Federalist* papers. Using the Bayesian method for calculating odds from these discriminations and using high-speed computers for many hours to make the calculations, Mosteller and Wallace were able to attribute all the disputed papers to Madison.

The first marker word test in this "Liberty or Death" authorship study used the list of "function" words compiled by Miller, Newman, and Friedman.[96] Function words are defined as those words traditionally called articles, prepositions, pronouns, numbers, conjunctions, and auxiliary verbs. The Miller-Newman-Friedman list of 363 function words is a useful starting point because the words selected are context-free and the set of function words is more resistant to innovation than is a set of content words.[97]

Three basic steps were used to identify marker words. First, the authors were paired. The marker words were words that distinguish Henry-Wirt, Henry-Tucker, Wirt-Tucker and not words that necessarily distinguish one author from *both* of the other two. Second, for each of the three author pairings a list was constructed of all words that mark one author over the other *and* occur at least once in the "Liberty or Death" speech. Third, a word was defined as a marker word if one of the three following criteria was met: (1) if a word does not occur in any of one author's texts, it must occur in 20 percent or more of the other author's texts; (2) if a word occurs in from 1 to 10 percent of one author's texts, it must occur in 40 percent or more of the other author's texts; (3) if the word occurs in 11 percent or more of one author's texts, the other author's percentage must be 30 percent or more greater for the word to be a marker word.

My analysis of the data used an approach similar in assumptions to Mosteller and Wallace. This study, however, did not use the complicated Bayesian analysis for computing probability. Instead, it used the basic probability equation where the probability $P(Ei)$ of a simple event Ei will be defined as a nonnegative number associated with a point Ei of sample space such that $P(E1) + P(E2) + \ldots P(En) = 1$, where the total number of points in the sample space is n. Although this looks complicated, this is the formula that tells a coin flipper that the odds of getting heads are 1:2 and the formula that tells a die thrower that the odds of getting the number five are 1:6. Odds that one of the paired authors was more likely to have written the "Liberty or Death" speech were computed by taking the ratio of one author's marker words probability to the other author's marker words probability. We would get high odds with other methods, too, but this approach is sufficient to clearly show authorship probability with the three authors compared in this study.

The examination of marker words from the Miller-NewmanFriedman function word list begins with the Henry-Wirt comparison. Sixty-one words from the list may be identified as marker words for Henry or Wirt.[98] Of these sixty-one words, seventeen occurred at least once in the "Liberty or Death" speech. Fifteen of the seventeen words were Wirt markers ($p= .88$); two were Henry markers ($p= .12$). In terms of probable vocabulary, the odds are 7.3 to 1 in favor of Wirt.

Patrick Henry fares even worse when we compare him with St. George Tucker. One hundred and nine words from the Miller-Newman-Friedman list may be defined as marker words for either Henry or Tucker.[99] Of these 109 marker words, twenty-nine occurred at least once in the "Liberty or Death" speech. Twenty-seven of the "Liberty or Death" markers were Tucker markers ($p= .93$); two markers were Henry markers ($p= .07$). In terms of probable vocabulary, the odds are 13.3 to 1 in favor of Tucker.

In terms of the function words that were marker words and that were also in the "Liberty or Death" speech, William Wirt beats Patrick Henry and St. George Tucker beats Henry. But how do Wirt and Tucker compare? Fifty-two words from the list were either Wirt or Tucker markers.[100] Eleven of those fifty-two words were in the "Liberty or Death" speech. Nine marked Tucker ($p= .82$); only two marked Wirt ($p= .18$). This gives odds of 4.5 to 1 in favor of Tucker.

The marker words from the Miller-Newman-Friedman list that also occur in the "Liberty or Death" speech show two definite patterns: (1) when Patrick Henry is compared with either of the other two authors, his vocabulary is less probable for the authorship of the "Liberty or Death" speech; and (2) when St. George Tucker is compared with the other authors, in every instance his function word vocabulary is more probable for authorship of the "Liberty or Death" speech.

The second general marker word test is to take the 462 unique words in the "Liberty or Death" speech as the initial word list and then use the marker word identification process described previously. One immediately disturbing piece of information shown by the initial search is that although the study identified 328,233 instances of

Henry, Wirt, and Tucker selecting words from their symbol systems (total words in the texts of known authorship), there are fifteen words in the "Liberty or Death" speech that none of the three authors ever used. The words are *basely, clanking, comports, disloyalty, forged, fulfil, hugging, implements, inviolate, irresolution, resounding, supinely, siren, temporal,* and *toward.* Nevertheless, the remaining words in the "Liberty or Death" speech do enable us to draw some firm conclusions about probable vocabulary for the three men.

The first comparison is between Patrick Henry and William Wirt. A total of fifty-seven words in the "Liberty or Death" speech mark the two authors. Of the fifty-seven markers, fifty-one mark Wirt ($p=$ .895) and six mark Henry ($p=$ .105). This gives odds of about 8.5 to 1 in favor of the vocabulary being more typical of Wirt than Henry.[101]

The comparison of Henry and Tucker is overwhelmingly in favor of Tucker. A total of eighty-nine words mark the two authors. Of the eighty-nine markers, eighty-five distinguish Tucker ($p=$ .955) and only four distinguish Henry ($p=$ .045). This gives comparative odds of probable vocabulary of 21.2 to 1 in favor of St. George Tucker.[102] The final marker word comparison is between William Wirt and St. George Tucker. A total of fifty-one words mark Wirt or Tucker. Seven of the fifty-one words distinguish Wirt ($p=$ .137); forty-four markers distinguish Tucker ($p=$ .863). So, in the comparison of the two men, each of whom scored considerably higher than Patrick Henry in terms of probable vocabulary, St. George Tucker is more probable than Wirt by the rate of 6.29 to 1.[103]

The final general marker word test measures normative patterns for the rate of occurrence of vocabulary. This adjusts for the difference in initial data bases among the three authors. It is more fair to Henry because the first two tests require him to use words in more texts to score high percentages and he made fewer total word selections than the other two authors. For each word that is a marker word for an author pair, the rate of occurrence (rate per 100 words) of that word in the texts of known authorship for each author was compared with the rate per 100 in the "Liberty or Death" speech. Using the rate-of-occurrence method, the odds that the vocabulary usage in the "Liberty or Death" speech are more typical of one author than the other are as follows: Henry-Wirt, 4.18 to 1 in favor of Wirt; Henry-Tucker, 3.45 to 1 in favor of Tucker; Wirt-Tucker, 5.38 to 1 in favor of Tucker.

On the basis of every marker word test (tests that are the most likely to expose attempted imitation), we may conclude that the vocabulary of the "Liberty or Death" speech is most typical of St. George Tucker's encoding norms.

Conclusion

Patrick Henry probably gave a speech on 23 March 1775 in St. John's Church to support his resolutions placed before the Virginia Convention. In that speech, he may well have spoken the phrase, "Give me liberty, or give me death." There is, however, no contemporary evidence to verify the wording of the speech. No stenographic notes were taken of the speech; Patrick Henry left no written account of the speech; no text of the "Liberty or Death" speech appeared during Henry's lifetime; and men who claimed to have heard the speech testified about the wording of the speech only after an account appeared in William Wirt's *Sketches of the Life and Character of Patrick Henry* (1816–17).

Scholars who have struggled with the question "Who really composed the text of the 'Liberty or Death' speech?" have generally sided with either Patrick Henry or William Wirt as the probable author. The attachment to Henry as the author appears more grounded in sentimental wishing than in historical fact. There is virtually no existing historical evidence that suggests that the wording of this speech is an authentic "transcript" of what Patrick Henry said on 23 March 1775. The claim for William Wirt as author is also suspect. Although the text of the "Liberty or Death" speech first appeared in the biography of Patrick Henry written by William Wirt, there is serious doubt that he composed the words of the speech. He did not ghostwrite other speeches for his biography of Henry and there is no evidence to indicate that he made an exception for this speech.

The preponderance of positive historical evidence strongly leads to the conclusion that St. George Tucker was the source for the text of the "Liberty or Death" speech. In a private letter dated 16 August 1815, William Wirt wrote to Judge Tucker, "I have taken almost entirely, Mr. Henry's speech in the convention of '75 from you." Additional evidence of Tucker's authorship may be found in Wirt's biography of Henry, including the preface and the footnotes concerning the "Liberty or Death" speech itself. St. George Tucker probably composed the text sometime between 31 January 1805 (when William Wirt requested from Tucker detailed information about Henry's eloquence) and 16 August 1815 (when Wirt thanked Tucker for providing details of Henry's speech at the Richmond Convention).

The computerized, quantitative analysis confirms St. George Tucker's authorship. The results of the linguistic stylistic tests and the marker word tests indicate that Tucker, imitating Patrick Henry's style as he remembered it, wrote the "Liberty or Death" speech and William Wirt then published Tucker's account.

The significant linguistic stylistic tests show that the "Liberty or Death" speech *is* similar in style to Henry's other communications. St. George Tucker, however, could use the same style he used in other works and produce the "Liberty or Death" speech's linguistic stylistic scores on six of the seven significant variables. The great difference between the linguistic stylistic test scores for the "Liberty or Death" speech and William Wirt's biography of Henry strongly suggests that the two works were not written by the same author.

On the basis of every marker word test, we may conclude that St. George Tucker is the most likely author to have written the "Liberty or Death" speech. Using the "Liberty or Death" vocabulary list, for example, the odds are 21.25 to 1 that Tucker wrote the speech, not Henry; the odds are 6.29 to 1 that Tucker wrote the speech, not Wirt. It does not matter whether we use the independent Miller-Newman-Friedman function word list or the actual vocabulary of the "Liberty or Death" speech, whether we identify marker words using the "at least once per text" counting method or the "rate of occurrence of the word" method—the vocabulary of the "Liberty or Death" speech is most typical of St. George Tucker.

So, who wrote the "Liberty or Death" speech? The preponderance of both historical and quantitative evidence presented in this study supports the claim that St. George Tucker was the composer of the "Liberty or Death" text. Unless substantive evidence can be found to refute that claim, one must conclude that the text of the "Liberty or Death" speech ought to be analyzed, interpreted, and criticized as a piece of early nationalist-period rhetoric, not as a piece of American revolutionary rhetoric.

Appendix A

After the texts were selected, they had to be encoded in machine-readable form (typed for computer processing). For the most part, the texts were typed exactly as they appeared in the original version. Exceptions included things like editorial comments written by others but appearing with the text, quotations, tables of contents, and so forth. The encoding conventions (typing instructions) for the texts were deliberately kept as simple as possible. This allows for faster text preparation, fewer encoder errors, and more reliable editing of the texts. The computer can be programmed to read the data accurately and make appropriate decoding decisions more easily than a typist can be trained to remember complicated encoding rules after five hours of typing!

Three programs were used to convert the textual data into formats amenable to variable measurements. The first program picked off words and did some other initial housekeeping. The second and third programs, modifications of John B. Smith's Random-Accessible Text System (RATS),[104] took the data and then arranged and stored the data in indexed files appropriate for the later variable measurements. Two data sets linked by pointers were created. The first data set, DICTIONARY, is a type file in which each unique word is listed alphabetically along with its frequency of occurrence and author designator letter (H, T, or W), and a pointer to the second file. A printout of this file with one record per line and spacing between record entries would look like this for the first five words of text in Henry's second ratification debate speech:

POINTER	FREQUENCY	AUTHOR	WORD
1	2	H	&C
3	1	H	'TIS
4	146	H	A
150	2	H	ABANDON
152	1	H	ABANDONED

The second data set, DATA, was a token data set of index information for each occurrence of each word in the text arranged in alphabetical order by word. Each record contained only numerical data indicating for each respective word that word's linear order number, the word's position in the sentence where it was found, and the length of that word. If printed, a DATA record might look like this: 1265410213. In this example, the word is the 12,654th word in the text; it is the 102d word in the sentence; and the word is 13 letters long. In order to reduce storage space, the word itself is not included in the DATA record; the pointer in the DICTIONARY file serves as the cross reference linking the DICTIONARY and DATA files.

The initial computer programs required considerable amounts of computer processing time, but once the DICTIONARY and DATA files were stored, subsequent analytic steps were very efficient. This may be demonstrated with two examples. First, suppose we wish to know whether Patrick Henry used the word *abandoned* in his second ratification debate speech. We could search the text word-by-word in linear order. If Henry never used *abandoned* in that speech, we would look at 8,105 words before we knew he never used the word. If we took a different approach and listed every word in the text in alphabetical order, we would have to examine 151 words (including 146 occurrences of *a*) before we discovered that Henry did use the word *abandoned.* With the RATS system, however, we need only retrieve the DICTIONARY file for text Henry 2 (which serves like a concordance), examine five records, and conclude that Henry used the word in that speech.

A second example illustrates the processing efficiency issue from a different perspective. Suppose we wish to know the mean letters-per-word in Henry's second ratification debate speech. We could count the number of letters as they occur sequentially (37,688), count the number of words (8,105), and divide the number of letters by the number of words—a total of 45,794 steps. (This, by the way, is exactly how the early scholars researching linguistic stylistics collected their data; it is little wonder that these studies took years to complete!) A more efficient alternative is to retrieve the DATA file for the text in question, compute the sum of the letters-per-word columns in each record, and divide by the number of records—a total of 8,106 steps. We can see from these two examples how the RATS system allows the researcher to store large volumes of data and then retrieve only those portions of the data that are appropriate for the particular analysis.

Notes

1. P. H. Fontaine, "New Facts in Regard to the Character and Opinions of Patrick Henry," *De Bow's Review* 7–8 (October 1870): 317.

2. Robert T. Oliver, *History of Public Speaking in America* (Boston: Allyn and Bacon, 1965), 62.

3. The text of the "Liberty or Death" speech was first published in William Wirt, "Legislature of Virginia. Debate on the motion offered by Patrick Henry, esq. in the year 1775, to put the colony of Virginia in a state of defence," *Port Folio*, 4th ser., 2 (December 1816): 460–68. The text was more widely circulated in the next year with the publication of William Wirt, *Sketches of the Life and Character of Patrick Henry* (Philadelphia: James Webster, 1817), 119–23.

4. Rt. Rev. Lewis W. Burton, "History of St. John's Church," in *Annals of Henrico Parish, Diocese of Virginia, and especially of St. John's Church, The Present Mother Church of the Parish, From 1611 to 1884,* ed. Josiah S. Moore (Richmond: Williams Printing, 1904), 24.

5. Peter Force, ed., *American Archives: Fourth Series, Containing A Documentary History of the English Colonies in North America, from the King's Message to Parliament, of March 7, 1774, to the Declaration Of Independence by the United States,* 6 vols. (Washington: M. St. Clair Clarke and Peter Force, 1837–46), 2: 165–68 (hereafter cited as 4 Am. Arch. There were 121 delegates elected to the convention by sixty-four county and city voting districts.

Although he was not an elected delegate, John Tazewell was elected clerk of the convention on 20 March 1775 (the first day of the convention), and I therefore included him in the total of participating members at the convention.

6. Wirt, *Henry*, 24. The description is that of Thomas Marshall, a delegate to the convention from Fauquier County, as reported to his nineteen-year-old son, John. The chief justice sent his father's description of Patrick Henry's speech to William Wirt after Wirt had sent his manuscript to the publisher, but before the first edition was actually printed. See also Leonard Baker, *John Marshall: A Life in Law* (New York: Macmillan, 1974), 25–26.

7. The first was the August 1774 convention held in Williamsburg to select delegates for the First Continental Congress.

8. Lord Dunmore dissolved the assembly on 26 May 1774 after learning it had passed a resolution setting aside 1 June 1774 as a day of "fasting, humiliation and prayer" in response to the British Coercive Acts. Lord Dunmore had summoned the assembly to meet on 11 August 1774, but prorogued it to 3 November. He continued postponing the session, first until 7 November, then to 10 November, and again until 1 February 1775. On 19 January 1775 Dunmore prorogued the assembly until the first Thursday in September 1775, but changed his mind on 12 May 1775 and called a meeting for 1 June 1775. The 1–24 June 1775 session of burgesses was the last to conduct business as an official Virginia colonial legislature. John Pendleton Kennedy, ed., *Journals of the House of Burgesses of Virginia 1773–1776. Including the records of the Committee of Correspondence* (Richmond: Colonial Pr., 1905), 132, 165–71, 283.

9. *Virginia Gazette* (John Pinkney), 26 January 1775, p. 3; The notice also appeared two days later in Dixon and Hunter's *Virginia Gazette*, 28 January 1775, p. 3; Peyton Randolph, the president of the August 1774 extralegal convention, sent the notice dated 20 January 1775 to Pinkney to print, but, as the newspaper publishing dates show, there was a one week delay before the notice appeared publicly.

10. Douglas Southall Freeman, *George Washington: A Biography*, vol. 3, *Planter and Patriot* (New York: Scribner's, 1951), 403.

11. Records of the convention's elections, appointments, and proceedings may be found in *4 Am. Arch.* 2: 165–72.

12. Burton, "St. John's Church," 21.

13. *4 Am. Arch.* 2: 167; Robert Douthat Meade, *Patrick Henry: Practical Revolutionary* (Philadelphia and New York: Lippincott, 1969), 22 (hereafter cited as Meade, *Henry* 2).

14. Burton stated that Patrick Henry "stood, according to tradition, near the present corner of the east transept and the nave, or more exactly, as it is commonly stated, in pew 47, in the east aisle of the nave, the third one from the transept aisle. He . . . faced the eastern wall of the transept. . ."; Burton, "St. John's Church," 23–24. A few historians have suggested that Henry's resolutions were not discrete resolutions, but were amendments to the Jamaica Petition resolutions. William Wirt Henry appears to be the originator of the amendment theory (William Wirt Henry, *Patrick Henry: Life, Correspondence, and Speeches*, 3 vols. [New York: Scribner's, 1891], 1: 257), and a recent biographer of Henry continued that interpretation (Meade, *Henry* 2: 28). Since the convention was operating under "the same rules and orders as are established in the House of Burgesses in this Colony," Peyton Randolph should have ruled Henry's resolutions as "out of order" if they were offered as amendments to the Jamaica Petition resolutions because they were not germane to the main motion before the convention. While unacceptable as amendments, Henry's resolutions would have been proper as a main motion.

15. Wirt, *Henry*, 119–23.

16. Wirt, *Henry*, 123–24.

17. Henry, *Henry* 1: 270.

18. Henry, *Henry* 1: 258.

19. *4 Am. Arch.* 2: 167–68; James Parker to Charles Steuart, 6 April 1775, quoted in A. Francis Steuart, "Letters from Virginia. 1774–1781," *The Magazine of History with Notes and Queries* 3 (March 1906): 158. James Parker was a merchant in Norfolk, Virginia. Unless new delegates were admitted to the convention but not recorded in the official proceedings, the 65–60 vote is incorrect because there were only 121 delegates. Parker provided his friend in England, Charles Steuart, with an unflattering description of Patrick Henry and his speech:

You never heard anything more infamously insolent than P. Henry's speech: he called the K——— a Tyrant, a fool, a puppet and a tool to the ministry. Said there was no Englishmen, no Scots, no Britons, but a set of wretches sunk in Luxury, they had lost their native courage and (were) unable to look the brave Americans in the face. . . . This Creature is so infatuated, that he goes about I am told, praying and preaching amongst the common people.

20. Bernard Mayo, *Myths and Men: Patrick Henry, George Washington, Thomas Jefferson* (Athens: Univ. of Georgia Pr., 1959; New York: Harper, Harper Torchbooks, 1963), 14. Although topped by the 61 percent who knew that Mae West said, "Come up and see me sometime," Henry fared better than Lincoln, Wilson, and the two Roosevelts in the public's identification of famous quotations from our history.

21. *Virginia Gazette* (John Pinkney), 30 March 1775, pp. 2–3; *Virginia Gazette* (Dixon and Hunter), 1 April 1775, pp. 2–3.

22. *4 Am. Arch.* 2: 516.

23. *Journal of the House of Burgesses 1773–1776*, 231–37.

24. *Virginia Gazette* (Alexander Purdie), 29 September 1775, p. 3; Philip Slaughter, "History of St. Mark's Parish," pt. 1, p. 47, and pt. 2, pp. 2–3, quoted in Baker, *Marshall*, 26–27. The motto "Liberty or Death" was not adopted by all the Virginia military companies. The Hanover Committee, for example, ordered that all its militia "tents, kettles, canteens, drums, fifes, and colours" be painted with the following motto on the side—"Virginia for Constitutional Liberty." *Virginia Gazette* (Alexander Purdie), 29 September 1775, p. 3.

25. William Wirt, "Legislature of Virginia. Debate on the motion offered by Patrick Henry, esq. in the year 1775, to put the colony of Virginia in a state of defence," *Port Folio*, 4th ser., 2 (December 1816): 460–68.

26. Jay B. Hubbell, *The South in American Literature, 1607–1900* (Durham, N. C.: Duke Univ. Pr., 1954), 240.

27. George Ticknor Curtis, *Life of Daniel Webster*, 2 vols., 3d ed. (New York: Appleton, 1870), 1: 585.

28. Norine Dickson Campbell, *Patrick Henry: Patriot and Statesman* (New York: Devin-Adair, 1969), 12n.11; Hubbell, *The South*, 240.

29. Campbell, *Henry*, 12; Robert Meade, *Patrick Henry: Patriot in the Making* (Philadelphia and New York: Lippincott, 1957), 50 (hereafter cited as Meade, *Henry* 1).

30. John P. Kennedy, *Memoirs of the Life of William Wirt, Attorney-General of the United States*, 2 vols., new and rev. ed. (Philadelphia: Lea and Blanchard, 1850), 2: 34. Wirt himself kept careful notice of criticisms and compliments and wrote to his wife, "I am quite ashamed of the magnificent eulogies which they are sounding here [Washington] on my talents, accomplishments, and all that; and in Philadelphia, the rapturous encomiums which they are bestowing on my book." William Wirt to Mrs. Wirt, 20 November 1817, in Kennedy, *Wirt* 2: 33.

31. See, for example, Jared Sparks, *North American Review* 6 (March 1818): 293–324; *Analectic Magazine* 10 (December 1817): 441–70; "P," *American Monthly Magazine* 2 (April 1818): 412–27; Oliver Oldschool, *Port Folio*, 4th ser., 2 (December 1816): 460; *Port Folio*, 5th ser., 4 (December 1817): 520–23; and *Virginia Evangelical and Literary Magazine* 1 (January, February, March 1818): 27–36, 74–80, 124–28.

32. Moses Coit Tyler, *Patrick Henry* (Boston: Houghton, Mifflin, 1898; Ithaca: Cornell Univ. Pr., Great Seal Books, 1962), iv.

33. Hugh Blair Grigsby, *The Virginia Convention of 1775. A discourse delivered before the Virginia Alpha of the Phi Beta Kappa society, in the chapel of William and Mary college, in the city of Williamsburg, on the afternoon of July 3rd, 1855* (Richmond: J.W. Randolph, 1855), 150. It is interesting to note the selective way in which Grigsby's footnote has been quoted. Moses Tyler, for example, quoted "much of the speech published by Wirt is apocryphal" (Tyler, *Henry*, 149). Robert Meade preferred a paraphrase: "it is not surprising that so friendly a critic as Hugh Blair Grigsby should state a half century after publication of Wirt's biography that 'much' of Wirt's text for the speech was 'apocryphal' " (Meade, *Henry* 2: 38). Neither historian included the beginning of the actual sentence: "Although it may well be doubted that . . ."

34. Judy Hample, "The Textual and Cultural Authenticity of Patrick Henry's 'Liberty or Death' Speech," *Quarterly Journal of Speech* 63 (October 1977).

35. David McCants, "The Authenticity of William Wirt's Version of Patrick Henry's 'Liberty or Death' Speech," *The Virginia Magazine of History and Biography* 87 (October 1979).

36. William Wirt, *The Letters of the British Spy* (Richmond: Samuel Pleasants, Junior, 1803); Kennedy, *Wirt* 1: 106, 119; Hubbell, *The South*, 237.

37. William Wirt to Dabney Carr, 8 June 1804, in Kennedy, *Wirt* 1: 116.

38. William Wirt to Thomas Jefferson, 18 January 1810, in Kennedy, *Wirt* 1: 251.

39. Wirt, *Henry*, vi–x; William Wirt to Dabney Carr, 9 August 1817, in Kennedy, *Wirt* 2: 23.

40. William Wirt to St. George Tucker, 31 January 1805, in Kennedy, *Wirt* 1: 121.

41. William Wirt to Thomas Jefferson, in Kennedy, *Wirt* 1: 302.

42. William Wirt to Dabney Carr, 12 January 1816, in Kennedy, *Wirt* 1: 352.

43. St. George Tucker to William Wirt, 4 April 1813, in Kennedy, *Wirt* 1: 316.

44. William Wirt to Dabney Carr, 20 August 1815, in Kennedy, *Wirt* 1: 345.

45. William Wirt to Dabney Carr, 12 January 1816, in Kennedy, *Wirt* 1: 352; The first three sections (chapters) of the manuscript were finished by 24 August 1816. Section 1 contains Wirt's account of Henry's speech in the Parson's Cause; section 2 contains Wirt's account of the Stamp Act debate. Additional portions of the book were completed about September 1816, and the final sheets of the "Sketches of Mr. Henry" were written by 23 October 1816. William Wirt to Thomas Jefferson, 24 August 1816, in Kennedy, *Wirt* 1: 361, and William Wirt to Thomas Jefferson, 23 October 1816, in Kennedy, *Wirt* 1: 363.

46. A strong, recent argument for this position may be found in Hample, "Textual and Cultural Authenticity."

47. William Wirt to Judge Carr, 20 August 1815, in Kennedy, *Wirt* 1: 345.

48. Wirt, *Henry*, 27–28; Wirt's treatment of the Parson's Cause speech is in Wirt, *Henry*, 19–31.

49. Wirt, *Henry*, 56–67; The only conflicting account of the wording of Henry's peroration was discovered in the archives of the Service Hydrographique de la Marine at Paris. An eyewitness account by a French traveler verified the "Caesar had his Brutus, Charles his Cromwell" wording, but added that Henry later apologized for the tone of his remarks. "Journal of a French Traveller in the Colonies, 1765, I," *American Historical Review* 26 (July 1921): 745.

50. Wirt, *Henry*, 139.

51. McCants, "Authenticity," 393.

52. Thomas Jefferson to William Wirt, 4 September 1816, in Kennedy, *Wirt* 1: 362.

53. William Wirt to Thomas Jefferson, 23 October 1816, in Kennedy, *Wirt* 1: 364; Thomas Jefferson to William Wirt, 12 November 1816, in Kennedy, *Wirt* 1: 365.

54. St. George Tucker to William Wirt, 25 September 1815, quoted in "William Wirt's Life of Patrick Henry," *William and Mary College Quarterly Historical Magazine* 22 (April 1914): 257 (hereafter cited as "St. George Tucker Correspondence"). Page 75 of Wirt's preliminary manuscript corresponds with page 116 in the first edition of the published manuscript; Tucker was correct about the wording, but Wirt failed to change the manuscript. Even Wirt's final revised edition (which was published two years after his death) continued to quote the resolution incorrectly.

55. Meade, *Henry* 2: 39; Richard R. Beeman, *Patrick Henry: A Biography* (New York: McGraw-Hill, 1974), 201n.20.

56. Henry S. Randall, *The Life of Thomas Jefferson*, 3 vols. (New York: Derby & Jackson, 1865), 1: 101–2; Edmund Randolph, *History of Virginia*, ed. Arthur H. Shaffer (Charlottesville: Univ. Pr. of Virginia, 1970), 212; William Winston Fontaine, "Diary of Col. William Winston Fontaine," *William and Mary College Quarterly Historical Magazine* 16 (January 1908): 157–58; P. H. Fontaine, "New Facts in Regard to the Character and Opinions of Patrick Henry," *De Bow's Review* 7–8 (October 1870): 817.

57. Fontaine, "New Facts," 816–17.

58. Wirt, *Henry*, 65. If John Roane actually heard the "Liberty or Death" speech, it was in the capacity of an observer at the convention because he was not an elected delegate. *4 Am. Arch.* 2: 165–67.

59. Tyler, *Henry*, 150; Campbell, *Henry*, 136–37; Meade, *Henry* 2: 39; Freeman, *George Washington* 3: 404n.56; William Wirt Henry, *Henry* 1: 261.

60. Kennedy, *Wirt* 1: 120–21; Wirt, *Henry*, 122.

61. Wirt, *Henry*, ix.

62. *North American Review* 6 (March 1818): 313.

63. Wirt, *Henry*, 122.

64. William Wirt to St. George Tucker, 16 August 1815, quoted in "St. George Tucker Correspondence," 251–52.

65. William Wirt to St. George Tucker, 31 January 1805, in Kennedy, *Wirt* 1: 123–24.

66. Henry St. George Tucker, "Patrick Henry and St. George Tucker," *University of Pennsylvania Law Review* 67 (1919): 70–73; William Wirt Henry, *Henry* 1: 264–65; McCants, "Authenticity," 395–96.

67. Freeman, *Washington* 3: 404 n.56; Freeman, *Washington* 3: 405n.58.

68. Wirt, *Henry*, 93–94; John Richard Alden, *The American Revolution: 1775–1783* (New York: Harper, 1954; Harper Torchbooks, 1962), 180.

69. Louis A. Mallory, "Patrick Henry," in *A History and Criticism of American Public*

Address, ed. William Brigance and Marie Hochmuth, 3 vols. (New York: Russell & Russell, 1943–55), 2: 590–91.

70. Campbell, *Henry*, 134–35.

71. Thomas Jefferson, *A Summary View of the Rights of British America. Set Forth in Some Resolutions Intended for the Inspection of the Present Delegates of the People of Virginia now in Convention* (Williamsburg: Clementina Rind, 1774), 11; "Declaration by the Representatives of the United Colonies of North America, now met in Congress at Philadelphia, setting forth the causes and necessity of their taking up arms," 6 July 1775, *4 Am. Arch.* 2: 1867–69.

72. Stephen T. Olsen, "Computerized Thematic Analysis of Selected American Revolution Pamphlets" (unpublished paper: Pennsylvania State University, 1973), 6, 17.

73. Mayo, *Myths and Men*, 16.

74. Aristotle, *The Rhetoric of Aristotle*, trans. Lane Cooper (New York: Appleton-Century-Crofts, 1932), 217; Cicero, *Cicero's Dialogues De Oratore: or, On the Character of the Orator*, trans. and ed. J. S. Watson (New York: Harper, 1878; reprint Carbondale: Southern Illinois Univ. Pr., 1970), 107–9, 199–202; Comte de Buffon, "Discours sur le Style," in *The Art of the Writer: Essays, Excerpts, and Translations*, ed. Lane Cooper (Ithaca: Cornell Univ. Pr., 1952), 153–54; Hugh Blair, *Lectures on Rhetoric and Belles Lettres*, ed. Harold F. Harding, 2 vols. (Carbondale: Southern Illinois Univ. Pr., 1965), 1: 183; Remy de Gourmont, *La culture des idees* (Paris: n.p., 1916), 9, translated and cited by Nils Erik Enkvist, "On Defining Style: an Essay in Applied Linguistics," in *Linguistics and Style*, ed. John Spencer (London: Oxford Univ. Pr., 1964), 21.

75. Enkvist, "On Defining Style," 28.

76. Frederick Mosteller and David Wallace, *Inference and Disputed Authorship: The Federalist* (Reading, Mass.: Addison-Wesley, 1964), 1.

77. The 500 words-per-unit criterion was adopted because the text needs to be long enough for the personal stylistic features to reveal themselves. Studies have been done with smaller samples (e.g., Andrew Morton and Michael Levison, "Some Indicators of Authorship in Greek Prose," in *The Computer and Literary Style*, ed. Jacob Leed [Kent, Oh.: Kent State Univ. Pr., 1966], 141–79), but confidence in the results increases with larger samples. The 100,000 word data base for each author was an adopted goal because some of the tests require counts approximating that figure for the statistics to be reliable, e.g., rank-frequency curves. See the journal debate by M., "Curves of Literary Style," *Science* 13 (April 1889): 269, and A. B. M., "Curves of Literary Style," *Science* 13 (March 1889): 226.

78. Henry's speeches were taken from Jonathan Elliot, ed., *The Debates in the Several State Conventions, on the Adoption of the Federal Constitution . . .* , 4 vols., 2d ed. (Washington: Jonathan Elliot, 1836); Henry's letters were taken from William Wirt Henry, *Patrick Henry: Life, Correspondence, and Speeches*.

Wirt's speeches were taken from David Robertson, *Reports of the Trials of Colonel Aaron Burr . . .* , 2 vols. (Philadelphia: Hopkins and Earle, 1808), and *An Oration Delivered in Richmond on the Fourth of July, 1800; the Anniversary of American Independence* (Richmond: Meriwether Jones, 1800); Wirt's writings were taken from Wirt, *The Letters of the British Spy* (Richmond: Samuel Pleasants, Junior, 1803); Wirt, *Sketches of the Life and Character of Patrick Henry*.

St. George Tucker, *Reflections on . . . Commerce . . .* (New York: Samuel and John Loudon, 1786); Tucker, *Letter . . . to Author of the American Universal Geography* (Richmond: Thomas Nicolson, 1795); Tucker, *A Dissertation of Slavery . . .* (Philadelphia: Matthew Carey, 1796); Tucker, *Letter . . . Respecting the Alien and Sedition Laws* (n.p., 1799); Tucker, *Reflections on the cession of Louisiana . . .* (Washington: Samuel Harrison Smith, 1803); Tucker, *Blackstone's Commentaries . . . With an appendix to each volume, containing short tracts . . .* , 5 vols. (Philadelphia: William Young Birch and Abraham Small, 1803); Tucker, *Liberty, A Poem on the Independence of America* (Richmond: Aug. Davis, 1788); Tucker, *The Probationary Odes of Jonathan Pindar, Esq. . . .* (Philadelphia: Benj. Franklin Balche, 1796).

79. A pioneering, yet still useful, statistical stylistic package program currently available is one written by George Borden and James Watts. The two main disadvantages of using that system for this kind of study are that the initial encoding of data to be processed is cumbersome and the package does require a great deal of core storage space. See George A Borden and James J. Watts, "A Computerized Language Analysis System," *Computers and the Humanities* 5 (January 1971): 129–41. Bell Laboratories Writers Workbench program, for example, is available on many college and university systems running the UNIX operating system. Bell Laboratories, Inc., UNIX Writers Workbench Software, 1982.

80. Lawrence Fellows, "Cleric Asserts Computer Proves Paul Wrote Only Five of Fourteen Epistles," New York *Times*, 7 November 1963, pp. 4, 13.

81. George Yule, "On Sentence-Length as a Statistical Characteristic of Style in Prose, with Application to Two Cases of Disputed Authorship," *Biometrika* 30 (January 1939): 363–90; William C. Wake, "Sentence Length Distribution of Greek Authors," *Journal of the Royal Statistical Society*, ser. A, 120 (1957): 343–45.

82. See, for example, Jane Blankenship, "The Influence of Mode, Sub-Mode, and Speaker Predilection on Style," *Speech Monographs* 41 (June 1974): 93–94.

83. T. C. Mendenhall, "A Mechanical Solution of a Literary Problem," *The Popular Science Monthly* 60 (December 1901): 104–5; Claude S. Brinegar, "Mark Twain and the Quintus Curtius Snodgrass Letters: A Statistical Test of Authorship," *Journal of the American Statistical Association* 58 (March 1963): 94.

84. John W. Chotlos, "A Statistical and Comparative Analysis of Individual Written Language Samples," *Psychological Monographs* 56 (1944): 41; Blankenship, "Influence," 59.

85. John Carroll, "Diversity of Vocabulary and the Harmonic Series Law of Word-Frequency Distribution," *The Psychological Record* 2 (December 1938): 379–86.

86. George Yule, *The Statistical Study of Literary Vocabulary* (Cambridge: Cambridge Univ. Pr., 1944), 47, 57; Paul E. Bennett, "The Statistical Measurement of a Stylistic Trait in *Julius Caesar* and *As You Like It*," *Shakespeare Quarterly* 8 (Winter 1957): 33–35.

87. Rudolph Flesch, *The Art of Readable Writing* (New York: Harper, 1949), 213–16.

88. Although word-category tests (numbers 10, 11, 12, and 13 in this study) have not been used in authorship studies, they have been used to compare psychotic patient documents with documents from normals and to compare real with simulated suicide notes. See Philip Stone et. al., *The General Inquirer: A Computer Approach to Content Analysis* (Cambridge, Mass.: MIT Pr., 1966).

89. Significance for type-of-sentence comparisons was determined using z-tests; p had to be greater than 0.025 to be significant. Rank-frequency curves were compared using the χ-square test. None of the data sets was closer than $p > 0.01$ when compared with the rank-frequency curve of the "Liberty or Death" speech.

90. Brinegar, "Snodgrass Letters," 87.

91. The twenty words that comprised the preposition list are those words identified as "commonly used prepositions" in John C. Hodges and Mary E. Whitten, *Harbrace College Handbook*, 5th ed. (New York: Harcourt, 1962), 467. Words for the other categories were taken from the *Harvard Third Dictionary* supplied as part of the Inquirer II content analysis system. For an explanation of the defensive quality measurement, see Philip Stone et al., *The General Inquirer*, 179.

92. William J. Paisley, "Studying 'Style' as Deviation from Encoding Norms," in *The Analysis of Communication Content: Developments in Scientific Theories and Computer Techniques*, ed. George Gerbner et al. (New York: Wiley, 1969), 134–35.

93. Tucker's *Probationary Odes of Jonathan Pindar* contains several instances of words used in a new sense to achieve either a satirical or poetic effect—for example, Tucker's references to Vice-president John Adams as "Daddy Vice, Daddy Vice" (21) and his reference to the moon as the sun's "sister-orb of night" (35). But this kind of word fabrication was rare in the texts analyzed for this study.

94. See, for example, Ellegard, *Junius Letters*; Mosteller and Wallace, *The Federalist*; Fellows, "Paul Wrote Only 5 of 14 Epistles,"; Nigel Hawkes, "New System Can Tell Who Didn't Write What," Wilmington Del. *Evening Journal*, 3 April 1976, p. 25.

95. It is interesting to notice that *whilst*, although not in the "Liberty or Death" speech, is a distinguishing word for St. George Tucker. Tucker used *whilst* in 76 percent of the texts analyzed, whereas Henry and Wirt only used *whilst* in 3 percent and 10 percent of their texts respectively.

96. G. A. Miller, E. B. Newman, and E. A. Friedman, "Length-Frequency Statistics for Written English," *Information and Control* 1 (December 1958): 376–77, 382.

97. See, for example, Mosteller and Wallace, "Deciding Authorship," *Statistics: A Guide to the Unknown*, ed. Judith M. Tanur (San Francisco: Holden-Day, 1978), 211–13. This essay provides a very readable introduction to the Mosteller and Wallace approach to authorship discrimination.

98. Henry marker words: *got, shall, yourselves*. Wirt marker words: *about, after, almost, along, always, around, awfully, before, behind, being, between, beyond, both, down, either, enough, even, ever, except, farther, first, forward, having, height, hence, himself, however, indeed, itself, just, lease, less, neither, nevertheless, next, nor, once, others, over, rather, same, second, since,*

sometimes, still, then, third, through, throughout, too, two, until, up, whether, while, whose, within, yet.

99. Henry marker words: *you, your.* Tucker marker words: *about, above, after, again, alone, already, although, always, among, amount, another, before, being, below, between, beyond, both, could, did, does, doing, down, during, each, eighteen, either, elsewhere, enough, even, ever, except, fairly, few, fifty, first, five, four, fourth, further, had, having, hence, her, himself, however, hundred, inasmuch, instead, its, itself, lease, less, likewise, might, moreover, neither, nevertheless, next, nor, often, once, others, otherwise, over, past, per, perhaps, rather, same, second, seven, she, since, six, somewhat, still, then, then, thereafter, thereby, therein, thereof, third, though, thousand, three, through, thus, thy, together, too, twenty, twice, two, unless, until, whatever, whenever, where, whereas, wherever, whether, whilst, whom, whose, within, yet.*

100. Wirt markers: *along, around, awfully, farther, throughout, while, you, your.* Tucker markers: *above, alone, amount, doing, during, each, elsewhere, except, five, four, further, inasmuch, likewise, moreover, neither, often, ought, past, per, perhaps, rather, real, shall, she, six, somewhat, ten, thereafter, thereby, therein, thereof, thereon, third, thou, though, three, thy, twice, unless, whence, whenever, whereas, whilst, whom.*

101. Marker words for Henry are *necessary, number, shall, trust, wish, yourselves.* Marker words for Wirt are: *after, argument, back, before, cause, character, considered, course, death, debate, disposed, enough, eyes, force, having, hear, heard, heaven, held, highly, himself, house, just, knew, less, life, light, love, man, moment, next, noble, others, over, produced, proper, question, same, spirit, storm, sweet, thought, through, too, towards, truth, until, up, whole, world, years.*

102. Henry marker words are *gentlemen, sir, you, your.* Tucker marker words are *above, actually, additional, after, alone, already, arrive, assign, avert, battle, before, besides, bound, Britain, British, capable, cause, character, considered, could, course, death, debate, did, different, enough, eyes, free, future, guilty, hand, hath, having, held, himself, insidious, its, land, less, life, light, longer, lying, means, meant, might, moment, nations, natural, nearly, next, object, obtained, offence, often, opinions, others, over, past, peace, possess, price, proper, proportion, purpose, reconciled, retire, same, she, shown, submission, terms, then, three, through, too, truth, until, use, whatever, whole, work, world, year, years.*

103. Wirt markers are *dear, gentlemen, pleased, retreat, storm, you, your.* Tucker markers are *above, actually, additional, almighty, alone, arrive, bound, chains, effectual, find, free, future, hands, hath, held, insidious, liberty, longer, means, meant, millions, nations, nearly, number, obtained, often, ought, past, peace, possess, preserve, price, proportion, purchased, salvation, shall, she, shown, ten, terms, three, trust, use, whatever.*

104. John B. Smith, "RATS: A Middle-Level Text Utility System," *Computers and the Humanities* 6 (May 1972): 277–83.

THREE

Justifying America: The Declaration of Independence as a Rhetorical Document

STEPHEN E. LUCAS

O<small>N JULY 2</small>, 1776, the Continental Congress voted in favor of Richard Henry Lee's resolution that "these United Colonies are, and, of right, ought to be, Free and Independent States; that they are absolved from all allegiance to the British crown, and that all political connection between them, and the State of Great Britain, is, and ought to be, totally dissolved."[1]

It was a momentous event. John Adams, who had helped lead the fight for independence, believed July 2 would henceforth be celebrated as the most glorious day in American history. "The Second Day of July 1776," he wrote to Abigail Adams, "will be the most memorable Epocha in the History of America. I am apt to believe that it will be celebrated, by succeeding Generations, as the great anniversary Festival. It ought to be commemorated as the Day of Deliverance by solemn Acts of Devotion to God Almighty. It ought to be solemnized with Pomp and Parade, with Shows, Games, Sports, Guns, Bells, Bonfires and Illuminations from one End of this Continent to the other from this Time forward forever more."[2]

Adams was remarkably prescient in describing how Americans would celebrate their divorce from England. What he did not foresee, of course, was that the festivities would take place on July 4 rather than on July 2. For the past two hundred years Americans have been celebrating Independence Day two days late. Congress's vote of July 2 in favor of Lee's resolution was the legal act of

67

separation from British rule. On July 4 Congress approved the Declaration of Independence, a formal announcement and justification of the decision made two days earlier. Because the Declaration was the first official news of that decision, Americans quickly equated it with the decision itself. They began to commemorate July 4 as early as 1777, and generation after generation has perpetuated the practice.[3]

Just as we have lost sight of the original Independence Day, so have we lost sight of the original Declaration of Independence. We have come to revere it as a charter of our political faith, as "a symbolic expression of national identity" whose timeless principles cannot be "abandoned or rejected without repudiating a national commitment." This apotheosis of the Declaration as a sacred creed is so deeply embedded in our national consciousness that we typically see its original purpose in universal terms almost totally divorced from the events of 1776. Abraham Lincoln said the Declaration was meant

to set up a standard maxim for free society, which would be familiar to all, and revered by all; constantly looked to, constantly labored for, and even though never perfectly attained, constantly spreading and deepening its influence, and augmenting the happiness and value of life to all people of all colors everywhere. The assertion that "all men are created equal" was of no practical use in effecting our separation from Great Britain; and it was placed in the Declaration not for that, but for future use. Its authors meant it to be . . . a stumbling block to all those who in after times might seek to turn a free people back into the hateful paths of despotism.[4]

This idealistic scenario suited Lincoln's purposes in the political debates of the 1850s, but it would have astonished the men who passed and signed the Declaration of Independence. It illustrates perfectly the enormous gulf between what we have made of the Declaration and what it was—and was meant to be—in its own time. On that subject there is no better witness than Thomas Jefferson, draftsman of the Declaration. Some years after the Revolution he explained that when the colonies were forced "to resort to arms for redress" in their struggle with England, "an appeal to the tribunal of the world was deemed proper for our justification. This was the object of the Declaration of Independence. Not to find out new principles, or new arguments, never before thought of, not merely to say things which had never been said before; but to place before mankind the common sense of the subject, in terms so plain and firm as to command their assent, and to justify ourselves in the independent stand we are compelled to take."[5]

As Jefferson made clear, the Declaration was a rhetorical document. Its immediate object was to persuade a "candid world" that the Americans were justified in seeking to establish themselves as an independent nation. The purpose of this essay is to explicate the Declaration as a discourse designed to meet the particular rhetorical situation faced by the American revolutionaries in July 1776. This will require close analysis of the Declaration's content, structure, and style and of the strategic interaction among them as the discourse unfolds. By probing the text microscopically—at the level of the sentence, phrase, word, and even syllable—we can, in effect, slow down its internal dynamics so as to allow more precise explication of its rhetorical artistry. To borrow Stanley Fish's analogy about the methods of reader-response criticism, "It is as if a slow-motion camera with an automatic stop action effect were recording our linguistic experiences and presenting them to us for viewing."[6]

Unlike a purely formalistic analysis, however, which is concerned with the relationship between the text and "the self considered in isolation," we are concerned with the relationship between the Declaration and its eighteenth-century audience. Thus we must set aside our twentieth-century notions about the Declaration and deal with it as a work written in "the lost language of the Enlightenment." Rather than imposing our own meanings on the Declaration, we must seek to recapture "the full wealth of association, implication and resonance, the many levels of meaning," it possessed for eighteenth-century readers.[7]

We must also deal with the Declaration as part of the ongoing dialectic of controversy between Great Britain and the colonies. Congress's assertion of independence was only one of hundreds of documents produced during the British-American conflict. Many of its claims and strategies can be understood only as extensions of or rejoinders to assertions made by previous writers and speakers on both sides of the controversy. Finally, we must view the Declaration within the framework of eighteenth-century genres of political discourse. The rhetorical conventions associated with those genres imposed powerful constraints on what Jefferson and the Congress said and on how they said it.

I

The Declaration of Independence, as Charles Warren stated, "has been the subject of more incorrect popular belief, more bad memory on the part of participants, and more false history than any other occurrence in our national life."[8] Before turning to the text of the Declaration, then, we need to set the record straight on how that text came into being.

Although the Declaration has become "the most sacred of all American political scriptures," there was no hint at the time that it would be more notable than any of the other sixteen state papers issued by the Continental Congress before July 4, 1776. Congress bore a monumental burden, a burden John Adams described this way: "When fifty or sixty men have a constitution to form for a great empire, at the same time they have a country of fifteen hundred miles extent to fortify, millions to arm and train, a naval power to begin, an extensive commerce to regulate, numerous tribes of Indians to negotiate with, a standing army of 27,000 men to raise, pay, victual, and officer, I shall really pity those men."[9] Given all their other chores, the members of Congress hardly regarded the Declaration of Independence as their leading item of business. They did not even regard it as the most important writing task associated with Richard Henry Lee's motion for independence. More important, in the eyes of most delegates, were composing a potential treaty of alliance with France and drawing up a plan of confederation for the soon-to-be-independent states of America. Both of these, the delegates assumed, would affect the fate of America long after the Declaration of Independence had fulfilled its immediate purpose. The first job fell primarily to John Adams, the second to John Dickinson.[10]

It is natural to assume that Thomas Jefferson received the "honor" of drafting the Declaration because of his great stature as a revolutionary leader. But his later fame as president has obscured the fact that he was not a pivotal figure in the Continental Congress. He was not among the seven men elected as Virginia's delegation to the first Congress in 1774. Nor was he among those chosen to represent the colony in the second Congress. He was sent to Philadelphia in June 1775 to replace Peyton Randolph, who rushed back to Virginia to preside over the House of Burgesses when it was reconvened by Governor Dunmore. When Jefferson took his seat in Congress on June 21, 1775, he was the second youngest member and stood very much in the shadow of such veteran Whig leaders as John Dickinson of Pennsylvania, Samuel Adams and John Adams of Massachusetts, Stephen Hopkins of Rhode Island, Roger Sherman of Connecticut, Christopher Gadsden of South Carolina, Samuel Chase of Maryland, and Patrick Henry and Richard Henry Lee of his own colony.[11]

At no time did Jefferson become deeply involved in the political maneuvering that preceded Congress's decision on independence. He stayed in Philadelphia until Congress adjourned in August 1775. He returned when it reconvened in October, but he left again in December and did not resume his duties until the second week of May 1776. Even when in attendance, Jefferson was what John Adams called a "silent member." "During the whole time I sat with him," Adams recalled, "I never heard him utter three sentences together" in debates on the floor of Congress.[12]

But Jefferson did acquire a reputation as a writer—partly for his 1774 pamphlet *A Summary View of the Rights of British America*, partly for his role in drafting two vital congressional state papers in 1775. The first of these papers, the Declaration of the Causes and Necessity of Taking Up Arms, was the most important document issued by Congress before the Declaration of Independence. As approved by Congress on July 6, 1775, it was the product of a collaborative effort by Jefferson and John Dickinson, the celebrated author of *Letters From a Farmer in Pennsylvania*. The second congressional paper that marked Jefferson as possessing a "masterly pen" was the Report on Lord North's Conciliatory Proposal. While in Virginia, Jefferson had written the House of Burgesses' widely acclaimed answer to the proposal. In Philadelphia he was tabbed to compose Congress's reply, and his draft was adopted on July 31 with only a few minor changes.[13]

Jefferson's success as a draftsman in his first congressional session marked him as a candidate for similar work in the future. When it became clear in June 1776 that Congress would soon vote to leave the empire, he was named as Virginia's representative on the Committee of Five assigned to prepare the Declaration of Independence. Richard Henry Lee, who had presented the motion for independence, would appear to have been the logical choice for Virginia's seat on the committee. But Lee, a dramatic orator whose speaking skills were matched only by Patrick Henry, had proved to be considerably less adept as a writer.[14] Besides, Lee wanted to return home to see his ailing wife and to attend the Virginia convention, which was creating a new state constitution. Jefferson would have liked to go with him, for, like Lee, he thought the business in Williamsburg more vital than that in Philadelphia. But having just returned to Congress in May, he could hardly leave again so soon.[15]

Jefferson was joined on the Committee of Five by John Adams, Benjamin Franklin, Roger Sherman, and Robert R. Livingston. At its first meeting the committee discussed the form and emphasis of the Declaration and selected Jefferson to draft it. Working in the second-floor parlor of a new brick house on the southwest corner of

Market and Seventh streets where he had rented rooms, Jefferson produced his first draft within a day or two. After presenting it to Adams and Franklin, who suggested a few minor changes, he made a number of additional revisions and prepared a fair copy that the committee reported to the whole Congress on June 28.[16]

On the morning of July 2, after voting in favor of independence, Congress began debate on the Declaration. For two days the delegates pored over Jefferson's draft and revised it to their satisfaction, making more than forty separate changes. Altogether they deleted 630 words and added 146, producing a final text of 1,322 words (excluding the title). With the exception of two major changes toward the end of the Declaration, most of the revisions were minor—a word here, a phrase there, to enhance clarity, tone, and emphasis.[17]

Jefferson sat quietly as Congress reworked his draft. "I thought it a duty," he explained years later, "to be, on that occasion, a passive auditor of the opinions of others, more impartial judges than I could be, of its merits and demerits." But quiet as he may have been, he was deeply disturbed by the "acrimonious criticisms" his manuscript met in Congress. On July 8 he sent Richard Henry Lee a copy of his draft along with the Declaration as agreed to by Congress so Lee could "judge whether it is the better or worse for the Critics." He also sent copies for the same purpose to George Wythe, Edmund Pendleton, John Page, and Philip Mazzei. Throughout the rest of his life he worked to keep his original text alive so it could be compared with the congressional Declaration. How important this was to Jefferson can be gauged by the fact that in his *Autobiography*, composed just five years before his death, he printed his original draft side by side with the Declaration as revised by Congress. To help readers compare the texts, he underlined those portions of his draft deleted by Congress and, in the margin, he inserted Congress's additions.[18]

Jefferson should not have been surprised by the extent to which Congress altered his draft. Of the sixteen state papers published by Congress before the Declaration, apparently only one, the 1776 Letter to the Inhabitants of Canada, had been approved without revision—sometimes substantial—by the whole Congress, and no fewer than five had been sent back to committee for complete rewriting before Congress would even consider them for adoption.[19] Although a few of Jefferson's colleagues agreed Congress had "mangled" his manuscript and altered it "much for the worse," the judgment of posterity is that "Congress left the Declaration better than it found it." "Congress," Julian Boyd explains, "was a fairly numerous body and included some men of very acute intelligence. . . . It is difficult to point out a passage in the Declaration, great as it was, that was not improved by their attention."[20]

In any event, for better or worse it was Congress's text that presented America's case to the world, and it is that text to which we now turn.

II

Every aspect of the Declaration was designed to create a favorable image of Congress and its actions. This was true even of the title. On the morning of July 4, immediately after the Declaration had been read aloud for the final time and approved, Congress directed the Committee of Five to superintend its printing. The first broadside of the Declaration was printed by John Dunlap and bore the same title as Jefferson's draft, "A Declaration by the Representatives of the United States of America, in General Congress Assembled." Two weeks later Congress ordered that the Declaration be retitled "The Unanimous Declaration of the Thirteen United States of America," which is how it has been officially known ever since.[21]

The claim of unanimity, however, was a facade. Six weeks before the vote on independence, several members of Congress had re-signed their seats in protest of Congress's controversial May 15 resolution that it was foreign to "reason and good Conscience" that Americans should continue to take the "oaths and affirmations necessary for the support of any government under the crown of Great Britain."[22] Even though they were replaced by more ardent Whigs, perhaps as many as a quarter of the delegates were still opposed to independence when it was approved on July 2. (Votes in Congress were cast by each colony's delegation, not by each individual delegate.) Moreover, the colonies continued to be divided by a host of long-standing political, economic, military, religious, geographical, and personal rivalries. These rivalries would plague Congress and the army throughout the war and would endanger the effective administration of government afterward.

Yet it was imperative that Congress present a united front to the world, no matter how sharply it divided behind the closed doors of its meeting hall. British leaders and American Tories had long claimed Congress did not represent the true wishes of most colonists, and Congress knew its enemies would condemn the quest for independence as a desperate measure forced on the majority of Americans by a handful of "artful, ambitious, and wicked men." If the charge took hold, it would alienate many citizens from Congress and "raise up such a Schism as would prove more dreadful than any outward Enemy."[23]

Keenly aware of the need for "the appearance of an unbroken Harmony in public measures," Congress had postponed a final decision on independence until July, even though a test ballot on June 10 had shown a majority of colonies in favor of leaving the empire. On July 2 every colony but one voted for Richard Henry Lee's resolution on independence. New York's delegates abstained, because they had not yet been authorized by their colony's convention to support separation. When that authorization arrived on July 15, the New York delegation announced its support of Lee's resolution and the Declaration of Independence. Four days later Congress changed the title of the Declaration to emphasize to the world that America was acting with one will in asserting its right to become an independent nation.[24]

III

The text of the Declaration can be divided into five sections—the introduction, the preamble, the indictment of George III, the denunciation of the British people, and the conclusion. Each section is designed to achieve a particular purpose within the overall strategic development of the Declaration, and each of the last four sections builds upon the preceding section to give the Declaration a cumulative persuasive power. Moreover, within each section there are important ideational, structural, and stylistic interactions that shape the meaning of the text and coerce the perceptions of readers as the text unfolds. Let us look at each section in turn.

The introduction consists of the first paragraph—a single, lengthy sentence:

When in the Course of human events, it becomes necessary for one people to dissolve the political bands which have connected them with another, and to assume among the powers of the earth, the separate and equal station to which the Laws of Nature and of Nature's God entitle them, a decent respect to the opinions of mankind requires that they should declare the causes which impel them to the separation.[25]

As Carl Becker noted in his classic study of the Declaration, this striking sentence, which was not revised by Congress, combines "simplicity of statement . . . with an urbane solemnity of manner in such a way as to give that felicitous, haunting cadence which is the peculiar quality of Jefferson's best writing."[26] Taken out of context, it is so general it could be used as the introduction to a declaration by any "oppressed" people. Seen within its original context, however, it is a model of subtlety, nuance, and implication. It teems with words and phrases that operate on several levels of meaning and allusion to orient readers toward a favorable view of America and to prepare them for the rest of the Declaration.

From its magisterial opening phrase, which sets the American Revolution within the whole "course of human events," to its assertion that "the Laws of Nature and of Nature's God" entitle America to a "separate and equal station among the powers of the earth," to its quest for sanction from "the opinions of mankind," the introduction elevates the quarrel with England from a petty political dispute to a major event in the grand sweep of history. It dignifies the Revolution as a contest of principle and implies that the American cause has a special claim to moral legitimacy—all without mentioning England or America by name.

Rather than defining the Declaration's task as one of persuasion, which would imply that there was more than one publicly credible view of the British-American conflict, the introduction identifies the purpose of the Declaration as simply to "declare"—to announce publicly in explicit terms—the causes impelling America to leave the British empire. This gives the Declaration, at the outset, an aura of objectivity that it will seek to maintain throughout. Rather than presenting one side in a public controversy on which good and decent people could differ, the Declaration purports to do no more than a natural philosopher (what we today call a natural scientist) would do in reporting the causes of any physical event. The issue, it implies, is not one of interpretation, but of observation.

In fact, of course, the purpose of the Declaration is to persuade "the opinions of mankind" that it is "necessary" for "one people" (the Americans) to separate from "another" people (the British). The first key word here is "necessary," which in the eighteenth century carried strongly deterministic overtones. It meant something was the "inevitable consequence" of irresistible causes. William Cowper captured this sense of the word perfectly when he stated, "Of causes, how they work By necessary laws their sure effects." To say an act was necessary implied that it was impelled by fate or determined by the operation of inextricable natural laws and was beyond the control of human agents. Thus Chambers's *Cyclopedia* defined "necessary" as "that which cannot but be, or cannot be otherwise." "The common notion of necessity and impossibility," wrote Jonathan Edwards in *Freedom of the Will,* "implies something that frustrates endeavor or desire. . . . That is necessary in the original and proper sense of the word, which is, or will be, notwithstanding all supposable opposition." Characterizing the Revolution as necessary suggested that it resulted from constraints which operated with lawlike force "throughout the material universe and within the sphere of human action." The Revolution was not merely preferable, defensible, or justifiable. It was as inescapable, as inevitable, as unavoidable within the course of human events as the motions of the tides or the changing of the seasons within the course of natural events.[27]

Investing the Revolution with connotations of necessity was particularly important because, according to the law of nations, recourse to war was lawful only when it became "necessary"—only when amicable negotiation had failed and all other alternatives for settling the differences between two states had been exhausted. Thus, for example, when Charles II declared war against the Low Countries in 1672, he claimed "nothing but inevitable necessity forceth Us to the resolution of taking up Arms." Similarly, George I justified war against Spain in 1718 as stemming from "a Necessity of providing for the Good and Safety of our Kingdoms," while George II portrayed the onset of war against France in 1756 as "indispensably necessary for the immediate Defense and Protection of our Subjects."[28]

Nor was the burden of necessity limited to monarchs and established states. At the start of the English Civil War in 1642, Parliament defended its recourse to military action against Charles I in a lengthy declaration demonstrating the "Necessity to take up Arms." Following this tradition, in July 1775 the Continental Congress issued its own Declaration Setting Forth the Causes and Necessity of Their Taking Up Arms. While that document characterized the establishment of an American army as "necessary," it also noted that "Necessity has not yet driven us into" the "desperate measure" of independence. When, a year later, Congress decided the colonies could no longer retain their liberty within the British empire, it followed long-established rhetorical convention by describing independence as a matter of absolute and inescapable necessity. Indeed, the notion of necessity was so important that in addition to appearing in the introduction of the Declaration of Independence, it was invoked explicitly twice more at crucial junctures in the rest of the text and appeared frequently in other congressional papers after July 4, 1776.[29]

The phrase "one people" also is laden with implication—as was seen immediately by loyalist writers. It is a "false hypothesis," said Thomas Hutchinson in his pamphlet attacking the Declaration, "that the Colonies are one *distinct people*, and the kingdom another, connected by political bands." There is only one political band, he argued, and that is the legislative authority of Parliament, which extends over the entire British empire. Charles Inglis, Anglican minister and devout loyalist from New York, was equally contemptuous of the notion that Americans constituted a separate people. "The Americans are properly Britons," he said. "They have the manners, habits, and ideas of Britons."[30]

The Declaration does not attempt to prove the Americans are "one people" and the British "another." This idea had developed steadily in Whig rhetoric since the Stamp Act crisis of 1765. Even as the Whigs acknowledged their subordinance to England before 1776, they often did so in language that disclosed their latent sense of American nationalism. When John Dickinson proclaimed in 1768 that the colonies were "as much dependent on *Great Britain* as a perfectly free people can be on another," he assumed the Americans constituted one people and the British another. By 1776 the revolutionaries had come to see America not just as distinct from but in many ways superior to the mother country. Time and again they contrasted the low state of the English, "a people stupefied by luxury and the opium *vice*," with the growing strength of the Americans, "a rough and hardy people, uneffeminated with luxury and uncontaminated with the vices that are preparing the inhabitants of the mother country to be slaves." Americans, they believed, were a robust and virtuous people blessed with powerful natural and moral resources and possessing a special destiny, bestowed by God, to preserve America as the world's "last asylum of truth, righteousness, and freedom." Josiah Quincy, Jr., mirrored the perceptions of most Whig leaders when he wrote from England that "corruption, baseness, fraud, exorbitant oppression, never so abounded as in this island. . . . Englishmen—that boasted race of freedom—are sunk—are sunk in abject submission." "The commonality in this country," he concluded, "are no more like the commonality in America than if they were two utterly distinct and unconnected people."[31]

Labeling the Americans "one people" and the British "another" performed several important strategic functions within the Declaration. First, because two alien peoples cannot be made one, it reinforced the notion that breaking the "political bands" with England

was a necessary step in the course of human events. America and
England were already separated by the more basic fact that they had
become two different peoples. The gulf between them was much
more than political; it was intellectual, social, moral, and cultural.
According to the principles of nature, it could no more be repaired,
as Thomas Paine said, than one could "restore to us the time that
is past" or "give to prostitution its former innocence." To try to
perpetuate a purely political connection would be "forced and unnatural," "repugnant to reason, to the universal order of things." "Nature hath deserted the connection, and Art cannot supply her
place."[32]

Second, once it is granted that Americans and Englishmen are
two distinct peoples, the conflict between them is less likely to be
seen as a civil war. The Continental Congress knew America could
not withstand Britain's military might without foreign assistance.
But they also knew America could not receive assistance as long as
the colonies were fighting a civil war as part of the British empire.
To help the colonies would constitute interference in Great Britain's
internal affairs. In the minds of many delegates this was the crucial
factor behind the decision for independence. They embraced it as
"the only means by which foreign Alliance can be obtained." As
Samuel Adams explained, "no foreign Power can consistently yield
Comfort to Rebels, or enter into any kind of Treaty with these
Colonies till they declare themselves free and independent." The
crucial factor in opening the way for foreign aid was, of course, the
act of declaring independence. But by defining America and England
as two separate peoples, Jefferson and the Congress may have sought
to reinforce the perception that the conflict was not a civil war,
thereby making it more "consistent with European delicacy for
European powers to treat with us, or even to receive an Ambassador."[33]

Third, defining the Americans as a separate people in the first
paragraph eased the task of invoking the right of revolution in
the second paragraph. That right, according to eighteenth-century
principles, could only be invoked in the most dire of circumstances—when "resistance was absolutely necessary in order to preserve the nation from slavery, misery, and ruin"—and then only by
"the Body of the People." It could not be invoked by a handful of
individuals; nor could it be invoked for private causes. If America
and Great Britain were seen as one people, Congress could not
justify revolution against the British government, for the simple
reason that the body of the people (of which the Americans would
be only one part) did not support the American cause. For America

to move against the government in such circumstances would not be a justifiable act of resistance, but "a sort of Sedition, Tumult, and War, proceeding from Malice, which is always detestable, aiming only at the satisfaction of private Lust, without regard to the public Good." By defining the Americans as a separate people, Congress could more readily satisfy the requirement for invoking the right of revolution that "the whole Body of Subjects" rise up against the government "to rescue themselves from the most violent and illegal oppressions."[34]

As the phrase "one people" implied much more than it actually said, so "the opinions of mankind" veiled the many layers of audience for the Declaration. To some extent, of course, the Declaration was literally addressed to the opinions of mankind. It was meant partly for America's friends in England, though Jefferson was not optimistic it would do much good there. More important, it was meant for the Spanish and especially the French, who, Congress hoped, would support America in its war for independence. Four days after the Declaration had been adopted, the Committee of Secret Correspondence sent a copy to Silas Deane, Congress's agent in France, with instructions to "immediately communicate the piece to the Court of France, and send copies of it to the other Courts of Europe. It may be well also to procure a good translation of it into French, and get it published in the gazettes."[35]

The Declaration was also meant for posterity. Congress knew that regardless of how the Revolution turned out, future generations would reach their own judgments about who was right and who was wrong. In doing so they would turn to the letters, speeches, essays, pamphlets, and state papers on both sides of the controversy. For this audience the Declaration of Independence would be a crucial part of the historical record. Given their repeated concern with the opinion of posterity throughout the dispute with Britain, we can confidently assume Jefferson and his colleagues saw the Declaration as a document that would justify the Revolution at the bar of history.

But important as these audiences were, they were not the readers for whom the Declaration was primarily intended. To interpret "the opinions of mankind" as meaning that the Declaration was written for a universal audience, or as a clarion call to "the liberal-minded everywhere,"[36] is to interpret the language of the eighteenth century by the standards of the twentieth. The first step to wisdom in this matter is to recognize that the Declaration of Independence fit the rhetorical conventions of declarations as a genre of seventeenth- and eighteenth-century Anglo-American public address. Such declarations were common on both sides of the Atlantic and often identified their audiences not just as interested parties in England or America but as "the world," "the whole world," "mankind," or "all of mankind."[37] Describing the audience as "the opinions of mankind" gave the Declaration a lofty tone and sense of serious purpose, but it should not be taken entirely literally. In this respect, as in several others, the Declaration merely adhered to the features of declarations as a genre of political discourse.

For whose opinions, then, was the Declaration primarily intended? The answer becomes clear when we turn to the records of the Continental Congress. No sooner had Congress adopted the Declaration on July 4 than it ordered that copies "be sent to the several assemblies, conventions and committees, or councils of safety, and to the several commanding officers of the continental troops; that it be proclaimed in each of the United States, and at the head of the army." Over the next few days John Hancock, president of the Congress, wrote to the states, urging them to publicize the Declaration "in such Way and Manner as you shall judge best." The importance of the Declaration, he said, "will naturally suggest the Propriety of proclaiming it in such a Mode, as that the People may be universally informed of it." Hancock also sent copies of the Declaration to Artemus Ward, commander of the American troops at Boston, and to George Washington, at his headquarters in New York, requesting that it be "proclaimed at the Head of the Army in the Way you shall think most proper."[38]

The Declaration was in turn sent to towns and villages throughout America, where, amidst a mix of pomp and hoopla, it was read aloud to the citizenry. The following account of the events at Huntington, Long Island, captures well what happened:

The *Freedom* and *Independency* of the Thirteen United Colonies was, with beat of drum, proclaimed at the several places of parade, by reading the Declaration . . . together with the Resolutions of our *Provincial Convention* thereupon; which were approved and applauded by the animated shouts of the people, who were present from all the distant quarters of this district. After which, the flag which used to wave on Liberty-pole, having *Liberty* on one side, and *George III* on the other, underwent a *reform*, i.e. the Union was cut off, and the Letters GEORGE III were discarded, . . . and then an effigy of the Personage, represented by those letters, [was] hastily fabricated. . . . The Whole, together with the letters above mentioned, was hung on a gallows, exploded and burnt to ashes.

To ensure that such ceremonies went as planned, the revolutionaries worked "to secure the attendance of as many as possible of the staunch friends of independence, so as to overawe any disaffected Tories" who might try to subvert the proceedings.[39]

These strenuous exertions by Congress and its supporters confirm that the key audience for the Declaration was not humanity in general but the people of America. This did not include Tories. They were already irrevocably opposed to independence, and, in any case, Congress by this time was more concerned with proscribing the Tories than with persuading them.[40] But if independence were to succeed, it would have to be accepted by a substantial portion of the other 70 or 80 percent of the colonists, who ranged from zealous backers of independence, to reluctant supporters, to middle-of-the roaders, to apathetic. It is easy today to forget that most Americans were not enthusiastic about independence in July 1776. Despite the fact that America had been at war with England since the battles of Lexington and Concord in April 1775, many colonists who supported the war did not believe it had to be or ought to be waged for independence but simply to force England to offer just terms for reconciliation within the empire. In some parts of America—especially the middle colonies of Pennsylvania, New York, New Jersey, and Delaware—anti-independence forces continued to hold the upper hand well into the spring of 1776. Joseph Reed echoed the thoughts of many advocates of independence when he complained that "notwithstanding the act of Parliament for seizing our property, and a thousand other proofs of a bitter and irreconcilable spirit, there is a strange reluctance in the minds of many to cut the knot which ties us to Great Britain."[41]

That reluctance may have been reinforced by Congress itself, which had repeatedly disavowed any "ambitious designs of separating from Great Britain and establishing independent states." By deciding to leave the empire, Congress reversed its long-standing public opposition to independence. In doing so it gave credence to the Tories' accusation that Congress had been scheming for independence from the very beginning and was just waiting for a propitious opportunity to take the final step. Thus even though pro-independence opinion had ripened markedly in May and June of 1776, Congress needed to justify its decision to its constituents as persuasively as possible. As Charles Pettit shrewdly observed, no matter how "determined the Congress may be to cut the Ligament, . . . the People at large must individually see and feel the Necessity and Propriety of it before they will give it such an Acquiescence as is necessary to ensure it success." Above all else the Declaration had to consolidate support for independence among the colonists. It had to present the case for independence so powerfully, so judiciously, so eloquently as to rally those Americans already committed to independence and to convince what Samuel Adams called the "timid" and the "doubting" of its justice and necessity. Its impact on mankind in general would be of little consequence if it failed to do its job in America.[42]

Before we leave the introduction of the Declaration, one more phrase requires attention—"the Laws of Nature and of Nature's God." Like much of the introduction, these words—perhaps borrowed from Bolingbroke or Pope—were rich in meaning for contemporary readers of the Declaration.[43] Their placement in the introduction is usually interpreted as grounding the whole matter of America's separation from Great Britain on principles of natural law. In fact, however, the only section of the Declaration based explicitly upon natural law is the preamble, in which Congress asserted the right of revolution against tyrannical authority. While that is the most famous section of the Declaration today, it makes up only 15 percent of the entire text and, as we shall see, was considerably less important in the eighteenth century than was the lengthy indictment of George III, which comprises almost 60 percent of the text. In that indictment Congress accused the king of violating not the colonists' natural rights, but their exercise of specific British constitutional rights. It did so, moreover, by emulating the rhetorical forms Englishmen had followed for centuries when deposing "tyrannical" monarchs and by arraigning George III for the same kinds of crimes against the constitution that had cost such rulers as Richard II, Charles I, and James II their thrones. Taken as a whole, the Declaration is much more a document of English constitutional principles than a statement of abstract, natural law.[44]

We should be wary, then, of reading too much into "the Laws of Nature and of Nature's God." In its original context the phrase is part of the clause, "to assume among the powers of the earth, the separate and equal station to which the Laws of Nature and of Nature's God entitle them." Read strictly within this context, "the Laws of Nature and of Nature's God" refers to the doctrine of eighteenth-century international law that all nations are by nature "free, independent, and equal" and entitled to the same rights and privileges.[45] By invoking this doctrine of the equality of states, the Declaration claimed for America the status accorded by natural law to sovereign states. This meant that America, no longer under the dominion of Great Britain, could lawfully make treaties and alliances with all other "powers of the earth," a provision of such great importance Congress would state it explicitly in the penultimate sentence of the Declaration.

IV

Although the introduction ends by stating that the aim of the Declaration is to declare the causes impelling America to seek independence, the next section—usually referred to as the preamble—does not deal with those causes. Like the introduction, it says nothing explicit about the British-American conflict. Instead, it presents a philosophy of government that makes revolution justifiable, even meritorious:

We hold these truths to be self-evident, that all men are created equal, that they are endowed by their Creator with certain unalienable Rights, that among these are Life, Liberty and the pursuit of happiness. That to secure these rights, Governments are instituted among Men, deriving their just powers from the consent of the governed. That whenever any Form of Government becomes destructive of these ends, it is the Right of the People to alter or to abolish it, and to institute new Government, laying its foundation on such principles and organizing its powers in such form, as to them shall seem most likely to effect their Safety and Happiness. Prudence, indeed, will dictate that Governments long established should not be changed for light and transient causes; and accordingly all experience hath shown that mankind are more disposed to suffer, while evils are sufferable, than to right themselves by abolishing the forms to which they are accustomed. But when a long train of abuses and usurpations, pursuing invariably the same Object evinces a design to reduce them under absolute Despotism, it is their right, it is their duty, to throw off such Government, and to provide new Guards for their future security.

Like the rest of the Declaration, the preamble is "brief, free of verbiage, a model of clear, concise, simple statement." It capsulizes in five sentences—202 words—what it took John Locke thousands of words to explain in his *Second Treatise of Government*. Each word is chosen and placed to achieve maximum impact. Each clause is indispensable to the progression of thought. Each sentence is carefully constructed internally and in relation to what precedes and follows. In its ability to compress complex ideas into a brief, clear statement, the preamble is a paradigm of eighteenth-century Enlightenment prose style, in which purity, simplicity, directness, precision, and, above all, perspicuity were the highest rhetorical and literary virtues. In keeping with Jefferson's ideas about tasteful and effective discourse, the preamble is "disfigured by no gaudy tinsel of rhetoric or declamation" and proceeds "without ever using a superfluous word."[46] One word follows another with complete inevitability of sound and meaning. Not one word can be moved or replaced without disrupting the balance and harmony of the entire preamble.

The preamble can be seen as a blend of what Jefferson later called "the simple and the sublime." The simple style, he said, was exemplified best by Thomas Paine, whom no one surpassed "in ease and familiarity of style, in perspicuity of expression, happiness of elucidation, and in simple and unassuming language." The sublime style, Jefferson thought, was characteristic of Bolingbroke, whose writings he deemed "the finest samples in the English language of the eloquence proper for the Senate. . . . The lofty, rhythmical, full-flowing eloquence of Cicero. Periods of just measure, their members proportioned, their close full and round. His conceptions, too, are bold and strong, his diction copious, polished and commanding as his subject."[47]

The stately and dignified tone of the preamble—like that of the introduction—comes partly from what the eighteenth century called "Style Periodique," in which, as Hugh Blair explained in his *Lectures on Rhetoric and Belles Lettres*, "the sentences are composed of several members linked together, and hanging upon one another, so that the sense of the whole is not brought out till the close." This, Blair said, "is the most pompous, musical, and oratorical manner of composing" and "gives an air of gravity and dignity to composition." The gravity and dignity of the preamble were reinforced by its adherence to the rhetorical precept that "when we aim at dignity or elevation, the sound [of each sentence] should be made to grow to the last; the longest members of the period, and the fullest and most sonorous words, should be reserved to the conclusion." None of the sentences of the preamble end on a single-syllable word; only one, the second (and least euphonious), ends on a two-syllable word. Of the other four, one ends with a four-syllable word ("security"), while three end with three-syllable words. Moreover, in each of the three-syllable words, the closing syllable is at least a medium-length four-letter syllable, which helps bring the sentences to "a full and harmonious close."[48]

It is unlikely that any of this was accidental. Thoroughly versed in classical oratory and rhetorical theory as well as in the belletristic treatises of his own time, Jefferson was a diligent student of rhythm, accent, timing, and cadence in discourse. This can be seen most clearly in his "Thoughts on English Prosody," a remarkable twenty-eight page unpublished essay written in Paris during the fall of 1786. Prompted by a discussion on language with the Marquis de Chastellux at Monticello four years earlier, it was a careful inquiry designed "to find out the real circumstance which gives harmony to English poetry and laws to those who make it." Using roughly the same system of diacritical notation he had employed in 1776 in his reading draft of the Declaration of Independence, Jefferson systematically analyzed the patterns of accentuation in a wide range of English writers, including Milton, Pope, Shakespeare, Addison, Gray, and Garth. Although "Thoughts on English Prosody" deals with poetry, it displays Jefferson's keen sense of the interplay between sound and sense in language. There can be little doubt that, like many accomplished writers, he consciously composed for the ear as well as for the eye—a trait that is nowhere better illustrated than in the eloquent cadence of his preamble in the Declaration of Independence.[49]

The preamble also has a powerful sense of structural unity. This is achieved partly by the latent chronological progression of thought, in which the reader is moved from the creation of mankind, to the institution of government, to the throwing off of government when it fails to protect the people's unalienable rights, to the creation of new government that will better secure the people's safety and happiness. This dramatic scenario, with its first act implicitly set in the Garden of Eden (where man was "created equal"), may, for some readers, have contained mythic overtones of man's fall from divine grace. At the very least, it gives an almost archetypal quality to the ideas of the preamble and continues the notion, broached in the introduction, that the American Revolution is a major development in "the course of human events."

Overtly, of course, the preamble consists not of a dramatic narrative but of a series of propositions that begins in the opening sentence: "We hold these truths to be self-evident, that all men are created equal, that they are endowed by their Creator with certain unalienable Rights, that among these are Life, Liberty and the pursuit of Happiness."[50] This is one of the best-known sentences in the English language. It has been studied and restudied by historians, critics, philosophers, and political theorists—usually in an effort to determine exactly what Jefferson and the Congress intended by such phrases as "created equal" and "the pursuit of Happiness." But there are no definitive answers—partly because Jefferson never explained what he meant, partly because the words of the Declaration did not mean the same thing to all members of Congress (or to all readers). Part of the rhetorical brilliance of the Declaration is that it was written so people who differed on a wide range of particular political issues could accept the general ideas stated in the preamble.[51]

In saying "all men are created equal," for example, the Declaration echoed a basic tenet of eighteenth-century enlightened thought. Almost all readers could agree, with Locke, that the "equality of Men by Nature" was "evident in itself, and beyond all question." The notion of a natural human equality was bruited by writers as diverse as the international revolutionary Thomas Paine ("all men are born equal") and the conservative English jurist William Blackstone ("all members of society are naturally equal"). What it meant, however, could vary greatly from person to person. One way of interpreting "all men are created equal" in the Declaration is to read it as being modified by the succeeding clauses in sentence one of the preamble. Given this reading, "all men are created equal" would mean that all men are endowed equally by their creator with basic unalienable rights, including the rights to life, liberty, and the pursuit of happiness. Such a reading would be consistent with Locke's dictum that men are "by Nature all free, equal, and independent . . . with a Title to perfect Freedom, and an uncontrolled enjoyment of all the Rights and Privileges of the Law of Nature, equally with any other Man."[52]

But the preamble need not be read this way. "All men are created equal" can also be taken as an independent clause whose meaning is not restricted by the succeeding clauses. In this case eighteenth-century readers would have interpreted "all men are created equal" in light of their own individual constructions of human equality. Those constructions would have included the notions that all men are equal insofar as they are members of the same species and have the same biological needs; that all men are equal since at birth the mind of every man is blank, a *tabula rasa* which is shaped and developed by the experience of the five human senses; that all men are equal insofar as they possess an innate moral sense that distinguishes them from the lower species; or that all men are equal before the law in rights, privileges, and legal capacities. One thing we can be sure of is that neither the Continental Congress nor contemporary readers of the Declaration would have taken "all men are created equal" to mean all people possess equal physical and intellectual endowments, or that all people are entitled to equal social status and material conditions regardless of their abilities and achievements.[53]

"The pursuit of Happiness" has been no less troublesome for modern students of the Declaration. Why did Jefferson add this phrase to life and liberty instead of reiterating the standard trilogy of "life, liberty, and property," which the colonists had invoked countless times in defending their rights during the previous eleven years? The most plausible answer is that to Jefferson, property (construed as a right to goods and estates) was not as fundamental a right as life, liberty, and the pursuit of happiness. Although Jefferson's surviving papers contain no direct comments on this aspect of the Declaration, he was consistent in not including property among humanity's most basic natural rights. In July 1789 the Marquis de Lafayette sent him a draft of a declaration of rights for France. In the draft Lafayette included "property" as one of the inalienable rights with which all men are born, but Jefferson urged him to omit it, leaving only "the care of his life, the power to dispose of his person and the fruits of his industry and of all his faculties, the pursuit of happiness and resistance to oppression."[54]

Whatever Jefferson's thinking in 1776, the immediate source for his phraseology most likely was George Mason's draft of the Virginia Declaration of Rights, which was published in the Philadelphia newspapers early in June of 1776. Jefferson's apparent indebtedness to Mason's work is especially evident when we compare it with the original rough draft of the Declaration of Independence:

Mason's Draft of the Declaration of Rights	*Jefferson's Draft of the Declaration of Independence*
All men are born equally free and independent, and have certain inherent natural rights, of which they cannot, by any compact, deprive or divest their posterity; among which are the enjoyment of life and liberty, with the means of acquiring and possessing property, and pursuing and obtaining happiness and safety.	All men are created equal and independent, that from that equal creation they derive rights inherent and inalienable, among which are the preservation of life, and liberty, and the pursuit of happiness.

While there is no way to know the extent to which Jefferson was influenced—either consciously or unconsciously—by Mason's document, the structure, language, and movement of thought in Jefferson's draft comports closely enough with Mason's to suggest that here, as in other aspects of drafting the Declaration, he drew upon existing public papers and adapted aspects of them to the rhetorical task of justifying independence.[55]

As puzzling as "the pursuit of Happiness" has been to twentieth-century commentators, it did not raise eyebrows in its own time. Happiness was a powerful concept in eighteenth-century thought and attracted the attention of the best minds of the age. It was a preoccupation of moral and political philosophers, who repeatedly dilated upon it, speculated about it, even reduced it to mathematical formulas. Men, they believed, were ordained by nature to pursue their own happiness, and the phrase "the pursuit of happiness" had been in wide use for at least three-quarters of a century before Jefferson placed it in the Declaration.[56] Happiness was also considered the supreme goal of civil society. As John Adams observed, "all speculative politicians will agree, that the happiness of society is the end of government, as all Divines and moral Philosophers will agree that the happiness of the individual is the end of man." Consequently, said Adams, "the form of government which communicates ease, comfort, security, or, in one word happiness to the greatest number of persons, and in the greatest degree, is the best." In April 1776, less than three months before the Declaration of Independence, Thomas Paine summarized the whole issue of America's position in the empire by saying, "the first and great question, and that from which every other will flow is *happiness*. Can this continent be happy under the government of Great Britain?" The Declaration of Independence provided Congress's answer to Paine's question, and although not all readers agreed with that answer, they could agree that the pursuit of happiness was an unalienable right and that "the happiness of the whole community is the ultimate end of government."[57]

Because of their concern with the philosophy of the Declaration, many scholars have dealt with the opening sentence of the preamble out of context, as if Jefferson and the Congress intended it to stand alone. Seen in context, however, it is no more than a preliminary move in Congress's effort to establish a philosophy of government that justifies the right of revolution against tyrannical authority. The core of that philosophy is presented in the first three sentences of the preamble in a series of five propositions that are characterized as self-evident truths, truths that, in Locke's words, would command "universal and ready assent upon hearing and understanding the terms."[58]

> Proposition 1: That all men are created equal.
>
> Proposition 2: That they [all men, from proposition 1] are endowed by their creator with certain unalienable rights.
>
> Proposition 3: That among these [man's unalienable rights, from proposition 2] are life, liberty, and the pursuit of happiness.
>
> Proposition 4: That to secure these rights [man's unalienable rights, from propositions 2 and 3] governments are instituted among men.
>
> Proposition 5: That whenever any form of government becomes destructive of these ends [securing man's unalienable rights, from propositions 2–4], it is the right of the people to alter or abolish it.

When we look at all five propositions, we see they are meant to be read together and have been meticulously written to achieve a specific rhetorical objective. The first three lead into the fourth, which in turn leads into the fifth. And it is the fifth, proclaiming the right of revolution when a government becomes destructive of the people's unalienable rights, that is most crucial in the overall argument of the Declaration. The first four are merely preliminary steps designed to give philosophical grounding to the fifth.

At first glance, these propositions appear to comprise what was known in the eighteenth century as a *sorites*—"a Way of argument in which a great Number of Propositions are so linked together, that the Predicate of one becomes continually the Subject of the next following, until at last a Conclusion is formed by bringing together the Subject of the First Proposition and the Predicate of the last." In his *Elements of Logick*, William Duncan provided the following example of a sorites:

God is omnipotent.
An omnipotent Being can do every thing possible.
He that can do every thing possible, can do whatever involves not a
    Contradiction.
Therefore God can do whatever involves not a Contradiction.[59]

Although the section of the preamble we have been considering is not a sorites (because it does not bring together the subject of the first proposition and the predicate of the last), its propositions are written in such a way as to take on the appearance of a logical demonstration. They are so tightly interwoven linguistically that they seem to make up a sequence in which the final proposition—asserting the right of revolution—is logically derived from the first four propositions. This is accomplished partly by the mimicry of the form of a sorites and partly by the sheer number of propositions, the accumulation of which is reinforced by the slow, deliberate pace of the text and by the use of "that" to introduce each proposition. There is also a steplike progression from proposition to proposition, a progression that is accentuated by the skillful use of demonstrative pronouns to make each succeeding proposition appear to be an inevitable consequence of the preceding propositions.

Having asserted the right of revolution, the preamble interjects a qualifier—"that Governments long established should not be changed for light and transient causes." In so stating, the Declaration reaffirmed the basic tenet of British revolutionary theory that obedience to lawful rulers was obligatory and that forceful resistance to government was warranted only when "the Mischief be grown general" and the tyranny or "Designs of the Rulers become notorious." It also implied that the Continental Congress would never promote revolution for anything less than the most serious and abiding causes. Like the rest of mankind, Americans were "more disposed to suffer, while evils are sufferable, than to right themselves by abolishing the forms to which they are accustomed." This, too, was a standard part of the Whig tradition and contains distinct echoes of Locke's statement, "Till the mischief be grown general, and the ill designs of the Rulers become visible, or their attempts sensible to the greater part, the People, who are more disposed to suffer, than right themselves by Resistance, are not apt to stir."[60]

"But . . ." the final sentence of the preamble begins, abruptly shifting the reader away from the qualifier introduced in sentence four to the forceful reaffirmation of the people's right and duty to "throw off" their government "when a long train of abuses and usurpations, pursuing invariably the same Object evinces a design to reduce them under absolute Despotism." In so stating, the Declaration recalled Locke's words that "if a long train of Abuses, Prevarications, and Artifices, all tending the same way, make the design visible to the People, . . . they should then rouze themselves, and endeavor to put the rule into such hands, which may secure to them the ends for which Government was at first erected."[61] It also followed English revolutionary tradition in stating that the people had not just a right but a duty to resist government when it deliberately sought to establish a despotic rule. The implication, of course, was that Americans had no choice but to seek independence. In this respect, too, the Revolution was a matter of "necessity."

It is also worth noting that this sentence, like the third sentence of the preamble, pronounces not just the people's duty to resist tyranny, but also their duty to institute new government to guard "their future security." This, of course, is precisely what America was doing in July 1776. When Richard Henry Lee introduced the motion for independence on June 7, he also proposed "That a plan of confederation be prepared and transmitted to the respective Colonies for their consideration and approbation."[62] At the very time Congress issued the Declaration of Independence, it was also developing the Articles of Confederation, which would result in a "Form of Government" quite different from the constitutional monarchy of Great Britain. By stressing the right of an oppressed people to establish new forms of government, the Declaration not only justified the Americans' efforts in this regard but also implied that the Revolution was not anarchic and that America could be regarded as a responsible member of the community of nations.

Although the preamble is the best-known part of the Declaration today, it attracted considerably less attention in its own time. It was debated but briefly by the Continental Congress, was given little heed by American loyalists or by English critics of the Declaration, and was all but ignored in America's early Fourth of July celebrations. For most people of the eighteenth century, it was an unobjectionable statement of commonplace political principles. As Jefferson explained years later, his charge in writing the Declaration was neither "to invent new ideas" nor "to offer no sentiment which had ever been expressed before." "All its authority," he said, "rests then on the harmonizing sentiments of the day, whether expressed in conversation, in letters, printed essays, or in the elementary books of public right, as Aristotle, Cicero, Locke, Sidney, etc."[63]

Far from being a weakness of the preamble, the lack of new ideas was perhaps its greatest strength. If one overlooks the introduction, the Declaration as a whole is structured along the lines of a deductive argument that can easily be put in syllogistic form:

Major premise:	When government deliberately seeks to reduce the people under absolute despotism, the people have a right, indeed a duty, to alter or abolish that form of government and to create new guards for their future security.
Minor premise:	The government of Great Britain has deliberately sought to reduce the American colonists under absolute despotism.
Conclusion:	Therefore, the American colonists have a right, indeed a duty, to abolish their present form of government and to create new guards for their future security.

As the major premise in this argument, the preamble allowed Jefferson and the Congress to reason from self-evident principles of government accepted by almost all contemporary readers of the Declaration.[64]

The key premise, however, was the minor premise. Since everyone agreed the people had a right to overthrow a tyrannical ruler when all other remedies had failed, the crucial question in July 1776 was whether the necessary conditions for revolution existed in the colonies. Congress answered this question with a sustained attack on George III. Unlike Jefferson's draft of the preamble, which passed through Congress relatively unscathed, the grievances against George III were intensely debated and closely edited. And when the Declaration was published, opponents of the Revolution took little notice of the preamble ("The truth is," said John Lind, "little or none does it deserve") and concentrated their firepower almost solely on Congress's charges against the king.[65]

V

The attack on George III marked a new direction in congressional rhetoric. Ever since the Stamp Act crisis, colonial protesters had claimed there was a conspiracy at the highest levels of British government to destroy American liberty. Congress had reiterated the claim in almost all of its state papers before the Declaration of Independence, but it had not implicated the king. It had followed the "ancient and fundamental maxim" of English politics that the king can do no wrong. This maxim held that in ordinary times any oppressive measures were blamed on the king's "wicked ministers" and "evil counsellors" rather than on the king himself. To accuse the king publicly of unconstitutional acts was to announce he had violated his compact with the people. Accordingly, even after the outbreak of war in April 1775, Congress had continued to attribute the "system formed to enslave America" to "the King's wicked counsellors," to Parliament's "intemperate rage for unlimited domi-nation," or to "the machinations of evil and abandoned Ministers." It had even portrayed the British troops as a "ministerial army" and had professed its abiding willingness to "cheerfully bleed in defence of our Sovereign in a righteous cause."[66]

By 1776, however, it was increasingly clear that the actions of Parliament and the ministry could not be dismissed as contravening the will of the king. George III's disregard of Congress's Olive Branch petition of July 1775, his proclamation of August 1775 for suppressing the American "rebellion," his sternly anti-American speech opening the new session of Parliament on October 26, 1775, his approval of the Prohibitory Act in December 1775—all led Congress to conclude that he was the guiding force behind England's quest to enslave America. This conclusion was reinforced in the spring of 1776 by the king's decision to hire Hessian mercenaries to help subdue the colonists. "We are told, and everything proves it true," Jefferson wrote to John Randolph, "that he [George III] is the bitterest enemy we have."[67]

But Jefferson and the Congress did not indict George III just because they were convinced of his guilt. According to Locke, the people could revolt against a tyrannical legislature as well as against a tyrannical monarch. But the colonies had already rejected the authority of Parliament. Ever since the Coercive Acts of 1774, American leaders had maintained the colonies were independent of Parliament and were bound to the empire solely through their allegiance to the king. In justifying independence Congress had to forswear allegiance to the king to break the last political link connecting America to the empire. The Declaration does not men-tion the ministry and takes note of Parliament only three times, and then not by name. It makes George III the sole agent responsible for England's oppression of the colonies.[68]

The indictment of George III begins with a transitional sentence immediately following the preamble:

Such has been the patient sufferance of these Colonies; and such is now the necessity which constrains them to alter their former Systems of Government.

Now, 273 words into the Declaration, appears the first explicit reference to the British-American conflict. The parallel structure of the sentence reinforces the parallel movement of ideas from the preamble to the indictment of the king. "Patient sufferance" refers back to the idea, stated in sentence four of the preamble, that governments should not be changed for "light and transient causes" and that "mankind are more disposed to suffer, while evils are sufferable." The "necessity which constrains" the colonists to change their government refers back to the "design to reduce them under absolute Despotism" mentioned in the last sentence of the preamble; because of that "design," the "evils" of British rule are no longer "sufferable." The use of "necessity" here also carries through the idea, broached first in the introduction, that the Revolution is consistent with the principles of international law and is the irresistible consequence of the specific "causes" detailed in the Declaration.

And so we come to the villain:

The history of the present King of Great Britain is a history of repeated injuries and usurpations, all having in direct object the establishment of an absolute Tyranny over these states.

This strong, direct sentence acquires added force on the heels of the more complex transitional sentence preceding it. It also provides a good example of how Congress improved Jefferson's draft of the Declaration. Here is how Congress edited Jefferson's fair copy to produce the sentence in its final form:

> The history of the present King of Great Britain is a history of
> repeated
> ~~unremitting~~ injuries and usurpations, ~~among which appears no solitary~~
>   having
> ~~fact to contradict the uniform tenor of the rest but~~ all ^have
> in direct object the establishment of an absolute Tyranny over
> these States.

"Repeated" is much better than "unremitting." It is less strident, less hortatory, more in keeping with the dignified tone of the rest of the Declaration. It is also more accurate. George III may have repeatedly injured the colonists, but he had not done so unremittingly. The second revision—in which Congress deleted fifteen words and changed "have" to "having"—greatly improved the economy, force, and cadence of the sentence. Like the first revision, it also eliminated the exclamatory tone of Jefferson's draft and removed the possibility that a reader could discredit the Declaration by scraping up just one "solitary fact" to contradict the claim that George III had sought to establish an absolute tyranny over the colonies.

In accusing George of "tyranny," Congress was not, as some writers have suggested, using language loosely for rhetorical effect. The charge of tyranny was the most serious that could be made against a British monarch. It meant, in Locke's words, "the exercise of Power beyond Right." "A Tyrant," Milton said, "is he who regarding neither Law nor the common good, reigns only for himself and his faction." In 1649 Charles I had been executed for "a wicked Design to erect and uphold in himself an unlimited and Tyrannical Power to rule according to his Will, and to overthrow the Rights and Liberties of the People." If George III had sought to establish a tyranny in the American colonies, it would mean he had violated his coronation oath to rule according to law and justice and had thereby forfeited his right to govern the colonies.[69]

The indictment of George III as a tyrant can be seen as a strategic response to the king's proclamation of August 1775 that American leaders were engaged in rebellion against the crown. He called them "dangerous and designing men" who "have at length proceeded to an open and avowed rebellion by arraying themselves in hostile manner to withstand the execution of the law, and traitorously preparing, ordering, and levying war against us." The best way for Congress to refute this charge was to indict the king as a tyrant, for in the eighteenth-century lexicon, opposition to "tyranny" could never be "rebellion." Rebellion meant forceful, unlawful opposition to government. But forceful opposition was unlawful only if the rulers fulfilled their obligation to uphold the constitution. When they did not, when they were unfaithful to their trust and tyrannically assaulted the people's lives, liberties, and estates, the people were justified in resisting the government and returning it to its original principles—just as the English people had done in deposing "tyrannical" kings on seven occasions since the Norman conquest. Each of those occasions had brought about a "revolution" in English government. But "revolution," unlike "rebellion," was not a negative term in the eighteenth century. In the broadest sense it meant simply the "course of anything which returns to the point at which it began to move," as in the revolution of the planets or the seasons. In a political sense it meant "a grand Turn or Change in Government," and was used by Englishmen and Americans alike to signify the Glorious Revolution in which William and Mary had replaced

James II on the throne. According to the American revolutionaries, they were no more guilty of rebellion in 1776 than Englishmen had been in 1689.[70]

Unlike the preamble, however, which most eighteenth-century readers could readily accept as self-evident, the indictment of the king required proof. In keeping with the rhetorical conventions Englishmen had followed for centuries when dethroning a "tyrannical" monarch, the Declaration contains a bill of particulars documenting the king's "repeated injuries and usurpations" of the Americans' rights and liberties.[71] The bill of particulars lists twenty-eight specific grievances and is introduced with the shortest sentence of the Declaration:

To prove this [the king's tyranny], let Facts be submitted to a candid world.[72]

This sentence is so innocuous one can easily overlook its artistry and importance. The opening phrase—"To prove this"—indicates the "facts" to follow will indeed prove that George III is a tyrant. But prove to whom? To a "candid world"—that is, in the eighteenth-century sense of "candid," to readers who are free from bias or malice, who are fair, impartial, and just. The implication is that any such reader will see the "facts" as demonstrating beyond doubt that the king has sought to establish an absolute tyranny in America. If a reader is not convinced, it is not because the facts are untrue or are insufficient to prove the king's villainy; it is because the reader is not "candid."

The pivotal word in the sentence, though, is "facts." As a term in eighteenth-century jurisprudence (Jefferson, like many of his colleagues in Congress, was a lawyer), it meant the circumstances and incidents of a legal case, looked at apart from their legal meaning. This usage fits with the Declaration's similarity to a legal declaration, the plaintiff's written statement of charges showing a "plain and certain" indictment against a defendant.[73] If the Declaration were considered as analogous to a legal declaration or a bill of impeachment, the issue of dispute would not be the status of the law (the right of revolution as expressed in the preamble), but the facts of the specific case at hand (the king's actions to erect a "tyranny" in America).

In ordinary usage, "fact" had by 1776 taken on its current meaning of something that had actually occurred, a truth known by observation, reality rather than supposition or speculation.[74] By characterizing the colonists' grievances against George III as "facts," the Declaration implies that they are unmediated representations of empirical reality rather than interpretations of reality. They are the objective constraints that make the Revolution "necessary." This is reinforced by the passive voice in "let Facts be submitted to a candid world." Who is submitting the facts? No one. They have not been gathered, structured, rendered, or in any way contaminated by human agents—least of all by the Continental Congress. They are just being "submitted," direct from experience without the corrupting intervention of any observer or interpreter.

But "fact" had yet another connotation in the eighteenth century. The word derived from the Latin *facere*, "to do." Its earliest meaning in English was "a thing done or performed"—an action or deed. In the sixteenth and seventeenth centuries it was used most frequently to denote an evil deed or a crime, a usage still in evidence at the time of the Revolution. In 1769, for example, Blackstone, in his *Commentaries on the Laws of England*, noted that "accessories after the fact" were "allowed the benefit of clergy in all cases." The *Annual Register* for 1772 wrote of a thief who was committed to prison for the "fact" of horse stealing.[75] There is no way to know whether Jefferson and the Congress had this sense of "fact" in mind when they adopted the Declaration. Yet regardless of their intentions, for some eighteenth-century readers "facts" may have had a powerful double-edged meaning when applied to George III's actions toward America.

The presentation of what Samuel Adams called George III's "Catalogue of Crimes" is among the Declaration's most skillful features. The grievances could have been arranged chronologically, as Congress had done in all but one of its former state papers. Instead they are arranged topically and are listed seriatim, in sixteen successive sentences beginning "He has" or, in the case of one grievance, "He is." Throughout this section of the Declaration form and content reinforce one another to magnify the perfidy of the king. The steady, laborious piling up of "facts" without comment takes on the character of a legal indictment, while the repetition of "He has" slows the movement of the text, draws attention to the accumulation of grievances, and accentuates George III's role as the prime conspirator against American liberty.[76]

Although one English critic assailed the Declaration for its "studied confusion in the arrangement" of the grievances, they are not listed in random order but fall into four distinct groups. The first group, consisting of charges 1–12, refers to abuses of the king's executive power (I have numbered the charges for ease of reference; they are not enumerated in the Declaration):[77]

He has refused his Assent to Laws, the most wholesome and necessary for the public good. [1]

He has forbidden his Governors to pass Laws of immediate and pressing importance, unless suspended in their operation till his Assent should be obtained; and
when so suspended, he has utterly neglected to attend to them. [2]

He has refused to pass other Laws for the accommodation of large districts of
people, unless those people would relinquish the right of Representation in the
Legislature, a right inestimable to them and formidable to tyrants only. [3]

He has called together legislative bodies at places unusual, uncomfortable, and
distant from the depository of their public Records, for the sole purpose of fatiguing
them into compliance with his measures. [4]

He has dissolved Representative Houses repeatedly, for opposing with manly
firmness his invasions on the rights of the people. [5]

He has refused for a long time, after such dissolutions, to cause others to be
elected; whereby the Legislative powers, incapable of Annihilation, have returned
to the People at large for their exercise; the State remaining in the mean time
exposed to all the dangers of invasion from without, and convulsions within. [6]

He has endeavored to prevent the population of these States; for that purpose
obstructing the Laws of Naturalization of Foreigners; refusing to pass others to
encourage their migrations hither, and raising the conditions of new Appropriations
of Lands. [7]

He has obstructed the Administration of Justice, by refusing his Assent to Laws
for establishing Judiciary powers. [8]

He has made Judges dependent on his Will alone, for the tenure of their offices,
and the amount and payment of their salaries. [9]

He has erected a multitude of New Offices, and sent hither swarms of Officers
to harass our people, and eat out their substance. [10]

He has kept among us, in times of peace, Standing Armies without the Consent
of our legislatures. [11]

He has affected to render the Military independent of and superior to the Civil
power. [12]

These were acts the king had committed himself, either by his
personal command, through his privy council, or by virtue of instructions to his royal governors in America. The substance of charges
5 and 9–12 had appeared in previous congressional state papers,
while charges 1–3, 5–7, and 11–12 had been adumbrated in Jefferson's 1774 pamphlet A *Summary View of the Rights of British America.*
In addition, charges 1 and 2 parallel the first two charges against
James II in the 1689 Declaration of Rights, and number 11 is
modeled closely on the first part of the fifth charge against James
II.[78] It is also worth noting that the average length of charges 1–7
is thirty-three words, while the average length of charges 8–12 is
only nineteen words. As an orator might follow a series of lengthy
passages with several short, sharp phrases for greater impact, so this
section of the Declaration picks up force and urgency by using
progressively shorter sentences.

With the exception of number 10, all of the first group of grievances are presented dispassionately, in legalistic prose, and do not
appear to be exaggerated for rhetorical effect. They look like factual

statements. In truth, though, like all of the Declaration's grievances, they reflect the revolutionaries' view of the conflict and are skillfully written to appear objective while placing George III in the worst possible light. Although the charges imply that George III had exceeded constitutional limitations on his authority, few of the charges actually represented usurpations of power by the king. Refusing assent to colonial laws, invoking the suspending clause, approving new legislative districts, dissolving legislative houses, setting dates for reconvening dissolved legislatures, and stationing regular troops in America during peacetime had long been recognized by most Americans as legitimate exertions of royal power in the colonies. The true source of America's discontent, British critics contended, was not that George III had overstepped the constitution but that the revolutionaries did not approve of his colonial policies.[79]

Moreover, several of the charges were overstated and, as Thomas Hutchinson complained, "most wickedly presented to cast reproach upon the King." As a case in point, charge 4 makes it sound as if George III had consistently and maliciously forced colonial legislatures to meet in "unusual, uncomfortable, and distant" locations. In fact, moving colonial assemblies from their normal meeting places occurred only in three colonies (Massachusetts, Virginia, and South Carolina) and happened more than once only in Massachusetts, where the legislature was convened at Cambridge, four miles outside Boston, from 1769 to 1772. Although this became a simmering dispute between the legislature and the governor, it came about initially because the legislature had refused to conduct business as long as British troops stood guard over the Court House in Boston. As for meeting in Cambridge, the legislature had voluntarily moved there in 1721 to escape the threat of smallpox in Boston, and again in 1747 following a fire in the Boston Town House.[80]

Similarly, the wording of grievance 8 implies that the king had repeatedly refused to establish law courts in America, leaving the colonists without any machinery for "the administration of justice." But all the colonies had courts, and there was only one instance in which George III disallowed a law establishing courts in a colony. That occurred in North Carolina, but it was part of a dispute between the legislature and the governor that stretched back into the 1750s. The disallowance took place because the legislature insisted on the right to attach the property of British debtors who had never resided in North Carolina, a provision without precedent in English common law. After disallowing the law, King George ordered the governor of North Carolina to establish courts of oyer and terminer on his own responsibility. The governor did so, but the legislature denied his authority and refused to appropriate salaries for the judges. A compromise was then worked out that allowed for the creation of inferior courts and courts of oyer and terminer, but neither side would budge on the attachment provision for superior courts. As a result, North Carolina remained without superior courts from 1773 to 1776, but it was hardly the fault of George III alone.[81]

Finally, consider grievance 10, the only one in the entire Declaration expressed figuratively. Its language is biblical and conjures up Old Testament images of "swarms" of flies and locusts covering the face of the earth, "so that the land was darkened," and devouring all they found until "there remained not any green thing in the trees, or in the herbs of the field" (Exodus 10:14–15). It also recalls the denunciation, in Psalms 53:4, of "the workers of iniquity . . . who eat up my people as they eat bread," and the prophecy of Deuteronomy 28:51 that an enemy nation "shall eat the fruit of thy cattle, and the fruit of thy land, until thou be destroyed: which also shall not leave thee either corn, wine, or oil, or the increase of thy kine, or flocks of thy sheep, until he have destroyed thee." For some readers the religious connotations may have been enhanced by "substance," which was used in theological discourse to signify "the Essence or Substance of the Godhead" and to describe the Holy Eucharist, in which Christ had "coupled the substance of his flesh and the substance of bread together, so we together should receive both."[82]

From the revolutionaries' view, however, the primary advantage of the wording of charge 10 was probably its purposeful ambiguity. The "multitude of New Offices" referred to the customs officials who had been appointed in the 1760s to control colonial smuggling. The "swarms" of new officers that were purportedly eating out the substance of the colonies' three million people numbered about fifty in the entire continent. But Congress could hardly assail George III as a tyrant for appointing a few dozen men to enforce the laws against smuggling, so it clothed the charge in vague, evocative imagery that gave significance and emotional resonance to what otherwise might have seemed a rather paltry grievance.[83]

This is not to say Jefferson and the Congress trumped up these charges or did not see them as genuine grievances. Although the Crown saw its order to convene the Massachusetts legislature at Cambridge as perfectly constitutional, the legislature saw it as a violation of "ancient usage and established law" designed to further Britain's "deep-laid and desperate plan of imperial despotism." Similarly, while the king and his advisors were legitimately concerned that North Carolina's attachment provision was contrary to English law, the lower house insisted it could not give up the provision "without at the same time abandoning the interest of their Constituents and the peace and happiness of this Colony." And as minor as it may seem to us today, the dispute over customs commissioners touched a deep nerve. To the revolutionaries, these "pitiful sycophants, court parasites, and hungry dependents" were controlled by the ministers who appointed them and would not think twice about sacrificing American rights and interests to "serve the ambitious purposes of great men at home." Thus while the British ridiculed grievance 10 as a serious issue only to colonial smugglers, the revolutionaries saw it as the entering wedge for an "unnecessary increase of Crown Officers" that one day "may ruin the liberties of America."[84]

The grievances in the Declaration of Independence reflected one side of the British-American conflict. The Declaration presented the truth as Jefferson and the Congress saw it, but it is the last place one should look for an evenhanded account of the American Revolution. Nor should one expect to find such an account in the writings of administration apologists like Lind and Hutchinson. The purpose of the Declaration was to present the case for revolution as persuasively as possible. Defenders of the British government could—and did—present a different view of the same issues.

The second group of charges, consisting of numbers 13–22, attacks the king for combining with "others" (Parliament) to subject America to a variety of unconstitutional measures:

> He has combined with others to subject us to a jurisdiction foreign to our constitution, and unacknowledged by our laws; giving his Assent to their Acts of pretended Legislation: [13]
>
> For Quartering large bodies of armed troops among us: [14]
>
> For protecting them, by a mock Trial, from punishment for any Murders which they should commit on the Inhabitants of these States: [15]
>
> For cutting off our Trade with all parts of the world: [16]
>
> For imposing Taxes on us without our Consent: [17]
>
> For depriving us in many cases of the benefits of Trial by Jury: [18]
>
> For transporting us beyond Seas to be tried for pretended offences: [19]
>
> For abolishing the free System of English Laws in a neighboring Province, establishing therein an Arbitrary government, and enlarging its Boundaries so as to render it at once an example and fit instrument for introducing the same absolute rule into these Colonies: [20]
>
> For taking away our Charters, abolishing our most valuable Laws, and altering fundamentally the Forms of our Governments: [21]
>
> For suspending our own Legislatures, and declaring themselves invested with power to legislate for us in all cases whatsoever. [22]

With the exception of number 13, which can be traced to Jefferson's *Summary View,* all these grievances had been complained of by Congress in previous petitions and addresses. Unlike earlier documents, however, the Declaration does not fault Parliament for its usurpations but blames the king for giving his assent to Parliament's "pretended Legislation." This phrase, which echoes the attack on James II's "pretended power" in the 1689 Declaration of Rights, was particularly galling to defenders of the king. For over a century, they noted, Americans had submitted to parliamentary authority. How, then, could Parliament's jurisdiction over the colonies be "foreign" to the constitution or "unacknowledged" by the colonists' laws? And how could the king be accused of tyranny for doing his duty in upholding the sovereignty of Parliament? To opponents of the Revolution, this was just another instance of the Declaration's "extravagance" and Congress's lack of "all sense of shame."[85]

To the revolutionaries, however, this group of charges was at the heart of the controversy. The proper scope of Parliament's authority had been the major issue in colonial protest rhetoric since the time of the Stamp Act. At first the Whigs had argued that Parliament could not tax the colonists; by 1774 they had moved to the more sweeping claim that Parliament could not make any laws for America—a claim as unacceptable to George III as it was to the House of Lords and the House of Commons. Moreover, in saying America was independent of Parliament but still connected to the empire by allegiance to the Crown, the Whigs had presupposed a dichotomy between the king and Parliament that did not exist in eighteenth-century British politics. As Blackstone explained, the king was a "constituent part" of Parliament. He called the houses together, he met with them (either in person or by representation) to open their sessions, he had the power of proroguing and dissolving them, and he had to assent to their legislation before it became law. Thus Tories had argued that in rejecting the sovereignty of Parliament the Whigs had rejected the king as well.[86] But American leaders held out against this interpretation of the constitution until the very end. It was only in the act of proclaiming independence, when they finally discarded the fiction that the king could do no wrong, that they linked the king with Parliament, and then they went to the other extreme of laying all responsibility for acts of Parliament on the shoulders of the king.

That grievances 14–22 had all been mentioned in earlier congressional papers reinforced the impression that America had repeatedly sought redress before resorting to revolution. Congress could hardly have demonstrated the colonists' "patient sufferance" or the "necessity" of revolution by coining a host of new grievances in the

Declaration. Nor were the "timid" and the "doubting" elements among the American population likely to support a war for independence on the basis of new grievances. By adducing old grievances the British government had insistently refused to redress, Congress strengthened its claim to having done everything possible to maintain American freedom within the British empire and made a strong appeal for support among those colonists who still needed convincing that independence was necessary in the face of England's deliberate assault on their rights and liberties.

As with other parts of the Declaration, the grievances are sometimes as interesting for what they omit as for what they include. Charge 20, for example, deals with the Quebec Act of 1774, which extended the boundary of Quebec to include the Old Northwest, provided for government by an appointed governor and council rather than by an elected legislature, and guaranteed freedom of religion to the province's French Catholics. Before 1776 Congress had often denounced the act for establishing "the Roman Catholic religion throughout those vast regions that border on the westerly and northerly boundaries of the free protestant English settlements." It was astonishing, Congress exclaimed in its 1774 Address to the People of Great Britain, that Parliament would establish in Canada "a religion that has deluged your island in blood, and dispersed impiety, bigotry, persecution, murder and rebellion through every part of the world." By such remarks Congress sought to exploit the deep Anglo-American hostility to Catholicism. But when Congress appealed to the people of Canada for support, it condemned the British government for not protecting "your priests" from "expulsion, banishment, and ruin, whenever their wealth and possessions furnish sufficient temptation," and labeled religious prejudice a "low-minded" infirmity that should not stand in the way of "a hearty amity with us." Similarly, the Declaration of Independence contains not a whisper of anti-Catholicism, for fear of jeopardizing the prospects for support from France or Spain.[87]

It is also worth noting that the second set of grievances, like the other sets, contains a substantial amount of strategic ambiguity. While the grievances have a certain specificity in that they refer to actual historical events, they do not identify names, dates, or places. This magnified the seriousness of the grievances by making it seem as if each charge against the king referred not to a particular piece of legislation or to an isolated act in a single colony, but to a violation of the constitution that had been repeated on many occasions throughout America.

The ambiguity of the grievances also made them more difficult to refute. In order to build a convincing case against the grievances, defenders of the king had to clarify each charge and what specific act or events it referred to, and then explain why the charge was not true. Thus it took John Lind, who composed the most sustained British response to the Declaration, 110 pages to answer the charges set forth by the Continental Congress in fewer than two dozen sentences. Although Lind deftly exposed many of the charges to be flimsy at best, his detailed and complex rebuttal did not stand a chance against the Declaration as a propaganda document. Nor has Lind's work fared much better since 1776. While the Declaration continues to command an international audience and has created an indelible popular image of George III as a tyrant, Lind's work remains a piece of arcana, buried in the dustheap of history.[88]

The third group of charges assails the king's violence and cruelty in waging war against his American subjects. They burden him with a litany of venal deeds that make him out as little better than the notorious Richard III, who had forfeited his crown in 1485 for "unnatural, mischievous, and great Perjuries, Treasons, Homicides and Murders, in shedding of Infants' blood, with many other Wrongs, odious Offences, and abominations against God and Man."[89]

He has abdicated Government here, by declaring us out of his Protection and waging War against us. [23]

He has plundered our seas, ravaged our Coasts, burnt our towns, and destroyed the Lives of our people. [24]

He is at this time transporting large Armies of foreign Mercenaries to complete the works of death, desolation and tyranny, already begun with circumstances of Cruelty and Perfidy scarcely paralleled in the most barbarous ages, and totally unworthy the Head of a civilized nation. [25]

He has constrained our fellow Citizens taken Captive on the high Seas to bear Arms against their Country, to become the executioners of their friends and Brethren, or to fall themselves by their Hands. [26]

He has excited domestic insurrections amongst us, and has endeavored to bring on the inhabitants of our frontiers, the merciless Indian Savages, whose known rule of warfare, is an undistinguished destruction of all ages, sexes and conditions. [27]

The immediate source for this set of grievances, as for the first two, was the draft of a new constitution for Virginia that Jefferson had written early in June 1776. In it Jefferson listed the "acts of misrule" by which George III had "forfeited the kingly office" within Virginia. Two weeks later Jefferson used that list as his model in composing the grievances against George III in the Declaration of Independence. With the exception of charge 26, which was added to the Declaration by the Committee of Five, all the war grievances were taken, in different order but with little change in wording, from Jefferson's draft of the Virginia constitution.[90]

This portion of the Declaration also had forerunners among earlier congressional documents. It contains ideas and snippets of prose from six papers composed since the outbreak of war—the Report on Lord North's Conciliatory Proposal (written by Jefferson), the Declaration of the Causes and Necessity for Taking Up Arms (coauthored by Jefferson), the 1775 Address to the Inhabitants of Great Britain, the Address to the People of Ireland, the Olive Branch Petition to George III, and the March 1776 Declaration on Armed Vessels.[91] Jefferson had likely drawn upon these papers in developing his war grievances for the Virginia constitution, which he subsequently transferred to his draft of the Declaration.

Although scholars often downplay the last five grievances as "the weakest part of the Declaration,"[92] they were extremely important to Congress and to the rhetorical strategy of the Declaration. They came last partly because they were the most recent of George III's "abuses and usurpations," but also because they constituted the ultimate proof of his plan to reduce the colonies under "absolute despotism." In the eyes of many moderate congressmen, as well as in the eyes of many citizens outside Congress, the king's acts of war proved to be the sword that finally severed the Gordian knot connecting the colonies to the empire.

Charge 23 is perhaps the most serious accusation in the Declaration. Its claim that George III "has abdicated Government here" parallels the charge of the Declaration of Rights that James II had "abdicated the Government" of England, while its accusation that George was "waging War" against his subjects saddles him with the same crime that had cost Charles I his throne in 1649. This charge, if accepted, put Congress squarely in the tradition of those seventeenth-century English patriots who had twice rescued the nation from monarchical tyranny. It meant that George III—like Charles I and James II—had "broken the original contract between king and people" by "not affording due protection to his subjects." Thus he could no longer claim authority over them, and they no longer owed obedience to him.[93]

The next four grievances amplify the "Cruelty and Perfidy" of King George's war measures. Number 24 refers to the burning of Falmouth, Charlestown, Norfolk, and Charleston by the British. The importance of this charge to the crystallization of support for independence was suggested by George Washington. "Such flaming arguments as were exhibited at Falmouth and Norfolk," he wrote in

January 1776, would help many colonists "decide upon the propriety of a separation." The hiring of Hessian mercenaries, condemned in charge 25, was even more telling. As Arthur St. Clair later explained, it "cast the die" for "many worthy men" who had heretofore argued for reconciliation but who now felt that "if foreign troops were employed to reduce Americans to absolute submission, . . . independence or any other mode was justifiable."[94]

Grievance 26 deals with a provision of the Prohibitory Act of December 1775 that empowered the British navy to capture American trading vessels and impress their crews into his majesty's service to fight against the colonies. Although the Continental Congress has often been criticized for exaggerating its grievances against the king, it was less harsh in expressing this charge than were members of the House of Lords who voted against the Prohibitory Act. They called its impressment provision "a refinement in tyranny" that obliged "the unhappy men who shall be made captives in this predatory war, to bear arms against their families, friends, and country; and after being plundered themselves, to become accomplices in plundering their brethren." Like many American leaders, John Adams believed this "piratical Act" effectually sundered America from Great Britain "forever."[95]

Grievance 27 is one of the most interesting and controversial of the entire Declaration. It actually contains three charges, as can be seen by looking at the revisions Congress made in Jefferson's fair copy. When this portion of the Declaration was reported to Congress, it read:

> He has endeavored to bring on the inhabitants of our frontiers the merciless Indian savages, whose known rule of warfare is an undistinguished destruction of all ages, sexes, and conditions of existence.
>
> He has incited treasonable insurrections of our fellow-citizens, with the allurements of forfeiture and confiscation of our property.
>
> He has waged cruel war against human nature itself, violating its most sacred rights of life and liberty in the persons of a distant people who never offended him, captivating and carrying them into slavery in another hemisphere or to incur miserable death in their transportation thither. This piratical warfare, the opprobrium of *infidel* powers, is the warfare of the *Christian* king of Great Britain. Determined to keep open a market where *Men* should be bought and sold, he has prostituted his negative for suppressing every legislative attempt to prohibit or to restrain this execrable commerce. And that this assemblage of horrors might want no fact of distinguished die, he is now exciting those very people to rise in arms among us, and to purchase that liberty of which he has deprived them, by murdering the people on whom he also obtruded them: thus paying off former crimes committed against the *Liberties* of one people, with crimes which he urges them to commit against the *lives* of another.[96]

Each of these charges attacked the king for inciting various groups in America to fight against the Revolution. The first charge, dealing with "the merciless Indian savages," surprises many modern readers, but it was fully in keeping with eighteenth-century attitudes and imagery.[97] The second charge, however, was potentially embarrassing to the revolutionaries. In attacking George III for inciting "treasonable insurrection of our [the colonists'] fellow-citizens," it referred to his efforts to enlist American loyalists in the British army. This put Congress in the awkward position of calling loyalists traitors and of attacking the king for encouraging them to remain loyal.

The third of Jefferson's grievances was even more troublesome. For years scholars have read it as an attack on the slave trade and on George III for not using his royal power to eliminate it. In fact, the real force of this grievance is in its last sentence, which indicts the king for exciting the slaves to "rise in arms" against their American masters—a reference to Governor Dunmore's proclamation of November 7, 1775, freeing Virginia slaves who joined the king's troops. This is especially evident when we look at other instances of colonial rhetoric. In March 1776 the Continental Congress condemned British leaders for "instigating negroes to murder their masters." Two months later William Henry Drayton told the grand jury of Charleston, South Carolina, that the "catalogue of our oppressions" included the fact that Southern governors "have enveigled negroes from, and have armed them against their masters." And when the Virginia Convention voted for independence on May 15, 1776, its official resolves berated Governor Dunmore for "carrying on a piratical and savage war against us, tempting our slaves by every artifice to resort to him, and training and employing them against their masters." Here, in all these documents, is the essence of the slavery charge without the tortuous prelude Jefferson added in the Declaration of Independence to obscure the irony of charging George III with the "crime" of manumission.[98]

As Garry Wills notes, "Congress had good reason to think Jefferson's longer, morally convoluted charge [on slavery] would just open it to ridicule," as would the charge that George III was violating the constitution by asking the loyalists to be loyal. Therefore, Congress struck both grievances and edited Jefferson's draft to read, "He has excited domestic insurrections amongst us, and has endeavored to bring on the inhabitants of our frontiers the merciless Indian Savages, whose known rule of warfare is an undistinguished destruction of all ages, sexes and conditions." The phrase "excited domestic insurrections amongst us" was meant to include both loyalists and slaves while making the Declaration less vulnerable to attack. This was unquestionably a salutary revision, but even the brief reference to "domestic insurrections" prompted a barrage of criticism from opponents of the Revolution, who scornfully dismissed the notion that enlisting the loyalists could be called insurrection and scathingly exposed the absurdity and hypocrisy of offering freedom to slaves as evidence of tyranny.[99]

Whatever they may have lacked in moral consistency, the war grievances expressed the revolutionaries' outrage over George III's behavior. Whereas the first two groups of grievances describe the king's acts with such temperate verbs as "refused," "called together," "dissolved," "endeavored," "made," "erected," "kept," and "affected," the war grievances use emotionally charged verbs such as "plundered," "ravaged," "burnt," and "destroyed." With the exception of grievance 10, which accused the king of sending "swarms of Officers to harass our people, and eat out their substance," there is nothing in the earlier charges to compare with the evocative accusation that George III was spreading "death, desolation and tyranny . . . with circumstances of Cruelty and Perfidy scarcely paralleled in the most barbarous ages," or with the characterization of "the merciless Indian Savages, whose known mode of warfare is an undistinguished destruction of all ages, sexes and conditions."

To some extent, of course, the emotional intensity of the war grievances was a natural outgrowth of their subject. It is hard to write about warfare without using strong language. Also, to many of the revolutionaries independence was at bottom an emotional—or sentimental—issue. It was folly, Thomas Paine argued in *Common Sense,* to talk of reconciliation with "that barbarous and hellish power, which have stirred up the Indians and the Negroes to destroy us." Our "affections" have been "wounded thro' a thousand pores," he exclaimed, and "never can true reconcilement grow where wounds of deadly hate have pierced so deep." To Paine, those wounds had broken the "last cord" with England:

There are injuries which nature cannot forgive; she would cease to be nature if she did. As well can the lover forgive the ravisher of his mistress, as the Continent forgive the murders of Britain. The Almighty hath implanted in us these inextinguishable feelings for good and wise purposes. They are the Guardians of his Image in our hearts. They distinguish us from the herd of common animals. The social compact would dissolve, and justice be extirpated from the earth, or have only a casual existence were we callous to the touches of affection. The robber and the murderer would often escape unpunished, did not the injuries which our tempers sustain, provoke us into justice.

A decade later, in his famous "Head and Heart" letter to Maria Cosway, Jefferson affirmed the supremacy of sentiment over reason and attributed the Revolution to the former: "If our country, when pressed with wrongs at the point of the bayonet, had been governed by its heads instead of its hearts, where should we have been now? hanging on a gallows as high as Haman's. You began to calculate and to compare wealth and numbers: we threw up a few pulsations of our warmest blood: we supplied enthusiasm against wealth and numbers: we put our existence to the hazard, when the hazard seemed against us, and we saved our country."[100]

In addition to reflecting the revolutionaries' "enthusiasm," the emotional pitch of the war grievances was probably designed to solidify support for independence in those parts of America that had yet to suffer the physical and economic hardships of war. As late as May 1776 John Adams lamented that while independence had strong support in New England and the South, it was less secure in the middle colonies, which "have never tasted the bitter Cup; they have never Smarted—and are therefore a little cooler." As Thomas Paine recognized, many colonists were untouched by the war; "the evil" was "not sufficiently brought to their doors to make them feel the precariousness with which all American property is possessed." In *Common Sense* Paine sought to bring the "evil" home to his readers by inducing them to identify with the "horror" inflicted on other Americans by the British forces "that hath carried fire and sword" into the land. He wrote: "If you say, you can still pass the violations over, then I ask, Hath your house been burnt? Hath your property been destroyed before your face? Are your wife and children destitute of a bed to lie on, or bread to live on? Have you lost a parent or a child by their hands, and yourself the ruined and wretched survivor?" In similar fashion the Declaration of Independence used images of terror to magnify the wickedness of George III, to arouse "the passions and feelings" of readers, and to awaken "from fatal and unmanly slumbers" those Americans who had yet to be directly touched by the ravages of war.[101]

After the last of the war grievances, the Declaration presents its final charge against the king:

In every stage of these Oppressions We have Petitioned for Redress in the most humble terms: Our repeated Petitions have been answered only by repeated injury. [28]

This is a very clever sentence. As the Declaration had earlier introduced the grievances against George III as "facts," here it summarizes them as "Oppressions." It then contrasts the king's "Oppressions" with the colonists' "humble" petitions for redress and claims those "repeated Petitions" had produced nothing but "repeated injury." The use of parallel structure and the reiteration of "repeated" accentuates the colonies' humility and England's malevolence. Coming immediately after the preceding twenty-seven grievances, this sentence emphasizes the colonists' "patient sufferance" through "every stage" of the Revolution and reinforces the point that they have been driven to independence as a last resort by the king's despotic ambition.

In saying America's requests for redress had been ignored, the Declaration struck a note that had been sounded in Congress's 1774 Petition to the King and in its 1775 Address to the Inhabitants of Great Britain. The former stated that "Humble and reasonable petitions from the representatives of the people have been fruitless," while the latter complained that "our late Petition to the Throne produced no other Effect than fresh Injuries." At no time, however, not even in 1776, did Congress accuse the British government of violating the Americans' "indubitable" right "peaceably to assemble, consider of their grievances, and Petition the King."[102] It charged merely that the government had refused to grant any of the Americans' requests for redress, that the colonists' "repeated Petitions" had produced "only . . . repeated injury." Even this charge was misleading, however, for though neither of Congress's petitions to the king had been successful, Parliament had repealed the Stamp Act in 1766 and in 1770 had retracted all of the Townshend duties save that on tea.

Although it has seldom been noticed, the final grievance does not explicitly mention the king. Instead of saying, "He has answered our repeated petitions only by repeated injury," which would have been consistent with the form of the earlier grievances, the Declaration uses a passive sentence that does not specify who is to blame for rejecting the petitions. This ambiguity was doubtless deliberate. Because the Continental Congress had not been formed until 1774, the "We" in "We have petitioned for redress" through "every stage of these Oppressions" cannot refer to Congress unless "these Oppressions" refers just to the war grievances. But it is hardly likely Jefferson and the Congress had this in mind, since the colonies had sent numerous petitions to England before 1774. So "We" must refer to the colonists in general and to the numerous petitions they had sent to England from 1765 onward. Yet most of America's efforts to obtain redress before 1774 had been directed to Parliament rather than to the king. Thus Congress could not overtly indict the king for rejecting America's petitions through "every stage" of the conflict; neither could it shift the focus at this point of the Declaration from the king to Parliament.

Congress solved this problem with the next sentence of the Declaration, which ended the indictment of the king:

A Prince, whose character is thus marked by every act which may define a Tyrant, is unfit to be the ruler of a free people.

The placement of this sentence immediately after "Our repeated Petitions have been answered only by repeated injury" not only reiterates the labeling of George III as a "tyrant," but strongly suggests it was George himself who had closed the door to reconciliation by rejecting all of the Americans' petitions. In this way Congress remained technically accurate while making its point no less effectively through implication. It also ended the attack on the king on a particularly personal note, attacking not just George III's policies but his "character," which it described as marked by "every act which may define a Tyrant."[103]

Finally, it is important to note that all of the Declaration's grievances indict only "the present King of Great Britain." They do not include any infringements of colonial rights that may have occurred before the reign of George III. Nor does the Declaration attack monarchy as an institution, despite the revolutionaries' belief that "Kings have been a curse to this and every other country where they have gained a footing." One of the great blessings of independence, they exulted, would be to free America from "that worst of plagues, the KING'S EVIL," which "will soon be [extir]pated from this otherwise happy land, and never more be suffered to infest it again."[104] But, of course, independence had to be won, and it was not likely to be won without support from European monarchies such as France and Spain, neither of which would be favorably impressed with a Declaration that inveighed against kingship. Thus even though Congress was committed to republicanism and was careful in the preamble of the Declaration to provide a justification for changing America's "Form of Government," it was equally careful not to betray antimonarchical sentiments. It renounced George III not for being a king, but for being a tyrant.

VI

In addition to petitioning Parliament and George III, Whig leaders had also worked hard to cultivate friends of the American cause in England. As part of this effort, Congress had sent two lengthy addresses to the British people, the first in October 1774 and the second in July 1775. These addresses detailed the colonists' grievances, warned that the plot against American liberty was just the first step in a design to reduce the people of England themselves to slavery, and appealed to the "voices of justice" to restore "harmony, friendship and fraternal affection" between the colonists and their "Friends, Brethren and Countrymen, on the other side of the Atlantic." "Permit us to be as free as yourselves," Congress urged, and "we shall consider your enemies as our enemies, and your interest as our own."[105]

But the British people had proved no more receptive to the Whigs than had the government, and so the Declaration follows the attack on George III by noting that the colonies had also appealed in vain to the people of Great Britain:

Nor have We been wanting in attentions to our British brethren. We have warned them from time to time of attempts by their legislature to extend an unwarrantable jurisdiction over us. We have reminded them of the circumstances of our emigration and settlement here. We have appealed to their native justice and magnanimity, and we have conjured them by the ties of our common kindred to disavow these usurpations, which, would inevitably interrupt our connections and correspondence. They too have been deaf to the voice of justice and of consanguinity. We must, therefore, acquiesce in the necessity, which denounces our Separation, and hold them, as we hold the rest of mankind, Enemies in War, in Peace Friends.

In Jefferson's draft this paragraph was three times as long as in its final version. Congress cut it by 229 words, almost all in two major deletions. The first removed Jefferson's statement that the settlement of the colonies had been

effected at the expence of our own blood and treasure, unassisted by the wealth or the strength of Great Britain: that in constituting indeed our several forms of government, we had adopted one common king, thereby laying a foundation for perpetual league and amity with them: but that submission to their parliament was no part of our constitution, nor ever in idea, if history may be credited.

The second excision included Jefferson's highly wrought condemnation of the British people for keeping in power "the disturbers of our harmony" and for "permitting" the king to send royal troops and foreign mercenaries "to invade and destroy us":

These facts have given the last stab to agonizing affection, and manly spirit bids us to renounce for ever these unfeeling brethren. We must endeavor to forget our former love for them. . . . We might have been a free and a great people together; but a communication of grandeur and of freedom it seems is below their dignity. Be it so, since they will have it. The road to happiness and to glory is open to us too. We will tread it apart from them.[106]

Although Jefferson never resigned himself to these "mutilations" of his manuscript, they substantially improved the Declaration from a rhetorical standpoint. For one thing, Jefferson's view of the colonies' historical claim to independence of Parliament from the very beginning of their settlement was questionable enough that including it in the Declaration would only have opened Congress to needless criticism. For another, the haughty tone of moral superiority in what John Adams called Jefferson's "oratorical paragraphs" about the colonists' "unfeeling brethren" was discordant with the rest of the Declaration. Jefferson claimed Congress struck "those passages which conveyed censures on the people of England" because many delegates were "still haunted" by "the pusillanimous idea that we had friends in England worth keeping terms with." Although Jefferson's explanation has been uncritically accepted by historians, it is suspect, for the simple reason that Congress did not eliminate his denunciation of the British people. It did, however, excise his hortatory prose—perhaps because the delegates thought it exhibited the deficiencies William Livingston had discerned in Jefferson's draft of the 1775 Declaration of the Causes and Necessity of Taking Up Arms: "Much fault-finding and declamation, with little sense or dignity."[107]

In its final version, the British brethren paragraph reinforces three crucial points made earlier in the Declaration—that the colonies have exhausted every avenue for reconciliation, that the Americans are a separate people from the British, and that independence is a matter of necessity. It is also one of the most artfully written sections of the Declaration. The first sentence, beginning "Nor . . . ," shifts attention quickly and cleanly away from George III to the colonists' "British brethren." The "have we" of the first sentence is neatly reversed in the "We have" at the start of the second. Sentences two through four, containing four successive clauses beginning "We Have," give a pronounced sense of momentum to the paragraph while underlining the colonists' active efforts to reach the British people. The repetition of "We have" here also parallels the repetition of "He has" in the grievances against George III.[108]

The fifth sentence—"They too have been deaf to the voice of justice and of consanguinity"—echoes the statement in Congress's Fast-Day Resolution of March 16, 1776, that the British had been "deaf to the voice of reason and humanity."[109] It contains one of the few metaphors in the Declaration and acquires added force by its simplicity and brevity, which contrast with the greater length and complexity of the preceding sentence. The final sentence unifies the paragraph by returning to the pattern of beginning with "We," and its intricate periodic structure plays off the simple structure of the fifth sentence so as to strengthen the cadence of the entire paragraph. The closing words—"Enemies in

War, in Peace Friends"—employ chiasmus, a favorite rhetorical device of eighteenth-century writers. How effective the device is in this case can be gauged by rearranging the final words to read, "Enemies in War, Friends in Peace," which weakens both the force and harmony of the Declaration's phrasing.

It is worth noting, as well, that this is the only part of the Declaration to employ much alliteration: "British brethren," "time to time," "common kindred," "which would," "connections and correspondence." The euphony gained by these phrases is fortified by the heavy repetition of medial and terminal consonants in adjoining words: "been wanting in attentions to," "them from time to time," "to their native justice," "disavow these usurpations," "have been deaf to the voice of." Finally, this paragraph, like the rest of the Declaration, contains a high proportion of one- and two-syllable words (82 percent). Of those words, an overwhelming number (eighty-one of ninety-six) contain only one syllable. The rest of the paragraph contains nine three-syllable words, eight four-syllable words, and four five-syllable words. This felicitous blend of a large number of very short words with a few very long ones is reminiscent of Lincoln's Gettysburg Address and contributes greatly to the harmony, cadence, and eloquence of the Declaration, much as it contributes to the same features in Lincoln's immortal speech.

VII

The British brethren section essentially finished the Declaration's persuasive work. The case for independence had been made. Congress had set forth the conditions that justified revolution and had shown, as best it could, that those conditions existed in Great Britain's thirteen North American colonies. All that remained was for Congress to conclude the Declaration:

We, therefore, the Representatives of the united States of America, in General Congress, Assembled, appealing to the Supreme Judge of the world for the rectitude of our intentions, do, in the Name, and by Authority of the good People of these Colonies, solemnly publish and declare, That these United Colonies are, and of Right ought to be Free and Independent States; that they are Absolved from all Allegiance to the British Crown, and that all political connection between them and the State of Great Britain, is and ought to be totally dissolved; and that as Free and Independent States, they have full Power to levy War, conclude Peace, contract Alliances, establish Commerce, and to do all other Acts and Things which Independent States may of right do. And for the support of this Declaration, with a firm reliance on the protection of divine Providence, we mutually pledge to each other our Lives, our Fortunes and our sacred Honor.

This final paragraph of the Declaration is highly formulaic. After professing the "rectitude" of the revolutionaries' intentions, a standard move in eighteenth-century political rhetoric, the conclusion affirms Congress's legitimacy as a representative body acting "in the Name, and by Authority of the good People of these Colonies." Because Congress was not a regularly constituted legislative body, it could not be presumed to represent the people of America in the same way Parliament could be presumed to represent the people of Great Britain. Most of its delegates had been chosen not by direct election of the people or even by the colonial legislatures, but by special provincial conventions created by the Whigs to safeguard the protest movement against the established colonial governments. Fully aware that Tories and British leaders would attack it on these grounds, Congress had included some kind of legitimating statement in most of its public papers before 1776. Such a statement was particularly important in the Declaration of Independence because, as we saw earlier, the right of revolution did not make it lawful for "a few Persons to oppose their Prince." Revolution was justified only when the "Body of the People" rose up to restore their most basic rights against an oppressive ruler.[110] By portraying itself as the agent of the American people, Congress helped forestall any possible challenges to its authority or to the legality of the Revolution. It also made clear to the nations of the world that it was the legitimate governing body of the "united States of America."

The main business of the conclusion—as in most political declarations of the time—was to announce (to "publish and declare") the policy to be followed in consequence of the claims advanced in the rest of the document. In this case, the statement of policy consisted of four propositions, the first three of which duplicated the exact wording of Richard Henry Lee's resolution for independence approved on July 2: "That these United Colonies are, and of Right ought to be Free and Independent States; that they are Absolved from all Allegiance to the British Crown; and that all political connection between them and the State of Great Britain, is and ought to be totally dissolved." Congress substituted Lee's resolution for Jefferson's wording, which, in addition to renouncing allegiance to the Crown, had also sworn off "all political connection which may heretofore have subsisted between us and the people or parliament of Great Britain."[111] Lee's resolution, like the rest of the Declaration, did not mention Parliament by name. Putting it in the conclusion kept the focus on the Crown and avoided the incongruity of rejecting America's subjection to a jurisdiction the Declaration had already dismissed as "foreign to our constitution and unacknowledged by our laws."

In addition to the propositions contained in Lee's resolution, the conclusion claimed for America all the powers of sovereign states under international law, including the power to "levy War, conclude Peace, contract Alliances, [and] establish Commerce." Here, it might be said, is the end to which the Declaration was the means. As we have seen, Congress believed America had to receive assistance from other nations if it were to win the war with Great Britain. Congress also knew America stood no chance of receiving assistance until it declared its independence from British rule. As Thomas Paine explained in January 1776, "under our present denomination of British Subjects, we can neither be received nor heard abroad: the custom of all Courts is against us, and will be so, until by an Independence we take rank with other Nations." Just as this was the climactic argument for independence in Paine's *Common Sense*, so is the assertion of America's right to "take rank with other nations" the climactic claim in the conclusion of the Declaration. Congress thereby sent a special reminder to European powers that they could lawfully establish commercial, military, and diplomatic alliances with the "Free and Independent States" of North America.[112]

In keeping with the rhetorical conventions of seventeenth- and eighteenth-century political declarations, the closing sentence of the Declaration of Independence claims the support of divine Providence and binds the members of Congress in a pledge of mutual support. Carl Becker, in discussing the literary qualities of the Declaration, deemed this sentence "perfection itself":

It is true (assuming that men value life more than property, which is doubtful) that the statement violates the rhetorical rule of climax; but it was a sure sense that made Jefferson place 'lives' first and 'fortunes' second. How much weaker if he had written "our fortunes, our lives, and our sacred honor"! Or suppose him to have used the word 'property' instead of 'fortunes!' Or suppose him to have omitted 'sacred!' Consider the effect of omitting any of the words, such as the last two 'ours'—"our lives, fortunes, and sacred honor." No, the sentence can hardly be improved.[113]

Becker is correct in his judgment about the wording and rhythm of the sentence, but he errs in attributing high marks to Jefferson for his "sure sense" in placing "lives" before "fortunes." "Lives and fortunes" was one of the most hackneyed phrases of eighteenth-century Anglo-American political discourse. Colonial writers had

used it with numbing regularity throughout the dispute with England
(along with other stock phrases such as "liberties and estates" and
"life, liberty, and property").[114] Its appearance in the Declaration
can hardly be taken as a measure of Jefferson's "peculiar felicity of
expression."

What marks Jefferson's "happy talent for composition" in this case
is the coupling of "our sacred honor" with "our lives" and "our
fortunes" to create the eloquent trilogy that closes the Declaration.
He may have been inspired by the Continental Association, in
which Congress pledged itself "under the sacred ties of virtue, honor
and love of our country," or by the Virginia nonimportation resolves
of 1770 and the Virginia Association of 1774, both of which bound
Virginians by the "sacred Ties of Honour and Love to our Country."[115] The concept of honor exerted a powerful hold on the eighteenth-century mind. Writers of all kinds—philosophers, preachers,
politicians, playwrights, poets—repeatedly speculated about the
sources of honor and how to achieve it. Virtually every educated
man in England or America was schooled in the classical maxim,
"What is left when honor is lost?" Or as Joseph Addison wrote in
his *Cato*, whose sentiments were widely admired throughout the
eighteenth century on both sides of the Atlantic: "Better to die ten
thousand deaths/Than wound my honour." The cult of honor was
so strong that in English judicial proceedings a peer of the realm did
not answer to bills in chancery or give a verdict "upon oath, like an
ordinary juryman, but upon his honour."[116]

By pledging "our sacred Honor" in support of the Declaration,
Congress made a particularly solemn vow. The pledge also carried
a latent message that the revolutionaries, contrary to the claims of
their detractors, were men of honor whose motives and actions could
not only withstand the closest scrutiny by contemporary persons of
quality and merit but would also deserve the approbation of posterity.
If the Revolution succeeded, its leaders stood to achieve lasting
honor as what Francis Bacon called "*Liberatores* or *Salvatores*"—men
who "compound the long Miseries of Civil Wars, or deliver their
Countries from Servitude of Strangers or Tyrants." Historical examples included Augustus Caesar, Henry VII of England, and Henry
IV of France. On Bacon's five-point scale of supreme honor, such
heroes ranked below only "*Conditores Imperiorum*, Founders of States
and Commonwealths," such as Romulus, Caesar, and Ottoman, and
"Lawgivers" such as Solon, Lycurgus, and Justinian, "also called
Second Founders, or *Perpetui Principes*, because they Govern by their
Ordinances after they are gone."[117] Seen in this way, "our sacred
Honor" lifts the motives of Congress above the more immediate

concerns of "our Lives" and "our Fortunes" and places the revolutionaries in the footsteps of history's most honorable figures. As a result
it also unifies the entire text by subtly playing out the notion that
the Revolution is a major turn in the broad "course of human
events."

At the same time, the final sentence completes a crucial metamorphosis in the text. Although the Declaration begins in an impersonal, even philosophical voice, it gradually becomes a kind of
drama, with its tensions expressed more and more in personal terms.
This transformation begins with the appearance of the villain, "the
present King of Great Britain," who dominates the stage through
the first nine grievances, all of which note what "He has" done
without identifying the victim of his evil deeds. Beginning with
grievance 10 the king is joined on stage by the American colonists,
who are identified as the victim by some form of first person plural
reference: The king has sent "swarms of officers to harass *our* people,"
has quartered "armed troops among *us*," has imposed "taxes on *us*
without *our* consent," "has taken away *our* charters, abolished *our*
most valuable laws," and altered "the Forms of *our* Governments."
He has "plundered *our* seas, ravaged *our* coasts, burnt *our* towns,
. . . destroyed the lives of *our* people," and "excited domestic insurrections amongst *us*." The word "our" is used twenty-six times from
its first appearance in grievance 10 through the last sentence of the
Declaration, while "us" occurs eleven times from its first appearance
in grievance 11 through the rest of the grievances.[118]

Throughout the grievances action is instigated by the king, as the
colonists passively accept blow after blow without wavering in their
loyalty. His villainy complete, George III leaves the stage and it is
occupied next by the colonists and their "British brethren." The
heavy use of personal pronouns continues, but by now the colonists
have become the instigators of action as they actively seek redress
of their grievances. This is marked by a shift in idiom from "He has"
to "We have": "*We* have petitioned for redress . . . ," "*We* have
reminded *them* . . . ," "*We* have appealed to *their* . . . ," and "*we*
have conjured *them*." But "*they* have been deaf" to all pleas, so "*We*
must . . . hold *them*" as enemies. By the last paragraph only the
colonists remain on stage to pronounce their dramatic closing lines:
"*We* . . . solemnly publish and declare. . . ." And to support this
declaration, "*we* mutually pledge to each other *our* Lives, *our* Fortunes, and *our* sacred Honor."

The persistent use of "he" and "them," "us" and "our," "they" and
"we" personalizes the British-American conflict and transfigures it
from a complex struggle of multifarious origins and diverse motives

to a simple moral drama in which a patiently suffering people courageously defend their liberty against a cruel and vicious tyrant. It also reduces the psychic distance between the reader and the text and coaxes the reader into seeing the dispute with Great Britain through the eyes of the revolutionaries. As the drama of the Declaration unfolds, the reader is increasingly solicited to identify with Congress and "the good people of these colonies," to share their sense of victimage, to participate vicariously in their struggle, and ultimately to act with them in their heroic quest for freedom.

VIII

It has become a commonplace of recent scholarship that the Declaration did not attract much interest in the 1770s. Contemporaries in France seldom mentioned the Declaration, though they studied and frequently cited the state constitutions and their accompanying declarations of rights. British officials in America treated its publication rather casually, neither the House of Lords nor the House of Commons said much about its substance during their lengthy debates on the American question in the fall of 1776, and in an age of intense political pamphleteering it provoked only two major pamphlet responses in England.[119] In America the Declaration was "hailed with acclamations," but it was hardly treated with awe or reverence. As Merrill Peterson has noted, neither Jefferson "nor anyone else realized the far-reaching implications of the document." Not until the burst of patriotic self-congratulation following the War of 1812 did Americans begin to regard the Declaration as a national treasure.[120]

Yet we should not conclude that the Declaration was unimportant or ineffective in its time. To understand its importance and effectiveness, however, we must disregard the aura that surrounds it today and recall that its original aim was to rally Americans in support of independence. In the weeks after July 4, thousands of Americans gathered in public ceremonies to hear the Declaration proclaimed, and many thousands more read it in the newspapers or on broadsides. Although it is difficult at times to distinguish between their response to the act of asserting independence and their response to the document justifying that act, the evidence seems clear that they attended closely to the words of the Declaration and responded enthusiastically to them.

In Philadelphia, for example, the Declaration was proclaimed publicly on July 8 to "a very large number of the inhabitants," who received it "with general applause and heart-felt satisfaction." When the Declaration reached New Brunswick, New Jersey, by express rider on July 9, it was read to the public "with grave deliberation and emphasis. At the close of the reading there was prolonged cheering." In Boston the Declaration elicited admiration "for its Comprehensive and calm Dignity" and seemed "to animate and inspire Everyone to support and defend the Independency he feels." According to Abigail Adams, "the multitude" who gathered to hear it proclaimed on July 18 gave "great attention . . . to every word." Afterward, "the Bells rang, the privateers fired, the forts and Batteries, the cannon were discharged, the platoons followed and every face appeared joyful." In Halifax, North Carolina, the Declaration was presented to an "immense crowd" by Cornelius Harnett. He read it "to the mute and impassioned multitude with the solemnity of an appeal to Heaven. When he had finished, all the people shouted with joy. . . . The soldiers seized Mr. Harnett, and bore him on their shoulders through the streets of the town, applauding him as their champion, and swearing allegiance to the instrument he had read." At Ticonderoga, Pennsylvania, the Declaration was read to the Continental troops by Arthur St. Clair. They "manifested their joy with three cheers. It was remarkably pleasing to see the spirits of the soldiers so raised after all their calamities; the language of every man's countenance was, Now we are a people! We have a name among the states of this world!"[121]

We could continue to multiply similar accounts. As one observer wrote from New York, the Declaration "was received everywhere with loud huzzas, and the utmost demonstrations of joy."[122] Once the news of independence spread, however, and the Declaration had been proclaimed and published in all parts of America, commentary about it virtually vanished from the press as well as from private letters. But the purpose of the Declaration was not to arouse debate on the propriety, merits, or timing of independence; not to spark dispute about the rights of man or philosophies of government; not to gain praise for its elegant diction or felicitous phrasing. Its purpose was to present the rationale for independence so clearly and so convincingly as to terminate public discussion of the issue. In this respect the Declaration can be contrasted with Thomas Paine's legendary *Common Sense*. Published in January 1776, Paine's tract was designed to provoke controversy over independence—to get it on the agenda of public debate, especially in the moderate middle colonies. The Declaration was designed to signal the end of debate over independence. Moreover, had the Declaration drawn attention to itself—either for its ideology or style—it would have drawn attention away from the war effort. Seen in this way, the Declaration was not designed to be memorable but to be forgettable, which is why, as Jefferson explained, it did not contain new ideas but expressed the "common sense" (that is, the commonly held ideas) about its subject. The lack of extended colloquy among Americans about the Declaration in 1776 is further testimony to its effectiveness. It allowed Congress to get on with the business of prosecuting the war, of seeking foreign alliances, and of developing a frame of government for the newly independent states.

It did so, moreover, with consummate rhetorical artistry. From its eloquent introduction, to its aphoristic maxims of government, to its relentless accumulation of charges against George III, to its elegiac denunciation of the British people, to its heroic closing sentence, the Declaration sustains an almost perfect synthesis of style, form, and content. Its solemn and dignified tone, its graceful and unhurried cadence, its symmetry, energy and confidence, its combination of logical structure and dramatic appeal, its adroit use of nuance and implication—all contribute to its rhetorical power. Above all, though, the Declaration is controlled by its sure sense of audience and purpose. Posterity has made the Declaration a timeless document, but Jefferson and the Congress were satisfied in 1776 that it be timely. Indeed, had it failed to be timely, chances are it would never have become timeless.

Notes

1. Worthington C. Ford, ed., *Journals of the Continental Congress, 1774–1789* (Washington, D.C.: Library of Congress, 1904–37), 5: 507. As with other quotations from eighteenth-century sources, I have modernized spelling and, when necessary for meaning, punctuation, but I have kept the original capitalization.

2. John Adams to Abigail Adams, 3 July 1776, in *Letters of Delegates to Congress, 1774–1789*, ed. Paul H. Smith (Washington, D.C.: Library of Congress, 1976–), 4: 376.

3. Charles Warren, "Fourth of July Myths," *William and Mary Quarterly* 2 (1945): 237–45.

4. Cecelia M. Kenyon, "The Declaration of Independence," in *Fundamental Testaments of the American Revolution* (Washington, D.C.: Library of Congress, 1977), 25; Abraham Lincoln, speech at Springfield, Illinois, 26 June 1857, in *The Collected Works of Abraham Lincoln*, ed. Roy P. Basler (New Brunswick, N.J.: Rutgers Univ. Pr., 1953), 2: 406.

5. Thomas Jefferson to Henry Lee, 8 May 1825, in *The Writings of Thomas Jefferson*, ed. Paul Leicester Ford (New York: Putnam's, 1892–99), 10: 343. On July 3, 1776, John Adams wrote to Abigail Adams, "You will see in a few days a Declaration setting forth the Causes which have impell'd Us to this mighty Revolution, and the Reasons which will justify it in the Sight of God and Man" (in Smith, *Letters of Delegates* 4: 374). See also Samuel Adams to John Pitts, ca. 9 July 1776, in Smith, *Letters of Delegates* 4: 417.

6. Stanley Fish, *Self-Consuming Artifacts* (Berkeley: Univ. of California Pr., 1972), 389.

7. Jane P. Tompkins, "The Reader in History: The Changing Face of Literary Response," in *Reader-Response Criticism: From Formalism to Post-Structuralism*, ed. Jane P. Tompkins (Baltimore: Johns Hopkins Univ. Pr., 1980), 210; Garry Wills, *Inventing America: Jefferson's Declaration of Independence* (New York: Doubleday, 1978), xiv; J. G. A. Pocock, *Politics Language, and Time: Essays on Political Thought and History* (New York: Atheneum, 1973), 12.

8. Warren, "Fourth of July Myths," 237.

9. Philip F. Detweiler, "The Changing Reputation of the Declaration of Independence: The First Fifty Years," *William and Mary Quarterly* 19 (1962): 557; John Adams to Abigail Adams, 24 July 1775, in Smith, *Letters of Delegates* 1: 657. For other comments on the heavy work load in Congress, see William Whipple to John Langdon, 10 June 1776, and John Adams to John Lowell, 12 June 1776, in Smith, *Letters of Delegates* 4: 185, 197; George Read to Gertrude Read, 6 December 1776, in Smith, *Letters of Delegates* 5: 582.

10. Edmund Cody Burnett, *The Continental Congress* (New York: Macmillan, 1941), 205–29; Wills, *Inventing America*, 325–33.

11. Henry S. Randall, *The Life of Thomas Jefferson* (Philadelphia: Lippincott, 1865), 1: 77–163; Dumas Malone, *Jefferson the Virginian* (Boston: Little, Brown, 1948), 169–214.

12. Charles Francis Adams, ed., *The Works of John Adams* (Boston: Little and Brown, 1850), 2: 511.

13. Adams, *Works of Adams* 2: 511; Julian P. Boyd, ed., *The Papers of Thomas Jefferson* (Princeton: Princeton Univ. Pr., 1950–), 1: 170–74, 187–219, 225–33.

14. In 1774 Lee had been assigned to compose the Address to the People of Great Britain, only to have Congress reject his work and assign someone else to redraft the paper (Burnett, *Continental Congress*, 51). Lee may have suffered a similar fate with respect to Congress's 1775 Address to the British People. See James H. Hutson, ed., *A Decent Respect to the Opinions of Mankind: Congressional State Papers, 1774–1776* (Washington, D.C.: Library of Congress, 1975), 100.

15. Malone, *Jefferson the Virginian*, 219.

16. Thomas Jefferson to James Madison, 30 August 1823, to John Vaughn, 16 September 1825, and to James Mease, 26 September 1825, in Ford, *Writings of Jefferson* 10: 267, 345–46; Adams, *Works of Adams* 2: 515. The most careful studies of the evolution of the Declaration from Jefferson's original draft through the version as reported to Congress are Carl Becker, *The Declaration of Independence: A Study in the History of Political Ideas* (New York: Knopf, 1933), 135–71, and Julian P. Boyd, *The Declaration of Independence: The Evolution of the Text* (Washington, D.C.: Library of Congress, 1943).

17. My count of Congress's additions to and deletions from Jefferson's draft are based on Jefferson's Notes of Proceedings in the Continental Congress, in Boyd, *Papers of Jefferson* 1: 315–19; my count of the final text is based on the version in Boyd, *Papers of Jefferson* 1: 429–32. I shall discuss Congress's revisions of the Declaration in the course of this essay.

18. Thomas Jefferson to James Madison, 30 August 1823, in Ford, *Writings of Jefferson* 10: 268; Jefferson to Richard Henry Lee, 8 July 1776, in Boyd, *Papers of Jefferson* 1: 455–56; Boyd, *Evolution*, 22; Wills, *Inventing America*, 307–8; Thomas Jefferson, *Autobiography*, ed. Dumas Malone (New York: Capricorn, 1959), 36–41.

19. For information about the drafting of Congress's pre-1776 state papers except the December 6, 1775, response to George III's Proclamation of Rebellion, see the editor's commentaries on the documents collected in Hutson, *Decent Respect*. For the evolution of Congress's response of December 6, 1775, see Ford, *Journals of Congress* 3: 353, 392, 408–12.

20. Richard Henry Lee to Thomas Jefferson, 21 July 1776, and Edmund Pendleton to Jefferson, 10 August 1776, in Boyd, *Papers of Jefferson* 1: 471, 488; Becker, *Declaration of Independence*, 209; Boyd, *Evolution*, 34. For other favorable comments about Jefferson's draft, see Josiah Bartlett to John Langdon, 1 July 1776, in Smith, *Letters of Delegates* 4: 351; John Adams to Timothy Pickering, 6 August 1822, in Adams, *Works of Adams* 2: 514n.

21. Historians have long maintained that, contrary to popular myth, the Declaration was not signed on July 4, 1776. Rather, they contend, the engrossed parchment copy, titled "The Unanimous Declaration of the Thirteen United States of America," was not ready for signing until August 2, 1776, at which time all of the delegates present affixed their signatures. Some, however, had already left for home and did not sign until they returned to Philadelphia later in the year. Moreover, because Congress had decided that everyone who served in Congress until the end of 1776 should sign the Declaration as a test of loyalty, six men signed who did not become delegates until after July 4.

Recently, however, this conclusion has been challenged by Wilfred J. Ritz, "The Authentication of the Engrossed Declaration of Independence on July 4, 1776," *Law and History Review* 4 (1986): 179–204. While Ritz agrees that as many as twenty-one signatures were affixed to the Declaration after July 4, 1776, he makes a plausible case that the Declaration was in fact engrossed and first signed on July 4, most likely by thirty-four members of Congress. In addition, he urges that the National Archives make a scientific documentary examination of the engrossed Declaration to determine exactly when it was signed.

There is also considerable scholarly debate over what time of day Congress approved the Declaration. Although most traditional accounts concur that it was approved in the afternoon or evening, Paul H. Smith, "Time and Temperature: Philadelphia, July 4, 1776," *Quarterly Journal of the Library of Congress* 33 (1976): 295–99, argues convincingly that it was adopted in the morning of July 4. Ironically, while Smith seconds the standard view that the Declaration was not signed until August 2, his account of its passage adds credence to the notion that it may have been engrossed and first signed on July 4. If the Declaration was approved in the evening of July 4, there probably would not have been time to prepare an engrossed parchment copy before Congress adjourned for the day. But if the Declaration was voted on in the morning of July 4, there would have been several hours in which to prepare an engrossed version for signing before adjournment.

22. Ford, *Journals of Congress* 4: 358.

23. Merrill Jensen, *The Founding of a Nation: A History of the American Revolution, 1763–1776* (New York: Oxford Univ. Pr., 1968), 484; "Machiavel," *Pennsylvania Chronicle*, 15 August 1768; Charles Pettit to Joseph Reed, 25 March 1776, quoted in Jack N. Rakove, *The Beginnings of National Politics: An Interpretive History of the Continental Congress* (Baltimore: Johns Hopkins Univ. Pr., 1979), 87.

24. John Dickinson to Samuel Ward, 29 January 1775, in Smith, *Letters of Delegates* 1: 303; Burnett, *Continental Congress*, 187–91.

25. All quotations from the Declaration as adopted by Congress are from Boyd, *Papers of Jefferson* 1: 429–32.

26. Becker, *Declaration of Independence*, 5.

27. "Necessary" in Samuel Johnson, *A Dictionary of the English Language: In Which the Words are Deduced from Their Origins and Illustrated in Their Different Significations by Examples from the Best Writers* (London: J. and P. Knapton, 1755); William Cowper, *The Task* (London: J. Johnson, 1785), 55; Ephraim Chambers, *Cyclopedia: Or, An Universal Dictionary of Arts and Sciences* (London: James and John Knapton, 1728), 2: 621; Jonathan Edwards, *Freedom of the Will*, ed. Paul Ramsey (New Haven: Yale Univ. Pr., 1957), 149; *Oxford English Dictionary* (Oxford: Oxford Univ. Pr., 1933), 7: 60–61.

28. *His Majesties Declaration against the States-General of the United Provinces of the Low-Countreys* (London: John Bell and Christopher Barker, 1672); "His Majesty King George the First's Declaration of War against the King of Spain, Published on December 17, 1718," in *A General Collection of Treatys, Declarations of War, Manifestos, and Other Publick Papers* (London: Andrew Bell and E. Sanger, 1710–32), 4: 378–81; *His Majestys Declaration of War against the French King* (New York: James Parker, 1756). On the importance of necessity as a justification for war among nations, see Tavers Twiss, *The Law of Nations Considered as Independent Political Communities* (Oxford: Clarendon Pr., 1863), 54–55.

29. Declaration of the Lords and Commons to Justify Their Taking Up Arms, August 1642, in *Historical Collections of Private Passages of State, Weighty Matters in Law, Remarkable Proceedings in Five Parliaments*, ed. John Rushworth (London: Robert Boulter, 1680–1722), 4: 761–68; Declaration of the Continental Congress Setting Forth the Causes and Necessity of Their Taking Up Arms, July 1775, in Hutson, *Decent Respect*, 89–98. The first additional invocation of the doctrine of necessity in the Declaration of Independence comes immediately after the preamble, when Congress states, "Such has been the patient sufferance of these Colonies; and such is now the necessity which constrains them to alter their former systems of Government." The second is at the end of the penultimate paragraph, in which Congress ends its denunciation of the British people by announcing, "We must, therefore, acquiesce in the necessity, which denounces our Separation, and hold them, as we hold the rest of mankind, Enemies in War, in Peace Friends."

30. [Thomas Hutchinson], *Strictures upon the Declaration of the Congress at Philadelphia . . .* (London: n.p., 1776), 9; [Charles Inglis], *The True Interest of America Impartially Stated . . .* (Philadelphia: James Humphreys, 1776), 52–53.

31. [John Dickinson], *Letters from a Farmer in Pennsylvania, to the Inhabitants of the British Colonies in America* (Philadelphia: David Hall, 1768), 7; London letter in *Pennsylvania Gazette*, 29 December 1768; "Rationalis," *Pennsylvania Evening Post*, 23 May 1775; Josiah Quincy, *Memoir of the Life of Josiah Quincy, Junior, of Massachusetts Bay, 1744–1775*, 3d ed.,

ed. Eliza S. Quincy (Boston: Little, Brown, 1875), 209, 259. For fuller discussion see Stephen E. Lucas, *Portents of Rebellion: Rhetoric and Revolution in Philadelphia, 1765–76* (Philadelphia: Temple Univ. Pr., 1976), 126–51.

32. [Thomas Paine], *Common Sense; Addressed to the Inhabitants of America . . .* (Philadelphia: Robert Bell, 1776), 41, 43, 59.

33. Richard Henry Lee to Landon Carter, 2 June 1776, in Smith, *Letters of Delegates* 4: 117; Samuel Adams to Joseph Hawley, 15 April 1776, in Smith, *Letters of Delegates* 3: 528; Thomas Jefferson, Notes of Proceedings in the Continental Congress, in Boyd, *Papers of Jefferson* 1: 312.

34. Jonathan Mayhew, A *Discourse Concerning Unlimited Submission and Nonresistance to the Higher Powers . . .* (Boston: D. Fowle and D. Gookin, 1750), 45; [John, Lord Somers], *The Judgment of Whole Kingdoms and Nations, Concerning the Rights, Power and Prerogative of Kings, and the Rights, Privileges and Properties of the People* (London: T. Harrison, 1710), par. 186; Algernon Sidney, *Discourses Concerning Government* (London: n.p., 1693), 181; John Hoadly, ed., *The Works of Benjamin Hoadly* (London: W. Bowyer and J. Nichols, 1773), 2: 36; "Pacificus," *Pennsylvania Gazette*, 14 September 1774. For fuller discussion see Pauline Maier, *From Resistance to Revolution: Colonial Radicals and the Development of American Opposition to Britain, 1765–1776* (New York: Knopf, 1972), 27–48.

35. Thomas Jefferson, Notes of Proceedings in the Continental Congress, in Boyd, *Papers of Jefferson* 1: 314; Committee of Secret Correspondence to Silas Deane, 8 July 1776, in Smith, *Letters of Delegates* 4: 405.

36. Howard H. Peckham, "Independence: The View from Britain," in *The Declaration of Independence: Two Essays* (Worcester, Mass: American Antiquarian Society, 1976), 37.

37. See, for example, A *Declaration of the Demeanour and Carriage of Sir Walter Raleigh. . .* (London: Bonham Norton and John Bill, 1618); Declaration of the House of Commons for Recovery of the Palatinate, 4 June 1621, in *Cobbett's Parliamentary History of England*, ed. William Cobbett (London: R. Bagshaw, 1806–20), 1: 1294–95; *An Humble Declaration of the Apprentices and Other Young Men of the City of London . . .* (London: n.p., 1642); Declaration of the Lords and Commons to Justify Their Taking Up Arms, August 1642, in Rushworth, *Historical Collections* 4: 761–68; William and Mary's Declaration of War against France, 7 May 1689, in A *General Collection of Treatys* 1: 281–83; George II, Declaration of War against Spain, 19 October 1739, in *Cobbett's Parliamentary History* 11: 3–6; Declaration of the Continental Congress Setting Forth the Causes and Necessity of Their Taking Up Arms, July 1775, in Hutson, *Decent Respect*, 89–98.

38. Ford, *Journals of Congress* 5: 516; John Hancock to New Jersey Convention, 5 July 1776, and to George Washington, 6 July 1776, in Smith, *Letters of Delegates* 4: 392, 397.

39. *New York Journal*, 8 August 1776; Hazelton, *Declaration of Independence*, 245.

40. John Adams, for example, wrote to John Winthrop on June 23, 1776, that one advantage of declaring independence was that the states "will establish Tests and ascertain the Criminality of Toryism" (in Smith, *Letters of Delegates* 4: 299). The attitudes of Congress toward the Tories can be gauged by its resolutions of January 2, 1776, in Ford, *Journals of Congress* 4: 18–21.

41. Joseph Reed to George Washington, 3 March 1776, in *Life and Correspondence of Joseph Reed*, ed. William B. Reed (Philadelphia: Lindsay and Blakiston, 1847), 1: 163.

42. Declaration of the Continental Congress Setting Forth the Causes and Necessity of Their Taking Up Arms, July 1775, in Hutson, *Decent Respect*, 96; Charles Pettit to Joseph Reed, 25 March 1776, in Rakove, *Beginnings of National Politics*, 87; Samuel Adams to Samuel Cooper, 30 April 1776, in Smith, *Letters of Delegates* 3: 601. In his *Strictures upon the Declaration*, Thomas Hutchinson said the purpose of the Declaration was "to reconcile the people of America to that Independence, which always before, they had been made to believe was not intended" (31–32).

43. Alexander Pope's *Essay on Man* contains the lines: "Slave to no sect, who takes no private road/But looks through Nature up to Nature's God." Bolingbroke says, "One follows Nature and Nature's God; that is, he follows God in his works and in his word." Jefferson was familiar with the writings of both Pope and Bolingbroke, and the latter was one of his favorite writers, as is explained by Merrill D. Peterson, "Thomas Jefferson and the Enlightenment: Reflections on Literary Influence," *Lex et Scientia* 11 (1975): 103–11. As a caveat, though, it must be recognized that phraseology linking divine law with natural law was common throughout most of the eighteenth century; Jefferson need not have turned to any particular writer for inspiration.

44. My argument here is consanguineous with that of John Phillip Reid, "The Irrelevance of the Declaration," in *Law in the American Revolution and the Revolution in the Law*, ed.

Hendrick Hartog (New York: New York Univ. Pr., 1981), 46–89, though Reid greatly overstates his case by suggesting that the preamble, too, was derived from British constitutional history. While Reid is correct that the right of revolution could be derived as readily from positive law and English precedent as from natural law, that is not how it is derived in the Declaration. The language of the preamble is altogether general and is much more in keeping with the language of natural law theorists than with the language of English jurisprudential writers. Reid acknowledges as much in his *Constitutional History of the American Revolution: The Authority of Rights* (Madison: Univ. of Wisconsin Pr., 1986), 91.

45. Emmerich de Vattel, *The Law of Nations* (Philadelphia: T. and J. W. Johnson, 1872), lxii. See also Edward Dumbauld, *The Declaration of Independence* (Norman: Univ. of Oklahoma Pr., 1950), 34–44.

46. Carl Becker, *Declaration of Independence*, 201; Jefferson, *Autobiography*, 114; Jefferson to John Adams, 14 October 1816, in *The Adams-Jefferson Letters*, ed. Lester J. Cappon (Chapel Hill: Univ. of North Carolina Pr., 1959), 2: 491.

47. Jefferson to Francis Eppes, 19 January 1821, in Ford, *Writings of Jefferson* 10: 183. Jefferson made no specific comments on the style of the Declaration and few on prose style in general. His ideas on the latter subject are explained by Stephen D. Cox, "The Literary Aesthetic of Thomas Jefferson," in *Essays in Early Virginia Literature Honoring Richard Beale Davis*, ed. J. A. Leo Lemay (New York: Franklin, 1977), 235–56. See also Robert Dawidoff, "Man of Letters," in *Thomas Jefferson: A Reference Biography*, ed. Merrill D. Peterson (New York: Scribner's, 1986), 181–98.

48. Hugh Blair, *Lectures on Rhetoric and Belles Lettres* (London: W. Strahan, T. Cadell, and W. Creech, 1783), 1: 206–7, 259.

49. "Thoughts on English Prosody" was enclosed in an undated letter of circa October 1786 to the Marquis de Chastellux. The letter is printed in Boyd, *Papers of Jefferson* 10: 498; the draft of Jefferson's essay, which has not been printed, is with the letter to Chastellux in the Thomas Jefferson Papers, Library of Congress. Julian P. Boyd, "The Declaration of Independence: The Mystery of the Lost Original," *Pennsylvania Magazine of History and Biography* 100 (1976): 455–62, discusses "Thoughts on English Prosody" and its relation to Jefferson's reading text of the Declaration.

50. Throughout all his drafts of this sentence, Jefferson had written of "inalienable" rights, and there is no record of Congress inserting "unalienable" during its debates on the Declaration. The change was made either by the congressional committee appointed to superintend the printing of the Declaration, or, more likely, as the result of a printer's error. Robert A. Rutland, ed., *The Papers of George Mason* (Chapel Hill: Univ. of North Carolina Pr., 1970), 1: 285, mistakenly says the change from "inalienable" to "unalienable" seriously altered the meaning of the Declaration. Citing the 1755 edition of Nathan Bailey's *New Universal English Dictionary*, Rutland contends "unalienable" meant that which "may not be altered," while "inalienable" meant that "which cannnot be alienated or transferred to another by Law." But this is the only major dictionary of the time to contain such definitions. In fact, Bailey's 1755 definition of "unalienable" as that which "may not be altered" is so idiosyncratic that one is inclined to suspect it may have resulted from a misprint in which "alienated" was erroneously rendered as "altered." This suspicion is strengthened by the fact that other editions of Bailey define "unalienable" as synonymous with "inalienable." Although "inalienable" appears to have been the term of choice, the lexicographical evidence points clearly to the conclusion that "inalienable" and "unalienable" were used interchangeably in the mid-eighteenth century. As careful as Jefferson was to record changes between his draft of the Declaration and the Declaration as passed and printed by Congress, he never commented on the shift from "inalienable" to "unalienable," which he surely would have done had the shift been of consequence.

51. For an interesting demonstration of how the Declaration meant different things to different people, see Barry Bell, "Reading and 'Misreading' the Declaration of Independence," *Early American Literature* 18 (1983): 71–83.

52. [John Locke], *Two Treatises of Government* . . . , ed. Peter Laslett (Cambridge: Cambridge Univ. Pr., 1964), book 2, secs. 5, 95, 87; Thomas Paine, "The Rights of Man," in *The Complete Writings of Thomas Paine*, ed. Philip S. Foner (New York: Citadel, 1969), 1: 274; Sir William Blackstone, *Commentaries on the Laws of England* (Philadelphia: Robert Bell, 1771), 1: 48.

53. See, for example, Merrill D. Peterson, *Thomas Jefferson and the New Nation* (New York: Oxford Univ. Pr., 1970), 93–94; Gordon S. Wood, *The Creation of the American Republic, 1776–1787* (Chapel Hill: Univ. of North Carolina Pr., 1969), 70–75; J. R. Pole, "Loyalists, Whigs, and the Idea of Equality," in *A Tug of Loyalties: Anglo-American Relations,*

1765–1785, ed. Esmond Wright (London: Athlone, 1975), 66–92; Jack P. Greene, *All Men Are Created Equal* (Oxford: Oxford Univ. Pr., 1976); Jack P. Greene, " 'Slavery or Independence': Some Reflections on the Relationship among Liberty, Black Bondage, and Equality in Revolutionary South Carolina," *South Carolina Historical Magazine* 80 (1979): 193–214; Forrest McDonald, *Novus Ordo Seclorum: The Intellectual Origins of the Constitution* (Lawrence: Univ. Pr. of Kansas, 1985), 53–55. The best-known statement of inequality in Jefferson's writings is his view of the inferiority of blacks, in *Notes on the State of Virginia*, ed. Thomas Perkins Abernathy (New York: Harper, 1964), 132–39.

54. Dumas Malone, *Jefferson and the Rights of Man* (Boston: Little, Brown, 1951), 223–24. See also Wills, *Inventing America*, 229–39; Morton White, *The Philosophy of the American Revolution* (New York: Oxford Univ. Pr., 1978), 213–21; Mortimer J. Adler and William Gorman, *The American Testament* (New York: Praeger, 1975), 37–41.

55. Mason's draft appeared in the *Pennsylvania Evening Post*, 6 June 1776, the *Pennsylvania Ledger*, 8 June 1776, and the *Pennsylvania Gazette*, 12 June 1776. For the evolution of Mason's document see Rutland, *Papers of George Mason* 1: 274–91; for Jefferson's rough draft of the Declaration see Boyd, *Papers of Jefferson 1*: 423–28. The question of whether Jefferson borrowed from Mason has been rehashed for decades by students of the Declaration, with no clear agreement. The various points of view are well represented by William F. Dana, "The Declaration of Independence," *Harvard Law Review* 13 (1900): 323–28; Boyd, *Evolution*, 21–22; David Hawke, *A Transaction of Free Men: The Birth and Course of the Declaration of Independence* (New York: Scribner's, 1964), 147–48.

56. Herbert Lawrence Ganter, "Jefferson's 'Pursuit of Happiness' and Some Forgotten Men," *William and Mary Quarterly* 16 (1936): 422–34, 558–85. As Ganter shows, writers who had used the phrase "pursuit of happiness" before Jefferson included John Locke, Samuel Johnson, Oliver Goldsmith, Francis Hutcheson, Richard Price, and Lord Kames. See also Howard Mumford Jones, *The Pursuit of Happiness* (Cambridge: Harvard Univ. Pr., 1953), 61–98; Arthur M. Schlesinger, "The Lost Meaning of 'The Pursuit of Happiness,' " *William and Mary Quarterly* 21 (1964), 325–27; Wills, *Inventing America*, 149–64, 240–55.

57. John Adams, "Thoughts on Government," in *Papers of John Adams*, ed. Robert J. Taylor (Cambridge: Harvard Univ. Pr., 1977–), 4: 86; [Thomas Paine], "The Forester," in *Pennsylvania Journal*, 24 April 1776; Joseph Priestley, *Essay on the First Principles of Government*, 2d ed. (London: J. Johnson, 1771), 57.

58. John Locke, *An Essay Concerning Human Understanding*, ed. Alexander Campbell Fraser (New York: Dover, 1959), book 1, chap. 2, sec. 18.

59. William Duncan, *The Elements of Logick* (London: R. Dodsley, 1748), 242. See also Isaac Watts, *Logick: or, The Right Use of Reason in the Enquiry After Truth*, 8th ed. (London: T. Longman, T. Shewell, and J. Brackstone, 1745), 304; [Henry Aldrich], *A Compendium of Logic*, 3d ed. (London: n.p., 1790), 23.

60. Somers, *Judgment of Whole Kingdoms*, pars. 83, 186; Locke, *Two Treatises*, book 2, sec. 230. In *Inventing America*, Wills argues that Jefferson was indebted to Francis Hutcheson and other Scottish common sense philosophers rather than to John Locke for the ideas expressed in the preamble. The textual parallels between Locke's *Second Treatise of Government* and the Declaration, however, are much stronger than those between Hutcheson's writings and the Declaration. This point is made emphatically by Ronald Hamowy, "Jefferson and the Scottish Enlightenment: A Critique of Garry Wills's *Inventing America: Jefferson's Declaration of Independence*," *William and Mary Quarterly* 36 (1979): 503–23.

As most scholars have recognized, the ideas of the Declaration cannot be traced to any single political, intellectual, or philosophical source. The revolutionaries themselves repeatedly stressed that the split from England was warranted by a wide range of doctrines, principles, and precedents, including, in John Adams's words, "the fundamental laws of the colonies and of the British constitution, by principles avowed in the English laws and confirmed by many examples in the English history, by principles interwoven into the history and public right of Europe, in the great examples of the Helvetic and Batavian revolutions, and many others, and frequently acknowledged and ratified by the diplomatic body, principles founded in eternal justice and the laws of God and nature" (Adams, *Works of Adams* 7: 398).

61. Locke, *Two Treatises*, book 2, sec. 225.

62. Ford, *Journals of Congress* 5: 425.

63. Thomas Jefferson to James Madison, 30 August 1823, in Ford, *Writings of Jefferson* 10: 268; Jefferson to Henry Lee, 8 May 1825, in Ford, *Writings of Jefferson* 10: 343. The only British writer I know of to focus exclusively on the preamble was "An Englishman," in *Gentlemen's Magazine*, September 1776, 403–4, and he was rebutted by "Philander" in the October issue of *Gentlemen's Magazine*. Thomas Hutchinson spent only two of the thirty-

three pages of his *Strictures on the Declaration* dealing with the preamble, while John Lind devoted only four and one-half pages to it in his 133-page *Answer to the Declaration of the American Congress . . .* , 5th ed. (London: J. Walter, 1776). On the disregard of the preamble in the early Fourth of July celebrations, see Detweiler, "Changing Reputation," 559–61.

64. Wilbur Samuel Howell, "The Declaration of Independence and Eighteenth-Century Logic," *William and Mary Quarterly*, 18 (1961): 463–84, claims Jefferson consciously structured the Declaration as a syllogism with a self-evident major premise to fit the standards for scientific proof advanced in William Duncan's *Elements of Logick*, a leading logical treatise of its time. However, as I argue in "The Rhetorical Ancestry of the Declaration of Independence" (paper presented to the International Society for the History of Rhetoric, Oxford, England, August 1985), there is no hard evidence to connect Duncan's book with the Declaration. Jefferson may have read the *Logick* while he was a student at the College of William and Mary, but we are not certain that he did. He owned a copy of it, but we cannot establish whether the edition he owned was published before or after 1776. We cannot even say with complete confidence that Jefferson wrote the words "self-evident" in the Declaration; if he did, it was only as an afterthought in the process of polishing his original draft. Moreover, upon close examination it becomes clear that the Declaration does not fit the method of scientific reasoning recommended in Duncan's *Logick*. Its "self-evident" truths are not self-evident in the rigorous technical sense used by Duncan; it does not provide the definitions of terms that Duncan regards as the crucial first step in syllogistic demonstration; and it does not follow Duncan's injunction that both the minor premise and major premise must be self-evident if a conclusion is to be demonstrated in a single act of reasoning. The syllogism had been part of the intellectual baggage of Western civilization for two thousand years, and the notion of self-evident truth was central to eighteenth-century philosophy. Jefferson could readily have used both without turning to Duncan's *Logick* for instruction.

65. Lind, *Answer*, 119.

66. Blackstone, *Commentaries* 1: 244–46; Hutson, *Decent Respect*, 55, 145, 91, 115, 151.

67. Jefferson to John Randolph, 29 November 1775, in Boyd, *Papers of Jefferson* 1: 269.

68. Locke, *Two Treatises*, book 2, secs. 221–22. The Declaration's first veiled reference to Parliament occurs in grievance 13 against the king, which says, "He has combined with others to subject us to a jurisdiction foreign to our constitution, and unacknowledged by our Laws; giving his Assent to their Acts of pretended Legislation." The second comes in grievance 22, which assails the act "declaring themselves [Parliament] invested with power to legislate for us in all cases whatsoever." The third is in the next-to-last paragraph: "We have warned them [our British brethren] from time to time of attempts by their legislature to extend an unwarrantable jurisdiction over us." For the development of American rhetoric declaring the colonies independent of Parliament after 1774, see Becker, *Declaration of Independence*, 80–134; Bernard Bailyn, *The Ideological Origins of the American Revolution* (Cambridge: Harvard Univ. Pr., 1967), 198–229.

69. Locke, *Two Treatises*, book 2, sec. 199; John Milton, "The Tenure of Kings and Magistrates," in *The Works of John Milton*, ed. Frank A. Patterson (New York: Columbia Univ. Pr., 1932), 5: 18; Rushworth, *Historical Collections* 7: 1396. The charge of tyranny particularly irritated the king's supporters. Was there a single instance, Thomas Hutchinson asked rhetorically, "in which the King has exceeded the just powers of the Crown as limited by the English constitution? Has he ever departed from known established laws, and substituted his own will as the rule of his actions? Has there ever been a Prince by whom subjects in rebellion have been treated with less severity, or with longer forbearance?" (*Strictures*, 30).

70. George III, Proclamation of 23 August 1775, in *English Historical Documents: American Colonial Documents to 1776*, ed. Merrill Jensen (New York: Oxford Univ. Pr., 1955), 850; "Revolution" in Johnson, *Dictionary*; Chambers, *Cyclopedia* 2: 1014; William H. Dunham, Jr., and Charles T. Wood, "The Right to Rule in England: Depositions and the King's Authority, 1327–1485," *American Historical Review*, 81 (1976): 738–61; Hannah Arendt, *On Revolution* (New York: Viking, 1963), 13–52.

71. The seven English kings dethroned since the Norman Conquest were Edward II (1327), Richard II (1399), Henry VI (1460), Edward V (1483), Richard III (1485), Charles I (1649), and James II (1689). In each case the deposition was accompanied by a public apologia detailing the crimes of the king and sanctioning a change in rulers. In a forthcoming essay I provide a detailed discussion of the parallels between the English deposition apologias and Congress's indictment of George III in the Declaration of Independence.

72. Jefferson had originally written, "To prove this, let facts be submitted to a candid world, for the truth of which we pledge a faith yet unsullied by falsehood" (Boyd, *Papers of*

Jefferson 1: 424). Congress wisely excised the lengthy final clause, which contained two unfortunate implications: first that Congress needed to pledge the truth of its statements; second, that there might be a tenable alternative interpretation of the Declaration's "facts."

73. "Declaration" in John Cowell, *Nomothetes. The Interpreter, Concerning the Genuine Signification of Such Obscure Words and Terms Used Either in the Common or Statute Laws of This Realm* . . . (London: Thomas Manley, 1684); M. Thomas Dyche and William Pardon, *A New General English Dictionary: Peculiarly Calculated for the Use and Improvement of Such as Are Unacquainted with the Learned Languages* . . . , 14th ed. (London: C. and R. Ware, 1771). For the requirements of legal declarations in various kinds of civil suits during the eighteenth century, see William Selwyn, *An Abridgement of the Law of Nisi Prius,* 4th ed. (London: W. Clarke and Sons, 1817).

74. "Fact" in Johnson, *Dictionary;* Dyche and Pardon, *General English Dictionary;* Thomas Sheridan, *A General Dictionary of the English Language* . . . (London: J. Dodsley, C. Dilly, and J. Wilkie, 1780).

75. *Oxford English Dictionary* 4: 11–12; Blackstone, *Commentaries* 4: 39; *The Annual Register, Or a View of the History, Politics, and Literature for the Year 1772* (London: J. Dodsley, 1773), 57.

76. Samuel Adams to John Pitts, ca. 9 July 1776, in Smith, *Letters of Delegates* 4: 417. The sole congressional paper before the Declaration of Independence to list grievances topically was the 1774 Bill of Rights (in Hutson, *Decent Respect,* 49–57), which, like the Declaration of Independence, was patterned at least partly on the 1689 English Declaration of Rights. Another possible model for the grievances in the Declaration of Independence was the 1769 petition of the Massachusetts House of Representatives for the removal of Governor Bernard, which indicted Bernard in a series of ten sentences, all beginning "He has." See Alden Bradford, ed., *Speeches of the Governors of Massachusetts, from 1765 to 1775* . . . (Boston: Russell and Gardner, 1818), 188–91.

77. Lind, *Answer,* 123. Because the charges are not enumerated in the Declaration, there has been a fair amount of disagreement over how many there are and how they should be numbered. I have followed Sidney George Fisher, "The Twenty-Eight Charges against the King in the Declaration of Independence," *Pennsylvania Magazine of History and Biography* 31 (1907): 257–303.

78. For previous expressions by Congress of the grievances in this section of the Declaration, see the 1774 Petition to the King (Declaration grievances 5, 9–12), the 1774 Bill of Rights (Declaration grievances 5, 9, and 11), and the 1774 Address to the Inhabitants of the Colonies (Declaration grievances 5, 9–12). Grievance 4 probably was added to Jefferson's draft of the Declaration by John Adams (Becker, *Declaration of Independence,* 155–56). Grievance 8 has no clear precedent in former congressional papers, though the phrase "the administration of justice" does appear in the 1775 Report on Lord North's Conciliatory Proposal. See Hutson, *Decent Respect,* for the congressional documents mentioned above, and consult Lois G. Schwoerer, *The Declaration of Rights, 1689* (Baltimore: Johns Hopkins Univ. Pr., 1981), 295–98, for the 1689 Declaration of Rights.

79. Leonard Woods Labaree, *Royal Government in America: A Study of the British Colonial System before 1783* (New Haven: Yale Univ. Pr., 1930), 179–88, 210–14, 223–67; Evarts Boutell Greene, *The Provincial Governor in the English Colonies of North America* (New York: Longmans, Green, 1898), 145–65; Oliver Morton Dickerson, *American Colonial Government, 1696–1765* (New York: Russell and Russell, 1962), 225–83; John Shy, *Toward Lexington: The Role of the British Army in the Coming of the American Revolution* (Princeton: Princeton Univ. Pr., 1965), 19–44; Lind, *Answer,* 13–55, 123–26.

80. Hutchinson, *Strictures,* 16; Donald C. Lord and Robert M. Calhoon, "The Removal of the Massachusetts General Court from Boston, 1769–1772," *Journal of American History* 55 (1969): 735–55; John F. Burns, *Controversies between Royal Governors and Their Assemblies in the North American Colonies* (Boston: Wright and Potter, 1923), 60–62, 185–210; John C. Miller, *Sam Adams: Pioneer in Propaganda* (Boston: Little, Brown, 1936), 242–50; Thomas Hutchinson, *The History of the Province of Massachusetts-Bay,* ed. Lawrence Shaw Mayo (Cambridge: Harvard Univ. Pr., 1936), 3: 370–404.

81. Jack P. Greene, *The Quest for Power: The Lower Houses of Assembly in the Southern Royal Colonies, 1689–1776* (Chapel Hill: Univ. of North Carolina Pr., 1963), 337–43, 420–24; Hugh T. Lefler and William S. Powell, *Colonial North Carolina: A History* (New York: Scribner's, 1973), 125–26, 256–57; Labaree, *Royal Government,* 373–419.

82. Ralph Cudworth, *The True Intellectual System of the Universe* (London: Richard Royston, 1678), 601; Richard Hooker, *Of the Laws of Ecclesiasticall Politie* (London: John Windet, 1594–97), 5: sec. 67, p. 178.

83. Between 1764 and 1766 England added twenty-five comptrollers, four surveyors general, and one plantation clerk to the customs service in America. It added seventeen more officials in 1767 with the creation of a Board of Customs Commissioners to reside in Boston. These appointments may also have generated a mild ripple effect, resulting in the hiring of a few lesser employees to help with office chores and customs searches, but there is no way to know, since the records are now lost. See Thomas C. Barrow, *Trade and Empire: The British Customs Service in Colonial America, 1660–1775* (Cambridge: Harvard Univ. Pr., 1967), esp. 186–87, 220–21.

84. *Journal of the Honorable House of Representatives of His Majesty's Province of the Massachusetts-Bay, in New-England, Begun and Held in Boston, in the county of Suffolk, on Wednesday the Thirty-First Day of May, Annoque Domini, 1769* (Boston: Edes and Gill, 1769–70), 139; W. L. Saunders, ed., *Colonial Records of North Carolina* (Raleigh: Josephus Daniels, 1886–90), 9: 581; Andrew Eliot to Thomas Hollis, 10 December 1767, in Massachusetts Historical Society *Collections*, 4th ser. (Boston: Little, Brown, 1858), 4: 420; House of Representatives of Massachusetts to Dennys De Berdt, 12 January 1768, in *The Writings of Samuel Adams*, ed. Harry A. Cushing (New York: Putnam's, 1904–8), 1: 146.

85. Lind, *Answer*, 121, 45. For congressional papers that expressed the substance of all or most of grievances 14–22 before the Declaration of Independence, see the 1774 Petition to the King, the 1774 Bill of Rights, the 1775 Declaration of the Causes and Necessity of Taking Up Arms, and the 1775 Report on Lord North's Conciliatory Proposal. See also the 1774 Association, the 1774 Address to the Inhabitants of the Colonies, and the 1774 Address to the People of Great Britain (all in Hutson, *Decent Respect*).

86. Blackstone, *Commentaries* 1: 153–89. For the Tory position see [Joseph Galloway], *A Candid Examination of the Mutual Claims of Great Britain and the Colonies . . .* (New York: James Rivington, 1775), 4–10; [Samuel Seabury] *The Congress Canvassed . . .* (New York: n.p., 1774), 26.

87. Hutson, *Decent Respect*, 76, 29, 86, 67. Although the Quebec Act had been mentioned time and again by Congress in its former state papers, Jefferson did not include it in his original draft of the Declaration but added it later, perhaps on recommendation of John Adams, whose colony had been particularly vociferous in censuring the act. Most historians have accepted the judgment of British apologists that Congress had no business complaining about what happened in a neighboring province, but Reid, "Irrelevance of the Declaration," 85, points out that there was precedent from English history for the Declaration's condemnation of the Quebec Act. One of the articles of treason stated by the House of Commons in 1667 against Edward Hyde, Earl of Clarendon, accused him of introducing "an arbitrary government in his majesty's foreign plantations." That the revolutionaries were familiar with Clarendon's impeachment is apparent from Joseph Warren's Boston massacre oration of March 5, 1772, in *Principles and Acts of the Revolution in America*, ed. Hezekiah Niles (Chicago: A. S. Barnes, 1876), 23.

88. See note 63 above for bibliographic information on Lind's pamphlet.

89. *Rotuli Parliamentorum; ut et petitiones placita in Parliamento* (London: n.p., 1783–1832), 6: 276.

90. For Jefferson's draft of the Virginia constitution and his use of its grievances in the Declaration, see Boyd, *Papers of Jefferson* 1: 337–47, 417–20. On the addition of grievance 26, see Boyd, *Evolution*, 30.

91. All of these documents except the last are in Hutson, *Decent Respect*; the Declaration on Armed Vessels is in Ford, *Journals of Congress* 4: 229–32. See also Congress's resolutions of January 2, 1776, in Ford, *Journals of Congress* 4: 21. Wills, *Inventing America*, 71, incorrectly claims that the war grievances did not have any forerunners in Congress's prior state papers.

92. Howard Mumford Jones, "The Declaration of Independence: A Critique," in *The Declaration of Independence: Two Essays* (Worcester, Mass., American Antiquarian Society, 1976), 7.

93. Declaration of Rights, in Schwoerer, *Declaration of Rights*, 296; sentence against Charles I, in Rushworth, *Historical Collections* 7: 1418–19; William Henry Drayton, speech to the Charleston grand jury, 2 May 1776, in Niles, *Principles and Acts*, 331–32.

94. George Washington to Joseph Reed, 31 January 1776, in *The Writings of George Washington*, ed. John C. Fitzpatrick (Washington, D.C.: Government Printing Office, 1931–44), 4: 297; Arthur St. Clair to William Allen, 1 September 1776, in *The St. Clair Papers: The Life and Public Services of Arthur St. Clair*, ed. William H. Smith (Cincinnati: R. Clarke, 1882), 1: 375–76.

95. Proceedings in the House of Lords, 15 December 1775, in *American Archives*, ed. Peter

Force, 4th ser. (Washington, D.C.: Clarke and Force, 1837–46), 6: 225; John Adams to Horatio Gates, 23 March 1776, in Smith, *Letters of Delegates* 3: 431.

96. Boyd, *Papers of Jefferson* 1: 317–18.

97. In his list of charges against George III presented to the Charleston grand jury in May 1776, William Henry Drayton accused the king of making "every attempt to instigate the savage nations to war upon the southern colonies, indiscriminately to massacre man, woman, and child" (in Niles, *Principles and Acts*, 329). Whig leaders, of course, had done their best to persuade the Indians to fight against the British. See, for example, Congress's Speech to the Six Confederate Nations, 10 May 1775, in Hutson, *Decent Respect*, 139–47.

98. Continental Congress, Declaration on Armed Vessels, 23 March 1776, in Ford, *Journals of Congress* 4: 229; William Henry Drayton, speech to the Charleston grand jury, 2 May 1776, in Niles, *Principles and Acts*, 329–30; resolves of the Virginia Convention, 15 May 1776, in Jensen, *English Historical Documents*, 867. The equivalent charge in Jefferson's draft of the Virginia constitution assailed George III for "promoting our Negroes to rise in Arms among us, those very negroes whom, by an inhuman use of his negative, he hath refused us permission to exclude by Law" (Boyd, *Papers of Jefferson* 1: 378). While this contained a codicil rebuking George III for allowing the slave trade to continue, it was considerably more straightforward than the version Jefferson drafted for the Declaration of Independence.

99. Wills, *Inventing America*, 71–74, esp. 72; Lind, *Answer*, 106–7. As Peterson notes, the slavery charge in Jefferson's draft "did not ring true. And Jefferson's bloated rhetoric gave it away" (*Jefferson and the New Nation*, 92). Sidney Kaplan, "The 'Domestic Insurrections' of the Declaration of Independence," *Journal of Negro History* 61 (1976): 243–55, mistakenly argues that the phrase "excited domestic insurrections amongst us" referred only to England's efforts to enlist colonial slaves.

100. Paine, *Common Sense*, 43, 59–60; Jefferson to Maria Cosway, 12 October 1786, in Boyd, *Papers of Jefferson* 10: 451.

101. John Adams to Benjamin Hichborn, 29 May 1776, in Smith, *Letters of Delegates* 4: 96; Paine, *Common Sense*, 40–42.

102. 1774 Petition to the King, 1775 Address to the Inhabitants of Great Britain, and 1774 Bill of Rights, all in Hutson, *Decent Respect*, 75, 105, 55.

103. This was probably the passage John Adams had in mind when he later said he thought calling the king a tyrant was "too personal; for I never believed George to be a tyrant in disposition and nature. I always believed him to be deceived by his courtiers on both sides of the Atlantic, and, in his official capacity only, cruel" (to Timothy Pickering, 6 August 1822, in Adams, *Works of Adams* 2: 514n.).

104. " A Republican," *Massachusetts Spy*, 8 April 1773; *Connecticut Gazette*, 7 June 1776. Also see Pauline Maier, "The Beginnings of American Republicanism," in *The Development of a Revolutionary Mentality* (Washington, D.C.: Library of Congress, 1972), 99–117; William D. Liddle, " 'A Patriot King or None': Lord Bolingbroke and the American Renunciation of George III," *Journal of American History* 65 (1979): 951–70.

105. Both addresses are in Hutson, *Decent Respect*, 21–32, 99–108.

106. Boyd, *Papers of Jefferson* 1: 318–19.

107. Jefferson to Robert Walsh, 4 December 1818, in Hazelton, *Declaration of Independence*, 178; Adams, *Works of Adams* 2: 515; Jefferson, Notes of Proceedings in the Continental Congress, in Boyd, *Papers of Jefferson* 1: 314; William Livingston to Lord Stirling, 4 July 1775, in Ford, *Journals of Congress* 2: 128n.

108. Jefferson had constructed a similar series of clauses beginning "We have" in his 1775 Virginia Resolves on Lord North's Conciliatory Proposal (in Boyd, *Papers of Jefferson* 1: 173).

109. Ford, *Journals of Congress* 4: 209.

110. Somers, *Judgment of Whole Kingdoms*, pars. 186, 83.

111. Boyd, *Papers of Jefferson* 1: 319.

112. Paine, *Common Sense*, 78.

113. Becker, *Declaration of Independence*, 197.

114. See, for example, Petition of the Stamp Act Congress to the House of Commons, in *Prologue to Revolution: Sources and Documents on the Stamp Act Crisis, 1764–1766*, ed. Edmund S. Morgan (Chapel Hill: Univ. of North Carolina Pr., 1959), 67; South Carolina Association, 3 June 1775, in "Miscellaneous Papers of the General Committee, Secret Committee, and Provincial Congress, 1775," *South Carolina Historical and Genealogical Magazine* 8 (1907): 141–42; Resolves and Association of the Virginia Convention of 1774, in Boyd, *Papers of Jefferson* 1: 137; 1775 Petition to the King, in Hutson, *Decent Respect*, 130;

Instruction of the Town of Boston, 23 May 1776, in Hazelton, *Declaration of Independence*, 390.

115. John Adams to Timothy Pickering, 6 August 1822, in Adams, *Works of Adams* 2: 513–14n.; Continental Association, in Hutson, *Decent Respect*, 9–19; Virginia nonimportation resolves of 1770 and Virginia Association of 1774, in Boyd, *Papers of Jefferson* 1: 45, 138.

116. See Douglass Adair, "Fame and the Founding Fathers," in *Fame and the Founding Fathers*, ed. Trevor Colbourn (New York: Norton, 1974), 3–26; Garry Wills, *Cincinnatus: George Washington and the Enlightenment* (New York: Doubleday, 1984), 109–48; Bruce Miroff, "John Adams: Merit, Fame, and Political Leadership," *Journal of Politics* 48 (1986): 116–32; and, for a broader discussion, Leo Braudy, *The Frenzy of Renown: Fame and Its History* (New York: Oxford Univ. Pr., 1986). The quotation about peers of the realm is from Blackstone, *Commentaries* 1: 402. During the reign of James I, debate arose as to whether members of the peerage should be allowed to continue the privilege of protesting "only upon their honours, and not to be put to their oaths, in suits, as ordinary subjects were." The lords responded by saying, "That they conceived protestation upon honour to bind them more than oath did; as being the same before God and before the world; and in regard to the trust given to their degree, a far greater charge" (*Cobbett's Parliamentary History* 1: 1202–3).

117. Francis Bacon, *The Essayes or Counsels, Civill and Morall . . .* (London: John Haviland, 1625), 313–14. See Adair, "Fame and the Founding Fathers," 114–15, for the importance of Bacon's essay on honor among the revolutionaries.

118. Cf. Robert Ginsberg, "The Declaration as Rhetoric," in *A Casebook on the Declaration of Independence*, ed. Robert Ginsberg (New York: Crowell, 1967), 228.

119. R. R. Palmer, "The Impact of the American Revolution Abroad," in *The Impact of the American Revolution Abroad* (Washington, D.C.: Library of Congress, 1976), 13; Peckham, "The View from Britain," 21–37.

120. Hazelton, *Declaration of Independence*, 254; Peterson, *Jefferson and the New Nation*, 92; Detweiler, "Changing Reputation," 555–74.

121. *Pennsylvania Journal*, 10 July 1776; Charles D. Deshler, "How the Declaration Was Received in the Old Thirteen," *Harper's New Monthly Magazine* 85 (July 1892): 168; Samuel Cooper to ?, 15 July 1776, in Hazelton, *Declaration of Independence*, 223; Joseph Warren to John Adams, 17 July 1776, in Warren, "Fourth of July Myths," 242n.; Abigail Adams to John Adams, 21 July 1776, in *The Book of Abigail and John: Selected Letters of the Adams Family, 1762–1784*, ed. L. H. Butterfield, Marc Friedlander, and Mary Jo Kline (Cambridge: Harvard Univ. Pr., 1975), 148; Joseph Seawell Jones, *A Defence of the Revolutionary History of the State of North Carolina from the Aspersions of Mr. Jefferson* (Boston: Charles Bowen, 1834), 269; *Pennsylvania Evening Post*, 15 August 1776. The best collection of reactions to the Declaration in America during July and August of 1776 is Hazelton, *Declaration of Independence*, 240–81.

122. Frank Moore, ed., *Diary of the American Revolution* (New York: Charles Scribner, 1860), 1: 270.

FOUR

Early Constitutional Rhetoric in Pennsylvania

CARROLL C. ARNOLD

IN NO OTHER of the first American states was establishing a permanent state constitution as prolonged a process as it was in Pennsylvania. Between 1776 and 1790 the character of a proper constitution was debated seven times. Three of these debates led to constitutional changes. The first state constitution was established in 1776, but the ratification in 1787 of the federal Constitution made alteration of the so-called Frame of 1776 inevitable, resulting in the state's adoption of the Constitution of 1790. Between these formal actions there were four unsuccessful attempts to alter the Frame of 1776, a document unique among constitutions anywhere in the world.

Records associated with these constitution-making and constitution-revising activities have been surveyed and resurveyed by expert historians for a century.[1] Historians have not, however, systematically studied the communicative qualities of the constitutional discourse embedded in the record. I therefore propose a qualitative interpretation of this discourse, viewing it as "a becoming, a development producing . . . 'realities' " for early Pennsylvanians.[2] Viewed in detail, the discourse reflects the truth of Richard A. Ryerson's trenchant observation that "in 1776 no one knew what it meant to establish a republic based on the sovereignty of the people, which is simply another way of saying that no one knew what a revolution was."[3] Viewed generally, the discourse reflects and projects two distinct conceptions of a "republic" and two evolving conceptions

131

of how "the sovereignty of the people" should be institutionalized in government.

Most North American colonies that declared their independence from England already had "mixed" republican systems of government. Their constitutional systems were such because of accidents, past experience, British traditions, and earlier rhetoric. By contrast, many leading advocates of independence in Pennsylvania were committed to a conception of democracy under "republican" principles that differed widely from views held by majorities in other states. The Pennsylvanians' unique conceptions were embodied in the Frame of 1776. Ardent defenses of that constitution and the distractions of war sustained the Frame for a dozen years, but in the end Pennsylvanians accepted the democratic-republican principles espoused by the federal Constitution. My object is to trace the rhetorical patterns that often restrained but eventually promoted this "becoming."

Creating the Frame of 1776

The events leading to creation of Pennsylvania's Frame of 1776 have been recounted many times. A very brief historical sketch will serve my purposes.

On 15 May 1776 the Continental Congress recommended that colonies lacking governments "sufficient to the exigencies of their affairs" create such governments. Advocates of independence in Pennsylvania immediately promulgated processes that culminated in a provincial conference that fixed a date and the conditions for election of a constitutional convention. Any "Associator" aged twenty-one years and a resident of the province for one year could vote for convention delegates if he would affirm that he did not hold himself bound to George III and that he would not oppose establishing a government "on the authority of the people only." Democratization of the electorate was thereby established, and since the war for independence was in progress, the test oath was considered essential even though it disfranchised Tories and a good many others who were hesitant about independence. It is evident from public and private statements that virtually everyone in the independence movement agreed that no independent government existed in the province.[4]

The constitutional convention was elected on 8 July 1776, and the convention met on 15 July. The conditions of suffrage assured that all delegates supported independence. No record of the convention's debates exists, but public letters and pamphlets addressed to the constitution makers show how visionary Pennsylvanians' theories of government were. During the first seven months of 1776, six major pieces of advice to the convention appeared in Philadelphia as pamphlets or letters to editors. Thomas Paine's *Common Sense,* published in January, contained a few pages of counsel on organizing governments. "Demophilus's" *Genuine Principles of the Ancient Saxon, or English Constitution* was specifically directed to the convention when published in pamphlet form by Robert Hall in July. It also purveyed the mythological vision of democracy that would, as I shall show, influence later discussions. At about the same time (16 July 1776) a long letter entitled "Hints for a Form of Government for the State of Pennsylvania, Submitted for the Consideration of the Convention Now Sitting in Philadelphia" appeared in the *Pennsylvania Evening Post.* Also in mid-July an anonymous pamphlet entitled *Four Letters on Interesting Subjects* was published by Styner and Cist. On 20 July the *Pennsylvania Evening Post* carried a letter by "Harrington," who argued on historical grounds for multichambered legislatures. On 30 July the same newspaper published extracts of a letter "From a Gentleman in a Neighbouring State." This letter offered a critique of the recently adopted constitution of New Jersey and counseled Pennsylvania's convention to avoid the flaws of that document.

Even though defense against English military actions was a paramount matter, these publications represent rather few reflections on what ought to be the form of a new state government. More important, however, was the speculative character of the essays. Pragmatics did not receive much attention.[5] The writers of the three letters just cited were most interested in the relative desirability of unicameral and bicameral legislatures, in limitations on executive powers, and in appropriate qualifications of office holders. Gentleman and Demophilus shared a conviction that towns or townships, rather than counties or districts, ought to be the basic units of government and representation. All three letter writers endorsed bicameralism, but Harrington alone provided extended argument. He stressed the "mischief" that single, unchecked legislatures had committed in ancient and modern times. All three letter writers explicitly or implicitly supported suffrage without property qualifications. No writer questioned the egalitarianism that the Provincial Conference had established for election of delegates to the convention. Each writer saw the convention's task as choosing among alternative ways of guaranteeing that relative to any and all governmental actions there should be continuous expression of the popular will.

The three pamphlets published during this period treated constitutional principles more deeply than the letters. It is universally agreed that the major rhetorical event of 1776, aside from the Declaration of Independence, was publication of Paine's *Common Sense,* which first appeared on 10 January 1776.[6] Of course, the work's importance lay much more in the case made for independence than in what it said about constitution making. However, Paine's views on creating new governments were especially likely to influence such convention delegates as Timothy Matlack, Benjamin Franklin, David Rittenhouse, James Cannon—who wrote and edited much of the new constitution—and George Bryan, who was widely believed to have had significant influence on the form of the new government even though he was not a delegate to the convention. Paine had worked closely with all of these men in promoting independence.

In dealing with forming new governments, Paine made the following claims:

1. Forming a democratic government is not a complex matter; all that is needed is to guarantee the natural rights of all and to fix the numbers and processes of representation and administration. In the expanded edition of his pamphlet Paine dispatched the entire subject of constituting a government for "the United Colonies" in seven pages.

2. "I drew my idea of the form of government from a principle in nature, which no art can overturn, viz. that the more simple anything is, the less liable it is to be disordered; and the easier repaired when disordered." This theme became a commonplace of postconvention defenses of the Frame of 1776.

3. A single, annually elected legislature is natural to a democratic state, since the check-and-balance system of the English constitution is in fact a system of monarchic tyranny and is incapable of securing the liberties of the people. (The author of *Four Letters* was to develop this theme more fully.)

4. The presiding officer of a state or nation should be "a President only," preferably chosen from and by the legislature.

Each of these propositions was observed in constructing the Frame of 1776, and each became a premise for subsequent argument in defense of the Frame.

The framers of Pennsylvania's first constitution adhered even more closely to principles expressed in *Four Letters on Interesting Subjects* and *Genuine Principles of the Ancient Saxon, or English Constitution.* The authors of these pamphlets insisted that a constitution differed from ordinary legislation because a constitution establishes

the basic law and the permanent forms and procedures of a government. More specifically than Paine, these two writers argued against
any overlap between executive and legislative powers. Significantly
for the future, however, neither author considered the difficulties of
effecting operational separation of powers. Both pamphleteers would
have placed some limit on the number of consecutive years an
elected officer could hold any given office, and both would have had
all officers elected annually. Both contended that legislatures should
submit all but emergency legislation to "public consideration" before
finally enacting measures. Both would have had any constitution
reviewed by a specially elected body every seven or ten years.

No one can say whether *Four Letters* or *Genuine Principles* persuaded any delegate to the constitutional convention, but each of
the above features existed in the Frame of 1776 as finally promulgated. At the least, the letter writers and pamphleteers identified and
articulated themes and values that were important to the majority in
the convention whom the writers expressly sought to advise.

On one point the writers of *Four Letters* and *Genuine Principles*
foreshadowed an enduring controversy: they disagreed on the relative merits of unicameralism and bicameralism. Demophilus urged
creation of a house of representatives and a council comprised
of wise and experienced men who would review and perfect the
representatives' enactments: "They [the council] will be more likely
to foresee the mischievous consequences, that might follow a proceeding, which at first view did not appear to have any thing
dangerous in it, to many honest men, who may however, be very
worthy of a seat in the house of representatives."[7] Demophilus was
not at all clear about how his council should be chosen or about its
powers. Nonetheless, he felt a need for some check on popular
legislators' possible shortsightedness. In this, his judgment paralleled
the judgments of most of those who refused to sign the Frame of
1776 and who formed the nucleus of a party for constitutional reform
that labored from 1776 to 1789 for constitutional changes, including
bicameralism.

The author of *Four Letters* presented standard arguments against
a bicameral legislature: "The notion of checking by having different
houses, has but little weight with it when inquired into, and . . . it
tends to embarrass and prolong business." He granted that "some
kind of convenience" occasionally arose from having a second house,
but delay, "petulances," multiplicity of parties, expense, and encour-
agement of divided interests were serious negative results of bicameralism. By contrast, said this author, a single legislative house works
against all of these disadvantages and will encourage political unity.[8]

Demophilus's imprecision about the qualifications of and the manner of selecting council members was symptomatic of a serious void in the thinking and argumentative resources of bicameralists in general. The author of *Four Letters* made a telling point when he said that the British justification for bicameralism rested on that nation's distinctions among "orders" in society. In America there were no such distinctions, so the basic reason for a bicameral legislature simply did not exist. Early bicameralists in Pennsylvania had no good counterargument here. Should they argue for property or other special qualifications for "councillors" or "senators," their contentions would fly in the face of the very popular principle of democratizing the new society. Bicameralists had not yet thought up good justifications for "checks" within democratically chosen legislatures.

As I have said, Demophilus also fostered a mythological view of governmental organization. About three-fourths of his forty pages were devoted to epideictic veneration of Saxon "democracy" and excoriation of the papal, Norman, monarchic, and ministerial corruption that had allegedly eviscerated the "Saxon and English Constitution." These themes were neither original with Demophilus nor unique to Pennsylvania rhetoric. Bernard Bailyn has pointed out that an image of "an ideal constitution based on an elected assembly in Saxon England" was frequently offered in revolutionary pamphlets.[9] Demophilus reaffirmed these notions and gave them ethnic and spiritual value at the time Pennsylvanians were framing their first constitution. He quoted extensively but selectively from "a certain very scarce book entitled an Historical Essay on the English Constitution." He said he was adding "improving observations our different circumstances may suggest, for the perusal of the gentlemen concerned in the arduous task of framing a constitution."[10] Having introduced his purpose and his source, Demophilus offered thirteen pages of largely quoted narrative-description of "that beautiful system, formed in the German woods." Applying that model to Pennsylvania, Demophilus insisted that the "Township" must be the basic "body politic." After recommending ways of electing local, representative officers and regulating their activities, he resumed his quotations, providing ten pages portraying the baleful influences of the clergy, of the Norman conquerors, of the ministerial system, and of royalty on liberties so carefully preserved by the pristine Saxon system. He closed by urging legislative dominance over executive branches of government, a constitution secured from easy alteration except by the people themselves, and preservation of "the advantage of such a communication of sentiments as will accrue from the establishment of frequent town meetings." This would prevent "our ever relapsing into a state of bondage and misery." The pamphlet's final pages were a brief discussion of the Declaration of Independence and a reprint of its text.

Demophilus gave the mythic Saxon model of governance a special, sanctified status. His method was epideictic in its strongest form. He invited readers to revere a tradition, to become spectators of the noble and excellent, to adopt a mood of remembrance. Such reverence for the beauty of the Saxon model, Demophilus seemed to think, would ennoble the convention delegates' deliberations as they worked out details of their new government.[11] He offered an ideological grounding for the direct democracy to which the majority of convention delegates were already committed. The simple directness of town- or tithing-based governance constituted an ethnic heritage to be restored in the present. Corruption of the system had begun with Norman taxation of individuals and with centralization of confederative authority. These were primary dangers to be avoided. The "mediocrity" of Pennsylvania already accepted the lesson Demophilus tried to teach; he gave those notions historic and ethnic nobility and his "truths" became commonplaces of debate when the Frame of 1776 needed defense. Only the alleged Saxon origins of the system disappeared from the pro-Frame rhetorical litany as constitutional debate continued through the next thirteen years.

Most of Demophilus's allegedly historic principles were observed in the Frame as finally written. Moreover, the theme that the Convention of 1776 had created a somehow sanctified system of government never disappeared from the rhetoric of the Frame's advocates. Only Demophilus's ambiguous recommendation for a bicameral legislature was ignored in the new scheme, and a week after the draft of the Frame was published Demophilus wrote that he was well pleased with it. His only additional hope was that in effecting election of representatives the state would be subdivided into shires and these into townships where inhabitants could meet about local matters and to choose representatives "in their little Conventions."[12] In fact, such practices of local governance within electoral districts were already being followed informally, and defenders of the Frame of 1776 would constantly extol the system as a "confederation" of "small republics" allied to express the wills of localities while restraining the powers of "rulers." As late as 1789 an obdurate defender of the Frame would picture the Convention of 1776 as providentially gathered at a unique moment when corruptive influences were at bay. They were thus able to conceive a pure democracy capable of thwarting juntos eager to "prevent the odious principles of equal liberty and equal privileges."[13] The allegedly historic principles of participatory democracy that Demophilus had so reverently portrayed became fundamental to all endorsements of the Frame of 1776, but therein lay seeds of ideological resistance to pragmatism in politics.

According to Bailyn, *Genuine Principles* and *Four Letters* were notable American tracts because they were among the few that explicitly faced the necessity of recognizing interests rather than orders as the elements to be harmonized in American government. Bailyn does not mention, however, that neither of the two pamphleteers nor the Pennsylvania Constitutional Convention conceptualized means by which the wishes of disparate interests could be bargained out *above* the level of electoral districts. In practice, the procedures of annual elections and "public consideration" of pending legislation fostered resistance to legislative compromise and always left the interpretation of the meanings of elections to whoever controlled the single-house legislature. Neither of these problems was clearly recognized in the public discussion that preceded formal enactment of the Frame on 28 September 1776.[14]

Between publication of a draft of the Frame and its final enactment, the most controversial feature of the constitution was inserted. This was a provision that no officer of the state be allowed to agitate for changes in the Frame. No one had publicly challenged the general notion that a constitution should be alterable only under special circumstances. The draft constitution provided that the Frame be subject to change only on recommendation of a directly elected Council of Censors chosen every seventh year. This drew no public outcry. But the Frame as finally enacted contained a further, unforecast provision against constitutional modification. Every officer of the state, including legislators, was required to swear or affirm "That I will be true and faithfull [sic] to the Common Wealth of Pennsylvania, And that I will not directly or indirectly do any any [sic] Act or Thing prejudicial or injurious to the Constitution or Government thereof as established by the Convention."[15] This prohibition against advocating change seemed to many an opprobrious restriction of personal freedom and of the representatives of the people. To make matters worse, the convention, acting as a legislature, made the same oath a condition for voting for officers of the new government.[16]

As J. Paul Selsam has pointed out, the proceedings of the convention imply that the final form of the constitution passed unanimously, yet only seventy-three of ninety-six delegates signed it.[17]

Clearly, there was a dissenting minority in the convention, but it is not known exactly what features of the Frame they objected to. Subsequent agitation suggests that the oath of allegiance to the Frame was a major irritant.

The first of four unsuccessful attempts to change the Frame of 1776 was mounted immediately upon publication of the final version. The general case against the Frame was epitomized by "Brutus": " Every man of sense in the state complains of [the Frame] . . . and yet in order to entitle himself to the privilege of an elector, he must swear or affirm that he will never 'directly' or 'indirectly' expose those imperfections, or propose an amendment to them. . . . Remember, my countrymen, that slavery is a potion equally bitter, whether it comes to us thro' the hands of Lord North, Lord Howe, or My Lords the Members of the Convention."[18] Of course, advocates of bicameralism treated the restrictions on constitutional amendment and the oaths as the kinds of excesses to be expected of an un-checked, single-house legislature. "Lucius" wrote an article of this sort in the *Pennsylvania Packet* (15 October 1776). He contended that oaths to treat constitutions as inviolate were "unknown in our former Constitution, and unpractised in any free country." By applying the oaths to both officers and voters, Lucius said, the convention overstepped its authority and imposed a suffrage restric-tion that was neither within the competence of a convention nor conformable to any previously confirmed laws.

This first attempt at constitutional modification showed at least two things about political thinking in Pennsylvania: (1) exactly how far the voice of the people was to be trusted was clear to no one on either side of the constitutional debate, and (2) advocates of change were decidedly reticent about just what they would change if they had the opportunity. The country was at war, but the challengers said nothing to show how changes would enhance the causes of independence and defense. A "mixed legislature" was demanded, but neither the distinctions between legislative houses nor their relations to one another was outlined by critics. Further reflecting the confusion among the challengers, for the first and only time, critics of the Frame urged that state officers be required to take an oath declaring their belief in the Trinity. Presumably this demand was made to enlist the support of religious conservatives, of whom there were many, but the proposal seemed calculated to debar from office the prominent deists among the Frame's friends, which sup-porters of the Frame were quick to point out. Perhaps most costly, however, was the fact that the critics of the Frame presented them-selves as a party led by persons who had been reluctant to support independence, "establishment men," and friends of Tories.[19] The *ethos* of this party was still further damaged when pseudonymous writers advocating change urged property qualifications for members of the legislature and said the "monarchic" American "genius" should be recognized by realigning executive powers. The elitism of at least some of the advocates of change was made clear when one proponent of amendment asserted that his side had "all rich great men and the wise men, the lawyers and doctors," as supporters.

In general, the rhetoric of critics in this period suggested that they were demanding a completely fresh start in constitution making and that the changes they sought were traceable to ambiguous, conservative, and perhaps antirevolutionary principles. The critics of the Frame could charge with considerable force that the Frame was ill conceived and unjust in several respects, but their overall case for change was without a clear, comprehensive, and consistent image of what they would put in the place of the Frame.

Issues relating to the oaths were prominent in this public debate. Opposition leaders accordingly proposed an alternative oath for voters and candidates for office. Their statement declared, "My sole intention in giving opposition to the Constitution . . . is to procure a free and good government," and concluded, "I will not directly or indirectly do any act . . . prejudicial to the independance [*sic*] of this State." This substitute oath and a series of resolutions were placed before a mass meeting convened 21 October and continued to the twenty-second in the State House Yard. The resolutions charged that the convention had exceeded its authority by legislating, had improperly constricted the process of amending the constitution, had violated the "rights of Freemen" by extending an unjustified oath to electors, and had failed to treat Christianity with "proper respect."

At the mass meeting John Dickinson and Thomas McKean were the chief speakers for the resolutions. Opposing were James Cannon, instructor in mathematics at the College of Philadelphia; Timothy Matlack, a radical who had risen to prominence through the forums of the militia; a "Colonel Smith," probably John Smith of York County; and Dr. Thomas Young, another ardent revolutionist. Cannon, Matlack, and Smith had been members of the constitutional convention; Dickinson and McKean had not. McKean had unassailable revolutionary credentials, but Dickinson did not. At this meeting as in the press, the proponents of change had less than ideal *ethos* for appealing to the "mediocrity" that needed to be won over.

The meeting was essentially an anti-Frame meeting; the majority of those present approved the resolutions and further declared that in the forthcoming election of legislators, electors should give only the alternative oath and that "no Counsellors [members of the Supreme Executive Council] ought to be chosen at the election to be held on the fifth day of November next." The essentially obstructionist posture of the critics was made clear by the last declaration. If insufficient members were elected to the Supreme Executive Council, there could be no functioning executive branch of the new government. As had been done repeatedly in colonial days, business would be brought to a halt until the majority accommodated the minority. The critics indicated that they wanted reconsideration of the Frame of 1776, either by the assembly or by a newly created constitutional convention, but neither move would be legal under the Frame.

In public at least, supporters of the Frame were reticent about the oaths of allegiance to the constitution. This matter was discussed in the press only in a satiric dialogue. The main thrust of pro-Frame arguments was against the critics' most vulnerable spot—their motives, including their revolutionary fervor. That line of attack had prompt effects.

The critics of the Frame quickly became defensive. At a public meeting and in a published broadside they insisted they were *not* Tories. Neither were they seeking a "House of Lords" or trying to restore colonial status. They were for independence; many of them had "exposed our lives" for the cause. They believed in the "sacred POWER of the PEOPLE," and they were simply appealing "from the tribunal of the Convention" to the tribunal of the people on behalf of a "mixed and tempered legislature."[20] In a belated indication of what they would do if they had their way, they promised voters they would retain those sections of the Frame that guaranteed freedom of press and conscience, annual elections, rotation of officers, and trial by jury. To the end of the campaign, however, the critics of the Frame failed to present either pragmatic reasons for *immediate* change or a comprehensive view of their plans for revising the government. Their call for a trinitarian oath for state officers was all too easily ridiculed, and it seemed extreme in a state whose colonial charter had required only that officers affirm belief in "one Almighty God and Creator." "A Real Friend to the Christian Religion" tellingly wrote that the history of Christianity was so filled with quarrels and even wars over interpretations of the Trinity that this alone should demonstrate the absurdity of insisting on that concept in any oath.[21]

The rhetoric of defenders of the Frame exhibited both much and little cogency. It generally followed the outline of a letter by

"Cincinnatus," who said that critics were "fanning the blaze of discord" in time of war, and doing so in the manner of "scoundrels void of every principle of virtue."[22] With less invective, he argued that the constitutional convention had been duly and representatively elected; that it had been wise to exclude the Executive Council from legislative powers, in view of the difficulties executive vetoes had caused in colonial times; that a radical change in government had been necessary because the Frame of 1701 had been a kingly document to "grant" rights that were God-given; and that the Frame of 1776 could be changed if and when experience had tested the whole of it.

The friends of the Frame had legal, rhetorical, and procedural advantages in this clash. It is not remarkable, then, that everywhere except in Philadelphia city and county they carried the election of legislators. Their opponents did, however, succeed in preventing election of enough Supreme Executive Council members so that the executive branch was disabled, and their minority in the elected assembly was sufficient to deny that house its required quorum— two-thirds of the total membership. Ironically, the movements of British troops and some constitutionally questionable actions by the pro-Frame majority ultimately put the government into effect.

Using their ability to prevent a quorum in the assembly and to prevent the executive branch from functioning, opponents of the Frame, under Dickinson's leadership, sought to force the assembly to call a new constitutional convention for January 1777.[23] However, fears that General Howe's troops would move across New Jersey to Pennsylvania caused the Continental Congress to flee to Baltimore and the Pennsylvania Assembly to disperse. After Washington's victories over the Hessians, the assembly reconvened in January 1777.

From this time it continued to act with regularity and apparent deliberation. As several opponents of the constitution refused to take their seats, the vacancies were filled by a new election, held under the authority of the Assembly itself. The failure to elect representative councillors from Philadelphia was remedied . . . by the election of Thomas Wharton, an active and patriotic Whig and Constitutionalist. On the 4th of March [1777] the Executive Council was organized by the election of Mr. Wharton as President and George Bryan as Vice-President, and thus at last the new government became complete.[24]

The colonial Whigs, once united in support of independence, were now irrevocably split, and the major issue dividing them was the "proper" structure of self-government. Having lost in the convention, the minority emulated colonial practice in Pennsylvania and tried to force change through deliberate obstructionism. Nor was it uncharacteristic of Pennsylvania politics that the majority should disregard legal technicalities to replace the obstructionists. What one finds missing from private letters and the public rhetoric are the notions that politics is the art of the possible and of rhetorical negotiation. The divisive constitutional issues remained, and the parties were seemingly innocent of negotiative spirit and rhetoric.

A New Thrust toward Change

When the state government began to function, a second attempt to alter the Frame was mounted, this time with a more promising rhetorical design. James Wilson led this campaign, first from his home in Carlisle, then from Philadelphia.[25] An Address to the Supreme Executive Council and to the Board of War (where support could be expected) was prepared and signed by forty-one prominent Philadelphians including Benjamin Rush, George Clymer, Daniel Clymer, George Ross, Thomas Fitzsimmons, Thomas and William Bradford, James Wilson, and Robert Morris. All of these were recognized critics of the Frame, but all save Morris had clear credentials as early advocates of independence. The Address was followed by a supportive Memorial addressed to the assembly, and slightly later a "Committee of Correspondence" published a Circular for distribution throughout the state.[26] All of these documents called for amendment of the Frame.

The government's supporters now designated themselves "The Whig Society" and issued their own Address to the assembly.[27] A supplementary statement to the public was published with this Address.

Under Wilson's leadership the anti-Frame faction's strategy was markedly changed from that of 1776 and early 1777. No extraconstitutional machinery was used, and there were no threats of obstruction. The faction for change sought to bring public pressure on and through agencies of government. They offered some relevant reasons why changes were needed immediately. Finally, in the "official" calls for change there was a general absence of rancor, though criticisms of past practices of the government were severe, with considerable reason. The Whig Society's responses were also relatively pragmatic in tone. The topics and issues raised by each side are summarized below:[28]

Leading Claims for and against Change, May and June 1777

FOR   AGAINST

Weakness and "languor" are every where in state government due to divided sentiments about the Frame. A clear majority-minority settlement is needed to restore energy and to prosecute war effectively.

SPECIFIC FAULTS IN THE FRAME AND ITS PRACTICALITY ARE EVIDENT. TO WIT:

Obstructionism by the minority produced whatever weakness and want of energy may have existed.

The Executive Council had to adjourn while action was needed in 1776.

This resulted only from refusal to elect councillors and the refusal of some to serve when elected.

The assembly and the Executive Council have been unable to control prices and back the state's credit.

It was complainants' opposition that prevented or slowed action.

The assembly couldn't organize as the Frame prescribed; required oaths had to be bypassed or ignored in many cases.

Oath requirements were altered in deference to the complainants. The oath is not "a necessary part" of the constitution. Abjuration of the king is enough.

The oath not to change the Frame disfranchises anyone with reservations about the Frame.

In fact, persons who objected to the oath were allowed to vote and serve in office.

The assembly violated the "public consideration" clause in enacting laws.

Where this happened exigencies of war and other emergencies existed and are excepted in the Frame.

Internal enemies go unpunished for lack of a "regular administration of justice."

(No direct, public replies are known.)

The above conditions show the need for the assembly to arrange for the election of a new convention for whom *all* can vote and which can alter or confirm the Frame "agreeable to the sentiments of a majority of the people."

The proposed actions would be unwise because: the assembly has no such powers; all attention should focus on the war; militiamen in the field would not be able to vote at this time; the Frame should be tested for a longer time.

Discourse concerning these claims and counterclaims was both reasoned and vituperative. The points made on both sides were founded on facts; however, the specific problems pointed to by advocates of change did not clearly affect the daily lives of electors. They were largely about technical and procedural matters, interesting chiefly to practicing politicians. Accordingly, the ensuing debate in the press focused on each side's competence to govern and on each side's general trustworthiness.

The Whigs said ambition and elitism motivated the agitators, and, indeed, some writings supporting change gave evidence that class distinctions were truly at issue. "Associator" said the Frame was the work of political innocents who had now "filled most of the offices" with "bankrupts, bullies, and blockheads."[29] "Ludlow," thought to be John Dickinson, said the Frame "supposes perfect equality" of possessions, wisdom, and virtue, which everyone knows is nonsense. The virtue of "mixed representation" was that property-based "natural distinctions" would win out over the "middling" and poorer interests.[30] Such claims impugned the trustworthiness of their authors, at least in the eyes of egalitarians. Other advocates of change charged the Whigs with being anti-intellectual. Justifiably, they cited James Cannon's letter to the electors of Bedford County, telling them to prefer "men of honesty, common sense, and plain understanding" over "gentlemen of the learned professions . . . generally filled with the quirks and quibbles of scholars."[31]

On the other side, "Common Sense" (Paine) responded to Ludlow chiefly with sarcasm. "Whitlocke" answered Ludlow saying, among other things, "To vest supreme rule in a few gentlemen of overgrown fortunes, and to render the first officers of the State wholly independent of the countroul of the people are the objects of your letters."[32] Whatever was true of the anti-Frame party in general, such letters as those by Ludlow continued to damage the perceived *ethos* of his party.

The campaign mounted by Wilson and his friends was generally more judicious than was Ludlow's support of it, and the campaign seems to have had significant influence. Wilson apparently believed at one point that the assembly might actually call a convention, on some terms. What negotiations took place is not clear, but the "Republicans," as the critics now called themselves, did have a meeting with a committee of the assembly on 9 July. We do not know what the Republicans expected, but the committee told them new dangers of invasion by the British made it impractical to recommend a convention at this time.[33] Wilson had foreseen that this was likely to be the outcome of his campaign; almost a week earlier he had written to Arthur St. Clair, "When an opposition has been twice set on foot, and has twice proceeded so far as to become formidable, he [General Howe] has twice, by his marches toward the Delaware, procured a cessation."[34]

From July 1777 to August 1778 British troop movements, including occupation of Philadelphia, stilled the war of words about the Frame. Once the military threat had diminished, Whigs and Republicans began their political campaigns in anticipation of the autumn election of 1778. Issues raised by the Republicans concerned chiefly the oaths of loyalty to the Frame and the management of government and defense during the previous year. Wilson seems, again, to have been the primary strategist. Whether he was the acknowleged leader or not, the Republicans' plan for constitutional reform was certainly one Wilson might have authored.

Internal Negotiations versus the Voice of the People

Burton A. Konkle estimates on the basis of voting records that the assembly elected in 1778 consisted of twenty-seven Republicans and thirty-one Whigs.[35] A push for constitutional revision began as soon as the new assembly convened. The nature of the behind-the-scenes maneuvering is not known, but on 28 November 1778 the assembly unanimously passed a resolution calling for a referendum in April 1779 to determine whether the voters of the state wanted a new constitutional convention to be called. If so, the convention would be directed to consider the following reforms: alteration of the unicameral system, changes in the functions of the executive branch, selection of justices and military field officers by appointment, abolition of the Council of Censors, fixed salaries for judges, permission for state executives and representatives to continue beyond three years in their offices if so chosen, and modification of the loyalty oaths. Despite the mystery about processes,[36] there were plainly new features in the strategy adopted in 1778: (1) for whatever reasons, a certain amount of bargaining had displaced ideological outcry respecting the Frame; (2) Republicans had become more explicit about the constitutional changes they wanted; and (3) an unchallengeable, although extraconstitutional, way had been found to inaugurate reconsideration of the Frame—asking the people to decide whether they wanted specially chosen convention delegates to consider a specific set of changes. These were moves the "democracy" would find it awkward to oppose.

This third attempt to secure changes ultimately failed. The Republicans appear to have made an egregious rhetorical/political error of omission. They did not mount an early, coordinated, and sustained campaign on behalf of the people's right to decide whether the Frame should be reconsidered. In December 1778 and January 1779 Republicans were silent in the public media.[37] Meanwhile, the Whigs were moving energetically to reverse the Assembly's resolution for a referendum in April. Robert L. Brunhouse aptly characterizes their activities:

> To negative the work of their enemies, the Radicals did not rely wholly on newspaper propaganda. They resorted to an old method which had often proved effective, that is, the use of petitions to the assembly to rescind its resolves. In these remonstrances one seeks in vain for good solid arguments against the call for a convention. The general line of reasoning was that designing persons sought to destroy the Constitution in order to introduce anarchy, that the assemblymen had disregarded their oaths to protect the Constitution, that the frame of government had already provided a Council of Censors to initiate any movement for reform, that the oath of allegiance taken by the people required them to defend the Constitution.[38]

In published letters the Whigs also insisted repeatedly that government under the Frame had worked successfully even under conditions of invasion, so no present crisis justified risking confusion by changing the established system.

It is amazing—and without explanation from the record—that until after the contest was ended no one ever argued publicly that letting the people decide through a referendum was more democratic and more equitable than trying to represent public opinion through petitions. There was no public appeal to the electorate to insist on their right to direct their legislative representatives by the same process through which they chose those representatives. From extant records there appears to have been no overall persuasive strategy among the Republicans. One can illustrate this by following the constitutional discourse in the important newspaper, the *Pennsylvania Packet*, from 1 December 1778 to 1 March 1779.

In support of Republican positions a long "Serious Address to the People of Pennsylvania, on the Present Situation of their Affairs" criticized the Frame of 1776, but it did not deal with the forthcoming referendum.[39] During January 1779 no constitutional commentary from either side appeared in the *Packet*. In February five anti-Frame authors published letters.[40] None discussed the pending referendum, and none took cognizance of the petition campaign the Whigs were carrying out. Two of the letters denied the wisdom of having popular representation in both houses of a bicameral legislature: the Republicans would formally recommend such representation the next month! Two of the five letters condemned the Frame because it did not allow representation of property as well as of persons. "A Political View" and "A Freeman" argued that the existing system was too costly. "A Whig" and "Machiavel" wrote satirically of the assembly's many violations of the Frame and suggested that since the Frame could be so easily disregarded, making "adjustments" ought to be easy. In sum, all Republican discourse in the *Packet* prior to March was highly individualistic, giving no evidence that the supporters of the referendum had any cohesive goals or that the writers shared interest in any of the specific topics the assembly had identified in its resolutions proposing the referendum.

The Whigs published little in the *Packet* from December to March, but what they did say focused directly on the claim that a change in governance was needed.[41] Two writers contended that no crisis existed and that government under the Frame had worked notably well under the most serious difficulties. A "Memorial" set forth the arguments of the petitions and remonstrances that Brunhouse summarized. But the Whigs' real attention was on collecting electors' signatures on petitions. Thereby, they caught the Republicans napping.

By the end of the first week of March 1779 some fifteen thousand signatures to petitions opposing the referendum had been filed with the assembly. This, said the *Packet* (11 March 1779) was a "greater number than were ever known to manifest their dislike for any public proceedings by this mode." As the petitions poured in, support for the referendum evaporated in the assembly, and on 27 February 1779 the assembly rescinded its resolutions concerning a referendum and did so with only seven abstaining members registering any dissent![42] There is no information about what behind-the-scenes maneuvering may have taken place, but outside the house the petition campaign decisively defeated the noncampaign for constitutional reconsideration.

Two aspects of the public rhetoric associated with this attempt at reform deserve special notice. The rhetoric of the Whigs' petition locked them into a political positon that was, and would remain, antidemocratic. On the other hand, when it was too late, the Republicans issued a platform that for the first time justified their proposals on strictly democratic grounds.[43] Ironically, it was a belatedly published platform of the "Republican Society" and an accompanying commentary that publicly moved the Republicans into a democratic position. An address to the public, probably written by James Wilson, and a supplementary statement signed by Benjamin Franklin's son-in-law, Richard Bache, were published about a month *after* the assembly's rescinding action. What was new in these documents was that the Republicans declared again for a bicameral legislature, but the members of both houses were to be popularly elected without distinction as to rank. The documents further contended that the Republicans belonged to no single social, economic, or professional class. The new position and claims could not help the anti-Frame cause in 1779, but they gave a new, nonelitist tone to reformism.

As Brunhouse indicates, the Whig petitions were absolutist. They insisted that the oaths of allegiance to the Frame of 1776 were permanently binding on every elector as well as on state officers, including assemblymen. This was perhaps a temporarily useful challenge to the assembly's resolutions for a referendum, but by being repeated in petition after petition the line of argument was made rigid and seriously diminished the Whigs' maneuvering room for the future. Whigs could no longer relax their interpretations of oaths as they had done in 1777. Further, the petitions committed the Whigs to a position asserting that the voters of the state did not have a right to instruct their electees even to consider altering the structure of government. This ideological posture of 1779 would enfeeble the Whigs rhetorically for almost a decade.

For a variety of reasons, most having little to do with the merits of the Frame, the Whigs increased their strength in the assembly and in the Executive Council in the elections of 1779 and 1780. Consequently, no new campaign for constitutional revision was mounted, and the Whigs were free to address such pragmatic issues as depreciated currency, abolition of slavery (passed in 1780), and punishment of alleged traitors and others who refused to support war efforts. From March 1779 until the elections of 1783 there was almost no discussion of constitutional issues in the press.

From 1780 to 1784 political power in Pennsylvania gradually shifted to the Republicans, but constitutional issues appear to have had little to do with the shift.[44] Republicans seemed content to work within the system set by the Frame. They appear to have enjoyed the almost untrammeled partisan advantages the Frame gave to clear majorities in the assembly. Furthermore, election of a Council of Censors was scheduled for 1783, and that was supposed to provide for a constitutional reevaluation of the Frame. In any case, constitutional discussion had chiefly to do with partisan attacks on and defenses of the ways the Republicans conducted legislation and administration once they had a majority in the assembly. There were, however, occasional essays and letters that dealt with whether the federal Constitution needed revision.

Experimentation with the Council of Censors

The Council of Censors was the single constitutionally authorized agency through which revision of the Frame of 1776 could be considered. Even under strict interpretations of the oaths of allegiance to the Frame, electors and officers were at this juncture free to campaign for changes as candidates sought election to the council. And since by 1783 the nation was at peace, it could no longer be said that altering the Frame would interfere with defense.[45]

Republicans presumably still wished for changes in the state government, but the rhetorical strategies they used could not promote change fully and strongly. They did not try to cultivate popular opinion across the state before the election of the council. This negligence is the more peculiar because securing changes through the censors had been made inherently difficult. Representation in the council was by counties, except for the city of Philadelphia, and action by the council could be effected only if supported by a two-thirds majority of the councillors.

Brunhouse says that "the Republicans contemplated the election [of censors] with enthusiastic optimism," but he cites no direct evidence of this.[46] I have found no such evidence, and it is difficult to see why the Republicans should have been optimistic. There would be twenty-six censors. At least Westmoreland, Northumberland, and Washington counties were certain to return opponents of constitutional change. Defenders of the Frame would need to carry only three more counties to prevent the two-thirds majority required to recommend changes and do so legally. In this situation, unless the Republicans became very active and very successful in preelection promotion of their cause, they would have little chance of achieving change through the council. Conceivably, though not demonstrably, this explains why they called no publicized meetings and published no prochange electoral appeals prior to the election of censors.

The election produced a thirteen to thirteen tie in the Council of Censors.[47] With a working majority of those present, the Republicans organized the council and, over the protests of the Whigs (now called "Constitutionalists"), they made altering the Frame the first order of business. By a vote of twelve to nine, the council on 19 January 1784 passed a report saying that changes were needed and a constitional convention ought to be authorized. The majority remained six votes short of the two-thirds necessary to give legal effect to the recommendation, so after some sparring with the minority, the majority adjourned the council to 1 June 1784. Presumably this action was intended to allow public consideration of the recommendation for a convention. Whig and Republican positions were set forth in an Address of the Minority of the Council of Censors and an Address to the Freemen of Pennsylvania. Both addresses were released for publication on 21 January 1784.

The majority's recommendations contained substantially the changes that had been proposed by the Republican Society in March 1779. A convention would be urged to create a bicameral legislature; members of a second house would be popularly chosen but from districts larger than those of members of the lower house; members of the second house would be chosen for three years rather than for the one-year terms of lower-house members; executive authority would lie with an annually elected governor having veto power over legislation, but subject to being overridden by two-thirds of both houses; judges would be appointed to serve during good behavior at fixed salaries, but be subject to removal by a two-thirds vote of the legislature; and rotation of officers would be eliminated. These proposals were familiar, but the majority also made proposals not before offered: (1) to insert in the declaration of rights a prohibition against *ex post facto* laws; (2) to alter residence requirements of electors from one to two years and provide that electors must vote in the districts of their residence;[48] (3) to eliminate the provision that every legislator "have the right to insert the reasons for his vote upon the Minutes if he desires it"; (4) to eliminate the Frame's provision that laws be published for "public consideration" before final passage.

The majority's Address offered these proposals in a generally restrained and reasonable style.[49] In contrast, the minority's Address was hyperbolic, defensive, addressed chiefly to questions of motive, and nowhere suggested that the signers would tolerate any alteration in the Frame. The absolutism of the petitions of 1778–79 was apparent throughout. Of Whig claims made in 1779, only reference to violation of oaths of allegiance was missing. Conspiracy themes dominated the minority's Address: a "disappointed spirit of domination is crawling from its lurking places"; the motive for proposing a second house was to enable "the better sort of people" to undermine democracy; the advocates of change were a faction that had refused to condemn Tories during the Revolution.

Amid such general, partisan attacks, the minority made some specific charges. (1) The majority had prevented the council from taking up its assigned tasks of inquiring into misfeasance and violations of the constitution. (2) The majority of twelve was actually fewer than half the total membership of the council, counting the absentees. (3) The proposed second house would be a "house of Lords." (4) Powers proposed for a governor should make the people "tremble." (5) Appointment of military and civil officers would create a patronage army impossible to oppose. (6) Abolishing rotation of officers was being proposed to preserve "faction." (7) Excluding reasons for votes from the minutes of the legislature was intended to "keep you in the dark" about legislation. (8) The proposed government would be unduly expensive and complex, whereas the Frame was a widely admired, sound, tested, and economical plan. (9) The majority were simply trying again what in 1779 they "had the mortification to find upwards of 16, 000 Whigs" opposed to.

It appears that after the council's temporary adjournment Benjamin Rush and John Armstrong of Carlisle tried privately but without success to persuade some Whigs to agree to a compromise on certain changes in the government, especially in the interest of establishing a bicameral legislature.[50] There were other behind-the-scenes attempts at promoting compromises, but they too were unsuccessful. However, the Republicans' lack of public activity during the council's recess is as perplexing as its inactivity prior to election of the council.

The entire matter of calling a constitutional convention was treated almost with indifference in the press. The *Freeman's Journal* was in this period normally a hotbed of political polemic from both Whigs and Republicans, yet between 24 March and 28 April 1784 more space was taken up by writers arguing the merits of Dr. Hugh Blair's newly published *Lectures on Rhetoric and Belles Lettres* than by discussions of all political topics taken together! The *Pennsylvania Gazette* was often a forum for Republicans, yet it carried only three significant letters on constitutional reform in February and March 1784. In the entire first half of 1784 only one writer in available Philadelphia newspapers offered any new line of argument on behalf of constitutional change. That writer signed himself "A Citizen of Pennsylvania" and published a long letter to "The People of Pennsylvania" in the *Pennsylvania Gazette* for 3 April 1784. He made four points that had not been made previously in proreform rhetoric. He contended that experience had shown that single legislative houses promote aristocratic domination by whatever party can sustain a majority in them; that the existing government left in doubt whether the state was to be governed by law or by men, since the bald idea of "one party triumphing over the other" gave no such stability as clear delineation of matched powers of different branches of government could promise; that the practices proposed by the majority of the council had all been validated in the experiences of other states; and that the continuous political warfare and eccentricity in Pennsylvania's political life under the Frame was deterring immigration into the state.

The most striking feature of Citizen's argumentation was that he buttressed each of his claims by arguing that each was justified by experience in other American states. This was the first time since the original constitutional convention had been elected that serious public attention had been given to the constitutional practices and experiences of other states. But Citizen's fresh, clear arguments evoked neither amplification nor rebuttal in the Philadelphia press. We cannot know whether this inattention bespoke indifference to constitutional discussion or belief on both sides that no changes were possible through the Council of Censors.

The Council of Censors reconvened, as scheduled, in June 1784. The members supporting change had been silent, and now one Republican had resigned and he had been replaced by George Bryan, dean of the radical democrats in Philadelphia. Two formerly absent friends of the Frame were now in attendance. Two Republicans absented themselves, again suggesting that the reformers saw no hope of success through the council's work. As the result of these shifts, the reconvened council consisted of fourteen supporters of the Frame of 1776 and ten critics of it. The reform movement, such as it had been, was dead, although there was a last gasp of prochange rhetoric when a petition from "Citizens of Philadelphia" was directed to the council and published in the press.[51] The petition urged the council to call for a constitutional convention—a thing the council as now constituted was certain not to do.

The Federal Constitution Becomes the Issue

The election of 1785 produced a virtual deadlock between the parties in the assembly. Fortunately, the deeply respected Benjamin Franklin was president of the commonwealth, and through his good offices the electors' oaths of allegiance to the Frame were revised, still leaving the vexatious oath for officers, including legislators. Also, direct concern with the Frame was now being displaced by concern about the constitution of the Confederation, and in 1786 the Republicans, now calling themselves "Federalists," won a clear majority in the assembly. With this political power they could respond forcefully to the national movement for a new constitution. Nor were they unaware that a new federal constitution would force constitutional revision in Pennsylvania.

The story of Pennsylvania's swift ratification of the federal Constitution has been told often; however, for want of detailed attention to the accompanying rhetoric, three important facts have been overlooked or discounted in a number of historical accounts. (1) Virtually all considerations relative to revising the structure of the Confederation were publicly raised in Pennsylvania well before the state ratified. (2) The legalisms and ideological stance of the Whigs, who now called themselves "Antifederalists," were rhetorically irrelevant in a situation where Federalists at long last had a strong majority. (3) Proratification rhetoric emphasized the expediency of changes in the national constitutional system. These three propositions are readily supported if one centers attention on the speaking and writing that hampered or facilitated change between 1786 and 1790.

By 1786, the leaders of both political parties in Pennsylvania granted that the Confederation required some reform. Even defenders of the Articles of Confederation admitted that a few changes were desirable—for example, strengthening the government's treaty-making powers and creating federal control over interstate and foreign trade regulations. Calls for federal change had appeared with increasing frequency in the Pennsylvania press since 1781, and, of course, comparable and often more vigorous agitation for change occurred in other states. A series of steps initiated in Virginia led to creation of a federal constitutional convention, which met in Philadelphia. The discussions of that body were secret, and the first knowledge the generality of Pennsylvanians had of the convention's proposal came when a draft of the new Constitution was read in the Pennsylvania Assembly on 18 September 1787. The reading was for information only, but the proposal was now a matter of public record. It came under public

discussion while the assembly continued with other business in anticipation of its scheduled, final adjournment on 29 September.

The Continental Congress, meeting in New York, debated the
convention's report on 26, 27, and 28 September. The Federalist
majority in the Pennsylvania assembly hoped for prompt congressional direction to the states to consider the Constitution, but the
majority was prepared to order election of a ratifying convention with
or without formal, federal direction. Accordingly, George Clymer
moved in the assembly on 28 September that a state convention be
called and election of its members scheduled. It was with this motion
that the last phase of constitutional controversy in Pennsylvania
began.

Clymer's motion was debated during the morning of 28 September 1787. The debate showed clearly (1) that both political parties
recognized that if a state convention were elected early, it would
certainly ratify the new Constitution; (2) that the real issue for
everyone in the assembly was the timing of a convention that
would have to be called sooner or later; and (3) that despite all
the casuistical and technical arguments that marked the debate,
everyone knew the issues on which ratification or rejection of the
proposed Constitution would hinge.

Given the history of parliamentary manipulations in the state, it
was almost predictable that this session of the assembly would end
with a comic-opera denouement deriving from the familiar tactic of
frustrating majority rule by invoking the Frame's requirement that
the assembly act only with at least two-thirds of its members present.
The famous bit of drama in which two protesting members were
physically forced to be present should not obscure the fact that the
pragmatic issue posed by Clymer's motion was simple and fully
understood by all. It was: Should those who disliked the proposed
federal Constitution have more than five to seven weeks to raise
sentiment against it? To answer in the negative, the Federalists
needed only to maintain a quorum in the house.

The debate on Clymer's motion and other public rhetoric treated
all of the major topics that would be discussed in the state's ratifying
convention, and most of the issues eventually raised in the ratifying
conventions of other states were touched on. This is a fact not noticed
by those historians who have implied or asserted that Pennsylvania's
ratification of the Constitution was hasty and/or ill advised.[52] The
facts are that each of the following contentions was made in the assembly on 28 September 1787 and/or was published in broadsides and in
the newspapers before 8 October—one month before delegates to the
Pennsylvania ratifying convention were elected.

Contentions Publicly Raised by 8 October 1787

FEDERALIST CONTENTIONS	ANTIFEDERALIST CONTENTIONS
The Articles of Confederation are inadequate to the nation's needs; hence the inadequate government should be altered as quickly as possible.	Some changes in the nation's Articles are needed, but the government that sustained us through war can sustain us through full deliberation on changes.
The new Constitution is needed to give government the "energy" to produce national prosperity and to conduct foreign affairs.	The proposed Constitution threatens to "sport away" the people's liberties.
The assembly has had the draft Constitution for "near a fortnight" and should be ready to act; the people will have ample time to consider if the election is set for early November.	The "back country" cannot be informed in time, and there must be time to explore alternatives to the new plan.
Federal and state conventions better express the will of the people than any machinery of the Confederation can; an elected state convention is the ideal voice of the people.	The federal convention exceeded its authority; to convene a state convention without congressional direction is to proceed unfederally.
Pennsylvania should lead in ratifying, for her own honor and to encourage other states to ratify.	There is no honor in haste; even with delay we will be in step with other states.
The federal convention represented the will of the people; no agency of the Confederation can so fully represent them.	Congress should take time to deliberate before authorizing state conventions; then the people must review, and if needed alter, the proposal.
The Constitution's great virtue is that it makes the Confederation into a *nation*.	The Constitution destroys the sovereignty of confederated states.
The ratification process is outside the prescriptions of the Articles; the convention and confirmation processes are new processes added by the Continental Congress.	The Articles still apply; hence, any action without congressional direction is improper. Ratification of the plan without all states concurring would be unconstitutional.

These contentions were all presented and publicized in late September and the first eight days of October. The question of whether a bill of rights was needed in the federal Constitution was not raised directly in the assembly debate until a compendium of rights to be guaranteed was offered but not debated in the final hours of the session. The minority's Address, published 6 October, gave the first strong emphasis to the importance of these safeguards.

Judged against political tradition in Pennsylvania, the heavy Federalist majority proceeded with restraint in the assembly, even though it passed Clymer's motion swiftly. Clymer had proposed that convention delegates be elected at the same time as assemblymen, on 9 October. Antifederalists objected, and the Federalists immediately agreed that a later date should be set. On whether the assembly should wait for formal directions from Congress, Clymer used a phrase his colleagues repeated: to wait would "be to attend to forms, and to lose the substance." Hugh Brackenridge of Pittsburgh, usually a stickler for parliamentary precision, gave the argument in support of Clymer's point:

If a thing, Sir, ought to be done, it is little matter whether it be from the reflection of Congress or the feeling and sensibility of the people; and I own that I always feel a contempt for those languid and trammeled sentiments which move but like a piece of mechanism. And what are the consequences of taking up the subject without waiting the result of Congressional deliberation? We lead the way, and do great honor to ourselves in marking the road to obtain the sense of the people on a subject that is of greatest moment to them and to their posterity.

Brackenridge and others further supported their position by insisting that the state had appointed its delegates to the Constitutional Convention before Congress formally called that convention; thus, Pennsylvania had from the beginning proceeded independently and by means beyond the provisions of the Articles of Confederation.

The gist of Antifederalist argument in the assembly was expressed by the always logically precise William Findley of Westmoreland County:

I have no doubt but a convention might be called, and will be called. That it ought to be called, and will be called, is seen so clearly, that I shall add nothing to enforce it; therefore I take it that the propriety of calling a convention is not the question before us. . . . I shall proceed, Sir, now to examine the ground on which we stand: I believe we stand on federal ground; therefore we are not in a state of nature. If we were in a state of nature, all the arguments produced for hastening this business would apply; but as we are not, I would observe that the most deliberate manner of proceeding is the best manner. . . . Now my opinion is, Sir, that we are on federal ground: that . . . [we should] have recourse to the confederation itself, and then to the law which appointed delegates to the convention, and let them decide whether we are on federal ground or not.

From this posture Findley and his colleagues would reason themselves into a position asserting that not even admittedly needed changes could be made in the national constitution without agreement of all the confederated states and that the proper way of proceeding was for Congress to receive recommendations for constitutional changes from the states and then refer these together with the proposed Constitution to a new federal constitutional convention.[53]

Besides seeming more interested in delay than in solving problems that they themselves admitted deserved attention, the Antifederalists were asserting that direct recourse to the people on issues of national governance was inappropriate. By the end of the assembly debate, the Federalists had at least tentatively taken democratic positions, whereas their opponents stood in firm defense of existing governmental institutions even where there existed a popular wish for change.

That a ratifying convention would be called in Pennsylvania was settled by a vote of forty-three to nineteen before noon on 28 September 1787. The date of an election of delegates and the date and place of their meeting remained to be acted upon. To frustrate settlement of these matters, the Antifederalists absented themselves from the assembly in the afternoon. For lack of a quorum, the majority was forced to adjourn to the following day. By the morning of 29 September, an unofficial copy of Congress's recommendation for state conventions had reached the Federalists,[54] but the Antifederalists were still absent from the assembly. The sergeant at arms was sent to seek the absent members and report receipt of the congressional directive.[55] The Antifederalists still refused to attend. Then a small mob, apparently led by a Colonel John Barry, seized assemblymen James M'Calmont (Franklin County) and Jacob Miley (Dauphin County) and delivered them to the assembly.

A charade of deliberation followed. Could the assembly have a quorum with two members present against their wills? Brackenridge made the telling parliamentary point that since M'Calmont had answered to his name in a roll call, he must be present and a quorum existed. Spectators helped to keep the reluctant members from leaving physically, and the assembly proceeded to some normal business. It then set the dates for electing and convening delegates to a convention directed to consider ratification or rejection of the new federal Constitution. Philadelphia was designated the site of the convention's sitting.

It is difficult to take seriously the tactical maneuverings in the last days of this assembly, but they should remind one that quorums and majorities of two-thirds had been prized since colonial times precisely because they allowed minorities to force a majority either to act as the minority wished or to cease functioning. All parties and factions had so used this device, giving it historic sanction but leaving ambiguous what was meant by "majority rule" and "the authority of the people."

A feature of the election of convention delegates reflected similar ambiguity concerning individual rights and privileges. No Federalist assemblyman stood for election to the convention, but several Antifederalists did. Evidence of the reasons for this is not conclusive, but it appears that the Federalists, who knew that the federal Constitution would force changes in the Frame, deliberately avoided the possibility that Federalists who voted to ratify the federal Constitution could later be charged with violating their officers' oaths to do nothing directly or indirectly to alter the Frame of 1776. Antifederalist assemblymen, who were determined to oppose ratification, apparently felt none of the Federalists' compunctions.[56]

Before election of delegates to the convention, Antifederalists tried in another way to constrain majoritarian decisions. They proposed in the new, twelfth assembly that the forthcoming convention be directed to adopt the assembly's two-thirds requirement for a quorum. The attempt failed, but Federalists had opportunity to point out the antidemocratic character of this sort of parliamentary requirement. Said Assemblyman William Lewis: "Let me . . . ask the advocates for this restriction, what may be the consequences if this doctrine is allowed? If they possess the right to say that two-thirds shall be a quorum, they possess the right of saying also that nine-tenths must be the number; nay, they may go further, and require the presence and consensus of every individual. And what consequences will result from a power of this nature? It will enable the legislature to defeat the intentions of the people."[57] Lewis might have added, as neither he nor any other Federalist did, that in free and open democratic government there ought always to be a presumption against the right of one representative body to set the rules for another. Pennsylvanians, however, had not yet learned fully the democratic principle that rules ought to facilitate majority action while protecting individual and minority rights.

The election on 6 November 1787 of convention delegates produced a majority of about two-thirds in favor of the new Constitution, but public debate on the merits of the proposal had begun immediately on the call for a convention. What may be thought of as the official Antifederalist and Federalist positions were stated upon adjournment of the eleventh assembly. These positions were expressed in the Address of the Seceding Assemblymen and in a Reply of Six Assemblymen. Both were published as soon as the

eleventh assembly adjourned.[58] Public meetings, letters, and essays
for and against the new plan competed for attention from 20 September onward. The arguments before, during, and within the convention can be readily summarized, for the arguments did not change.
The substantive contentions were as follows:

FOR THE CONSTITUTION	AGAINST THE CONSTITUTION
The plan is brought forward under congressional direction, and the present issue is whether to ratify or reject the plan the federal convention offered and the Congress chose to submit for consideration by the people of each state. Inadequacies of government under the Articles are admitted by all.	The proper procedure is to collect suggestions for alterations of govern- ment and then have Congress call a second convention to reconsider and resubmit a plan.
The federal convention was legitimately authorized and chosen. It said that a wholly new plan was needed. The issue is not the propriety of their action but whether their proposal is or is not acceptable.	The federal convention should have confined itself to empowering the Confederation to regulate foreign relations more fully, to settle maritime issues, and to regulate currency and imposts.
The proposed system is unique; it depends on and preserves the sover- eignty of the states while creating responsive government capable of forwarding diplomatic, economic, and military "energy."	It is a system of "consolidation," not "confederacy"—which is the only known system for governing large areas comprised of "republics." Consolidation destroys the sovereignty of subsidiary states.
Government of a nation must extend to and be responsive to the people, who are the ultimate source of all au- thority; states or other subordinate entities are not such authorities.	The taxing and other powers of the proposed system extend to the "lives of individuals," which means there is power to destroy the rights of persons.
States must continue to exist, for they create segments of the national government and they have first responsibility for electoral processes; they train and staff the military.	Sovereignty of the states will be "annihilated" by national power to regulate elections, direct military movements, and otherwise act directly on the people instead of on the states.
The system is feasible and safe because individual rights are guaranteed by the states; making their restatement unnecessary;	The Confederation and the Frame are better models because the new system provides no bill of individual rights, as in the Frame.

"Mixed" powers assigned to elements of government yield checks on each element except the House of Representatives, the popular house; powers and checks are all clearly specified.

The system of "mixed" powers and checks is unworkable and leads to complexity and undue expense. The principle that powers should be separated is ignored.

All elements of government are directly or indirectly responsible to the people; Senate and president are checked by each other, by the representatives, and by the electoral processes.

The system is "aristocratic," especially in empowering the Senate and president and in eliminating rotation in offices.

Standing armies are essential to defense, already exist, and are subject to refunding every two years. Judicial authority is duly limited.

The plan promises tyranny by creating standing armies and extending judicial power beyond maritime and similar purely national concerns.

Representation is reasonable and is more direct than under the Articles. The plan also provides for amendments.

Representation favors small states in the Senate and gives too few representatives in the House.

The slavery clause is the best that could be achieved and is at least a step against this institution; nothing in the plan endangers Pennsylvania's prohibitory legislation.

The slavery clause makes slavery permanent and endangers Pennsylvania's legislation providing for slavery's abolition.

The system is the best that serious delegates could work out in the face of differing interests that had to be accommodated.

An "aristocratic sett of men" proposes this system to establish means by which they can permanently and despotically control the people.

In view of the fact that virtually everyone conceded that some changes in national government were needed, the Antifederalist arguments and claims had an enfeebling weakness as rhetoric. They attacked features of the proposed Constitution but offered as an alternative only continuance of admitted shortcomings under the Articles of Confederation. Furthermore, under the Antifederalists' very strict interpretation of the Articles, whatever needed to be done with the Articles could only be done by using a very laborious and time-consuming set of procedures. Such an option could not be attractive to the various groups of Pennsylvanians who were impatient with some or all of such federal difficulties as money policies, responses to the depredations of Barbary pirates, inability to establish foreign credits, interstate trade barriers, and lack of a judicial system capable of resolving interstate conflicts. Nonetheless, in the press and in the convention Antifederalists uniformly defended the flawed status quo against an alternative that was at least coherent and promised some prospect of useful governmental action at home and abroad.

Inherently and by design, Federalist rhetoric fit the political and rhetorical situation. They defended their plan in ways that emphasized the coherence of the entire scheme and invited attention to alleged superiorities of the Constitution over the status quo. They not only had a powerful majority in Pennsylvania; they also had the more appealing response to the exigencies of the day. In the past they had not established a compelling need for changing the Frame of 1776, but now the need for change in national government was granted. They could amplify difficulties the existence of which few could deny. Most importantly, the Federalists were now in full possession of all persuasive themes arising out of the American commonplace that legitimate governance exists "by authority of the *people* only."[59] Antifederalists' commitment to existing institutions prevented them from associating major arguments with the virtues of direct, democratic responsiveness. Their basic position was that the United States was, and for reasons not discussed should remain, a confederation of states, not of peoples or of the people of a nation. Federalist rhetoric attached the virtues of strength and unity to the concept of nationhood, but given their absolutist stance relative to the concepts of confederation and state, Antifederalists could take no advantage of "nationhood" as a theme.

Between the formal call for a ratifying convention and the convention's conclusion on 15 December 1787, much was written in the press and much said at public meetings for and against the Constitution. On the Antifederalist side the chief writings during this period were the Address of the Seceding Assemblymen; three letters by Centinel, appearing in the *Independent Gazetteer* on 5 October and 8 and 30 November; and a letter by "An Officer of the Late Continental Army" published in the *Independent Gazetteer* on 6 November.[60]

The major addresses and writings from Federalists were the Reply of Six Assemblymen; three letters signed "An American Citizen," published in the *Independent Gazetteer* on 26, 28, and 29 September;[61] a speech by James Wilson to a mass meeting at the State House on 6 October and reported, among other places, in the *Pennsylvania Packet* on 10 October; a reply to Centinel's first letter, appearing in the *Independent Gazetteer* on 10 October; and a reply by "Plain Truth" in the *Independent Gazetteer* on 10 November, answering "An Officer of the Late Continental Army."

There were, of course, many more letters, essays, and public speeches, but the rhetoric contained in this sample of sources fairly represents the arguments, appeals, and styles of both sides.[62] Major parts of the convention's proceedings were also published; the convention's sessions were open to the public and appear to have been well attended.

All of this rhetoric fell on the ears and eyes of a population the majority of which had endorsed federal change as they chose their assemblymen and their convention delegates in October and November 1787. At least some in that electorate were aware that if they favored the federal Constitution, they were in effect paving the way for major changes in the Frame of 1776. Antifederalists sometimes used this fact as an argument against ratification; the Federalists were generally silent about it although they fully understood it.

Judge George Bryan of Philadelphia had been and continued to be one of the staunchest advocates for Pennsylvania's Frame of 1776 and an opponent of the proposed federal Constitution. His estimate of the state of public opinion at the time of ratification was not likely, therefore, to be biased in the Federalists' favor, but he wrote:

The Cincinnati were in support of it [the Constitution]. The civil officers were threatened in newspaper publications, if they should oppose, and were mostly in favor of it. Monied men, and particularly the stockholders in the bank were in favor of it. The merchants [were] in favor of it. Lawyers—the greatest part in favor of it. Divines of all denominations, with very few exceptions, in favor of it. They had suffered by paper money. Men of letters, many of them, were opposed to it. Whigs—the majority of whom opposed to it. Tories—almost all for it. The women—all admire Genl. W[ashington]. Mechanics—such as depend on commerce and navigation, in favor. The others divided. . . . Sea-faring men followed the mercantile interests and were strenuous in favor of it. Creditors were influenced in favor of it by their aversion to paper money; yet some were opposed to it. Debtors are often creditors in their turn and the paper money had great effect on men's minds. . . . The counties nearest the navigation were in favor of it generally; those more remote in opposition. The farmers were perhaps more numerous in opposition than any other set of men. Most townsmen were for it. The foreigners were chiefly connected to the mercantile people and were in favor of it. Even the foreign seamen were made useful in support of it in Philadelphia.[63]

Bryan's Antifederalist colleagues presumably knew their vote-getting difficulties as well as he. Their most practical strategy both in and out of the ratification convention was to introduce whatever delay they could while making a rhetorical record that might influence the progress of ratification at home and in other states. What they did and said *after* Pennsylvania had ratified was thus about as important to their aims as what they said and did before.

Although their cause was effectively won with the election of the ratifying convention, Federalists proceeded as though they genuinely intended to persuade—with an eye to citizens of other states as well as to Pennsylvanians. The three most important features of Federalists' rhetoric between late September and formal ratification in mid-December 1787 were these: (1) although they argued diligently, the Federalists were thoroughly bested by the Antifederalists on the issue of whether a formal bill of rights was necessary and desirable in the new Constitution; (2) under James Wilson's leadership the Federalists completely displaced the Antifederalists as the exponents of democratic self-government; and (3) in organization and style the written and oral rhetoric of the Federalists (except on the Bill of Rights) was effectively designed to keep adherents and gain new ones—in and out of Pennsylvania.

The Antifederalists' insistence on the need to add a bill of rights began with the Address of the minority of the eleventh assembly; there, however, the demand appeared only at the conclusion of a long section of complaints against procedures of the assembly. The Federalists' basic reply was first outlined by James Wilson at the State House on 6 October. Wilson argued that individual rights were guaranteed by the laws of the states and that sovereignty of the states was preserved in the new Constitution. To enumerate those same rights in the federal document would be redundant, he said. As an example, he pointed out that stipulating freedom of the press would make sense only if the federal Constitution contained some regulation of literary output in the way that it authorized federal regulation of interstate commerce. There was no such regulation of oral or written words, so there was no point in stipulating freedom of the press.[64]

"An Officer of the Late Continental Army" picked up this topic on 6 November, and Centinel addressed it in his letter of 8 November. Both contended that, in fact, the sovereignty of the states would be destroyed and the security of individual rights lost thereby. Officer insisted that the entire thrust of "consolidation" and centralization was inimical to individual liberty. Centinel characteristically alleged that the whole plan was part of a conspiracy to crush "equal liberty," and that was why "an odious bill of rights" was being avoided. Significantly, neither writer suggested that the plan would be acceptable if a bill of rights were added. "Plain Truth" replied, repeating Wilson's claim that enumeration would be redundant and adding that to enumerate rights in the Constitution might "grant, by implication, what was intended to be reserved" to the states and the people.

The most revealing exchange concerning a bill of rights occurred in the ratifying convention on 28 November. Antifederalists had insisted that a bill of rights was traditional and essential in any and all constitutions. Wilson replied as he had before, but in the course of debate, which lasted several days, he took a confusing variety of positions and even made mistakes concerning facts relative to guarantees of individual rights.[65] His strongest argument was that "We the people of the United States do ordain" in the preamble "is tantamount to a volume, and contains the essence of all the bills of rights that . . . can be devised." But John Smilie, former assembly-man, censor, and member of the state's Executive Council, caught Wilson and his colleagues on a trilemma from which they never escaped. Smilie insisted (1) that precedents for listing rights were both British and American, as the Frame of 1776 and other state constitutions showed; (2) that "the supreme authority naturally rests in the people, but does it follow that therefore a declaration of rights would be superfluous?" and (3) that the precedents are wise, and superfluity cannot be claimed "unless some criterion is established by which it could be easily and constitutionally ascertained how far our governors may proceed, and by which it might appear when they transgress their jurisdiction."[66]

No Federalist writer or speaker successfully refuted or evaded even one of Smilie's claims. Wilson tried to evade the net by saying that to enumerate some rights would imply that those not listed were not retained by the people. But Smilie, Findley, and Robert Whitehill (Cumberland County) responded that precisely this kind of exclusory process was already begun in the Constitution when it guaranteed the rights of habeas corpus and trial by jury in criminal cases. From 28 November to the final vote on ratification, the Federalists were on the defensive whenever the issue of a bill of rights was raised. When Wilson lamely said that no delegate to the federal convention had thought about a bill of rights until three days before adjournment, the Antifederalists were quick to seize on this admission as proof of their contentions that the Constitution was not well thought out and that reconsideration was necessary.

The extent to which Federalists in other states drew lessons from their friends' embarrassments on this issue in Pennsylvania is not known precisely. It is striking, however, that in no later convention did Federalists refuse to consider the possibility of adding a bill of rights once the basic Constitution was ratified. The Antifederalists in Pennsylvania made enumeration of rights a major feature of their postconvention rhetoric. It is possible that their continued agitation contributed to the fact that nine of the first ten amendments ultimately adopted dealt with rights first formally proposed by Antifederalists as the Pennsylvania convention closed.

On all other issues the Federalists' rhetoric in and out of the convention was markedly superior to their opponents'. Federalists were more comprehensive and had better theoretical and empirical grounding, and most individual contributions to the debate were coherent and cogent, as was their overall case. The most effective rhetor in the press was the author of letters by "An American Citizen" that appeared in September. In the convention, Wilson and his chief lieutenant on the floor, Thomas McKean, were the leaders. They sometimes veered toward superciliousness, but for the most part they addressed issues rather than personalities. Wilson's intimate knowledge of the law, his part in drawing up the Constitution, and his expository skill made him a powerful spokesman. McKean functioned as his aide, offering careful arguments on points of law and political theory, but he seldom pursued topics to first principles as Wilson did. Thomas Hartley of York County also spoke in disciplined fashion, confining himself largely to point-by-point replies. Jasper Yeates and Timothy Pickering spoke occasionally, reasoning closely about specific points. Both in the convention and at public meetings, Benjamin Rush seems to have attempted grandiloquence. Reporters several times referred to his speaking as "metaphysical" or "pathetic." The most heated and personality-oriented speaker for the Federalists was Stephen Chambers of Lancaster. In the press there were also a few publications that were more vindictive and personal than substantive, but in the main Federalist discourse was thoughtful and deliberative. Throughout, the pillar of strength in Federalist rhetoric was Wilson.

The Federalists needed to show that their plan met needs beyond those conceded by the Antifederalists, and they needed to show that their plan facilitated democratic government without undue dangers. They needed to do these things to hold and strengthen local, favorable views but, perhaps even more importantly, because theirs was the first comprehensive debate on ratification their strengths and weaknesses could influence opinion in other states. The best Federalist speakers and writers focused sharply on these two crucial tasks. Perhaps the most important rhetorical achievement in Pennsylvania was that James Wilson comprehensively showed there was a grand democratic base in the proposed new government. In the convention he did this most forcefully near the end of a major speech on 26 November. He said in part:

In all governments, whatever is their form . . . there must be a power established from which there is no appeal, and which is therefore called absolute, supreme, and uncontrollable. The only question is, where that power is lodged?—a question that will receive different answers from the different writers on the subject. . . .

But were we to ask some politicians who have taken a faint and inaccurate view of our establishments, where does this supreme power reside in the United States? they would probably answer, in their Constitutions. This however, though a step nearer to the fact, is not a just opinion; for in truth, it remains and flourishes with the people; and under the influence of that truth we, at this moment, sit, deliberate, and speak. . . . That the supreme power . . . should be vested in the people, is in my judgment the great panacea of human politics. It is a power paramount to every constitution, inalienable in its nature, and indefinite in its extent. For I insist, if there are errors in government, the people have the right not only to correct and amend them, but likewise totally to change and reject its form; and under the operation of that right, the citizens of the United States can never be wretched beyond retrieve, unless they are wanting to themselves. . . . To obtain all the advantages, and to avoid all the inconveniences of these governments [monarchic, aristocratic, and democratic] was the leading object of the late convention. Having therefore considered the formation and principles of other systems, it is natural to enquire, of what description is the constitution before us? In its principles, Sir, it is purely democratical; varying indeed, in its form, in order to admit all the advantages, and to exclude all the disadvantages which are incidental to the known and established constitutions of government. But when we take an extensive and accurate view of the streams of power that appear through this great and comprehensive plan, when we contemplate the variety of their directions, the force and dignity of their currents, when we behold them intersecting, embracing, and surrounding the vast possessions and interests of the continent, and when we see them distributing on all hands beauty, energy and riches, still, however numerous and wide their courses, however diversified and remote the blessings they diffuse, we shall be able to trace them all to one great and noble cause, THE PEOPLE.[67]

This passage constitutes the précis of Wilson's total case for ratification, phrased in the philosophical tone and weighty but not stolid style of his best discourse. The Constitution was "democratical"—but with safeguards. Around this premise the entire Federalist case in the ratifying convention was built. Time would show that not every Federalist in Pennsylvania admired the plan's thoroughly "democratical" features, but during the ratification debate the ultra-conservative Federalists held their tongues in and out of the convention. At long last, the friends of constitutional change had presented a unified and democratic front.

The worst-case scenarios conjured up by Antifederalists were answered by pointing to the internal and electoral checks of the proposed government. To claims that officers would continue too long in power, Federalists replied that occupation of office was everywhere subject to popular consent or the consent of other elected officials. Federalists made much of the fact that the exclusive power of the purse was vested in directly elected, two-year representatives, and they insisted that "touching the lives of individuals" was precisely the way to maintain democracy in a governmental system. Charges that the system was "aristocratical" were similarly met by pointing again to popular control of the purse and to the states' control over elections of senators and the president. Federalists showed further that federal influence over elections was expressly limited to cases where states failed to exercise their authority. They did not need to mention specifically the Confederation's continuous and well-known troubles with recalcitrant Rhode Island.

In the convention, Wilson dealt a fatal blow to the commonplace that standing armies were universally to be feared. He pointed out that some always-available military force was inevitably necessary to defense. Still more tellingly, he pointed to the Confederation's own military force sitting at that moment on the Ohio River to defend western Pennsylvania and adjacent areas. Here and elsewhere, most pro-Constitution rhetoric aimed at allaying fears and establishing the reasonableness of the proposed plan. Such admittedly unfortunate features as continuance of slave trade were excused on pragmatic grounds: they were inescapable accommodations to special interests of different sections of the nation, and their presence showed a proper deference to the sovereignty of the several states.

In sum, the standard Federalist *topoi* of argument were: what was probable, what was practically feasible, and how, in operational terms, one force or agency of government would probably act on others. The result was a systematic defense of the Constitution embodying strongly supported claims that the system had unique, positive features.

Except on the issue of a bill of rights, Antifederalist rhetoric from October through December 1787 lacked coherence and pragmatism. What Judge Bryan wrote of Antifederalists nationally was true of his friends in Pennsylvania: "Those in opposition . . . seem to have had no pre-concert, nor any suspicion of what was coming forward. The same objections were made in different parts of the Continent, almost at the same time, merely as though they were obviously dictated by the subject. Local ideas seem to have entered very little into the objections."[68] In and out of the convention, Antifederalist rhetoric in Pennsylvania was similarly piecemeal and reactive, giving no evidence of any concerted program for solving problems—except through delay. In only three ways did local considerations enter into this rhetoric. Pennsylvania's large size relative to Rhode Island, New Jersey, and other states was made ground for claims that Pennsylvania would be underrepresented in the Senate. The Frame of 1776 was repetitiously offered as the ideal model for a government, but no one spelled out the practical advantages of applying that model on a national scale. Moreover, the Antifederalists in the convention chose not to challenge the Constitution's bicameralism and use of a single executive; as a result, the relevance of the Frame as a model was undermined. Third, the commonplace that "the junto" was once more conspiring to seize despotic power was amplified again and again, especially by the chief Antifederalist writer, Centinel; but this theme had become hackneyed by repeated use in the earlier debates about altering the Frame. Until the very end of the convention, the stance of the Antifederalists was that the new Constitution was entirely unacceptable. Almost all of their rhetoric asserted or implied that the process of constitutional revision should be started over, with the purpose of limiting changes to those that would enlarge Congress's powers in international affairs and taxing imports. Such urgings were foredoomed. The citizens of the state had elected friends of the Constitution to their assembly and then to the convention. Perhaps it was out of frustration that the Antifederalist writers spent most of their space on denouncing, generally and individually, the proponents of ratification.[69] When not denouncing, they excoriated the idea of "consolidation" and enumerated ways in which centralized powers were being vested in the national government at the expense of individuals and the states. One of the few times an Antifederalist writer dealt in any way with the need for change occurred when Centinel, at the end of November, contended that people were too swiftly and thoughtlessly making "the needless sacrifice" of supporting the Constitution simply because it seemed to rectify a few things that genuinely needed to be changed.[70]

As I have indicated, the most striking ideational feature of Antifederalist rhetoric in Pennsylvania was that these sometime revolutionists and ultrademocrats continued to argue themselves into fundamentally antidemocratic positions—positions from which an escape was possible only by conceding the Federalists' basic point that the people always have the right to alter their forms of government. Were that conceded, of course, most of the machinery restricting change in the Frame of 1776 would be indefensible.

The three Antifederalist speakers in the ratifying convention took the position that the people had no legal right to form a new kind of national government. On 28 November, John Smilie said the proposed plan represented "the manifest subversion of the principle that constitutes a union of States, which are sovereign and independent, except in the specific objects of confederation. . . . The plan before us, then, explicitly proposes the formation of a new constitution upon the original authority of the people, and not an association of States upon the authority of their respective governments."[71]

On these premises "the people" could not begin again to create a government, even by the same convention and ratification processes they had used in creating their first government. William Findley, always the most philosophical Antifederalist in the state, put the issue in the language of political theory: "In the Preamble, it is said, 'We the People,' and not 'We the States,' which therefore is a compact between individuals entering into society, and not between separate states enjoying independent power and delegating a portion of that power for their common benefit."[72] Anthony Wayne's notes record Findley as giving his argument precisely the Lockean base he had used in the assembly, where he had said, " 'We the people,' not 'the people of the United States,' supposes us in a state of nature, and to a stranger it would appear that no states were in existence."[73] Of all Antifederalist spokesmen, Findley was the most precise and most candid. We must therefore take what he said as Antifederalist theory, not rhetorical enthusiasm. Robert Whitehill was more given to hyperbole. His version of the doctrine ran that the "We the people" phrase "shows the old foundation of the union is destroyed . . . and a new and unwieldy system of consolidated empire is set up, upon the ruins of the present compact between the states."[74] Findley and Whitehill did not document their claims, as they might have, by citing Robinson, Fitzsimmons, and Brackenridge, who had said in the eleventh assembly that the Confederation was indeed dead.

It appears that Smilie, Findley, and Whitehill were the only Antifederalists to speak in the ratifying convention, and according to all three the confederative structure of the nation stood and must continue to stand between the people and their right to alter their own government. Whitehill was explicit: "[If four states were to refuse to ratify] would they not still be entitled to demand performance of the original compact between the states? Sir, these questions must introduce a painful anticipation of the confusion, contest, and a civil war, which, under the circumstances, the adoption of the offered system must produce."[75]

The Antifederalist ideal was of a confederation of "small republics" loosely allied in order to act concertedly where absolutely necessary but with the tightest of reins on elected "rulers." Only the Saxon element of Demophilus's mythology was missing from Antifederalist themes in the convention. Liberty was secured by what Whitehill called a "permanent land-mark," and that "landmark" was the Articles of Confederation—a bulwark against even the popular will. Following ratification, Centinel would use the Frame of 1776 precisely as other Antifederalists had used the Articles: the Council of Censors was a wisely created guard against "ever restless designs of ambition, on one hand, and credulity of the people on the other." Constitutional change should not hinge on "the breath of an annual Legislature."[76] More and more, the "permanent land-marks," the Articles of Confederation and the Frame of 1776, were rhetorically portrayed as protections *against* popular self-government. Meanwhile, under James Wilson's leadership, the justifications for changes were being firmly rooted in "the authority of the people only." The Federalists were making a clear record on behalf of democratic representation and responsibility, and the Antifederalists were adamantly making a record on behalf of repressing the popular will.

Predictably, the Pennsylvania convention ratified the federal Constitution by a two-to-one majority, and by the end of 1787 three of the required nine states had ratified. The Pennsylvania forums for further constitutional discussion were now public meetings of protest and celebration and the press. Federalists interested themselves chiefly in the progress of ratification in other states and in defending themselves against personal and partisan attacks by their opponents. Nothing was added to the case for the Constitution, nor was the Frame as yet made a public issue by the Federalists. Among the Antifederalists, confusion reigned for a time; then two distinctive strands of discourse emerged.

An Address and Reasons of Dissent of the Minority of the Convention of the State of Pennsylvania to Their Constituents formed the base-point for orthodox, postconvention, Antifederalist rhetoric.[77] This Dissent mingled complaints, hyperbole, and interpretations of the Constitution with advocacy for the bill of rights that Antifederalists had offered at the end of the convention. According to the Dissent, every procedure giving rise to the Constitution and ratification was illegal, therefore null and void. Such claims, however, were largely irrelevant in the rhetorical situation existing after Pennsylvania's ratification. There were no means of adjudicating issues of legality, and the prescribed ratification process was being followed in other states. What the Dissent did accomplish, however, was to give high visibility to the proposed bill of rights and to provide the first hints that at least some Antifederalists might reconcile themselves to the Constitution if a bill of rights were appended.

The fifteen amendments proposed by Whitehill in the convention were presented as "propositions" in the Dissent. They were followed by this statement: "After reading these propositions, we declared our willingness to agree to the plan, provided it was so amended as to meet those propositions, or something similar to them; and finally moved that the Convention adjourn, to give the people of Pennsylvania time to consider the subject, and determine for themselves; but these were all rejected, and the final vote was taken."[78] The statement left moot whether reconciliation could actually be brought about, but the possibility was at least hinted at. For the most part, however, the tone of the Dissent was absolutist. The *Independent Gazetteer* (22 January 1788) summarized and editorially reflected the general frame of mind of opponents of the Constitution:

The minority of the state Convention . . . have declared in their protest, that the continental convention have no power to annihilate the old articles of Confedration without the consent of every one of the thirteen states . . . ; that two members of the late Assembly . . . were forcibly dragged to the House for the purpose of making a quorum to call a convention, whereby the proceedings of such an assembly are by no means binding upon the people; and that the constitution of the State . . . cannot be set aside although nine states should agree to the ratification of the new constitution. In these opinions they are supported not only by their constituents but by a very considerable part of the whole body of the people of Pennsylvania, who, it is expected, will soon confederate under these sentiments. It would be the part therefore of wisdom in some of the states who have not yet adopted the new constitution, to pause a while before they proceed to the ratification of it. A civil war with all its dreadful train of evils will probably be the consequence of such a proceeding. Whereas if we have patience we may at a more convenient opportunity determine upon some alteration in government which will be peaceably adopted by the people.

Without any real alternative to offer, and having insisted that the entire constitutional process was illegal, some Antifederalists saw nullification of Pennsylvania's ratification as their best alternative.

Nullification was attempted, without success. John Nicholson, comptroller general of the state, and some colleagues from Philadelphia tried to mount the kind of petition campaign that had successfully induced the assembly to reverse itself on calling a state convention in 1779. Nicholson's petition asked the assembly to bring "to account" the Pennsylvania delegation to the federal Constitutional Convention, to refuse to "confirm" the new Constitution, and to instruct its delegates to Congress to prevent the Constitution's adoption there. Assemblymen were also reminded that they had sworn to do nothing "prejudicial or injurious" to the Frame of 1776, and the Frame would certainly be "violated or subverted" by the federal Constitution. The petitions were circulated between 2 January and 29 March 1788. There was a striking absence of rhetoric in the press supporting the petition, and by 29 March only about six thousand signatures had been collected. It was plain there was no groundswell of anti-Constitutional feeling.[79]

Nullification had failed, but the war of words did not stop. Jensen has accurately described the overall character of the hundreds of rhetorical appeals. Four topics dominated discussion: (1) the need for amendments to the Constitution; (2) charges that the post office prevented the distribution of Antifederalist material through the mails; (3) charges that men such as Robert Morris were corrupt and supported the Constitution in order to escape paying the debts they owed to the United States; and (4) the publication of fake letters by Federalists and Antifederalists alike to discredit their opponents.[80] By September 1788, however, another strand of Antifederalist rhetoric could be discerned. It was pragmatically conciliatory, in contrast to the intransigent character of orthodox Antifederalism. To illustrate the two patterns, I shall focus on the writings of the prolific Centinel, an extreme Antifederalist, and the more pragmatic Antifederalist rhetoric that began to appear with what was known as "The Harrisburg Convention."

Centinel's was the longest and most comprehensive series of constitutional essays published in Pennsylvania. Eighteen Centinel essays appeared between 5 October 1787 and 9 April 1788. Six more appeared in September through November 1788.[81]

Centinel was an orthodox exponent of concepts that had held sway in the state constitutional convention of 1776, except that Centinel drew on Roman historical analogies—also largely mythic—rather than on Anglo-Saxon mythology. He presupposed that for a large area, one and only one kind of government was desirable: a confederation of towns or "communities" through which limited powers were granted to delegates who periodically assembled to transact inescapable, collective business according to instructions from their respective "republics." This being the ideal state, its structure must be treated as permanent, at least in principle. Movements for change must be guarded against because they might introduce "impurity" into the system. In the nature of things, "ambitious men" would continually seek to introduce change because the ideal system debarred them from power.[82]

Like the writers of the Frame, Centinel believed a special, political "purity" resided in the class of persons variously called "plebeians" or "the mediocrity." Providentially, this class of persons had dominated the Constitutional Convention of 1776. Their special patriotism gave them confidence in the prospects of independence, while the "natural aristocracy" of wealth, higher education, and birth held back, waiting to see on which side "ambition" would be more richly rewarded.[83] To secure themselves against the "aristocracy," the "mediocrity" had happily instituted the principles of rotation in office, "public consideration" of pending legislation, strict accountability to the people in all branches of government, rigid separation of powers between legislative and executive branches, and procedural security against all but the most cautious and deliberate governmental changes. Centinel saw the first constitutional convention as having established a "state of political society," discontinuing the "state of nature" into which dissolving all bonds to England had momentarily thrust the American colonies.[84]

In orthodox Antifederalist rhetoric, *simplicity* was exalted as a major virtue in governmental organization. Its opposite was *complexity*, and complexity was associated with intellectualism "of the schools" and with intertwining functions of the branches of government. As Antifederalists worked out these formulations, another antidemocratic stance emerged. Complexity must be avoided not just because simplicity was better, but because complexity was desired by the predatory aristocracy in order that they might befuddle the populace and take away their liberties. The ironic implication was that the pure "mediocrity" was incapable of understanding self-government fully. Centinel opened this possibility in his first letter:

> The highest responsibility is to be attained, in a simple struction [sic] of government, for the great body of the people never steadily attend to the operations of government, and for want of due information are liable to be imposed on. If you complicate the plan by various orders, the people will be perplexed and divided in their sentiments about the source of abuses or misconduct. Some will impute it to the Senate, others to the House of Representatives, and so on, that the interposition of the people may be rendered imperfect or perhaps wholly abortive. But if, imitating the constitution of Pennsylvania, you vest all power in one body of men . . . elected for a short period . . . you will create the most perfect responsibility.[85]

Denigration of the "mediocrity's" wisdom was certainly implicit here, and when there appeared to be strong popular sentiment for revising the Frame of 1776, Centinel carried his premise to its logical conclusion: Pennsylvania's "invaluable constitution" had the special virtue of recognizing and making difficult expression of the "wickedness and imbecility of mankind which continually endanger the best governments."[86] From such a position it was impossible to defend any institution on grounds of its democratic responsiveness. Centinel and other orthodox Antifederalists were led to claim that both the Articles and the Frame had special merit because they prevented direct responses to the people's wishes. This was also a logical extension of the Antifederalists' enthusiasm for two-thirds majorities and quorums.

Another basic assumption of orthodox Antifederalists led to antidemocratic rhetorical positions. Like a good many of his friends, Centinel accepted it as a truism that all societies are naturally divided into a predatory "aristocracy" of wealth and breeding and a "mediocrity" of public spirit and common sense. But the theory that evil lay with a natural aristocracy and good with the common people created two philosophical problems as arguments developed in Pennsylvania. First, since class distinctions were qualitative, the numbers of persons belonging to either class were irrelevant in calculating where political "good" lay. Majoritarianism thus had no presumptive moral or practical standing. As majorities came to favor constitutional changes, a serious result emerged in Antifederalist rhetoric. The letters of Centinel illustrated what must be said, given his premises, if large numbers of the mediocrity disagreed with an orthodox rhetor.

Majorities of the electors supported the Federalists in 1786, 1787, 1788, and 1789. In Antifederalist lore, the Federalists represented an "aristocratic junto." But now the mediocrity was agreeing with that junto. Centinel at first explained that the virtuous "democracy" was seeking to strengthen the Confederation but mistakenly overlooking the sacrifice of liberty that was exacted by the proposed Constitution.[87] It was harder, however, to explain how heroes of the "democracy," such as George Washington and Benjamin Franklin, could support the federal Constitution. Said Centinel, the "bare possibility" of anarchy trumpeted by the junto must have misled these *"preeminent* men."[88] But Centinel's logic carried him further: that such men could be misled "raises a blush for the weakness of humanity" and teaches that each man must judge for himself and eschew the advice of leaders. And when, in the autumn of 1789, the assembly seemed preparing to call a convention to reform the Frame of 1776, Centinel was led to challenge even that bulwark of libertarian government, the annually elected legislature. Change, said Centinel, must always be hedged against in order to forestall the "ever restless designs of ambition . . . and credulity of the people."[89] Two months later, Centinel was making a final argument for rotation of officers. He pointed to an assemblyman from Dauphin County who had been elected to four successive terms despite the fact that he consistently voted against the four Antifederalist legislators from his county. Centinel asked how such a renegade could ever be ousted from the assembly without the Frame's provision that no one could serve more that four successive terms in the assembly.[90] In other words, the voters of Dauphin County needed institutional protection against their electoral folly. There was considerable justice in the claim of "A Citizen of Philadelphia" that whenever the electorate disagreed with Centinel, he was reduced to threatening civil war unless the electorate reformed.[91] From a rhetorical point

of view, the most significant thing about orthodox Antifederalists'
threats when outnumbered at the polls is that it was the inevitable,
logical outcome of their original, absolutist defense of the Frame of
1776 as a "pure" creation, based on "pure republican principles,"
applied by an especially "pure" convention comprised of "the democracy" of the state. From a mythologized conception of "democracy"
in 1776, they had drifted into such an idealization of the Frame and
the Articles of Confederation that those instruments were now
treated as sacred. When "the people" began to turn elsewhere, the
only rhetorical choices possible were to denounce "the people" or
to resort to force—unless one retreated pragmatically and acquiesced
in "the people's" wishes.

There were pragmatists among the Antifederalists, and they gradually did retreat. Once the federal Constitution was ratified, the
most practical politicians began to develop conciliatory rhetoric—
tentatively at first, it is true. The new style appeared in the call for
the Harrisburg Convention to be held 3–6 September 1788. A
circular letter invited Antifederalists to send delegates to Harrisburg
to consider means of securing "requisite amendments in the said
constitution."[92] Thirteen counties and the city of Philadelphia sent
thirty-three delegates. The invitation had said that the federal Constitution "having been adopted by eleven of the States, ought . . . to
come into operation, and have force until altered in a constitutional
way." Albert Gallatin submitted resolutions proposing that the convention cooperate with like-minded groups in other states, but his
resolutions did not pass. The resolutions that passed asserted the
delegates' belief that the new Constitution would obviate "most of
the inconveniences" of a too-weak Confederation, and they expressed a desire to "harmonize with our fellow citizens." Their goal,
said the delegates, was to make the new system such as would gain
"the approbation and support of every class of citizens."[93]

Conciliatory ideas based on expediency had seldom before come
from the Pennsylvania Antifederalists. It is not remarkable that
Federalists did not know what to make of the new tone coming
out of Harrisburg. Privately they worried; publicly they cautioned
listeners and readers not to succumb to what seemed a strategy of
dissembling.[94]

The Harrisburg Convention spurred Federalists to move systematically to nominate candidates for federal representatives and for
presidential electors. There was also some hyperbolic and satirical
Federalist rhetoric, as when "A Freeman to the Citizens of Pennsylvania" poured out his wrath: "Behold them assembled for the diaboli-
cal purpose, at Harrisburg, the pandemonium of Pennsylvania. Be-

hold them, under the specious pretext of deliberating on *amendments* endeavoring to sap and undermine that constitution which has hitherto baffled their open attacks, and withstood all their collected fury! Behold them in ambuscade, collecting their shattered forces, once more, to try their bankrupt fortune at the approaching elections of state and federal representatives."[95] Most Federalist rhetoric was less apocalyptic. "Lucullus" was typical in challenging the political credibility of the opposition. He attacked the Antifederalist candidates for federal office by saying that the ticket was made up of the same men who had "violated the *rights of conscience*" by imposing "a wicked and tyrannical test law" on Pennsylvania's pacifists, had supported paper money and otherwise ruined the state's credit, had "violated the constitution by seizing the endowments of the College of Philadelphia," and had opposed the federal Constitution "by an attempt to excite a CIVIL WAR."[96]

Collectively, the Federalist rhetoricians made four main points as the federal elections neared: (1) opponents of the Constitution were not the proper people to activate the new government; (2) amendment ought not be the first order of business, for amending should occur only after experience had taught what was needed; (3) proposals for a mixed ticket consisting of persons from both parties were ruses intended to divide the eastern vote; and (4) Federalist nominees had been chosen by a publicly selected nominating conference, whereas Antifederalist nominees were chosen in secret by self-appointed nominators.

Two "official" pieces of campaign rhetoric for the parties were James Wilson's public report on the "Lancaster ticket"and an Antifederalist address by "A Friend to Liberty and Union to the Freemen of Pennsylvania."[97]

Wilson spoke at the State House on 23 November 1788 to report the Lancaster ticket and encourage its support. He described the nominating conference, stressing its representative nature and its high degree of unanimity. Having announced the nominees, he pled for unity of all Federalists in opposition to what "has been named 'the amendment ticket.' " He did not descend to personalities; however, he did say:

I make no observations that are personal, but I submit it whether some of those, whose names are to be found in that ticket are not the same whom many of you now present heard about twelve months ago, most warm, most earnest, and most anxious to obtain the rejection of that system of government. You will recollect this, gentlemen, for you heard the debates within these walls. Now say, is it natural that those who were for the rejection of this system, should be its supporters? Or ought such to be appointed to carry it into execution? I think it is not natural on

their part to expect it: but it would certainly be more unnatural for its friends to
throw it into their hands.

No doubt, gentlemen, the pretense of amendment is a specious one. It is well
known, that everything *human* is *capable* of being amended; it may therefore be
said, and said truly, that this system, like every other production of the human
mind, is capable of improvement. But let me ask, who is most likely to improve
it, its friends or its opposers? This question is easily answered, and upon that answer
your votes will be formed. . . . Each will say, let the Constitution be fairly carried
into execution, by those who are not its enemies, then such amendments as
experience may discover to be necessary, can be made without tearing the whole
to pieces. And the United States may reasonably hope to enjoy that happiness,
which, I trust, is destined for them under every administration of their government.[98]

The Antifederalist address by "A Friend to Liberty and Union"
was equally well mannered. The author denied personal or political
ambition and began by recounting his version of recent history.
Despite the war, states had framed wise constitutions for themselves,
but "only one defect remained. The general government of the
continent . . . was too feeble to secure the safety of the people."
The late Continental Convention framed a new government, but
"whether . . . it was the effect of accident or design, most glaring
defects appear in the Constitution which they have proposed."
Excessive powers given to Congress would cause the states to crum-
ble, but effective government could be had without these undue
powers. "Equally alarming" was the absence of a bill of individual
rights, but this fault could be removed by amendment directly
expressing the authority of the states to protect citizens' rights.[99]

In this conciliatory but not obsequious vein the author said that
the "wisest and best of the people" now acquiesced in the new
government "from the hope of obtaining those amendments, which
the Constitution itself has provided for the attaining." Two points
were clear, said "A Friend": "We must have a continental government or we are an undone people," but at the same time, "we ought
to preserve our liberties." So believing, a number of Pennsylvanians
proposed a ticket of "friends to the new Constitution" who wished
for amendments. The address closed with the names of eight candidates for the House of Representatives. Significantly for the outcome
of the election, the ticket carried the names of two Germans: Daniel
Hiester and Peter Muhlenberg.[100]

The general air of conciliation was enhanced when "A German
Federalist" proposed that since the Federalist ticket nominated only
one German and the Harrisburg ticket proposed two, a fair representation of German citizens could be achieved by voters' substituting
Daniel Hiester and Peter Muhlenberg for two non-Germans on the

Federalist ticket, John Allison and Stephen Chambers.[101] Federalist leaders did not accede to this suggestion, but it was promoted in the press by several writers who endorsed broader ethnic representation.[102] When the ballots were cast, the winning representatives were six Federalists, including F. A. Muhlenberg and Hiester and Peter Muhlenberg from the Harrisburg ticket.[103]

The outcome of this election showed that several changes had occurred in Pennsylvania politics. It was now possible for ethnicity to operate as a more powerful appeal than party loyalty. Second, despite fulminations of orthodox Antifederalists, practical politicians who had opposed the Constitution and adamantly defended the Frame of 1776 now were willing to participate in establishing the new government in spite of common knowledge that the Frame would have to be changed also. Third, new coalitions were beginning to form, based on geographical, local, ethnic, and other pragmatically significant considerations.[104] With these shifts the way was opening for political bargaining and for diminished doctrinal differences. Effectuation of an efficient and responsive but safe government was becoming an immediate rhetorical exigence for the majority of political leaders and electors. Moreover, the fact that under the Frame Pennsylvania simply could not carry out its functions as a state within the newly organized Union made reform of the Frame far less controversial than it had been.

Alteration of the Frame of 1776

Federalists once again won a strong majority in the assembly elected in 1788. Their tactical problem was to secure needed changes in the Frame without incurring the difficulties of dealing with the Council of Censors. Under the Frame, the council was not authorized to write a new constitution, and the council represented counties, not the general population of the state. Accordingly, Wilson and his friends devised a plan that was constitutionally irregular but entirely defensible on democratic grounds.[105] On 24 March 1789, G. Wynkoop moved and George Clymer seconded an assembly resolution saying, among other things, that the "burdens" of the present government were heavy and "various instances occur wherein this form is contradictory to the constitution of the United States." Yet, all state officers had now sworn to uphold this federal Constitution. The difficulties, continued the resolution, would not "admit of the delay of the mode prescribed by the [state] constitution"; that is,

having recourse to the Council of Censors. The citizens of the
state should therefore be asked whether a constitutional convention
should be chosen at the next election, "it being the right of the
people alone to determine on this interesting question ."[106] Wynkoop's resolution passed by a vote of forty-one to seventeen and was
published for "public consideration."

The resolution and the machinery it would set in motion were
shrewdly conceived as political strategy and rhetoric. Immediate
need for change was asserted, and no one could deny that there were
"contradictions" between the Frame and the federal Constitution.
For example, the federal Constitution clearly presupposed bicameral
legislatures and state executives with powers not granted to Pennsylvania's Supreme Executive Council. More importantly for political
persuasion, the resolution reiterated the Federalist theme that "the
people alone" had authority to determine the conditions of self-
government. This theme was now astutely presented on the authority of both the federal Declaration of Independence and the Declaration of Rights section of the Frame of 1776.

While the resolution was under "public consideration," the Federalists took the familiar step of launching a petition drive in support
of the resolution. The Antifederalists were ill organized, and their
responses lacked cohesion and originality. A few remonstrances were
filed from public meetings in counties, but Antifederalist writers in
the press said little about the pending resolution. For example,
between 1 July and 1 December 1789, the *Pennsylvania Gazette*
printed the text of Georgia's newly revised and now *bicameral* constitution and two letters touching on Pennsylvania's constitution. In
the *Independent Gazetteer,* Centinel denounced the federal Constitution in a series of letters but only interrupted this series on 8
September to deal with "an alarming attempt making to annihilate"
the "invaluable" constitution of the state.[107] He had waited until
the very week in which the assembly began to assess public reaction
to its resolution.

The Federalists produced some nine thousand signatures favoring
a convention, and they claimed in the assembly that they had
directly consulted their constituents and could therefore speak with
authority concerning their districts' wishes. This kind of claim to
speak directly for constituents was new in Pennsylvania politics.
Centinel, not very cogently, said such claims were made by "prosti-
tuted minions of venality, who have obtruded themselves on the
people."[108] He and others derided the petitions the Federalists had
filed, but that was scarcely telling because the number of signatures
to the petitions exceeded the number of votes cast for the most

popular candidate in the recent elections of federal representatives.[109]

The new resolution calling for election of a state convention was, itself, a masterful bit of rhetoric. It said in part:

[H]aving taken effectual measures for satisfying themselves of the sense of the good people of this commonwealth thereon, they [the assembly] are well assured, from the petitions referred to them, from the enquiries made, and from information given by the several members, that a large majority of the citizens of this state are not only satisfied with the measures submitted to them by the house at their last session, but are desirous that the same should be carried into effect, in preference to the mode by the Council of Censors, which is not only unequal and unnecessarily expensive, but too dilatory to produce the speedy and necessary alterations, which the late change in the political union and the exigencies of the state require: And as the bill of rights declares it to be "An indubitable, unalienable and indefeazible right of the community, to reform alter or abolish government, in such a manner as shall be by that community judged most conducive to the public weal," so on this occasion your committee [of the whole assembly] are perfectly satisfied, that a great majority of them are desirous to exercise that right by the mode proposed.[110]

Using article 5 of the Frame's Declaration of Rights to justify an otherwise unauthorized course of action was a new strategy and especially astute. This article had never before been called in to service by advocates of constitutional change, even though it had always existed, at odds with the complicated amending processes built into the Frame. Not even Centinel had an answer to this reclamation of the people's right to design and redesign their governments.

Obstructionism could no longer serve the purposes of constitutional doubters. When Albert Gallatin tried to organize a bloc of Antifederalist leaders to boycott the election of delegates to the state convention, he failed. In the end, he himself stood successfully for election as a delegate.[111] Only a few writers other than Centinel continued to oppose the convention, and they did not make clear just what features of the Frame deserved most protection. In general, the election of delegates evoked surprisingly little rhetoric in the press. The *Pennsylvania Journal* carried no comment on constitutional issues between 1 July and 1 December 1789. The *Independent Gazetteer*, which frequently published Antifederalist material, printed the Centinel letters, six other letters opposing change, and two letters favoring constitutional change.

The Pennsylvania Constitutional Convention of 1789–90 secured a quorum on 25 November 1789, the day after it first convened. It was overwhelmingly Federalist, and almost all the non-Federalists were committed to some degree of change in the Frame. That meant that for the first time since 1776 there could be genuine deliberation and bargaining about a constitution. Albert Gallatin, originally opposed to the Convention, remembered later:

It was one of the ablest bodies of which I was a member, or with which I was acquainted. . . . But the distinguishing feature of the convention was that, owing perhaps to more favorable times, it was less affected by party feelings than any other public body that I have known. The points of difference were almost exclusively on general and abstract propositions; there was less prejudice and more sincerity in the discussions than usual; and, throughout, a desire to conciliate opposite opinions by mutual concessions. The consequence was that, though not formally submitted to the ratification of the people, no public act was ever more universally approved than the constitution of Pennsylvania at the time when it was promulgated.[112]

The convention also had members of considerable political experience. Four delegates had sat in the Convention of 1776 and also in the ratifying convention of 1787. An additional ten had been in the ratifying convention.

William Findley, John Smilie, and Robert Whitehill were once more the leaders and spokesmen for the Antifederalists. They were aided behind the scenes by Albert Gallatin. James Wilson was once more the chief spokesman and strategist for the Federalists, but the debates would show that his party was divided into a conservative wing led by William Lewis and Timothy Pickering and a democratic wing led by Wilson, sometimes McKean, and by two new men: Samuel Sitgreaves of Northampton County and James Ross of Allegheny County. Differences of opinion between Federalists and Antifederalists were already eased on two major issues. The three Antifederalist leaders had publicly decided not to oppose bicameralism or designation of a single executive officer.

The convention's most serious deliberations occurred in the Committee of the Whole, which was open to the public but not reported in great detail. Agreements reached in committee were ratified without much debate in formal, fully reported sessions. The outlines of deliberations can nonetheless be discerned from the records.

For the first time in Pennsylvania, the agenda was set by bipartisan planning. How and why this came about was later recounted by William Findley.[113] According to Findley, the convention began with much "declaiming" against the Frame of 1776. Wilson was "considered the most able politician in the state," but he took no part in these criticisms. Findley therefore "took him aside" and explained that this sort of rhetoric could only rekindle "the old party jealousies." Findley suggested that out of respect for those who were friends of the Frame because it had "carried them through the war" and because it continued respected features of "Penn's Constitution," the best way of proceeding would be to propose "resolutions of amendment to the constitution," making it clear that the whole of the Frame was not going to be uprooted. According to Findley, Wilson endorsed this strategy, so Findley proposed that he, Findley, "open the way" with a "preparatory discourse," and that Wilson then present specific resolutions concerning what was to be amended and on what principles. The plan was agreed upon and, wrote Findley:

> In the preparatory discourse which was pretty long I took a view of Penns [sic] Government with all its perfections and defects and of the then present Constitution in the same manner, and concluded by showing that even though the present const [sic] might be good in theory yet so many deviations had been made from it, so great difference of opinion had always existed about it, and that the voluntary election of the present convention was such a testimony of want of confidence in it, that it was vain to think of restoring its energy without essential alterations. This discourse had perhaps the greatest influence in reconciling parties of any ever I made. The consequence of it was that resolutions for two branches of the Legislature, a qualified negative by the governor, and greater Independance [sic] of the Judiciary was [sic] carried with very few dissenting votes, and that in a committee of nine members elected by ballot to digest a plan I alone had every vote but my own.

Findley's role and influence probably did not diminish in his telling, nor does his account recognize that Wilson and his friends had, over the years, formed precise and feasible means for instituting the changes on which he and Findley now agreed. In any case, the most significant rhetorical feature of the plan of presentation was that it put each leader in a rhetorical role for which he had been preparing himself for more than a decade: Findley could speak as political philosopher and peacemaker, and Wilson could speak as a democratic pragmatist and expert legal expositor.

Findley had been in the councils of the state since its beginning. He had been proposed but declined to be a candidate for election to the convention that wrote the Frame. Whether in majority or minority, acerbity had never been his mode unless crossed on a point of fact or authority. He was admired by all. In private correspondence both Federalists and Antifederalists referred to him with such terms as "winning," "ablest," "intelligent," and "honest." He had consistently voted with the friends of the Frame and had functioned as their most thoughtful leader. No one would question his loyalty to Antifederalism, but neither would anyone question his reflectiveness and fairness. In short, he had built a vast reservoir of *ethos* which, under the Findley-Wilson strategy, he could now spend lavishly to create a climate of opinion in which Antifederalists could view change without completely denying their former loyalties to the

Frame and its tradition. No man could so fittingly "open the way" for moving resolutions of amendment of the Frame.

James Wilson, newly appointed associate justice of the United States Supreme Court, had since 1777 been thinking out and polishing precisely the amendments he and Findley wished now to propose. A fortuitous event made it still easier for the Findley-Wilson strategy to work. Congress had just passed the first ten amendments to the federal Constitution, and this Bill of Rights was before the states as the Pennsylvania Constitutional Convention opened.[114] In these amendments were nine of the fifteen guarantees the Antifederalists had demanded since the conclusion of the state's ratifying convention. Here was proof that Antifederalists' views could influence Federalist majorities.

The outcome of the Findley-Wilson strategy is clear. On 1 December 1789 the convention adopted the principle that altering, not replacing, the Frame would be the goal. The convention then began sitting as a Committee of the Whole to consider which alterations should be made. The general kinds of changes were agreed to on 9 December. Three of the changes had been urged by Federalists for almost a decade: the legislature would be bicameral, the executive would be a single person with a "qualified negative" over legislation, and the judiciary would be peopled by judges serving during good behavior and "independent as to their salaries." The fourth change had been a favorite of the Antifederalists: the Declaration of Rights in the Frame would be retained, and it would now declare that the "rights of the people" were "reserved and excepted out of the general powers of government." If, as Federalists had argued, the states were the guarantors of individual rights, this statement would be a further protection against federal encroachments.

Final votes on the four kinds of change showed that the old party divisions no longer held and that the course of national events and the Findley-Wilson strategy had softened Antifederalist allegiance to the doctrines of 1776. The principle of having a single executive and the proposed modification of the Declaration of Rights passed without a dissenting vote. The idea of a qualified executive veto passed 60–4, the dissenting votes coming from Antifederalists. Bicameralism was endorsed 56–5; among those favoring were Antifederalist leaders Smilie, Findley, and Gallatin, but Whitehill cast one of the negative votes. Judicial reform carried 56-8. The nays were cast by Antifederalists, but Whitehill and Findley were among the affirmatives.[115] Federalists voted in favor of all of these resolutions, but disagreements on how to effect the principles soon appeared.

Among the most telling arguments in favor of bicameralism were those having to do with dubious actions that had been taken by the unicameral assembly. The character of discussion on the subject is suggested by a "Letter from a Member of the State Convention to his Friend in Pittsburgh": "Perhaps our western constituents may be surprised that a greater stand was not made for a single branch; I would only suggest to them that every check that had been devised . . . [has on some important occasion] given way to party rage."[116] A later letter bearing the same title reviewed the familiar arguments on behalf of a unicameral legislature but concluded, "Those who are still in favor of a single legislature, offer no new guards, and I can offer none."[117] No doubt, too, the bicameralism of the federal Constitution and the operations of "upper houses" in other states had influence. In any case, when the convention got to details, the presumed virtues of unicameralism were no longer topics of discussion.

With general policy lines settled, the convention elected a drafting committee. Both Findley and Wilson were chosen. The committee submitted a draft of constitutional revisions on 21 December, and on 23 December it reported out the proposed revisions of the Declaration of Rights. Debate on details began at the latter date and ran through 23 January 1790. The most heated divisions occurred among Federalists. The "aristocratic" inclinations of some Federalists came into view in discussions of the character of the second legislative house. Among ultraconservatives' proposals were property qualifications for senators and an electoral college to choose senators. It was on this issue that James Wilson's unique fitness as a leader and constitutional expert became vital to maintaining the nonpartisan character of the convention's work.

Ever since the Address of the Republican Society in 1779, Wilson had been amplifying his contention that since ultimate authority lay with the people, representation in a second house must be either direct or indirect representation of all the people, without regard to property, rank, or any other qualifications beyond those applied in electing members of the "lower house." Now, in the convention of 1789–90, Antifederalists discovered somewhat to their surprise that Wilson really meant what he had said so often about the roots of democratic systems.

The best available account of the debate on senatorial representation comes from Alexander Graydon's *Memoirs*. Graydon entered the convention on 31 December 1789 as the replacement for a deceased delegate from Dauphin County. "Construction of the Senate" was the order of business when he arrived:

A committee . . . had reported an outline of the constitution; and that part of the report, which recommended the choosing of Senators through the medium of electors, was under discussion. Mr. Wilson took the lead in opposition to the report; Mr. [William] Lewis in support of it. It was urged by the latter and his co-operators that the Senate should be so constituted as to form a check upon the house of representatives; and, as in the proposed mode of creating it through the alembic of electors, it would be purged of the impurities of an immediate election by the people, the *desideratum* would be obtained:—that being chosen by a selected few, it was presumable, it would be more wise, more respectable, and more composed of men of wealth, than if chosen by the multitude; and hence, it was inferred, that it would partake, in no inconsiderable degree, of the proper qualities of an Upper House—of an house of lords, it might have been said, if the idea had been endurable. [118]

William Lewis's proposals expressed precisely those "lordly principles" against which Antifederalist rhetors had railed for years. But Wilson exercised the full force of his leadership and rhetoric to defeat the proposals.

Wilson insisted that direct election was the only way "the authority of the people only" could be expressed in government. In this he had the full support of Antifederalists and of a majority of his fellow Federalists. He argued, further, that the checks of one house on another could be gained without any distinctions of rank between members of the houses. His detailed arguments were not reported, but Graydon described them thus:

Wilson, in defence of his plan [for popular election of senators chosen from large electoral districts], was for resting the chance of the two bodies being sufficient checks upon each other, upon the circumstances of their different spheres of election; of their sitting in different chambers, which would produce, he contended, an *esprit du corps* in each; and their being chosen for different periods, the representatives for one year, the senators for four years. . . . As the debate seemed to turn upon the idea, that this was a contest between the principles of democracy and aristocracy, and that great advantages would be gained to either that might prevail, a considerable degree of heat was engendered; and Wilson, hitherto deemed an aristocrat, a monarchist, and a despot, as all the federalists were, found his adherents on this occasion, with a few exceptions, on the democratic or anti-federal side of the house. In this list of exceptions I was. [119]

Among Wilson's private papers there exists a draft speech, presumably prepared for the three-day debate on senatorial representation. Parts of the draft suggest that Wilson planned some attempt at grandiloquence—a style in which he was never at his rhetorical best. The following excerpt, however, suggests his force and reasoning in direct argument: "Will the choice of the people be less disinterested than the choice of the Electors? Interest will probably be consulted in both choices. But, in the first, the interests of individuals, added together, will form precisely the aggregate interest of the whole; whereas, in the last the interests of the Electors added together will form but a small part of the interests of the whole and that small part may be altogether unattached, nay, it may be altogether repugnant, to the remainder."[120] The surprised respect that Wilson's defense of democracy earned among Antifederalists is reflected in "A Letter from a Gentleman in Philadelphia to his Friend in New York." After the usual condemnations of "ambition" among the "well born" who sought special standing for the senate, this writer said: "[B]ut to my, and to your also, astonishment be it known, that he [Wilson] stepped forward in defence of the people's rights, and by the weight of a powerful and honest argument crushed the sophistical bellowings of his colleague L[ewis]."[121]

The division among Federalists on the issue of representation was further evidence that practicalities and political principles, not party alliances, were the foci of this convention. Other actions showed the same. When a young Federalist, James Ross, proposed to reduce the size of the house of representatives, he was defeated twenty-one to thirty-eight with Wilson and a number of other Federalists opposing him. But when Gallatin and Smilie wanted to increase the size of the same house, they had so little support, even from Antifederalists, that their motion lost without a call for the yeas and nays. A major outcome of the convention was that the kind of democracy with checks and balances that Wilson espoused won overwhelmingly and displaced for good the confederative mythology formerly so dear to Antifederalists.

The convention issued its proposed constitutional revisions for "public consideration" on 27 February 1790, having adjourned to 9 August 1790. The shape of the document had been argued out through truly deliberative and candid debate; rhetorical charade and obstructionism had no place in its development. The Findley-Wilson strategy created a new reality in the state; it facilitated a coalition of democratic opinion that had never before been seen in constitutional debate in Pennsylvania. This had been Findley's aim. And for the future of political rhetoric in the state it was no small thing that the convention had struck procedural blows for majoritarianism. Its rule that a simple majority of members constituted a quorum was given the qualification that members must obtain leave of absence from the house if they could not attend. Even Wilson had to secure temporary leave when he went to New York to assume his seat on the Supreme Court! In the convention's procedures and in the constitution it constructed, majority rule was established as a norm. For the first time in Pennsylvania, a governmental body committed itself in advance to the proposition that deliberative business must be forwarded according to the wishes of the majority, following full and free debate.

After allowing the public to consider its work for four months, the convention reconvened to reconsider.[122] There had been very little public debate about the revisions, and the convention had only a few, minor second thoughts. The revised constitution was formally adopted by a vote of forty-seven to zero and constitutional eccentricity was ended in Pennsylvania.

Conclusions

Pennsylvania's unusual Frame of 1776 was created by Whigs who in most cases were new to self-government and who had risen to public influence through displaying leadership in mass meetings, in public committees, and in democratized and politicized militia companies. All had been active in resisting the British. With them in the first state constitutional convention sat other Whigs who can be loosely thought of as "establishment men" whose influence derived from their wealth, learning, colonial political activity, and family connections. These, too, were active resisters. Both groups held Whiggish, class-oriented conceptions of political society: societies were normally and naturally comprised of an actual or incipient "aristocracy" and a "democracy" or "mediocrity." What divided the "new men" from the "establishment men" was their understanding of the implications of this natural division. A major factor that eventually allowed these parties to establish an effective state government was abandonment of this view as a fundamental principle of political organization.

According to the received beliefs of most "establishment men" in 1776, a "natural aristocracy" tended to be created by education, wealth, and breeding, and it could and should rise to authority in any rightly conceived system of self-government. But according to those who actually wrote the Frame of 1776, it was the nature of aristocracies to seek social control "ambitiously," at the expense of "the liberties of the people." Aristocracies' pursuit of power must, therefore, be vigilantly guarded against by ensuring that the authority of "the democracy" was protected both institutionally and through active use of all political powers available. Such, said the authors of the Frame, was the lesson of history—especially of Saxon-English and Roman history. These basic, Whiggish differences were at the root of the fourteen years of constitutional controversy peculiar to Pennsylvania.

In the course of the protracted argument, those who were originally inclined toward elitism gradually evolved, articulated, and finally established a conception of democratic, representative, majoritarian government. During the same time, the political mythology that accounted for the Frame's unique features became rhetorically hardened into political doctrine that justified rejecting even "the democracy's" voice in order to retain protections against "ambition." These differences could occur because the positions of many elitists were based on pragmatic considerations, whereas the initial positions of the Frame's authors and friends were mythological and doctrinaire. The elitists' practical views were subject to adjustments as society changed. The Constitutionalists' initial view of social forces was insisted upon as a "true," "pure," and final view of political reality. The more it was articulated in debate, the more it congealed rhetorically until not even the "voice of the people" could be entertained if critical of inherited, doctrinaire views.

The Frame's authors undertook to establish their ideal and pure democratic system as permanently as possible. They expressed that determination by repeatedly declaring that the Frame and its procedures were to last "forever"; by establishing an extraordinarily complicated set of procedures for altering any part of the Frame; and by introducing oaths of allegiance to the Frame as it was initially written. They thus committed themselves to opposing governmental change as a matter of principle. Pro-Frame rhetoric eventually extended this commitment to the Articles of Confederation. Given this framework of thought, it was almost preordained that not until 1788 would ideas of bargaining, compromise, and expediency became significant *topoi* in the discourse of friends of the Frame.

The rhetoric of "establishment men" asserted the superiority of the well educated, the wealthy, and the well born less and less strongly. The sometime elitist Whigs came to call themselves "Republicans," and they placed themselves under the leadership of a self-made, somewhat pragmatic lawyer-politician, James Wilson. Under his tutelage and by virtue of his skill as an expositor and arguer, the Republican-Federalist segment of political opinion eventually came to articulate and then formally to advocate uniformly democratic-representative principles. Once they endorsed a popularly elected, bicameral legislature in 1779, most of their public rhetoric ceased to assert the superiority of any class; indeed, it stressed the classlessness of the American society. Later controversy showed that some Republican-Federalists did not, in fact, abandon class-oriented conceptions of "good government"; nonetheless, the party's public self-presentation disregarded, even denied, class distinctions.

One cannot say that the antidemocratic rhetoric of the Antifederalists and the concomitant rise of democratic themes in Federalists'
rhetoric accounted for the corresponding rise of Federalists' popularity in Pennsylvania from 1785 through 1790. The electorate was
probably more sensitive to pragmatic needs than to philosophical
shifts. What study of the parties' public rhetoric does show, however,
is that changes did occur in self-presentations and that the Federalists' rhetoric came gradually to offer clear and inviting ways of
organizing government while Antifederalists' persistent loyalty to
existing systems disregarded the pluralistic interests of Pennsylvania's citizenry.

No amount of research is likely to tell us when or how Pennsylvanians would have changed their constantly violated and inadequate
Frame of 1776 had not the inefficiency and weakness of the Confederation become a serious and immediate problem. The rhetorical
case that carried the day for Pennsylvania's Constitution of 1790
rested heavily on the brute fact that the federal Constitution rendered the Frame all but inoperable. Rhetoric per se could only
intensify a sense of need for constitutional change and open the way
for exploring practical alternatives. In this the Federalists were
perhaps fortunate. They had never mustered an effective, comprehensive case stressing the need and the expediency of altering the
Frame. Such a case was always possible from 1776 onward, but the
case was never made. The Frame provided no methods of interpreting the results of the vaunted periods of "public consideration";
there was no clear way of supervising the administration of justice;
obviously unjust procedures were countenanced, including impeachment of officers no longer in office, enactment of *ex post facto* laws,
and infringements on rights of conscience; recourse for persons
who believed their guaranteed rights were abridged was obscure;
congressmen served without specified terms and could be dismissed
at the whim of the assembly; no public officers served at fixed
salaries, so all were beholden to a legislature that changed annually.
These and other dangerous features provided ample material with
which to build a coherent case for the need of constitutional
change—a case based on the interests and safety of all Pennsylvanians. But the faults of the existing system were never brought together
into a coherent challenge. Each time the critics of the Frame
mounted a rhetorical effort, they called for sweeping changes without showing what specific needs and benefits to individual voters
those changes could provide. By 1788 the new federal Constitution
made the need for changes so evident that detailed argument on the
point was scarcely needed. Under those conditions William Findley's

"preparatory discourse" in the Convention of 1790 could subtly make the case for change on pragmatic grounds, and Findley succeeded almost beyond his expectations.

It is not clear why popular interests were never comprehensively invoked in appeals for altering the Frame prior to 1787. The occasional superciliousness of Republican-Federalist rhetors may have reflected a degree of self-satisfaction that blinded them to the necessity of engaging the interests of the populace. That they treated calls for a bill of rights as though the demand raised a nonissue seems to have reflected an insensitivity to popular, personal interests. It took Antifederalists to address these interests, and John Smilie's claim that superfluity would be no fault in such a serious matter must have made sense to a populace conditioned since the Charter of 1701 to enumerating individual rights in all basic formulations of governmental organization. It is at least thinkable that Republican-Federalists' pride in their natural right to lead blinded them to individual concerns. The notion of a "natural aristocracy" never disappeared from private correspondence among leading Federalists—even though the concept largely disappeared from their public rhetoric after 1779.

Finally, Richard A. Ryerson's observation that no one really knew how to make a revolution or a system of self-government springs again and again to the mind of one who reads the plethora of constitutional speaking and writing in Pennsylvania's early years of statehood. Political spokesmen did not know initially "what it meant to establish a republic based on the sovereignty of the people."[123] They were struggling for reasonable answers to that problem. The majority began with a vague, mythic, anachronistic model positing social orders. They possessed a patchwork of partial theories of government. Catchwords did for theory much of the time: authority of the people, aristocracy, democracy, mediocrity, confederation, consolidation, republic, liberties, "sett of men," ambition, rulers, checks, house of representatives, "upper house," state of nature, compact, faction, patriotism, treason. Each such term stood ambiguously for some fragment of social or political conceptualization, but no comprehensive theory of republican government existed by which to explore the concepts' implications and to order, sift, and integrate those fragments. The supposition that the well endowed and the less well endowed must be adversaries informed most early political thinking. On this premise the authors and defenders of the Frame of 1776 conceptualized a confederative, representative "republic" structured specifically and primarily to exclude "aristocracy."

The constitutional rhetoric of 1776 to 1790 in Pennsylvania reflects and projects the reality of slowly growing awarenesses: (1) that a free people can share enough interest in political efficiency, energy, and responsiveness to render safe a government that can also take initiatives, and (2) that for representative democracy to work, deliberative bodies must be organized and disciplined in ways that effect the will of the popular majority after clear and fair consideration of alternative views. Put differently, the Pennsylvanians' problem was to evolve operational meanings for selected catchwords of 1776. The British model of self-government was acceptable to no one. Revolutionary rhetoric had wedded that system to "ministerial arrogance," undemocratic class distinctions, and repression, so a different system had to be created. Oddly, the Pennsylvanians paid little attention to the experiences of their sister states. Instead, they experimented with a mythic, Saxon-English-Roman model that failed the tests of practice. The fundamental question confronting all Pennsylvania politicians between 1776 and 1790 was: What constitutes the fairest, safest, and most functional "translation" of "government by authority of the people only"? Republican-Federalist rhetoric offered features of a strong answer, but a fully coherent answer had to come from the federal Constitutional Convention where the concepts of checks and balances were operationalized by men who practiced the arts of the possible and who established accommodation within the canon of deliberation.

The discourse I have explored in this essay was a mass of description and critique of alternative ways of invoking "the authority of the people only." It shows that Pennsylvania rhetoricians were not sophisticated enough to bring efficiency and justice to their first experiment at self-government. Beyond their own thought and utterance, they needed the external impetus given by national deliberation to aid them in establishing the desiderata of a democratic-republican government.

The early constitutional rhetoric of Pennsylvania is a record of men gradually learning how to create and use constructive forms and procedures of government. Once Pennsylvanians were their own "rulers," they had to learn how to contain within disciplined, democratic procedures their familiar tools of resistance such as obstructionism and unrestricted exercise of raw political power. They also had to learn that if those who legislate are to contribute to the common good, they must place practical values of efficiency and productiveness above legalisms and doctrinal generalities. In Pennsylvania early constitutional rhetoric exhibits the processes of trial and error by which men finally taught themselves that a reality of democratic self-government is that the end of parliamentary procedures is to generate creative responses to the will of the popular majority, after terminable consideration of alternatives.

Vituperation and supercilious attacks and defenses did not end with the Constitution of 1790, but conciliation, responsiveness to popular opinion, and regard for pragmatic necessities were by 1790 raised to high status among political values. In the evolution of these values two figures stand out as the readiest learners and most skillful teachers of lessons about self-government—James Wilson of the city of Philadelphia and William Findley of Westmoreland County. Although they were antagonists until 1789–90, each displayed from the beginning of his career personal integrity, respect for the legitimating powers of political procedures, and greater concern for ideas than for personalities. By these qualities they became models and leaders for their peers. In 1789 they epitomized in rhetorical and procedural strategies the lessons of fourteen years. They quietly devised a shrewd, pragmatic, conciliatory strategy of speech and action by which representatives of all the people could gain respectful hearing and share in creating a stable and efficient state within the United States of America. Had traditional political conceptions been less doctrinaire, these master rhetors might well have effected deliberative collaboration much earlier.

The final product of fourteen years of constitutional controversy was the Pennsylvania Constitution of 1790. It lasted for more than forty years without major change. Through it, a new reality was established. The state's political institutions were harmonized with those of other states, with new federal institutions, and with principles of stable, representative democracy. From external events and from years of sometimes obstructive and sometimes constructive rhetorical exercise, Pennsylvanians finally learned and established "what it meant to establish a republic based on the sovereignty of the people."

Notes

1. In 1888 John B. McMaster and Frederick D. Stone published all pertinent records then available in their *Pennsylvania and the Federal Constitution* (Lancaster: Historical Society of Pennsylvania, 1888). In 1976 Merrill Jensen and his associates published *The Documentary History of the Ratification of the Constitution* (Madison: State Historical Society of Wisconsin, 1976) in two volumes. Volume 2 of this work covers Pennsylvania's ratification debates in and out of government. In the same year Jensen and Robert A. Becker published *The Documentary History of the First Federal Elections: 1788–1790* (Madison: Univ. of Wisconsin Pr., 1976). Chapter 4 of the first volume presents the existing major documents relative to

the first federal elections in Pennsylvania. Earlier stages of constitutional debates have been treated by J. Paul Selsam, *The Pennsylvania Constitution of 1776* (1936; reprint New York: Octagon, 1971); Theodore Thayer, *Pennsylvania Politics and the Growth of Democracy: 1740–1776* (Harrisburg: Pennsylvania Historical and Museum Commission, 1953); and Robert L. Brunhouse, *The Counter-Revolution in Pennsylvania: 1776–1790* (Harrisburg: Pennsylvania Historical and Museum Commission, 1971). I depend for texts of articles, speeches, and letters on these sources and my own searches of newspapers and minutes and journals of public bodies.

2. My "Debates in the Constitutional Conventions: Constitutional Eccentricity" and "Debates in the Constitutional Conventions: Ritual and Deliberation," constitute chapters 4 and 5 of DeWitte Holland and Robert T. Oliver, eds., *A History of Public Speaking in Pennsylvania* (Philadelphia: Pennsylvania Speech Association, n.d.). These essays treat the rhetoric of the formal conventions but configuring external rhetoric was not explored. I borrow the conception of rhetoric as formative of historical realities from Eugene E. White, "Rhetoric in Historical Configuration," in *Rhetoric in Transition: Studies in the Nature and Uses of Rhetoric,* ed. Eugene E. White (University Park: Pennsylvania State Univ. Pr., 1980), 7–20.

3. Richard A. Ryerson, *The Revolution Is Now Begun* (Philadelphia: Univ. of Pennsylvania Pr., 1978), 248n.4.

4. The provincial assembly was seen as an agency of colonialism, had most reluctantly agreed that its congressional delegates could vote for independence, and had on 14 June 1776 adjourned to the following August despite the exigencies of war (Peter Force, *American Archives* , 4th ser., 6 : cols. 859–66). From mid-June, advocates of independence could very plausibly claim that the state had no provincial/state government.

5. The wisdom of resistance and independence were, of course, the primary topics of political rhetoric between January and July 1776. When the convention sat, newspapers reported its various enactments when it assumed the role of the state's legislative body. Prior to 10 August these were the only accounts of the convention's activities. On 10 August the *Evening Post* reported, "The Convention . . . have resolved that the future Legislature of this state consist of one branch only, under proper restrictions." Texts of the newly formed constitutions of New Jersey, Virginia, and Connecticut were published during July and August, and the *Evening Post* published two letters (1 and 13 August) that dealt with the general qualities that deserving public office holders should have.

6. For an important discussion of the rhetorical impact of *Common Sense* see Stephen E. Lucas, *Portents of Rebellion* (Philadelphia: Temple Univ. Pr., 1976), 167–75. My quotations are from the second, enlarged edition of *Common Sense,* first published on 14 February 1776. See Thomas Paine, *Common Sense,* ed. Isaac Kramnick (New York: Penguin, 1982). Pagination cited is that of this source.

7. *Genuine Principles,* 37.

8. *Four Letters,* "Letter IV," 19–21.

9. Bernard Bailyn, *The Ideological Origins of the American Revolution* (Cambridge, Mass.: Belknap Pr., 1967), 80–85. Bailyn identifies James Otis, James Wilson, John Adams, Charles Carroll, Maurice Moore, and others as using or commenting on this alleged tradition (81–83n.26).

10. *Genuine Principles,* 4. *An Historical Essay* (London, 1771) was published anonymously, presumably by one Obediah Hulme. It was a propaganda tract of the British Society for Constitutional Information. The Society was generally favorable to the colonies and it identified its members as "Real Whigs," but its concerns were chiefly with parliamentary reform in England and other internal political affairs. Demophilus could scarcely have known the author of this tract because Obediah Hulme was publicly credited with its authorship only in 1791. See Caroline Robbins, *Eighteenth-Century Commonwealthmen* (Cambridge: Harvard Univ. Pr., 1959), 324, 363–64, 369. As Demophilus said, he was adapting some of the arguments of this tract to Pennsylvania's circumstances.

11. Lawrence W. Rosenfield has penetratingly discussed the character of strong forms of epideictic address; see his "The Practical Celebration of Epideictic," in White, *Rhetoric in Transition,* 131–55.

12. "Demophilus," *Pennsylvania Packet,* 17 September 1776.

13. "Centinel Revived; Letter XXXVI," *Independent Gazetteer,* 28 October 1789.

14. Bailyn, *Ideological Origins,* 294–301. The public was given eighteen days to consider this draft. During that time public pressure led to two changes. To the religious oath for office holders, initially reading "I do believe in one God the Creator and Governor of the Universe," there were added, seemingly at the behest of Demophilus, (*Pennsylvania Packet,* 17 September

1776), the words "the Rewarder of the Good and Punisher of the Wicked." In response to private persuasion by Protestant ministers, a guarantee of "Privileges, Immunities and Estate" was inserted protecting religious societies and corporations for the advancement of learning. See letter by the Reverend Henry Melchior Muhlenberg, dated 2 October 1776 and published in "Notes and Queries," *Pennsylvania Magazine of History and Biography* 22, no. 1 (1898): 129–31.

15. From "Section the Fortieth" of the text of the Frame reprinted from the original in Thayer, *Growth of Democracy*, 225.

16. Selsam, *Pennsylvania Constitution*, 164.

17. Selsam, *Pennsylvania Constitution*, 164–65. Selsam infers that "those who opposed . . . withdrew, as was the practice then" (165). Later scholars seem to have found no better explanation for the disparity between the number of delegates and the number of signers.

18. "Brutus," *Pennsylvania Journal*, 2 October 1776. The 9 October 1776 issue of this paper carried a reply from "A Friend to Truth and the People" in which it was said that Brutus ignored the sanctity of the Declaration of Rights of the Frame and its provision for amendment on recommendation of the Council of Censors.

19. John Dickinson was the most prominent spokesman for the critics. He had refused to sign the Declaration of Independence. Another whose enthusiasm for independence was doubted was Robert Morris. There were, of course, unquestionable supporters of independence who publicly advocated change. They were, however, "establishment men" such as George Clymer, Benjamin Rush, John Bayard, George Ross, Joseph Parker, and Samuel Morris. Plausible attacks on the motives of such leaders could easily be made, and they were.

20. I am citing an "Address" signed by Samuel Howell and published in the *Pennsylvania Packet* for 5 November 1776 and also printed elsewhere. The document was issued on behalf of those who attended a public meeting on 2 November.

21. Penn's Charter of 1701 accorded the vote (though not office) to all who, given other qualifications, would "acknowledge one Almighty God and Creator, upholder and Ruler of the world." The text of this charter is reprinted from the original in Thayer, *Growth of Democracy*, 206. The Convention of 1776 essentially reproduced this oath.

"A Real Friend" wrote two and one-half columns of closely reasoned support for the convention's emergency legislation, caution against letting legislatures alter constitutions, and criticism of the call for a trinitarian oath. *Pennsylvania Packet*, 29 October 1776.

22. *Pennsylvania Packet*, 22 October 1776.

23. For details of this power struggle see Selsam, *Pennsylvania Constitution*, 226–30.

24. Albert S. Bolles, *Pennsylvania: Province and State*, 2 vols. (Philadelphia: John Wanamaker, 1899), 1: 467.

25. Charles Page Smith, *James Wilson* (Chapel Hill: Univ. of North Carolina Pr., 1956), 112.

26. The Address was dated 6 May 1777. It was published in the *Pennsylvania Packet* on 20 May and in the *Pennsylvania Journal* the following day. The Memorial was published with the Address. The Circular appeared in the *Journal* on 28 May and was also distributed as a broadside.

27. It was published in the *Pennsylvania Journal* on 21 May 1777.

28. I have collated the position statements of the critics from their Address, Memorial, and Circular, and from a letter signed "Addison," presumed to be James Wilson, published in the *Pennsylvania Packet* beginning 27 May and concluding 3 June 1777. The Whig case is drawn from their Address and their supplementary statement of 21 May 1777.

29. *Pennsylvania Journal*, 21 May 1777.

30. These claims, among many others, appeared in letters signed "Ludlow" in the *Pennsylvania Journal*, 21 and 28 May and 4 June 1777.

31. *Pennsylvania Journal*, 26 March 1777. Cannon admitted to the words but insisted that in context they were reasonable.

32. *Pennsylvania Packet*, 10 June 1777.

33. Smith, *James Wilson*, 115. That the British fleet was perhaps destined for Philadelphia was widely and genuinely believed.

34. Letter dated 3 July 1777, in Smith, *James Wilson*, 399n.46.

35. Burton A. Konkle, *George Bryan and the Constitution of Pennsylvania, 1731–1791* (Philadelphia: William J. Campbell, 1922), 163. Assemblymen were not officially identified by party, hence Konkle has calculated probable party allegiance by members' votes on a series of divisive issues.

36. Brunhouse, *Counter-Revolution*, 56, 247n.13. Brunhouse thinks a deal was made whereby Republicans would support Joseph Reed for president of the commonwealth in return

for the promise of a referendum. He grants he can find no direct evidence for this. Konkle (*George Bryan*, 163) and Smith (*James Wilson*, 123–24) merely attribute the action to the Republicans' gains in the election of 1778. Most historians pass over the matter without comment.

37. Smith says, "Wilson and his fellow Republicans . . . worked assiduously in the early months of 1779 to rally voters to their cause. But the Constitutionalists were once more ahead of them"; *James Wilson*, 129. Smith cites no instance of this early activity, and I can find reports of none in the press or in private letters brought to public attention since 1956. The first public letters supporting constitutional revision appeared in the press in February, and they give no sign of being parts of a coordinated, coherent program of persuasion. Newspapers carried no accounts of Republican public meetings or "resolves." No official appeals to voters by Republicans appeared in the press until late March. I cannot think they "worked assiduously."

38. Brunhouse, *Counter-Revolution*, 58.

39. This letter was begun in the *Packet* on 1 December and continued in several later but not consecutive issues during the month.

40. The letters were "A Political View of the State of Pennsylvania, by a Foreigner, translated into English," 2 February 1779; "A Freeman," 4 February; "Agricola," begun 6 February and concluded 13 February; "A Whig," 20 February ; and "Machiavel," 25 February.

41. Two letters and a "Memorial to the Assembly, now Circulating" were published in the *Pennsylvania Packet*: "Remarks on the Calling of a Convention," 29 December 1778; "A Faithful Patriot," 4 February 1779; and the "Memorial," 9 February 1779.

42. The dissenters were Robert Morris, George Clymer, Samuel Meredith, Thomas Mifflin, George Woods, Bernard Dougherty, and Thomas Sloan. The first four were from Philadelphia and the last three from Bedford County.

43. Edwin Black has stressed the ways rhetors engaged in continuing debates frequently constrict their rhetorical options for the future when they express themselves in doctrinal rather than pragmatic terms; *Rhetorical Criticism* (New York: Macmillan, 1965). He has developed this point further in his "Ideological Justifications" (paper presented at the 68th annual meeting of the Speech Communication Association, Louisville, Ky., 5 November 1982). In the present case the Whig arguments closed off pragmatic arguments and negotiations, and they equated Whig feelings about Republican intentions with proofs of bad intentions and of the virtue of whatever Republicans criticized.

44. The political changes and reasons for them are well discussed in Brunhouse, *Counter-Revolution*, 120–21.

45. "Authentic Copies of the Preliminary Articles of Peace" was published in the *Pennsylvania Packet* on 10 April 1783, putting an end to rumors.

46. Brunhouse, *Counter-Revolution*, 156.

47. Brunhouse (*Counter-Revolution*, 278) rightly counts Baltzer Gehr of Berks County as a member more likely to vote with the Whigs than with the Republicans. Some other historians have recorded Gehr as a Republican and so concluded that the division was fourteen Republicans and twelve Whigs or "Constitutionalists."

48. Principally because of the movements of militia companies during the war, this provision had not been proposed before. With peace, voting in one's home district was feasible.

49. Unable to resist one gratuitous jab at the Frame and its adherents, the majority did assert that their recommendations were somewhat disorganized because of the "confused manner in which the constitution is thrown together."

50. Brunhouse, *Counter-Revolution*, 156–59.

51. The petition was published in the *Pennsylvania Gazette* on 16 June 1784 and in the *Pennsylvania Journal* three days later. The *Journal* editorially urged others to circulate like petitions to the council, but it was, of course, too late to raise influential public pressure.

52. Two historians directly asserting this position are Jackson Turner Main, *The Antifederalists* (Chapel Hill: Univ. of North Carolina Pr., 1961), and Carl Van Doren, *The Great Rehearsal* (New York: Viking, 1948). Main says the Federalists acted in "almost desperate haste" (187–88). He cites as evidence a letter from David Redick to General William Irvine, but both of these men were adamant defenders of the Frame and ardent Antifederalists. Van Doren opens description of Pennsylvania's ratification with, "The conflict between the two instinctive parties was put quickly, and too hastily to the test in Pennsylvania" (180). My contention is that if there was opportunity to raise and consider all relevant issues and arguments, there was ample deliberation, given that two elections just before the convention had produced Federalist majorities known to favor ratification.

53. This and other quotations and summaries of the debate come from the assembly's Minutes. For a detailed account see either Jensen, *Ratification of the Constitution* 2: 68ff., or McMaster and Stone, *Pennsylvania and the Federal Constitution*, 27ff.

54. *Pennsylvania Gazette*, 3 October 1787.

55. These episodes are recounted in many sources. I am using the assembly records as reproduced in McMaster and Stone, *Pennsylvania and the Federal Constitution*, 63–70.

56. The facts I have described are confirmed by Jensen's documentation; *Ratification of the Constitution* 2: 128–29. That concern about the officers' oaths of allegiance to the Frame influenced the Republicans is my own conjecture.

57. My discussion of the assembly debate on this issue is based on the *Minutes* in Jensen, *Ratification of the Constitution* 2: 266–78. Lewis's remarks appear at 2: 276–77.

58. The Address is known to have been published twelve times in newspapers and broadsides in Pennsylvania and sixteen times in other states (Jensen, *Ratification of the Constitution* 2: 128). The Reply was dated 6 October 1787 and appeared in the *Pennsylvania Packet* on 8 October. For texts see Jensen, *Ratification of the Constitution* 2: 112–20.

59. James Wilson made central to the Federalists' case for ratification the claim that the Constitution was *democratic*. He is thought to have written the "Republican Party's" belated Address published 25 March 1779. In that Address popular election of both houses of the legislature was recommended. In the federal Constitutional Convention, Wilson had repeatedly argued that authority for the new government must flow directly from "the people." He urged, but failed to carry, popular election of the federal Senate and president. See Smith, *James Wilson*, chap. 15, esp. 220–26, where Smith draws on Wilson's private notes. In the state ratifying convention Wilson led in arguing that the fundamental thing justifying the new plan was that the people controlled all parts of the system, indirectly when not directly.

60. Jensen says this letter "was allegedly written by William Findley"; *Ratification of the Constitution* 2: 216. I do not know who made that attribution, but I suspect it. The style of the letter resembles nothing that is known certainly to have come from Findley's pen or mouth. In any case, the document had more than passing importance in the flow of argument, for it was several times reprinted and was widely circulated in other states as well as in Pennsylvania.

61. Jensen agrees with other historians that these letters by Tench Coxe "were the first major defenses of the Constitution published in the United States"; *Ratification of the Constitution* 2: 138. Jensen has found, further, that the letters were reprinted at least three times in Pennsylvania's English newspapers, at least once in a German newspaper, and in expanded form in an anthology titled *Addresses to the Citizens of Pennsylvania*, published 21 October 1787. Texts of the original three letters appear in Jensen, *Ratification of the Constitution* 2: 138–46.

62. Jensen and his associates have sought to identify all extant publications of this sort, and Jensen says, "While the Antifederalists published more major items than the Federalists, the latter had the advantage in the greater number of squibs and short items containing optimistic reports of the prospect of ratification in various states"; *Ratification of the Constitution* 2: 180. Despite Antifederalists' complaints that their propaganda was suppressed by publishers and those in charge of the postal system, it appears they had ample access to the press in the last quarter of 1787.

63. From a private memorandum quoted in Konkle, *George Bryan*, 304–5. At the time, Bryan was widely thought to be the author of the Centinel letters. They are now believed to have been written by his son, Samuel Bryan.

64. My source is Wilson's speech as excerpted in the *Pennsylvania Packet*, 10 October. About a fifth of the address, as published, was spent on these points.

65. On 28 November Wilson treated as mistaken John Smilie's claim that Virginia's constitution had a bill of rights (McMaster and Stone, *Pennsylvania and the Federal Constituton*, 253). On 30 November, Smilie presented a full printing of the Virginia constitution, complete with its bill of rights. On 8 December, Wilson and McKean challenged Findley's statement that trial by jury had formerly existed in Sweden. On 10 December, Findley presented his sources, including entries from Blackstone's *Commentaries*. Findley noted sarcastically that apparently the state's leading attorney (Wilson) and the state's chief justice of the Supreme Court (McKean) could not recognize citations from Blackstone. Since the Federalists' case against adding a bill of rights was fundamentally technical, these embarrassments of their convention leaders made their position on rights seem even worse.

66. Smilie's speech was made on 28 November 1787. The same arguments also came up later. See McMaster and Stone, *Pennsylvania and the Federal Constitution*, esp. 250–51 and 254–56.

67. From the text as in McMaster and Stone, *Pennsylvania and the Federal Constitution*, 229–31.

68. Quoted in Konkle, *George Bryan*, 306.

69. Most of the Address of the Seceding Assemblymen condemned the procedures in the assembly. Centinel's letter of 8 November was almost entirely a diatribe against Federalists and their alleged motives. In October "A Constant Reader" denounced Wilson's speech at the State House as incompetent, but he offered no direct refutation of it. "An Officer of the Late Continental Army" spent almost a fourth of his letter attacking Wilson's person, loyalty, "patrician interest," and his alleged hostility to any "popular measure."

70. *Independent Gazetteer*, 30 November 1787.

71. From the text as in McMaster and Stone, *Pennsylvania and the Federal Constitution*, 268.

72. Findley in convention, 1 December 1787. Quotation is from a summary of the speech that appeared in the *Pennsylvania Herald*, 5 December 1787, reproduced in Jensen, *Ratification of the Constitution*, 2: 447–48. Italics in original.

73. See Wayne's notes, reproduced in Jensen, *Ratification of the Constitution* 2: 446.

74. Whitehill in convention; text as in McMaster and Stone, *Pennsylvania and the Federal Constitution*, 256.

75. Whitehill in convention; text as in McMaster and Stone, *Pennsylvania and the Federal Constitution*, 257.

76. "Centinel Revived, Letter XXXI," *Independent Gazetteer*, 12 September 1789.

77. The Dissent was published in the *Pennsylvania Packet*, 18 December 1787, three days after the convention's adjournment. It was also circulated as a broadside, was reprinted in at least three other English and two German newspapers in Pennsylvania, and was "circulated throughout the country in newspaper, broadside, and pamphlet form" (Jensen, *Ratification of the Constitution* 2: 617). The Dissent was reputedly written by Samuel Bryan.

78. From the Dissent as reprinted in Jensen, *Ratification of the Constitution* 2: 625.

79. The effort seems to have been selective. Jensen says no petitions were sent to Lancaster County, a Federalist stronghold, and no petitions were returned from Philadelphia City or County, or from Bucks, Chester, York, Berks, or Washington counties; *Ratification of the Constitution* 2: 709. Allegedly, petitions signed in Huntingdon County were prevented from reaching the assembly. Doubtless the campaign was disadvantaged by the fact that during the petition drive Georgia, Connecticut, and Massachusetts ratified, bringing to six the number of states having ratified.

80. Jensen, *Ratification of the Constitution* 2: 642. Jensen and his associates have located well over four hundred printed items from the heated and often scurrilous paper war between 15 December 1787 and early summer 1788 (2: 645). Even this material was only a part of the rhetoric circulated in the state during this period.

81. Morton Borden, *The Antifederalist Papers* (East Lansing: Michigan State Univ. Pr., 1965), 14.

82. In Centinel's view a relatively ideal system in Rome was destroyed by the rise of an aristocracy over the plebeians. The parallel with Demophilus's version of how Saxon democracy was corrupted is plain. For discussion of the Roman changes see Theodor Mommsen, *The History of Rome*, abridged ed. (New York: Philosophical Library, 1959), 65–67.

83. "Centinel Revived," *Independent Gazetteer*, 28 October 1789. The parallel with the ten-year struggle for plebeian rights in Rome between 377 and 367 B.C. was clearly in Centinel's mind.

84. The Lockean concepts of "state of perfect freedom" and the state of having assigned certain powers "up into the hands of the community" were not specifically defined by Centinel; they were treated as concepts of common knowledge. Their roots lie in Locke's *Essay Concerning the True Original Extent of Civil Government*, esp. chaps. 2 (section 4) and 7 (section 87).

85. "Centinel," *Independent Gazetteer*, 5 October 1787.

86. "Centinel Revived, Letter XXXI," *Independent Gazetteer*, 12 September 1789.

87. "Centinel," *Independent Gazetteer*, 30 November 1787.

88. "Centinel," *Independent Gazetteer*, 16 January 1788. Emphasis in original. Other Antifederalists at first claimed the two leaders signed the Constitution *pro forma* without actually approving of it, but this claim did not hold up to the facts.

89. "Centinel Revived, Letter XXXI," *Independent Gazetteer*, 12 September 1789.

90. "Centinel Revived, Letter XXXVII," *Independent Gazetteer*, 11 November 1789.

91. "A Citizen," published in the *Pennsylvania Gazette*, 23 January 1788, replied specifically to Centinel in the *Independent Gazetteer* of 16 January 1788. Citizen's charge was defensible

because Centinel had more than once written that if the Constitution were ratified, rebellious warfare could be expected.

92. Resolution No. 4 of the *Circular Letter* as reproduced in McMaster and Stone, *Pennsylvania and the Federal Constitution*, 556.

93. Gallatin's resolutions appear in McMaster and Stone, *Pennsylvania and the Federal Constitution*, 557–58. Resolutions that passed appear at 558–64.

94. In *First Federal Elections*, Jensen and Becker reprint a number of private letters exchanged among puzzled, suspicious Federalists. In response to the Harrisburg documents, Tench Coxe published and sent to James Madison for further dissemination an essay signed "A Federal Centinel"; see *Pennsylvania Gazette*, 10 September 1788. Other Federalist reactions ranged from "Civis's" "agreeable disappointment" at the "moderation" of the Harrisburg Convention (*Pennsylvania Packet*, 19 September 1788) to "Cassius's" claim that the Antifederalists' "insidious efforts" resembled those of the Borgias, who made "a feeble attack, in order that by a feigned reconciliation" they could disarm their adversaries and so "secretly and safely" destroy them; *Federal Gazette*, 9 October 1788.

95. *Federal Gazette*, 8 October 1788. The first part of this letter had appeared in the same paper on 6 October.

96. *Pennsylvania Gazette*, 5 November 1788. Jensen and Becker say Lucullus was "almost certainly Dr. Benjamin Rush"; *First Federal Elections* 1: 331. Centinel replied to Lucullus as though he were Rush. In any case, the Lucullus letter was more incisive and closely reasoned than Rush's "metaphysical" and "pathetic" outpourings in other precisely identified speeches and private letters.

97. Federalist candidates were nominated at an open conference in Lancaster. The Harrisburg ticket or "Amendments ticket" may or may not have been agreed to at the Harrisburg Convention, but Federalists alleged it was created there, in secret and by unelected delegates. "A Friend's" address was printed in English and in German several times during mid-November 1788. Its author is not known. The essay is reprinted in Jensen and Becker, *First Federal Elections* 1: 332–35. It seems to have been the main instrument for disseminating knowledge of the Harrisburg ticket.

98. From the text as reproduced in Jensen and Becker, *First Federal Elections* 1: 324–27.

99. There is interesting adaptation here. In this document the Antifederalists were accepting Wilson's argument that individual rights were guaranteed by the states. Instead of insisting on appending a bill of rights, the Antifederalists here asked only for an amendment explicitly assigning protection of individual rights to the states. Ultimately, in the Convention of 1789–90, they accepted the same kind of statement as appropriate modification of the Frame's Declaration of Rights. The position may have reflected deference to Wilson's arguments.

100. "Hiester" was sometimes spelled "Heister." The former spelling was used in the Harrisburg ticket.

101. *Pennsylvania Packet*, 25 November 1788.

102. Jensen and Becker reprint several proposed slates of candidates for representatives; *First Federal Elections* 1: 365. "A Spectator" urged election of two, and preferably three, Germans; *Independent Gazetteer*, 25 November 1788. It appears that Benjamin Rush tried to promote addition of German candidates to the Federalists' slate. Other writers similarly urged better ethnic balance than the Lancaster slate provided.

103. Proceedings of the Supreme Executive Council for 31 December 1788, in Jensen and Becker, *First Federal Elections* 1: 376–77. P. Muhlenberg and D. Hiester each outpolled Allison and Chambers by some four hundred votes, and F. A. Muhlenberg received the highest number of votes cast for any candidate.

There may even have been confusion about the political partisanship of Daniel Hiester and Peter Muhlenberg. Their names first appeared on the Harrisburg ticket, but discussions of them in the press stressed the fact that they were Germans and, without identifying them as Antifederalists, called them men who favored the Constitution but wanted amendments.

104. In his "Partisanship and the Constitution: Pennsylvania 1787," Owen Ireland reports a detailed study of voting patterns of members of the Pennsylvania Assembly in 1787–88. He concludes, "A broad coalition of Republicans, Constitutionalists, and the formerly nonaligned combined to support ratification while a *segment* of the Constitutional party provided the bulk of the opposition" (my emphasis). Ireland argues that new coalitions were already beginning to form at the time when the Constitution was placed before the state for ratification; *Pennsylvania History* 45 (October 1978) : 315–32.

105. C. P. Smith reconstructs the planning, drawing on Rush's *Autobiography* and William Maclay's *Journal*; *James Wilson*, 297. Both of these men were parties to the plans.

106. *The Pennsylvania Convention, 1789. Minutes of the Convention* (Philadelphia : Zacharia

Poulson, 1789). The relevant minutes of the assembly are bound with the minutes of the convention in this edition.

107. *Independent Gazetteer*, 8 September 1789. Centinel published four pieces during this week, two against holding a state convention and two against the federal Constitution. He insisted that assemblymen would violate their oaths of allegiance to the Frame if they allowed a convention, belittled petitions as a reflection of public opinion, attacked the rights of assemblymen to pretend to speak for their constituents, and accused "the junto" of financial and political corruption. Three other writers who published Antifederalist letters during this week denied the need for changes in the Frame, belittled the petitions, and charged that calling a convention would be "treason" to the Frame. Given the Antifederalists' petition drive of 1779, it was especially ironic for their partisans to belittle the Federalists' petitions.

108. "Centinel Revived, Letter XXXII," *Independent Gazetteer*, 15 September 1789.

109. F. A. Muhlenberg received 8, 726 votes. Jensen and Becker, *First Federal Elections* 1: 377.

110. Resolution dated 15 September 1789. Reprinted in *Pennsylvania Convention, 1789*.

111. Henry Adams, *Life of Albert Gallatin* (New York: Peter Smith, 1943), 79–80.

112. Gallatin to Charles Brown, dated New York, 1 March 1838, in *The Writings of Albert Gallatin*, ed. Henry Adams, 2 vols. (New York: Antiquarian Pr., 1960), 2: 523.

113. Findley wrote a long account to William Plumer, who was preparing a history of America. The account is published in "William Findley of Westmoreland, Pa.," *Pennsylvania Magazine of History and Biography* 5 (1881) : 440–50. Passages I summarize and excerpt appear at 444–46.

114. Seven states had ratified the amendments by the time the Pennsylvania Constitutional Convention adjourned its first session.

115. Voting data and other material here are from *Pennsylvania Convention, 1789*.

116. Letter dated 5 December and published in the *Pittsburgh Gazette*, 26 December 1789.

117. Letter dated 23 December 1789 and published in the *Pittsburgh Gazette*, 9 January 1790.

118. This and later excerpts are from [Alexander Graydon], *Memoirs of a Life Chiefly Passed in Pennsylvania within the Last Sixty Years* (Harrisburg, Penn.: John Wyeth, 1811). This passage appears at 317–18. Graydon misstates the origin of Lewis's proposals. They were not in the committee's report but were offered as amendments to that report.

119. Graydon, *Memoirs*, 318. Graydon seems to exaggerate the closeness of the contest. Popular representation in the Senate carried by a vote of forty-eight to eleven according to the published *Minutes*.

120. Smith, *James Wilson*, 302. Smith quotes from the draft and from Graydon in his reconstruction of this speech, 301–3.

121. Letter dated 11 January 1790 and published in the *Pittsburgh Gazette*, 27 February 1790.

122. The device of "public consideration" was not included in the revised constitution, but the convention observed that principle scrupulously while functioning under the Frame of 1776. In doing so, it gave the public the longest time it had ever had prior to a formal, constitutional enactment.

123. Ryerson, *The Revolution Is Now Begun*, 248n.4.

FIVE

The Rhetorical Birth of a Political Pamphleteer: William Cobbett's "Observations on Priestley's Emigration"

JAMES R. ANDREWS

I⊤ WAS A RIOTOUS, tumultuous, earth-shattering time as the last decade of the eighteenth century opened. In France the world was turned upside down when the brooding symbol of princely pride and terror, the Bastille, was stormed by a Paris mob. The old regime crumbled as each day seemed to bring dramatic changes in the way the ancient and proud monarchy was to be governed.

In the midst of these upheavals, the *Mary*, an American merchant ship, set sail from Le Havre, landing in Philadelphia in October 1792. On board the little vessel was a young Englishman who was to place himself at the center of political controversy for the next four decades. At times an exile, ultimately a member of Parliament, William Cobbett was destined to become one of the most famous journalists and reformers of the nineteenth century. It was in England, as editor of the *Political Register*, author of the *Rural Rides*, and radical pamphleteer in behalf of parliamentary reform, that Cobbett did most of his work. But it was in America, with the publication of his *Observations on Priestley's Emigration*, that Cobbett's polemical career was launched. This thundering broadside deserves close rhetorical explication because the source of its power, the source of Cobbett's immediate and lasting power, is its ability to cut through the tangled complexities of the times and create a clear vision of his reality.

Revolutionary events in France eventually brought that country into the conflict with England that prompted Cobbett's hurried departure for the United States. At first, however, the strivings of the French people against autocracy struck responsive chords in liberal English hearts. Sir Samuel Romilly "rejoiced at the revolution which has taken place," and the intrepid Major Cartwright, tireless advocate of parliamentary reform, was of the opinion that the "heart which expands not with sentiments of delight at what is now transacting in the National Assembly of France" must indeed be "degenerate." The major was sure that the French people stood proxy for all mankind; they were "asserting not only their own rights," but were "also asserting and advancing the general liberties of mankind."[1]

The positive English reaction to the French Revolution was epitomized in a sermon by the Unitarian minister Richard Price. On 4 November 1789, the Reverend Dr. Price appeared before a meeting of the Society for Commemorating the Revolution in Great Britain at the meeting house in Old Jewery to deliver a "Discourse on the Love of Our Country." The revolution being commemorated by the society, of course, was the Glorious Revolution of 1688 in which the Stuart kings were driven from the English throne and by which, according to prevailing mytho-history, English liberties were forever established. Price could not confine himself, however, to events of a century ago, nor to the blessings that flowed from it, nor even to the actions necessary to complete it. The news of the present day was too pressing, too obviously relevant to be ignored. "What an eventful period is this! I am thankful that I have lived to see it; and I could almost say, *Lord now lettest thy servant depart in peace, for mine eyes have seen thy salvation.*" In a passionate peroration, Price saw "kingdoms . . . starting from their sleep, breaking their fetters, and claiming justice from their oppressors!" With dark foreboding he admonished tyrants: "tremble all ye oppressors of the world! Take warning all ye supporters of slavish governments, and slavish hierarchies! . . . You cannot now hold the world in darkness. Struggle no longer against increasing light and liberty. Restore to mankind their rights; and consent to the correction of abuses, before they and you are destroyed together."[2]

Destruction came soon enough. The revolution in France, threatened by the autocratic forces of Austria and Prussia, rose to defend its frontiers and to crush its enemies at home. The moderates lost all control. The Marquis de Lafayette, a symbol in America of French sympathy with its own revolution, was exiled; the mob in Paris rose in the bloody indulgence known as the "September Massacres," slaughtering aristocrats, and, in an infamous act of fury, mutilating the murdered Princesse de Lamballe in order to wave her head on a pike beneath the windows of her friend, Marie Antoinette. The inexorable tide of vengeance, let loose by the breaking of the centuries of damming oppression, flowed without abate. The king and queen were executed and terror reigned.

As the Revolution progressed, its supporters abroad reacted in various ways. Liberals like Romilly, put on the defensive, looked for the good that transcended the evils in France. His opinion, he declared, was "not in the least altered," and, although he was driven to "lament sincerely the miseries which have happened," he could still console himself "with thinking that the evils of the revolution are transitory, and all the good of it is permanent." For others, disillusionment was bitter. Engaging as it did their humane and romantic impulses, the brutality of the real revolution dashed the hopes of sympathizers like Wordsworth. He saw the erstwhile heroic revolutionaries "become oppressors in their turn . . . losing sight of all which they had struggled for." Hope was replaced by despair as he "read her doom, with anger vexed, with disappointment sore."[3]

As the tragedies and triumphs were played out with rising intensity in France, English conservatives took increasingly uneasy notice. The initial rhapsodies of liberals had not, quite naturally, been shared by the upper classes of Great Britain. Yet, neither were the aristocratic governors especially hostile. Indifference was a more characteristic response—indifference and instinctive Francophobia. Lord Grenville observed rather languidly to the Marquis of Buckingham that "one ought to be much more interested than I feel myself in the event of these disputes, not to be heartily tired of hearing of them"; but, he was able to add, "The main point appears quite secure, that they will not for many years be in a situation to molest the invaluable peace which we now enjoy."[4] As much as its romantic supporters, the natural enemies of the Revolution were disappointed and distressed by the turn it took, and with each report from across the channel disdainful nonchalance transformed to alarm. The growing militancy of the Revolution was matched by intensified reaction.

Liberals fighting a rearguard action against the conservative reaction were swamped. Charles James Fox, struggling to avert the suspension of habeas corpus in 1794, might proclaim that "meetings of the people . . . for the discussion of public objects, were not merely legal, but laudable," and that the intention of people "to hold a meeting for the purpose of obtaining parliamentary reform" was hardly "just ground for demolishing the constitution of England." But such protestations were in vain when answered by the charge that "the words parliamentary reform were used by the seditious societies . . . as a mask for their real intention of a total annihilation of all property, constitution, and religion." William Windham, voicing conservative sentiments, answered Fox with the claim that the "tenor of their proceedings and resolutions" made it "plain as the sun that what they meant by reform was the wildest anarchy."[5]

Authority, of course, had ample reason to fear crowds and their potential to become "mobs," given the examples afforded by riots in England itself, let alone demonstrations of the fury of the Parisian mobs. In the turmoil of the early 1790s, however, one of the most famous riots was motivated ostensibly by support of the government against the radicals.[6] The Birmingham riots, or the Priestley riots as they are often called in recognition of their most famous victim, Joseph Priestley, occurred in July 1791 following a dinner held in honor of Bastille Day. This "Church and King" riot was aimed largely at prosperous Dissenters who not only supported the French Revolution, but who also—and perhaps even more importantly— openly attacked the Established Church of England and pressed for repeal of the Test and Corporation Acts that severely restricted non-Anglicans from political and civil participation. Dr. Joseph Priestley, the scientist and Unitarian minister, with his house, laboratory, and chapel destroyed by the rioters, contended that his "real crime" was not "sedition or treason." No, in his opinion, the "crime" was his "open hostility to the doctrines of the established church, and more especially to all civil establishments of religion whatever." Others, however, like the pious and conservative Hannah More, believed that "certain opinions in politics have a tendency to lead to certain opinions in religion" and distrusted attempts to discriminate between the two. She concluded "that the same impatience of restraint, the same contempt of order, peace, and subordination which makes men bad citizens, makes them bad Christians; and that to this secret, but almost infallible connection between religious and political sentiment, does France owe her present unparalleled anarchy and impiety."[7]

Some believed that Priestley had but received his just desserts. George III himself observed that "Priestley is the sufferer for the doctrines he and his party have instilled," although the king was disapproving of the mob's "having employed atrocious means of shewing their discontent." That the government disliked Priestley and his ilk was apparent; nevertheless, they cannot be said to have been entirely pleased with the riots. Former Home Secretary William Grenville probably voiced the view of the affair that was shared by most of those in authority when he wrote to Lord

Auckland, "I do not admire riots in favour of Government much more than riots against it." And in fairness to the authorities— at least the authorities in London; the actions of the local magistrates are more dubious—they acted speedily and decisively to quell the disturbances.[8]

In the next few years, however, official resistance to dissent of any kind intensified, and by 1794, with habeas corpus suspended and England at war with France, Dr. Priestley fled "from ill treatment in my native country, on account of my attachment to the cause of civil and religious liberty." On 4 June 1794 he arrived in New York, where he found himself "cheerfully welcomed" by "persons of sentiments similar to my own."[9]

America at this time may have been separated widely in time and space from Europe, but it was no more immune to the repercussions of continental struggles than were France's nearer neighbors: the United States could not avoid the political and intellectual turmoil even if its relative isolation spared it from the immediate effects of direct physical confrontation.

The fruits of the American Revolution were ripening into a new and experimental government that presented, according to its first president, "an ocean of difficulties," not the least of which was the contrary political philosophies of his own cabinet ministers.[10] Washington detested the seeds of partisanship growing into Hamiltonian or Jeffersonian "factions," and events in France exacerbated this contentious spirit that he so abhorred.

Americans might naturally feel kinship with a France that had come to their assistance in the war for independence from Britain, even though it was monarchical France serving its own interest in opposing Great Britain. Americans, too, while they at first paid respect to Louis XVI, could understandably feel some of the proselyte's pride in the flattering spectacle of a great and cultured nation following their revolutionary example.[11] In any event, pro-French sentiments, while by no means universal, were extravagant.

In 1794, for example, the Massachusetts Constitutional Society passed a resolution professing that a triumphant French Revolution would bring happiness to "the *whole world of Mankind.*" The death of the king of France, formerly a venerated figure, did not have the revulsive impact in America that it did in Great Britain. It even provided a clever exhibitor in Philadelphia with the opportunity to put Yankee ingenuity to work to turn a profit. The execution of Louis XVI was recreated for anyone with three shillings to pay to see it: "the executioner drops the knife, and severs the head from the body in one second; the head falls in a basket, and the lips which

are first red, turn blue; the whole is performed to the life by an
invisible machine, without any perceivable assistance."[12]

Not all demonstrations of the "French frenzy" were so bizarre.
Nevertheless, it was clear that a considerable body of American
opinion looked with favor on the march of the French Revolution.
Of course, the French Revolution did not *cause* the formation of
two distinct American parties; lines of division had been drawn from
the establishment of the Constitution. Yet, as the historian R. R.
Palmer points out, "While Americans were thus becoming divided,
on purely domestic grounds, France was invaded and became a
republic, and then went to war with Britain. Americans took sides,
for Britain or for France, to a degree never paralleled in connection
with any later war or revolution in Europe."[13]

By the time Joseph Priestley set foot on American soil the intemperate French ambassador, Citizen Genet, had been recalled after an
effort to appeal to the American people, over the head of President
Washington, to join France in its war on the enemies of liberty.
Active in stirring up pro-French and antigovernment sentiment,
Genet was also instrumental in encouraging the formation of "democratic societies" that looked to some suspiciously like the Jacobin
clubs that had animated the French Revolution. Washington was
disapproving and alarmed. "I early gave it as my opinion," the
president wrote in 1794, a year after the founding of the Pennsylvania Democratic Society, ". . . that if these societies were not coun-
teracted . . . or did not fall into disesteem from the knowledge of
their origin and the views for which they had been instituted by
their father, Genet, for purposes well known to the government,
that they would shake the government to its foundation."[14] The
societies did not disappear with Genet; they were active when
Priestley arrived and were prominent among those who provided
the "cheerful welcome" for which he was so grateful.

Also resident in America, however, was another Englishman,
one who decidedly was not among those who held "sentiments
similar" to Dr. Priestley's. For William Cobbett, the landing in New
York of "the famous Unitarian Doctor, fellow of the *Royal* Society,
London, *citizen* of France, and delegate to the *Grande Convention
Nationale* of notorious memory," was "nothing to me, nor to anybody
else." But, Cobbett explained, "the fulsome and consequential addresses sent him by the pretended patriots, and his canting replies,
at once calculated to flatter the people here, and to degrade his
country and mine, was something to me. It was my business, and
the business of every man, who thinks that truth ought to be
opposed to malice and hypocrisy."[15] In response to the declarations

welcoming Priestley and to Priestley's response to those declarations, Cobbett launched a stinging attack, his first real effort at political pamphleteering, *Observations on Priestley's Emigration.*

William Cobbett, born in rural England—the market town of Farnum in western Surrey—was the son of a tavern keeper who provided what formal education William ever was to have.[16] The lure of London drew young William from the farm in 1783, but he was not happy as a lawyer's clerk and in 1784 joined the army. He rose to the rank of sergeant major and served with his regiment in Nova Scotia. Upon his return to England, he resolved to right wrongs done to the ordinary soldier by officers who swindled them of their pay; but the army was too formidable an establishment to yield easily to the naive attacks of a young noncommissioned officer, and Cobbett soon realized that his crusade for justice had put him in personal danger. With his young wife, he left England for France. After only a year there, however, the threat of war between France and England justifiably alarmed him, and he took ship for America. After a brief sojourn in Wilmington, where his principal occupation was teaching English to French émigrés, he removed to Philadelphia. He had previously published his translation of the proceedings against Lafayette, but his long and stormy career really began with the pamphlet on Priestley.

It was only after some negotiation that Cobbett found a publisher for his article; the printer William Bradford would have been happier if Cobbett could have made the piece "a little more popular." Cobbett, however, was never "of an accommodating disposition," and the sole concession he would make was to delete the original title, *The Tartuffe Detected,* and keep only the subtitle, although, he grudgingly observed, "the *Tartuffe Detected* should have remained; for the person on whom it was bestowed, merited it much better than the character so named from Moliere."[17]

This first polemic launched the career of an agitational genius. Cobbett's opinions might change, but, then, circumstances change, and Cobbett would dismiss with contempt "the doctrine of *consistency*" as "the most absurd that ever was broached." His pungent rhetorical stance, style, and strategy was ever that of the passionate mover and not the reflective thinker. Crane Brinton might indict him for his failure to "use his intellect to correct, build up, and render systematic" his prejudices and his thought, but Brinton does recognize that Cobbett "could be interesting because he could use hard, tangible phrases that got to work at once on the senses of his readers. He could move men because he felt as they did."[18]

The *Observations* is a stunning polemic. Polemical rhetoric may encourage tunnel vision, but the tunnel is one at whose end a light can clearly be discerned. The pamphleteer may be condemned as a demagogue and be accused of oversimplification, but the true polemicist attempts always to make real people—perplexed, confused, and limited—see their world in a way that will induce belief and inform action. At this, Cobbett was a master.[19]

Cobbett begins his work with a justification of his own decision to enter the fray, a justification based largely on his reaction to the acclaim Priestley received from the democratic societies and the doctor's reactions to these flattering addresses. Cobbett professes to welcome him "to the shores of peace" and to wish him "what he certainly ought to have wished for himself, a quiet obscurity." As an emigrant seeking only repose, Priestley would not have attracted Cobbett's attention. Priestley, however, by his answers to the addresses presented to him, surrendered immediately the right to exemption from public scrutiny. Once he had made his opinions public and once he attempted "to make converts," then "his opinions, his principles, his motives, every action of his life, public or private, become the fair subject of public discussion." Given Priestley's actions, then, Cobbett feels that his own "observations need no apology."[20]

In his opening Cobbett reveals his basic stance. He is called to the fray not by personal aversion to Priestley, but by the public effort to canonize him. A man's opinions are his own property and should be respected; once they become the vehicle of influencing others, however, those opinions elicit response. Cobbett rises to the occasion as a defender of public debate and as an interrogator seeking to uncover the real meanings and implications behind Priestley's words and actions.

Cobbett also establishes the ground for investigation in his first strategic choice. His latitude is sweeping: every action of Priestley's life is open to discussion. Cobbett, of course, will not delve into every action, but he seizes the ground of his own choosing, thus asserting the legitimacy of whatever line of argument he pursues.

The next paragraph moves immediately to a forceful personal denunciation of Priestley and shows why Cobbett was so eager to label Priestley as Tartuffe, that prince of hypocrites, in the disallowed title of the pamphlet. For this section, strong language sets out Cobbett's premises without ambiguity. Priestley's answers "are calculated to mislead and deceive"; he "endeavours to impose himself on them for a sufferer in the cause of liberty," and his profession of moderation is a "canting one." Indeed, his claims are "in direct contradiction to his whole life" (152).

Here, then, is the clear indication of the strategy that will govern Cobbett's choices: Priestley's image as a martyr to liberty, a moderate reformer, and a sufferer at the hands of both an unruly mob and his own government will become the subject of refutation. Cobbett turns Priestley's praise for America back on Priestley as an insult to American intelligence: "he must certainly suppose" that no news from Europe "ever reaches this side of the Atlantic, or that the inhabitants of these countries are too dull to comprehend the sublime events that mark his life and character." Assuming the persona of the intelligent and fair-minded American people, Cobbett opines, "Perhaps I shall show him that it is not the people of England alone who know how to estimate the merit of Doctor Priestley" (152).

Cobbett sets as the initial issue for investigation whether or not the charge leveled in Priestley's response to the societies—his hope to find in America "that protection from violence which laws and government promise in all countries, but which he has not found in his own"—be "just or not" (152). The extended argument which follows, and which is the heart of the *Observations*, blends several important argumentative and stylistic choices that make up Cobbett's strategy. Essentially, he looks to Priestley's own behavior as a cause of the riots; the nature of the government's responses to the riots; the logical justification of the riots from Priestley's own political and philosophic premises; and, most tellingly and most significantly for Cobbett's strategy, the comparison of events in Birmingham and the nature of English justice with the situation in revolutionary France.

Cobbett does not deny the fact that "an unruly mob" in Birmingham "set fire to [Priestley's] house and burnt it, together with all that it contained." But "in the relation of facts, circumstances must not be forgotten." It is crucial to Cobbett's argument at this stage that he be allowed to "take a retrospective view of his [Priestley's] conduct, and of the circumstances that led to the destruction of his property" (152). In short, the technical guilt of the mob is to be balanced against the provocative sins of Dr. Priestley. Now this particular tactic is a common and powerful one. It has been used most reprehensibly to justify the outrages of a lynch mob or the vicious attack of a rapist; on the other hand, the concept of "mitigating circumstances" has always had some claim on popular attention and sympathy and has found its way in various forms into the law. For Cobbett, the "common sense" of such an approach is its principal appeal. The tactic is especially important to Cobbett, for to advance his argument he must show the facts not to be the *cause* of Priesley's emigration, but, rather, the *effect* of Priestley's previous actions; he must, in other words, refocus the perception of events in order to create the reality that Cobbett himself sees.

Cobbett goes back twelve years to the time when Priestley "began to be distinguished among the dissenters from the established church of England." Cobbett disdainfully pictures the "kind of deism" Priestley preached. Unitarianism, a doctrine "which nobody understood, and which," Cobbett adds as a direct attack on Priesley's vaunted intellect, "the Doctor understood full as well as his neighbors," never "rose into consequence" and had become out of date when the French Revolution came to give both the doctor and his "sect" a "short respite from eternal oblivion" (153).

Cobbett attempts to blend religious and political dissent, to demonstrate the relationship between efforts to undermine both religion and the state, in order that readers may see a long pattern of subversion of traditional values. "Those who know anything of the English dissenters," he asserts, "know that they always introduce their political claims and projects under the mask of religion." And Priestley led the dissenters—through his "inflammatory discourses, called sermons"—to attack openly the English constitution. From his meeting house, Dr. Priestley "beat his drum ecclesiastic, to raise recruits in the cause of rebellion." By a description of the formation of revolutionary societies after the model of Jacobin clubs, the proliferation of revolutionary propaganda, the initiation of "federation dinners, toasts, sermons, prayers, in short, every trick that religious or political duplicity could suggest," Cobbett paints a picture of the concerted attack by Priestley and his Unitarian followers on "a constitution which has borne the test, and attracted the admiration of ages" (153–54).

Here is presented a scene of wanton disregard not only for what is sacred to many, but is, in its essence, good. What Priestley and his followers would destroy was the constitution that protected the people and "with it their happiness." Even this monstrous assault, Cobbett alleges, was greeted only with "contempt" until the last straw was loaded on the unhappy camel's back: the "public notice of a feast, to be held in Birmingham, in which they intended to celebrate the French revolution." Local citizens, writes Cobbett, were "scandalized" that the commemoration of "events that were in reality a subject of the deepest horror," was to be held in their town. What is of particular interest is Cobbett's vivid descriptions of how these townsmen felt, what they believed, and what they proposed to do. He projects for the reader a set of motives, vis-à-vis the victims, that cast the action not only in a reasonable, but even a commendable, light. Birminghamites found "their understandings and loyalty insulted." As a result, the actions they took, as described in Cobbett's vivid language, take on the aura of avenging angels descending justly on the wicked malefactors; as Cobbett puts it, they "prepared to avenge themselves by the chastisement of the English revolutionists, in the midst of their scandalous orgies" (154). "Chastisement" clearly implies a just and proper punishment such as might be meted out to an errant child or a wayward sinner; and, most surely, those reveling in "scandalous orgies" have scant grounds upon which to appeal to the sympathy of the righteous. Even so, Cobbett emphasizes, the mob did not act against the persons of the revolutionaries, contenting themselves in devastating the tavern in which the dinner was held after the celebrants had left it. Cobbett cannot forbear to add that it might have been well if the mob *had* "vented their anger on the revolutionists" by throwing them in a horse-pond or tossing them in a blanket. With that out of their system, the rioters might have stopped there.

Of course, the riot did not end with the destruction of the tavern. What followed was the demolition of the Unitarian meeting house, an act that Cobbett cannot bring himself to condemn since "the destruction of this temple of sedition and infidelity would have been of no great consequence" in itself. The mob continued its depredations, however, burning down the houses of members of the club, including Priestley's house—and with it his laboratory and scientific instruments. This wanton attack on private property Cobbett does not defend. But the entire movement of this argument has been in the direction of the clear culpability of the victims of the riot in bringing such actions upon themselves: "when that many-headed monster, a mob, is once roused and put in motion, who can stop its destructive steps?" (154–55). That the monster was roused by Dr. Priestley, Cobbett is content that he has made clear. He then proceeds to consider the role played by the government in reacting to the riots.

During a relatively brief description of the progress of the riots Cobbett points out, in passing, what is later to be a major matter: "not a single person was killed or wounded, either willfully or by accident, except some of the rioters themselves." He goes on to detail the exertions of the local officials and the arrival, on 18 July, of a detachment of dragoons, asserting that "responsible persons" were "indefatigable in their endeavours to put a stop to the depredations" (155–56).

Turning to Priestley's charges that the law did not protect him, Cobbett reacts with vivid indignation. The government, he points out, brought prosecutions against eleven of the rioters, it being impossible, of course, to "imprison, try, and execute the whole of a mob." The results were that seven were acquitted and four found guilty, two of whom "suffered death." It is all very well to complain that juries were too lenient, but there could be no grounds for arguing that the government did not vigorously apply the laws against those who had injured Priestley. Further, the laws, Cobbett argues, "rendered him strict justice" in the civil suit that he brought against the city of Birmingham. In a careful reckoning of Priestley's demands and the ultimate award made by the jury, Cobbett declares that he got "more than he had a right to expect." Cobbett asks what more could be done: "If he had been the very best subject in England, in place of one of the very worst, what could the laws have done more for him?" Cobbett neatly sums up his argument to this point by skillful use of ironic contrasts:

Nothing certainly can be a stronger proof of the independence of the courts of justice, and of the impartial execution of the laws of England, than the circum- stances and result of this cause. A man who for many years had been the avowed and open enemy of the government and constitution, had his property destroyed by a mob, who declared themselves the friends of both, and who rose up against him because he was not. This mob was pursued by the Government, whose cause they thought they were defending; some of them suffered death, and the inhabitants of the place where they assembled were obliged to indemnify the man whose property they had destroyed. (156–58)

The striking justice of these events as Cobbett capsulizes them allowed him to turn to Priestley's own political and philosophic opinions and the relationship between those opinions and the course of the French Revolution. Priestley's complaint that he was not afforded protection and justice by the law permits Cobbett to ask darkly what Priestley wanted: "Would nothing satisfy him but the blood of the whole mob?" Cobbett can then swiftly connect Priest- ley's dissatisfaction with the slaughter in France: "Did he wish to see the town of Birmingham, like that of Lyons, razed, and all its industrious inhabitants butchered, because some of them had been carried to commit unlawful excesses, from their detestation of his wicked projects?" What saved the people of Birmingham from bloody retribution, Cobbett is eager to point out, was that "there was no National Convention, Revolutionary Tribunal, or guillotine, in England" (158–59).

The excesses in France, of which Cobbett planned to say much more later, and the excesses in Birmingham, lead Cobbett to a telling point that depends on the effective use of a tactic designed to turn the tables on Priestley. The mob, after all, "did nothing that was not perfectly consonant to the principles he had for many years been labouring to infuse in their minds." The revolutionists maintained that they were exercising their rights as free men to assemble, and, even if they had been acting illegally, it was the role of proper officials to intercede: liberty could not exist when a mob was allowed to supersede the law. Cobbett pounces on this argument: "That is what the Doctor has been told a thousand times, but he never would believe it." Quoting Priestley, Cobbett points to the irony of the statement that "when the majesty of the people *is insulted,* or they feel themselves oppressed by *any set of men,* they have the power to redress the grievance." Cobbett suggests that the revolutionists are caught in their own trap. "So the people of Birmingham, feeling their majesty insulted by a *set of men . . .* who audaciously attempted to persuade them that they were '*all slaves and idolators,*' and to seduce them from their duty to God and their country, rose '*to redress the grievance.*' " Contrast, clear, sharp and dramatic, is one of Cobbett's most striking tools as he attempts to keep the choices between the France admired by the revolutionaries and the England they seek to reform. What if the mob had acted as urged by the supporters of insurrection, Cobbett wonders: "had they burnt the churches, cut the throats of the clergy, and hung the magistrates, military officers, and nobility to lamp-posts, would he not have said they exercised a sacred right?" (160–62).

The starkest of contrasts, however, is yet to come. "What we celebrate we must approve," Cobbett writes; since the purpose of the meeting disrupted by the rioters was to commemorate the French Revolution, the club members must assuredly approve of the Revolution. Complaints have been lodged against the mob of Birmingham; very well, "Let us see, a little, how mobs have acted under the famous government that the Doctor so much admires" (163). The comparisons that Cobbett proceeds to lay out are overwhelming.

In Provence, Avignon, Languedoc, and Roufillon, "towns and villages were sacked, gentlemen's seats and castles burnt, and their inhabitants massacred; magistrates insulted, beat, and imprisoned, sometimes killed; prisoners set at liberty, to cut the throats of those they had already robbed." When this is set against the events in Birmingham, "The amount of damages sustained in property, was perhaps a hundred thousand times as great as that sustained by the revolutionists at Birmingham." And what of redress for these depredations? When a delegate attempted to bring the horrifying events occurring throughout France to the attention of the National Assembly in Paris, the assembly "passed a censure on him, for having slandered the patriots" (163–64).

Cobbett then asks, "Does the Doctor remember having heard

anything about the glorious achievements of the 10th of August, 1792? Has he ever made an estimate of the property destroyed in Paris on that and the following days?" The rhetorical questions are driven home: "let him compare the destruction that followed the steps of that mob, with the loss of his boasted apparatus" (164).

On the September Massacres Cobbett dwells at length. A long passage relates the eyewitness account of Doctor Moore, who tells of bodies being nonchalantly piled in carts by a young boy; of a man standing smoking with a human hand stuck on the point of his sword and another walking about with an arm impaled on his. Moore describes the fate of newly transported prisoners waiting in fetters at the door of the prison, set upon and hacked to pieces while their guards watched with unconcern. It is with profound psychological truth that Cobbett observes, "From scenes like these, the mind turns for relief and consolation to the riot at Birmingham. That riot, considered comparatively with what Doctor Priestley and his friends wished and attempted to stir up, was peace, harmony, and gentleness" (165–67).

Cobbett's powerful contrasts seem designed to force a moral decision, and with contrasts he continues to press his readers to choose among Priestley's supposed choices. Priestley had said in response to the addresses that his country afforded him no protection and was oppressive. "Would he really prefer," Cobbett asks, "the proceedings of a *revolutionary tribunal* to those of a court of justice in England?" The doctor is then asked if he envies "the lot of his colleagues Manuel, Lacroix, Danton, and Chabot," all of whom had been summarily arrested. As in the case of the mob comparison, Cobbett uses a vivid and horrifying example, given in some detail. "How would he look at a tribunal like that of the Princess de Lamballe, for example?" Cobbett luridly describes the "unfortunate lady" being dragged before her judges, who sat drinking wine and damning those that literally lay dead before them. "Their shirtsleeves were tucked up to their elbows; their arms and hands, and even the goblets they were drinking out of, were besmeared with human blood." Picturing the "blood-freezing sight of these hell-hounds," Cobbett rises to a pitch of indignant horror when he contemplates that "this was a court of justice, under that constitution which 'the friend of human happiness' wanted to impose on his countrymen" (168).

The final contrastive assault is launched against the supporters of parliamentary reform. This new argument harks back to Cobbett's initial one in which he pictured Priestley as the cause of his own miseries. It is an argument that pits the abstract against the practical.

Cobbett takes to task the "visionary delusions" that afflict reformers. In the very practical terms of a very practical man he argues that reformers "do not consider what *can* be done, but what they think ought to be done." They do not determine before they launch their proposals "whether a reform will cost them more than it is worth. . . . They do not sit down to count the cost." Because the object of their efforts is "desirable, the means are totally disregarded." The sharp contrasts between what the French reformers wanted and the cost of their actions is then portrayed with vivid specifics: "To save a tenth of their income, they have given the whole, or rather it has been taken from them"; "To preserve the life of a person now and then unjustly condemned, they have drenched the country with the blood of the innocent"; the Bastille was razed and the two state prisoners incarcerated in it freed, and the reformers, "to deliver these two prisoners, and to guard others from a like fate, have erected bastilles in every town and in every street"; whereas "before the revolution there were only two state prisoners, there are now above *two hundred thousand.*"

Cobbett then calculates the cost of parliamentary reform, offering the argument accepted in conservative circles that it was but the opening shot that would be followed by a bloody fusillade. He advances this argument with a short fable demonstrating that "some trifling innovation always paves the way to the subversion of a government." He relates the story of the axe who "humbly besought" a small piece of wood from the mighty forest to make a handle. The forest, with so many trees, did not refuse the "humble" request. But "the handle once granted, the contemptible tool began to lay about it with so much violence, that in a little time not a tree, not even a shrub, was left standing" (169–70).

A long section of Cobbett's argument is then directed at proving that Priestley stands convicted by his own words of hoping to change the entire form of government and not simply to bring about mild reform, and to point to the similarities between the English government that Priestley detests and the American one to which he has fled (170–78).

The remainder of the pamphlet is virtually a catalogue of Priestley's infamies, hypocrisies, and failings. Each one is presented by first laying out the flattering words of the democratic societies and Priestley's replies. The addresses "dun our ears with *French Liberty.*" French liberty, Cobbett asserts, is worse than the Inquisition. What, Cobbett asks, is "their own definition" of liberty? Quoting Barrère to the National Convention, Cobbett writes, "Liberty, my dear fellow citizens, is a privileged and general creditor; not only has she the right to our *property* and *persons,* but to our *talents* and *courage,* and even to our thoughts!" Cobbett's response to such a definition is a horrified one: "Oh, liberty! what a metamorphosis hast thou undergone in the hands of these political jugglers!" (179).

The Tammany Society speaks of "a sentiment of free and candid inquiry," while Doctor Priestley "professes to wish for nothing but toleration, liberty of conscience." But what, Cobbett asks, does Priestley say to the persecution of the Catholic clergy in France? Contrasting Priestley's treatment with theirs, Cobbett observes, "He talks of persecution, and puts on the mockery of woe: theirs has been persecution, indeed. Robbed, dragged from their homes, or obliged to hide from the sight of man, in continual expectation of the assassin's stab; some transported like common felons, for ever, and a much greater number butchered." The phrase by which the Tammany Society affirms that Doctor Priestley has "long disinterestedly laboured for his country" is pounced upon by Cobbett and used as the occasion to impugn Priestley's motives. Cobbett refers to Priestley's sermon on the Test laws in which the Unitarian preacher proposed "to set apart one church for the Dissenters in every considerable town, and a certain allotment of *tithes* for their Minister, proportioned to the number of Dissenters in the district." A suggestion that a portion of the taxes raised to go to the church be given to dissenting clergy, Cobbett finds "Astonishing disinterestedness!" "After all his clamour against tithes, and his rejoicing on account of their abolition in France, he has no objection to their continuing in England, provided he came in for a share" (180–84).

Much of what remains in the polemic is a direct assault on every aspect of Priestley's character. His "metaphysical reveries" would lead him, to Cobbett's way of thinking, to be as detested in America as he was in England; his "scientific productions," Cobbett claims, have been repudiated by the Royal Society; even his "talents as a writer" were "far below mediocrity," for not only was his style "uncouth and superlatively diffuse . . . even in point of grammar he is very often incorrect." No matter what kind of style he affects, the doctor is to Cobbett a demagogue, and "God knows, there were too many of this description in America before the arrival of Doctor Priestley." Cobbett can see no use for Doctor Priestley in America: "Of all the English arrived in these States (since the war) no one was ever calculated to render them less service than Doctor Priestley" (191–93, 195, 198).[21]

Cobbett's parting shot caps a persistent theme that runs through the *Observations* and is a critical one in understanding Cobbett as an exponent of the pamphleteer's art. In describing those emigrants who are truly useful to America, Cobbett chooses "mechanics" as a prime example. "Perhaps a cobbler, with his hammer and awls, is a more valuable acquisition than a dozen philosophi-theologi-political empirics, with all their boasted apparatus" (198). Running through the entire work is a sustained attack on the "philosophers." Priestley becomes the embodiment of those social experimenters whose theories result in disastrous consequences. An attack on Priestley is an attack on the entire ethos of the revolutionary thinkers. Such an assault provides a tangible object for Cobbett to sink his teeth into and makes the abstractions underlying revolutionary changes concrete realities, easily perceived by masses of men.

Priestley and his fellow "philosophers" are heaped with scorn. Cobbett does not enter into long disputations on natural right or the rights of man; rather, he intertwines doctrine and persona; Cobbett is living proof of Wendell Phillips's observation that "the great mass of people can never be made to stay and argue a long question. They must be made to feel it through the hides of their idols."[22] And *feel* Cobbett does; no one can read Cobbett without experiencing the heat of his passion and the depth of his scorn. The philosophers would destroy a time-tested system and "establish in its place a new system, fabricated by themselves" (154). He contends that Doctor Priestley's dissatisfaction with the action taken against the mob would have been answered by razing the town of Birmingham as Lyons had been razed: this would have satisfied the "charitable modern philosopher" (158). Priestley's supposed duplicity in giving the loyal toast in England and in condemning monarchy in America is but proof that "philosophers are but mere men" (171). And these men would impose "a system that never was, and never can be, brought into practice" (170). Indeed, the "system-mongers" would create a model government that practical men know could not be since events and circumstances make up a long process that forms a government "little by little." The result "when completed . . . presents nothing like a *system*; nothing like a thing composed, and written in a book" (172). The effects of imposing abstract theory on real life are the opposite of the philosophers' benevolent intentions since the practical result is "opulence reduced to misery." Nonetheless, this unhappy outcome appears "delectable to a modern philosopher" (173).

Even allowing for the forceful and vituperative style of the typical eighteenth-century political pamphlet, Cobbett's *Observations* stands out. In this work, Cobbett's polemical nativity, he shows the force of contrast in presenting clear moral choices, demonstrates the power of reducing complex ideas to concrete experience, and exhibits the potential impact on the sense and the senses in merging individual ethos with the ethos of an entire movement. Again, Phillips put it quite well when he said of the agitator: "He is not always right. He may often be wrong. He may say the very worst thing that can be said, but he says something that stirs the whole atmosphere."[23] Cobbett stirred the atmosphere. He fixed on the inescapable chink in the armor of democrats when he so brilliantly contrasted the results of the workings of the system they attacked with the horrifying excesses of the French Revolution. Of course, it wasn't that simple; but Cobbett forced moral and political simplicity on events and thus his rhetoric created a reality against which events could be judged.

Cobbett's tract was but the opening gun and not the last word. His salvo brought heated fire in return and ultimately caused him to launch the famous *Peter Porcupine* series—and to continue to fight battles with words for the rest of his life. It was with the *Observations* that his journalistic apprenticeship began, and in it may be seen the roots of his long rhetorical career. From defender of the Tories he eventually became their bane. "A journalist of genius," Cobbett was, through all his political fluctuations, as G. D. H. Cole and Raymond Postgate remark, "the most powerful political pamphleteer in English history," and his first efforts in America show the signs and the promise of that rhetorical power.[24]

Notes

1. Letter to M. Dumont, 28 July 1789, in *Memoirs of Sir S. Romilly*, 2 vols. (London, 1840), 1: 356; letter to the President of the Committee of the Constitution of the States General, 18 August 1789, in *Life and Correspondence of Major Cartwright*, ed. F.D. Cartwright (London, 1826), 182.

2. Richard Price, *A Discourse on the Love of Our Country* (London, 1789), 50–51.

3. Letter to Madame G ——— , 15 May 1792, *Memoirs of Sir S. Romilly* 2: 1–2; William Wordsworth, *The Prelude*, ed. Jonathan Wordsworth, M. H. Abrams, and Stephen Gill (New York: Norton, 1979), 401–3.

4. Grenville to Marquis of Buckingham, 14 September 1789, in Duke of Buckingham, *Courts and Cabinets of George III*; quoted in *The Debate on the French Revolution*, ed. Alfred Cobben, 2d ed. (London: Adam and Charles Black, 1960), 443.

5. Debate in the House of Commons, 17 May 1794, *Parliamentary History* 31 (1794): 559–60, 546–47.

6. Much has been written on the nature and operations of the "mob." G. F. Rude, *The Crowd in History: A Study of Popular Disturbances in France and England, 1730–1848* (New York: Wiley, 1964), is a particularly important study. For a full discussion of sources related to riots in this period see John Ehrman, *The Younger Pitt: The Reluctant Transition* (Stanford, Calif.: Stanford Univ. Pr., 1983), 656–57. Ehrman's chapters on the "Dimension of Unrest" in 1792 (91–171) provide an excellent and comprehensive analysis of popular disturbances in England at this time.

It was always difficult to fathom the *precise* motives of mobs in the eighteenth century:

economic, social, political, and religious factors made up the volatile mix that produced riotous explosions. See Ehrman, *The Younger Pitt*, 131–34.

7. Joseph Priestley, "Preface to the Fast Sermon of 1794," in *Memoirs* (London, 1806), 145; "Remarks on the Speech of M. Dupont," in *The Works of Hannah More*, 18 vols. (London, 1818), 6: 322.

8. Ehrman, *The Younger Pitt*, 132, 134. Ehrman points out that when the riot began local authorities "were curiously slow to act," and may have "countenanced the burning of chapels." But Ehrman's examination of the sequence of events leads him to conclude that charges that the government deliberately ignored the victims "cannot be sustained." *The Younger Pitt*, 132–33.

9. William Cobbett, "Addresses to Doctor Priestley," in *Porcupine's Works*, 12 vols. (London, 1801), 1: 129, 134.

10. Washington to General Knox, quoted in Samuel Eliot Morison, *The Oxford History of the American People* (New York: Oxford Univ. Pr., 1972), 317.

11. This point is made and developed by George Spater, *William Cobbett: The Poor Man's Friend* (Cambridge: Cambridge Univ. Pr., 1982), 44.

12. R. R. Palmer, *The World of the French Revolution* (New York: Harper, 1971), 226; Spater, *William Cobbett*, 45.

13. Palmer, *The World of the French Revolution*, 223–24.

14. Quoted in James Thomas Flexner, *George Washington: Anguish and Farewell (1792–1799)* (Boston: Little, Brown, 1969), 64.

15. William Cobbett, *The Life of William Cobbett By Himself* (London, 1809), 36–37.

16. There is a wealth of biographical material on Cobbett. W. Reitzel edited Cobbett's own scattered fragments of autobiography in *The Autobiography of William Cobbett, the Progress of a Plough-Boy to a Seat in Parliament* (London: Faber & Faber, 1947). The standard biography remains G. D. H. Cole, *The Life of William Cobbett* (London: Collins, 1924). A short biographical essay that relates major events of Cobbett's life is Asa Briggs, *William Cobbett* (Oxford: Clarendon Pr., 1967). Still the best account of Cobbett's career in America is Mary Elizabeth Clark, *Peter Porcupine in America: The Career of William Cobbett, 1792–1800* (Philadelphia: Univ. of Pennsylvania Pr., 1939).

17. Cobbett, *Life*, 38–39.

18. Quoted in Spater, *William Cobbett*, 4; Crane Brinton, *English Political Thought in the Nineteenth Century* (New York: Harper, 1962), 74, 64.

19. I have used "polemicist" in the traditional sense of one who engages in controversy with an aim to refuting or attacking a specific opinion, doctrine, or the like. The etymology of "polemic" is especially appealing in this case: "polemic" is from the Medieval Latin *polemicus*, "controversialist," from the Greek *polemikos*, "of war, hostile, opposed," from *polemos*, "war"; William Morris, ed., *The American Heritage Dictionary of the English Language* (Boston: American Heritage and Houghton Mifflin, 1969), 1014. Cobbett the polemicist does battle with words: he does not merely dispute with an atagonist, he wages verbal war.

It will be apparent to rhetorical critics that the polemicist, of course, shares some of the characteristics of the agitator. John Bowers and Donovan Ochs, *The Rhetoric of Agitation and Control* (Reading, Mass.: Addison-Wesley, 1971), hold the generally agreed upon perception of the agitator as one "outside the normal decision-making establishment," but they are focusing on contemporary agitation, and it would be hard to define the "decision-making establishment" in the same way in eighteenth-century America; in any event, Cobbett certainly can be seen to employ the agitational tactics of "polarization" (26) and "derogatory jargon" (28). Further, the "particular rhetorical style" that Mary McEdwards describes in "Agitative Rhetoric: Its Nature and Effect," *Western Speech* 32 (1968): 37, might well be applied to Cobbett. But I am not attempting here to make a case for Cobbett as an "agitator" in the sense it has been delineated by contemporary critics. When I use the word in this study, I simply mean it in its broadest sense as one who stirs things up, who "agitates."

20. William Cobbett, "Observations on Priestley's Emigration," *Porcupine's Works* 1: 151–52. Volume 1 of this work is hereafter cited in the text.

21. Conservatives were often to return to the attack on "philosophers"—and implicitly on Thomas Jefferson—as impractical and even absurd dreamers whose ideas were unpolluted by common sense. A prime, and very entertaining, example is David Daggett's 1799 Fourth of July oration, "Sun-Beams May Be Extracted from Cucumbers, But the Process Is Tedious." A condensed version of the speech is in Ernest Wrage and Barnet Baskerville, eds., *American Forum: Speeches on Historic Issues 1788–1900* (New York: Harper, 1960), 37–49.

22. Quoted in McEdwards, "Agitative Rhetoric," 38.
23. Quoted in McEdwards, "Agitative Rhetoric," 59.
24. J. H. Plumb et al., *The English Heritage* (Arlington Heights, Ill.: Forum, 1978), 269; G. D. H. Cole and Raymond Postgate, *The British Common People* (New York: University Paperbacks/Barnes and Noble, 1961), 183.

SIX

Central Park and the Celebration of Civic Virtue

LAWRENCE W. ROSENFIELD

IN THE NORTHEASTERN CORNER of New York City's Central Park, in a section seldom frequented by tourists these days, lie the exquisite Conservatory Gardens. They can be entered at East 105th Street through the wrought-iron Vanderbilt Gate. It is unfortunate that these replicas of eighteenth-century formal gardens are not well known, since they come close to revealing for the visitor the character and function of the park as a whole and through it, the enduring fabric that weds rhetoric and the visual arts. Strolling in their midst, one is struck by the incongruity of locating a product of aristocratic enlightenment on what is today the boundary of two distinct racial and class neighborhoods, the one black and Spanish Harlem, the other the affluent Silk Stocking district, home to international celebrities and financiers. Yet within the gardens themselves one loses any sense of the sharp cleavages and tensions just outside the gate. The pathways, vegetation and fountains of the garden evoke a sense of peacefulness and well-being that leave the visitor with a more benevolent outlook toward one's fellows than one ordinarily has upon entering the park. If the thrust of this essay is correct, that is exactly the experience for which Central Park was intended, and we should be able to uncover those rhetorical elements of park design that continue to make such an evocation possible.

My aim in this essay is to establish a background against which it will be possible to read the park as a text whose web of significant meaning can be analyzed to disclose larger patterns cohering in culture and society. This is not an intellectual history of parks as such or of Central Park in particular. I propose rather to consider what the cultivated or built park owes to an earlier art of rhetoric. The legacy goes beyond the transference of formal design principles; it borrows as well from the functions rhetorical arts performed in republican civic life. My ultimate claim is that the public park served for nineteenth-century urban democracy much the same function that civic oratory or eloquence served in traditional republican societies: to celebrate institutions and ideological principles thought to be the genius of those cultures.

Central Park and Republican Virtu

Central Park, the first urban park expressly constructed for general public use, exemplifies as well as any the membrane of republican motifs woven into its aesthetic. Its founders and early supporters quite explicitly recognized its political significance. The park was built during an era of democratic humanism, and it reflects that spirit. The ideology of the times held that, given the proper institutions and environment, all persons, regardless of birth or social standing, were capable of becoming active and valued participants in republican government. They needed only the educational opportunities (both formal and informal) that would enable them to develop the appropriate republican habits.

Public schools, parks and gardens, art galleries and museums, Sunday schools and tract societies all represented attempts to extend the sphere of republican instruction in the principles of social order and virtue to the maximum number of citizens; to counteract the turbulence and corruption of American life by improving the social environment and establishing monitors over it.[1]

Public parks were manifestly suitable socializing vehicles for the democratic experiment. Americans distrusted elitist "fine arts," such as painting, opera, and ballet, that smacked of European debauchery and religious sectarianism. Yet they still required means to bend the imaginations and loyalties of individuals from a bewildering variety of cultural backgrounds to democratic principles. They sought an aesthetic of public taste that could inform democratic institutions and activities, could rehearse newcomers in proper republican conduct, and could compare favorably with the finest artworks of more elitist societies. Central Park was one of the first and most spectacular of these vehicles. Its sheer size made possible its recreational use by literally masses of individuals. At the same time, its advantages in encouraging republican modes of socialization among its users were recognized and proclaimed from the outset.[2]

A. J. Downing, the horticulturist who first proposed the park's construction, foresaw its value in fostering republican virtue. For one thing, the park would be a focal point of civic pride, a creation accomplished by the cooperation of all for the benefit of all. As a public works project, its magnitude befitted a dynamic and prosperous people. More important, it would demonstrate that a republic gave highest priority to general happiness and commonwealth rather than private well-being. "The true policy of republics is to foster the taste for great public libraries, parks and gardens which *all* may enjoy, since our institutions wisely forbid the growth of private fortunes sufficient to achieve these desireable results in another way."[3] Downing's commitment to republican sharing-in-common is echoed by early park enthusiasts, such as Clarence Cook. "The Central Park is the pleasure ground of the chief city in a great republic. It has not been set apart by any privileged class . . . but is the creation of the whole people . . . for their enjoyment, and with a large hospitality, they invite the rest of the world to share it freely with them on equal terms."[4] Cook went on to note that the cooperative character of the park is emphasized by its various entry gates, named to honor diverse occupations and classes (immigrants, farmers, merchants, women, seamen, and so forth).[5] It may be a bit hard to realize that public facilities welcoming all social strata was once a novel idea.

A second function served by the park was to afford the opportunity for mingling among those of differing economic classes and cultures. Were such interaction to occur in a benign recreational setting in which amicable cooperation by all would be of benefit to all, it would hopefully encourage the kind of orderly goodwill and toleration of differences essential for republican practice. To this end, drives, walks, paths, and commercial passageways were constructed in and through the park at different levels; they cohered by an ingenious system of tunnels and bridges. This remarkable innovation allowed a free flow of different types of traffic, and it enabled people of all social stations to make common use of the park in each other's presence without interfering with one another. In this instance the symbolism was obvious.[6]

Hanging over the entire operation of Central Park was a novel ideal in the history of republics: if diverse people showed a modicum of consideration for each other in spite of personal or class differences or aims, and if under such circumstances all could sense the benefit derived from the orderly use of a large landscape, then they might carry such benevolence over into the daily functioning of other, more fractious republican institutions. In Olmsted's words:

Consider that the New York [Central] Park and the Brooklyn [Prospect] Park are the only places in those associated cities where, in this eighteenth hundred and seventieth year after Christ, you will find a body of Christians coming together, all classes largely represented, with a common purpose, not at all intellectual, competitive with none, disposing to jealousy and spiritual pride toward none, each individual adding by his mere presence to the greater pleasure of all the others, all helping to the greater happiness of each. You may thus often see vast numbers of persons brought closely together, poor and rich, young and old, Jew and Gentile.[7]

Cooperation and corruption, sharing and selfishness, decency and mendacity, common wealth and private avarice—these are the polarities within which the republican mythology was always articulated.[8] In this dramatic schema, Central Park served as both a monument and medium of indoctrination for the new democratic masses. It held out the promise that republican ideals could contribute to the pursuit of the general public happiness.

In addition to instilling pride and providing opportunities for harmonious social interaction, a third, more comprehensive element of republican virtue was associated with the park's design. The park's amenities, including space and vistas, hygienic facilities, natural beauty, and educational features, items all formerly the exclusive possessions of the propertied classes, were reminders to the working classes of their entitlement to the better things in life. Space, for instance, was equated with a sense of freedom. People who could lift their eyes to a panoramic horizon could give range to their vision and thus lift their spirits and aspirations for liberty.[9] Devices for hygiene had similar connotations in this period. The contrast between the discomfort, filth, monotony, poverty, and squalor of urban tenements and the order, sanitary wholesomeness, and natural abundance of a well-regulated republic was a Victorian aesthetic commonplace.[10] To emphasize this benefit, fountains with fresh running water, bathing and exercise facilities, meandering paths for leisurely strolls, even gazebos where a family could sleep to escape the summer heat, were strewn throughout the park.[11] Again, the emphasis was on the ready availability of such facilities for the common person.

Of course, the age of Darwin and Ruskin was fascinated with natural science, whose pursuit had until then been largely the hobby of nobility. Central Park was an ideal place to popularize the close observation of natural phenomena—flowers, plants, soils, animals—in what was at the time a reasonably natural setting. Efforts were made to satisfy botanical and biological interests with provisions for a zoo, a dairy, a greenhouse conservatory, a modest natural history collection, and the planting of a generous assortment of clearly labeled botanical specimens.[12]

But the park's aim was not primarily pedagogical, nor was such education as might occur intended to take a didactic form. The park's foremost goal was to ennoble its users through recreation.

The great danger is, lest the Park should come to be looked upon merely as a place wherein are collected, a large number of curious and rare, or pretty things, which . . . is not proper to a park. A park is a place of rest and recreation for mind and body; and while nature soothes and tranquilizes the mind, and thus gives the body the repose it needs, pretty objects, merely curious or pleasing, distract the thoughts and fret the nerves.[13]

Clearly, the sort of recreation envisioned was not the escapism of *panem et circenses*. The park invited serendipitous learning about natural science as a side effect of its primary purpose: to engage the visitor's body and soul in pleasurable rediscovery of the freedom that was natural to man, and through this realization, to evoke in everyone a common civic pride and a sense of the satisfactions afforded by life in public institutions. What was intended was no less than to inculcate a passion for republican virtue.[14]

Moreover, the park served as a continual reminder of another tenet central to republican virtue, common sense. The twin objectives of the park's design were to encourage in the public a consensus on the character of natural beauty and to rehearse them in judicious social conduct. The ability to educate morals presupposed the individual's cultivating a sensuality that took judicious account of public opinion. Indiscriminate indulgence in any and all pleasures led to the vice of preciosity; it rendered the individual unfit to be truly cultured—that is, to be entrusted with the care of the civic legacy. In contrast, moral sentiments, the appreciation of community standards of beauty and pleasure, were more likely to be on the whole more genuinely gratifying. Since they integrated sensuality with prudential judgment and respect for public taste, such sentiments on matters aesthetic prefigured the *sensus communis* presumed by political activity in a republic.[15]

Readers familiar with eighteenth-century aesthetics will recognize here the influence of the notion of *taste*. Central Park, along with public education, represents an early large-scale application of taste to universal moral uplift. The park set forth the natural ideal, and it offered all visitors the opportunity to cultivate their sensibilities and rehearse their conduct in public. Henceforth, "good taste" would no longer be the monopoly of a privileged few of society. The trustees of taste would be determined neither by birth nor rank, but only by their capacity to set aside narrow interest and personal preference in favor of a cultivated sensitivity to that which was "naturally" beneficial.

The form and substance of Central Park were thus meant to address republican aspirations. The question that remains is, what features of the republican heritage suggested to nineteenth-century democrats that a park was an appropriate instrument to promote civic virtue? Since evolution of the public park from its origins in the Italian Renaissance is well documented, another detailed chronicle of those developments is unnecessary.[16] What is lacking in the welter of documentation on the historical record is the Rosetta Stone provided by rhetorical theory, the set of principles linking the garden's symbolic code with the visitor's experience. Our task is to look to the rhetorical dimension to examine how the tradition of park design came to surmise that character traits, such as pride, cooperation, dignity, and common sense, could be instilled and enhanced by visiting a garden landscape. To investigate this development, we must reach back to the Italian Renaissance and beyond to the murky beginnings of Western culture in ancient times. There we may discern the establishment of the iconic vocabulary and the celebratory rituals that became the foundation for republican political practice.[17]

The Rhetorical Arts

The confluence of garden artworks, celebrations, and republican *virtu* came about under the sway of Renaissance rhetorical theory. Renaissance thinkers saw close affinities among the rhetorical, poetic, and visual arts. In the Middle Ages the arts were classified by a three-tiered hierarchy. At the top were those arts that appealed to reason (grammar, rhetoric, logic). The lesser poetic and imaginative arts, which imitated the sensate world, occupied the middle. Because they were both carnal and sensory, the musical and visual arts, considered the basest of art forms, resided at the bottom of the hierarchy. The Italian Renaissance tended to dissolve these hierarchical distinctions, and the verbal, visual, musical, dramatic, and political arts drew substantially from each others' theories.[18]

The blurring of distinctions among the arts was justified using the

cryptic Horatian formula *ut pictura poesis* ("as is painting so is poetry"). It was ordinarily glossed to read, "Painting is mute poetry
and poetry a speaking picture." This rubric gave Renaissance practitioners of one art form—architecture, for instance—license to
appropriate other arts such as sculpture or painting or poetry.[19]
Typical of the trading back and forth among art theories was Leon
Battista Alberti's *Della pittura*, a 1436 treatise on the application of
perspective to painting. Not only did Alberti define painting as a
liberal art, an unusual claim for the time, he also drew specific
comparisons among painting, poetry, grammar, rhetoric, and logic,
including them all in the general purview of eloquence.[20] Highlighting the interrelationship of the arts, Alberti called on the theoretically grounded painter to associate with orators, because they would
provide him with subject matter and arrangement schemes for his
compositions.[21]

In all such discussions rhetorical theory integrated and gave status
to the other arts. Thus, emerging art forms, such as civic pageants,
the emblem arts, architecture, masques and carnivals, mime arts,
and rulebooks for courtesy and etiquette, all borrowed liberally from
standard rhetorical canons. Indeed, rhetoric served as a wellspring
for more than the decorative arts. Its influence was felt throughout
the domain that would come to be called "the humanities."[22]

When the early humanists wanted a term to describe themselves as a class . . . the
word they generally used was *orator*, or occasionally *rhetoricus*. . . .[23] By this they
meant not that they made a living by the teaching or practice of oratory, but that
they wished to be known as men of eloquence. An "orator" could have made his
career in government, in the Church, in leisured study and collecting, in teaching
or writing or scholarship. He might have written poetry or history. . . . The orator
was, by definition and inclination, a non-specialist.[24]

The blending of arts and letters with rhetoric as the centerpiece
had numerous ramifications. To mention only one, rhetorical
theory and practice was no longer confined to the creators of
artistic works. The liberal arts were both created and consumed
by a public lettered in rhetorical principles. The recognition that
the consumer of art versed in rhetorical precepts found his
satisfaction thereby enriched prompted Castiglione to sketch the
conduct of the gracious courtier as well as the responses with which
the courtier's audience should properly reward his performance.
Similarly, dramatic theorists, such as Castelvetro and Robertello,
bemoaned playgoers' limitations: their lack of memory or imagination and their ignorance of rhetoric hindered their full enjoyment
of theater.[25] In such typical fashion rhetorical theory permeated
much of cultural activity in the Renaissance.

Rhetoric's enfranchisement as the theoretical foundation of the arts and letters resulted at least in part because the Renaissance arts performed rhetorical functions. Since Cicero's day, rhetoric had been synonymous with civic philosophy, the theory of conduct in political contexts. In contrast to neo-Aristotelians, who saw rhetoric as a technical or "rational science" of communication, Ciceronians, the bulk of medieval and Renaissance authors, saw eloquence as the engine that gave force to political and moral action in public affairs. Rhetorical works consequently became organs to express standards of socially appropriate conduct; they acted to inculcate in the public the mores (*virtu*) necessary to sustain the political fabric. In a word, by legitimizing community mores through their display, rhetoric "civilized" the citizenry.[26] And all arts which contributed to this task of publication joined with rhetoric in a reciprocal alliance with political affairs.

State and church supported the arts, and artistic patronage became an arm of government. Visual arts especially benefited from the union: beguiling impressions were thought to have the most powerful impact on the minds and passions of those classes most likely to be unruly because they had the smallest stake in the republic's security and prosperity. In return for support, the arts were expected to validate church and state. Hence, state and religion came to employ beauty as a political tool.[27]

However, artistic patronage suggested nothing so simple as bribery of artisans or propaganda. Artistic sanctioning of established institutions undeniably involved celebration of the prevailing political powers. This was most blatant in Venice, where commissioned art was an implement of policy; the political ethic celebrated in the art accentuated obedience more than it did communal pride or responsibility. But evidences of art's role in promoting the status quo pervaded Renaissance Italy.[28]

And this artistic validation was neither craven nor casuistic. Artists, rhetoricians, and humanists of all stripes saw themselves joining with statesmen, clerics, and moralists in the exaltation of virtue; and the *virtu* of all citizens consisted in their display of civic pride through their works and deeds. To pay tribute to the glory of the *civitas* which was their common home, to show gratitude for the *beneficia* of the people's good fortune in sharing a blessed republican life, and, not least, to harbor a taste for the public glory an urban audience could grant in its delight with their works, these were honorable civic activities.[29] So it was that all arts were valued whose practice contributed to the beauty, honor, and fame of the city.

Especially prized were those arts which fashioned arenas and theaters in which individual civic virtuosity might appear and be displayed.

The setting of civil life . . . embraces the "magnificence of spacious edifices," the dignity of the magistracies, the solemnity of divine worship and the spendour of living of the private citizens. City walls, "sacred temples," private dwellings, "by which the dignity of man is appropriately embellished," squares, bridges, ceremonial processions and religious observance, which "makes the city more magnificent when it is celebrated marvelously and solemnly," should all combine to form a proper stage for the exhibition of the civic virtues.[30]

Alberti was among those who advocated the construction of places for public gathering and activity as part of every urban plan. "The People, by thus meeting frequently together at publick Feasts, might grow more humane, and be the closer linked in Friendship one with another. So I imagine our Ancestors instituted publick Shows in the City, not so much for the Sake of the Diversions themselves as for their Usefulness."[31] There was a consensus that the architecture of a city contributed to its social life, expressing its dignity and aspirations and serving as a constant reminder of the rewards of shared communal action.[32] The "stages" thus produced by artworks held in common were nothing less than the body of shared memories, attitudes, and references that comprised the common sense of the community.

Eloquence was essential to the texture of the Renaissance *sensus communis*. It contributed materially in constituting the platforms where people gathered to socialize. It also comprised the product they displayed therein, the symbolic validations which demonstrated the vitality of that network of "theatrical" ties known as meaningful communal life.

Ritual transformed anger and individuality into friendship and community. Participation forced unity upon participants by committing them to the public show of solidarity with their . . . group or person and with the saint. They then spent the next year living up to the public actions. . . . Just as form generated such inner states in private relationships, so it did in public ritual.[33]

In both cases, the Italian city-states made pervasive use of rhetorically grounded civic arts to promote the harmony of their institutions and to reinforce republican principles.

Lauro Martines summarizes the ways in which eloquence, in alliance with political power, enriched the spirit of common sense and republican consenses in a typical instance, Florence.

1. In a time of great political and social distress for Florence, guilds and patriciate plunged into the vigorous support of major commissions. . . . All were produced

or started in an atmosphere of civil tension and fiscal sacrifice, and all involved the civic pride of the Florentines, who soon boasted about them.

2. Using the dignity of the state and exploiting traditional animosities such as against Pisa and Lucca, the ruling group sought to unify Florence, while being itself often divided in its views of foreign dangers, taxation, and the Florentine middle classes. The result . . . was an ideology of militant republicanism with a note of universality. . . .

3. Florence was caught up in the fusionist process of having recourse to ideals that seemed to overcome rifts in the body politic and served to defend the community from external threat. Artists also were caught up in the civic fervor.[34]

So artists generated symbols for the benefit and glory of the state: to remind the citizenry of its heritage, to encourage through civic celebration pride in the commonwealth and the consensus that supported it, to repudiate potential adversaries and those who would dishonor republican institutions, and to turn the attention of rival internal factions to the advantages of civic harmony.[35]

Renaissance rhetorical works were thus valued for their *civilizing* influence on the body politic. Eloquence was thought to have the power to shape and sustain society, to dissolve bellicosity, fickleness, and obduracy, to rehabilitate the populace into a public at once more gentle and joyous than their lowborn natures would ordinarily allow. Echoing a traditional commonplace, Thomas Wilson articulates this objective when he traces the rise of culture to its origins in eloquence.

Whereas men lived brutishly in open fields, having neither house to shroud them in, nor attire to clothe their bodies, nor yet any regard to see their best avail, these [orators] appointed by God called them together by utterance of speech and persuaded them what was good, what was bad, and what was gainful for mankind. And . . . being somewhat drawn with the pleasantness of reason, and the sweetness of utterance . . . after a certain space they became . . . of wild, sober: of cruel, gentle: of fools, wise: and of beasts, men: such force hath the tongue, and such is the power of Eloquence and reason, that most men are forced, even to yield in that which most standeth against their will.[36]

Boccaccio even sought to expropriate this civilizing power of eloquence exclusively to the poetic arts with the dubious philological argument that the term *poetry* meant "exquisite discourse" in Latin.[37]

The Ends and Means of Celebration

All of the rhetorical functions discussed above employ forms of celebration. The branch of rhetoric devoted to celebration is epideictic. And it was to epideictic that the Renaissance turned to determine how to teach and inspire, how to dispose people to act according to principles of decorum and to derive gratification from looking to the common well-being.[38] Epideictic precepts explained how to glorify and promote, how to render public celebrations so as to achieve desired ends. Wilson again voices Renaissance humanism when he attributes to poetry the supreme task of eloquence, *laudandi vituperandique peritus* (skill in congratulation and reproach).[39] So it is to epideictic theory that we now turn to deepen our understanding of the rhetorical roots of celebration through the medium of garden artwork.

EPIDEICTIC RECREATION

To understand how Renaissance epideictic theory could beget garden art we must digress briefly to contrast Renaissance thought on the matter with the embryonic Greek concept of celebration. This topic has been examined more fully elsewhere;[40] here we need only sketch its outlines and note how the Greek heritage was modified by Roman, Byzantine, and Renaissance theorists. The changes caused a "degeneration" of epideictic which in turn opened it up to new aesthetic possibilities for both the theory and practice of celebration, among them the garden as a medium of epideictic ceremony.

The epideictic category is formalized with Aristotle. For him it is an enactment that conjoins the sense of beholding wonder (*thaumadzein*) that envelopes one privileged to witness the revelation of Being (*alethaeia*). The wedding of these two features, reality's disclosure and the sense of admiring gratitude at what is for what it is, results in a psychological precipitate variously characterized as benevolence, goodwill, expansiveness, jubilation, generosity of spirit.

However we label it, students of celebration realized that when our wonder at what is brims over in elation, we are seized with a desire to testify, to bear witness, to ratify, to give voice to our heartfelt appreciation of what is *as it is*, to put into words what is presented to our consciousness for recognition, without naming, rating, analyzing, or otherwise investigating it.[41]

Such an act of authentic "re-creation" lacks elements of self-display or vanity. Rather, classical pantheism presumed an animistic cosmos, one literally "in-spired" by some primordial breath of life, a cosmos in which being pulsed out to the receptive as a kind of radiance. The orator fortunate to be so touched or inspired by such revelations engages in *emphasis*, a sharing with the community at large his own wonder-at-what-is, at the sheer miracle of human being. Unlike the arguer who forces the audience to submit to the power of cold logic, the epideictic orator charms his listeners. He enchants them so that they, like him, are drawn to embrace reality in a mood of thankfulness at the divine mysteries revealed by the discourse to the contemplative mind.[42]

But a paradoxical ingredient pervades the epideictic experience. Reality, as confronted by the human witness, always exhibits an evasive quality: it concurrently invites recognition and veils or conceals itself. Even as the enigmas of being reveal themselves to the beholder, they are at the same time disguising and withholding themselves from the sacrilege of the brazen stare.[43] Reality is not so much capricious as it is flirtatious. Its luster hints at the full glory of what is, but its modesty affords the spectator only the faintest glimpse of itself before it returns to its origins in oblivion and the taken-for-granted. The insensitive bystander is only brushed by the disclosure. In the headlong rush to file these experiences among the predictable categories of daily existence, he or she ignores reality's call or is at most momentarily puzzled by it, as by a vaguely recalled dream, before thrusting it aside and returning to the comfortable banality of the common-place, the familiar world of convention. What is lacking in such a life is appreciation, the coming together of care for the world and mindfulness of it.

The act of celebration is thus one of memorialization. By words and rejoicing the beholder seeks to crystallize the nobility, the excellence, the sacredness fleetingly revealed. And through his or her voice, the beholder affords that radiance a permanent abode in the world constituted of the sensibilities of the assembled community. To witness the sacred appreciatively is to become enraptured with the *mousike* of a cosmic order as both reciter and listener share in the lyrical spell of recreation.[44] Our "memorialization" is intended neither to meet the ritual needs of a festival nor to reinforce pieties. We commemorate instead the gift of having been privileged to dwell together with and to become custodians of the luminosity that was unexpectedly revealed to us in our releasement. Our task as celebrants is to preserve those precious revelations by committing to memory and to the fabric of our thought what has been illuminated in the testimonial. Our satisfaction in such an encounter is the revitalization experienced by the celebrants in their own reconciliation with "human being" when the beholding is genuine.[45]

EPIDEICTIC REPRESENTATION

When living organisms decay, they often become brittle. A similar fossilization seems to overcome meanings subjected to overuse; they are reduced to empty rituals and clichés. Repetition makes them hollow.

> As soon as speech acts get "passed on" . . . as soon as speech acts are translated from acts in the form "I say that . . . into the forms "It is said that . . ." they undergo a degradation. They empty their meaning, they seem now to articulate a general form of the world and no longer only the singular situation of the speaker, but in reality they function now to cover over and conceal the singular lines of reality.[46]

When celebration loses its essence as a personal epiphany, a gift from the beholder to the community at large, it is often replaced with a more passive, opaque state of mind. Celebration begins to forego recreation in favor of greater representation of the formal components of the ritual.

> It is the fixing of the symbol that makes both a separation from the living insight and utilization of the product of that insight without reactivating it anew possible. When the symbol is reproduced, it, to be sure, reawakens its corresponding significance. But it can do so merely passively. . . . Communication then occurs on the level of the detached symbols, and not on the level of the living insights. It substitutes passive recall for the reactivation of insight. . . .[47]

And with this change, epideictic discourse no longer serves to inspire but comes now to observe and give honor in a detached, even platitudinous spirit. Such, in brief, was the fate of celebration and the epideictic theory that characterized it from the time of the Greeks until the Italian Renaissance.

Succeeding centuries saw the understanding of recreational celebration undergo codification and embellishment at the hands of Greek, Roman, Byzantine, and Renaissance rhetoricians. Taken as a whole, their program changed what was originally considered a divine gift into a *techne* (procedure) whose mastery was open to all. Insofar as it survived, recreational epideictic was increasingly relegated to the realm of mystics; it remained largely outside established religious, political, and educational systems.[48]

Several consequences followed from the demystification and formalization of commemoration. For one, in the gradual coagulation of its artistic rules, celebration as an ecstatic experience gave way to a set of norms thought to govern festivity. Second, the end of celebration became more and more a matter of satisfying evermore complex formulas for proper conduct. Inspiration and recreation were consequently lost sight of, and art became the moral arbiter of conduct.[49] Finally, it was inevitable that these reciprocal processes of erosion and sedimentation should turn epideictic from an experience into an aesthetic, a formal art through which one learned how to behave in rituals. Acting replaced direct involvement. What originated as an effort to penetrate the veil of reality in a spirit of thankfulness and reverence had become, by the Renaissance, rules of etiquette for ceremonies, a code of culturally sanctioned customs. *The* routine became *a* routine, a staged act.

RENAISSANCE REPRESENTATION

J.W. O'Malley has performed a valuable service by constructing a model of the epideictic paradigm that dominated the Italian Renaissance. Six of the ingredients he identifies are of interest for our purposes, for they laid the foundation for the newly developing art of the garden.

First, epideictic shifted from meditative activity to a form of display oratory. As with much modern entertainment, artful construction of a ceremonial address came to be almost an end in itself. The listener was reduced to a passive role. His function was to enjoy the beauty of the oration rather than to affirm his own recreation.[50] In its inception, as already noted, the epideictic experience was the commonly shared moment of appreciation of human being. Such display as existed was incidental to the subject's luminosity; both performer and listener entered equally into the rejuvenating enchantment. The rise of formal *techne* for the ceremonial genre shifted focus to the artistic qualities in the discourse that induced pleasure in the audience. Far from disappearing unobtrusively behind his work, the artist was seen as the genius of the work's radiance.

Second, epideictic became more dogmatic; prior agreement with the orator's claims by the audience was assumed. Correspondingly, because the orator sought to intensify attitudes already held and to evoke them more vividly for the celebration, controversial or provocative assertions were avoided. In their place trite, widely held bromides (often hortatory in tone) were refurbished.[51]

Third, the religious use of illustrations in sermons influenced secular epideictic practice. Because epideictic oratory was a mainstay of ceremonies, there was seldom an immediate "inspiring" event to relate. Orators were obliged to warm over miracles, such as Christ's resurrection, that were probably familiar to auditors only through previous rehearsals of the narration. The task was to vitalize incidents that were widely known but nevertheless not experienced at first hand. A common strategy was to compare the events with similar ones and rate them. As a consequence, epideictic tactics once intended to promote appreciation for reality (what *is*) came to take on a prescriptive character, recommending what ought to be and repudiating what ought not be.

A body of historical materials (*res gestae*) grew up to facilitate such comparisons, as did a repertory of illustrations (*istoria*) that could be used to highlight the importance of the memorialized deeds.[52] The incidents being amplified thereby took on the character of Aristotelian examples: They were literally "paradigms," exceptional instances that stood so far afield from ordinary events that they could serve as guides to ideal conduct. Stories told in a recreational setting become the stuff of legends; when such stories must serve as well to instruct and uplift, miracles must predominate. Where once epideictic had emphasized a sense of beauty and meaningfulness, it now also reviewed catalogues of virtue. Almost as a by-product of the exemplars used to illustrate, ceremonies turned from the act of embracing what *is* and trained the audience to submit to the authority and moral superiority of what once *was*.

A fourth element in this rhetoric was its elevation of its audience by stimulating in them the will to feel beneficent emotions. This seeming paradox (to "will" to feel a certain way) depended on a notion of psychological interlinking between discourse and auditor. Through lively retelling of a subject, the speaker created a gift for the audience. As with other gifts, the appropriate response to the bestowal of the *ars laudandi* were feelings of gratitude and pleasure at the gift as gift. From the evocation of these feelings, it was a short step to *imitari*, the desire to imitate what is enjoyed, in this case the epideictic lesson. In turn, the impulse to emulate engages the will: the listener resolves to act more virtuously. O'Malley sums up the process rather well.

> The "perfect epideictic" will be an oration whose purpose is to evoke sentiments of admiration, gratitude, and praise, which in turn will lead to a desire for imitation. The materials most appropriate for exciting such sentiments are great deeds . . . presented to the listener in the most visual and graphic fashion possible . . . and made relevant to the lives of the listeners. . . . The high purposes of epideictic mean that its vocabulary and syntax will be dignified, but its congratulatory mood allows, even enjoins, at least moments of lyric.[53]

Note that O'Malley, perhaps sensing some lack in this account of arousal, speaks of sentiments rather than feelings. In all likehood this psychological theory was one for the invoking of sentiments, fabricated emotions, in the absence of direct involvement in the events being memorialized. In any case, the potential of moving an audience from lively entertainment to a resolve to act in certain ways abides in the contemporary fear of pornography and televised violence.

Fifth, the psychological account of how *istoria* mediated to move the auditor's soul depended upon the special interior and detached viewpoint the auditor was conceived to hold. Ceremony had once sought to bring the participants closer to reality; historical factors too complex to trace here now worked to detach celebrants aesthetically and emotionally from direct experience. What matters for our purposes is that detachment prompted a *visual* mode of consciousness.

> Epideictic wants as far as possible to present us with words and deeds . . . *for viewing.* The epideictic preacher consistently invites his . . . audience . . . to "look," to "view," to "gaze upon," and to "contemplate." . . . "Look," demands Lodovico da Ferrara, the Dominican procurator general, "for I cannot *explain.*" What is at stake is clearly seen in the meaning which the verb *contemplari* always conveys in the epideictic context. It never means "to think" or "to consider" or "to meditate." It always means "to gaze upon."
>
> These verbs of seeing relate directly to actions and deeds. Though one may eventually reflect upon an action, one must first see it with one's own eyes or hear it described in words.[54]

In its genesis, epideictic opened its audience to a replenished sense of human being. In its evolved form, epideictic amplification internalized the discourse in imagined experience nested in the auditor's soul.[55] For the pantheist, who believes himself at least potentially at one with nature, celebration is a kind of welcome home. For the Christian, whose soul is a filter and precondition of moral action and whose body is a relentless enemy of the soul, ceremony enlisted a passive, visual imagination. In the new psychology of detached cognition, the effective ceremony induced a state we might today call reverie. Where once *phronesis* (readiness for judgment and prudential action) held sway in human affairs, the new psychology exalted self-consciousness. Its external manifestation was *maraviglia* (delighted astonishment), a yearning to be impressed.[56]

The sixth and final feature of this epideictic model that concerns us pertains to the metaphysics underlying the ceremonial enterprise. For the Greeks, reality was a tantalizing luster that called forth acknowledgement. Renaissance epideictic had at its core a *faith*: beneath external enigmas in the apparent world, the earthly universe was governed by coherent, harmonious forces. Epideictic was in fact a mode of inquiry that functioned to make intelligible the divine cryptogram that is the world. Reality was no longer flirtatious; it had become God's message. Although it remained exceedingly perplexing and fraught with obscurity, reality was knowable in principle to the believer.[57] Ceremonial discourse sought to decode facets of this mystery to display the "loving connectedness" by which God linked the Christian to every other constituent in his universe. Epideictic theory, along with its newly devised implement, the emblem book, proffered iconographically suitable symbols and forms to decode the clouded or forgotten wisdom thought to be contained in community ritual. The task was always to confirm the faith that being and appearance, while distinct, were nonetheless parallel. One had only to know how to decifer the enigmas that constitute appearance to affirm the eternal truths of God's will. Thus did disclosure become doctrine.

Here in sum are the six characteristics prominent in Renaissance epideictic theory that were to give rise to the main rhetorical aspects of public garden art:

1. The discourse itself exhibited pleasing traits apart from the holiness of the subject being discussed.

2. Ceremonial discourse avoided controversial topics. It concentrated on rehabilitating and making vivid commonly held memories regarding the subjects memorialized.

3. Rhetorical devices such as *ekphrasis*, were used to produce "paradigms" of excellence, beauty, and virtue. These exemplars in turn served educational and moral aims; they affirmed conventional morality.

4. When the "gift" of epideictic depiction was effective, it entertained. That is, it triggered sentiments as well as a desire to emulate the worthiness of the subject of the celebration.

5. Memory, formerly the keystone of epideictic mental faculties, was partially eclipsed by visual imagination as the synthesizing agent. The extension of the interior mental landscape and the enhanced legitimacy of self-consciousness widened the rift between mind and matter. Instead of reconciliation, epideictic now acted to represent reality in the plenum of the auditor's soul. In turn, the socially appropriate response of discourse that bridged this chasm was to marvel at the rhetorical spectacle displayed.

6. The foregoing rhetorical activities were meaningful in the context of a universe that was itself intelligible and ordered. In a cosmos of apparent paradoxes, epideictic was a means of inquiry that uncoded the appearance of things and made comprehensible

the innate harmony linking the parallel domains of the divine, the earthly world (i.e., deeds, flesh), and the universe of discourse.

To this point I have argued for the centrality of rhetoric in the Renaissance scheme of the arts. More particularly, I have claimed that epideictic ministered as a theoretical cornerstone for many of the arts which had ceremonial or entertainment functions. I have also traced briefly epideictic's origins as a communal means of recreating human being's commemoration. It is obvious that those lofty beginnings were eroded by centuries of technical refinement in rhetorical theory. Intent on penetrating the festival experience in a rude search for formulaic explanations that would assist in the composition of ceremonial utterances, pedagogues succeeded in codifying procedures but transmuted the nature of epideictic from a recreative to a representational art. Their quest culminated in the Italian Renaissance's elaborate rules for managing ritual.

We are now in a position to specify with more detail the influence of epideictic theory during the fifteenth and sixteenth centuries in the emergence of an art dedicated to glorifying republican political ideals through the medium of the garden and the park design.

Repose

The garden as an art form is a creation of the Italian republics. Although the ancients (among them Plato, Cicero, Virgil, Longinus, and Saint Augustine) had known and commented on the bucolic pleasures, it fell to the Florentines to turn gardening into a fine art with political overtones.[58] In 1417 Cosimo de Medici had purchased a country house at Careggi and set about improving its grounds; but although Careggi was ostensibly designed as a retreat from the pressures of Florentine business and social life, by Lorenzo's time, it would become a gathering place for lively conversation. A circle of talented individuals—including Marsilo Ficino, Giovanni Pico della Mirandola, Poliziano (the Medici family tutor), and the artist Giorgio Vasari—was known to gather in the garden with some regularity to enjoy companionship, wine, and stimulating discussion. Soon thereafter (around 1440) the nobleman Luc Pitti commissioned the architect Brunelleschi to build for his Pitti Palace across the Arno from Florence a grounds that would a century later (1550) be adorned with one of the most magnificent landscapes of the age, the Boboli Gardens.

Finally, in 1458 Giovanni de Medici, Cosimo's younger son, engaged Michelozzo to build what was to become the first recognizably modern garden as part of a new villa at Fiesole. By now the craze in garden planning had taken firm hold in Florence. Soon after, it spread to Rome and thereafter, well into the sixteenth century, the fashion for garden artwork spread swiftly throughout Italy.[59]

The rapid development of the art form, with little or no foundering, suggests that it was drawing its principles whole from other art theories rather than groping by trial and error for its own aesthetic. Inasmuch as rhetoric was an acknowledged reservoir for art theory of the time, it is reasonable that artists would borrow from rhetoric to aid them in the new medium of the natural landscape.

One of the clearest rhetorical extensions relates to the purpose for which gardens were ostensibly built: to provide convenient shade from the midday Mediterranean sun.[60] Yet shade and cool breeze could be achieved by several means. Latent in this aim was a larger rhetorical ideal, the Ciceronian *utile dulci* (both useful and agreeable), the orator's practical need for relief from the physical and emotional fatigues of daily affairs. In contrast to mass culture's idea of rest as distraction, the Romans sought a particular sort of leisure, the repose of *otium* (tranquility). The goal of *otium*, to restore the man of affairs to a condition of mental contentment, was well served by a bucolic spot filled with reminders that the dweller was momentarily without occupation.

Orators needed temporary respite from the cares of events, not to rest but to rejuvenate themselves. Hidden from public view behind wall, fence, trees, and shrubs, even the cloistered monk had relished the solace and temporary suspension of responsibility signaled by earth, plant, and water. These pastoral reminders of life outside the city had traditionally acted as an invitation to inconsequence. Unobserved, the restraints of everyday decorum could be relaxed, and the garden dwellers might put themselves at ease.[61] Repose had metaphysical significance. It was not a matter of killing time. The garden revitalized its user for a return to public activity. Thus, the rhetorician Pico della Mirandola astutely remarked on the good fortune of one who could repair the breach between physical and spiritual self by temporarily setting aside public business to dwell in a holy shrine amidst sacred groves.[62] Nor was the garden's purpose tied to the Greek notion of *paedaeia* (active leisure); gardening itself was labor, not leisure.

Here we are reminded of a major distinction between Greek and

Renaissance epideictic theory. For the Greeks, restoration consisted of opening oneself to an intensified awareness of reality. For Renaissance Christians, it demanded calling forth interior resources in the solitude of a meditative moment.[63] Such recuperation was focused inward; it required a carefree place where one felt free to rid oneself of the anxieties that disrupt the mind and hinder the capacity for true eloquence. The place best suited to achieve this effect was one decorated with symbolic reminders, to which we shall shortly turn, of the essential fecundity and mercy of the world.

Rhetorical Sensibility

Had gardens given the orator only escape from daily cares, they would hold no more interest than their prosaic descendents, weekend "change of pace" escapes to resorts. But an age which esteemed rhetorical conduct treasured the garden, and later the park (from the Persian *paradise*—"pleasure place"), for its promotion of what we might call rhetorical sensibility.

Renaissance thinkers saw the landscape as potentially a living mirror of human consciousness. Thus, Petrarch drew the parallel.

In this function of reflecting the soul, nature itself possesses . . . reflected reality. Nature is not sought and represented for its own sake; rather, its value lies in its service to modern man as a new *means of expression*, for the liveliness and the infinite polymorphism of his inner life . . . [L]andscape loses its independent value and its own *content*. The feeling for nature . . . becomes the mere foil for self-awareness . . . Nature cannot be understood, felt, and enjoyed *per se*, but only as a dark or light background for the Ego.[64]

So too was architecture prominent in the period as a discipline that displayed the parallels between human *arche* (excellence) and constructed shapes.

A building is a model both of the human intellect and of the cosmos. Designing and erecting a building helps us understand the way we think and act. These activities also help us understand the way God thought and acted when he created the universe and mankind . . . By imposing mathematical form on matter, whose natural state is formlessness, man imitates God and struggles against what might be called the entropy of material creation . . . [O]ne might even define civilization itself as man's making an architecture out of a chaos.[65]

Similar functions were served by palaces, monuments, and loggias.[66]

The paradox of rhetorical sensibility is that it inevitably entails a "give-and-take" of mutual influence: the orator influences the audience by adapting to it. The Renaissance garden also fostered mutual dependence. The garden exhibited its owner's mastery or "domestication" of his property in much the same way as artists of all sorts were expected to master their materials for poetic ends.[67] But equally important was how the garden replenished its users and restored its owner's mind and spirit to a condition fitting his station. "The garden models the way in which the mind conceives its relation to the world external to itself; but gardens . . . become arenas in which the externality of the world is at least temporarily overcome, a truce proclaimed in the continual battle between the shows of things and the desires of the mind."[68] The effective oration was supposed to mirror the general structure and working of its auditors' thoughts. By the same token it would of necessity mirror its creator's mind as well. So it might be with the semiotics of the book of nature as represented in the garden.[69] This fabricated earth symbolized the interior landscape. Its ensemble of icons operated on our soul, according to Comito, in the same ways as does the sweetness of effective rhetoric.[70] To this end, a stroll through the garden landscape became a metaphorical journey of instruction in how one might, by "imitating" the garden (that is, by comparably arranging and tending to one's own mind), guarantee an interior peace and satisfaction like that experienced in the senuous terrain of the garden.[71]

By the late eighteenth century, such notions as these would start to be articulated as a distinct discipline of psychology under the influence of Ramus and Locke. But in the Renaissance proper, they were still understood as extensions of rhetoric. It stood to reason that rhetorical theory permeated garden design. "The garden evolved into a series of separate yet interconnected intellectual and physical experiences which required the mental and physical cooperation of the visitor as he moved through them."[72]

Much the same was true of other architectural forms. Cathedrals, for instance, were designed to encourage the worshiper to discover unrecognized inner spiritual resources. And because the garden incorporated the ultimate worldly matter (earth, water, atmosphere, life), it was a richer place to reenact theatrically (in imitation) the experience of one's interplay with the world. At the same time the emblem system it made available furnished an "ideal temple of the human mind."[73]

The contrast between Renaissance and medieval gardens is instructive. The medieval gardens were largely turned inward, ordinarily consisting of a small interior or cloistered space with an encircled or protected perimeter.[74] The Italian Renaissance garden turned outward to face, subdue, yet remain adapted to and on harmonious terms with its surroundings. Hence, villa gardens often merged inconspicuously into their "natural" environs. They opened outward like ripples of water, progressing from more formal and obviously artificial arrangements near the villa and gradually spreading into less formal, more natural features toward the edges of the property.

The garden thus illustrated the quest for the bridge between nature as flesh and those coherent principles of order that underlay it. Such a representation paralleled the "civil" office of those who exercised rhetorical sensibility to repeatedly bring public harmony out of discord.[75] It is no accident that when the dialogue participants in Castiglione's *Courtier* reach an impasse in the conversation, they take refuge in the delights of "delicate breeze and murmuring woods." As they yield to new rhetorical possibilities, their need is to search out the soul's natural tabernacle, union with the cosmos. Properly composed, the landscape can instruct. It holds out to the mind a blueprint for the soul.[76]

Emblem and Allegory as Rhetorical Utensils

The pleasure that attended rhetorical sensibility in the garden was in the main epideictic. The garden dweller was no judge: he neither decided on a course of action nor modified his behavior. In the garden the will was momentarily disengaged and one became a spectator who celebrated the glories of human being.[77] The garden dweller's "task" was to behold and take to heart what the garden disclosed. And what was displayed was the epideictic enigma: revelation of what is coupled with the subtlety of its veiling. This system of seeming contradictions was contained in the emblem code governing Renaissance garden design. To cite but one example from among many:

> Water, and especially the play of water in fountains, becomes . . . the sensible measure of the vitality of the antique world. This intuition is worked out most elaborately . . . at the Villa d'Este, where water playing from the grotto of a many-breasted Diana of Ephesus originally made harmonies on the famous water organ, and streams flowing from a hundred fountains connect the Fountain of Tivoli, where a sibyl pays tribute to the lord of the villa, with that of a reborn Roma Triumphans.[78]

However, where modern symbols tend to be arbitrary (the "corporate logo" acts more as an official seal than a symbol), Renaissance emblems assumed a more talismanic embodiment of the ideas and moods they evoked. In this they remained true to their medieval iconic heritage and its "semiotic of things." "Man-as-body is involved in erotic relationships with God, Nature, and himself—all of which are in some hidden way look-alikes: those who know can discern images of man's physique in all of them."[79] The forms employed bore an idolic character which hinted at the full revelation beneath their display. The *ars emblemata* incorporated a vast substructure of allegorical signification which both represented and was concealed from its audience.[80] As a matter of style, emblem artists, like their medieval forebearers, preferred icons, metaphors, and analogies to direct narrative. In lieu of explicit denotation, the vernacular of all the arts featured an ongoing commentary on the entire political and social fabric.[81]

Two factors contribute to this effort to replicate in symbol the germinal epideictic tension between expression and concealment. For one thing, those who were indifferent to the iconic richness of reality would not, indeed should not, enjoy its disclosure.

Important truths . . . must be concealed from the vulgar . . . not that the vulgar would despise them, but that they would corrupt and distort them. . . . The ancients, by wrapping the kernal of truth in a husk of fable, enabled it to pass unchanged through many minds of various quality. The ignorant could enjoy merely the outer layer, the literal story, the more intelligent and virtuous the moral meaning as well, and the few sages could add to these the allegorical meanings.[82]

Beyond the effort to exclude those who could not fully profit, there was also the entertainment factor, the desire to lend added satisfaction for those equipped to pierce the artwork's membrane of symbolism and uncover its deeper meaning. In this respect, the art represented or "imitated" the primal experience of beholding being as a human being in the cosmos. Hence, decoding the art was in itself pleasurable insofar as it stimulated the imagination. Of course, botanical examples of such symbolic allusion abound. Among other meanings triggered by the presence of a plane tree, for instance, might be reminders of Plato and Cicero discussing the rhetorical arts, the notion of a bachelor (because, unlike the elm, the plane does not support a vine), Christ's charity (since the tree covered the earth with its merciful shadow), virginity (the plane tree grows near water, which in this conjunction might connote frigidity), and an angel's virtue (a biblical reference: "the plane trees were not higher than he" [Ezek. 31:8].[83] So reading garden artwork became a game of "sight and insight."[84]

This dual aim could be achieved because epideictic rhetoric, with its reliance on illustration, invested the particular object or detail with "fabulous" significance. Events were portrayed as exemplars of traits, experiences, or virtues absent the logical proofs demanded of more action-oriented rhetorical genres. Obscure or figurative emblems intimated richer, more fabulous meanings which listeners were prompted to explore along internal "picturesque" mental paths. Which is to say, knowledgeable viewers could engage with their imaginations fables and other allusions presented by the Renaissance garden or discourse. The resultant enlarged and illuminated experiences were known as *picturae*. The attractive surface delighted one and all. But for those literate in the iconic code, delight was a prelude to a process of discovery which culminated in the cultivation of *virtu* (a process based on the importance of being "re-minded" of the vision of ideal virtue) in its recipient.[85]

Examples of this simulation through the imagination abound. Thus, it was common to reproduce in the garden legendary quandaries to vividly "re-present" them to the marveling gaze of the visitor. "A grotto of Venus, symbol of voluptuous pleasure, for instance, is placed in juxtaposition to one of Diana, symbol of virtuous pleasure and chastity. Groupings of opposites such as these made the visitor himself experience the choice of Hercules."[86] Again, gardening manuals of the period remind us that moral precepts pertain to gardens as well as life. "There are always weeds to be rooted out, trees to be 'reformed' by 'good government,' walls to be held firmly against a world of invaders. This is a rigid and emblematic use of nature."[87]

Terry Comito more than most scholars understands that the experience of garden dwelling celebrated a more profound habitation. "What art repairs is not the recalcitrance of matter itself (withered branches or guarded roots), but simply ignorance, forgetfulness of the possibilities the world continues to offer. Many great men . . . have hitherto 'Not known either what to choose, or what to desire.'"[88] Nature's fecundity points to a more copious vision. The garden dweller was led neither to action nor judgment but to a fuller appreciation of potentialities abiding always in the world and his or her own mind.

Thus far I have described the delight available to one who frequented a Renaissance garden as three-tiered. First, the visitor found a temporary repose, a respite necessary to restore the mental calm and sense of equanimity always held hostage to the cares of the world. Second, the semiotic of the "things" of nature ready at hand in the garden—water, soil, rock, tended plant, life, shade, aroma—

comprised an ensemble paradigmatic of a well-ordered, peaceful, beautiful cosmos, a reminder that we might order our souls and minds just as we might our property, and so increase our satisfactions. Third, the garden entertained: one familiar with the iconic code could be drawn into a state of alertness and discovery by the cryptic puzzles adorning the landscape, memorials to the beauty and latent meaning in the world in which we all must make our home. These were three inventional functions served by garden artwork in a republic.

Yet it was not sufficient that a garden excite emotions. To serve a moral function, the garden, no less than any other type of eloquence, needed to stimulate the *appropriate* feelings. And it was to achieve these more specific rhetorical goals that the Renaissance made use of the canons of memory, style, and deployment in ways that proved seminal to both the verbal and the visual arts. So it is to the extension of these three canons to garden artworks that we shall now turn.

Memory and the Two Dimensions of Consciousness

For the Renaissance, the line from passion to moral virtue led through the memory. At least since 1416, when the Florentine town fathers had placed Donatello's freestanding statue of David triumphant over Goliath in the Palazzo Vecchio in anticipation of the visit of a foreign diplomatic delegation, the power of civic-patriotic symbols had been used as an instrument of public policy. Similarly, the well-planned garden was a means of transport to a mental realm where iconic images and moral ideals of nobility and honor were fused with the solder of memory.[89]

The first advantage the garden had in this fusion process, one it shared with pageants and processions and carnivals, was the spectator's movement. As the visitor wandered in the garden, a series of symbolic tableaus were encountered from which one could serendipitously draw meaning. This contrasted with the static condition between reader and text or picture, a situation that smacked more of formal instruction. Walking encouraged contemplation (from *contemplare*, "to gaze" at the marvelous), because it corresponded more closely to the process of rhetorical invention, that mental search in which the orator ransacked the *topoi* (storage bins) of the memory for ideas.

Though planned, such flexible arrangement of material gave the walker wider latitude to grasp the meaning of what was beheld in his or her own fashion. "Any stone or tree trunk or flower can become without warning an appropriate space on which another order of signs supercedes nature's original significance."[90] Instead of forcing the walker's mind to a conclusion (as in a disputation), such highlighting tended to lead him or her toward a more quiescent and personal realization. When we "come home" to Nature, we rediscover our own nature. It was thus no accident that Ficino inscribed the following epideictic sentiment on his garden wall. "All things are directed from the good to the good. Rejoicing in the present you must not prize wealth or desire dignity. Flee excess, flee affairs, rejoicing in the present."[91] Rejoicing in the present, being present to what is as it is, that is the epideictic ideal. Celebration is of itself not abstract. It calls beholders to entertain (hold in their attention) what is presented to them. One must remain present to what is presented or represented.

Because epideictic does not prove, but rather presents, displays, and illuminates, selectivity of material is a vital concern. The rhetorician must capture the topic's essentials in a few instantly recognizable, highly suggestive strokes which concentrate and visualize the totality of the subject's *virtu*. Incomplete or equivocal emblems may leave a residue of confusion for the beholder and dim the subject's glory or brilliance.

Likewise, the garden dweller was expected to move among and pause to gaze at a series of scenes whose mimetic features and continually altered aspects would bring vividly to mind ancient legends and reminders of noble deeds. The initial images ordinarily began with more public or "theatrical" vistas (as in the Boboli Gardens) and gradually became more intimate and fecund as the wanderer moved closer to some *locus amoenus* (pleasant spot) such as a grotto or a *giardino segreto* (trysting place). There the soul, sensitized to the rich implications strewn along the path taken, encountered some such representation of the world's potency and love as a sculpture of Venus. The rapture felt in that spot was the reward for those who had prepared themselves by opening their imaginations to the suggestiveness of the park's delights.[92]

The tableaus and panoramas did not function simply to aid recall. We have all had the experience of listening absentmindedly, hearing words devoid of meaning which we could later spew back by rote. Such absentmindedness is a denial of epideictic celebration; the latter calls for a taking to heart, a focus on the present in the moment. Such hearing is not recall but remembrance. And remembrance is a form of consciousness in which two facets of mind, imitation and association, operate.[93]

Ernst Gombrich takes note of this dual operation in his examination of Renaissance symbolism.

We may call it the principle of intersection—having in mind the use of letters and numbers arranged on the sides of a chequerboard or map which are used conjointly to plot a particular square or area. The Renaissance artist or artistic advisor had in his mind a number of such maps, listing, say, Ovidian stories on one side and typical tasks on the other. Just as the letter B on such a map does not indicate one field but a zone which is only narrowed down by consulting the number, so the story of Icarus, for instance, does not have one meaning but a whole range of meaning, which in its turn is then determined by the context.[94]

Memory: imitation and association; art: verisimilitude and paradigm; conduct: decorum and glory. All unfold in a flash as the two modes of knowledge, mimetic and associational, intersect simultaneously in the mind of the receptive spectator. Verbal discourse may be too clumsy for such knowledge; revelation calls for the gentle *coup*, the loving spirit typical of visual art. "This doctrine of the two modes of knowledge is the correlate of the doctrine of the two worlds . . . Thus seeing becomes, by virtue of its speed and immediacy, a favored symbol of higher knowledge."[95] Perhaps the seeming paradox of activating two such distinct memory trains as these in generating meaning adds to the mystery of epideictic.

On the one hand, the injunction to the artist to "imitate nature" invites him or her to mirror or directly replicate ordinary appearance. Hence the art exhibits resemblances from history and mythology. On the other hand, associational memory has its own logic. Giving the imagination free reign may produce unexpectedly seminal insights which embellish the mental region. This will be especially true of the poetic arts, whose basic aim is acknowledgment and glorification and whose pragmatic correlate is emulation. It appears to have been just such a conjoining of poetic elements, with fragments of idiosyncratic imagery blended into more traditional literary and historical allusions, that have made gardens such as the one at Bomarzo (begun in 1567 by Pier Francesco "Vicino" Orsini, an eccentric retired *condottiere*) so puzzling and bizarre to modern visitors who lack the capacity to read the "text" of the landscape.[96]

Where mimetic images might instruct in the details of conduct, associations can inflame the imagination, filling it with resolution to emulate the glory of virtuous men. This dual mental configuration characterized *marviglia*, the sudden surrender to astonishment, of being overwhelmed with the recognition of one's own partaking in the glory and memorability of human destiny.[97]

Statuary and reflecting pools were of particular help along these dual avenues to remembrance. Statues commemorated ancient or legendary fame. *Fama* means "to be talked about," as in everyday conversation. Statues furthered the fame of their subjects by prompting talk of deeds and virtues that outlasted mortal life. Unlike our modern "celebrity", fame was limited to those items of common knowledge that inspired admiration. Shameful events smacking of notoriety, brazen conduct, or scandal were consigned to silence and oblivion. Typical of this usage are the five paths of the Regio Parco near Turin. The statues alongside each path symbolize the senses (amidst ditches and inclines), the liberal arts, productive arts, mathematical sciences, and theology; each path is a way of life.[98]

Imitation engaged memory by versimilar depiction, portraying in familiar form the commonly known details of the heroic deed. O. B. Hardison sees the artistic sequence of such conventional portrayal as fourfold, roughly paralleling J. W. O'Malley's ordering of the elements of visual cognition needed for celebration.

The poetic hero is usually described as an "image," "pattern," or "example" of virtue. . . . In order to make the "example" attractive the poet clothes it with "magnificence" which . . . can be created by elevated conception or ornaments of style or both. This creation in turn arouses "admiration"—a term which . . . was early associated with literary matters in a discussion by Cicero of the effects of an epideictic speech. Finally, admiration begets "emulation" or the desire to "imitate" the poet's hero by conforming to the pattern of virtue which he exemplifies.[99]

So, artistic representation arouses imitation in the viewer. And since imitation calls forth imitation in response, verisimilitude, the picturesque mirroring of traits in the exemplar, becomes a major artistic ideal. Thus does action become "an act," a noble gesture of the sort that was eventually catalogued in etiquette books.[100]

Pools were another garden feature that enforced memorability. The pool literally mirrored aspects of the garden, including the viewers themselves, in its still water and sometimes in conjunction with shifting shadows. These reflections and silhouettes of particular scenes, at times with reversed or otherwise altered perspectives, were "re-minders" meant to lend emphasis to verisimilitude. They invited the viewers not to disregard what presented itself to them. Reflections and silhouettes petition the visitor to see *through* the appearances to the *nature* being thus manifested. Both depiction (statue) and emphasis (mirror) concentrated the spectator's attention on the enigmas of human being. In their mindfulness they thus bore witness to the true worthiness of glory.[101]

This dual operation of memory combines a political dimension (conventional imitation, resemblance, allegory) and a psychological one (association, suggestion, the urge to emulate). Together, they perform the epideictic function of investing the symbol cluster with significance. They also generate a tension between two stylistic tendencies: the impulse to decorum, order, and restraint, and the impulse to ornament, copiousness, and inspiration. It is in this tension that the Renaissance foreshadows the principle of taste. We turn now to sketch this schema and show how the canon of style expresses itself in the celebration of garden art.

ORNAMENTATION: THE ENRICHMENT OF MEMORY

Copiousness was a Renaissance stylistic ideal. The artist tried to assist nature to augment its variety. All Renaissance arts, therefore, stressed the artwork's surface or facade. Rhetorical theory also laid emphasis on elaborate style through its figurative *colores*. Ornamental variety was employed in both rhetoric and garden design for dual purposes: to make the viewer receptive and to allow for a gradual unfolding of the artist's theme or motif which conformed to the oblique workings of consciousness.[102]

The initial rhetorical phase was ornamental beauty, which attracted the audience. Like modern store window displays, the outer decorative cover enthralled the senses. Once attuned sensually, the auditor's memory would respond to the adornment by envisioning still further embellishment. So did art and recipient join in creating a "story" in space and time.[103]

This flowering of detail which ornamentation elicited from the viewer became especially prominent in the theatrical use of adornment in baroque gardens. There, for instance, broad public spaces devoid of pretty detail contrasted with highly ornamented and formal features close to the villa. As visitors struck by the variation plumbed their memories to complete associational chains prompted by decorations, they became aware of the artifice employed as well as the interior origins of their own contributions to the meaning. Thus did the *colores* both delight spectators and heighten their self-consciousness of the *colores'* conjoint working with their own minds.[104]

Copiousness as a stylistic ideal often entailed a kind of fecund variety, a surplus overflow that suggested the subject's vitality; The garden's parallel for the copious was the fruitful, the abundant; growth and fertility metaphorically reminded the participant of the liveliness of inspiration. Architectural variety contributed to the impression.

Steps and stairways are features intensely alive and varied. There are the stately moving steps of Torlonia and the fanciful steps of Crivelli; there are the ramps of Este that flow down and of Palieri that sweep up to the terrace. In the Vatican the steps are grave and dignified; at Spello yawning and full of laughter. At Tremezzo they echo the ripples playing across the lake.[105]

But the most spectacular ornamental reminder of abundance was likely the artful use of moving water, in cascades and freestanding fountains. Ranging from quiet pools designed for peace and reflection, to trickling basins, to rushing streams meant to create rustling sounds amidst foliage, to the cool splashing effects of fountain sprays, to the "supreme achievement" of a sparkling, roaring cascade.[106]

Comito argues convincingly that Renaissance artists turned the classical rhetorical concept of "place" back upon its metaphorical origins in order to better apply the concept of *loci* to the ideal of a lush and fertile garden.

In the *Orator*, Cicero explains that the places were devised by Aristotle not for subtle analysis but to provide his students with "copiam rhetoricum" (14.46), a rhetorical abundance, which like nature's own—Cicero is here urging the necessity of judgment as well as invention—must be used with discretion: "just as fruitful and fertile fields produce not only crops but harmful weeds, so sometimes from these categories arguments are derived which are inconsequential, immaterial, or useless" (15.48). . . . [T]he real seriousness behind Cicero's gardens . . . [is] a feeling that intellectual action canot be divorced from its cosmic scene and that, if the first is to be communicated, the second must somehow be reconstituted. . . [T]here is in living thought, beyond any conceptual abstraction, some residue of intuition, of vision, and this is what one means by being inspired by the deities of a place.[107]

The notion of rhetorical *loci* thus implies the profusion of a copious mind; it nourishes both the canon of invention and of style. The garden, as the epiphany of consciousness and not merely a repository of data, was intended to replicate that procreative interior and remind the spectator that moods of confusion or depletion can give way to renewal if one searches inventively among the ample resources husbanded in one's soul.

In sacred places man discovers a special bond with the world. But if the royal garden celebrates man's power in this encounter, the enhancement and perfection of his being, in gardens of love the imagination concedes the helplessness of its rapture and the strangeness of its discovery. . . . [S]uch spots are not just conveniences for lovers but incitements to love, centers of a sometimes dangerous power. . . . Circe hopes to persuade the jaded Encolpius, "ambushed in the grass," to feel "the strange insensible power of some god, drawing us together." Calypso's wiles are paradigmatic for such enchantresses, but even without their mediation, the charm of the place itself often serves to melt away all the determination of prudence or fixed intention.[108]

So beneath the topic system there evidently lay a more animistic sense of the potency of place, an energy that can erupt in the abundance and variety of things that flourish in such space. The well-equipped orator made discoveries in the mental inventory of rhetorical invention. The garden visitor simulated that experience of reawakening as he or she explored the garden places containing natural and artificial reminders of a fertile consciousness.[109] Here the canons of invention and style were reunited; in the flash of insight wisdom and eloquence became one.

PERSPECTIVE: THE DIGNITY OF ORDER

Unlimited adornment led to stylistic excess. Copiousness had to be balanced by another rhetorical ideal: decorum, the harmonious and appropriate arrangement of details to lend a proper sense of dignity. Dignity is a necessary precondition for civic life in a republic. The citizens' *dignitas* was the garment of respect that enveloped them when they took part in discourse with their fellows. Like a badge of membership, it was their guarantee that they would be accorded the honor due them as citizens and without regard to matters of personal liking or disliking. Dignity allowed for a certain detached view partitioning who people were in intimate moments from their roles or offices in the company of others.

Gardens expressed these qualities of dignity by using the newly discovered principles of visual perspective. The viewer/auditor needed a certain distance with which to discern the overriding formal pattern governing the profusion of detail.

"The soul is delighted by all copiousness and variety," Alberti says, but copiousness "without dignity" is a "dissolute confusion"; and his prescriptions for villa gardens include, along with suggestions for pavement, statues, and artificial grottoes, rules for the proper order—no random grove—in which trees should be planted. The insistence on both *copia* and *ordo*, on sensuous variety and intellectual precision. . . .[110]

Surrender to participation in nature must, therefore, be balanced with the detachment typified by objective observation. "Order is discovered in the sensuous experience only as we move away from that experience: an order less of *res* than of *verba*. . . . [Peter] adheres more rigidly to the rhetorician's paradigm, rejecting all the seductions of narrative that might sink him in mere repetition."[111]

Submission to the onslaught of adornment is the beginning. If it is to truly commemorate, the surrender must culminate in introspection or withdrawal inward. For it was in one's internal representation that the spectator recognized the formal order paralleled in garden and soul.[112]

Comito cites the medieval monk Basil as one who anticipated the link between gardens and epideictic rhetoric. "You would have thought that all the elements were keeping solemn festival, *renewing*, so to speak *their own natures*. . . . The earth, lately stripped of its adornments by the thieving winter, through the generosity of spring, donned a purple tunic of flowers, that it might not, inglorious in ragged vestments, appear to the young virgin unbecomingly."[113] Comito's gloss on the notions of adornment and order contained in Basil is worth repeating.

The concern is with the renewing of distinctive properties, and it is this concern that defines the import of the garment that is taken on. This whole complex of ideas is in fact embodied and perpetuated in the word with which Basil describes the earth's new robe, *kosmos*, which signifies at once ornament and order, cosmetics and cosmos.

The essential discovery is that to adorn a world is precisely to beworld it, to clothe it in its proper virtues and operations, to bring it to completion. . . . Basil's image of the earth's new garb simply takes advantage of the pun implicit in *kosmos* to represent investiture, as the ceremonial or baptismal assumption of proper dignities. . . .[114]

Cosmic order was typically rendered in the garden by two means: (1) the use of repetition to lend a sense of harmony, and (2) efforts to "fit" adornment to circumstance and mores so as to compose perspectives appropriate for commemoration.

Symmetry was of course a Renaissance hallmark. The garden layout did not follow the terrain as faithfully as it would in later Romantic styles. It sought instead to dominate the landscape, to subordinate it to a unified and harmonious plan. At the very least, the formal gardens, the series of walks interconnecting in complex geometrical patterns, together with carefully trimmed hedges bordering the walks, called attention to the formality of inventional procedures. The orator used intricate topical pathways to inventory possible lines of argument in his or her mind. Similarly, the walker in the Borghese formal gardens, for instance, obtained perspectives from a sufficient variety of directions by following the paths that he or she could inventory the garden's delights comprehensively. Indeed, it was the mark of the "courtly" man of affairs that he would devote just such systematic and detailed consideration to matters of status and decorum in order to prevent elements of the haphazard and unpredictable from dislocating his public conduct.[115]

The ability to alter one's point of view by searching through an inventory of the mental topic system had been a cornerstone of traditional rhetoric. To it the Renaissance added an innovation uniquely suited to commemorative meditation: the capacity to widen the spectators' perspective and to make them aware of the vistas and horizons that deepened their vision. In this regard, the visual arts likely extended epideictic theory in ways that have continued to influence literary and entertainment theory to our own day.

According to Alberti, the core of art was the science of perspective, of the relative order and position of parts in a proportion as they *appeared* in nature. Hence, the artist's province was form rather than substance. The artist did not create nature; he or she illuminated it. When we notice symmetrical order retreating in perspective, we are led to contemplation; our "gaze" is drawn deeper into the subject and our mental "vision" is correspondingly enlarged. Depending upon their relative positions, certain geometrical combinations might prompt corresponding "sequences of emotions and thoughts."[116]

Gardens made extensive use of the new principle to invest their artifices with metaphysical significance.[117] Thus, for example, some pathways might wander in seemingly aimless fashion only to burst forth suddenly onto an exciting panorama. (One such illustration that comes to mind is the meandering ramble leading to the Belvidere castle in the Boboli Gardens.) The walker, like his counterpart in rhetorical invention, might, in the course of his investigation, discover unexpected viewpoints which gave added meaning to objects, locations, and details he might otherwise overlook were he to stick to more conventional paths. The effortlessness and surprise of the discovery only enriched the delight.

Yet novelty was not the criterion of such artifice. What mattered was that the perspective conform to standards of decorum, to what was fitting to the circumstances.[118] In the realm of speech and manners this meant reliance on courtesy books, and conformity to standards of courtliness and correctness. Manley characterizes this principle as "a highly rhetorical conception of human personality."[119] Comparable standards pertained to landscape art. Not all perspectives were of the panoramic variety; other emotions and thoughts called for different sorts of deepened vision.

The *guardino segreto*, the spot sheltering the temple of Venus, was ordinarily hidden by dense foliage from the view of those unaware of its location. The few who found their way there discovered a dark, quiet, secluded space. Its cylindrical perimeter was surrounded by soft, yielding moss growing on rocks over which trickled gentle, dewlike water. In the center of this still clearing stood a statue of the nude Venus. What better place to ripen a romantic vision for a couple coming upon this erotic setting and realizing the full import of the "temple of Venus" rendered before their eyes?

The lover's "desirying" is simply the inwardness of his seeing, the mode of his involvement with the world; and its repetition marks the incremental claims his vision makes upon his behavior. A rhetorician would describe the situation by saying that the stir of potencies . . . is an *argumentum a tempore*. . . . [A]nd the garden argues in the same way. It is not a neutral scene, but a place considered . . . as a probable opportunity, an occasion . . . an invitation to our own imaginations. . . . It is a space alive with potential meanings, a picture that speaks, a place that becomes, quite literally, the *domicilium argumentorum*.[120]

In such a setting, decorum dictated erotic vision and passion. Here the lines from James Thompson's *The Seasons* (1730) rang as true as they would for later inhabitants of English parks:

And all the Tumult of the guilty World,
Tost by ungenerous Passions, sinks away:
The tender Heart is animated Peace.[121]

Although intimate settings were appropriate for intimate passions, it is the grand vista that puts all the works of human artifice into their proper proportion in that enormous sweep of vision that the Renaissance most prized. Oddly enough, decorum prescribed that a fitting reaction to such a vision be melancholy, because one was expected to be reminded by such a perspective of the frailty of human works.[122] "The new art of perspective . . . is a way of looking . . . that discovers the structure of the real immanent in experience itself. . . . Once the only limit is the horizon, one is forced to admit . . . that any "center" is merely subjective. Place itself (*locus*) becomes merely location (*locatio*), the mind's determination for its own ends."[123] The loss of a "sense of place" that accompanied dramatic perspective also transformed the witness into an observer. All that remained of contemplation was cognition. Spontaneous feeling abdicated in favor of a pose, the appropriate sentiment.

Manley's "highly rhetorical" conception of human personality alluded to earlier grew directly out of the new inventional concern for perspective. The Renaissance was an age which held that the emotions *displayed* should conform to what was fitting for the social circumstances and one's station in life ("Keep a stiff upper lip"). Passions performed became sentiments, the handy props in portrayal of status. Likewise, as garden vistas were planned and choreographed so as to achieve the maximum dramatic impact, a curious line was crossed; spectators came to the scene as theater-goers. Their commemoration consisted of expecting to *see* things freshly, to feel them more fully. As the visual arts led rhetorical theory toward increased union with the theory of perspective, the ground was set for the excesses of the baroque.

A Commonwealth of Yeomen

There has been a recent flourishing of scholarly literature detailing the place of rhetorical theory and practice in Italian Renaissance republics.[124] Rhetoric's pervasive influence seems beyond question. More problematic has been the relation between the *vita activa* and the *vita contemplativa,* the civic life and the withdrawn, private, philosophical life. J. G. A. Pocock comes closest to this study's position. The humanist was ambivalent as between action and contemplation; it was his *métier* as an intellectual to be so, and he could practice it perfectly well within the framework of the republic.[125] The parallels between gardens and eloquence lead one beyond Pocock; they suggest that contemplative life was an indispensable counterweight to civic life in the republic. It was thus as necessary to set aside spaces for meditation as it was to build forums if public discussion was to thrive.

Although historical documentation concerning the functions to which gardens were put in this period is incomplete, recent scholarship has uncovered a fair amount concerning the activities in one Florentine garden, the Orti Oricellari on the Via della Scala. From these records it is possible to see something of the epideictic character of the garden and its social activities. It was purchased in 1482 by a wealthy wool merchant and financier, Bernardo Rucellai, who set about developing it (perhaps with some help from Alberti) into what would become by 1498 a renowned gathering spot for a group of important humanists, historians, political figures, and aristocrats. First Bernardo then his son Cosimo and grandson Cosimino hosted these groups, which met off and on until 1522. At that time, several of the younger members of the Orti circle were implicated in an ill-fated republican conspiracy against Cardinal Guilio de Medici, and the meetings came to an abrupt end. Today the Orti Oricellari is remembered due to the fame of one of its visitors, Niccolo Machiavelli; he is believed to have given an initial reading of his play *The*

Mandragola there. He also honored his host, Cosimo, by making the gardens the setting for his treatise, *The Art of War*, and he dedicated his *Discourses* to several members of the Orti circle.[126] The little we know of the garden's layout suggests how well it would have contributed to the epideictic atmosphere and conversation that is alleged to have taken place there.

The garden was praised as particularly cool and shady. Rucellai himself had super-vised its arrangement and had imported a number of rare plants, with an eye to have represented all the species mentioned in classical literature. Along the paths were mounted the busts of famous men of the classical world—emperors, statesmen, poets and thinkers. A summer house and marble benches, placed under the larger trees, invited quiet reading, serious conversation or discussion in larger groups.[127]

Although the exact content of the garden discussions remains vague, most historians are agreed that they were neither idle chatter nor strictly abstract and philosophical in nature. Rather, they combined literature, culture, and political theory in a form that historians unfamiliar with epideictic theory seem at a loss to explain. Thus, Delio Cantimori refers to an oratory of "parade," of ceremony, in which "rhetorical" issues concerning language and discourses are always flung into a political context.

The meetings of the *Orti Oricellari* bring to a close a long tradition in Florence of literary and political conversations. This tradition begins with the talks upon moral, philosophical, and political themes recorded in the *Paradiso degli Alberti* and with the debates upon the relative merits of the active and contemplative life collected in Landino's *Disputationes Camaldulenses*. It . . . finally reappears in a livelier and more insistent form towards the end of Florence's independent life as a literary and religious centre, in the decades which precede . . . the fall of the last Florentine republic.[128]

Groping toward a correct analysis, but lacking the vocabulary of epideictic theory, Cantimori nevertheless intuits the inspirational function of "representation" to inspire and commemorate events and times in danger of fading from the cultural consciousness.

Brucioli, and probably the other young men of the *Orti Oricellari* circle, thus intended to diffuse as widely as possible the study of languages and those subjects of learning which would teach and develop the civic virtues. . . . This aim . . . was similar to that which underlay the training of young citizens in the use of arms, namely, to find a means of educating more and more sections of the people in virtue and thus to give the greatest possible force to the "Republic." In the minds of these young men, who were seriously and passionately interested in philosophical and political problems full of . . . moral enthusiasm for "virtue" so characteristic of humanism, the "rhetorical" style which "makes the best things more beautiful and suppresses the others," became one with that most political of instruments, arms. Rhetoric and politics were for the humanists . . . one and the same thing since both were founded upon ethics. And from these political passions, this ethical and educational enthusiasm, the Florentine humanists and literati returned, towards the sunset of Humanism, to "rhetorical" problems—literary, philological, linguistic—but always with a political preoccupation. The project of achieving the civil and political education of the people.[129]

Felix Gilbert, too, comes close to the mark, although lacking the necessary vocabulary; he resorts to such terms as "idealistic," "ideological," and even "nostalgic." He notes that the Orti discussions went through two stages, the earlier ones given over to establishing general ideals (looking to such norms as the Roman and Venetian republics and employing the method of historical example) for a virtuous republican commune, while the later period was more devoted to application of the ideals to an examination of the contemporary Florentine political scene (which, from this "conservative" viewpoint was in danger of the erosion of republican tradition by de Medici princely ambition). Yet Gilbert stops short of claiming these discussions were deliberative, as they would be were they part of a political conspiracy. Instead, this "expression of aspirations . . . never passed from the stage of nostalgia to that of deliberate planing."[130] And Gilbert also acknowledges the otherwise curious fact that both aristocrats and humanists seem to have been caught up in a kind of "enthusiasm" for republican political ideals. So the conversations worked to commemorate and inculcate republicanism among a diverse social group who shared the "common sense" necessary for the epideictic experience to be meaningful: good will toward one another and an attachment to the common wealth that was their joint heritage in the form of Florentine political and social traditions.[131]

But to recognize the need for distinct arenas for public affairs and repose is not to say that politics and philosophy stood opposed to each other. They were related, and the ground of their relationship was rhetoric. From the time of Aristotle it had been understood that life in a *polis* or republic was fulfilled in direct association with one's neighbors, in conversation. It was also realized that such activity was fatiguing, that rhetoric depleted the individual, deprived one of those "virtues" essential for prudential conduct. "In the civic humanist ethos, then, the individual knew himself to be rational and virtuous . . . knew himself to be a citizen and knew how to play his role and take decisions within . . . a republic."[132] The aim was always "civic humanism," to be a fully human participant in the body politic. Such a condition called for two distinct rhetorical activities: thought and discourse to carry on the public business, and thought and discourse to celebrate life in the republic. It fell in large measure to the visual arts, with their theoretical foundations in epideictic rhetoric, to accomplish the latter task.

So we return again to the rhetorical dimension in garden and park design. The rhetorical goal of the Renaissance garden was epideictic: to enhance the garden dweller's capacity for full participation in the republic. The form given to the garden by the epideictic semiotic emphasized the typically Renaissance interest in representation instead of the more primal search for recreation. This semiotic produced a multi-layered iconic code intended to be suggestive for an exclusive initiated nobility, those leaders and courtiers who were directly involved in civic activity. As such, the code offered only a hollow shell of appeal to the general run of people. As previously mentioned it was felt that "important truths . . . must be concealed from the vulgar."[133]

It fell to such commemorative arts as literature, painting, and landscape design to incorporate the cryptic symbolism in their productions.[134] Whereas ordinary rhetorical discourse is bound by time and context and so needs to express itself in a manner adapted to a parochial audience, celebratory artworks had a wider scope. They endured: as such, they needed to preserve a suitable tribute though their users might bring to the engagement a variety of temperaments and training. The symbolism employed had to ensure preservation of the commemoration, "and when a nation passed through a period of cultural decline and intellectual tradition dies out . . . the fables, still containing their hidden though forgotten truths, would be preserved by the ignorant common people for posterity."[135] Like seeds preserved for a later planting, memorializing artworks carry their meaningfulness forward in aesthetic forms. The art forms, faithfully repeated by later generations that might reverence the past even if they only dimly comprehended it, became vehicles for preserving the significance resting dormant in the iconic code.

This is likely what befell garden design in the eighteenth and nineteenth centuries. Adherents to notions of "good taste" incorporated the old symbols, their significance now largely forgotten, because good taste dictated that an aesthetic heritage entrusted to one generation be passed on to later generations.[136] And it was this republican patrimony of style that ironically was passed through the hands of the despised English aristocrats on to America, the new yeoman's commonwealth. "The agrarian and civic ideal is presented as occupying a 'middle landscape' between the extremes of wilderness savagery and metropolitan corruption. The image of the polis is therefore always in part Arcadian."[137] By remaining faithful to the tradition of garden and park design, the builders of Central Park may well have created better than they realized.

They intended a monument to republican vitality. By hearkening back to a much earlier, long-neglected theory of the relation between gardens and republican practice to determine the formal and material character of the park, they in fact built a monument to and a vehicle for the full scope of republican activity. The original import of the artistic vocabulary used by the park's designers had been concealed amidst the debris of antiquity. Nevertheless, what remained in the aesthetic shards wrenched from their original political context was remarkably appropriate for the needs of a commonwealth now expanded to include its entire populace. It is in this spirit that such institutions as Central Park have much to teach us about the family ties that abide among rhetoric, republicanism, and commemoration.

Acknowledgments

Much of the work for this project was initiated during a 1981 National Endowment for the Humanities Summer Seminar at Ohio State University under the masterful direction of Professor E. P. J. Corbett. Its completion was facilitated by a sabbatical fellowship awarded by Queens College for 1985–86. Grateful acknowledgment is also due Dr. Barbara Waxenberg, whose influence is evident throughout this essay: *volo ut sis*.

Notes

1. J. F. Kasson, *Civilizing the Machine: Technology and Republican Values in America, 1776–1900* (New York: Viking, 1976), 63.

2. Kasson, *Civilizing the Machine*, 143–46.

3. Cited in C. C. Cook, *A Description of the New York Central Park* (1869; reprint New York: Benjamin Blom, 1979), 16.

4. Cook, *Description*, 199; E. Barlow et al., *The Central Park Book* (New York: The Central Park Task Force, 1977), 20.

5. Cook, *Description*, 199; G. Blodgett, "Landscape Design as Conservative Reform," in *Art of the Olmsted Landscape*, ed. B. Kelly, G. T. Gillet, and M. E. Hern (New York: Arts Publishers, 1981), 115.

6. Cook, *Description*, 46–47; B. Kelly, "Art of the Olmsted Landscape," in *Olmsted Landscape*, ed. Kelly et al., 59.

7. E. L. Olmsted, *Public Parks and the Enlargement of Towns* (1870; reprint New York: Arno, 1970), 18. See also Henry James's comments on the popular character of the park as a social experiment, in Barlow et al., *Central Park*, 121; Cook, *Description*, 204.

8. L. W. Rosenfield, "The Terms of Commonwealth: A Reply to Arnold," *Central States Speech Journal* 28 (Summer 1977): 86–91.

9. Cook, *Description*, 73–80; Sir Joshua Reynolds, in *Discourses on Art*, ed. R. R. Wark (1797; reprint San Marino: Huntington Library, 1959), 131–34; C. Thacker, *The History of Gardens* (Los Angeles: Univ. of California Pr., 1979), 230; E. W. Manwaring, *Italian Landscape in Eighteenth Century England* (New York: Oxford Univ. Pr., 1925), 124; Kelly, "Olmsted," 26.

10. See P. Smith, *Disraelian Conservatism and Social Reform* (London: Routledge and Kegan Paul, 1967), 218–32; Blodgett, "Landscape Design," 122.

11. Cook, *Description*, 115–16.

12. Cook, *Description*, 101–7; Thacker, *Gardens*, 235.

13. Cook, *Description*, 81. See also Barlow et al., *Central Park*, 36–42; A. Fein, "The Olmsted Renaissance," in *Olmsted Landscape*, ed. Kelly et al., 100.

14. See E. T. H. Brann, *Paradoxes of Education in a Republic* (Chicago: Univ. of Chicago Pr., 1979), 42–48; Blodgett, "Landscape Design," 112.

15. L. W. Roper, *FLO: A Biography of Frederick Law Olmsted* (Baltimore: Johns Hopkins Univ. Pr., 1973), 136–37; H. Arendt, *Between Past and Future* (1954; reprint New York: Viking, 1968), 215–16; R. Smithson, *The Writings of Robert Smithson*, ed. N. Holt (New York: New York Univ. Pr., 1979), 117–28; J. D. Scheffer, "Vico's Rhetorical Model of the Mind," *Philosophy and Rhetoric* 14 (Summer 1981): 163; H. G. Gadamer, *Truth and Method* (New York: Continuum, 1975), 34; Manwaring, *Italian Landscape*, 150; Reynolds, *Discourses*, 235–40; Fein, "Olmsted Renaissance," 102; H. Arendt, *Lectures on Kant's Political Philosophy*, ed. R. Beiner (Chicago: Univ. of Chicago Pr., 1982), 66–73.

16. See Thacker, *Gardens*; Manwaring, *Italian Landscapes*; A. O. Lovejoy, *The Great Chain of Being* (1936; reprint Cambridge: Harvard Univ. Pr., 1964), 15–16; R. Strong, *The Renaissance Garden in England* (London: Thames and Hudson, 1979); G. F. Chadwick, *The Park and the Town: Public Landscape in the Nineteenth and Twentieth Centuries* (New York: Praeger, 1966).

17. H. F. North, *From Myth to Icon* (Ithaca: Cornell Univ. Pr., 1979), 135–76; H. Caplan, *Of Eloquence* (Ithaca: Cornell Univ. Pr., 1970), 190–95.

18. R. McKeon, "Rhetoric in the Middle Ages," in *Critics and Criticism, Ancient and Modern*, ed. R. S. Crane (Chicago: Univ. of Chicago Pr., 1952), 260–96; G. A. Kennedy, *Classical Rhetoric and Its Christian and Secular Tradition from Ancient to Modern Times* (Chapel Hill: Univ. of North Carolina Pr., 1980), 215.

19. J. Graham, "Ut Pictura Poesis," in *Dictionary of the History of Ideas*, ed. P. P. Wiener, vol. 4 (New York: Scribner's, 1973), 465–68; B. Weinberg, "Castelvetro's Theory of Poetics," in *Critics and Criticism*, ed. Crane, 357; R. W. Lee, *Ut Pictura Poesis: The Humanistic Theory of Painting* (New York: Norton, 1967), 3; R. S. Nichols, *Italian Pleasure Gardens* (New York: Dodd, Mead, 1928), 87.

20. C. W. Westfall, "Painting and the Liberal Arts: Alberti's View," *Journal of the History of Ideas* 30 (1969): 492–505; F. Borsi, *Leon Alberti*, trans. R. G. Carpanini (New York: Harper, 1977), 293; Lee, *Ut Pictura*, 70–71; J. R. Spencer, "Ut Rhetorica Pictura: A Study in Quattrocento Theory of Painting," *Journal of the Warburg and Courtauld Institutes* 20 (1957): 26–44, does us a special service in demonstrating that Alberti's theories were composed in an ambience favoring a rhetorical rather than a poetical basis for all the arts. Spencer goes so far as to trace Alberti's notions to specific Ciceronian concepts, through the influence of his mentor, the noted Ciceronian scholar Gasparino Barzizza of Padua. A similar point is made in passing by E. B. MacDougall, who notes that rhetoric "was considered the proper goal of all forms of art"; "Imitation and Invention: Language and Decoration in Renaissance Gardens," *Journal of Garden History* 5 (1985): 131.

21. Graham, "Ut Pictura," 468. See especially the seminal work by W. Trimpi, "The Meaning of Horace's Ut Pictura Poesis," *Journal of the Warburg and Courtauld Institutes* 36 (1973): 1–34. Trimpi is at pains to set the Horatian formula in its rhetorical context.

22. E. Muir, "Images of Power: Art and Pageantry in Renaissance Venice," *American Historical Review* 84 (1979): 36; M. Levy, *High Renaissance* (New York: Penguin, 1975), 141–46; R. J. Clements, *Picta Poesis: Literary and Humanistic Theory in Renaissance Emblem Books* (Rome: Teni e Testi, 1960), 64–65; T. C. Burgess, *Epideictic Literature*, University of Chicago Studies in Classical Philology, vol. 3 (Chicago: Univ. of Chicago Pr., 1902), 140; W. A. Reborn, *Courtly Performances* (Detroit: Wayne State Univ. Pr. 1978), 28–40; R. H. Brown, "Theories of Rhetoric and the Rhetorics of Theory: Toward a Political Phenomenology of Sociological Truth," *Social Research* 50 (1983): 132; L. Manley, *Convention*, [1500–1750] (Cambridge: Harvard Univ. Pr., 1980), 114; J. W. Holme, "Italian Courtesy Books of the

Sixteenth Century," *Modern Language Review* 5 (1910): 145–66; H. Maguire, *Art and Eloquence in Byzantium* (Princeton: Princeton Univ. Pr., 1981); O. B. Hardison, "The Orator and the Poet: The Dilemma of Humanist Literature," *The Journal of Medieval and Renaissance Studies* 1 (1971): 43; A. L. DeNeef, "Epideictic Rhetoric and the Renaissance Lyric," *The Journal of Medieval and Renaissance Studies* 3 (1973): 206; Lee, *Ut Pictura*, 16–17; Spencer, "Ut Rhetorica," 26.

23. M. Baxandall, *Giotto and the Orators* (New York: Oxford Univ. Pr., 1971), 1.

24. H. Gray, "Renaissance Humanism: The Pursuit of Eloquence," *Journal of the History of Ideas* 24 (1963): 500. See also P. O. Kristeller, *Eight Philosophers of the Renaissance* (Palo Alto, Calif.: Stanford Univ. Pr., 1964), 153.

25. G. Holmes, *The Florentine Enlightenment, 1400–1450* (New York: Pegasus, 1969), 224; Baxandall, *Giotto*, 124–27; Weinberg, "Castelvetro," 351–54; B. Weinberg, "From Aristotle to Pseudo-Aristotle," in *Aristotle's Poetics and English Literature*, ed. E. Olson (Chicago: Univ. of Chicago Pr., 1965), 196–97; J. R. Woodhouse, *Baldesar Castiglione: A Reassessment of "The Courtier"* (Edinburgh: Edinburgh Univ. Pr., 1978), 178–87.

26. O. B. Hardison, *The Enduring Monument: A Study of the Idea of Praise in Renaissance Literary Theory and Practice* (Chapel Hill: Univ. of North Carolina Pr., 1962), 20–21; Vito R. Giustiniani, "Homo, Humanus, and the Meanings of 'Humanism'," *Journal of the History of Ideas* 49 (1985): 189–93; Manley, *Convention*, 38–40; DeNeef, "Epideictic," 225–26; M. B. Becker, *Florence in Transition*, 2 vols. (Baltimore: Johns Hopkins Univ. Pr., 1968), 2:4–16.

27. Muir, "Images," 18,51; Westfall, "Painting," 502–4; J. B. Riess, "The Civic View of Sculpture in Alberti's *De re aedificatoria*," *Renaissance Quarterly* 32 (1979): 1–17; Hardison, "Orator," 38; J. W. O'Malley, *Praise and Blame in Renaissance Rome*, Duke Monographs in Medieval and Renaissance Studies, vol. 3 (Durham: Duke Univ. Pr., 1979), 49; J. B. Spencer, "Introduction," in Leon Battista Alberti, *On Painting* (New Haven: Yale Univ. Pr., 1956), 18–25 J. Berger, *Ways of Seeing* (New York: Penguin, 1977), 83–112.

28. Muir, "Images of Power," 37–42; Becker, *Florence* 2:28–35; R. C. Trexler, *Public Life in Renaissance Florence* (New York: Academic, 1980), 216–23.

29. Reborn, *Courtly Performances*, 30–44; O'Malley, *Praise* 239–42; Becker, *Florence*, 20–23; North, *Myth*, 233; R. Price, "The Theme of *Gloria* in Machiavelli," *Renaissance Quarterly* 30 (1977): 588–631; B. Berenson, *The Italian Painters of the Renaissance* (Ithaca: Cornell Univ. Pr., 1952), 10–11; H. W. Janson, "The Image of Man in Renaissance Art: From Donatello to Michaelangelo," in *The Renaissance Image of Man and the World*, ed. B. O'Kelly, Ohio State Conference on the Humanities, vol. 4 (Columbus: Ohio State Univ. Pr., 1961), 91–97; A. J. Close, "Commonplace Theories of Art and Nature in Classical Antiquity and in the Renaissance," *Journal of the History of Ideas* 30 (1969), 485–86; M. B. Becker, "The Republican City State in Florence," *Speculum* 35 (1960): 39–50.

30. Holmes, *Enlightenment*, 168; E. Muir, *Civic Rituals in Renaissance Venice* (Princeton: Princeton Univ. Pr., 1981), 185–211.

31. Riess, "Civic View," 2–6; L. Alberti, *Ten Books on Architecture,*. trans. J. Leoni (New York: Transatlantic Arts, 1966), 175–82; Price, 608–11; Reborn, *Courtly*, 168–71.

32. J. B. Spencer, "Introduction," 28; Holmes, *Enlightenment*, 170; Borsi, *Alberti*, 326–27; Janson, "Image" 92; E. F. Gombrich, *Symbolic Images: Studies in the Art of the Renaissance* (London: Phaidon, 1972), 8. Castelvetro stands as a rare exception to this moralistic tone; see Weinberg, "Aristotle," 354–55; Trexler, *Florence*, 277.

33. Trexler, *Florence*, 270; Reborn, *Courtly*, 24–29; Nichols, *Pleasure Gardens*, 79; Manley, *Convention*, 49; Janson, "Image," 79; Becker, *Florence*, 44.

34. L. Martines, *Power and Imagination: City-States in Renaissance Italy* (New York: Knopf, 1979), 253.

35. Martines, *Power*, 251–52; Janson, "Image," 87; H. Decker, *The Renaissance in Italy* (New York: Viking, 1969), 32.

36. T. Wilson, "The Arte of Rhetoric," in *English Literary Criticism: The Renaissance*, ed. O. B. Hardison (New York: Appleton-Century-Crofts, 1963), 27. See also Manley, *Convention*, 47; Hardison, "Orator," 34–36.

37. G. Boccaccio, *Genealogia Deorum Gentilium*, trans. C. G. Osgood (1930); reprint New York: Bobbs Merrill Library of Liberal Arts, 1956), 40–41.

38. Boccaccio, *Genealogia*, 32; Burgess, *Epideictic*, 166–67; Hardison, *Monument*, 26–38; V. Branca, *Boccaccio*, trans. R. Monges (New York: Harvester, 1976), 223–27; Plato, *The Laws*, trans. T. J. Saunders (New York: Penguin, 1970), vii, 801.

39. O'Malley, *Praise*, 39: Hardison, "Orator," 36; B. Hathaway, *Marvels and Commonplaces: Renaissance Literary Criticism* (New York: Random House, 1968), 154–57.

40. L. W. Rosenfield, "The Practical Celebration of Rhetoric," in *Rhetoric in Transition*, ed. E. E. White (University Park: Pennsylvania State Univ. Pr., 1980), 131–53.

41. I am indebted to Professor Parke Burgess for clarification of this point in a personal communication, 30 March 1981. See also H. Plessner, *Laughing and Crying*, trans. J. S. Churchill and M. Grene (1961; reprint Evanston, Ill.; Northwestern Univ. Pr., 1970), 71.

42. Kennedy, *Classical Rhetoric*, 67; O'Malley, *Praise*, 49; Hardison, *Monument*, 24–25; O. Barfield, *Saving the Appearances* (New York: Harcourt, 1965), 28–45; M. Warnock, *Imagination* (Berkeley: Univ. of California Pr., 1978), 109; A. Broyard, "Reading and Writing," *New York Times Book Review*, 14 June 1981, 39; K. Dockhorn, "Hans-Georg Gadamer's *Truth and Method*," *Philosophy and Rhetoric* 13 (1980): 177; E. Cassirer, *The Individual and the Cosmos in Renaissance Philosophy*, trans. M. Domandi (Philadelphia: Univ. of Pennsylvania Pr. 1964), 149–51; Longinus, *Peri Hupsis*, trans. T. S. Dorsch (Baltimore: Penguin, 1965), chap. 35.

43. Burgess, *Epideictic*, 96; J. Briggs, "Unshrouding the Muse: The Anatomy of Inspiration," *Art News*, April 1980, 53–55; R. Weaver, *Ideas Have Consequences* (1948; Chicago: Univ. of Chicago Pr., 1976), 26–28.

44. DeNeef, "Epideictic," 228; Levy, *High Renaissance*, 213–14; Hardison, *Monument*, 35; Cassirer, *Renaissance Philosophy*, 159–61; E. Havelock, *Preface to Plato* (New York: Grosset and Dunlap, 1967), 146–53.

45. The intimate connection of commemoration to being accounts for at least some of the confusion surrounding the "art imitates Nature" saw over the centuries. See Close, "Commonplace," 469–80; Cassirer, *Renaissance Philosophy*, 148; G. W. Pigman, "Versions of Imitation in the Renaissance," *Renaissance Quarterly* 33 (1980): 1–32. It goes without saying that the obverse of acknowledgment is, *mutatis mutandis*, disparagement. Where celebration calls men to appreciate reality and become its custodians, invective voices disgust as a way of repudiating evil and cleansing from the communal consciousness the banal, the sham, the frivolous, and the mindless. Thus, the primary epideictic strategies are *both* magnification and minification. The latter is the procedure for making our impressions insignificant and superficial in the scheme of our lives. In this essay I treat the epideictic tactics for glorification and celebration with the understanding that society also employs discourse which fulfills the thankless task of removing the offal elements that would otherwise confuse, distract and clog communal sensibilities. See DeNeef, "Epideictic," 229; Broyard, "Reading," 39; Becker, *Florence*, 9.

46. A. Lingus, "Abject Communication," in *Interpersonal Communication: Essays in Phenomenology and Hermeneutics*, ed. J. Pilotta (Washington: Univ. Pr. of America, 1982), 165.

47. Lingus, "Communication," 167.

48. DeNeef, "Epideictic," 209–11; Hardison, *Monument*, 33; Kennedy, *Classical Rhetoric*, 108–19, 190–215; J. de Romilley, *Magic and Rhetoric in Ancient Greece* (Cambridge: Harvard Univ. Pr., 1975), 9–38; C. B. Watson, *Shakespeare and the Renaissance Concept of Honor* (Princeton: Princeton Univ. Pr., 1980), 71; N. Cohn, *The Pursuit of the Millenium* (New York: Harper, 1961).

49. Reborn, *Courtly*, 184–92; Hardison, *Monument*, 60–61. David Summers offers a splendid case study of the congealing of a single stylistic canon in his "Contrapposto: Style and Meaning in Renaissance Art," *The Art Bulletin* 59 (1977): 336–61.

50. O'Malley, *Praise*, 40; Hardison, *Monument*, 43. Thus Alberti's project for glorifying and propagating "the fame of great exploits" through civic statues; see Riess, "Civic View," 8–9.

51. O'Malley, *Praise*, 64–65; DeNeef, "Epideictic," 220; Maguire, *Byzantium*, 13. A number of striking parallels exist between O'Malley's model and the dogmatism typical of so much contemporary public address. See F. G. Bailey, *The Tactical Uses of Passion* (Ithaca: Cornell Univ. Pr., 1983), 123–43.

52. O'Malley, *Praise*, 40–41; Hardison, *Monument*, 53–56; MacDougall, "Imitation," 131–32.

53. O'Malley, *Praise*, 71; J. B. Spencer, "Introduction," 24–26; Borsi, *Alberti*, 293; Hardison, *Monument*, 52.

54. O'Malley, *Praise*, 63. See also Becker, *Florence*, 249; Barfield, *Appearances*, 126–29. This visual emphasis held sway in western thought until it was itself fragmented with the rise of Cubism. See M. Praz, *Mnemosyne: The Parallel between Literature and the Visual Arts*, Bollingen Series, no. 35 (Princeton: Princeton Univ. Pr., 1970), 207. The beginnings of the transformation from rhetorical concepts into a vocabulary for the visual arts is discussed by M. Baxandall, *Painting and Experience in Fifteenth Century Italy* (Oxford: Clarendon Pr., 1972).

55. See G. Murray, *The Classical Tradition in Poetry* (1927; reprint New York: Vintage, 1957), 38–42; J. Bialostocki, "Iconography," in *Dictionary*, ed. Wiener, 2:529.

56. J. B. Spencer, "Introduction," 25; Becker, *Florence*, 254–55; T. O. Sloan, "Rhetoric and Meditation: Three Case Studies," *The Journal of Medieval and Renaissance Studies* 1 (1971): 49–52; K. E. Cool, "The Petrarchan Landscape as Palimpsest," *The Journal of Medieval and Renaissance Studies* 11 (1981): 84. On the matter of *maraviglia* see Reborn, *Courtly*, 47–51, and Weinberg, "Castelvetro," 367, with special attention to the role of paradox as an element that befuddles the intellect while releasing the spirit of enthusiasm. The political consequences of the drift away from *phronesis* are documented by N. Rotenstreich, "Prudence and Folly," *American Philosophical Quarterly* 22 (1985): 93–104.

57. O'Malley, *Praise*, 125–29.

58. It is worth recalling at this point both the traditional relation of gardens to rhetorical literature and the radical transformation garden design underwent in the Renaissance. References to gardens and natural settings occupy a central place in classical rhetorical theory. This may seem surprising inasmuch as we anticipate that matters rhetorical are limited to the forum. Yet the dramatic settings for both Plato's *Phaedrus* and Cicero's *De Oratore* (to mention only two of the more obvious examples) rely heavily on awareness of natural vegetation. Of course the garden was known long before the Renaissance, reaching back into the Old Testament and the Roman Empire and extending forward in time to the voluptuous "paradise" gardens of the Moorish rulers of Spain in the late Middle Ages. However, these earlier gardens had been primarily refuges, bastions of seclusion and settings for private pleasures. It was only in the Italian Renaissance that the foundations for the modern public park space were established, for it was then that rhetorical principles came to influence garden design and so to expand the concept of the park from a cloistered space to one that would encourage more public recreational activity. These matters are treated at greater length by several historians of garden art. See E,. Battisti, "Natura Artificiosa to Natura Artificialis," in *The Italian Garden*, ed. D. R. Coffin (Washington: Dumbarton Oaks, 1972), 136; Thacker, *Gardens*, 95–112; J. Lehrman, *Earthly Paradise: Garden and Courtyard in Islam* (Berkeley: Univ. of California Pr., 1980); J. S. Berrall, *The Garden: An Illustrated History* (New York: Viking, 1966); D. Clifford, *A History of Garden Design* (1963; reprint New York: Praeger, 1966), 17–47. What is crucial for our purposes is that in the place and period we are examining, little was known about garden decoration, so Renaissance garden designers came to their projects with a freshness and willingness to adopt rhetorical canons to their work. See MacDougall, "Imitation," 119–22.

59. H. I. Triggs, *The Art of Garden Design in Italy* (London: Longmans Green, 1906),24; J. C. Shepherd and G. A. Jellicoe, *Italian Gardens of the Renaissance* (1925; reprint New York: Architectural Book Publishing, 1966), 12; G. B. Tobey, Jr., *A History of Landscape Architecture: The Relationship of People to Environment* (New York: Elsevier, 1973), 98–101; Berrall, *Garden*, 112–15. That these developments were not happenstance can be seen from Michelozzi's instructions in the building of the Villa Fiesole, which were, according to Tobey (98), to create a villa serving the purposes of Pliny the Younger's villa in ancient Rome, as set forth in Pliny's letters.

60. Clements, *Pieta* 119; Shepherd and Jellicoe, *Gardens*, 42.

61. Shepherd and Jellicoe, *Gardens*, 12; Clements, *Picta*, 119; T. Comito, *The Idea of the Garden in the Renaissance* (New Brunswick: Rutgers Univ. Pr., 1978), 69–79; H. Wolfflin, *Renaissance and Baroque*, trans. K. Simon (1961; reprint Ithaca: Cornell Univ. Pr., 1979), 148; N. Miller, *Heavenly Caves: Reflections on the Garden Grotto* (New York: Braziller, 1982), 41–43.

62. Comito, *Idea*, 88. It goes without saying that gardens also contained "public" areas and that rejuvenation encompassed activities in the company of others. Modern cocktail parties or golf outings may supply opportunities for transacting business, but they, like gardens, are understood to be "informal." See Miller, *Caves*, 80; Boccaccio, *Genealogia*, 56–57.

63. See Sloan, "Rhetoric," 46–51; Boccaccio, *Genealogia*, 54–55.

64. Cassirer, *Renaissance Philosophy*, 143–45. On the etymology of garden terms, see Anne Van Erp-Houtepen, "The Etymological Origin of the Garden," *Journal of Garden History* 6 (1986), 227–31.

65. G. L. Hersey, *Pythagorean Palaces: Magic and Architecture in the Italian Renaissance* (Ithaca: Cornell Univ. Pr., 1976), 34.

66. Comito, *Idea*, 183; W. Lotz, *Studies in Italian Renaissance Architecture* (Cambridge: MIT Pr., 1981), 126–155.

67. Cool, "Landscape," 83–84.

68. Comito, *Idea*, xii.

69. Cassirer, *Renaissance Philosophy*, 160; Cool, "Landscape," 88–94.

70. Comito, *Idea*, 81. See also L. Puppi, "The Villa Garden in the Veneto from the Fifteenth to the Eighteenth Century," in *Italian Garden*, ed. Coffin, 81–114.

71. Cool, "Landscape," 96; Comito, *Idea*, 115, 182. See also Levy, *High Renaissance*, 213–14; F. A. Yates, *The Art of Memory* (Chicago: Univ. of Chicago Pr., 1966), 143–45; E. MacDougall, "Ars Hortulorum: Sixteenth Century Garden Iconography and Literary Theory in Italy," in *Italian Garden*, ed. Coffin, 52–53. Perhaps the most stunning instance of this trait, although it is somewhat later than the focus of the present study, are the royal gardens at Caserta, begun in 1753. It is instructive to learn that the rhetorician Giambattista Vico was court historiographer to Charles of Bourbon, the garden's developer. G. L. Hersey, "Ovid, Vico, and the Central Garden at Caserta," *Journal of Garden History* 1 (1981): 3–34, provides important insights into the psychological and metaphysical significance to one who experienced walking the full length of the main pathway past the various clusters of statues, reliefs, and tableaus of mythical events. It seems apparent that a Vician interpretation of key passages from Ovid makes comprehensible a metaphorical journey into mankind's past and into the depths of the individual's soul as one strolls along what might otherwise seem a long, tedious trek.

72. Strong, *Renaissance Garden*, 20. See also J. D. Hunt and P. Willis, eds., *The Genius of Place: The English Landscape Garden, 1620–1820* (New York: Harper, 1975), 33–41.

73. Comito, *Idea*, 162–63. See also Strong, *Renaissance Garden*, 10–17; Yates, *Memory*, 129–40; Praz, *Mnemosyne* 85; F. B. Artz, *From the Renaissance to Romanticism* (Chicago: Univ. of Chicago Pr., 1962), 81.

74. See T. McLean, *Medieval English Gardens* (New York: Viking, 1980).

75. Wolfflin, *Renaissance*, 147; Shepherd and Jellicoe, *Gardens*, 28; Levy, *High Renaissance*, 231–32; T. Comito, "Renaissance Gardens and the Discovery of Paradise," *Journal of the History of Ideas*, 32 (1971): 487–88.

76. Artz, *Renaissance*, 225; Strong, *Renaissance Gardens*, 43; Boccaccio, *Genealogia*, 24; F. A. Yates, *Giordano Bruno and the Hermetic Tradition* (1964; reprint Chicago: Univ. of Chicago Pr., 1979), 191–92; B. Castiglione, *The Book of the Courtier*, trans. G. Bull (New York: Penguin, 1976), 345; J. Burckhardt, *The Civilization of the Renaissance*, trans. L. Geiger and W. Gotz (1929; reprint New York: Harper, 1958), 378.

77. Hunt and Willis, *Genius*, 11.

78. Comito, *Idea*, 166. On the similar use of "classical ruins" to evoke past glories, see Artz, *Renaissance*, 173–81; Cool, "Landscape," 98; G. Masson, *Italian Villas and Palaces* (New York: Abrams, 1966), 249; T. Whately, "The Progress of Gardening," in *Genius*, ed. Hunt and Willis, 305.

79. Hersey, *Palaces*, 90. See also Levy, *High Renaissance*, 166–68; Yates, *Bruno*, 331–35; L. Puppi, "The Giardino Bararigo at Valsanzibio," *Journal of Garden History* 3 (1983): 296.

80. Clements, *Picta*, 227; See also North, *Myth*, 207–50; Bialostocki, "Iconography," 529–30; Miller, *Caves*, 35; Yates, *Memory*, 165–70.

81. Clements, *Picta*, 228; Muir, "Images," 50; Boccaccio, *Genealogia*, 79–80; Janson, "Image," 80–92; C. Condren, "Authorities, Emblems, and Sources: Reflections on the Role of a Rhetorical Strategy in the History of History," *Philosophy and Rhetoric* 15 (1982): 174.

82. D. P. Walker, "Esoteric Symbolism," in *Poetry and Poetics from Ancient Greece to the Renaissance*, ed. G. M. Kirkwood (Ithaca: Cornell Univ. Pr., 1975), 225.

83. M. L. D'Ancona, *The Garden in the Renaissance: Botanical Symbolism in Italian Painting* (Florence: Okschki, 1977), 307–18. See also Battisti, "Nature," 20–24; MacDougall, "Hortulorum," 37–60.

84. Cool, "Landscape," 90. See also Graham, "Ut Pictura," 470; Lee, *Ut Pictura*, 19; Close, "Commonplace," 480–86; Yates, *Memory*, 251–59. Particularly helpful in his treatment of dissimulative imitation is Pigman, "Versions," *passim*.

85. DeNeef, "Epideictic," 219; Hardison, *Monument*, 60–65; Yates, *Bruno*, 264–66; V. Cronin, *The Flowering of the Renaissance* (London: History Book Club, 1969), 167; MacDougall, "Imitation," 127; M. J. Darnall and M. S. Weil, "Il Sacroi Bosco di Bomarzo," *Journal of Garden History* 4 (1984): 72–74; R. P. Knight, "Picturesque Taste and the Garden," in *Genius*, ed. Hunt and Willis, 349–50; Praz, *Mnemosyne*, 4; Graham, "Ut Pictura," 469; Bialostocki, "Iconography," 528; J. B. Spencer, "Introduction," 24–25; Yates, *Memory*, 154–57.

86. Strong, *Renaissance Garden*, 21. See also R. L. Colie, *Paradoxia Epidemica: The Renaissance Tradition of Paradox* (Princeton: Princeton Univ. Pr., 1966), 3; Reborn, *Courtly*, 46–49; Miller, *Caves*, 60; MacDougall, "Imitation," 128–29.

87. Comito, "Renaissance Gardens," 502.

88. Comito, "Renaissance Gardens," 504.

89. Janson, "Image," 87; North, Myth, 223; Decker, Renaissance, 32; Comito, Idea, 71; Hersey, Palaces, 21, 60; Watson, Shakespeare, 68–73; Shepherd and Jellicoe, Gardens, 20; Yates, Bruno, 191–92.

90. Cool, "Landscape," 93. See also Kelly, "Olmstead Landscape," 28.

91. Ficino, cited in Comito, Idea, 79.

92. O'Malley, Praise, 78–79; DeNeef, "Epideictic," 220–21; Cronin, Flowering, 157; Hersey, Palaces, 35; Thacker, Gardens, 96–100; Strong, Renaissance Gardens, 203; Nichols, Pleasure Gardens, 79–83; Decker, Renaissance, 32ff.; Comito, Idea, 164–65; Yates, Bruno, 282–87; Shepherd and Jellicoe, Gardens, 32–33. Contrast this meditative experience of being (which can still be felt in Italian Renaissance gardens) with the wholly different mood experienced in such thoroughly "modern" gardens as those designed by Roberto Burle Marx throughout Brazil. Marx's landscapes induce feelings of serenity, joy, and/or playfulness, but seldom that meditative celebration we are here considering. Their appeal seems to be precisely their existence in an enduring present moment, and their consequent disconnectedness from any past more remote than European cubism or dadaism. These "modern" gardens bespeak formalism for itself, devoid of meaning or significance beyond their immediate beauty. See F. L. Motta, Roberto Burle Marx e a Nova Visao da Paisagem (Sao Paulo: Livraria Nobel, 1984).

93. Artz, Renaissance, 169; Yates, Bruno, 298–99; Comito, "Renaissance Gardens" 493–504; Miller, Caves, 78.

94. Gombrich, Images, 8.

95. Gombrich, Images, 147. See also O'Malley, Praise, 65.

96. Martines, Power, 260; Whately, "Progress," 305; Close, "Commonplace," 469–72; Muir, "Images," 34; Sloan, "Rhetoric," 57; Hardison, Monument, 37. For a fascinating instance of the sort of scholarly furor that can arise from this ambiguous process, see Darnall and Weil, "Bosco," 1–91; J. B. Bury, "Bomarzo Revisited," Journal of Garden History 5 (1985): 213–23.

97. Watson, Shakespeare, 68; Thacker, Gardens, 97; Berenson, Painters, 6–10; Holme, "Courtesy Books," 46; Praz, Mnemosyne, 82; Hersey, Palaces, 21; Reborn, Courtly, 47–51; Hardison, Monument, 39; Weinberg, "Castelvetro," 357.

98. MacDougall, "Imitation," 120–22. See also Riess, "Civic View," 3–9; Janson, "Image," 98–100; Hardison, Monument, 95.

99. Hardison, Monument, 52. See also Lee, Ut Pictura, 74–75.

100. Knight, "Taste," 349; Manley, Convention, 114–15; Lee, Ut Pictura, 33; Reborn, Courtly, 12–14; Holme, "Courtesy Books;" G. P. Mohrmann, "The Civile Conversation: Communication in the Renaissance," Speech Monographs 39 (1972): 193–204.

101. Martines, Power, 257–60; Cool, "Landscape," 98; Shepherd and Jellicoe, Gardens, 46; Riess, "Civic View," 7; Hardison, Monument, 59; Comito, Idea, 78–79.

102. Clements, Picta, 64; Hunt and Willis, Genius, 119; R. Wittkower, Architectural Principles in the Age of Humanism (New York: Norton, 1971), 74.

103. Graham, "Ut Pictura," 460, 466–68; Hardison, Monument, 65; Wittkower, Principles, 33–34.

104. Wolfflin, Renaissance, 151; Artz, Renaissance, 227; Sloan, "Rhetoric," 48–52; Manley, Convention, 114–15.

105. Shepherd and Jellicoe, Genius, 46.

106. Wolfflin, Renaissance, 154–55; Shepherd and Jellicoe, Genius, 20; Puppi, "Giardino," 292.

107. Comito, Idea, 72.

108. Comito, Idea, 90.

109. Comito, Idea, 52–53, 60–62; Miller, 11. See also L. W. Rosenfield, "Rhetorical Criticism and an Aristotelian Notion of Process," Speech Monographs 33 (1966): 1–16.

110. Comito, Idea, 167.

111. Comito, Idea, 169.

112. Comito, "Renaissance Gardens," 500; W. Tatarkiewicz, "Form in the History of Aesthetics," in Dictionary, ed. Wiener, 2: 218.

113. Cited in Comito, Idea, 130.

114. Comito, Idea, 130–32.

115. Shepherd and Jellicoe, Genius, 28–29; Wolfflin, Renaissance, 150; W. Paatz, The Arts of the Italian Renaissance (New York: Abrams, n.d.), 83–85; Reborn, Courtly, 192; Burckhardt, Civilization, 382.

116. Westfall, "Painting," 495–97; G. de Santillana, Reflections on Men and Ideas (Cambridge: MIT Pr., 1968), 158–59; Hersey, Palaces, 35.

117. DeNeef, "Epideictic," 227–28; Comito, Idea, 28.

118. Gombrich, Images, 7; Strong, Renaissance Garden, 202–3; Artz, Renaissance, 182; Cool, "Landscape," 96; Lee, Ut Pictura, 35–37; MacDougall, "Imitation," 122. The ethical parallel to decorum was prudence, man's capacity to fuse reason and action in a fashion appropriate to the circumstances. This becomes all the more fascinating since, as decorum was to give way to imagination in the sixteenth century, so would the value society placed in prudential wisdom erode in favor of the fancy and theatricality of the Baroque, See V. Kahn, "Giovanni Pontano's Rhetoric of Prudence," Philosophy and Rhetoric 16 (1983): 20–23.

119. Manley, Convention, 112–13.

120. Comito, Idea, 105–6.

121. Cited in Hunt and Willis, Genius, 195.

122. Comito, Idea, 158; Sloan, "Rhetoric," 50–51; Hardison, Monument, 100–101.

123. Comito, Idea, 159.

124. See H. Baron, The Crisis of the Early Italian Renaissance (Princeton: Princeton Univ. Pr., 1966); H. Baron, From Petrarch to Bruni: Studies in Humanistic Political Literature (Chicago: Univ. of Chicago Pr., 1968); J. E. Seigel, Rhetoric and Philosophy in Renaissance Humanism: The Union of Eloquence and Wisdom (Princeton: Princeton Univ. Pr., 1968); N. S. Struever, The Language of History in the Renaissance: Rhetoric and Consciousness in Florentine Humanism (Princeton: Princeton Univ. Pr., 1970); C. Trinkhaus, In Our Image and Likeness: Humanity and Divinity in Italian Humanist Thought, 2 vols. (London: Constable, 1970); D. Weinstein, "In Whose Image and Likeness? Interpretations of Renaissance Humanism," Journal of the History of Ideas 33 (1972): 165–76.

125. J. G. A. Pocock, The Machiavellian Moment (Princeton: Princeton Univ. Pr., 1975), 59.

126. Battisti, "Natura," 15–30; Berrall, Garden, 111–12; D. Cantimori, "Rhetoric and Politics in Italian Humanism," Journal of the Warburg Institute 1 (1937): 83–102; F. Gilbert, "Bernardo Rucellai and the Orti Oricellari," Journal of the Warburg Institute 12 (1949): 101–36; P. Villari, The Life and Times of Niccolo Machiavelli, trans. L. Villari, 2 vols. (1892; reprint New York: Greenwood, 1968), 2: 284–89; J. R. Hale, Machiavelli (New York: Collier, 1963), 148–85.

127. Gilbert, "Rucellai," 114.

128. Cantimori, "Rhetoric," 87.

129. Cantimori, "Rhetoric," 100–101.

130. Gilbert, "Rucellai," 127.

131. Gilbert, "Rucellai," 119–27.

132. Pocock, Moment, 150.

133. Walker, "Symbolism," 225. See also Bialostocki, "Iconography," 529.

134. See W. Tatarkiewicz, "Classification of the Arts," in Dictionary, ed. Wiener, 1: 460.

135. Walker, "Symbolism," 225.

136. Bialostocki, "Iconography," 531–32.

137. Pocock, Moment, 540.

SEVEN

The Politics of Prayer: A Case Study in Configurational Interplay

MARTIN J. MEDHURST

In his seminal essay "Rhetoric as Historical Configuration," Eugene E. White describes what he calls the "exigential flow" of historical causation.[1] All rhetoric, White argues, is part of a chain stretching back through history in a neverending cycle of cause and effect. Rhetoric, properly understood, is to be considered both cause and consequent, both antecedent and outcome. Specific rhetorical events, White reminds us, come about because particular configurations of historical/rhetorical forces exist at a certain point in time. But to evaluate adequately the rhetorical potency of any given speech, campaign, social movement, or event, the critic must look beyond the moment, must expand the scope of investigation to encompass both antecedents and consequents of the rhetorical phenomenon being examined.

White's notion of rhetoric in configured interplay is an important adjunct to our knowledge about how the historical, situational, and generic dimensions of discourse influence rhetor invention and potential audience response. Recent contributions to critical theory have aided our understanding of how the past shapes the present and prefigures the future. Kathleen Jamieson has shown how preexisting rhetorical forms shape and constrain subsequent inventional behavior. G. P. Mohrmann and Michael Leff have demonstrated how proper generic classification can lead to more accurate rhetorical prediction and greater critical understanding. Others have illumined

267

the utility of generic and situational factors for understanding particular forms of discourse.[2]

White's notion of historical forces in configured interplay is an
important contribution to critical theory precisely because it encourages the critic to remember that all rhetorical acts are but scenes in
an ongoing play. "Any rhetorical act," says White, "is not so much
a being as a becoming, not so much an entity as a historical development and flow."[3] It is this idea of the historical flow that helps
to extend our knowledge and understanding of particular types of
discourse.

White defines the flow as "the cyclical historical movement, or
antecedents-events-consequences, that provides both the matrix for
the speech and the speech itself. Thus the exigential flow is at once
the cause, context, and product of rhetorical action, as well as the
potential provoker of further responding actions in a continuing
cycle of antecedents and consequences." To examine the flow of
events, White suggests that the critic explore "the configurational
playing of regularized forces."[4] These forces, says White, are of three
basic types: contextual, processual, and correlational.

By examining the *context* (both historical and contemporary)
within which a rhetorical act occurs, the *process* that leads up to
and culminates in the act, and the *correlation* of the act to actual or
potential audience response, the critic is able to fashion a richer
statement about the various factors that affect the creation and
reception of the message. It is this task—the explication of context,
process, and correlation within a particular scene—that I now propose to undertake. If my argument about the utility of White's
approach to rhetorical criticism is to be validated, the reader should
emerge with a heightened understanding not only of a particular
message and scene, but also of the antecedents and consequences
giving rise to and issuing from that scene.

Rhetorical Antecedents to Inaugural Prayer

The scene I have chosen to examine is ritualistic in nature, epideictic
in form, and confirmatory in effect. Every four years the people of
the United States inaugurate a president. For most of the twentieth
century this ritualistic act of inauguration has involved the offering
of prayers on behalf of the nation and in support of the new leader.
The practice of offering prayer at the inauguration, like all rhetorical
rituals, has antecedent forms that, through their historical evolu-

tion, have created commonplaces, molded rhetor attitudes, and shaped audience expectations. The "presentness of the past"[5] lurks in inaugural prayers, conjuring, as it were, the spirits of rhetorical forms now deceased or deformed.

To call forth the ancestors of inaugural prayer, one must return to the early Middle Ages, to fourth-century France, where, for perhaps the first time in recorded history, the office of military chaplain was established. The term "chaplain," derived from the Latin *cappellani*, originally referred to those priests who guarded the cape of Saint Martin. The cape was carried into battle by the kings of France as a sign of divine approval. The "chapel," or *cappela*, was the house in which the cape was kept during times of peace. Establishment of a military chaplaincy was, of course, an extension and institutionalization of the ancient custom of the wise man, prophet, or mystic blessing the troops before they did battle.

Institutionalization was important because it gave form to practice. The institution of the military chaplaincy evolved from fourth-century France to medieval Britain, and it was from his knowledge of British battle practices that George Washington, in the midst of fighting the French and Indians, requested that a chaplain be appointed to his regiment. The year was 1756. Eighteen years later, in September 1774, the First Continental Congress appointed Jacob Duché as their chaplain, preparing, it seems, for the battle that lay ahead.[6]

The evolution from prophet to military chaplain to congressional chaplain forms the genealogical tree of inaugural prayer, for it was from the congressional chaplaincy that the first inaugural clergyman emerged at the 1789 inauguration of George Washington. The practice of offering prayer at the inaugural ceremony then disappeared for nearly one and one-half centuries, eventually reemerging at the 1937 inauguration of Franklin D. Roosevelt. Prayers have been offered at every presidential inauguration since 1937.

When Franklin D. Roosevelt reinstituted the practice of prayer at his second inauguration in 1937, he did so by clinging to the past with one hand and reaching for the future with the other. He selected *two* clergymen to pray. One of the reverends, ZeBarney T. Phillips, was chaplain of the Senate, but the other, the Right Reverend John A. Ryan, was a civilian clergyman distinguished primarily by his stout advocacy of Roosevelt's social revolution.[7] With one stroke, Roosevelt effected the evolution from an official, appointed clergyman (the Senate chaplain) to an unofficial, invited one. The change was significant for it opened the door for clergymen, distinguished by their performance in the religious life of the nation, to participate rhetorically in the civic ritual of inauguration. It also opened the door for astute politicians to stage clergymen for personal or partisan gain, as well as for status-minded religious leaders to use the state to secure recognition and approbation for their particular group or cause.

The history of inaugural prayer is replete with politicians and clergymen using one another to gain their own ends. Rather than chronicle these events from 1937 to the present, I propose to examine the role of prayer in one inauguration—the forces that shaped it, the constraints that influenced it, and the rhetorical choices that emerged from it. I have chosen the 1965 inaugural of Lyndon Baines Johnson. After examining the rhetorical processes that shaped the form of the ceremony, I will then focus on one of the prayers delivered at Johnson's inauguration, its evolution, its reliance on antecedent forms, and its rhetorical invitations to the listening audience.

The Johnson Inauguration

> *We who hold public office are enjoined by our*
> *Constitution against enacting laws to tell the people*
> *when or where or how to pray. All our experience and*
> *all our knowledge proves that injunction is good. For, if*
> *government could ordain the people's prayers,*
> *government could also ordain its own worship—and*
> *that must never be.*
> —LYNDON BAINES JOHNSON, 1964[8]

Lyndon Johnson was the first president to exercise direct pressure in an effort to shape the content of inaugural prayer. Though Johnson ostensibly believed that government ordination of prayer was wrong, he himself engaged in such "ordaining." The occasion was the 1965 inaugural ceremony and the prayers were those offered by the invited clergy. Johnson, assisted by his speechwriting staff, required prior submission of clerical prayers, made suggestions for deletions and additions to those prayers, and gave final approval to the prayers before they could be uttered.

On the surface, such a brash act of interventionism might seem strangely out of place, if not with the spirit of the ceremony itself, then at least with the doctrine of separation of church and state. But the act was not out of character for Johnson. Quite the contrary, it would have been unusual if he had not tried to control the rhetorical output of the inaugural ceremony, for Johnson had long displayed a deep-seated desire, perhaps even a need, to control. He sought to control every facet of his existence—his family, his friends, his possessions, even the information he received. Control, for Johnson, meant power and power meant the ability to fulfill his vision.[9]

At the Democratic convention in July 1964 the Johnson hand was omnipresent. "Johnson's grip was so unyielding," wrote Alfred Steinberg, "that an advance tape recording of the keynote address had to be sent him, the content of the convention's souvenir book required his approval, and the cover picture of himself would be one he selected." Eric Goldman recalled that "LBJ was like the mother of the bride, considering, controlling, fussing over every detail. This was to be *his* convention, leading to *his* triumph. He personally chose where his aides would stay . . . and he supervised bloc by bloc the allotment of spectator's seats in the auditorium."[10] In addition to providing more evidence of Johnson's great ego, this fascination with personal prior inspection of convention discourse prefigured similar behavior at the 1965 inaugural.

The events leading up to the 1965 inauguration and Lyndon Johnson's response to them were part of a long line of consistent actions. Though ostensibly believing in the sanctity of prayer and the separation of church and state, Johnson nevertheless acted in such a manner as to subvert his profession of belief. The president invited four clergymen to participate in the inauguration ceremony, but not until he had thoroughly considered the strategic advantages to be gained through their participation and the rhetorical tone to be set by their prayers. By focusing first on the selection procedure that brought Rabbi Hyman Judah Schachtel to the inaugural platform and then on the editing process that lay behind the Reverend George Davis's prayer, I will show how knowledge of context, process, and correlation broadens one's understanding of the strategic functions of public prayer.[11]

SELECTING INAUGURAL CLERGY

Since Franklin D. Roosevelt's reintroduction of clerical participation at the 1937 inaugural ceremony, political expediency and rhetorical effect had dominated the selection of clergy. The inauguration in 1965 was no exception. If anything, the politics of prayer were even more confusing than usual, for in 1965 special interest groups, realizing the potential of inaugural prayer to legitimate religious factions, petitioned the White House for the opportunity to participate. In years past, Catholics, Jews, and Greek Orthodox had fought to gain access to the inaugural platform. By the mid-1960s, the process had evolved to the point where subgroups within each tradition were fighting among themselves for the "honor" of representing the group at the inaugural ceremony.

In 1965, the Jewish community in general, and its Orthodox wing in particular, caused concern within the White House and among members of the speechwriting staff. The process started on 2 November 1964, when Rabbi Abraham N. AvRutick wrote to Senator Abraham Ribicoff of Connecticut. "Because of our long and warm friendship," the rabbi wrote, "I want to share with you confidentially a matter that is currently being discussed among leaders of Orthodox Jewry. . . . It has been customary to have outstanding religious personalities of the various faiths take part in the Inauguration. In the past the Reform and Conservative segments of the Jewish community were represented at the inauguration of a President. The Orthodox Jewish community has never had one of its spiritual leaders participate. It seems to many of us that the honor in 1965 should be accorded to an Orthodox leader."[12] Rabbi AvRutick concluded by recommending the selection of Rabbi Samuel Belkin, president of Yeshiva University.

On 4 November, two days after receiving the rabbi's letter, Senator Ribicoff wrote to President Johnson. After congratulating the president on his victory, Ribicoff concluded: "I am enclosing the original of a letter received from Rabbi AvRutick, head of the Rabbinical Council of America. May I respectfully submit that his suggestion is worthy of your consideration." Senator Ribicoff went on to point out that "the Orthodox Jewish community is the largest group—with two thousand Rabbis and some three thousand Congregations."[13]

To make sure the letter reached the hands of the president, Ribicoff channeled it through presidential assistant Jack Valenti with the comment that "the suggestion is not only a sound one but eminently fair in meting out honor to the people of the Jewish faith." On 9 November, Valenti wrote back to the senator, assuring him that both his letter and that of Rabbi AvRutick would receive "proper consideration."[14]

While Rabbi AvRutick's request was being considered, another communication reached the White House. Written by Rabbi Israel Miller and directed to special counsel Myer Feldman, this letter also pleaded for an Orthodox representative and suggested the name of

Dr. Belkin. From the similarity of language, arguments employed, and letterhead used, it was clear that a campaign of sorts was under way to secure the selection of Rabbi Belkin. A day after receiving the Miller letter, Feldman sent a memo to the president recommending Dr. Belkin for the honor of participating in the inaugural.[15]

Not everyone, however, wanted Dr. Belkin to be the Jewish representative. Other names were also suggested by people outside of the administration, including that of Rabbi Max Schenk, president of the New York Board of Rabbis. Unbeknownst to the letter writers, President Johnson preferred inviting his old friend from Houston, Rabbi Hyman Judah Schachtel. But there was a problem. Schachtel was a member of the Reform branch of Judaism and would not be acceptable to the Orthodox rabbis. By 21 November the problem had reached the president, who directed Bill Moyers to study the situation and pick the "best one."[16] The criteria for "best" were left ambiguous.

ENTER MOYERS AND VALENTI

Bill Don Moyers was, as one writer put it, "the President's 'good angel, representing his conscience when there's a conflict between conscience and expediency.' " Moyers was one of several clergymen who served in the Johnson White House. A graduate of Southwest Baptist Seminary, Moyers had spent a year at Edinburgh studying "the relationship of church and state in Western civilization."[17] He was the logical choice to investigate what, at one level at least, was a confrontation between religious interest groups.

Feldman was already on record as favoring Dr. Belkin. Before Moyers could complete his investigation, Jack Valenti declared himself in favor of the selection of Hyman Judah Schachtel, a fellow Texan and close friend of the president. Not only did Valenti make a recommendation, but he listed for Johnson four reasons why Schachtel was the best choice. First, said Valenti, "he knows you, loves you, and has for some years." Second, he continued, "he is a man of unmatched eloquence." Third, "he is an intellectual . . . who has published four books—one of which was a best seller." Finally, Valenti concluded, "I think it good that the President's choice for a rabbi in the ceremony is someone who is not only a man of broad and distinguished talents in the Jewish community, but one who is his friend and supporter and loyal admirer."[18]

Valenti's memo was instructive for it served as a partial listing of the criteria that one should consider when making the choice of an inaugural clergyman. Although none of the topics was specifically concerned with the content of prayer, several of them suggested a sensitivity to rhetorical concerns such as the relationship between the speaker and the audience. A man who had written a best-seller would be more likely to appeal to a wider cross-section of the listening audience than would, say, a college president. Likewise, a man who knew and loved the president and who was a loyal supporter probably would not say anything to subvert or challenge presidential authority.

A day after Valenti sent his memo, Bill Moyers filed his report with the president. Concentrating on Schachtel, Moyers cautioned that he should be considered in the light of three circumstances. First, Schachtel was a Reform rabbi while Orthodox and Conservative Jews were in the majority. Second, Schachtel had once been associated with the viewpoints promulgated by the American Council for Judaism, a group opposed to the establishment of the independent state of Israel. Moyers noted: "I have been unable to find out whether Rabbi Schachtel belonged or belongs to this minority group. If he does, it would be inadvisable to have him participate in the Inauguration."[19] Third, wrote Moyers, a Reform rabbi participated in Kennedy's inaugural.

Moyers's memo deserves note for it, too, provided criteria for the selection of an inaugural clergyman. Moyers implicitly stated that the person should represent a majority of the religious group from which he came. The clergyman should not be involved in any controversial political issues within his religious community, and concern for equal representation among factions of the same religion should be considered. Of the three factors cited, Moyers spent twice as much space on the political controversy as on the other two issues combined. Both Moyers's and Valenti's memos were forwarded to Myer Feldman who, on 9 December, summarized the arguments in a memo to the president.

Feldman's memo was noteworthy not so much for its content as for the point of view it assumed. "The selection of Dr. Schachtel," wrote Feldman, "would be understood by everyone on the ground that he is a friend and the President is entitled to the request that the prayer be offered by a friend." Thus, Feldman assumed a distinctly rhetorical point of view in which audience perception was paramount. Feldman was concerned with how a certain man's appearance would be understood. He was concerned with the message that would be conveyed by his selection. After pointing out that Congressman "Abe Multer and Abe Ribicoff have both urged that Dr. Belkin be designated," Feldman closed by observing: "Although it would be appropriate to select Dr. Schachtel, I believe it would be even better to select Dr. Belkin."[20]

On 14 December, the issues surrounding the selection of inaugural clergy reached a climax. Valenti sent a memo to the staff that simply said, "May we meet on the entire problem of who prays at the Inaugural ceremony?"[21] The meeting took place within days of the Valenti memo and from it emerged the slate of inaugural clergy. Also from this meeting, the exact date of which is not known, emerged the plan to require prior submission of each sacred discourse.

SUBMISSIONS, SUGGESTIONS, AND REVISIONS

The staff meeting resulted in the selection of Hyman Judah Schachtel as the Jewish clergyman. But a problem still remained. Schachtel was from Texas. So too were the Catholic representative, Archbishop Robert E. Lucey, and the Protestant representative, the Reverend John Barclay. Only the Greek Orthodox representative, Archbishop Iakovos, was a non-Texan. Thus emerged another critical topic, geographical representation. The Johnson staff was concerned that the inauguration not be perceived as a regional affair. Johnson was president of all the people, not just Texans. Hence, geographical balance was believed to be necessary for the projection of a correct image. To solve the problem, the staff decided to drop Dr. Barclay and replace him with Dr. George R. Davis, minister of the National City Christian Church in Washington, D.C. On 27 December, Valenti phoned Dr. Barclay and informed him that he would give a prayer not at the inaugural ceremony as originally planned, but at the luncheon immediately following. In his report to Johnson, Valenti wrote, "I explained to him [Barclay] that Dr. Davis ministers to the President all during the year and that he [Davis] will give the prayer at the inauguration."[22] Valenti, it seems, clearly misled Barclay about the true reason for the change.

Also in the Valenti report were the results of his conversations with the other clergymen. In reference to Schachtel, he wrote: "Told him that the President wanted him to give the prayer. . . . Pledged him to secrecy." Valenti went on to note, "I have told Schachtel and Manatos [the White House contact with Archbishop Iakovos] a limit of 200 words and *to have the actual prayer to me no later than Jan. 5*" (emphasis added). Thus, by 27 December the decision had been made to require prior submission of the prayers. It was not clear who initiated the idea of prior submission, but a note dated 31 December and written on top of the Valenti report seemed to indicate that the president had knowledge of, and thus approved, the submission of the prayers. The note, initialed HB (Horace Busby), said: "Told JV [Jack Valenti] to call Lucey (for details following up Pres's talk). Also to contact Davis for prayer."[23] Thus Busby, following a conversation with the president, instructed Valenti to secure copies of clerical prayers.

Cooperative Clergy: The Case of George Davis

The first clergyman to submit his prayer was George Davis. As early as 22 December, Davis had written to the president at the Texas White House, "I will go to work on the request you made of me, and if you wish would be glad to let you see a copy in advance of the time and place you wish it used."[24] By 5 January 1965, the deadline specified by Valenti, all four clergymen had submitted their prayers. The following day Valenti delivered the prayers to the president.

On 6 January, the same day that his original submission reached the president's desk, George Davis wrote to the chief executive and included two versions of his prayer: a short form and the longer one which he had sent to Valenti. In an addendum he wrote: "Please feel free to offer any suggestions, even to my doing it over again. As I [sic] usual rule I do not give prayers in that way, but it seems to me this is so important, your judgment is needed, in any way you desire to give it." It did not take long for the "judgment" to come. Two days later, on 8 January, Valenti wrote to Davis: "May I suggest to you for whatever the judgment is worth that you may want to consider the shorter prayer for the Inaugural ceremony." Bill Moyers was even more direct. In a note to an aide he wrote, "Call Davis, tell him please to use the short version."[25]

One factor in the staff preference for the shorter prayer was the tight schedule for the inauguration. A second factor, however, was the difference in content between the two prayers. Furthermore, it was clear from the correspondence that Davis would have preferred to use the longer prayer "because of the 'poetic sentences' in it." In more than one piece of correspondence Davis observed that he had "read the longer version of this prayer over again and again at a less rapid speed than I usually use and it comes within 2½ minutes."[26] If the longer prayer fell within the allotted time limit, why did the staff insist on the use of the shorter form? An analysis of the Davis prayer and the changes it underwent from version one (long form) to version two (shorter form) to version three (first revision) to version four (final draft) may provide part of the answer as well as lend insight into the evolution of the rhetorical invitation being offered to the audience.[27]

Each version of the prayer had three paragraphs. By examining the changes, paragraph by paragraph, across the versions, I will show how changes in form affected the rhetorical invitation being offered to the listeners.

Paragraph 1   Versions one and two were sent to the president simultaneously, and it was version two that Jack Valenti favored. Even from a comparison of the opening paragraphs one clear difference between the first two versions can be discerned. Version two was considerably shorter. Upon inspection it was obvious that Davis simply removed sentences two, three, and four from the first draft to which he referred in his letter of 6 January. In addition to being "poetic," however, these sentences also alluded to the myth of destiny and to the divine nature of the ceremony.

The first paragraph of version three, sent to the White House a few days after versions one and two, was different from the second version in only one major respect. Davis added to the end of sentence one the phrase, "and this exciting yet profound event is of God as well as of men." This idea hearkened back to the first version and reinstated the invitation to view the ceremony as a divine enactment.

The final version, although retaining overtones from the first three versions, actually introduced several new words and phrases not found in any of the previous efforts. First, the adjectives describing God as eternal, loving, and invisible were dropped. Instead, Davis began with the myth-of-state commonplace, "God of our fathers," followed by the ascription, "to whom persons are of supreme importance." He completed his first sentence by bringing the phrase "a man to be set apart in a special way" from the middle of version three to the top of the final version.

Sentence two of the final version, although retaining words and phrases from version three, rearranged the phrases in such a manner as to change their meaning. Whereas in version three "this historic

VERSION 1

Eternal, and loving, though invisible Friend, God of our Fathers, we believe with calm and deep assurance that Thou art involved in this historic and exalting ceremony. We believe what is taking place here to be divine as well as human, of God as well as of man. Surely the destiny of this great nation is on Thy heart, and our origins, our story of splendor, our imperishable dreams matter to Thee. For not even a leaf flutters in the breeze, no rain drop falls upon the earth, no snow flake glistens in the winter sky apart from Thy awareness. Therefore to Thee, to Whom persons are of supreme importance, we lift up this day in our love and prayers a man to be set apart in a very special way. We commend him, and the Vice-President, and their families, their comrades, colleagues, and advisors, to Thy strong help, and unfailing mercy.

Bless, guard, and keep Thy servant, Lyndon Baines Johnson, that he may prosper in the glorious task to which he has been called by the decisive will of the people, and by the Providence of God. We thank Thee for his magnificently significant service to his Nation and the world, which the years have already inscribed on the scroll of history. We thank Thee that we have already witnessed his gallantry and stability, in times of gravest peril, and dire tragedy, as well as in the daily routine of unending duties. We thank Thee for his careful preparation for such a time as this, by hard discipline, rugged testing, tireless attention to detail. For all of his skills in the political sciences and arts, for his insights into our patterns of doing the business of government, we stand in appreciation to Thee O God who giveth such gifts to men. Let no weariness of spirit or body defeat him, no shadows of doubt engulf him. Let no merely human ambition take his eyes from the true course he has set. And let no humiliation of temporary failure or defeat which are the lot at times of all Thy children, great and small, cause him to stumble.

Help our President, O God, to help us keep remembering that we are one family as a Nation, and that we are but one nation in a family of Nations, so that our dreams, our goals, our ambitions, our efforts, and our sacrifices may have universal purpose. Help him, O God, to help us to be able increasingly to reason together, to seek and find worthy consensus, to live in our diversity with stable unity. Help him, O God, to help us, to move onward toward a great and desirable society of men and nations. We ask all of this, together with those genuine though unspoken yearnings of our spirits, in the Name of him who is the Wonderful Counsellor, the Mighty God, the Everlasting Father, the Prince of Peace.

VERSION 2

Eternal, and loving, though invisible Friend, God of our Fathers, we believe with calm and deep assurance that Thou art involved in this historic and exalting ceremony. Therefore to Thee, to Whom persons are of supreme importance, we lift up this day in our love and prayers a man to be set apart in a very special way. We commend him, and the Vice-President, and their families, their comrades, colleagues, and advisors, to Thy strong help, and unfailing mercy.

Bless, guard and keep Thy servant, Lyndon Baines Johnson, that he may prosper in the glorious task to which he has been called by the decisive will of the people, and by the Providence of God. We thank Thee for his magnificently significant service to his nation and the world, which the years have already inscribed on the scroll of history. We thank Thee that we have already witnessed his gallantry and stability, in times of greatest peril and dire tragedy, as well as in the daily routine of unending duties. We thank Thee for his careful preparation for such a time as this, by hard discipline, rugged testing, tireless attention to detail. For all of his skills in the political sciences and arts, for his insights into our patterns of doing the business of government, we stand in appreciation to Thee O God who giveth such gifts to men.

Help our President, O God, to help us keep remembering that we are one family as a Nation, and that we are but one Nation in a family of nations, so that our dreams, our goals, our ambitions, our efforts, and our sacrifices may have universal purpose. Help him, O God, to help us to be able increasingly to reason together, to seek and find worthy consensus, to live in our diversity with stable unity. Help him, O God, to help us, to move onward toward a great and desirable society of men and nations. Our prayer we offer in the Redeemer's name.

VERSION 3

Eternal, and loving, though invisible Friend, God of our Fathers, we believe with calm, deep assurance Thou art involved in this historic and exalting ceremony, and this exciting yet profound event is of God as well as of men. Therefore, to Thee, to Whom persons are of supreme importance, we lift up this day in our love and prayers a man to be set apart in a special way. We commend him, and the Vice-President of the United States, and their families, their comrades, colleagues and advisors, to Thy strong help and unfailing mercy.

Bless, guard, and keep Thy servant, Lyndon Baines Johnson, that he may prosper in the glorious task to which he has been called by the decisive will of the people, and by the Providence of God. We thank Thee for his magnificently significant service to his Nation and the world, which the years have already inscribed on the scroll of history. We thank Thee that we have already witnessed his gallantry and stability, in times of greatest peril and in dire tragedy, as well as in the daily routine of his unending duties. We thank Thee for his careful preparation for such a time as this, by hard discipline, rugged testing, and tireless attention to detail. For all of his skills in the political sciences and arts, and for his insights into our patterns of doing the business of Government, we voice our gratitude to Thee O God, who giveth such gifts to men.

Continue Thy help to our President, O Father of Truth and Light, that he may in turn help us not to forget we are one family of people as a nation, and that we are but one of many nations in a family of nations. For thus our dreams, our goals, our ambitions, our efforts, and our sacrifices may be redeemed to have universal meaning and purpose. Support our President that he may inspire us to be able increasingly to reason together, to seek and to find worthy consensus, to live in our strange and wonderful diversity, with stable unity. Uphold him, O God, that he may urge us onward toward a great and desirable society of persons who desire goodness, and Nations whose God is the Lord. In the name of the Wonderful Counsellor, The Mighty God, The Everlasting Father, The Prince of Peace. Amen.

VERSION 4

God of our fathers, to whom persons are of supreme importance, we lift up, this day, a man to be set apart in a special way. In our love and prayers, through this historic and exalting ceremony, we lift him up, as we do the Vice-President and their gracious families. To Thy strong help we commend them and all men and women in all areas and branches of our Nation's life who share the terrible splendor of leadership and authority.

Bless, guard and keep Thy servant, Lyndon Baines Johnson, that he may prosper in the sacred task to which he has been called by the decisive vote of the people and by divine providence. We thank Thee for his magnificently significant service to his Nation and the world, already written on history's scroll. For his gallantry and stability, seen in times of greatest peril and in dark tragedy, as well as in the daily routine of his never-ending duties, we thank Thee. For his careful preparation for such a time as this, by hard discipline and patient attention to details, we thank Thee. For all of his skills in the political sciences and arts, and for his insights into the ways of government, we voice our gratitude to Thee, Giver of all gifts to men.

To the President and the Vice-President, continue Thy help, and to all those whose judgments and loyalties they must be able to rely upon. Grant our President not to grow weary, as he must remind us that we are one people and that we are but one of many worthy nations in an aspiring family of nations. For us, God of all the worlds, our dreams, our efforts, and our sacrifices, Thou wilt redeem to give them universal meaning and purpose. Uphold him, that he may encourage us to be able increasingly to reason together, to seek an essential consensus, to live in our strange and wonderful diversity with stable unity. Uphold our President, O God, as he leads us onward to that desirable society of persons who seek real worth, a society in which none shall live in fear, because justice, mercy, and brotherhood, will flourish on the earth. This we pray in the name of Him who is the Wonderful Counsellor, the Mighty God, the Everlasting Father, and the Prince of Peace. Amen.

and exalting ceremony" was linked with the "deep assurance Thou art involved," in the final version the historic and exalting ceremony was the medium through which "we lift him up" to God in prayer. Thus, once again the direct involvement of the divine in the ceremony was lost.

Davis inserted the modifiers "gracious," referring to the families, and "strong," referring to God's help, in the final version. In addition, he dropped the reference to "unfailing mercy" and replaced his long list of those being commended by a general petition for "all men and women in all areas and branches of our Nation's life." This change shifted the focus from people working for Johnson to people working on behalf of the nation.

Davis also added a phrase not found in any of the first three versions, but well established in the history of inaugural prayer. He referred to those "who share the terrible splendor of leadership and authority." To judge from preceding inaugural prayers, it was a rhetorical necessity to testify to the terrible hardships and difficulties faced by a new president.[28]

Paragraph 2   The differences between the second paragraphs of versions one and two can be easily discerned. The last three sentences of the first version were simply dropped. Unlike the deletion in paragraph one, however, these sentences were not "poetic," but implicitly confessional. The deleted lines were: "Let no *weariness* of spirit or body *defeat* him, no *shadows* of *doubt* engulf him. Let no *merely human ambition* take his eyes from the true course he has set. And let no *humiliation* of temporary *failure* or *defeat* which are the lot at times of all Thy children, great and small, cause him to *stumble*" (emphasis added).

The deleted lines asked for God's protection from the temptations, doubts, and defeats that humans experience. The lines were implicitly confessional in that they admitted the possibility of human frailty, a possibility that Johnson seldom, if ever, admitted.

There was no direct evidence to indicate that the confessional lines in paragraph two were the prime concern of the Johnson staff. Nevertheless, it was true that Davis preferred version one and that Valenti "suggested" he use version two—a version that was subsequently revised two more times. In none of the other versions did confessional language appear.[29]

Versions two and three of the second paragraph were identical. The final version, version four, revealed several minor changes both in word choice and rhythm.

VERSION 3	VERSION 4
"glorious task"	*"sacred* task"
"decisive *will* of the people"	"decisive *vote* of the people"
"dire tragedy"	*"dark* tragedy"
"unending duties"	*"never-ending* duties"
"rugged testing"	deleted
"patterns of doing the business of Government"	*"the ways* of Government"
"O God, *who giveth such gifts to men"*	*"Giver of all good gifts to men"*

The most significant change was the movement from a "glorious" task to a "sacred" one. One can be glorified in purely human fashion, but "sacred" connotes ultimate values. Coming from the lips of a clergyman the term would tend to connote a religious significance as well. Having deleted his earlier reference to the ceremony as a divine enactment, Davis recaptured the essence of the idea through a single word change.

The rhythm of paragraph two was also altered in the move from version three to version four. The first three versions used the phrase "we thank Thee" as an *introduction* to specific assertions. The rhythmical pattern developed was:

> *"We thank Thee . . ."*
> *"We thank Thee . . ."*
> *"We thank Thee . . ."*

In the final draft, however, the rhythmical pattern changed to:

> *"We thank Thee . . ."*
> *"For . . . we thank Thee."*
> *"For . . . we thank Thee."*

Thus, Davis moved from the rhetorical technique of epanaphora to that of epistrophe, thereby allowing him to highlight the presidential qualities of "gallantry," "stability," and "careful preparation."[30]

Paragraph 3   The final paragraph underwent more change, perhaps, than either of the previous two. The first and second versions of paragraph three differed only in the construction of the last sentence:

Version 1.   "We ask all of this, together with those genuine though unspoken yearnings of our spirits, in the name of him who is the Wonderful Counsellor, the Mighty God, the Everlasting Father, the Prince of Peace."
Version 2.   "Our prayer we offer in the Redeemer's name."

The shorter ending was not any more "positive" than that found in the first version. Version two changed only the title of the Deity and eliminated a rather ambiguous and perhaps autobiographical phrase about "unspoken yearning."

In the movement from version two to version three, however, substantial changes occurred. Instead of the petition, "help our President," Davis wrote, "Continue Thy help to our President." Thus, the minister emphasized the ongoing nature of divine assistance by inserting the word "continue," a term which presupposed past action. In addition, Davis inserted the title "Father of Truth and Light" into the first petition. The title functioned to call attention and lend support to the truths that "we are one family of people as a nation" and "one of many nations in a family of nations."

Although the family metaphor has long appealed to the American people,[31] Americans have not always been willing to extend membership in the family to those outside of the United States. While paying homage to the *idea* of a family of nations, Americans have steadfastly held to the myth of special destiny with its connotations of superior moral quality. Hence, Davis appealed through the "Father of Truth" first to a proposition widely held and then to one less widely held.

By accepting Davis's assertion concerning the family of nations, the audience could enjoy the satisfaction of knowing they were participating in an enterprise of "universal meaning and purpose." The universalism of Davis's prayer was in marked contrast to many previous prayers that located America's meaning and purpose in its status as a redeemer nation specially chosen by God as a blueprint for the nations of the world.[32] Indeed, Davis's conception of universal meaning predicated on familial relationship flew directly in the face of both Archbishop Lucey's and Archbishop Iakovos's prayers.

For both Lucey and Iakovos, America's calling was clear. She was to be the instrument of God's salvation. Archbishop Lucey prayed, "In Thy divine providence, O Heavenly Father, the moral leadership of the world has been entrusted to us; the fate of humanity is in our hands; the nations look to us for survival; Western civilization stands or falls with America."[33]

America's calling was not predicated on participation in a family of nations, but rather upon God's preordained choice. As Archbishop Iakovos affirmed: "From the time of the Pilgrims and the Founding Fathers of our Nation, and throughout the course of our entire history, Thou has been our guiding light, our constant inspiration and illumination, and an inexhaustible source of reinforcement and fortitude. Having our trust in Thee, we have raised under the splendor of Thy skies the Stars and Stripes of our exalted ideals and national pursuits, and in the measure of Thy loving kindness, we selflessly serve the spiritual as well as the material welfare of our fellow man at home and abroad."[34]

Having alluded to a universalism seldom found in official prayer, Davis then applied his new paradigm to an old myth-of-state commonplace. He prayed, "Uphold him, O God, that he may urge us onward toward a great and desirable society of persons who desire goodness, and Nations whose God is the Lord." The common formulation was "that Nation [singular] whose God is the Lord." Davis rejected such an ambiguous construction as he intentionally inserted the plural form of the word. As he later testified: "That's why I spoke about the family of nations. . . . That's one of the things I wanted to avoid in this prayer."[35]

Unlike some of his clerical predecessors, Davis actualized his universal concept through changes in word choice, as demonstrated in the third version. He returned to the original ending by listing the titles of the Holy One of Israel found in the Book of Isaiah.

The final version of the prayer continued to show change as Davis rearranged phrases, adding and deleting at several points. In addition to asking help for the president, Davis requested that aid he extended "to all those whose judgments and loyalties they must be able to rely upon." Davis again moved from an audience action to a presidential action when he substituted "he must remind us" for "help us not to forget." "Reminding" pictured the president seizing the initiative while the earlier phrase connoted a secondary reaction.

Continuing his universal emphasis, Davis inserted the modifier "worthy" into the last version when he observed that "we are but one of many worthy nations in an aspiring family of nations." As if to further emphasize this universalism, Davis inserted the title "God of all the worlds." The title functioned to lend support and authority to Davis's assertion of universal meaning and purpose.

A phrase that originated in version one and survived, virtually intact, to version four was the petition for help to "reason together, to seek an essential consensus, to live in our strange and wonderful diversity with stable unity." The only change in this petition was the substitution of "essential" for "worthy" consensus. It was part of the Johnson image or political myth that he was a consensus seeker. Johnson explained his consensus politics when he observed: "The biggest danger to American stability is the politics of principle, which brings out the masses in irrational fights for unlimited goals, for once the masses begin to move, then the whole thing begins to explode. Thus it is for the sake of nothing less than stability that I consider myself a consensus man."[36]

It was obvious that Davis was familiar with Johnson's view of himself and incorporated that view into his prayer. It was not by accident that the terms "consensus" and "stable" occurred in such close proximity. One source of invention for Dr. Davis, as for previous inaugural clergy, was the dominant political image associated with the chief of state. Davis's allusion to "reasoning together" was another example of invention arising from political image. On more than one occasion Johnson said, "I want all of us to constantly bear in mind the biblical injunction by the prophet Isaiah, 'Come now, let us reason together.' " The scripture was, in fact, a constant refrain in his quest "to make all men think alike, or reasonably so."[37] To the extent that inaugural prayers reflected the dominant political stance of the chief executive, the prayers functioned as reinforcement and legitimation for an image already formed, a myth already extant.

In the final version Davis dropped "great and desirable society" for "desirable society." In doing so he eliminated the Johnson slogan but retained the implied argument that Johnson's great society was indeed a desirable one. Davis deleted the reference to "nations whose God is the Lord" in the final version, but substituted for it another biblical allusion. He prayed for "a society in which none shall live in fear, because justice, mercy, and brotherhood will flourish on the earth." Though he eliminated one part of his universal appeal by this deletion, Davis succeeded in adding a note of hope through the allusion to the ancient prophecy. That Davis believed the prayer "should have a note of hope in it" accounted perhaps for the scriptural change.[38]

Davis concluded his prayer with the list of divine titles from Isaiah. Only version two failed to contain this ending, indicating that Davis strongly preferred it to any other. Even in version two, Davis avoided a strictly Christological conclusion, opting instead for "the Redeemer's name." When questioned about his use of the Isaiah passage and his failure to use Christological terminology, Davis replied: "Well, that closing I often use. . . . It's a quotation from scripture. I think it did grow out of when I was traveling widely with the National Conference of Christians and Jews. I like this closing. It was in reference to Christ, at least Christians interpret it that way from the Old Testament. So instead of saying 'in the name of Christ,' I said, 'We ask it in the name of Him who is the Wonderful Counsellor, the Mighty God, the Everlasting Father, the Prince of Peace.'. . . I still have this consciousness of the broader scope when you're in a different situation."[39]

Although there is no direct evidence linking specific White House suggestions with specific changes in content, it is clear that version two was preferred over version one and that this preference was communicated to Dr. Davis. It is also clear from the foregoing analysis that the final prayer resembled version two (the White House preference) more than version one (Dr. Davis's original preference). Furthermore, the only confessional passages, found exclusively in version one, were eliminated because of Davis's adherence to White House guidance. This is not to say that Davis would not have eliminated those passages himself as he "struggled over the language,"[40] but it is to contend that his choice in the matter was effectively negated by the presence of White House "suggestions."

Since Dr. Davis, when interviewed in 1979, did not recall any of the events surrounding the submission and subsequent revisions of his prayer, it was difficult to assess with any accuracy the specific effect of the White House. When contacted about his role in the prayer debate, Bill Moyers replied, "You have drawn a total blank with me; I simply can't remember."[41] Hence, the actual effect of prior submission and oversight may never be known, but the very fact that submissions were required, suggestions made, and revisions scrutinized testifies to the ease with which inaugural prayer could be turned to partisan political ends.

Generic Characteristics of Inaugural Prayer

George Davis's prayer was not appreciably different from dozens of others that had been delivered in the thirty years preceding the Johnson inaugural. It followed the prescribed form of address to the Deity ("God of our fathers"), ascription to the Deity ("to whom persons are of supreme importance"), assertion ("we are but one of many worthy nations in an aspiring family of nations"), petition ("Grant our President not to grow weary"), and conclusion ("We pray in the name of Him who is the Wonderful Counsellor, the Mighty God, the Everlasting Father, and the Prince of Peace. Amen."). There were no explicit supports or warrants for assertions in this prayer, though reference or allusion to Scripture is often employed by inaugural clergymen. Structurally, the prayer was similar to those that had preceded it and those that would follow.[42]

Likewise, in terms of its rhetorical appeals, the Davis prayer conformed to the overall pattern evidenced over the past fifty years. Davis appealed to the nature of the presidential character, office, and program ("We thank Thee for his magnificently significant service to his Nation and the World, already written on history's scroll. For his gallantry and stability, seen in times of greatest peril and in dark tragedy, as well as in the daily routine of his never-ending duties, we thank Thee"); to the nature of the Deity ("Giver of all gifts to men"); to the nature of the relationship of the Deity to America and her people ("For us, God of all the worlds, our dreams, our efforts, and our sacrifices, Thou wilt redeem to give them universal meaning and purpose"); to unity and national solidarity ("that he may encourage us to be able increasingly to reason together, to seek an essential consensus, to live in our strange and wonderful diversity with stable unity"); and to self-understanding ("to that desirable society of persons who seek real worth, a society in which none shall live in fear, because justice, mercy, and brotherhood, will flourish on the earth").

If Davis's rhetoric was neither structurally nor substantively different from other instances that preceded and followed it, wherein lies its importance as a rhetorical artifact? What do we learn from study of this one prayer that we could not learn from examination of any one of a dozen others? The answer, I believe, lies in the notion of configurated interplay, the particular constellation of elements that at one point in time conspired to allow *this prayer* to be given by *this clergyman* at *this ceremony* under *these particular circumstances*.

ELEMENTS IN CONFIGURED INTERPLAY

The importance of Davis's prayer is not in the rhetoric per se, but in the contextual, processual, and correlational features that called it into being, shaped it, and modified it in line with existing exigencies. Study of the prayer is important because it helps to unmask the forces operating in the processes of invention, arrangement, style, and delivery.

The process by which the prayer was called into being originated centuries prior to this enactment. Hence, the potential for modification within the provoking urgency was slim to none. Inaugural prayer was an institutionalized ritual whose antecedent forms allowed certain pragmatic and functional objectives to be achieved.

For inaugural planners and political strategists, prayer functioned rhetorically to identify the incoming leader with goodness and righteousness. It was an explicit sign that the president believed in God, prayer, and institutionalized religion. It was an implicit testimony to the rapprochement that occurred between civil and religious authorities shortly after the official separation of church and state. It was, in short, good politics.

For the clergymen who participated in events of state, prayers functioned to remind the civil authorities of their exercise of power *under* God. Participation was a way of redeeming, if only symbolically, the power and prestige that once accompanied high ecclesiastical office. Though personal power was often highly circumscribed, clerical participation functioned to remind the audience, both political and lay, of the institutional importance of organized religion. As the political strategists gained a rhetorical advantage from clerical participation, so the clerics and their institutions gained the credibility that inevitably accompanies those perceived to be close to the sources of power.

For the audience members, the prayers functioned as rhetorical legitimators of American myths of state, of uncontested propositions to which Americans had traditionally paid obeisance: that the leader was blessed by God; that American ideals were lofty and unblemished; that Americans were God's people; that America had a responsibility to provide moral leadership to the world. These were propositions to be honored and remembered, not debated, for such is the nature of epideictic discourse.

Lawrence W. Rosenfield has noted that epideictic evokes "a distinctive form of understanding" that "differs from inferences and judgments more common to public controversy. Epideictic's understanding calls upon us to join with our community in giving thought to what we witness, and such thoughtful beholding in commemoration constitutes memorializing."[43]

The rhetoric of inaugural prayer functions as a memorial of the past, a confirmation of the present, and a vision for the future. Its purpose is to weave together the threads of history that constitute the meaning of America, and to do so under the rubric of address to God.

From the point of view of inaugural planners the question was not, therefore, whether there should be a prayer, for perceived political advantage already dictated that answer. The question, instead, became what sort of prayer should be delivered and by

whom? When the Johnson staff was faced with the decision concerning the Jewish representative a whole set of criteria were already in
existence, albeit implicitly, to help them make an informed choice.
By applying the criteria to the case at hand, the question as to which
clergyman was "best" answered itself.

Likewise, the contextual nature of an inaugural ceremony virtually dictated the form the prayer would take. Prayers, like public
speeches, have conventional forms: beginnings, middles, and end-
ings. A prayer that failed to address the deity, petition the deity, or
conclude with an explicit or implicit reference to the deity would
fail the structural tests of the genre. An inaugural prayer is even
more circumscribed, requiring recognition of the occasion, a blessing
upon the president, and renewed vision for the future of the nation.
Given these strictures, the capacity of the listener to do anything
more than recognize and appreciate the myths was, again, slim to
none.

Participants in epideictic, including the audience, are usually
predisposed to accept the vision offered. Listeners are ready to hear
the story of the beginning, the fight against overwhelming odds, the
momentary setbacks, the seeming defeat but eventual triumph over
evil, and finally the rebirth in a new and better world. Just as the
potential to correlate epideictic oratory with specific behavioral
change is minimal, so readiness to hear, understand, and accept is
at a maximum. The orator presents a familiar story in a familiar
form. The audience, drawing on a communal consciousness, reani-
mates the heroes of the republic and reaffirms its commitment to
national ideals and its loyalty to the bearer of those ideals, the new
president.

The relation of the clergyman to the entire ceremony is not
as predictable as one might expect, however. The case of the
clergymen at the Johnson inauguration notwithstanding, the
history of inaugural prayer demonstrates that individual clergymen
have, on occasion, been able to exert the force of their own beliefs,
personalities, and agenda into the prayer moment. Contextual and
procedural factors have not always determined specific content.
Yet, in the case of the Johnson inaugural, processual considerations
largely subsumed other factors. If there were any differences
between the purposes of the clergymen and the purposes of those
who chose them, such differences were homogenized in the
editorial process.

The symbolic inducements offered by the Reverend Davis and
the other clerics at the 1965 inaugural not only conformed to the
contextual and processual requirements, but also conformed to the

political and personal requirements of Lyndon Johnson. It was not enough that the prayers drew upon the cultural mythology or the structural antecedents. They had also to bear the imprimatur, the personal stamp of approval, of Lyndon Baines Johnson. In the case of the Davis prayer this resulted in a discourse less confessional in nature, more laudatory of the president, and less focused on the nature and attributes of the Deity. Processual factors, more than context, antecedent forms, or the speaker's belief, attitude and value structure, influenced specific aspects of invention.

Conclusion

The exigential flow, of which the Johnson inaugural was but one word in a long book extending back into antiquity, continues to invite discourses that reflect the human propensity to encompass the world in civil-religious terms. Antecedents helped to shape the prayers and those prayers, in turn, became part of the flow, creating ever-new urgencies, potential for modifications, and constraining influences.

The short-term consequences of the processual modifications introduced by Johnson appeared four years later at Nixon's first inauguration. Clerical selection was based not only on personal loyalty and geographical representation as it had been during the Johnson ceremony, but also on race and politics. Speaker invention functioned not only as secondhand apologia for the Nixon administration, just as it had for Johnson, but also as rhetorical foil and instrument of division. Rhetorical invitations emphasized not only the unity of the people—as had nearly all the inaugural prayers from Roosevelt to Johnson—but also the distinctiveness of race, class, and philosophical commitment.[44]

Pieces of rhetoric viewed in isolation are mere travelers in time; momentarily meaningful, lost, forgotten, only to rise again clothed anew and seeking adherence. From the city-states of ancient Greece to the medieval churchmen to the English Puritans arriving on the shores of the New World, civil-religious rhetoric has flowed and ebbed but never disappeared.

Study of one event within the historical flow hardly merits the space occupied, for such events are but a frame in time, a deformity, a lie. Yet it is from the study of such lies, and the urgencies which call them into being, that we realize anew that ideas and their expression do have consequences and that those consequences can have profound implications for the study of humanity. By expanding our gaze beyond the moment to encompass the contextual, processual, and correlational dimensions of discourse, we are better able to discern cause and consequent where before we could find "nothing but" rhetoric.

Notes

1. Eugene E. White, "Rhetoric as Historical Configuration," in *Rhetoric in Transition: Studies in the Nature and Uses of Rhetoric*, ed. Eugene E. White (University Park: Pennsylvania State Univ. Pr., 1980), 7–20.

2. Kathleen M. Hall Jamieson, "Generic Constraints and the Rhetorical Situation," *Philosophy and Rhetoric* 6 (1973): 162–70; Jamieson, "Antecedent Genre as Rhetorical Constraint," *Quarterly Journal of Speech* 61 (1975): 406–15. For an application of these ideas in critical practice see Kathleen Hall Jamieson, "Interpretation of Natural Law in the Conflict Over *Humanae Vitae*," *Quarterly Journal of Speech* 60 (1974): 201–11. G. P. Mohrmann and Michael C. Leff, "Lincoln at Cooper Union: A Rationale for Neo-Classical Criticism," *Quarterly Journal of Speech* 60 (1974): 459–67; Martin J. Medhurst, "American Cosmology and the Rhetoric of Inaugural Prayer," *Central States Speech Journal* 28 (1977): 272–82; Kurt W. Ritter, "American Political Rhetoric and the Jeremiad Tradition: Presidential Nomination Acceptance Addresses, 1960–1976," *Central States Speech Journal* 31 (1980): 153–71; Ruth Ann Weaver, "Acknowledgment of Victory and Defeat: The Reciprocal Ritual," *Central States Speech Journal* 33 (1982): 480–89.

3. White, "Historical Configuration," 17.

4. White, "Historical Configuration," 14, 15.

5. Jamieson, "Generic Constraints," 165.

6. Martin J. Medhurst, "From Duché to Provoost: The Birth of Inaugural Prayer," *Journal of Church and State* 24 (1982): 573–88.

7. For a discussion of Ryan's relationship with Roosevelt see Martin J. Medhurst, "Argument and Role: Monsignor John A. Ryan on Social Justice," *Western Journal of Speech Communication* 52 (1988): 75–90. Ryan's works which relate most directly to the Roosevelt revolution are *A Living Wage* (New York: Macmillan, 1906); *Distributive Justice—The Right and Wrong of Our Present Distribution of Wealth*, 3d ed. (New York: Macmillan, 1942); and *Seven Troubled Years* (Ann Arbor, Mich.: Edwards Brothers, 1937). See also Francis L. Broderick, *The Right Reverend New Dealer: John A. Ryan* (New York: Macmillan, 1963); and Patrick W. Gearty, *The Economic Thought of Monsignor John A. Ryan* (Washington, D.C.: Catholic Univ. Pr., 1953).

8. Lyndon Baines Johnson, "Remarks at the Twelfth Annual Presidential Prayer Breakfast," 5 Feb. 1964, in *Public Papers of the Presidents of the United States, 1964* (Washington, D.C.: Government Printing Office, 1965), 261.

9. Rowland Evans and Robert Novak, *Lyndon B. Johnson: The Exercise of Power* (London: George Allen and Unwin, 1966), 4. See also Kathleen J. Turner, *Lyndon Johnson's Dual War: Vietnam and the Press* (Chicago: Univ. of Chicago Pr., 1985).

10. Alfred Steinberg, *Sam Johnson's Boy: A Close-up of the President From Texas* (New York: Macmillan, 1968), 681; Eric F. Goldman, *The Tragedy of Lyndon Johnson* (New York: Knopf, 1969), 190.

11. I have chosen to focus first on Rabbi Schachtel then on Reverend Davis for purely pragmatic reasons. Even though several different religious groups have, through the years, waged campaigns to gain admittance to the inaugural platform, I have significant documentary evidence for only this one case. Likewise, though all four clergymen at the Johnson inaugural were required to submit their prayers for review, I have been able to obtain sequential drafts only for the Davis prayer.

12. Rabbi Abraham N. AvRutick to Senator Abraham A. Ribicoff, 2 Nov. 1964. President's Personal File (PPF), Lyndon Baines Johnson Library, Austin, Texas.

13. Senator Abraham A. Ribicoff to Lyndon B. Johnson, 4 Nov. 1964. PPF.

14. Senator Abraham A. Ribicoff to Jack Valenti, 4 Nov. 1964; Jack Valenti to Senator Abraham A. Ribicoff, 9 Nov. 1964. PPF.

15. Rabbi Israel Miller to Myer Feldman, 16 Nov. 1964; Myer Feldman to Lyndon B. Johnson, 17 Nov. 1964. PPF.

16. Rabbi Harold H. Gordon to Lyndon B. Johnson, 16 Nov. 1964; Jack Valenti to Bill Moyers, 21 Nov. 1964. PPF.

17. Quoted in Charles Roberts, *LBJ's Inner Circle* (New York: Delacorte, 1965), 53; Roberts, *Inner Circle*, 56–57.

18. Jack Valenti to Lyndon B. Johnson, 4 Dec. 1964. PPF.

19. Bill Moyers to Lyndon B. Johnson, 5 Dec. 1964. PPF.

20. Myer Feldman to Lyndon B. Johnson, 9 Dec. 1964. PPF.

21. Jack Valenti to Bill Moyers, 14 Dec. 1964. PPF.

22. Jack Valenti to Lyndon B. Johnson, 27 Dec. 1964. PPF.

23. Jack Valenti to Lyndon B. Johnson, 27 Dec. 1964; Horace Busby, note written on top of Valenti to Johnson, 27 Dec. 1964. PPF.

24. Rev. George Davis to The President and Mrs. Johnson, 22 Dec. 1964. PPF.

25. Rev. George Davis to Lyndon B. Johnson, 6 Jan. 1965; Jack Valenti to Rev. George Davis, 8 Jan. 1965; Bill Moyers to Hayes written on top of George Davis to Bill Moyers, 6 Jan. 1965. PPF.

26. Rev. George Davis to Lyndon B. Johnson, 6 Jan. 1965; Rev. George Davis to Bill Moyers, 6 Jan. 1965. PPF.

27. It should be noted that documents obtained from the Johnson Library in Austin, Texas, do not indicate whether the Iakovos and Lucey prayers were revised, but it was clear that both were submitted on 5 January as requested.

28. In 1945, John A. Ryan prayed, "The tasks which he [Roosevelt] faces are supremely difficult; the responsibilities which he assumes are weightier and more complex than those that burdened any of his predecessors." At the 1953 ceremony Archbishop Patrick O'Boyle petitioned the Deity for divine aid which would "make bearable the great burdens of his high office." And in 1957 Edward Cardinal Mooney concluded by asking God to bless the "Chief Executive as he assumes for another term the heavy responsibility of the Presidency in a troubled and confused world."

29. When later asked about the possibility of his prayers being submitted prior to the inaugural, Dr. Davis denied that any such thing ever took place. "I was very close to Jack Valenti when he was in the White House and the time since he left it," said Davis, "and nothing like that was ever said to me. . . . They didn't know any more about the content of the prayer than anybody in the audience did."

Davis vigorously defended the Johnson White House and especially Jack Valenti. "I just don't think he [Valenti] would have done that," said Davis. "His wife was a member of the Christian Church," he continued, "he was a Catholic. Valenti was very wise and shrewd politically and I think he was very aware of the stupid things ministers can do sometimes. . . . They do have an unusual opportunity to take advantage of the situation. I think he may have foreseen, but I don't think he did anything. I just know Jack Valenti, I know Bill Moyers well enough, I knew Watson well enough, I just don't believe those men would have presumed to have said that. And if they did, Johnson would not have listened to them."

After being confronted with the correspondence cited above, as well as with his own letters, Davis had to admit that his memory had failed him. "Well," he said, "I can honestly say that for the life of me I do not remember that. If I did that, I'm lost in the passing of years. But I have no recall of it at all. . . . Maybe I wanted to lose sight of it. Some things you don't want to remember you forget. So maybe I forgot it because I wanted to." Telephone interview with Rev. George R. Davis, 4 Aug. 1979; tape recording in author's possession.

30. The rhetorical figure of *epanaphora* is defined as "the repetition of the same word at the beginning of successive clauses or verses." *Epistrophe* is defined as the "repetition of a closing word or words at the end of several clauses, sentences, or verses." See Richard A. Lanham, *A Handlist of Rhetorical Terms* (Berkeley: Univ. of California Pr., 1968), 42, 8, 45.

31. Metaphors connoting familial relationships were an integral part of Pilgrim and Puritan thinking. God was the "Father" and men and women were his "children." Believers were all part of God's family according to the doctrine of relatives. See Edmund S. Morgan, *The Puritan Family* (New York: Harper, 1966), 1–28.

32. See Ernest Lee Tuveson, *Redeemer Nation: The Idea of America's Millennial Role* (Chicago: Univ. of Chicago Pr., 1968).

33. Archbishop Robert E. Lucey, quoted in the *Congressional Record—Senate*, 91st Congress (1965), 984.

34. Archbishop Iakovos, quoted in the *Congressional Record—Senate,* 91st Congress (1965), 986.

35. Interview, George Davis.

36. Lyndon B. Johnson, quoted in Doris Kearns, *Lyndon Johnson and The American Dream* (New York: Harper, 1976), 154.

37. Lyndon B. Johnson, "Remarks upon Receiving a Citation from the Disciples of Christ Historical Society," *Personal Papers, 1964,* 507; Hugh Sidey, *A Very Personal Presidency: Lyndon Johnson in the White House* (New York: Atheneum, 1968), 45.

38. Interview, George Davis.

39. Interview, George Davis.

40. Interview, George Davis.

41. Bill Moyers to the author, 14 Aug. 1979.

42. Martin J. Medhurst, "God Bless The President: The Rhetoric of Inaugural Prayer" (Ph.D., diss., Pennsylvania State University, 1980). See especially 554–600.

43. Lawrence W. Rosenfield, "The Practical Celebration of Epideictic," in *Rhetoric in Transition,* ed. White, 133.

44. In addition to the rhetorical considerations that Johnson used when making his clerical selections, Nixon employed race, class, and political philosophy as criteria. He invited the first black clergyman, Bishop Charles Ewbank Tucker of the African Methodist Episcopal Zion Church. He also invited evangelist Billy Graham, the quintessential representative of the great American middle class. All five clerics at the 1969 Nixon inauguration were well-known conservatives and at least two—Tucker and Graham—had campaigned actively for Nixon's election. For more detail see Medhurst, "God Bless the President," 383–403.

EIGHT

Rhetoric as a Way of Being

THOMAS W. BENSON

THIS ESSAY IS an inquiry into rhetoric as a way of being. Every rhetorical and communication theorist who attempts a comprehensive description of human symbolic behavior must address the complex of issues surrounding human agency in discourse.[1] Most theorists agree that discourse is produced by human agents and addressed to other human agents. Other theorists go further and insist that discourse constitutes those agents and their relationships to one another. In this essay I shall pose, as briefly as possible, what I take to be a central question in the theory of rhetoric as being, and explore the question through a close reading of one rhetorical event.

Modern rhetorical theorists tend to regard as outmoded a conception of speaker and audience that describes the two as if they were made of different materials—one a manipulator, the other a passive object; one a cue and the other a billiard ball; one a hypodermic syringe and the other a patient. Rhetorical theory as a humanistic discipline has emphasized that both speaker and audience are human agents. Modern theory has also emphasized the extent to which human reality is constructed through symbols, which leads to the view that *being* exists in and through symbolic behavior. But if this is so, are not speaker and listener once again reified into separate beings? From this apparent contradiction comes the question to which this essay is addressed: How, if at all, is it possible to describe the actions of speaker (or writer) and listener (or reader) in a way that acknowledges the extent to which the *being* of each is constituted by their interaction but which also acknowledges that both are human agents? A theoretical question would seem to require a theoretical reply, but I shall move as quickly as possible from theory to criticism, since the details of a case are likely to present a necessary challenge to theoretical oversimplification.

The concept of rhetoric as a way of being suffers from some of the same conceptual difficulties as the concept of rhetoric as a way of knowing.[2] It may be argued that *all* human being is rhetorical, in that human personality and our awareness of it are constituted and transmitted through symbolic behavior. Or we may take the matter of rhetorical being more narrowly, arguing only that in strictly rhetorical situations the issue of who is speaking and who is listening is both relevant to and constructed in the rhetoric. Even in the narrowest sense, at least the following elements of being are present:

—the speaker as known to the hearers before the encounter
—the speaker as perceived by the audience during the act of speaking
—the personality of the speaker as it influences rhetorical choices
—the predispositions of the audience, singly and together, before the encounter
—the audience as known to the speaker before the encounter
—the speaker as a self-constructed symbolic entity in the speech
—the audience as it is invited to perceive itself in the speech

In theory, most contemporary students of rhetoric and communication seem to agree that speaker and listener are mutually interacting agents, each the center of his or her own perceptions. Carroll C. Arnold puts the matter clearly:

Any speaker with rhetorical intent acts, first projectively and then actually, as his own protagonist in an interaction with fellow human beings who, on their parts, see *themselves* as both chief protagonists and directors in the relationship. The conditions being those of orality, something resembling the speaker's script is to be played ensemble, despite the fact that no one engaged in the personalized, rhetorical situation can be cast as a minor actor within *his* dramatic world. In speech the physical person and the existential self are invested—in what is prepared to be spoken, in what is spoken, and in the instant-by-instant *being* of speaking. Listeners expect it to be so, and, if they listen, they ready themselves to close on instigated but private messages, all the while regarding the speaker as an "other" who seeks a role within their worlds.[3]

Arnold appears to take a firmly centralist position on the matter of speaker-listener relations. In theoretical debates over the past thirty or so years, the extremes on this issue have tended to overstate each others' positions, if not their own; parodies of the two extremes, as stated by their opponents, would run something like this: To the far right, the variable testers seek the invariable laws that govern what they truly believe must, if they could but generalize broadly enough, and free of confounding variables, describe the technology of belief. These seekers after the law somewhat disguise their position by referring to the objects they are attempting to control as subjects, but the only subjectivity in this universe is regarded as sentimentality or bad science. To the far left of the center are those who conceive of purposive, public discourse as an offense against the warm bath of intimacy in which every free creature is to be left to do its own thing.

In practice, few academic theorists have ever been so far out on either of these limbs, and I have no wish to slander with a *reductio ad absurdum* either those theorists who have sought, in the last decade, to find a language that would enable them to describe the relationship between speaker and listener as something more balanced than "who" speaking to "whom," or those who have sought to introduce the rigor of quantitative investigation into the study of communication. Still, at their most extreme, the far left and right positions on communication theory become no communication at all. One side distrusts communication as manipulation and opts instead for communion, empathy, and affinity that are not based on the restrictions of symbolism, tact, or competing interests. And the other side seeks not communication but control, wherein purpose, message, transmission, and response are part of a totally predictable process of management.

Among the utopians, Arnold is not simply a moderate. His position allows him radical forays to both left and right in search of the variety of human symbolic collaboration as rhetoric. Because of the way we have posed the problem thus far, it may appear that Arnold offers, as against the extremes of determinism and privatism, an insipid centralism. But Arnold goes beyond saying that the truth is somewhere in between. Arnold does, it is true, suggest that rhetorical situations constrain the choices open to speakers and listeners, and he does note the personal risks of public action. But it is a special quality of Arnold's conception that he avoids reifying the speaker and listener.

Speakers and listeners are not two different materials or species. As Arnold is careful to note, a speaker is a person acting. "It appears to me that a basic characteristic of rhetorical engagement or relationship under conditions of orality is that each party retains its dominion over self but commits himself to ally (often fitfully) with the other in closure-encouraging, closure-making activity. Because the alliance is sustained orally, the burden of sustaining it to the listener's satisfaction falls upon the person-as-action of the speaker."[4] It is characteristic of Arnold's writing that he slows the reader down by refusing to hurry along with the convenient formulas that are often mistaken for clarity in academic writing. For Arnold, the speaker is not one thing and the listener another thing. Rather, both are persons-as-actions—an awkward phrase, it may seem at first, but one that forces the reader to pause. Arnold's speaker and listener, to paraphrase Buckminster Fuller, seem to be verbs.[5]

If speaker and listener are regarded as indissoluble elements precipitated out of the rhetorical situation, or as incompatible species of a common genus, then they are trapped into an at least metaphorical otherness, an otherness that is liable to deny their common human agency and to lead to a rhetorical theory that emphasizes the manipulation of objects. A more satisfactory view is suggested by Arnold: rhetorical being is a mode of action. The terms *speaker* and *listener* are only a shorthand for persons-as-actions, persons speaking and listening. Or, as Kenneth Burke has put it, speaker and listener are roles or stances enacted by human beings with a common human sub-stance. Action and substance are inseparable.[6]

The way of addressing rhetorical being that Arnold suggests has an important consequence for ways of thinking about rhetoric. Traditional rhetorical theory asked how human being can be employed as a resource for proof in rhetorical transactions: the speaker constructs an image of himself, draws proof from received opinion about how people can be expected to behave, and appeals to the conjectured feelings and beliefs of an audience. The question for such theories is, how can the resources of human being be drawn upon in the given case to gain an end desired by the speaker? But, as Arnold reminds us, another question must always run parallel to the first: how can the resources of rhetorical interaction contribute to human being? Arnold is too pragmatic and too devoted to the public uses of discourse to suggest a shift in focus from rhetoric as proving to rhetoric as experience, but he does insist that any account of rhetorical events is incomplete if it does not account for the human experience as well as the pragmatic outcome of persuasion.

Critics and teachers of speech communication have been attempting in recent years to reframe their conceptions of relations between speakers and audiences. Undergraduate courses in speech communication were at one time concerned primarily with the speaker as the agent in rhetoric, leaving the audience as, at best, something to be analyzed, convinced, persuaded. In recent years, new courses have been developed that attempt to focus attention on the listener as a fully participating agent in the transaction. But simply shifting attention from a "speaker-centered" to a "listener-centered" approach will not, in itself, lead to a satisfactory account of rhetoric as a way of being. Courses that address students in their roles as listeners tend to fall into six patterns: (1) Students are taught to comprehend and remember; these are the listening and study skills courses. (2) Students are taught to "appreciate" an art form, such as film, television, or orally interpreted literature. (3) Students are told to be "good listeners," meaning that they should observe the decorum of the classroom and provide sympathetic support for their fellow speakers. (4) Students are taught to be judges of the truth-value of public speaking, which in practice means learning to apply a handbook of logical fallacies and propaganda tricks to the study of texts. Such inquiries, for better or worse, teach the student that a case can be made for any proposition and, worse, that all public discourse is, strictly speaking, fallacious. Always. This approach is usually interpreted by students to mean that all decision making that is not purely technical is irrational, so that in public situations their own prejudices are just as good as anyone else's. (5) Drawing upon the current enthusiasm for the consumer-protection movement in this country, students are imagined to be consumers of discourse. In practice, this approach uses the materials from the fourth approach and adds to them some information on the critical sociology of communication and an interest in the mass media and popular arts. But the analogy to consumerism is misleading, from a rhetorical point of view, because it draws students further into the mode of acquisitive narcissism that a "listener-centered" approach was designed to combat in the first place. It is as if one were to introduce an overprivileged American adolescent to the theme of economic and social justice by giving him a subscription to *Consumer Reports*. (6) Students are taught to be rhetorical critics. This is at least an intellectually respectable enterprise, and it may well teach students to think more fully about rhetorical interaction. Depending upon how it is taught, it may, however, enrich students' appreciation of their own and others' roles as speakers and listeners, or it may encourage them to stand apart from speakers and audiences as disinterested but disabled third parties. In each of these six "listener-centered" approaches, students are not simply taught to do something, but also to be something: sucessful exam takers, appreciators, polite supporters, logic choppers, consumers, or critics. It is not clear which approach will teach students to be effective and responsible social actors.

It is my purpose in the remainder of this essay to examine in detail a particular speaking-listening event as a collaboration between speakers and listeners to constitute a satisfactory "fusing" of "person and personality with a conceptual message."[7] The rhetorical event I propose to examine took place on 11 May 1972, in State College, Pennsylvania, and on the adjacent campus of the Pennsylvania State University, as several thousand antiwar demonstrators blocked a major highway and threatened to disrupt the operations of the Ordnance Research Laboratory. In examining these events, I will focus exclusively on the actions of speakers, listeners, and other relevant agents as they bear upon the question of rhetoric as a way of being. How did the speakers attempt to draw upon images of themselves, their listeners, and other human agents to achieve their ends? What actions did listeners take to constitute themselves in the situation? What evidence does the transaction provide as to the ways in which rhetoric can function as a way of being?

Implicit in the analysis that follows will be a theory and a method often espoused and demonstrated in the work of Eugene E. White. White's work in rhetoric has consistently demonstrated an attempt to relate theory to practice and to root the analysis of a text in a thorough understanding of the "configuration" of historical forces that unfold in a rhetorical event.[8]

I

The month of May 1972 saw one of the last great national waves of antiwar protest of the Vietnam era. Leaders of peace groups organized a national moratorium for 4 May, the second anniversary of the killings at Kent State University. The concept of a moratorium had first been employed by moderate peace groups in October and November 1969, and since that time there had been a rapid and steady decline in support for the continuation of the American venture in Southeast Asia.[9]

On 4 May, a group of about three hundred people turned out for a demonstration at the Pennsylvania State University. The group marched through the town of State College and across the campus, carrying a coffin in remembrance of the Kent State victims and calling for an end to the bombing of Vietnam. During the march, the demonstrators stopped for a time in front of the Ordnance Research Laboratory and sang "Give Peace a Chance" (figure 8–1).

Figure 8-1. Pennsylvania State University and vicinity

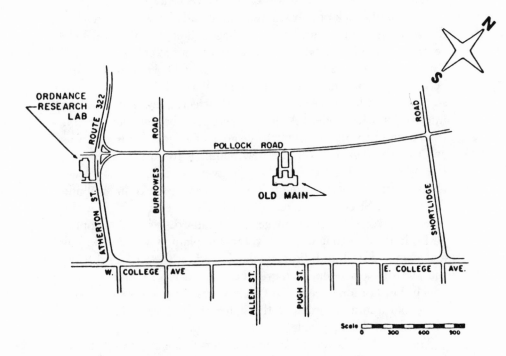

The Ordnance Research Laboratory had often been the focus of antiwar demonstrations at the university. The laboratory was known to conduct classified weapons research for the United States Navy and was famous for its Garfield Thomas Water Tunnel, a test facility for torpedoes and other underwater vehicles. As at other universities, Penn State antiwar protesters had called for an end to the ROTC program and the war, but at Penn State every list of demands seeking an end of complicity with the defense establishment had also called for the abolition of the Ordnance Research Laboratory and the Garfield Thomas Water Tunnel. At the end of the 1960s, a student underground newspaper was called *The Garfield Thomas Water Tunnel*, and many students in May 1972 remembered that in early 1969 the university administration had attempted to censor the newspaper, and that State College borough police had arrested people selling the newspaper on the grounds that it was obscene.[10]

The demonstrations of 4 May 1972 were mild. At a university of thirty thousand students, a peaceful march by three hundred demonstrators was news but not a large distraction, and certainly not a disruption. On campus there were a few discussion groups at the student union, but these were overshadowed by the feeling that with the coming of warmer weather fraternity parties could move outdoors. Spring Weekend was only two weeks away.

The relative lack of political tension in early May can be read in the activities surrounding State College's "People's Park." Three years before, in Berkeley, California, an attempt to create a People's Park in an abandoned university parking lot had led to bitter clashes between students and police. In State College a fire in a downtown storefront had left an open lot on Allen Street, a few doors from its intersection with College Avenue, where town bordered university. In the early spring the lot was cleared of major debris and was awaiting the construction of a new building. In April and May, a loosely organized group of faculty, university students, and local children began to clean it up. One morning pedestrians walking down Allen Street to the main entrance of the university at the intersection of Allen and College saw a small wooden sign: "People's Park." In the days that followed, volunteers planted trees and flowers and even laid fresh sod. From a pile of debris at the back of the lot, the park makers rescued charred beams and cinder blocks, from which they fashioned benches. One university professor spent a day laying out a formal garden in the shape of the "peace sign," using old bricks for his materials.

The mood of the People's Park builders was earnest and festive by turns. There was a general sense that the work could proceed communally but without any hierarchy of leadership. But the response of the townspeople was equally significant. The middle-aged shoppers and business people, as well as faculty and students, who passed the site seemed to regard it not as a revolutionary incursion on private property or as a hippie invasion, but as something akin to a Cub Scout cleanup campaign. Sidewalk superintendents called their appreciation, and one matron commented that it was "so nice that these children are doing something to improve the town."

But on 8 May, a Monday, the mood in State College—and the country—changed. In a televised address, President Nixon announced an intensified campaign of bombing in North Vietnam, concentrating on Hanoi and the major port city of Haiphong. In addition he announced that Haiphong harbor had been mined and that the United States Navy had been instructed to blockade the port, preventing the delivery of any materials that would support the war.[11]

In the context of an essay on rhetorical being, it is worth noting that Nixon used the bombings, and his speech, to construct himself, to assert his power over foreign policy, his determination not to lose in Indochina, and his willingness to be irrational. In the 8 May speech, Nixon asserted his dominance over Henry Kissinger in every reference to him ("I sent Dr. Kissinger"; "I instructed him"; "I authorized Dr. Kissinger"). In his memoirs, Nixon quotes from a memorandum to Kissinger, "I cannot emphasize too strongly that I have determined that we should go for broke. What we have got to get across to the enemy is the impression that we are doing exactly that. . . . He has now gone over the brink *and so have we.* . . . I have the *will* in spades. . . . For once, I want the military and I want the NSC staff to come up with some ideas on their own which will recommend *action* that is very *strong, threatening,* and *effective.*[12]

Soon after Nixon finished his speech, students knocked on doors in the dormitories on the Penn State campus, calling for a demonstration at the Ordnance Research Laboratory (the ORL) at 7:30 A.M., Tuesday, and for a noon rally at the student union, the Hetzel Union Building, usually called the HUB.

According to the campus newspaper, the *Daily Collegian,* at 7:30 A.M. on Tuesday, 9 May, about eighty-five demonstrators engaged in peaceful picketing of the ORL, then left at 8:30 A.M. A noon rally at the HUB heard calls for larger demonstrations.

On Wednesday, 10 May, more than two thousand people marched in protest against the war. Various streets in downtown State College were blocked by protesters following a noon rally. Large numbers of people sat down on Atherton Street at the intersection with Pollock Road, just opposite the ORL. Several students were hit by cars pushing through the crowd, and at one point several students were injured when a flatbed truck carrying five men wielding lead pipes plowed through the crowd. The behavior of the large crowd of demonstrators, though obstructive, was peaceful. The relatively small forces of the campus and borough police were tentative and not aggressively hostile. Where possible they routed traffic around the demonstration to avoid confrontations.

I saw one incident in which a woman in a car with her small child was unable to proceed because of the crowd of students. The woman was obviously panicky. The students around and in front of her car did not in any way threaten her, though it was clear that she was frightened, angry, and almost hysterical. And yet no student came forward to talk to her, to calm her fear, or to explain the purposes of the demonstration. They were against the war, and they had lent themselves to the only action in town, but not many students were taking any initiative to talk to stalled drivers about their views. At 6:30 P.M., a rumor circulated that Lieutenant Governor Ernest Kline had arrived in town to confer with the president of the university, John Oswald. News also circulated that the governor, Democrat

Milton Shapp, had sent a telegram to President Nixon opposing the
renewed bombing, the mining, and the blockade. Many students
left the demonstration as evening settled in, but some students
stayed for an all-night vigil at the ORL. The evening papers reported
that massive antiwar demonstrations were taking place at many
colleges and universities and in cities all across the country.

On Thursday, 11 May, a crowd estimated by the *Daily Collegian*
at 5,500 was assembled in front of the ORL, once more completely
blocking North Atherton Street. But the new day brought something more than the largest antiwar demonstration ever at Penn
State. In a couple of places stones had been thrown through the
large glass windows through which the water tunnel itself could be
seen. Uniformed campus patrolmen guarded the doors of the building. In a parking lot next to the ORL, and just to the southeast,
were three busloads of state police. They were clearly visible to the
demonstrators, and it was reported later that the state police had
been issued riot gear and ordered to remove all identifying insignia.
Many in the crowd expected to be teargassed, and small knots of
people shared what little they knew about the situation, about how
to avoid the worst effects of the tear gas, and about what was
happening around the country. It was a feisty crowd, not especially
belligerent, but almost jubilant that such a large number of people
had turned out to protest the war. Occasionally there were isolated
calls to "trash the ORL," but most of the crowd seemed determined
to avoid violence. At no time was it clear that the large crowd was
under the leadership of any particular individual or group.

But the presence of the riot police seemed ominous to the crowd,
as, no doubt, the occasional calls of "trash the ORL" seemed ominous
to the police. It was the sort of situation in which a few wrong
choices could have turned the day into another Kent State. Then
there was a flurry of activity at the corner of the intersection next
to the ORL building. A knot of people had gathered, and someone
tested a bullhorn.

II

In the moments that followed, three people spoke to the crowd: the
lieutenant governor of Pennsylvania, Ernest Kline; the president of
the Penn State student government, Mike Shields; and a faculty
member, the advisor of the campus chapter of Students for a Democratic Society (SDS), Wells Keddie. The speeches were all directed

to a similar end, but the first two were dangerous failures and the third an immediate if ambiguous success. What follows is a transcript of the speeches taken from a tape recording. I will present the transcript in its entirety and then propose an analysis of the event. Because the crowd clearly rejected the first two speakers and accepted the third, we are presented with a more than usually sensitive transcript by which to read the probable responses of the audience. But we are interested in more than rhetorical success or failure; rather, I propose to inquire into the rhetorical event as an ongoing experience, for speakers and listeners, of what it meant to be a human agent in this situation. For this reason, our analysis will proceed as a fairly detailed explication, attempting to render a sense of speaking/listening as an unfolding of the process of rhetorical being.[13.]

SHIELDS:
Lieutenant Governor Kline has a statement to make. (*Applause*)
KLINE:
Is this all right, can you hear? ("Louder!") I've been here since last evening observing what's been going on. Oh, you can't? All I said was, I've been here since last evening, and observing what's [been?] going on, and I met earlier with a group of representatives who explained to me what they felt were some of the major reasons that you were conducting this demonstration. I spoke with the governor a few minutes ago for about fifteen minutes. I did not speak with Dr. Oswald, he did, in what was represented as a three-way conversation. The result of that conversation is this. First of all, the governor wishes me to convey to you, for himself and also for me, his feeling that he is in undoubted general sympathy with your attitude toward the actions of the president recently. . . . (*Applause*) Really [briefly?] I want you to understand this clearly because it's essentially on the request of the governor, not necessarily an order but one in which the university has agreed to comply, but only upon the strong request of the governor, that is in an effort to demonstrate our feelings and we hope to demonstrate the feelings you share, the Ordnance Research Laboratory operation, not just the building, operation, will be closed down tomorrow. (*Applause, cheers.* "How long? How long?") The request, the request was made that it be closed tomorrow. That's the message. (*Shouts from the crowd*) Wait a minute, that's not it, now wait a minute, it's not it. And the other part of the it is, that when I came

back to these people who represented you, I had no conditions
to lay down for them to meet. That's it. ("Throw him a fish!"
Shouts, chanting. "One, two, three, four, we don't want your
dirty war!")

SHIELDS:

I hope everyone understands that what this is doing is shutting
down the operation of the ORL. ("For one day!") Tomorrow is
Friday, and it will be shut down Saturday and Sunday. (*Shouts,
boos*) . . . I know what it means. I think you all know what it
means. (*Pause. Shouting.* "We want Wells back!") By shutting
down the operation of the Ordnance Research Laboratory, we
have achieved what we set out to do. (*Shouts*) What we are
asking (*shouts*), what we are asking now is that we continue this,
the ORL is shut down, and we continue this and move onto
campus now. ("Why?" *Shouts.* "Genocide." *Pause, then cheers*)

KEDDIE:

Now look, I'm not sure you can all hear me, because I was back
there and I couldn't hear much of what was being said. I know,
louder. (*Shouts*) Look, one of the things that we've been trying
to do is to get some kind of indication that somewhere along the
way we're going to start separating this university from the war
machine. We've never had a goddamn prayer in hell before and
you people have done it. Now, think about that for a minute. A
lot of you are quick to think that a three day, by the way, they
work this Goddamn place seven days a week so don't, don't sell
yourselves short what you got here. A three-day shut-down is
obviously not going to stop the university's complicity in the
war. One . . . yeah, I know, we are all here, we're trying to do
something about it. But one thing we've done that we have
never been able to do is to stop the whole goddamn thing for
three days and that really means something. If you want to sell
yourselves short and say, as usual, we didn't get it all, go ahead.
But I think we've really got some start here. (*Cheers, applause*)
So what happens after three days, the question is. (*Shouts.* "We
come back!") Wait a minute. What happens after three days,
what happens after three days is that if you spend the next three
days getting your analysis together and figuring out what to do
you can begin to dig this goddamn military machine out of here.
(*Cheers, applause*) Now wait a minute. Yeah, but, I know, it's
goddamned easy to stand out there and yell we're going to take
it, and take it, and take it, but we are not going to do it that
way. We've done it this way, we've done it more than we've
ever done before. Now we've got to get people like me to stop

doing this goddamn military research. We've got to get out there and do a job on these people and talk to them and talk to them and be here and make them explain why they are working on this war machine until they are so goddamn sick of it they stop. (*Applause.* "All right!") We've got to keep this thing going. And you can't keep it going sitting in the streets. We know that already. The only next step, the only next step from right here is to have a fight. Right? If some of you want it, then I don't. And you know I don't and I'm not trying to talk you out of it. If you want to have a fight there's lots of people ready. But you've won something, God almighty. The governor of this state, who has never before intervened in a positive manner, such as [Shapp has?]—I'm talking about the governor's office—has never before intervened in a positive manner—we have some examples of nonpositive interventions from the Republicans before—my gosh, let's see if we can keep this particular precedent going. We've won something. God almighty! Eight thousand people have brought this university to its knees, and shut the damn thing down, but President Oswald said he wouldn't do it. (*Applause*) We've won a battle. But we haven't won the war, and we haven't won the war until two things have happened. This university stops being part of the war machine and until that war in Vietnam and every place else has stopped we are going to have to keep fighting battles. But you don't fight the battles all the same way. Now's the tough part, right? Today we had it good. Eight thousand people, for the first time on this campus, we've won, now we've got to get back on that campus and we've got to talk to every goddamn person who isn't here and we've got to start talking to the faculty. Where are those sons of bitches, anyway? (*Cheers, applause.* "All right!") Well, well, by [thank?] God, we won't have to do anything. Right? But some of them want to, some of them are not sons of bitches, and we've got them on our side. There's a meeting of faculty tonight, and don't you believe that this is going to give them a lift? They're going to be on the upgrade for the first time since I've been here. You wait. Those people are going to be working. But you've got to get to those faculty. You've got to find out from every faculty member you know why they are doing this goddamn kind of research, if they are. And don't let them push you around, for God sakes. You're the university as much as they are. Let's get back on that campus. We've got a victory march ahead of us. Then let's organize ourselves. By God, you've got the beginnings of a student union here that will really show them something. (*Applause, cheers, chant.* "We want Keddie back.")[14]

III

As Keddie concluded, the enormous crowd cheered and, within a few minutes, dispersed. A potentially violent and destructive confrontation had been avoided. How can we explain the crowd's unwillingness to disperse after listening to Kline and Shields and its enthusiastic compliance with Keddie? The reasons are to be found, I believe, in the circumstances of the occasion but, more importantly, in the way the crowd, Kline, Shields, and Keddie defined themselves and their relationships.

At the moment when Shields introduced Lieutenant Governor Kline there was a wave of surprise and anticipation in the crowd. But the moment came with little preparation. Most in the crowd had no orientation to any particular leaders of the demonstration and knew nothing of the negotiations that were going on among the governor's office, the university administration, and student "leaders." Shields's introduction was made to an excited crowd that had a strong sense of its power, an uneasy awareness of its vulnerability to police attack, and a very unclear idea of what might happen next. Certainly it had no anticipation that it was about to hear any speeches.

Shields's announcement that Kline would speak was followed by applause, the tone of which, to judge from the context, was not applause for Kline but for the fact that the crowd's actions had made it necessary for the government to make some response to them. So Kline's speech was preceded by a whiff of victory for his audience. That the lieutenant governor came was a sign, if not of his sympathy, at least of what students had so passionately requested, then demanded, of the generation of their parents and teachers: meet with us, talk with us, negotiate with us. But as the lieutenant governor began to speak, the police were visible in the background. Would he simply read an order for the students to disperse?

Kline's speech appears to be a slightly awkward but otherwise straightforward narrative. But at every step, Kline's remarks called into question the relationships of the relevant participants in the drama. Kline confirmed that he had been in town since the previous evening. Then he went on, ". . . and I met earlier with a group of representatives who explained to me what they felt were some of

the major reasons that you were conducting this demonstration."
What representatives? Kline did not say and the crowd could not
have known. Were the "representatives" student government leaders, who are held in general contempt on most college campuses, or
antiwar activists? Although there had been some organizing activities to initiate the demonstrations in State College on 4 May and
again on 9 May, there was very little sense, from the crowd's point
of view, that it was "represented." There was no continuing public
platform of any significance from the period of 3 May to 11 May,
with the possible exception of the workshops in the HUB on 4 May,
and a diffuse series of meetings after 8 May. Hence, the lieutenant
governor's mention of "representatives" must have seemed ambiguous. That he met with students at all might have been regarded as
a concession, and it may have been impressive to the crowd to hear
Kline's narrative of the behind-the-scenes events of the past hours.
But the crowd was also alert to the possibility of a sellout by those
suddenly invented "representatives," and it still had no notion of
Kline's attitude toward what was happening.

Kline proceeded, not having named the "representatives" or having described where he met them, how many he spoke to, or what
they had said about "some of the major reasons you are conducting
this demonstration." The nature of human agency in this situation
was clouded by Kline's reference to "representatives," and it became
more obscure as he went on.

Kline continued, "I spoke with the governor a few minutes ago
for about fifteen minutes." Clear enough. "I did not speak with Dr.
Oswald, he did, in what was represented as a three-way conversation." Here the narrative loses clarity and seems to be carefully
shaded to avoid misattribution of responsibility. It is not clear
whether the conversation between Shapp and Oswald came before
or after Kline's conversation with Oswald. Who was it who "represented" these events as "a three-way conversation"? The passive
construction here introduces a mysterious other who is never identified, and the correction by Kline supposes a previous report that the
crowd had certainly not heard. In context, of course, it appears that
someone in the press must have alleged that there was a three-way
conversation, and Kline's correction, since it was not needed by the
audience standing in front of him, who had no previous information
about the conversation, seems to be directed at members of the press
listening to this speech. If Kline seemed to be speaking to the press,
and for the record, that would disrupt his implied contract to speak
directly to the audience before him and would, even if slightly, fan
the suspicion that a platform was being laid down for later reference.

Paranoid? Yes, but the students who had disrupted a community, who could see riot police over the speaker's shoulder, who could remember Kent State, and many of whom had personal recollections of the feelings of bad faith growing out of Penn State demonstrations of 1969 and 1970, might well be expected to be suspicious and particularly alert for any signs of a sellout or a setup.

Kline proceeded with another ambiguous description of human agency: "First of all, the governor wishes me to convey to you, for himself and also for me, his feeling that he is in undoubted general sympathy with your attitude toward the actions of the president recently. . . ." The substantive kernel of this sentence was met with enthusiasm: the governor was against the war, against Nixon, and was willing to identify himself publicly with the views of the students. But the grammar of the sentence is odd. Kline represented himself here as the governor's messenger, conveying, on the governor's orders, the governor's and Kline's feeling. Kline might have said, but did not, that he was conveying the governor's feelings and his own. Rather, Kline's feelings were filtered. They arose from Kline, went through the governor, and then were delivered by Kline as a subordinate aspect of the governor's feelings. Kline divided himself in half. There was the Kline who had an attitude toward the president's actions, and there was a different Kline, present before the immediate audience only in his role as lieutenant governor and the governor's messenger. Clearly, Kline was not present to negotiate or even to speak for himself, but to convey. His appearance before the audience was not marked by the same degree or kind of personal presence brought by the audience and did not, apparently, present any grounds upon which inter-action between Kline and the audience could occur.

Kline exercised considerable tact, though he may have made a mistake in doing so. He failed at several points in his speech to elaborate with details that might have illuminated what was happening, or brought the audience into a more sympathetic identification with his position. His reference to his and Shapp's "undoubted general sympathy with your attitude" was apparently deliberately vague. A strong statement against the war at this point would have had an electrifying effect upon the crowd, but Kline carefully did not go beyond the merest indication of support. Shapp had already sent a telegram of protest to Richard Nixon, and Kline might have quoted it to good effect. For the audience at the ORL, Kline's tact may well have seemed an attempt to protect his flanks, to express "general sympathy" but not to express antiwar sentiments that might alienate Pennsylvania citizens to whom his remarks would be reported. Of course, if the students sensed such caution it would have seemed to qualify Shapp's and Kline's move toward identification with the taint of hypocrisy.

Of course, Kline's tact could have been read another way, and was, I think, designed to be. Kline's speech asked nothing of the audience, and Kline did not enter into direct substantive interaction with the audience. To this rhetorical critic, with leisure to examine Kline's remarks after the fact, it appears that Kline was taking considerable pains to concede to his audience its responsibility for what it did. He offered "facts" for its consideration, but he did not ask the crowd to do anything, nor did he risk the charge of attempted co-optation by asking the crowd to accept him as an antiwar leader. He may have been moved by respect for the citizens he was addressing, but we cannot know whether he was, and that is a matter of psychobiography rather than rhetorical criticism in any case. What we do know is that the crowd did not respond to Kline with uncritical enthusiasm, and our interest as rhetorical critics is in trying to construct a reading of the speech that explains most fully what we can find in the situation, the speech, and the audience's response.

Kline continued, and once again the nature of human agency constituted the essential context of his remarks. "I want you to understand this clearly because it's essentially on the request of the governor, not necessarily an order but one in which the university has agreed to comply, but only upon the strong request of the governor, that is in an effort to demonstrate our feelings and we hope to demonstrate the feelings you share, the Ordnance Research Laboratory operation, not just the building, operation, will be closed down tomorrow." Kline said he wanted the crowd to "understand this clearly," but his description is both subtle and ambiguous. It might at first appear that the sentence indicates the governor's support: "on the request of the governor"; "only upon the strong request of the governor"; "to demonstrate our feelings." But Kline also seems to be spreading the responsibility for closing the ORL. He clearly does not indicate that the ORL was being closed in response to student demands; rather, it was being shut down "in an effort to demonstrate our feelings," and only after that was it "we hope to demonstrate the feelings you share." The responsibility for closing the ORL was not upon President Oswald, who was depicted as acting "upon the strong request of the governor." But the responsibility was also not entirely the governor's, since he was depicted as conveying a "request . . . not necessarily an order."

Furthermore, the elaborate way in which Kline diffused the responsibility for closing the ORL, excusing President Oswald and the governor, put a further strain on the directness of his relation with his audience. There was no particular reason for Kline to be so elaborate for the crowd. For them, he could simply have said something along the lines of, "To demonstrate their sympathy for your protest, the governor and President Oswald have decided to close the ORL for three days." But such a sentence would have had the effect of asserting a double responsibility, whereas Kline's way of putting it was a way of denying responsibility. And it was clear, if only implicitly, that such an elaborate avoidance was not needed so much by the student protesters as by the press and by other constituencies and agencies not present. The students were being granted a concession—for which they had not negotiated—but the concession was partly robbed of its moral force by being hedged and compromised in its very announcement: Kline was talking over the heads of the crowd to the public record. Kline was not there to negotiate with his audience, and to a large degree he was not talking exclusively and directly to them, but to an absent public. Any response the crowd made to Kline at this point would be partly a matter of whether it was willing to adopt the role Kline offered it in the drama his speech implied.

There was a moment of elation when Kline said that the ORL would be "closed down tomorrow." Then some members of the crowd sensed the ambiguity of the announcement. Did "closed down tomorrow" mean that the laboratory was to be closed, permanently, as of tomorrow? Clearly, most of the crowd at first interpreted Kline's words as indicating a permanent closing, but almost at once came the shouted question: "How long? How long?" The elation gave way to doubt and to a disappointment exaggerated by the fantasy that the demonstration had succeeded in abolishing the ORL, as Kline continued: "The request, the request was made that it be closed tomorrow." The repetition of "the request" conveys Kline's attempt to swim upstream against the growing current of doubt and frustration spilling from the audience before him. And then Kline seemed to want to end his talk: "That's the message."

Kline's announcement of the closing of the ORL, at first taken to mean a permanent closing, was a climax immediately followed by an equal and opposite anticlimax as the crowd realized that it was being offered a one-day closing of the ORL. And Kline's "that's the message" came with an abruptness that fanned the suddenly growing sense of outrage that his ambiguity had needlessly sparked, seeming to cut off discussion and reminding his audience of his status as a messenger.

Kline seemed to have finished, but as the shouts of protest continued, he seemed to have another thought, and struggled to regain his listeners' attention. "Wait a minute, that's not it, now wait a minute, it's not it." Again the repetition, struggling to overcome the noisy confusion spreading through the crowd. He realized that his first announcement had not worked and that he had lost whatever ground he had gained early in his speech with his reference to Governor Shapp's "undoubted general sympathy." Now things seemed to be worse than before he started. He tried again, the crowd noises now somewhat diminishing. "And the other part of the it is, that when I came back to those people who represented you, I had no conditions to lay down for them to meet. That's it." Once again the reference to "representatives" who, so far as the crowd was concerned, had no representative status. Why this postscript to Kline's message, this "other part of the it"? The announcement was clearly meant, and must have seemed, an attempt to indicate good faith; it was also the first indication that perhaps the police were not going to be ordered to attack the crowd. But if there was no demand from Kline for a *quid pro quo*, where did that leave things? An appeal, even implicit, that he was acting in good faith, and that he had no demands to make, put the question of Kline's good faith and of a possible *quid pro quo* on the agenda.

As Kline finished, with no indication that he wanted any further part in the events of the day, a heckler shouted, "Throw him a fish!"—implying that Kline was simply a trained seal, a stooge, a contemptible non-agent.

Kline had spoken to the crowd without any indication that he was asking anything of them, and yet why would he speak if he were not asking something of them? The crowd seemed to sense that it was being offered a deal. But the context was unclear. The announcement from Kline had come out of the blue.

And then Mike Shields began to speak. Shields was not well known to most of his audience. The student government at Penn State, as at most colleges and universities, was a plaything for its officers and their hangers-on, but not a vital or continuously visible part of the ongoing life of the academic or social community. Shields had only recently been elected president. In a front-page story in the *Daily Collegian* on 4 May, Shields was quoted as calling himself a "street waif," influenced in his social attitudes by Timothy Leary and the Berrigans. Shields had first enrolled at Penn State while serving a term at the nearby Rockview State Penitentiary for robbery, but by 1972 had been released and was a full-time student.[15]

Shields spoke in a high-pitched and slightly quavering voice. It soon became clear what Kline had meant when he said that he had no demands. Shields began without preamble, but his "I hope everyone understands" indicates that he thought the crowd had somehow not understood how it ought to be acting. Hence, he began by placing himself in a position that was both critical and doubtful of the crowd, implicitly aligning himself, at least partially, with Kline or with some agreement he had previously made with Kline. The crowd sensed Shields's admonitory tone and would have none of it. Shields's reminder that the ORL was to be shut down was met with loud objections: "For one day!" The crowd, which presumably understood itself to have taken "action," in the vocabulary of protest, was being fobbed of with a "symbol." Shields replied to the shout of "For one day!"—with all its implications that one day was not enough—by attempting to maximize the importance of the shutdown. He chose an absurd way to amplify his point in response to the objections of the crowd: "Tomorrow is Friday, and it will be shut down Saturday and Sunday." So the laboratory was not to be shut down for just one day, but, if we count the weekend, for three. In his first two sentences, Shields had lost the crowd. Then he made the situation worse.

The crowd now began to dismiss Shields. His attempt to personalize the issue came too late: "I know what it means. I think you all know what it means." There was another pause and various segments of the crowd began to start protest chants. Note the use of pronouns in Shields's next two sentences: "By shutting down the operation of the Ordnance Research Laboratory, we have achieved what we set out to do. (*Shouts from the crowd*) What we are asking (*shouts*), what we are asking now is that we continue this—the ORL is shut down—and we continue this and move onto campus now." In the first sentence "we"—meaning Shields and the protesters, evidently—have shut down the ORL, but the crowd shouts its denial that a one-day shutdown is all that it set out to accomplish. In the second sentence, "we" changes, presumably into some unknown group of "representatives" and Kline, and asks the first "we" to continue "this" on campus. The *quid pro quo* has finally come. Now it is clear to everyone in the crowd that some sort of deal has been struck between Kline and some "representatives" and that the crowd is being asked to go along, without having been told about the negotiations or asked to comment on them. Under the circumstances, it sounded like a sellout. Shields's quavering voice, his shifting pronouns, his failure to provide adequate rhetorical amplification, his oddly patched-together sentences that weakly overstated and restated, his introducing Kline, and then following Kline's no-deal speech with a clear indication that there was, indeed, a deal—all of these bespoke confusion of role, both his own and his listeners.

If the aim of the speeches by Kline and Shields had been to get the 5,500 demonstrators out of the intersection, they had failed. And not only had they failed to disperse the demonstration, they had, by their failure, made it difficult for anyone else to do so. Starting from scratch, Shields might have spoken of the demands, the negotiation, the concession, the victory, and he might have called for a specific time and place at which the crowd could meet to consider its next actions. But now he had not only failed, he had, as had Kline, called into question the definitions that the crowd must make of itself, of its "representatives," of Kline, and of Shields. Kline was a messenger, and Shields was apparently acting by prearrangement, so that his being in the situation was at least compromised. The crowd clearly felt that if it dispersed, it would not only be doing so without a good reason, it would be doing so in response to an implicit deception: it was being asked to be a collection of dupes.

IV

After a delay of approximately a minute following Shields's speech, there were cheers from the crowd, and Wells Keddie appeared with the bullhorn. Keddie was an assistant professor of labor studies and the advisor to the Penn State SDS. Keddie was well known on campus not only through his own involvement with the antiwar protests of preceding years, but because of the announcement, the year before, that he would be denied tenure and that his employment would be terminated at the end of the 1972 academic year. Keddie, claiming that his dismissal was politically motivated, appealed the decision through the university structure and eventually in court. Large numbers of students signed petitions asking President Oswald to rehire Keddie, and there were frequent stories about him in the *Daily Collegian*. And so as Keddie began to speak, he was well known, had impressive credentials as an antiwar activist, and was obviously not a creature of the university.

Keddie began by showing concern for whether his listeners could hear him, as Kline had done. But Keddie's first sentence also said much about his relation with the crowd and with the first two speakers. He indicated that he "was back there," deep in the crowd, when Kline and Shields spoke, implying that he was part of the crowd rather than part of a prearranged slate of speakers. As part of the crowd, Keddie "couldn't hear much." And as he finished the sentence, having established his identity as part of the crowd, Keddie avoided mentioning the speakers by name, or even by allowing them to become the subjects of his last clause: Keddie said he "couldn't hear much of what was being said," instead of "I couldn't hear much of what Lieutenant Governor Kline and Mike Shields said."

Keddie's arguments, and his stylistic choices, indicate a remarkable sensitivity to the audience's need to find an acceptable definition of itself, and an acceptable meaning for its actions.

Keddie proceeded by a temporal pattern, which he employed twice. He described what the antiwar forces had tried to achieve in the past, what they had accomplished with the three-day shutdown of ORL, and what they ought to do next. Then he repeated the same pattern again. Hence:

Past: We've tried to separate the university from the war machine.
Present: You've done it, for the first time.
Future: Either stand here and fight, thus throwing away the meaningfulness of your victory and admitting defeat, or go back and plan your next moves, which should include (1) separating the university from war research, (2) talking to the faculty, (3) starting a student union, and (4) staging a victory march.

The logic of Keddie's argument turned around the impression that had been left by the pairing of Kline and Shields. Kline and Shields seemed to say that the state and the university had made a concession and that the crowd should be willing to admit that the concession was enough to satisfy its demands. But Keddie reversed that logic. As he presented the case, the crowd had won an important victory, and to proceed with the demonstration against ORL, or to escalate to violence, would be to admit defeat.

Keddie presented the crowd with an opportunity to construe its actions as a victory, to write its autobiography in its deeds. It is Keddie's special gift to the participants in the actions of 11 May 1972 that he was able to interpret a movement away from violence as a move forward, not as a retreat.

Keddie's argument hinged upon redefining the meaning of the facts of the case, but not upon the case as external to the people who were involved. Categorical notions of ethos and pathos are inadequate to explain the relationships of the agents in the drama, though they do provide a beginning. Keddie's argument was more persuasive because it was he who made it and because he presented himself as part of the antiwar movement. And it could be argued that he played upon the emotions of the crowd, stirring up their hostility to the war and the university and then channeling that hostility into a dispersal of the demonstration. These observations are accurate as far as they go, but they do not do justice to the complexity of the relations between agent and agent since they suggest, as critics employing Aristotle's *Rhetoric* often do, that apart from the case itself (logos), persuasion is a matter of the perceived identity of the speaker (ethos) and the emotional predispositions and responses of the auditors (pathos).[16] Keddie defined his audience not as pathetic objects but as active agents, and the audience accepted that definition.

Keddie's definition of himself was complex: he was part of the crowd, but a speaker; he was a protester against war-related university research, but also a faculty member. Implicitly, and perhaps at least as important in the crowd's decision to agree with him, he was a victim who had been defeated by the university's tenure process and who was now asking the crowd to confirm that the closing of the ORL was a victory over the university. For the crowd to disagree with Keddie would have meant that it was telling him he had been defeated twice. He had been rejected by the university, and his rehiring was one of the issues raised by the protesters of May 1972. Could the crowd that had protested his rejection by the university also reject him?

Keddie's pronouns reflect his complex relationship with his audience. By far the largest number of personal pronouns were the first person plural *we* (73, or 57 percent). And in his use of the first person singular (*I, me, my*), Keddie almost always referred to himself as on the side of the crowd, with the sole exception of some part of the crowd that might have wanted violence. Judging from the context, in which Keddie linked himself to the crowd, the references to the crowd (*I, we, you*) total 111, or 86.7 percent of the personal pronouns in the speech. Similarly, Keddie referred with his pronouns primarily to collective action rather than to the actions of single, separate persons: plural pronouns accounted for a total of 113, or 88.3 percent of personal pronouns (table 8–1). Overwhelmingly, sentences referring to Keddie or the crowd were in the active voice, subjective case, as opposed to passive or objective.[17] Keddie and the crowd were depicted as acting, rather than acted upon.

Keddie's references to the third person, though often oppositional, were not belligerent. All sixteen uses of the third-person plural (*they, them*) referred to university faculty and staff, and in every reference *they* were portrayed as either sympathetic or corrigible.

Table 8-1 Personal Pronouns in Wells Keddie's Speech

First person singular (I, me, my)	14	(10.9%)
Second person singular (you)	0	
Third person singular (he)	1	(0.78%)
First person plural (we, our, us)	73	(57.0%)
Second person plural (you, your)	24	(18.8%)
Third person plural (they, them)	16	(12.5%)
Total	128	

Unlike *we,* however, *they* were often acted upon: *they* was used eight times (50 percent), *them* eight times (50 percent).

Keddie was part of the antiwar protest: "Look, one of the things that *we've* been trying to do is get some kind of indication that somewhere along the way *we're* going to start separating this university from the war machine." In this sentence, Keddie not only placed himself in the collective *we* of antiwar protest, but he also reminded his audience that the protest had been going on for years—since before many in the crowd were at Penn State. The *we* had roots in the past, and created an obligation for the *we* of the present. "A lot of *you* are quick to think that a three-day, by the way, they work this goddamn place seven days a week so don't, don't sell *yourselves* short what you got here." Keddie had an authority that neither Kline nor Shields had, to divide the crowd, isolating those ("a lot of you") who might want to stay and start a fight. But Keddie apparently thought better of his attempt to divide the crowd, because he revised his sentence at the first comma, and did not complete the thought. He came back to the idea later in the speech, however: "The only next step, the only next step from right here is to have a fight. Right? If some of you want it, then I don't. And you know I don't and I'm not trying to talk you out of it. If you want to have a fight there's lots of people ready. But you've won something, God almighty."

Just as he was of and not of the crowd, Keddie was of and not of the faculty. He said: "Now we've got to get people like me to stop doing this goddamn military research." The shifting of Keddie's identity from crowd to speaker to faculty was consistent with his message that the job to be done was one of persuasion. Faculty, crowd, and Keddie were all human agents, and it was the job of the crowd to persuade the faculty to oppose the war and the university's cooperation with the war. As human agents, the faculty could be persuaded; as human agents, the students could succeed.

And so Keddie created a definition of his audience as active human agents and invited them to identify with that idea of themselves. He advanced this idea in his use of personal pronouns and in his arguments. Throughout the speech he argued that the active next step was to reorganize, analyze, and embark upon a further campaign of persuasion. To remain at the intersection would be passive, an implicit rejection of Keddie's appeal to conceive of themselves as active agents. "We've got to keep this thing going. And you can't keep it going sitting in the streets. We know that already."

V

Rhetoric is a matter of choices made before, during, and after an interaction by all participants. What each participant chooses to do limits and partially defines the meanings of the actions of all the other participants. It may be idle to speculate about what might have been had other choices been made, but it is important to remember that the actions taken on 11 May 1972 were not inevitable, that they were influenced by but not determined by the preexisting constraints of the rhetorical situation.

The ORL demonstration could have developed as another Kent State. The restraint of the Penn State demonstrators, the expression of sympathy from the governor, the willingness of the state and university to offer a concession, the presence of Wells Keddie to recall the demonstrators to their political task—all of these elements contrast with what happened at Kent State in May 1970.[18]

The choices made by Keddie and the crowd's willingness to disperse at the end of his talk, rather than stay to fight or talk further, were also not inevitable. There is a mythology of crowd dispersal that runs entirely counter to what happened at Penn State. The police theory of "riot control," demonstrated in the streets throughout the 1960s and early 1970s, called for the swift and brutal application of force through tear gas and club-swinging police.[19]

The nearest thing in our popular mythology to dispersing a hostile crowd is the well-known scene from American Western movies where a sheriff turns back a lynch mob. A classic variation on the lynch-mob scene occurs in John Ford's *Young Mr. Lincoln,* where Henry Fonda stands at the jailhouse door to save two young men from the mob. An analysis of Fonda's speech by the editors of *Cahiers du Cinema* shows how different was Keddie's approach. Among the rhetorical tactics cited by the editors of *Cahiers du Cinema* are these: (1) Lincoln displays personal, physical courage in challenging the crowd to single combat with him; (2) Lincoln employs humor to change the mood of the crowd; (3) Lincoln singles out one man in the crowd and appeals to him on the basis of religious conviction; (4) Lincoln shows the crowd that once lynching begins it could attack any one of them.[20]

Keddie's rhetorical approach depended, as does Lincoln's, upon definitions of personal identity in the crisis situation, but differed in that Keddie (1) specifically identified with the crowd; (2) employed a serious tone throughout; (3) appealed to the crowd as a social entity rather than as a group of individuals; (4) based his appeal on political grounds rather than personal conscience or divine law.

It is perhaps a paradox of the situation that Keddie's speech depended for its success on an existential, phenomenological approach, in that it offered the crowd an identity it could accept. And yet the identity Keddie offered was a rhetorical one, as opposed to the readily available roles of existential heroes or villains.[21] And he convinced his audience that to stay and fight was to define themselves as losers, whereas to leave and reorganize was to define themselves as winners.

VI

In another essay I argued that rhetoric is a way of being, a way of knowing, and a way of doing.[22] Rhetorical being, knowing, and doing are simultaneous and overlapping actions that together constitute rhetorical action: discourse is fabricated, judgments are made, understandings are shared, agents move others and are themselves moved to belief and action, and identities are revealed and created. Each of the subordinate actions is carried out in and through the others. I have argued here that insofar as rhetoric is a way of being, it is ideally a collaboration between speaker and listener to find a mutually satisfactory notion of themselves as interacting agents.

The case of the demonstration at the Ordnance Research Laboratory in 1972 is an especially useful one for a critic, since three speakers who were seeking the dispersal of a crowd achieved obviously different results, because they defined themselves, their listeners, and the action they recommended so differently. The audience rejected the identities offered to it by Lieutenant Governor Kline and by Mike Shields, but accepted the identity offered by Wells Keddie. And the demonstrators, by their unwillingness to disperse at the invitation of Shields and their later acceptance of Wells Keddie's invitation to leave the intersection as victorious, active agents, tell us something about the phenomenal world of crowds. The crowd is not necessarily a formless mass of chaotic and irresponsible beings; it may prefer to think of itself as exercising choice as to its character, its actions, and its definitions of other human agents. This crowd rejected an exchange but accepted an opportunity to continue its opposition to the war. Given a choice, this crowd accepted the alternative that offered the promise of further rhetorical interaction. Not only did each speaker make a commitment to the listeners and the listeners consider a contract with the speakers, but each listener made a contract with the other listeners, from moment to moment and as part of a national effort of protest. It would be merely a political slander to reduce the crowd's sense of shared identity to "peer pressure" or "mob psychology."

As a drama, the ORL demonstration displays unmistakably the demand of an audience that a speaker collaborate with them in rhetorical being. But it may be that the victory of the demonstrators should be regarded with a pinch of skepticism. The Ordnance Research Laboratory reopened on the Monday after the demonstration and is still in business, though with a cosmetic change in name to the Applied Research Laboratory. Wells Keddie was fired. Though two thousand demonstrators started a protest march on Monday, 15 May, they were soon reduced to a core of four hundred by a thunderstorm, and even at their largest must be compared to the twenty thousand enthusiasts who showed up on Saturday, 13 May, to cheer for the football team's annual spring scrimmage. And in the week that followed, the protests disappeared, their place taken by Spring Weekend and the culture of beer, frisbees, and rock music.

Social theorists at the end of the 1960s often worried about the consequences for democracy of the mass demonstrations protesting against the war in Vietnam. Public policy, they warned, could not be made in the streets. Then came the White House tapes, and it became possible to assess the quality of talk that led to presidential decisions. Critics had long since given up reading the *Congressional Record* for enlightenment about public policy, and there is a consensus among liberal intellectuals that television, from which most Americans appear to derive their political intelligence, is shallow and misleading. It is perhaps still possible to retain the faith that the real decisions are made by calmly deliberating experts in committee rooms, though what few reports we have about committees, boards,

and bureaus have undermined that faith, and professional intellectuals who have spent any time in faculty meetings can hardly believe
that academic decision making is very much more enlightened than
what is likely to be found in business or government.

And so, if we are tempted to dismiss the ORL demonstrators as
fickle, we should at least remember with what sorts of deliberations
we are comparing them. Rhetorical talk is designed to cope with
situational adversity; that is its reason for being. At a moment of
crisis, the demonstrators insisted on being their best.

Speakers and writers, acting rhetorically, create not only themselves, but their audiences. That creation is an act of rhetorical
being and an invitation to rhetorical being. Listeners and readers
engage in rhetorical action of their own—being, knowing, and
doing with the speaker and other listeners, accepting or refusing to
accept the images offered by the speaker, enacting or declining to
enact the role of the public.

Rhetorical being is an action, not an essence; it is public, not
private. Rhetorical being is being with, carried out through symbols.
Rhetorical being is public even when it occurs as an inner reflection
or a dialogue, in that it draws upon a shared system of public symbols.
A listener or reader is a *who*, not a *whom*. Rhetorical being is a
becoming, both the revelation of an inner condition and the ongoing
creation of interacting selves. And rhetorical being is an action
performed collaboratively by both speakers and listeners. Hence,
listening is a kind of speech, which is not the same thing as saying
that silence is speech. Perhaps it is time to learn to listen to the
listener. Just as the speaker creates the listener, the listener creates
the speaker. If speakers and writers are the authors of speeches and
books, it is equally true that listeners are the authors of their responses to speeches and books. Hence, if we may criticize the speech,
speaker, and listener that are constructed by the speaker, it follows
that we may criticize the speech, speaker, and listener constructed
by the listener, as well as the listener's other relevant actions.

Just as rhetoric displays and creates that to which it refers for
judgment, it displays and creates the experience of being human.

Notes

1. And every communicator also employs, at least implicitly, a theory of human agency
in discourse. See Eugene E. White, "Solomon Stoddard's Theories of Persuasion," *Speech
Monographs* 29 (1962): 235–59; Bonnie Johnson, "Images of the Enemy in Intergroup Conflict," *Central States Speech Journal* 26 (1975): 84–92; Thomas W. Benson, "Implicit Commu-

nication Theory in Campaign Coverage," in *Television Coverage of the 1980 Presidential Campaign*, ed. William Adams (Norwood, N.J.: Ablex, 1983), 101–14.

2. For a recent review of rhetoric as epistemic, see Michael C. Leff, "In Search of Ariadne's Thread: A Review of the Recent Literature on Rhetorical Theory," *Central States Speech Journal* 29 (1978): 73–91. There is a growing body of literature on rhetoric and the self. For a sample, consult Edwin Black, "The Second Persona," *Quarterly Journal of Speech* 56 (1970): 109–19; Wayne C. Booth, "The Rhetorical Stance," in *Now Don't Try to Reason with Me* (Chicago: Univ. of Chicago Pr., 1970), 25–33; Kenneth Burke, "Antony on Behalf of the Play," in *The Philosophy of Literary Form*, 3d edition (Berkeley: Univ. of California Pr., 1973), 329–43; Kenneth Burke, *A Grammar of Motives* (Berkeley: Univ. of California Pr., 1969); Kenneth Burke, *A Rhetoric of Motives* (Berkeley: Univ. of California Pr., 1969); Elias Canetti, *Crowds and Power*, trans. Carol Stewart (New York: Continuum, 1981); Maurice Charland, "Constitutive Rhetoric: The Case of the *Peuple Quebecois*," *Quarterly Journal of Speech* 73 (1987): 133–50; Richard B. Gregg, "The Ego-Function of the Rhetoric of Protest," *Philosophy and Rhetoric* 4 (1971): 71–91; Michael Halloran, "Doing Public Business in Public," in *Form and Genre: Shaping Rhetorical Action*, ed. Karlyn Kohrs Campbell and Kathleen Hall Jamieson (Falls Church, Va.: Speech Communication Association, [1978]), 118–38; Richard L. Johannesen, "Attitude of Speaker toward Audience: A Significant Concept for Contemporary Rhetorical Theory and Criticism," *Central States Speech Journal* 25 (1974): 95–104; Richard L. Johannesen, "The Emerging Concept of Communication as Dialogue," *The Quarterly Journal of Speech* 57 (1971): 373–82; Henry W. Johnstone, Jr., *The Problem of the Self* (University Park: Pennsylvania State Univ. Pr., 1970); David S. Kaufer, "Point of View in Rhetorical Situations: Classical and Romantic Contrasts and Contemporary Implications," *Quarterly Journal of Speech* 65 (1979): 171–86; Michael C. McGee, "In Search of 'The People': A Rhetorical Alternative," *The Quarterly Journal of Speech* 61 (1975): 235–49; Walter J. Ong, "The Writer's Audience Is Always a Fiction," in *Interfaces of the Word* (Ithaca: Cornell Univ. Pr., 1977), 53–81; Lawrence W. Rosenfield, "The Practical Celebration of Epideictic," in *Rhetoric in Transition: Studies in the Nature and Uses of Rhetoric*, ed. Eugene E. White (University Park: Pennsylvania State Univ. Pr., 1979), 131–55.

3. Carroll C. Arnold, "Oral Rhetoric, Rhetoric, and Literature," *Philosophy and Rhetoric* 1 (1968): 201.

4. Arnold, "Oral Rhetoric," 201.

5. Buckminster Fuller with Jerome Agel and Quentin Fiore, *I Seem to Be a Verb* (New York: Bantam, 1970).

6. "A doctrine of *consubstantiality*, either explicit or implicit, may be necessary to any way of life. For substance, in the old philosophies, was an *act*; and a way of life is an *acting-together*; and in acting together men have common sensations, concepts, images, ideas, attitudes that make them *consubstantial*" Kenneth Burke, *A Rhetoric of Motives*, 21. See also Burke, *A Grammar of Motives*, 21–23, where Burke points out that *substance* "would refer to an attribute of the thing's *context*, since that which supports or underlies a thing would be a part of the thing's context. And a thing's context, being outside the thing, would be something that the thing is *not*" (23). Hence, speaker and listener are substantiated in the context of a rhetorical situation.

7. Arnold, "Oral Rhetoric," 201.

8. See especially Eugene E. White, "Rhetoric as Historical Configuration," in *Rhetoric in Transition*, ed. White, 7–20.

9. See Paul Hoffman, *Moratorium: An American Protest* (New York: Tower, 1970); William E. Jurma, "Moderate Movement Leadership and the Vietnam Moratorium Committee," *Quarterly Journal of Speech* 68 (1982): 262–72.

10. A remarkable and detailed documentary film describes these and other events of 1969 at Penn State. P. J. O'Connell produced the two and one-half hour film *The Year Behind, The Year Ahead* for the university's public television station, WPSX-TV, but it was never broadcast. In her analysis of student demonstrations and administrative response at Penn State, 15–23 April 1970, Anderson reports that the ORL was an issue. See Carolyn Gilpin Anderson, "Students and Administrators: Confrontation and Communication" (M.A. thesis, Pennsylvania State University, 1972), 69–81. The account herein also draws upon various issues of the Penn State student newspaper, the *Daily Collegian*, and the local daily paper, the *Centre Daily Times*. The author was an eyewitness to and sometime participant in the events at Penn State in the spring of 1972.

11. A transcript of Nixon's speech appears in "Address to the Nation on the Situation in Southeast Asia," 8 May 1972, *Public Papers of the Presidents of the United States: Richard Nixon, 1972* (Washington: Government Printing Office, 1974), 538–87.

12. Richard M. Nixon, *The Memoirs of Richard Nixon* (New York: Grosset and Dunlap, 1978), 606–7. Nixon often spoke of the necessity to convey to his adversaries the impression that he was so crazy he might do anything. See William Shawcross, *Sideshow: Kissinger, Nixon, and the Destruction of Cambodia* (New York: Simon and Schuster, 1979), 90, 260.

13. For an interesting and early attempt to monitor the process of ethical proof as it is experienced by listeners during a speech, see Robert D. Brooks and Thomas M. Scheidel, "Speech as Process: A Case Study," *Speech Monographs* 35 (1968): 1–7. On the importance of detailed explication in rhetorical criticism, see Hermann G. Stelzner, " 'War Message,' December 8, 1941: An Approach to Language," *Speech Monographs* 33 (1966): 419–37.

14. The transcript is taken from a tape recording made by the author and Andrew Ferullo. In the transcript, all matter in parenthesis refers to responses from the audience.

15. *Daily Collegian*, 4 May 1972, p. 1.

16. I do not think Aristotle saw persuasion in such a mechanical fashion, but I am a Greekless reader, possibly prone to project his own interpretations of what Aristotle might have said or "should" have said into someone else's translation; see Thomas M. Conley, "The Greekless Reader and Aristotle's *Rhetoric*," *Quarterly Journal of Speech* 65 (1979): 74–79. But I am here addressing not Aristotle's theory so much as the use made of it by critics who too often confine themselves, I believe, to a model that depicts listeners as substantively different from speakers.

17. "Voice is technically and grammatically a property of verbs alone, but actually it controls the whole pattern of a sentence by determining its subject—what it shall be written about"; Wilson Follett, *Modern American Usage* (New York: Hill & Wang, 1966), 346.

18. For an account of Kent State, see James A. Michener, *Kent State: What Happened and Why* (New York: Random, 1971); Phillip K. Tompkins and Elaine Vanden Bout Anderson, *Communication Crisis at Kent State* (New York: Gordon and Breach, 1971).

19. There is a vast literature on police tactics, but for a discussion of those tactics as they relate to a total public experience, see Norman Mailer, *The Armies of the Night* (New York: New American Library, 1968); Norman Mailer, *Miami and the Siege of Chicago* (New York: New American Library, 1968); Daniel Walker, *Rights in Conflict* (New York: Bantam, 1968).

20. The Editors of *Cahiers du Cinema*, "John Ford's *Young Mr. Lincoln*," in *Movies and Methods*, ed. Bill Nichols (Berkeley: Univ. of California Pr., 1976), 515. For an example of a lynch scene ineptly handled by the speaker at the jailhouse door, see Fritz Lang's *Fury* (1936). William Wellman's *The Ox-bow Incident* (1943) also revolves around a lynching. Leslie Halliwell lists several other American films with lynching scenes: *They Won't Forget* (1937); *Storm Warning* (1951); *The Sound of Fury* (1951); *The Sun Shines Bright* (1952); *Rough Night in Jericho* (1968); Leslie Halliwell, *The Filmgoer's Companion*, 4th ed. (New York: Avon, 1975). Films have also peopled our imaginations with a variety of crowds from Lang's *Metropolis* (1926) to the films of Sergei Eisenstein and Leni Riefenstahl. For audiences in the early 1970s, images of crowds and violence had been derived from television and print journalism as well as from fiction films. The civil rights movement had shown black Americans attacked by police with fire hoses and snarling dogs; the antiwar movement had given us police riots at the Democratic National Convention in Chicago in 1968; other reports featured urban rioters and student protesters. See Todd Gitlin, *The Whole World Is Watching: Mass Media in the Making and Unmaking of the New Left* (Berkeley: Univ. of California Pr., 1980); Thomas W. Benson, "Violence: Communication Breakdown?" *Today's Speech* 18 (Winter 1970): 39–47; Thomas W. Benson and Bonnie Johnson, "The Rhetoric of Resistance: Confrontation with the Warmakers, Washington, D.C., October, 1967," *Today's Speech* 16 (September 1968): 35–42.

21. For discussions of the relations of personal and public identities in American life, see Christopher Lasch, *The Culture of Narcissism: American Life in an Age of Diminishing Expectations* (New York: Norton, 1978); Richard Sennett, *The Fall of Public Man* (New York: Knopf, 1977).

22. "Rhetoric and Autobiography: The Case of Malcolm X," *Quarterly Journal of Speech* 60 (1974): 1–13.

NINE

Administrative Rhetoric and Public Opinion: Discussing the Iranian Hostages in the Public Sphere

GERARD A. HAUSER

> *If a president's policy is right, debate will strengthen the national consensus. If it is wrong, debate may save the country from catastrophe.*
> —*Sen. Edward M. Kennedy,*
> *Georgetown University Address, 1980*

> *There's only one poll that counts, as my wife said on the "Today" show this morning, and that's the final vote.*
> —*Jimmy Carter, "Remarks to Gannett Newspaper and Broadcast Executives," 13 December 1979*

THIS IS AN essay about public opinion: about how politicians frame it, respond to it, misconstrue its character, and ultimately get trapped by it. The essay questions whether the data reported by polls—those taps on the mercurial fluctuations of popular mood—are really *public* opinions. In the following pages I try, through innuendo as well as explicit argument, to aggravate the reader into thinking about the nature and function of public opinion in a nation like the United States, especially with respect to the "publicness" of it—where public opinion is formed, how it is influenced, and what it represents.

The perspective I adopt toward public opinion places rhetoric, not survey research, in focus. I assume that "the public" is a rhetorically based concept, not an aggregate to be measured nor the ideal community envisioned in the liberal-democratic tradition of political philosophy.[1] Hence, I assume that publics emerge insofar as enfranchised citizens, out of concern for the common good, engage in dialogue on the issues that touch our lives; and further, that individual publics are not conceptual but real—although not ideally real.[2] To render these assumptions intelligible, I begin by sketching a framework rhetoricians might employ in studying a public's opinion.

323

This framework will then be brought to bear on a specific case that illustrates a number of problems with our understanding and use of public opinion in American politics. The framework I discuss is that of the public sphere, and the illustrative case I explore is the Carter administration's rhetoric concerning the Iranian hostage affair.

The Public Sphere

The history of public rhetoric is clear in its lesson that political communication requires a functioning open forum where private individuals can unite as a public through the exchange of ideas. Without this condition propaganda prevails and public opinion becomes managed in ways that deny its significance in shaping institutional policies. In other words, for opinion to be more than nominally public, citizens require a vibrant public sphere.

By *public sphere*, I refer to a discursive realm in which individuals and groups may step beyond their private concerns to interact freely in ways conducive to forming a public opinion. This sphere exists between the private realm of personal, business, professional, and special interests on the one hand, and the domain of governmental action on the other. In this realm, citizens voice their common concerns, discover their generalized interests, galvanize themselves into a public, and pursue modes of action to secure their common interests. As the German sociologist Jürgen Habermas points out, whenever private citizens assemble to form a public body, some portion of the public sphere is made manifest in their conversation.[3]

This definition points to several conditions that are essential to the smooth functioning of the public sphere. First, it must be accessible to all citizens. Whenever individuals or groups are denied the opportunity to participate actively in discussions that affect their lives, they are left to the mercy of special interests or institutional powers. Second, there must be access to information. Without access to information, the citizenry can neither conduct intelligent discussions nor form balanced opinions. They are vulnerable to control. Third, specific means for transmitting information must be accessible to those who can be influenced by it. Historically, the means for transmitting information have been open discussions undertaken by individuals in town meetings or by representative agents like newspapers. In contemporary industrial societies, these means are the mass media.

To illustrate, Habermas cites the example of Paris during 1848, where "every halfway eminent politician organized his club, every other his journal: 450 clubs and over 200 journals were established there between February and May alone. Until the permanent legalization of a politically functional public sphere, the appearance of a political newspaper meant joining the struggle for freedom and public opinion, and thus for the public sphere as a principle."[4]

Opinions formed in a public sphere have consequences only when some agency with power to act takes them seriously. Unless legislative and administrative bodies subordinate the exercise of political control to the demand for public access to information, the public sphere remains impotent.[5] Hence, citizens may be guaranteed access to the public sphere while the public sphere itself is simultaneously fettered with legal, economic, psychological, informational, or like restraints. As Habermas notes, after a constitutional state was established in France, the press was relieved of its burden to establish freedom. It could and did concentrate instead on its commercial potential,[6] resulting in a transformation of the public sphere through an influx of private interests. With the generalizable interests of the public no longer dominant, special interests arguing for their partisan advantage diminished the attention of the public sphere to the common interest, which produced a steady deterioration of the public itself.[7]

Habermas's example of the press's role in the French struggle for a constitutional state suggests a fourth feature of the public sphere: there must be institutional guarantees for the public sphere to exist. But his characterization of this feature requires a significant modification. Habermas presents the public sphere as an *ideal* and *counterfactual* construct. It is ideal because his theoretical definition of the public sphere stipulates the conditions for a perfect public sphere. But his theory is counterfactual because in practice such conditions are contrary to the ones under which any particular public sphere actually exists. His theory thus addresses the ways in which actual practice introduces distorting influences,[8] consistent with the emancipative aims of his critical theory. So Habermas recognizes that there are various types of public spheres, with few, if any, free from domination or constraints by special interests. Habermas's solution to the problem of domination stresses the necessity of institutional guarantees for the public sphere. Hence, his diagnosis of any given instance is guided by institutional conditions controlling the public sphere's existence, nature, and function. His emphasis on institutional constraints is reinforced by his claim that a principle of the public sphere can exist without a formal institution of the public sphere only when the functioning of public opinion is guaranteed by three guidelines: general accessibility, elimination of all privileges, and discovery of general norms and rational legitimations.[9]

The importance Habermas attributes to institutional features is not to be underestimated; institutional factors are undeniably essential features of any public sphere. However, they are not so by virtue of their institutional character but because of their discursive character. Institutional constraints are significant because they regulate the kinds of content and presentation permitted in and excluded from a public's realm of discussion: hence, the active consideration and role of these forms in shaping a public opinion.

My point is illustrated by Hannah Arendt's discussion of the French resistance. In *Between Past and Future* she considers the meaning French people found in opposing the Nazi regime. By joining the resistance they had created a "public realm where—without the paraphernalia of officialdom and hidden from the eyes of friend and foe—all relevant business in the affairs of the country was transacted in deed and word."[10] Matters of personal interest were weightless by comparison with the circumstances they confronted together. Whereas their private lives had been empty, though filled with self-centered concerns, as public actors their lives took on a transcendent meaning. Men and women in the public realm were able to discover their individuality and, related to this, discover an inner strength in the sincerity of their actions. Arendt observes:

They had been visited for the first time in their lives by an apparition of freedom, not, to be sure, because they acted against tyranny and things worse than tyranny—this was true for every soldier in the Allied armies—but because they had become "challengers," had taken the initiative upon themselves and therefore without knowing or even noticing it, had begun to create that public space between themselves where freedom could appear.[11]

The link between the resisters' positive self-awareness and their existence as a public is not incidental. Acting together in a public realm, they could enrich their lives through the experience of working together on issues beyond the merely individual. The fact that the resisters' underground public realm lacked institutional guarantees and yet produced an opinion of genuinely public character and evoked communal conduct in the pursuit of a common interest underscores the point that institutional guarantees are not significant in and of themselves. These guarantees have meaning insofar as they relate to discourse and the actions resulting therefrom. Indeed, even in the absence of institutional guarantees, it is possible for a public realm to form and a community to act in ways responsive to human needs.[12] The resisters' unity of interests was unveiled through their common experience of words supported by deeds. This was a discursive experience of a *public* relationship, on which their trust and spirit of reciprocity—in short, their community—rested.

When the discursive element of the public sphere is emphasized, the experiential nature of "publicness" comes to the fore. The public sphere emerges as the framework of ideas and deeds encountered, participated in, discussed, and shared by whatever segment of society we are inspecting. This discursive realm can be added to, distracted, redirected, repressed, or energized by the patterns of stimuli from outside. The public sphere's contours provide the overall pattern of awareness at any given time of those at whom we are looking.

Those in the public sphere at whom we are looking are the participating, judging—in a dynamic sense—persons who are actively involved in shaping the ways social wheels turn. Rhetorical and social critics alike (indeed, they are frequently the same) need a concept that deals with the working part of society engaged in creating policies and evaluating deeds. The concept we reserve for them is that of a public, which is defined as that part of the populace engaged in evolving opinion.[13] This notion of a "public" is not synonymous with that of a "populace." "Populace" is altogether general, including all citizens, regardless of interests, level of participation, receptiveness to stimuli, and like states pertinent to the discussions that transpire in the public sphere.

As witnesses to words spoken and deeds enacted in the public sphere, members of the public stand in contrast to those who reject alternatives out of hand or by doctrine. The public is active and creative; it weighs and exchanges. The totally "knowing" are not part of a "public" because they are closed. They may vote and shout but they do not shape; they shove and claim. Publics discuss; special interests ejaculate.

Thus, I would agree with Habermas and others that a public sphere requires a common space where people can meet. However, the significance of this space is neither that it affords visibility to the persons in it nor that it receives institutional recognition, but that it provides witnesses for public actors. These witnesses form a public. Ideally, a public serves as a source of opportunity and a testing agency for public behavior. Its members act as judges who certify the public worth of ideas and emotions performed before them. A smoothly functioning public sphere thus demands rhetor-listeners who are afforded institutional freedoms and guarantees, or who—through subterfuge or even happenstance—create conditions that will permit a rhetoric able to evoke deep and moving response. Consequently, in addition to the aforementioned conditions for the existence of a structurally ideal public sphere, the framework I am espousing requires the absence of restraints on discourse *and* the presence of rhetor-listeners who are critically sensitive to rhetoric.

Finally, the product of the public's discursive interaction is *public opinion,* by which I mean the evolving judgment of the public on issues and concerns in the public sphere.[14] This opinion is marked by intensity and duration; it is anchored by the discursive experiences of the public realm; and it is expressed in the public's words and deeds. Significantly, it is not represented by public opinion polls.[15]

There are several problems with opinion polling that bear on the relevance of such data to an understanding of *public* opinion as distinct from *popular* opinion.[16] First, public opinion polls are designed to provide a statistical measure of what a sample of people thinks, at a given moment, about a subject not necessarily of their own choice. Hence, polls may indicate what is momentarily popular or what the general populace momentarily holds. But they do not mine the vein of opinion of the active, creative segment of society evolving a view on the course that institutional representatives should follow. Even if polls could measure such "evolution," as statistical instruments they could do so only after the fact. Through their focus on preselected problems, opinion polls create specific "issues" without regard to the people's hierarchy. Although polls may indicate what issues are responded to, they do not reveal why people find these issues salient nor do they afford guidance on ways to resolve them. Moreover, polls substitute the number found on each side of a question for intensity or durability of responses. Because they measure responses of the moment to matters on which someone else (a pollster) chooses to focus attention, and because they poll all parts of the populace, including those that are not "evolving" anything, opinion polls obscure in the aggregate the opinions of those actively shaping the ways social wheels turn.

Public opinion is formed through the give and take of discussion; its form and quality are influenced significantly by the contours of the public sphere and the characteristics of those active in it. Thus, the study of public opinion requires an understanding of the conditions that shape the discursive environment in which a public emerges and evolves opinions.[17] In sum, the study of public opinion is properly a rhetorical study, not a statistical one.

The conditions I have been enumerating under the heading of "the public sphere" are seldom, if ever, fully realized in practice. But as a *counterfactual ideal,* the idea of a public sphere can be of great critical utility by providing a framework in which to consider how public opinion is formed.[18] Specifically, it provides a rhetorical framework for examining a discursive realm—the information available to it, the personae of speakers therein, the roles participants suggest to the public, the media functions prevalent within its domain, and the types of opinions that emerge. Studies of the ways in which the public sphere is managed and constrained may provide a useful index to how public opinion is shaped and social will formed in complex, industrialized, Western nations.

In the remainder of this essay, I wish to explore public opinion more concretely by bringing this framework to bear on a test case. My observations are intended to be provocative in developing an interpretation of how public opinion was formed, understood, and used in a contemporary political crisis.

Transforming Victims into Heroes

On 4 November 1979 Iranian militants stormed the American embassy in Tehran as a protest against the United States granting the deposed shah entrance to its territory for medical treatment. The resulting Iranian hostage affair became a national preoccupation fraught with competing impulses that galvanized a nation and eventually helped to unseat a president. Here was a situation in which more than sixty Americans fell victims to an angry mob which stormed the United States embassy compound in Tehran, took the officials and staff prisoners, held them as hostages while issuing various demands to the government of the United States, and kept fifty-two of them incarcerated for more than a year. The public exchanges between the two governments instantly precipitated and then sustained an international crisis that remained in the glare of public light for the episode's duration. When the hostages were finally released, these apparently innocent victims—individuals who prior to captivity were engaged in the "normal" activities of embassy personnel—returned home to a heroes' welcome. But the president who negotiated their release had already been turned out of office. I propose to focus upon the Carter administration's rhetoric concerning the hostages so that I can explore why Americans responded by lionizing their captive countrymen and women while rejecting the president who secured their release.

In the first part of my analysis, I will explore some ways in which the Carter administration's rhetoric encouraged the formation of a heroic view of the Tehran captives. My intent is to explain how this opinion was formed and how to assess its character. The second part of my analysis will explore how Carter, armed with a particular conception of public opinion, made rhetorical choices that eventually contributed to his loss of the presidency. My intent is to explain how Carter's rhetorical choices were guided and to assess the consequences of these choices on the public's confidence in his leadership.

Why were the returned embassy personnel given heroic treatment when those held captive in similar cases, such as the *Pueblo* and *Mayaguez* incidents, were not? Why were these apparently innocent victims, who had engaged in no extraordinary acts on behalf of their nation treated heroically, while returning veterans and prisoners of war from Vietnam—men and women commissioned to risk their lives and subjected to much greater physical danger—were and still are treated as outcasts? Among the hypotheses advanced to explain the returned hostages' reception, we cannot discount the likelihood that the rhetoric of the Carter administration insinuated itself into the public sphere—molded it, constrained it, and thereby influenced the formation of public opinion concerning the hostages and the American values they represented.[19] That is the first hypothesis I shall explore.

Several dimensions of the Carter administration's rhetoric are noteworthy. I shall discuss three. First, the administration seemed to go out of its way to impress upon the American public that securing the hostages' release was a matter of preeminent significance. The event naturally attracted attention and concern; an embassy seizure is, after all, an international news item. However, seizure of the Dominican embassy in Colombia on 27 February 1980 received far less public attention despite the fact that Americans, including Ambassador Diego C. Asencio, were taken hostage. Indeed, a search of the *Department of State Bulletin* and the *Weekly Compilation of Presidential Documents* failed to locate even a short press statement announcing Ambassador Asencio's release after sixty- one days in captivity. The qualitative difference in the Iranian hostage matter was our government's willingness to participate with the Iranian parties in an exchange of a series of public acts.[20] In the immediate aftermath of the embassy takeover, these acts heightened the drama of the event, riveted continual attention on it, and suggested that the hostages' incarceration was a matter of sustained national emergency.

Dramatic events came in rapid succession. The interim government of Iranian Prime Minister Mehdi Bazargan fell. Ayatollah Khomeini refused to meet with presidential envoys Ramsey Clark and William Miller. Crowds took to the street, creating the recurring spectacle of multitudes chanting anti-American slogans and hectoring foreign reporters. Iranian militants were televised using the American flag to haul garbage. Sketchy information created ambiguity about the numbers actually held hostage, and anxiety over this was compounded by the militants' threatened actions against the hostages. Six hostages escaped with the aid of Canada, signaling an interim victory over a clearly defined villain.

In response there was the drama of American action: the United Nations Security Council resolutions and the plea to the World Court. Adding to the drama's intensity were the personal acts of Carter: the stopped delivery of $300 million in spare military parts bought from the United States by the shah, issuance of a deportation order for Iranian students with visa irregularities, suspension of importation of Iranian oil, dispatch of the carrier Midway to the Arabian Sea, and the freezing of $8 billion in Iranian assets. These events attracted attention and kept it focused on the affair. The reciprocation of hostilities confirmed that these hostages were extremely important.

The perception of the hostages' significance was reinforced by the administration's communication to the American people. It proclaimed that the crisis stood at the center of American foreign policy. Though the administration initially called for quiet, patient diplomacy, for restraint and firm negotiation, its practice was just the opposite. The United States cajoled other nations to line up either "with us or against us." The White House issued a river of words informing Americans about its responses and initiatives, indicting and denouncing Iran, and otherwise publicizing the hostages' plight.

Nothing communicated urgency more than the president's own behavior. In the early going Jimmy Carter appeared to be a virtual recluse at the White House, as meetings abroad and at home were canceled. Soon the president announced that he was canceling his political activities to stay close to the scene.[21] As the primary election season arrived, Carter's preoccupation with remaining in Washington mushroomed into his celebrated "Rose Garden strategy." The style of his conduct sent Americans an unmistakable message: the Iranian situation was so volatile, required so much executive attention, was so important to the nation, that the president could not leave his post. In the phrase often repeated by the administration, it was his "abiding concern." By word and by deed the White House kept the Iranian affair in the glare of public light and thereby sustained its importance in the public realm.[22]

The precise importance of the hostages was asserted by the Carter rhetoric, which repeatedly linked them to national character and honor. The nation was told that these "American citizens continue to be held as hostages in an attempt to force unacceptable demands on our country"; that our concern was for the "lives of these brave hostages—our nation's loyal citizens and faithful representatives"; and that our national response was not just anger, outrage, and concern, but "pride in their great courage." The significance of their detainment for the nation was stressed: "No single situation so aggravates the American people, so tests our maturity, so tries our patience, so challenges our unity, as does the continued captivity of American hostages in the Tehran Embassy." And as if presenting them as the heroic symbol of national character were not enough, their meaning was magnified in a textbook example of condensation when the president proclaimed, "The lives of over 50 innocent people are at stake; the foundation of civilized diplomacy is at stake; the integrity of international law is at stake; the credibility of the United Nations is at stake. And at stake, ultimately, is the maintenance of peace in the region."[23]

Thus the course of events and the behavior and rhetoric of their leaders told the American people that this was a singularly important episode; that its significance was no less than the honor and character of the nation itself; that the foundations of civilization and of peace were symbolized by their brave and faithful representatives; and that this matter of grave import presented Americans their opportunity to rededicate themselves to the ennobling principles of freedom and decency through national unity, resolve, sacrifice, and support of a dauntless leadership.

Had the Carter administration adopted a policy of quiet diplomacy and done all within its means to minimize public preoccupation with the hostages, its behaviors and rhetoric might have projected other matters into the limelight of national discussion, leaving the hostage taking for necessary but perfunctory news releases. But the opposite decision was firmly made—a decision, in the words of Cyrus Vance, that "as long as their cruel torment continues, this matter will remain in the forefront of our national agenda."[24] The administration placed this incident within the public sphere and made it uniquely salient matter for public opinion. This choice made it necessary to keep that opinion solidly unified behind the president and to focus attention on issues that would serve the administration in its attempts to secure the hostages' release. To these ends the Carter administration attempted to manage topics admitted into the public sphere, with the result that the information made accessible to the public contributed to their perception of the hostages as heroes. This is the second feature of Carter's rhetoric that contributed to the formation of the public's opinion.

For the most part, the president wished the public to entertain certain obvious topics that, predictably, worked to the administration's favor. There were the official acts: the United Nations resolution, the World Court proceedings, the freezing of assets, the deportation of Iranian students, the embargo on Iranian oil, the wavering of diplomatic relations, and other actions of an official nature. There were also strategies to place pressure on Iran: the principles that would guide the administration's responses to the situation were publicized, attempts were made to solidify foreign support through common deeds, and ominous references were made to unspecified military options. Attempts to negotiate a settlement were reported in releases laced generously with descriptions of weird politics involving the street, the embassy, and a strange ménage of militant-president-mosque-parliament-potentate-minister. Politics of this sort soon appeared to be "typically" Iranian.

But there were also topics of a less obvious nature. For example, the commonplace of American unity was reiterated. Citizens were repeatedly reminded that they were in "unanimity," "galvanized" in "public unity," "dedicated to the principles and honor of our nation," standing "as one people."[25] In the words of United Nations Ambassador Donald McHenry:

> There is in the United States a unity of purpose, a disciplined sensitivity to the needs of peace, a determination to search out all peaceful means to bring this dispute to a just conclusion, and also a determination to do what must be done to protect our fellow citizens and the rule of law. That unity of purpose is shared by all Americans. But make no mistake. Beneath that discipline is a seething anger which Americans properly feel as they witness on daily television new threats and outrages against their fellow citizens. The hostages must be freed.[26]

Like the folk in *Network*, the citizenry was portrayed as ready to pull up windows and shout, "I'm mad as hell and I'm not going to take it anymore!" According to the administration, these hostages had given the country a renewed sense of patriotism. With hindsight we can see how rhetoric that stressed the people's renewed sense of national pride led to lionizing the symbols who evoked that patriotism.

A more peculiar topic was that of America's energy needs. National energy problems were repeatedly associated with the hostage taking. To the Thirteenth Constitutional Convention of the AFL-CIO, Carter stated, "The developments in Iran have made it starkly clear to all of us that our excessive dependence on foreign oil is a direct, physical threat to our freedom and security as Americans."

But, he continued: "Our love of freedom will not be auctioned off
for foreign oil. Hundreds of thousands of our forebears gave their
very lives for our freedom. Our freedom is not for sale—now or ever
in the future."[27] Two weeks later, the president linked energy to the
hostage issue when he proclaimed, "We stand as a nation unified,
a people determined to protect the life and the honor of every
American. And we are determined to make America an energy
secure nation once again. It is unthinkable that we will allow
ourselves to be dominated by any form of overdependence at home
or any brand of terrorism abroad. We are determined that the freest
nation on earth shall protect and enhance its freedom." To the
lawmakers of the nation Carter's State of the Union address continued this theme, claiming that the events in Iran and Afghanistan
dramatized the fact that a clear and present danger to national
security was created by our excessive dependence on foreign oil.[28]

The implications of these references to America's energy needs
were twofold: our energy dependence kept us vulnerable to future
humiliation by unstable OPEC regimes, and it jeopardized national
freedom. The issue of national security was thereby inserted into
the public sphere as related to the hostages' status. Not only was
Carter using the hostage crisis to support his energy program, but
he was also making support of energy conservation and related
legislation appear a patriotic duty that would somehow assist in
securing the release of the hostages and defend the nation's honor
and security.[29]

Equally interesting are topics Carter did *not* wish to open for
discussion. From the outset he determined that grievances voiced
by Iranians against the shah were inappropriate matters for public
discussion. When asked why he had reversed a previous decision
not to grant the shah entrance to the United States, his pithy
response was "for humanitarian reasons": he was a sick man and "I
took the right decision. I have no regrets about it nor apologies to
make because it did help to save a man's life, and it was compatible
with the principles of our country." When the press asked if the
United States would assist in the investigation of serious charges
against the shah, Carter declined to comment on any role the
government might play in such proceedings. He said he "didn't
know of any international forum within which charges have ever
been brought against a deposed leader who has left his country,"
and he added as a gratuitous afterthought that no such forum would
listen anyway, as long as Iran held the hostages. Following a meeting
with the hostage families he asserted, "I am not interested in trying
to resolve whether or not the Shah was a good or bad leader or the

history of—[applause]—or the history of Iran." And again, at his news conference of 13 February 1980, he was asked if he thought it proper for the United States to restore the shah to the throne in 1953. He responded, "That's ancient history, and I don't think it's appropriate or helpful for me to go into the propriety of something that happened 30 years ago." Considering that the militants, the official representatives of Iran, and the spokesmen for Khomeini were harping on the shah's sins as their major issue, Carter's response had the domestic effect of a rebuttal to the Iranians' complaint.[30]

The president was equally reluctant to entertain any discussion of American responsibility for events in Iran. Thus, Carter maintained that the embassy's fall was not our fault: the Iranian government had given assurances that the embassy would be protected; the changes in Iran had occurred so rapidly that "no one on Earth predicted them"; and he was uninterested in "public debate, at this time, with former Secretary Kissinger about who is or who is not responsible for the events that took place in Iran."[31] Intended or not, the effect of this reluctance was to nip in the bud any suggestion of American culpability for this frustrating event. It kept the target of public discussion clear: the illegal holding of American citizens.

Consonant with his aversion to questions that criticized the United States, Carter was quick to chastise anyone who dared to entertain them. When former United Nations Ambassador Andrew Young suggested that to the Iranians "our protecting the Shah is about like our protecting Adolf Eichmann," National Security Adviser Zbigniew Brzezinski was sent to instruct Young graciously but clearly "to stop talking about it for the duration of the crisis."[32] Senator Kennedy's ill-timed December attack on admitting the shah into the United States met with disbelief and then quick condemnation from the White House. Perhaps the most blatant attempt to quash criticism came in response to Ramsey Clark's participation in the May 1980 Tehran meeting that castigated the United States for its interference in Iranian internal affairs. Armed with his recent ban on travel to Iran, the president vented his aggravation before the press, denounced Clark's participation, and indicated that he favored the Justice Department's proceeding with a civil suit. His exasperation was heightened when he was informed of Secretary of State Edmund Muskie's comment that the purpose of this ban was to keep Americans from traveling to dangerous places, not to punish them. Carter shot back, "I don't think Ed Muskie has any legal responsibility for determining whom to prosecute or not to prosecute." For that matter neither did the president, a point former attorney general Clark was only too willing to make.

In fact, on his behalf Clark cited the Constitution, Supreme Court decisions, and Carter's own human rights posture toward the Soviet Union's repression of the rights to travel by political dissidents.[33] In general, however, the Carter administration was successful in minimizing discussion of Iranian complaints.[34]

Finally, the administration did not welcome discussion of topics that could lead to public exploration of its options. Obviously, no party to hostilities wishes to reveal in advance its retaliatory plans. But Carter was willing to insinuate his retaliatory possibilities into the public realm in ways that asked for blind acceptance of America's potential to act. For example, early in the crisis Carter informed the American people that he was sending naval forces to the Arabian Sea to prevent injury to the hostages. And when the possibility of placing the hostages on trial was raised, Carter ominously warned, "We are prepared to take action that would be quite serious in its consequences for Iran."[35]

On these and other occasions when the administration did not wish Iran to ignore the specter of armed intervention, the president and his staff were naturally reluctant to specify time, place, and manner of action. However, the speculative and even unrealistic character of these threats invited questions of clarification from the American press and people. The policy of publicly raising the possibility of armed intervention and then closing discussion was nothing less than a pronounced effort to keep the threat alive for the Iranians. But, trumpeted on the public stage, it kept the threat alive for the domestic audience as well. Thus on 13 April, Deputy Secretary of State Warren Christopher, appearing on "Issues and Answers," proclaimed that the United States had military options. When asked how viable these were, since they lacked definition, Christopher responded that the government was not going to tele-graph its decisions. Pressed on how the administration had any realistic military options, since the embassy walls apparently had been equipped with explosives, he answered that they had to weigh these threats carefully but would make no comment on military options.[36]

This strategy of keeping alive the possibility of armed intervention collapsed when the ill-fated rescue attempt of 25 April was aborted after mechanical failures and then pilot error resulted in the death of eight American servicemen. Later that day Secretary of Defense Harold Brown held a news conference at which he refused to outline the rescue plan beyond the point at which it aborted. He asked, in effect, that the American people take his word that it would have worked. The press then questioned why this act would not have increased tensions since Iranians would have been confronted and possibly killed. His response was reminiscent of Nixon on the 1970 Cambodia incursion.[37] He asserted that this was not a military action but a rescue attempt. When asked if there remained viable military options, he refused to discuss the matter, simply stating that the administration was keeping all options open. The press incredulously inquired how he could claim not to rule out *any* options, since the United States had just blown one. To this he merely repeated his previous position.[38] Two days later, on "Issues and Answers," Brzezinski had this to say about the disastrous mission: "I believe that one of the very important lessons to be drawn from the events of the last few days, by everyone concerned, is that the United States, and the President of the United States, is prepared to do all that is necessary to obtain their release and will persist in these efforts; I repeat will persist in these efforts." The panel refused to buy this attempt to transform a disaster into a bald assertion of power and wondered whether this failure had not effectively ended any prospect for the hostages' early release. Brzezinski replied that this mission sent a very important message to Tehran: "Do not scoff at American power, do not scoff at American reach." He followed this comment with a stream of ambiguous characterizations of possibilities but refused to discuss specific military options.[39]

These three topics had enormous potential to redirect public attention from the plight of the fifty-two persons held hostage to matters of the nation's conduct in Iran, both before and during the hostage crisis. Had grievances against the shah, or America's responsibility for events in Iran, or alternatives to the administration's chosen options become subjects for public deliberation, public opinion might have swung in another direction, seeing the hostages as victims of misguided American policy. As long as Carter could insulate the government from criticism, then clearly America appeared as an aggrieved, innocent nation, and the hostages' role as heroic representatives of American honor was solidified. As Carter was fond of repeating, "We have done nothing for which any American need apologize."[40]

Third, and finally, the public's perception of the captives as heroes was distorted by the administration's depiction of the Iranians. Four days into the crisis, Secretary Vance stated, "It is a time not for rhetoric, but for quiet, careful, and firm diplomacy."[41] Yet American officials portrayed Iran in a manner that could serve only to sustain national outrage, maintain support for the Carter initiatives, and prevent the hostages from appearing as victims of any force except Iranian malice.

There is no denying that the incident called for stern language in official public statements. It shocked no one to hear Iran depicted as violating international law and defying world opinion. It followed that the Iranians would be characterized as isolating themselves from the community of nations and as setting a precedent that undermined the assumed sanctuary of diplomatic missions and the diplomatic process. So much was inevitable. The tone of public discourse that Vance called for was exemplified by his own testimony before the Senate Foreign Relations Committee. In March 1980 he explained: "International condemnation of Iran and the economic measures which have raised the cost to Iran of their illegal actions are bringing home to Iranians the fact that the holding of the hostages is harmful to their interests and to the success of their revolution. But divisions within Iran have prevented progress."[42]

However, Vance's quiet restraint was not representative of the administration's rhetoric. Daily fare for the American people characterized Iran as an "irrational opponent" in "arrogant defiance of world community." Iran was contemptuous of international law and international diplomatic structures. She continued to "flaunt [sic] with impunity the expressed will and law of the world community," issuing a "drum-fire of propaganda out of Tehran." Her act was an "abhorrent violation" of moral and ethical standards. Iranian officials and militants were called kidnappers, blackmailers, criminals, terrorists, international terrorists, zealots, and political and moral bankrupts. Through innuendo it was suggested that the Iranian leaders permitted the hostage crisis to drag on so as to divert their people from internal problems. Iran was depicted as a nation in chaos; it lacked cohesive leadership; its rulers were opportunists; and it was on the verge of collapse.[43] Indeed, in a remarkable exchange reflecting a prophet's zeal for predicting demise, Zbigniew Brzezinski proclaimed:

B.
The country is gradually disintegrating.
Q.
Now you have said that for a long time.
B.
Its peripheries are falling apart.
Q.
Excuse me, you've said that for a long time.
B.
Its enemies are gathering force.[44]

The inflammatory nature of these characterizations and the repeated references to the motivations of Iranian leadership could only narrow public perceptions and subsequent discourse in the public sphere. How could Americans seriously entertain any assertions of legitimate grievance from people who clearly were mad? Seething anger seemed the only appropriate response. At a time when the United States was once again put up against the wall by a small nation, seething anger was also a politically useful response. Without it the public might well have lapsed into the post-Vietnam syndrome of presuming American guilt for interfering in the affairs of another nation. Then the fate of these hostages, like that of Vietnam veterans, might be perceived as made in America. Rather than heroic symbols of national honor, the hostages might have been seen as pitiful victims of American diplomatic bankruptcy.

While we currently lack sufficient documents to determine whether the patterns I have been discussing were planned, their cumulative effects remain no less apparent.[45] There is no denying that the outpouring of emotion and the euphoric festivity permeating the hostages' return were indicative of the symbolic value Americans placed on the detained embassy personnel. In retrospect one might question whether "heroic" accurately describes the hostages' ordeal. But in the context of their 444-day captivity, the Carter administration's rhetoric surely encouraged the nation to perceive it as "heroic." By word and deed Carter invested these men and women with a significance reserved for heroes: important symbols of American honor and character. Further, the administration explicitly urged Americans to share in the captives' sacrifices by restraints of policy and conduct. The hostages united the nation in a common bond by asserting what it stood for—even if what America stood for was expressed only by what it opposed. Supporting the hostages was thus a patriotic act evoking national identification, which befitted paying the source of such unity the homage due a hero. Moreover, since the administration suppressed alternative interpretations or consideration of related issues, perspectives and information that might have encouraged different perceptions were unavailable. Finally, the characterizations of Iranians served to strengthen domestic opinion. Administration rhetoric celebrating the captives' bravery in the face of a maniacal and malevolent foe galvanized the public's perception of their heroism. Cast as symbolic representatives who opposed the forces of wickedness and injustice, they functioned to certify national worth. Insofar as the administration's rhetoric helped shape the public sphere, this rhetoric was a source of narrow and unbalanced discourse among the populace. The evidence is plain that the public sphere was distorted in a way that encouraged Americans to perceive their captive countrymen as heroes.

And what of the public? If public expression by a people may serve as evidence of the emergence of a public and of the opinions it holds, then there is no denying the facts of the hostages' welcome home. A public did find itself and form an opinion. However, this opinion was significantly colored by administration attempts to craft unified public opinion. The public located itself not only in the officially provided characterizations of its mood and temper, but in interactions among the populace evoked by officialdom's rhetoric. If anything, the Carter administration's rhetoric was too successful at planting a seed crystal around which fragmented popular thought could solidify. These captives appeared to embody a common interest of all Americans. Carter's use of the heroism theme provided a rhetoric suited to gradually transforming disparate groups into a single body shouting abhorrence and intolerance at the events in Tehran and newfound pride in American bravery.

This patriotic expression was no less than a public opinion, but it was an opinion of special cast. The public's image of the hostages' heroism was akin to what the ancient Greeks termed *doxa*, "opinion," which was contrasted with *episteme*, "knowledge." Moreover, it was a special type of opinion—a form of thought that typifies an unqualified state of mind.[46] The public discussion of the hostages encouraged formation of an opinion about the ethos of the hostages—an opinion that was personal and bimodal. They were *our* hostages; they represented America as a put-upon nation. Iran was a clear enemy, personified by the cartoonlike image of a Draconian cleric. Judging from the euphoria publicly displayed upon their return, one would have to conclude that this state of *doxa*—simplified, clarified, and polarized—was widespread.[47]

Obviously, other important factors contributed to the public's pouring of honor on the returning hostages. Media coverage certainly contributed, as did Iran's own conduct and her manners of publicizing the matter. It would be simplistic to seek the full account for the people's response in any single doorway. My aims are more modest: to set forth the reasonable beginnings for an account of how American officials contributed to evoking, sustaining, and managing this aspect of public opinion by constraining the public sphere.

Public Opinion as Technological Constraint

Thus far I have been concerned with public opinion from the vantage point of the public. I began with the empirical datum of a widespread public response and inquired into how administration rhetoric contributed to its formation. My orientation assumed that public opinion was a product of discourse and, further, that the character and quality of this opinion could be gauged by examining the discourse to which the public was exposed. I concluded that the Carter administration succeeded in encouraging the public to perceive the hostages as heroes. In fact, as I noted at the conclusion of the previous section, Carter may have been too successful. The American public accepted his interpretation of the hostages' character, but they also rejected the president in his reelection bid.

How could this same public, so supportive of its president through most of this crisis, come to reject Jimmy Carter at the polls? In the judgments of campaign braintrusters like Robert Strauss and Patrick Caddell, the voters did so precisely because of the hostage affair.[48] Why was this so? How could the administration succeed so well in shaping some perceptions of the hostages and yet fail so emphatically in the same arena at the end? We may gain insight into this matter and into the troublesome nature of public opinion in the public realm by examining how Carter and his lieutenants thought about public opinion. This will require a different perspective on public opinion in the public sphere than that employed in the foregoing analysis of the "hostages-as-heroes" theme. Whereas the earlier analysis focused on how discourse shaped opinion, now the focus will be on how an administration's perception of public opinion influenced the shape of presidential rhetoric. I intend to show how Carter's political staff misconceived public opinion as a technological construct rather than as a discursive product. I intend, further, to show how this misconception resulted in ill-conceived rhetoric by the president.

In *Toward a Rational Society*, Jürgen Habermas writes:

The choice that interests us is not between one elite that effectively exploits vital resources of knowledge over the heads of a mediatized population and another that is isolated from inputs of scientific information, so that technical knowledge flows inadequately into the processes of political decision-making. The question is rather whether a productive body of knowledge is merely transmitted to men engaged in technical manipulation for purposes of control or is simultaneously appropriated as the linguistic possession of communicating individuals.[49]

In other words, when a technology is put in the hands of a few while made inaccessible to the community at large, the few may use technology as a means of mass manipulation and control. Habermas's point bears on the contemporary meaning of public opinion. Histori-cally, "public opinion" has referred to community-based views. But in the comparatively recent past, this concept has been technolo-gized to refer to data acquired in opinion polls.[50]

Public opinion polls technologize public opinion in two ways: they technologize what counts as knowledge of public opinion and they technologize the way public opinion is produced. First, opinion polls change what counts as theoretical knowledge of public opinion by substituting the data of survey research for the processes and outcomes of rhetoric. Survey research adheres to the guidelines of social scientific methodology in seeking factors that are related in some statistically significant fashion. Therefore, opinion polls attempt to elicit responses to a set list of questions administered to a random sample of a stipulated population. By definition, this methodology substitutes the general populace for the active portion of the citizenry that constitutes a particular public. It substitutes randomness for discrimination in determining whose opinion should be counted as bearing on public questions. It substitutes statistical quantification for intensity and duration in deciding the weight to ascribe to a reported view. In these ways, public opinion is trans-formed from a discursive phenomenon studied critically to a statisti-cal phenomenon studied scientifically.

Second, opinion polls technologize the way public opinion is produced. Survey research can reveal what is popular at any given moment. It can reveal, as well, selected factors that enhance or diminish an item's popularity. But, as conditions change, the popu-larity of persons, programs, issues, and so forth may alter so drasti-cally as to vanish from view. In the hands of the powerful (and assistants to the powerful), a technologized view of public opinion encourages emphasis on the popular, stresses the efficacy of themes that accentuate popularity, and promotes keeping "helpful" concerns before the citizenry as long as possible. It does not project the public as an active audience but as an incremental assemblage of responses to be arranged and rearranged in various combinations that may suit the ends of those in power.

This transformed sense of the "public" highlights the danger of technologizing public opinion. Even in the hands of well-inten-tioned leaders, the frequent measurement of opinions on policies, programs, job performance, and the like, may distort their percep-tions. Polls may suggest it is necessary to tell the public what it wants to hear in order to secure election and then reelection. This can result in a philosophy of pragmatic deception for noble ends: "I can't do good unless I'm elected, I can't be elected unless I say what they want to hear, thus I'll speak their mind rather than my own."[51] When the violent fluctuations of popular attitude, as measured by opinion polls, are taken for public opinion,[52] evanescent factors like mood intimidate public officials. Intimidation minimizes open debate and deprives the community at large of a vibrant public sphere. If anything, the Carter administration fell prey to this pragmatic view. It misconceived the Iranian hostage affair as a source of opportunity to be interjected into the president's reelection campaign. That is the second hypothesis I shall explore.

Political observers, not to mention Carter's opponents, were quick to comment on the president's attempts to exploit the political cash value of the hostage situation. But more can be said than this easy generalization. Close examination of the timing and content of Iran-related statements by Carter and of public opinion data reveals an intriguing pattern. The president or his staff apparently selected items to discuss and times to discuss them by referring to popular attitudes revealed by his personal pollster's data on opinions about Iran and other salient matters.

To set the president's political uses of public opinion data on the hostage affair in perspective, two observations are germane as background. First, the Carter administration was calculatingly sensitive to the symbolic value of projecting a presidential image suited to the nation's mood. Witness Carter's "plain-folks" inaugural stroll down Pennsylvania Avenue hand in hand with Mrs. Carter; or the initial banning of "Hail to the Chief" as too imperial and its subsequent revival after intense criticism of his administration's competence; or his attempted emulations of FDR's fireside chats, embellished with the "down-home" casualness of cardigan and jeans. Indeed, two of the more prominent White House advisers were technologists who specialized in political images—Patrick Caddell and Gerald Rafshoon. Politicians doubtless have been concerned with their public image since Cleon was emboldened to declare that he spoke for the city. However, Carter's embrace of the data provided by technological advances in polling and media techniques represented a qualitative leap in a new direction. Not only did he use technologically derived data as a guide for crafting messages, he then extended these technologically grounded images into areas of substantive decision.

For better or worse, Carter did not capriciously place confidence in the work of his political technologists. This was especially true in respect to Caddell's polling data. During the 1980 campaign, Caddell's polls provided several levels of information. Like others of his fraternity Caddell would administer the standard questions asking whom the electorate favored. Answers to these questions of preference indicated whether a candidate was ahead or behind and by how many points. But Caddell hypothesized that when voters cast their actual ballots, they carefully weigh a variety of factors that lie beneath the surface and remain untapped by standard questioning.

To discover the underlying factors, Caddell administered additional questions employing a semantic differential. Then through regression analysis he located salient factors that voters weighed in arriving at their final judgments. He discovered, for example, that when voters opposed to Carter were reminded of his deeds that corresponded favorably with positive factors, a significantly different set of results emerged. Voters switched choices along lines of thought they might follow when weighing all factors in their own final balloting.[53]

The significance of Caddell's polling techniques are most apparent in their relationship to voter behavior. Voters sometimes seize primary elections as opportunities to express protests. Ballots for a challenger may represent attempts to send an incumbent a message. In general elections, voters appear to be more deliberate, taking stock of a candidate's personal attributes as well as policy commitments when deciding whom they wish to have in office. Polling data that revealed a candidate's perceived strengths and weaknesses would therefore be most useful in laying tactics designed to encourage voters to ballot "correctly." For a sitting president, the obvious rule of thumb is to minimize protest votes by encouraging voters to think of the primary as if it were the general election.

This more elaborate polling technique also provided data that permitted Caddell to make revised estimates of the point differences between candidates. The "second cuts" proved to be unnervingly accurate in telling the candidate precisely how matters stood going into the election—sometimes, as in the New York primary, forecasting an outcome opposite from that indicated by preferential polls.

Caddell's polls played a significant role in Carter's use of the hostage affair because they provided the president with indexes of popular sentiment relating to the presidential race and suggested times when positive steps by the president might prove politically useful.

A second background observation concerns the strategy Carter aides had mapped for the reelection campaign prior to the embassy takeover. Hamilton Jordan, Carter's White House chief of staff, had examined strategies and their consequences in previous presidential campaigns. Among his conclusions were that incumbents erred if they did not plan for opposition and attempt to defeat opponents soundly from the outset; that incumbents erred if they ignored the advantages of incumbency for securing endorsement; that incumbents erred if they did not campaign from the White House, using it rather than the campaign trail to present their messages. In October 1979, Carter gathered with his strategists at Camp David. Jordan's observations on incumbency were incorporated as major features of the Carter primary campaign plan. Carter would make Senator Kennedy chase him, would use incumbency to secure endorsements, and would emphasize his leadership abilities by tending to the business of the White House.[54]

As the Carter forces left Camp David, public perceptions of the president's leadership were their chief concern. Caddell's polls showed that on questions of character, Carter had a decisive edge over Kennedy. And the Carter people were confident that the president's use of discretionary federal funds for well-placed and well-timed executive grants would garner the endorsements of mayors, governors, and other party regulars who were opinion leaders. But Caddell's polls also showed Kennedy with a decisive edge in leadership. Carter's problem was that he did not act in ways that appeared "presidential."[55]

Shortly thereafter the American embassy in Tehran was seized. Its importance to the campaign was recognized instantly. Elizabeth Drew reports these reactions by Carter strategists:

One of the decisions made at the Camp David meeting was that the most important thing for the President to do to enhance his chances of renomination was to be seen as being "Presidential." One of the participants at the meeting says, "There was acceptance of the idea that Carter would win or lose based on how he was seen doing his job in the White House, far more than on what he did on the campaign trail." The following week—on November 4th, one year before Election Day—the hostages were seized in Iran. One of Carter's strategists says, "The perception of his handling of Iran and Afghanistan had more impact than anything we could have done—tripled or squared."[56]

Incumbency assuredly provides political aspirants the great advantage of opportunities to appear fit for office, especially for incumbent presidents. They can to some extent command events and to a greater extent command the news media. Presidents can open relations with previously hostile nations, arrange and attend summits, dispense discretionary favors, initiate legislative proposals, sign bills, hold "nonpolitical" press conferences, and in it all appear most "presidential." Certainly no one should have expected Jimmy Carter to be above exploiting the unique opportunities incumbency provided. But less predictable was his repeated reliance on the Iranian crisis to boost his reelection bid.

Carter vehemently denied charges that he was playing politics with the hostage crisis. Assertions like "I've never used the hostage issue for political purposes and never will," and "I do not make, and have not made, and will not make decisions nor announcements concerning the lives and safety of our hostages simply to derive some political benefit from them"[57] were typical and often repeated. Whether this was sincerely the case may never be known, since it raises a question of motivation.[58] Nonetheless, there were political benefits to be derived from this situation, and they were not entirely fortuitous. To reap them, the Carter strategists apparently believed the president must be seen handling the crisis; conducting the nation's business would display his "presidential" attributes.[59] Of course, this conviction committed the Administration to the delicate course of weaving the hostage affair into the campaign—not as an issue but as the foundation of an image. And it committed the president to respond less to the informed opinion of the public sphere than to the image of that sphere projected by the technology of opinion polls. This latter commitment was not without baggage, since acts intended to create an image might actually set policy and since Iranian actions beyond Carter's control might actually undermine the campaign itself—if, for example, the Iranians' intransigence should stymie "presidential" initiatives.

Within the context of Carter's reelection strategy, the concerns of Americans about hostages were addressed at propitious moments during the campaign: that is, when the polls coincidentally showed that the Carter candidacy could use a boost. Moreover, the hostage question was addressed in several ways that fitted into the overall campaign strategy I have briefly outlined. I will comment on three of these campaign tactics designed to enhance the presidential image of Jimmy Carter.

First, Carter's operatives were quick to employ the Iranian crisis as a shield with which they could protect the president's administration from scrutiny while simultaneously displaying him in a leadership role. Although Carter had no control over the timing of events in Tehran, a quick glance at Carter's standings in the polls suggests that the embassy seizure could not have occurred at a more opportune political moment. The opinion polls of late summer 1979 did not bode well for the president. In August, the Yankelovich, Skelly, and White survey showed that among Democrats 62 percent favored Kennedy for nomination, whereas only 24 percent favored Carter. More telling, their poll revealed a dismal level of confidence in the president's ability to perform his job, with one-third to nearly one-half of the respondents expressing no confidence in his ability to deal with the economy, conduct foreign policy, appoint the right people to office, or manage domestic affairs. One month later, the AP-NBC News Survey showed that only 19 percent of Americans thought Carter was doing an excellent or good job. By the end of October, as Kennedy's announcement for candidacy appeared imminent, the race for the nomination took on more realistic proportions, but Carter still trailed 39 percent to 49 percent in the Yankelovich survey.[60] At the very best, the president appeared to have a serious fight on his hands. This was especially so because the economy was suffering a recession, with interest rates and inflation at record highs and unemployment climbing. These were Kennedy issues that placed the president in apparent jeopardy of losing an economic debate and the nomination.

The seizure of the Tehran embassy provided an overwhelming diversion from these problems. Hostage developments were dramatically played out on the public stage and embedded in the electorate's consciousness as a very important matter, contributing to the swift swing in national concern from economic matters to diplomacy and Carter's handling of this foreign crisis. The nation's concern only intensified when the Soviet Union invaded Afghanistan in late December, thereby posing a serious threat to American oil interests in the Mideast. In terms of the campaign, the immediate issues suddenly swung in Carter's favor and, for all practical purposes, Kennedy was left without salient issues to discuss.

Most importantly, the crisis provided a perfect excuse for Carter to remain aloof from the partisan politics of the campaign: not only from the stump speeches and the debates but also from the risky scrutiny of his whole administration that such encounters would have involved. If the press had been given the chance to report on normal campaign speeches defending his record, they could have zeroed in on matters where he was weakest. And Kennedy's remorseless hammering at Carter's poor performance in dealing with the economy and at an alleged absence of leadership would only have intensified the electorate's focus on Carter's record as the issue. As long as he could remain above the fray, he would continue to appear presidential and the issue would be whether Kennedy was fit to serve. This was precisely what the Carter forces wanted, since "fitness to serve" was not a substantive issue that challenged the Carter record but one of image, hinging on the perceived character of the candidates; and it was Kennedy's weak suit.[61]

The celebrated Rose Garden strategy was nothing less than a decision to sustain this shield, a decision that appears to have been the result of poll data reflecting increased Carter strength as a result of the patriotic surge following the embassy's fall.[62] Indeed, two days into the crisis, with the president trailing Kennedy in the polls, he agreed to the Des Moines *Register* debate scheduled for mid-January. By 29 December having overtaken Kennedy and with 66 percent of the electorate rating his handling of the crisis as "just right," he withdrew.[63] Martin Schram reports a senior adviser as explaining, "Things were going well for us in the polls. . . . By being president, by leading, he could do more for himself than by campaigning. . . . We had nothing to gain by Carter debating." Carter himself acknowledged as much to his staff. "Look, you guys," Jordan quotes him as saying, "if I go out to Iowa to debate Ted Kennedy, I go out there as a President and return as just another political candidate." Schram also suggested that the Iowa debate bail-out was part of the larger scheme of keeping the president at home. Indeed, one Carter aide confessed that even though the president was preoccupied by the crisis he could still have campaigned through January and into February, which is when serious decisions on negotiations were being made.[64]

If these attributions to and by Carter insiders are to be trusted, then more than foreign crisis kept the president in his Rose Garden. Had this been generally perceived, cynicism might well have eroded the support Carter was gaining in the public opinion polls and in his renomination bid. The president therefore acted to squelch possible negative repercussions that might follow his withdrawal from the Iowa debate by receiving a memo from Press Secretary Jody Powell outlining the arguments of Carter's campaign advisers on why he should go through with the debate. Carter then dutifully penned: "I can't disagree with any of this; but I cannot break away from my duties here, which are extraordinary now and ones which only I can fulfill. We will just have to take the adverse political consequences and make the best of it. Right now both Iran and Afghanistan look bad, and will need my constant attention." Then the orchestrated memo plus Carter's handwritten response were leaked to the Los Angeles *Times* by Powell.[65]

In the short run, the Rose Garden strategy worked. It put Kennedy in a very weak campaign posture and virtually assured the renomination of Jimmy Carter as the Democratic candidate. However, the strategy had only short-term value. Early on Powell recognized that criticism of Carter's handling of the crisis was inevitable, but he anticipated it would not come until the general election, and that was not his problem at the moment.[66] More than this, the Rose Garden strategy created a trap. Since the president gave the hostage affair as the reason for not debating, it became all the more important that he not be seen making other political appearances. But what was he to do if the hostage situation lingered and the polls reflected impatience with him? No plans were laid for resolving this problem, and thus Carter himself became a political prisoner of sorts.

That Carter settled on the Rose Garden strategy for the political gain of appearing presidential is indicative of his flawed conception of the public. The embassy seizure raised a number of serious questions, most of which went begging for answers through sheer lack of information: Who were these people demonstrating on the streets of Tehran? Who was the shah? Who were the hostages? Who were the activists? What did the shah do to make Iranians want to kill him? And, perhaps most fundamentally, there was the frustrated question of Stephen Smith, Kennedy's campaign director. "In the end, the basic question about the Iranian crisis is whether it was necessary for the Shah to be here. Obviously, there will be a rather careful examination of all that. I don't know why he's here. Do you?"[67]

Since Carter chose not to answer these questions, the primary data at the public's disposal were not about the issues, but about events. Americans were being held hostage by fanatical Iranians in apparent contravention of international law; and the president was acting presidential by attending to the crisis through initiatives in the United Nations and the World Court, by levying economic sanctions, and by rallying the nation to lend support and remain temperate.

As the campaign season rolled into late winter, basic questions remained unanswered, the Americans were still held hostage, and disenchantment with the president's conduct started to mount. Nothing captures the reversal more clearly than the shift in reporting by *Time*. In the 18 February 1980 issue, Hugh Sidey defended the Rose Garden ploy by proclaiming, "A President cannot run his country properly from Air Force One. . . . The White House, with its ready access to information and people, with its tensions and moods and direct lines to friends and critics, with its tradition and reminders of duty, is needed by any President in critical times." One month later, *Time* took off its gloves and reported, "He has been holed up in the White House for more than three months now. He has given only two press conferences since October, and only a few aides see him regularly. He summoned 300 business leaders and prominent citizens last week to consult on the galloping inflation rate, but chose not to meet with them. While an aide chaired one of the sessions, Jimmy Carter was in the garden with his grandson Jason, 4. Together they built a snowman." The story continued, detailing how the Rose Garden strategy began accidentally but was adopted as a way of life as Carter rose in the polls and racked up primary victories. The report concluded that recent blunders suggested the president was now isolated, out of touch, and not doing a good job.[68]

The disenchanted perception of Carter's handling of the presidency was not foreign to an electorate who had to view with suspicion a president now reportedly spending every spare minute phoning local Democratic politicians and functionaries in primary states. Carter was actually campaigning with great energy even though he presented himself in public as above politics and as acting presidential during this time of crisis. By spring, his apparent inconsistency of behavior became a recurrent theme in his press interviews.[69]

Unable to free himself from the Rose Garden but needing to campaign, unwilling to discuss Iran as a legitimate issue in the public sphere and yet interjecting it into the public sphere as a shield against the issue of his stewardship, Carter was encountering the long-term weakness of his appearance as presidential. It was inevitably perceived as a ploy, a course chosen on the strength of a shallow image of the public—a technological mirage. The Rose Garden strategy was merely a political response to a momentary opportunity: it could have no staying power before an audience capable of perceiving virtuosity and hypocrisy. Not surprisingly, Carter's projection of himself as presidential proved evanescent, failing to produce the concrete results that might have substantiated it.

How had Carter led Americans to form their expectations about his leadership abilities? Shielded from the criticisms of press and opponents, Carter used the Iranian issue as an impenetrable sanctuary from which he could speak without fear of attack and from which he could attack without fear of retaliation. In effect, the president freed himself from the need to debate the issue by appropriating unto himself the turf of the Iranian crisis. As a second tactic exploiting the hostage affair, Carter made it a one-sided issue that only he might legitimately manage, and then exploited the press's insatiable desire to cover the event and its management. He thereby had the press carry his presidential image to the people.

Americans became familiar with Carter's presidential quality through a montage of scenes that uncritically suggested that he was a leader of stature: scenes of the president huddled with his aides or taking a lonely stroll in the Rose Garden, always looking concerned; scenes of televised epideictic, like the nonlighting of the White House Christmas tree at the 1979 ceremony, that showed Carter leading the nation in its somber vigil awaiting the hostages' release;[70] scenes of Carter addressing groups of legislators or the hostage families, his remarks covered but no questions permitted; scenes from backgrounders at which the president or one of his aides would talk to the press about coming events or the president's thoughts, later dutifully reported as news from "sources close to the President"; scenes of brief presidential statements announcing another sanction or initiative designed to bring Iran to its senses, broadcast from the Oval Office and without opportunities for questions. In these ways Carter made his views known without subjecting them to interrogation. He also portrayed himself thereby in a most presidential manner.

When the President did open himself to scrutiny, it was at a news conference or interview in which, inevitably, the subject of Iran was featured and the questions generally friendly. Such press events also provided a convenient forum in which the president assumed the role of leader—the area of Carter's "negatives," according to Caddell's polls—by emphasizing his unique responsibilities during the crisis.

Americans were reminded that he was not campaigning "in order to stay close to the scene here where constantly changing events could be handled by me as President," and that "there is only one spokesman for our Nation." The Iranian crisis gave Carter opportunity to say how important it was for all Americans "to realize that almost all of the complications that address our society today eventually wind up on my desk in the Oval Office. And I think it's important for the American people to realize that I'm there on the job."[71]

Press events also were convenient forums in which to remind opponents and the public that it was unpatriotic at this time not to support Carter's actions. So, while restricting his own political activities, he called "on those who might be opposing me in the future for president to support my position as President and to provide unity for our country and for our nation in the eyes of those who might be looking for some sign of weakness or division in order to perpetuate their abuse of our hostages."[72]

Through publicity of this sort, the president used his power to command the media in ways that kept attention focused on Iran and off domestic issues. He also kept attention on himself in his leadership role, showing Americans that at least some of the time he could act presidential. Furthermore, he undermined the substantive and symbolic base of Kennedy's challenge, since in the face of a foreign crisis, economic matters engendered neither enthusiasm nor interest.

Kennedy himself noted the enormous advantage in media coverage and in shaping of national consciousness afforded the president by the Tehran captivity. While assessing his devastating loss in Iowa, he commented:

Just every single evening there was [sic] twelve, fifteen, eighteen minutes of national television focused on the hostages and the administration's reaction to it. It was the dominance of that issue in the news, and not just any issue but an issue of foreign policy that touched the hearts and souls of the American people, and also reached the matter of national honor and national prestige as that prestige and power is institutionalized in the presidency. . . . And of course as one who shared those same kinds of emotions, I probably didn't anticipate it could be that divisive in terms of the political implications vis-a-vis the administration and myself.[73]

Indeed, the senator's final observation on the divisive impact of the issue is especially pertinent since the official rhetoric, cast in terms of the nation's honor with Jimmy Carter as its sole trustee, left Kennedy little room in which to demonstrate leadership in the Iran game unless he wished to risk his own credibility as a fit leader by challenging the president's concentration on the hostages.

When Kennedy decided to run that risk, the press conference served as Carter's vehicle for publicly castigating his opponent as irresponsible at best, and perhaps even unpatriotic.[74] For example, following Carter's State of the Union address on 23 January, Kennedy made aggressive moves to force Carter to debate the issues. On the twenty-eighth Kennedy delivered a strong speech at Georgetown in which he put his claim to attention squarely:

Forty years ago, when the Nazis swept across the Low Countries and France, a far more urgent threat to our security, there was no suspension of the public debate— or the presidential campaign [between Roosevelt and Wilkie]. If we could discuss foreign policy frankly when Hitler's panzers were poised at the English Channel, surely we can discuss foreign policy when the Soviet Union has crossed the border of Afghanistan.

If the Vietnam war taught us anything, it is precisely that when we do not debate our foreign policy, we may drift into deeper trouble. If a President's policy is right, debate will strengthen the national consensus. If it is wrong, debate may save the country from catastrophe.[75]

Two weeks later, voters in Maine showed signs of responsiveness to this appeal as Kennedy ran a close second in the municipal caucuses, taking 39.4 percent to Carter's 45.2 percent. Two nights after the Maine contest Kennedy pressed his attack on Carter's foreign policy. He asserted that "no president should be reelected because he happened to be standing there when his foreign policy collapsed around him," and that "the last gasp of a failed foreign policy is war." Again he called upon Carter to debate, interpreting the results in Maine as a warning that "the Presidency can never be above the fray," and that "a President cannot afford to posture as the high priest of patriotism."[76]

Kennedy's attacks seemed to be working. As the New Hampshire primary neared, Caddell's adjusted figures indicated that the president's lead was only five points; Kennedy's campaign was gaining strength and voters were thinking of the election as a primary, where protest votes are more likely to occur. Carter had to reach New Hampshire voters; he had to allay their fears about his action on Afghanistan and convince them that he was not hiding out, as Kennedy was charging; and he also had to undercut his opponent.

Carter found his opportunity to address these needs when he held a press conference on 13 February, his second since the embassy seizure. After using carefully chosen language to deal with negative voter perceptions on other issues, he turned to Kennedy. The senator had accused the administration of endorsing a United Nations commission on Iran only because Kennedy had urged the formation of such a body. The president used this topic as a point of departure for a general attack on Kennedy's offensive. Carter angrily denounced him for this charge of stealing Kennedy's foreign policy ideas. "His statements have not been true, they've not been accurate, and they've not been responsible, and they're not helping the country." And later, "This thrust of what he has said throughout the last few weeks is very damaging to our country, and to the establishment of our principles and the maintenance of them, and the achieving of our goals to keep the peace and to get our hostages released."[77]

Elizabeth Drew comments on the connection between Carter's attack and the Caddell polls: "Carter's anger was real anger, apparently, but the demonstration of it was calculated. Caddell's figures showed afterward that Kennedy's 'negatives'—questions about his credibility and dependability—went up."[78]

Through publicity of this sort, the president used his power to command the media in ways that admirably suited his polling data. Carter was extremely vulnerable on domestic economic issues. By keeping attention riveted on Iran well into the primary season, he sustained the single most unifying factor working in his favor while diverting attention from his major substantive weaknesses. The hostage crisis also proved to be an antidote for those aspects of Caddell's polls that showed the weak impression voters had of the president's leadership abilities as a substantial Carter negative. By emphasizing his unique responsibilities at this time, as well as through the announced measures he was pursuing, he made the hostage affair became a conduit for projecting himself as presidential.

The unifying influence of the hostage crisis on national attitudes and its convenience as an opportunity for Carter to demonstrate his presidential stature also indicate the precarious and artificial nature of Carter's popularity during the primaries. Developments in Iran (and to some extent Afghanistan) permitted him to undermine the substantive basis of his opponent's challenge and simultaneously to deflect attention from his own record, but what was he to do if the crisis was resolved, or if the public's patience grew short, or if either Kennedy or Ronald Reagan found a political vulnerability on Iran? Clearly as the crisis lingered, its political capital diminished. Further, the press's insatiable appetite for the story threatened to sustain an impression Carter increasingly did not desire—that his management of the Iranian matter indicated how well he functioned as a leader.

Thus, as spring arrived and the American hostages remained incarcerated, the press started to raise doubts: Were there, in fact, realistic military alternatives? What were the positive results of his embargo measures? Was he timing his statements in harness with the primary schedule? Was the job of being president too large for any individual?[79] At the very least, these and similar queries reflected a tacit skepticism about Carter's leadership ability. And if the American electorate was even moderately attentive to such questions, the administration's evasive explanations of the attempted rescue and Carter's punitive reaction to Ramsey Clark's travels to Tehran could only reinforce the impression that the president was less the leader than his media image projected. In fact, he appeared reckless, mean, and opportunistic.

The administration's decision to use Iran as Carter's exclusive domain and to exploit for political gain the media's interest and the public's emotional susceptibilities was a self-constructed trap. The administration had sealed off the national debate for which Kennedy had called, thereby denying itself an informed consensus. It had manipulated press events to convey a hyperbolized image that distorted perceptions of the type of problem the incarceration represented and the type of leader required to resolve it. And it had committed itself to managing Carter's image as leader according to the dictates of polling data. However, once the president quit the Rose Garden to deliver his message personally to the people, there was no effective way to remove the Iranian matter from the public sphere, nor to open the affair to debate, nor to restrict the power he gave the press and television to keep attention focused on the incident, nor to reduce the salience of video images as the basis for judging Carter's presidential stature. In the end, even the images of Carter acting presidential served as subtle reminders that as a leader he was seriously flawed, as this recollection by Robert Strauss of the Sunday before the election testifies:

Let me tell you the final straw for me, when I almost felt like throwing it in. We finally staged it: the President flies back on Sunday morning of the hostage thing. He's got his message, he comes back from the campaign, he helicopters in to the White House, and he takes a long stroll by himself, not even with his wife with him, so he'll look dramatic. Here's this man dealing with the issue. I'll be a dirty son of a bitch if in the middle of the television screen I'm looking at, and thinking how good it's looking, out runs Brzezinski, puts his arm around him, and hands him a paper. And the two of them walk off together talking about the paper. He [Brzezinski] put the negative touch on that, a great scene, a poignant scene. So he killed that morning. The news could have been good. It turned out to be a negative instead of a positive. That's the story of the campaign there.[80]

Strauss's comments, in addition to their analysis of how the president's campaign of images returned to haunt him, reflect how thoroughly the Carter camp had entrenched its thinking about the public in a technological mold. The public—the voters of the nation—was neither an aggregate with shared interests nor an aggregate discursively formed and identified by consensus; it was seen as a quantity assembled in bits and pieces by projecting orchestrated images before voters to excite "positive" and "negative" impressions. This mode of thinking governed the Carter campaign generally, and it even governed treatment of what had been built up as the most solemn of all issues, the problem of freeing the hostages. We can see most clearly how such thinking apparently led Carter to exploit the Iranian affair by exploring a third trait of his campaign rhetoric. The president, through word and deed, inserted Iran into the campaign precisely when opinion polls suggested it would be politically efficacious.

From the beginning, White House political advisers realized that galvanizing American public opinion around Iranian events worked in Carter's favor. The liabilities of three years were swept aside. Economic woes, fits and starts of foreign policy, and controversial management of his own staff and cabinet would be forgotten as each new development in the Iranian situation triggered a positive image

of the president. Early developments—such as official acts of retaliation against Iran; the World Court and United Nations initiatives;
the shah's departure from New York and locating a haven in Panama
when Mexico denied him refuge in Cuernavaca; the ominous response when Iran threatened to place the hostages on trial—all
these were reflected in the public mood, as an AP-NBC News poll
revealed. Over 70 percent believed Carter was doing everything in
his power to release the hostages, and two-thirds opposed extraditing
the shah. By the end of November, he had edged ahead of Kennedy
in the ABC News-Lou Harris poll for the first time, 48 percent to
46 percent.[81]

Carter displayed the hostage issue prominently in early December
as he announced his candidacy for a second term. Not only did he
call for unity and support during his absence from the campaign trail,
but he magnified the crisis—and his leadership—by comparisons to
World War II and to Abraham Lincoln. Indeed, Carter proclaimed,
"At the height of the Civil War, President Abraham Lincoln said,
'I have but one task, and that is to save the Union.' Now I must
devote my concerted efforts to resolving the Iranian crisis." Shortly
thereafter Carter's lead over Kennedy grew to eight points in the
Gallup poll. Later in December, after the shah left the United
States and Iran called for trials of the hostages, Carter responded by
appealing for United Nations sanctions. Yankelovich, Skelly, and
White showed that his lead increased to twenty points.[82] As these
trends continued and the president retreated into the Rose Garden,
he seemed to send out timely reminders and announce developments
that coincided with the polling data on his reelection chances.

Iowa came first, scheduled for 21 January. As this test drew
near, Carter called in a small group of columnists and television
commentators for a backgrounder. There he in effect wrote his own
news story, although under White House rules the material was not
attributed to him. The Soviet Union's invasion of Afghanistan, in
tandem with the Iranian crisis, had the potential to emphasize
America's Middle Eastern plight and the president's leadership in
framing an effective response. Haynes Johnson gives this account:

The stories said the President was prepared to take any action, including war, to
block Soviet aggression in the Mideast after the invasion of Afghanistan; that he
would cancel U.S. participation in the Summer Olympic games scheduled for
Moscow, and that he was planning a new, tough speech to the nation outlining a
"Carter doctrine" for the Mideast.

The stories were a trial ballot for Carter, and they made him appear strong just
at a time when the first critical primary contests with Kennedy loomed.[83]

Less disguised was Carter's outmaneuvering of Kennedy the day before the Iowa caucuses when, on 20 January, Carter appeared on "Meet the Press." His appearance was tantamount to inserting his leadership role into the public's consciousness in a way that could only aid his chances in the Iowa caucuses and damage Kennedy's. An internal memo written by a Washington *Post* reporter assigned to Kennedy depicts Carter's exploitation of the hostage issue this way:

I often get the feeling that this election campaign is being run of, by, and for the TV networks, and so it was fitting that it was a TV show that perfectly crystallized Ted Kennedy's dilemma. The show was the January 20 edition of ABC's "Issues and Answers," on which Kennedy appeared only after he was turned down in an effort to worm his way onto "Meet the Press" for a joint appearance with Carter. (Must note there the utterly brazen arrogance of Carter agreeing to go on that show one day before the Iowa caucuses after he had said in writing that he would have to forego personal appearances until the Tehran hostages were freed.) Kennedy's whole campaign has been upstaged by Carter's handling of the Mideast situation, and sure enough, his appearance on "Issues and Answers" was interrupted twice by news bulletins reporting what Carter was saying at the same time on "Meet the Press."[84]

Iowa, of course, went two to one for the president in their caucuses, and his campaign was off to a strong if not decisive beginning. The next primary, New Hampshire, was in Kennedy's backyard, and the Carter people were concerned that a Kennedy rebound might reverse his faltering campaign start. As discussed earlier, when Caddell's polls indicated that these fears were justified, Carter held a news conference, attacking Kennedy's statements on Iran and thereby directing attention to Kennedy's negatives—credibility and dependability. The desired outcome, of course, was for voters to perceive Kennedy's character, not Carter's record, as the overriding concern in casting their votes.

Carter won the New Hampshire primary and a string of others in quick succession. Voters were perceiving him as the clear winner and started to cast votes on a primary basis of "let's send him a message" rather than on a general election basis of "I want this person in office." New York was a clear case that gave Carter a warning of trouble. After Ambassador McHenry voted for a United Nations resolution sanctioning Israel, the Carter campaign in New York started to slip. Preferential polls showed him with a substantial lead (on the Friday before the primary, the Harris polls gave Carter a twenty-seven-point lead), but Caddell's figures proved the contrary. In fact, six days before the primary Carter trailed in his own pollster's adjusted figures, and the bottom was dropping out of "character" as a significant issue in New Yorkers' minds. Discontent over the economy and the lack of development in Iran started to take hold, and Kennedy eventually trounced Carter, 59 percent to 41 percent.

Carter was facing a similar problem in the Wisconsin primary. While the preferential polls showed a sizable Carter lead, Caddell's adjusted figures indicated that Kennedy was moving closer. Matters were compounded by recent losses in New York and Connecticut. Another defeat could make these look like a trend rather than exceptions. Appearances here were especially important, with the Pennsylvania primary just ahead and not looking secure for the President. In Caddell's view, "The Iranian thing was clearly a problem. . . . The President's ratings on his handling of it were declining."[85] Carter again played his Iranian card.

For some time Hamilton Jordan had been involved in secret negotiations with go-betweens approved by the Iranians.[86] They had worked out a scenario for transferring the hostages from the militants to the government, scheduled for 29 March. There were delays, but news reports raised speculation that some movement on the crisis was likely soon. On 1 April, the day of the Wisconsin primary, the president appeared before the television news cameras at 7:20 A.M., just in time to make the morning newscasts, to announce the "positive step" that President Bani-Sadr had declared the intent of the Iranian government to take control of the hostages—a report that subsequently proved false. But in the context of the Wisconsin primary, the weekend speculation and Carter's primary morning message proved significant. According to Caddell, "When it was made clear over the weekend that there was going to be some progress, that bumped the race for us. It went from a lead of 15 to 18 points to a win of almost 30 points. Wisconsin was the only state where we ever got the undecided to go for us in the end."[87]

Carter paid a price in the long run, however, for the 1 April announcement. The press was alienated by its impression of his apparent willingness to manipulate Iranian news to gain campaign advantages. Having used the press to shape popular opinion by controlling the information released into the public sphere, Carter now had to contend with the license he issued the press to cover the story. As the public's main source of information, the press could and did adopt a more critical attitude toward Carter's handling of the crisis, presenting a less favorable view of his presidential timber than he and his staff desired. In the words of a senior adviser, "That 7 A.M. thing crossed the line. Carter no longer seemed decent and honorable, but manipulative." Then, in admission that the intent behind the Wisconsin announcement was misconceived, he observed, "Ironically, it probably had no impact—usually it takes a 24-hour gestation period for big events to have an impact on the public."[88]

The observations on "crossing the line" were not without foundation. Shortly after Wisconsin, the apparent progress toward securing the hostages' release went up in smoke, and the public's impatience with Carter's handling of Iran began to grow. For the first time he received a negative rating on the hostage affair as a *Newsweek*-Gallup poll showed 49 percent to 40 percent disapproved.[89]

Carter made a concerted effort in the Pennsylvania primary to remind voters of Kennedy's character and to keep the press's remorseless questioning of his timing of Iranian announcements from casting doubts on his own character. And at that, he only managed a near draw, actually losing the delegate count by one to Kennedy.

It was becoming clear that while Carter was going to win the nomination, he did not have deep support. His aides warned him to end his self-imposed seclusion in the White House and go on the campaign trail lest he face grim consequences in the fall. But the problem created by the Rose Garden strategy remained. Carter had made a point of giving his word not to campaign until the Iranian crisis was resolved. Against this backdrop, Carter made his most dramatic move on Iran, the rescue attempt.

In the middle of April a decision was made to attempt the rescue, with Carter's people well aware of the political risks the mission involved. Germond and Witcover report Jody Powell's recollection of a prophetic conversation among the cabinet members after being briefed on the planned raid. "Somebody said on the way out, 'God, I hope to hell this works.' To which a Cabinet member replied: 'Well, if it doesn't it could be the end of the Carter presidency.' "[90]

The political risks weren't the only ones. The mission did not have a high probability of success without significant casualties. Indeed, the Central Intelligence Agency prepared a secret report on the prospects of the mission and presented it to CIA Director Stansfield Turner on 16 March 1980. The pertinent portion of the report begins with item six.

6. The estimated percentage of loss among Amembassy hostages during each of the five major phases was:
   (a) Entry/Staging   :   0%
       Assumes no loss of cover
   (b) Initial Assault   :   20%

Assumes . . . immediate loss of those under
State FSR and FSS cover and others
(c) Location/Identification   :   25%
     Loss of State personnel before full
     suppression of resistance. Problem
     accentuated since Amembassy hostages
     not collocated.
(d) Evacuation to RH–53s   :   5%
     Assumes loss from snipers, from inside and
     outside Amembassy Compound, and AT and
     Apers mines.
(e) Transfer—RH–53s to C–130s   :   0%
     Assumes maintenance of site security.

7. The estimate of a loss rate of 60% for the Amembassy hostages
   represents the best estimate of CA & M7P Staff.[91]

One can only speculate whether the president would have ordered
a rescue attempt that his own intelligence service predicted would
result in the deaths of 60 percent of those it was attempting to
liberate were he not involved in a presidential campaign apparently
headed for trouble.[92] The facts remain that he did order a raid of
precisely this nature under precisely these circumstances. Moreover,
despite aborting the attempt because of mechanical failure and the
subsequent loss of eight lives when an RH–53 and G–130 collided,
Carter gained the political support a president predictably receives
in a moment of crisis. His ratings rose in the polls. Caddell explains,
"People wanted the President to do something, and something
happened. It's that simple. It dissipated the growing anger and
pressure over the crisis. It's the one reason no one in the country
cared whether Cyrus Vance was leaving—especially once Muskie
was chosen."[93]

But the support Caddell points to was gained in a negative way,
fashioned out of the deaths of eight servicemen and another failure
by the president to free the hostages. If anything, the popularity of
the attempted rescue reflected the frustrations of the electorate.
Moreover, the event raised the danger that their frustrations could
turn to cynicism toward Carter for his exploitation of the hostages'
plight, suggesting the error of regarding the public as a technological
concept expressed by polling data and managed through incremental
assembly.[94]

Ironically, even the polling data began to reflect the futility of
crafting policy in line with quantified reflections of the public. By
mid-March, a Time poll showed only 14 percent optimistic about

the future (versus 47 percent early in Carter's administration); 74 percent considered inflation our number one problem (versus 50 percent in January); over 50 percent thought Carter was too soft in dealing with Iran; and only 17 percent thought his handling of Afghanistan enhanced United States prestige abroad. One month later, on the very day that the aborted rescue mission was announced, an ABC-Harris survey showed Ronald Reagan now leading Carter by 42 percent to 33 percent. In February, Carter had led Reagan by 64 percent to 32 percent.[95]

Having failed to create a consensus on Iran, and having responded to the image of the public projected by the technology of opinion polls, Carter now found himself entrapped as a result of doing and saying what his polls suggested was politically expedient. He had no political alternative to placing distance between himself and the hostage issue and trying to redirect the nation's attention. On 29 April, in response to a planted question at a briefing for civic leaders,[96] Carter offered the awkward ad lib that "none of these challenges [Iran and Afghanistan] are completely removed [sic], but I believe they are manageable enough now for me to leave the White House for a limited travel schedule, including some campaigning if I choose to do so. . . ."[97]

The transparent implausibility of this remark escaped no one, including the president's advisers, who grumbled about it for weeks afterward.[98] And if anyone had not been listening closely, Kennedy was only too ready to render a verdict on the matter. "We have had a failed military intrusion into Iran. [Carter] has lost five of the last seven primaries [and state caucuses] and now he is willing to come out of the White House. I think the decision is quite clearly a political judgment."[99]

Nor was the public's cynicism abated by the treatment Carter gave Iran in the public sphere once he started campaigning. Specifically, the hostage matter was dropped as an issue. Apart from the Ramsey Clark incident, the White House initiated little if any discussion of Iran from May until September. One finds very few remarks on the subject in the *Department of State Bulletin* for this period. The statements that do appear are usually those of Secretary Muskie, who all but displaced Carter as the American spokesperson on the matter. Moreover, the press cooperated by providing limited coverage during this time.[100] For six months Americans had been asked to think of nothing but the hostages. After the failed rescue mission left no room for bold new moves to secure their release, the public was asked to forget them. At the very least, the sudden silence spoke loudly as reinforcement to a growing public perception of

Carter as incompetent. To the more contemplative observer, and perhaps the more skeptical, Carter's sudden silence on the hostage situation had the air of a strategy to jerk the public around by gearing events and information flow about Iran to political ends. In brief, voters sensed that "they'd been had."[101]

Iran resurfaced as a topic in the fall. As the election campaign broke into full stride, there was growing discussion that the president would secure the hostages' timely release just before the election.[102] But these discussions were not of the president's doing. Since the Clark incident, Carter had commented on the Iranian situation only when asked, responding almost always with the same *topoi*— America's policy, national honor, and safety of the hostages; they are daily in my thoughts and prayers; the nation should not raise expectations falsely; there is no promise of early release; it would be inappropriate to comment on possible actions; shame on my opponent for interjecting the hostage matter into the campaign. Under the circumstances Carter plainly was not interested in reinitiating discussions of the hostages: any mention of contact with Iran fueled speculation that they might be returned soon, and also evoked suspicion that he had used earlier discussions for political ends. Since there were no new sanctions to impose or bold rescue missions to undertake, the president was at the mercy of Iranian will to negotiate—as, quite probably, he always had been. And since there had been no public debate on the matter, Jimmy Carter became the focal point for the frustration and rage promoted in the early stages of the crisis. However cautious and however responsive his public comments now were to actual events in Tehran, his use of the crisis in the primaries had led to a widespread suspicion that administration hints at an impending resolution were calculated for political gain.

The Republicans fueled this perception by repeated mention of an "October surprise." They suspected Carter was going to stage a last-minute return of the hostages and that the emotions of this event could cost Reagan the election. Elaborate plans were laid for appearances on televised news forums by former president Gerald Ford and his secretary of state, Henry Kissinger, and for speeches by Reagan to indict the president for playing politics with the hostages. To ensure that their message would be accurately received they talked incessantly about the October surprise, planting the idea in the public sphere and raising the electorate's expectations that it would happen.[103] If it did, Carter would seem to be continuing his manipulation of crisis events for political gain; if not, it would appear as another indication of Carter's ineptitude.

Nothing captured Carter's bind more clearly than the last weekend of the campaign. Trailing in the polls and almost certain to be defeated, he found the hostage issue once more thrust upon him as the Majlis, Iran's parliament, finally acted by issuing the conditions for the hostages' release. Carter hastily flew from Chicago to Washington; his arrival received much coverage. He strode boldly from the helicopter to the White House, looking presidential and weighted with responsibility, but the earlier-cited image Robert Strauss described appeared on Americans' television screens. The adviser Americans saw as most deviously calculating, Zbigniew Brzezinski, came rushing to Carter's side.

Later that afternoon, Carter interrupted the Sunday football telecasts to announce "a significant development" that provided a "positive basis" for negotiating the hostages' release, but, he said, he would not broker a deal for his own political advantage. That evening the networks ran specials on the full year of captivity. The public sphere was saturated with reminders of the hostage affair and of the president's failure to return these "heroes." Two days later, one year after the embassy was overthrown, the voters removed Jimmy Carter from office.

The significance of Carter's technologized conception of a public and its opinions had a profound influence on the president's rhetorical choices. The foregoing analysis suggests that these choices often were ill conceived. Certainly it was a mistake to exploit the popularity of a strong, visible stand against the Iranians when the president could not control how they responded. It was no less mistaken to publicize the event and promote press coverage since there were no available means of silencing the press if the incident became protracted. It was equally ill advised to capitalize on the populace's susceptibilities to hopeful news and willingness to rally in support of elected leaders during a crisis, since the president lacked the power to transform hopeful news into concrete results that would end the crisis.

In committing these errors, Carter and his staff constrained and distorted the public sphere, much as they had in their management of the "hero" theme. The public sphere was narrowed and contoured through a one-sided portrayal of Jimmy Carter's presidential qualities while resolving the crisis. But it must be added that even though the public sphere was distorted by the president, he was considered by its inhabitants on his own terms.

Jimmy Carter went into the 1980 election campaign without a broad base of political or popular support. Regardless of the stature of his accomplishments, Carter was not particularly eloquent in his own defense and had not enjoyed significant success at presenting his stewardship in the best light. In his eyes, his lack of popular support was most tellingly portrayed in opinion polls that indicated a sizable portion of Americans thought he lacked leadership ability. Carter persistently analyzed his problem as one of weak image, as if failed policies or misconceived programs were not relevant to American voters. The strategy-setting Jordan report and Caddell memo—both prior to Carter's reelection bid announcement—indicate that the president did not envision a campaign of issues but a campaign of images. From the outset a hard-nosed pragmatism marked his mapping of a reelection strategy that would exploit his strengths and his opponents' weaknesses of image. There was also every indication of willingness to capitalize on the opportunities of incumbency to enhance the appearance of leadership, where Carter's image was most vulnerable.

Carter's perspective on the American voters did not project them as weighing issues but as responding to appearances: they were, in this perspective, interested in the semblance of honesty, compassion, decency, pacifism, strength, and so forth. Indeed, this is precisely the data Caddell's polls provided, a technologist's portrayal of audience. Cadell's approach assumed that voters are passive and impressionable. Reminded of the right qualities, each subset of the electorate would fall into line with a positive image of Carter, a negative image of his opponent, and a ballot for the president's reelection. It was as if this technological epistemology could not conceive of an active electorate capable of judging on the basis of conduct. Carter's embrace of a technologized image of the public is no exception among contemporary politicians; that he is representative in his reliance on polling data makes his rhetoric on the Iranian matter all the more telling. Given the way Carter and his strategists defined the campaign—as image making, not issue resolving—the exploitation of the hostage crisis was predictable. Saddled with a "weak leader" image as his major campaign problem, nothing could have been more opportune than this foreign development. It diverted attention from issues to image and allowed a demonstration of bold leadership and presidential stature.

Telling the American people that he could not campaign because of the crisis could only communicate the incident's importance and enlarge perceptions of Carter's role. When subsequent polling data showed Carter surging ahead of Kennedy, they were reason enough to exploit this fortuitous shield against debating the issues. Surely the spotlight on Carter's presidential initiative was intensified by the press coverage he encouraged throughout most of the primary season, especially since he claimed the exclusive role of America's only qualified voice. Considering that he went so far as to remind other politicians that it was their duty to support him and to question the patriotism, judgment, and motives of those who criticized him, what else could Americans conclude but that this incident was of extraordinary significance and required an extraordinary leader to handle it? Cast as the sole spokesperson for his country, Carter encouraged a lofty image of his leadership qualities and also the high expectations that accompany such an image. Even though his polls showed Carter enjoying initial success by gearing announcements and initiatives to mesh with the campaign needs of caucuses and primaries, the fact remained that eventually he had to produce some tangible accomplishment. After all, the hostages were not images; they were real and they were still incarcerated on election day.

For all of Carter's image building, he did not succeed in convincing the electorate that his true presidential stature was backed by deeds. Thus, we must conclude that the technologically constructed public Carter imagined never formed. The reason it never formed lies ultimately in the Carter people's mistaken belief that a public was a constellation of opinions pieced together or "constructed" by telling people first this bit, then that bit, depending upon what the polls' quantification showed they wanted to hear. But a public is more profound and intelligent and stable than a nose-count can reveal. It is that portion of the populace who are joined through their mutual experiences of actively weighing and judging partisan appeals on an issue. The Carter campaigners' conception of public opinion doomed them from the start. Their technological approach, which revealed only what was popular, lacked the potential for indicating rhetorical strategies and appeals with enduring suasory potential.

Certainly other factors were at play in Carter's loss of the 1980 election. The condition of the economy, the scandals in his administration, a general swing to the political right, and Ronald Reagan's own campaigning skills contributed in large measure. But there is no denying that the hostage affair loomed throughout as an issue Carter himself defined as an important index of his presidential qualities. In retrospect one might question the wisdom of this as the litmus test of his administration, since there were accomplishments of economic, social, and diplomatic substance of which he could have boasted. And a review of the campaign rhetoric during the 1980 general election will show that Carter did point to his accomplishments. However, in the context of national concern for the hostages' return, his earlier appearance as "Jimmy One-note" served to sustain interest in and fuel public frustration over the hostage situation well past the point where it served a politically expedient end for the president. Harsh as the American public may appear for judging Carter's capacity to lead by his failures with an intractable and irrational foe, that test was one of his own making in significant ways.

Conclusion

The Carter rhetoric on the hostage affair appears, at one level of inspection, to contain few surprises. Certainly it is no surprise to find political leaders exploiting emotional issues for political gain. The news in this study, however, is in what it tells us about the public sphere and about public opinion through a president's failed attempt to control both.

Perhaps most obviously, Carter's rhetoric on the hostage situation served to distort the public sphere. Administration depictions of the hostages as heroes, rhetorical hyperbole in accounts of the event's significance, linkages with national honor, closing of debate, and vilification of Iran encouraged an ideological perception of the issue in nationalistic terms. Certainly the actions of the Iranian militants were inexcusable; but Iranian culpability was complemented by the public's distorted awareness of the causes behind the affair.[104] Americans saw the issues as the illegal detention of the hostages, not the repressive regime of the shah; as the violation of international law by Iran, not the historical pattern of illegal intrusions by the United States in Iranian affairs. The whole affair was reduced first to an American perspective, and then, as the White House effectively silenced the opposition by wrapping Carter in the flag at the slightest hint of criticism, to a sitting president's perspective. The point is not that Carter would have had greater political success by discussing American faults. Rather it is that close observation of the administration's rhetoric reveals the way in which Americans were stimulated by their leaders to see the hostage taking as one set of issues rather than some other, to feel one set of emotions rather than some other, to give a particular set of responses rather than some other. The inevitable distortions of the public sphere from some ideal communicative realm provide an important index to the character of publics that actually form.

Moreover, the public sphere was distorted by the interjection of the issue into the election campaign. Rather than treating the public sphere as a discursive place in which the public would form its own opinion, Carter treated it as a behavioral space to be mechanically fashioned by reflecting back to it a composite image attuned to the polls' quantifications of popular mood. In its polling data, the Carter campaign perceived a productive body of knowledge that those engaged in the technological manipulation of the president's image might use for purposes of control. The data bore no relevance to shaping issues and arguments, serving instead as a guide to what would produce predictable behavior. The concern for predictability, in turn, guided how these data were used in crafting the president's rhetoric.

Carter's tactics led to an irreconcilable tension implicit in his conception of the public sphere. On the one hand, Carter came before Americans to establish his virtuosity as a leader.[105] By repeatedly invoking the Iranian situation in ways that made it symbolic of his presidential qualities, Carter was attempting to improve his image with an audience who would soon test both his qualifications as an official and his chosen path of leadership. Yet he never went so far as to permit these judges freedom of thought in rendering their verdict.

Carter's references to the hostages did more than invoke a potent image that Americans were predisposed to adopt: it also invoked an image of Americans as passive and restrained.[106] They were simultaneously whipped into a state of seething anger and denied any legitimate outlet in word or deed, save one—supporting the president. By this reduction Jimmy Carter became the sole active agent representing national concerns in the high drama of securing the hostages' release. While on the one hand he required affirmation of his virtuosity as a leader, his contrived monologue on leadership meant he either satisfied the conditions he himself set: secure liberation of these heroes—or be judged a failure.

Thus Carter had a dilemma: if he talked about the importance of his single-handed leadership, then the only reasonable inference was that the hostages were so important that to fail in securing their release was to fail as a nation. On these terms, Carter was vulnerable to rejection as a fit leader. The alternative, given the constraints he imposed on the public sphere, was to confine and even repress as much as possible any public consideration or discussion of the incident, and, in the ensuing silence, repress also his opportunity to appear presidential.[107]

Having made the commitment to interject the hostage matter into the public sphere, Carter acted not out of concern for the underlying issues about American foreign policy but out of hope for political gain. And he got caught at it. Instead of soliciting through open deliberation a verdict on his leadership abilities, he appropriated the entire matter to himself. By squelching debate, he lost his lone opportunity to demonstrate that his actions were reasonable, were in the nation's and the hostages' best interest, and were all that could be done under the circumstances. He also denied himself the opportunity to frame an informed consensus in his support.

Consequently, what he responded to were images: polling data could tell him that the people were frustrated, that they were growing impatient, that they wanted him to do something. But polling data could not tell him how to solve problems the polls revealed—neither the material one of securing the hostages' release nor the public relations one of placating an increasingly hostile electorate. In a political monologue, the value of policies tends toward positive or negative extremes insofar as they produce results. They lose the distinct advantage of comparative measure that derives only from open debate.

The different responses to Carter's rhetoric—the acceptance of the hostages as heroes and the rejection of Carter as leader—are also revealing. They tell us something important about public opinion. In the case of the hero image, a public opinion did form, but it was not particularly well informed or balanced. Like the Greek concept of *doxa*, it was a mere belief and tended to be extreme in its comprehension of the affair. Certainly public opinion was not shaped exclusively by the words and deeds of Jimmy Carter, but he did play a significant role in shaping that opinion. Importantly, that opinion did not derive from an informed debate, but from the managed cues that bombarded the public through the entire affair. It was, in the final analysis, an opinion of an image, though the image seems to have resulted inadvertently from the way the administration handled the issue.

The president's reliance on polls reflected a second vision of public opinion. Carter considered the public to be a quantity assembled incrementally by appealing to people's susceptibilities. Carter and his staff perceived public opinion as a quickly changing attitude or mood that could be focused on a candidate's beauty marks and an opponent's blemishes, thereby altering a candidate's image and a "public's" response. Each of Carter's attempts to control public opinion ultimately failed because the judging and acting portion of the citizenry saw it for what it was: a tactic to sustain an image of Carter as presidential.

Carter did not, in fact, respond to the public but to an image of the public reflected by his polls. The public, after all, never gets to speak *its* mind in a poll. A technician (pollster) determines what is to be asked. He or she determines the *topoi.* Thus, the individuals who may be included in the sample are required to offer an opinion about an issue not of their choosing and in a manner that is preselected to serve the needs of data analysis. Whatever the quantified totals represent, that representation is at best an imitation of the public.

Further, in this case one might say that Carter effectively denied himself anything more than a false image of the public since, by closing off debate, he never allowed a vibrant public sphere to materialize on the hostage issue. When the public sphere is technologized, its discursive quality is diminished, and with the diminishing of open deliberation, leaders lose their sense of what the public wishes them to do to solve problems. In the place of public opinion, a technologized public sphere offers public moods—at best reflecting what the public sees as a problem, not what it wishes done. Its wishes are not examined because, in the absence of open deliberation, they remain unknown. Informed public opinion exists only where there is open deliberation.

Although the president's technologized conception of public opinion may have misled his rhetorical efforts, his rhetoric nonetheless galvanized a public. Emerging on election day, the public responded to his invitation to view him in personal terms. Since he emphasized throughout that the crisis was his alone to resolve, he assumed the burden of personal responsibility. From the beginning of Jimmy Carter's appearance as a national leader, there was more than a trace of paternalism in his appeals to "trust me." In his handling of the hostage crisis, Carter relied even more heavily on the image of himself as the authority figure who would set things right. Without public deliberation to clarify the pros and cons of American actions, there was no objective measure to test Carter's appearance as presidential. Instead, the themes of Carter's personal stewardship, lacking any effective counterbalance, invited the public to focus on Carter's persona rather than on issues. Carter's rhetoric accentuated this invitation, aiming so narrowly at personal positives and negatives that it could do little but emphasize the image of the president as a caring and powerful father to the American populace. And it also elicited a personal response of blaming him when events repeatedly turned sour.

At the beginning of this essay I maintained that the public provides an audience that judges virtuosity. Open debate links virtuosity to the effectiveness of each voice in establishing the truth. But a rhetoric of persona measures virtuosity in terms of personal worth.

When the worth of the authority is found lacking, the only way for the public to affirm truth is through the negative act of rejecting the authority figure. Perhaps one reason for the profound effect of the Iranian hostage affair on American perceptions of Jimmy Carter is that it served as a metaphor for his administration.[108] Initially, he appeared to be the fatherly authority who asks his children to trust him. But as the crisis unfolded by dynamics beyond Carter's control, the image of Carter as father came increasingly into focus as neither powerful nor kindly. In fact, unlike a genuine father who places his children's welfare to the fore and nurtures their growth and development, Carter was seen—whether fairly or not—as self-serving and manipulative in his use of the crisis to advance his political fortune. If the public wished to purchase truth, it could do so only by rejecting the president. Thus, more than mandating new leadership, the 1980 election may be seen as a negation: the psychological rejection by the public of the paternal authority Jimmy Carter attempted to exercise during his presidency.

Finally, the public's behavior raises this interesting consideration. It would appear that Carter was mistaken in treating the public as a passive entity. Students of political communication may be tempted to claim that the public is never thus: it is active in its ability to partake in the experience of discursive give and take, ebb and flow, that culminates in public opinion. But one can hear echoes of more hardened observers suggesting there is only romantic idealism in that view. Nonetheless, Carter's miscalculation in this case is doubly informing.

Carter treated the public as passive by projecting before it images he thought it desired while avoiding discussion of issues. When the electorate saw through this, they became active in terms of their vote. But more than this, they became active in seeing the management of the hostage affair as a ruse to keep them distracted from the issue of Carter's record. While the general public apparently did not get beyond the bimodal image of the Iranian affair itself, it is significant that they saw Carter's use of it as image projection. Their awareness suggests that in a mass society, the public can become active whenever it is able to penetrate the projected images of their leaders and perceive the hidden issues. At the level of issues, they are ready for informed discussion and affirmative judgments of virtuosity. But there is in this a corollary suggestion that if images are fulfilled by actions, the public can be led. One cannot help but wonder whether the electorate would not have judged Jimmy Carter differently on 4 November 1980 had he secured the hostages' release.

Appendix I

CHRONOLOGY OF HOSTAGE DEVELOPMENTS

The following chronology is based on articles appearing in the *Department of State Bulletin,* January 1980 through February 1981.

22 Oct. 1979	The deposed shah of Iran, Mohammed Reza Pahlavi, enters the United States for medical treatment.
4 Nov.	Iranian students seize U.S. embassy in Tehran and hold one hundred hostages (sixty-five Americans), demanding that the deposed shah be returned to Iran to stand trial.
5 Nov.	Press Secretary Jody Powell says the U.S. will not return the shah. He is here for medical treatment. He indicates U.S. desire to negotiate a settlement with Iran.
6 Nov.	Prime Minister Bazargan's provisional government dissolves, yielding power to the Islamic authority of Ayatollah Ruhollah Khomeini and his secret Revolutionary Council.
	Former Attorney General Ramsey Clark and William Miller, U.S. Senate committee senior staff official, leave Washington carrying a message from the president to Iranian officials.
7 Nov.	Khomeini rejects talks with Clark and Miller.
8 Nov.	President Carter postpones Canada visit until 1980.
9 Nov.	U.S. suspends deliveries of about $30 million in military equipment and spare parts to Iran.
10 Nov.	Carter directs Attorney General Civiletti to deport any Iranian student who is in the U.S. illegally.
	Abolhassan Bani-Sadr becomes Iran's Acting Foreign Minister and reaffirms Iran's demand that the U.S. return the shah.
12 Nov.	Carter orders suspension of purchase of Iranian oil by U.S. Iran announces it is cutting petroleum shipments to the U.S.
13 Nov.	American naval vessels start maneuvers in the Arabian Sea. Iran charges U.S. with threatening war.

14 Nov.	Bani-Sadr announces Iran will withdraw its funds from American banks. Carter acts to block all official Iranian assets in the U.S.
16 Nov.	Iranian militants threaten hostages if the shah is allowed to go anywhere but to Iran.
17 Nov.	Khomeini orders the militants to release all women and blacks among the hostages.
18 Nov.	Khomeini declares hostages face being tried as spies.
19 Nov.	Three of the hostages—two black marines and one white secretary—are released.
20 Nov.	Ten more Americans are freed. U.S. suggests to Iran that it might resort to military force if the remaining hostages are not freed. Carter orders a second naval task force into the Indian Ocean.
21 Nov.	Militants warn that all hostages will die and the embassy will be blown up if the U.S. attacks.
25 Nov.	U.N. Security Council session is called by Secretary General Waldheim because Iran fails to respond to an appeal to release U.S. hostages. It is only the second time in nineteen years that a secretary general has requested such a meeting.
27 Nov.	Hospital officials announce that the shah is able to leave the hospital and return to Mexico within the week.
28 Nov.	Bani-Sadr is dismissed as Iran's acting foreign minister. Sadigh Ghotbzadeh is named in his place.
29 Nov.	U.S. initiates action against Iran in the International Court of Justice. Mexico announces it will not renew visa for the shah.
30 Nov.	Carter postpones six-state political tour because of Iranian crisis.
1 Dec.	U.N. Security Council begins debate on the hostage affair.
2 Dec.	Carter gives shah temporary sanctuary at Lackland Air Force Base Hospital in San Antonio, Texas.
12 Dec.	U.S. orders expulsion of 183 Iranian diplomats in retaliation for continued detention of the hostages. They must leave in five days.
15 Dec.	International Court of Justice orders Iran to immediately release all hostages. Shah leaves U.S. for residence in Panama.

16 Dec.	President Carter proclaims 18 December National Unity Day to demonstrate support for the hostages.
18 Dec.	Carter administration reports it is seriously considering "nonviolent" military action if hostages are put on trial.
21 Dec.	Carter decides to ask U.N. Security Council to impose economic sanctions against Iran.
27 Dec.	The Soviet Union invades Afghanistan.
1 Jan. 1980	Waldheim arrives in Tehran to seek negotiations for release of the hostages.
3 Jan.	Khomeini refuses to meet with Waldheim.
8 Jan.	U.S. wins approval from other major industrial countries on new financial sanctions against Iran.
13 Jan.	Security Council votes thirteen to two (USSR and East Germany) on a draft resolution calling for economic sanctions against Iran.
14 Jan.	The Revolutionary Council orders all U.S. news correspondents to leave Iran because of their "biased reporting."
15 Jan.	U.S. files its memorial with the World Court on the merits of the U.S.-Iran hostage case.
25 Jan.	Bani-Sadr wins Iran's first presidential election.
29 Jan.	Six U.S. embassy employees who had been hiding in the Canadian embassy escape from Iran.
6 Feb.	U.S. delays imposing formal economic sanctions against Iran to avoid upsetting possible chances for settling the crisis.
13 Feb.	Carter approves of an international commission of inquiry into Iran's grievances.
14 Feb.	Bani-Sadr states that hostages could be freed within forty-eight hours if Carter agrees to conditions approved by Khomeini.
20 Feb.	At Iran's request, U.N. inquiry commission delays trip to Tehran for three days.
23 Feb.	Commission arrives in Tehran, but Khomeini issues a statement saying the fate of the hostages should be decided by the new parliament to be elected March/April.
10 March	Commission of inquiry departs Iran after failing to see the hostages.
23 March	Shah departs Panama for Egypt.
25 March	Ayatollah Mohammed Beheshti, leader of the Is-

lamic Republican party, announces he favors holding trials for those hostages accused of espionage if the shah is not returned to Iran to stand trial.

30 March   U.S. and its Western allies are said to make major efforts to pressure Iran to take steps to release hostages.

31 March   U.S. gives Iran until 1 April to announce steps to remove hostages from militants' control or face new U.S. economic and political retaliations.

1 April   Bani-Sadr offers to take custody of the hostages if the U.S. agrees to a truce in its "war of words" and in its economic and political pressures on Iran. Carter, regarding this as a "positive development," defers plans to impose new sanctions against Iran.

2 April   Carter publicly pledges silence to Iran about hostages as long as progress is being made to resolve the crisis.

7 April   Khomeini rules that hostages must remain in hands of the militants. U.S. breaks diplomatic relations with Iran and imposes a formal embargo on U. S. exports.

13 April   Eight Common Market countries announce they would withdraw their ambassadors temporarily from Iran in protest against the holding of U.S. hostages.

18 April   Carter orders new economic sanctions against Iran and indicates that if Iran does not release the hostages, military action will be the next step.

20 April   Public notice is issued restricting the use of U.S. passports for travel to, in, or through Iran.

21 April   Secretary of State Cyrus Vance submits a letter of resignation to Carter stating that he could not support the president's decision to attempt a rescue mission of the hostages in Iran.

22 April   Common Market foreign ministers vote unanimously to impose full economic sanctions against Iran on 17 May unless "decisive progress" is made in freeing the hostages.

25 April   A mission to rescue the hostages is aborted by President Carter because of equipment failures.

28 April   Carter accepts Vance's resignation.

29 April   Senator Edmund S. Muskie is named to succeed Vance.

24 May	International Court of Justice rules that Iran must immediately release all U.S. hostages.
June 2	Despite Carter's ban on travel to Iran, Ramsey Clark leads a ten-member group to an Iranian-sponsored conference on U.S. "intervention in Iran."
10 July	Khomeini orders the release of hostage Richard Queen, for reasons of health.
20 July	Majlis, Iran's parliament, takes over legislative power from the Revolutionary Council.
22 July	Bani-Sadr takes formal oath of office as Iranian president.
27 July	Shah dies in Cairo.
10 Aug.	Muskie says U.S. is considering new diplomatic initiatives for the release of the hostages.
12 Sept.	Khomeini sets four conditions on which the hostages are to be released.
18 Sept.	Carter rules out an apology to Iran as a prerequisite to releasing the hostages.
19 Sept.	Air and ground battles break out between Iran and Iraq.
16 Oct.	Prime Minister Rajai leaves Tehran for New York to attend a U.N. Security Council meeting on the Iran-Iraq war.
18 Oct.	Rajai says a decision on the release of the hostages is "not far away."
20 Oct.	Carter says he will lift U.S. sanctions against Iran if the hostages are freed.
31 Oct.	Despite numerous delays by Majlis, administration officials appear optimistic that Iranian authorities seem to have committed themselves to releasing the hostages.
2 Nov.	Majlis sets first official release terms.
3 Nov.	Militants turn jurisdiction of hostages over to the Iranian government but not the hostages themselves.
5 Nov.	Carter administration officials suggest that the president will agree to conditions if Iranian authorities accept a "narrow interpretation" of the Iranian parliament's demands.
10 Nov.	Deputy Secretary of State Christopher begins U.S. negotiations with Algerian intermediaries.
20 Nov.	The U.S. confirms that it has accepted in principle

the four conditions "as a basis for resolution of the crisis."

18 Dec.	Iran's new terms for release of the hostages are delivered to Algerian intermediaries.
20 Dec.	U.S. views Iran's conditions as unacceptable.
30 Dec.	U.S. gives Algerians a "reformulation" of American proposals.
8 Jan. 1981	President-elect Reagan states he could honor any agreement with Iran made by President Carter but also says he reserves the right to draw up new proposals if the crisis is not settled by 20 Jan.
18 Jan.	U.S. and Iran sign final documents agreeing on central issues and issue a final declaration for release of the hostages.
20 Jan.	After 444 days in captivity, hostages are freed.

Appendix II

CHRONOLOGY OF THE 1980 CAMPAIGN

7 Nov. 1979	Senator Kennedy announces his candidacy.
4 Dec.	President Carter announces his candidacy.
28 Dec.	Carter cancels Des Moines *Register* debate scheduled for early January.
21 Jan. 1980	Iowa caucuses, won by Carter.
23 Jan.	Carter delivers State of the Union address.
28 Jan.	Kennedy delivers campaign address at Georgetown, crisply attacking Carter's foreign policy.
12 Feb.	Kennedy delivers campaign address at Harvard, sustaining his attack on Carter's foreign policy.
13 Feb.	Carter holds a press conference, using it to refute Kennedy's attacks.
26 Feb.	Carter wins New Hampshire primary.
18 March	Carter wins Illinois primary.
25 March	Kennedy wins New York primary.
1 April	Carter wins Wisconsin primary.
3 June	Final primary date.
14–17 July	Republican National Convention, Ronald Reagan nominated.
11–14 Aug.	Democratic National Convention, Jimmy Carter nominated.

4 Nov.   General election, won by Reagan.
20 Jan. 1981   Inauguration Day.

Acknowledgment

This project was funded in part by the Office of the Associate Dean for Graduate Research in the College of the Liberal Arts at the Pennsylvania State University. An earlier version was presented at the Speech Communication Association meeting in Anaheim, California, November 1981. Comments by Thomas Farrell on an earlier draft were most helpful in my thinking about Carter's rhetoric. Finally, the assistance of Carole Blair is gratefully acknowledged.

Notes

1. The rhetorical character of publics has come under scrutiny from a variety of perspectives. A sampling of positions may be found in Lloyd F. Bitzer, "Rhetoric and Public Knowledge," in *Rhetoric, and Philosophy, and Literature: An Exploration,* ed. Don M. Burks (West Lafayette, Ind: Purdue Univ. Pr., 1978), 67–95; Thomas B. Farrell and G. Thomas Goodnight, "Accidental Rhetoric: The Root Metaphors of Three Mile Island," *Communication Monographs* 48 (1981): 271–300; Gerard A. Hauser, "Common Sense in the Public Sphere: A Rhetorical Grounding for Publics," *Informatologia Yugoslavica* 17 (1985): 67–75; Gerard A. Hauser and Carole Blair, "Rhetorical Antecedents to the Public," *Pre/Text* 3 (1982): 139–67; Michael Calvin McGee, "In Search of 'The People': A Rhetorical Alternative," *Quarterly Journal of Speech* 61 (1975): 235–49; Michael Calvin McGee and Martha Anne Martin, "Public Knowledge and Ideological Argumentation," *Communication Monographs* 50 (1983): 47–65.

2. Real publics are not ideally real in the sense that their existence is always beset by constraints or marked by flaws that prevent them from existing in an ideal or perfect manner. See Hauser and Blair, "Rhetorical Antecedents," 161–63.

3. See Jürgen Habermas, "The Public Sphere," *New German Critique* 3 (1974): 49; Hannah Arendt, *The Human Condition* (Chicago: Univ. of Chicago Pr., 1958); Hauser, "Common Sense."

4. Habermas, "The Public Sphere," 53.

5. See John Dewey, *The Public and Its Problems* (1927; reprint Chicago: Swallow, 1954), 27ff.

6. Habermas, "The Public Sphere," 53.

7. Richard Sennett, *The Fall of Public Man* (New York: Vintage, 1978), 224–37.

8. Habermas's theory of systematically distorted communication is discussed in several places, but his essential position can be found in Jürgen Habermas, "On Systematically Distorted Communication," *Inquiry* 13 (1970): 205–18. Discussion of the emancipatory interests of critical theory pervade Habermas's writings. It is considered thoroughly in Habermas, *Knowledge and Human Interest* trans. Jeremy J. Shapiro (Boston: Beacon, 1971).

9. Habermas, "The Public Sphere," translator's note 3, p. 50.

10. Hannah Arendt, *Between Past and Future* (New York: Penguin, 1977), 3.

11. Arendt, *Between Past and Future,* 4.

12. The resistance of Polish workers who are part of Solidarity provides ample support for this observation. While open deliberation appeared to characterize their mode of securing unity prior to the Polish government's imposition of martial law (December 1981), even subsequent repressive acts have not been successful (as of this writing, spring 1988) in

squelching the ongoing dialogue among Poles searching for freedom: they have merely forced it underground. The union's continued ability to invoke strike action and widespread public resistance, not to mention the Polish government's fear of relaxing martial law, is testimony to the public realm that Solidarity has forged and the vibrancy of that realm as the locus where Polish public opinion is being formed in the face of oppression.

13. In terms of this dynamic view of a public, with its implication that publics come into being and pass away as they are engaged by the issues and events that occupy a public sphere, I am in agreement with the analysis of "the public" in Herbert Blumer, "The Mass, The Public, and Public Opinion," in *Reader in Public Opinion*, ed. Bernard Berelson and Morris Janowitz, 2d ed. (New York: Free Pr., 1966), 43–50.

14. For a historical overview of the concept "public opinion," see Hans Speier, "Historical Development of Public Opinion," *American Journal of Sociology* 55 (1950): 376–88.

15. This is not to say that survey research is illegitimate, but that it requires a larger theoretical frame for its data to take on meaning. See, for example, Elisabeth Noelle-Neumann, *The Spiral of Silence: Public Opinion—Our Social Skin* (Chicago: Univ. of Chicago Pr., 1984).

16. See Robert Nisbet, "Public Opinion versus Popular Opinion," *Public Interest* 41 (Fall 1975): 166–92. Nisbett follows the classical position set forth in Lawrence A. Lowell, *Public Opinion and Popular Government* (New York: Longmans, Green, 1914), a view implicit in the indictment of the public in Walter Lippman, *Public Opinion* (New York: Free Pr., 1922).

17. Supporting evidence for this claim may be found in the studies reported in Noelle-Neumann, *Spiral of Silence*.

18. The counterfactual character of the public sphere is discussed at greater length in Hauser and Blair, "Rhetorical Antecedents."

19. There were suggestions that the welcome was a form of catharsis. The whole nation had been held hostage. Thus there was the need to celebrate the release of 220 million Americans. A milder version held that the celebration was a way of demarcating the end of a state of emergency. The welcome was a collective sigh of relief. Others claimed that it allowed a clean cut between capture and return. Americans lacked such a break in the wars in Korea and Vietnam, as both actions merely trickled off. Some believed that Americans needed heroes; the captives satisfied this need. And there were psychologists who viewed the nation's euphoria as a form of overcompensation; it arose from a need to hide a collective sense of humiliation. These and other hypotheses were discussed in national television and newsweekly commentaries and interviews immediately prior to and following the hostages' release.

20. Despite the claim by Hamilton Jordan that from the start it was not possible to reduce the glare of public attention on the hostage affair, the administration adopted a volatile rhetorical posture in attacking Iran publicly, as his own account illustrates; Hamilton Jordan, *Crisis: The Last Year of The Carter Presidency* (New York: Putnam's, 1982), 55–56. But see also 44–45, 64–65; and Cyrus Vance, *Hard Choices* (New York: Simon and Schuster, 1983), 380.

21. "News Conference of November 28," *Department of State Bulletin* [DOSB] 80 (January 1980): 2.

22. Here and throughout this essay it is important to bear in mind the multiple roles of the press. Obviously it serves as a conduit of information between institutional representatives (here, the Carter administration) and the reading, listening, and viewing audience. But equally obviously the press can (and, in this case, did) act as an active agent, shaping audience perceptions through choices of what to cover and how to present it. Further, it can act as the public's agent and representative when it questions officials and probes beneath the surface of events to reveal information salient to framing sound opinion. Finally, it can provide the critic with an indication of public opinion by reflecting concerns being voiced in the community.

From the vantage point of the public sphere, a public in a mass society receives its information on public affairs largely through the mass media. Hence, the reporting of this affair cannot be divorced from the analysis of Carter's rhetoric. With each piece of evidence examined, important critical distinctions must be drawn in terms of the press's function. Since my interest here is with Carter's rhetoric as a force molding public opinion, I have concentrated on administration statements that would have received press coverage. The reader will note, however, that I have relied extensively on government records, not press reports, for evidentiary sources of what was actually said. Later in this essay, when the roles of the press as a source of opinion formation or as the public's agent and representative are raised, I have attempted to be clear on how that role was linked as a source of opportunity or limitation to the administration's rhetoric. Of significance here, the administration did not discourage press coverage in the early going.

23. "President's Announcement, November 12, 1979," *DOSB* 79 (December 1979): 50; "Remarks at the Thirteenth Constitutional Convention of the AFL-CIO, in Washington D.C. on November 15, 1979," *DOSB* 79 (December 1979): 18 ("lives of these brave hostages . . ." and "pride in their great courage"); "U.S. Course in a Changing World [Remarks to the American Society of Newspaper Editors in Washington, D.C. on April 10, 1980]," *DOSB* 80 (May 1980): 3–4; "U.S. Seeks Sanctions Against Iran [Remarks to Reporters Assembled in the White House Briefing Room, December 21, 1980]," *DOSB* 80 (February 1980): 53.

The concept of *condensation* as a use of language to distort perceptions is discussed in Herbert Marcuse, *One Dimensional Man* (Boston: Beacon, 1964). See especially chap. 4, "The Closing of the Universe of Discourse." *Condensation* refers to a linguistic style in which the syntax of an utterance pushes ideas together in a way that leaves no "space" for qualifications, contrast, differences, explanation—in short, for *meaning*—to develop. Marcuse identifies this style particularly with the discourse of bureaucracies in large Western societies.

24. "U.S. Foreign Policy: Our Broader Strategy [Statement before the Senate Foreign Relations Committee, March 27, 1980]," *DOSB* 80 (May 1980): 17.

25. A sampling of these comments by Carter and administration spokespersons may be found in "President's Announcement, November 12, 1979," 50; "Ambassador McHenry, November 27, 1979 [Remarks to the U.N. Security Council]", *DOSB* 80 (January 1980): 49; "Ambassador McHenry, December 1, 1979 [Remarks to the U.N. Security Council]," *DOSB* 80 (January 1980) 51; and "Hostages in Iran [Remarks by the President at a White House Briefing for Members of Congress, January 8, 1980]," *DOSB* 80 (March 1980): 33.

26. "Ambassador McHenry, December 1, 1979," 52.

27. "Thirteenth Convention," 19.

28. "News Conference of November 28," 1; "State of the Union Address [January 23, 1980]," *DOSB* 80 (February 1980): C.

29. The patriotic responses to Carter's pleas for conservation of oil and for his imposed embargo on Iranian oil—like the general linking of the hostages and energy—were not fortuitous. Rosalyn Carter reports asking with some incredulity whether the United States was still using Iranian oil. "I don't know anybody in the United States that wants to use Iranian oil," she reports telling the president. A few days later the oil embargo was imposed. *First Lady from Plains* (Boston: Houghton Mifflin, 1984), 311. And Jordan reports the president saying about his tough talk to the AFL-CIO: "You know, I've got to give expression to the anger of the American people. I guarantee that if I asked the people of Plains what I should do, every last on of them would say 'Bomb Iran!' I've got to keep a lid on their emotions. If they perceive me as firm and tough in voicing their rage, maybe we'll be able to control this thing"; Jordan, *Crisis*, 57. Whether Carter's assessment of his impact on defusing emotions is correct, the fact remains that he was clearly making a link to patriotism in linking the hostages to energy policies.

30. "News Conference of November 28," 1–2, 4; "President Carter, December 7, 1979 [Remarks Made to State Department Employees in the Lobby at the State Department]," *DOSB* 80 (February 1980): 55; "President Carter's News Conference, February 13," *DOSB* 80 (March 1980): C.

Carter's reluctance to discuss past American involvement in Iran was not completely without concern for his own part in supporting the deposed shah's regime. Indeed, the diplomatic corps received with raised brows his Tehran toast to the shah on 31 December 1977. He therein proclaimed: "Iran, because of the great leadership of the Shah, is an island of stability in one of the more troubled areas of the world. This is a great tribute to you, Your Majesty, and to your leadership and to the respect and the admiration and love which your people give you." Then, "The cause of human rights is one that also is shared deeply by our people and by the leaders of our two nations." Finally, "We have no other nation on earth who is closer to us in planning for our mutual military security. We have no other nation with whom we have closer consultation on regional problems that concern us both. And there is no leader with whom I have a deeper sense of personal gratitude and personal friendship." Quoted in Pierre Salinger, *America Held Hostage* (Garden City, N.Y.: Doubleday, 1981), 4–5. In light of Carter's human rights policy and the shah's notoriety as a repressive monarch, the president's words could have encouraged some sympathy for the militants' claim of American culpability in the shah's practices.

31. "News Conference of November 28," 1–2.

32. *Newsweek*, 26 November 1979, 23.

33. *Time*, 30 June 1980, 10.

34. The general posture with regard to not entertaining the Iranian point of view reflects an ethnocentric bias that not only delegitimated the Iranian side of the story but also distorted the cultural differences at play in all phases of the affair. To a domestic audience ignorant of Iranian culture, an imposed American perspective as the only perspective made the Iranian actions seem all the more insane. See Patricia J. Higgins, "Anthropologists and Issues of Public Concern: The Iran Crisis," *Human Organization* 43 (1984): 132–45, for a summary of important cultural differences that were at play in the negotiation process with Iran and the Carter administration's reluctance to engage experts on these differences as aides in interpreting the other side.

35. " 'Meet the Press' Interview [January 20, 1980]," *DOSB* 80 (March 1980): 31; "Interview for NBC News [January 7, 1980]," *DOSB* 80 (March 1980): 32.

36. "Deputy Secretary Christopher Interviewed on 'Issues and Answers' [April 13, 1980]," *DOSB* 80 (May 1980): 25.

37. See Washington *Evening Star*, 1 May 1970, for a text of Nixon's remarks on American involvement in Cambodia. A critical analysis of this speech may be found in Richard B. Gregg and Gerard A. Hauser, "Richard Nixon's April 30, 1970 Address on Cambodia: The 'Ceremony' of Confrontation," *Speech Monographs* 40 (1973): 167–81.

38. "Secretary Brown's News Conference,' April 25, 1980 (12:15 P.M.)," *DOSB*, 80 (June 1980), 39–41.

39. "National Security Adviser Brzezinski Interviewed on 'Issues and Answers' [April 27, 1980]," *DOSB* 80 (June 1980): 47–48.

40. "Thirteenth Convention," 19.

41. "Secretary's Statement, November 8, 1979," *DOSB* 79 (December 1979): 49.

42. "U.S. Foreign Policy: Our Broader Strategy," 17.

43. See, for example, *Time*, 19 November 1979, 26; "Vice President Mondale, December 5, 1979 [Remarks Made to Reporters Assembled in the White House Briefing Room]," *DOSB*, 80 (February 1980): 55; "U.S. Seeks Sanctions against Iran," 53; "Interview for NBC News [January 7, 1980]," 32; "Hostages in Iran," 33; " 'Meet the Press Carter' [January 20, 1980]," 30–31; "U.S. Course in a Changing World," 4.

44. " 'Issues and Answers' [April 27, 1980]," 47.

45. Despite the appearance of books by the major administrative players, the intent behind public statements remains ambiguous. As one would expect, the beleaguered Carter principals write defensively about a press out to get them and in a manner that casts glowingly on their own "nonpolitical" motivations at every step along the hostage affair trail. As we will see in the next section of this essay, other observers of the Carter White House held a different view. Regardless of intent, however, the point here has to do with public rhetoric that galvanizes common perceptions and, eventually, a public opinion. In addition to memoirs by Rosalyn Carter, Hamilton Jordan, and Cyrus Vance cited above, see Zbigniew Brzezinski, *Power and Principle: Memoirs of the National Security Advisers, 1977–1981* (New York: Farrar, 1983); Jimmy Carter, *Keeping Faith: Memoirs of a President* (New York: Bantam, 1982); and Jody Powell, *The Other Side of the Story* (New York: William Morrow, 1984).

46. *Episteme* is the ancient Greek term for knowledge. In Greek philosophy it is contrasted with *dionoia*, which refers to informed opinion, and *doxa*, which refers to uneducated opinion lacking in the supports of evidence, reasoning, or qualification. See Eric Havelock, *Preface to Plato* (New York: Grosset & Dunlop, 1967), 251n.1.

47. However, see "Letters" in *Time*, 16 and 23 February 1981, for some statements questioning the "heroism" of the Tehran hostages.

48. Jack W. Germond and Jules Witcover, *Blue Smoke and Mirrors* (New York: Viking, 1981), 294.

49. Jürgen Habermas, *Toward a Rational Society*, trans. Jeremy J. Shapiro (Boston: Beacon, 1971), 79.

50. See Noelle-Neumann, *Spiral of Silence*, and Speier, "Public Opinion," for overviews of the concept "public opinion."

51. *New Yorker*, 12 May 1980, 32.

52. See Nisbet, "Public Opinion."

53. These views and their supporting data are presented in two of Caddell's memos to Jimmy Carter reprinted as appendices in Elizabeth Drew, *Portrait of an Election* (New York: Simon and Schuster, 1981), 388–439.

54. Discussions of the Carter strategy going into the 1980 campaign may be found in David Broder et al., *The Pursuit of the Presidency 1980* (New York: Berkeley, 1980); Drew, *Portrait*; and Germond and Witcover, *Blue Smoke*.

55. Drew, *Portrait*, 124.

56. Drew, *Portrait*, 124.

57. "Flint, Michigan: Interview with Joe Stroud and Remer Tyson of the Detroit Free Press, October 1, 1980," *Weekly Compilation of Presidential Documents* [WCPD] 16 (1980): 2013; "The President's News Conference of April 17, 1980," *WCPD* 16 (1980): 710.

58. Despite protests to the contrary, the intersection of the public management of the affair with Carter's reelection bid was a continuing preoccupation. Especially illuminating in this regard is Jordan's *Crisis*, which is peppered throughout with calculations on the impact the hostage's detention was having on the presidential campaign; see 45, 55, 65, 98–99, and 285 for a random sampling of such reflections.

59. See Caddell's "Memorandum I," quoted in *Drew*, Portrait, 388–409 *passim*.

60. *Time*, 10 September 1979, 10–11; *Time*, 24 September 1979, 14; *Time*, 12 November 1979, 22.

61. Edward Kennedy was particularly vulnerable to questions of character on at least two counts. His marriage to Joan Kennedy was subject to press scrutiny when the couple separated. Joan Kennedy had publicly acknowledged that she had an alcohol dependency, for which she received treatment. She was also disenchanted with the rigors of campaigning and her statements of independence, such as living apart from her husband to pursue an advanced degree, suggested she did not find the spousal demands of one married to a public figure of Kennedy's stature conducive to her own personal growth. Speculation about the senator's unsettled marital status were constantly fueled by the specter of the Mary Jo Kopeckne drowning. Ms. Kopeckne, a campaign worker for the slain Robert Kennedy, was alone with Senator Kennedy on the evening of 18 July 1969 when he drove off a narrow bridge on Martha's Vineyard. The midnight incident received considerable public attention at the time and for years afterward. Throughout the 1980 campaign, references to "judgment" were taken as code to remind voters that in the Chappaquidick incident, Kennedy seemed to panic under pressure. Beyond this, there remained unanswered questions and ugly speculations about Kennedy's relationship to Ms. Kopeckne, his state of sobriety on the night of the accident, his intentions upon departing with Kopeckne, the implausibility of his making a wrong turn accidentally, and his motivations in leaving the scene of the accident.

On another plane, Kennedy was suspect as trading on his brothers' reputations without meriting his leadership role through strength of ideas or performance. A most damaging blow to his campaign came when, in a CBS interview with television correspondent Roger Mudd, he was unable to explain why he wanted to be president. The Mudd interview left the impression that Kennedy wanted the nation's highest office but did not have a program of leadership to enact. The Mudd interview is discussed in greater detail in Germond and Witcover, *Blue Smoke*, 48–78.

62. The "Rose Garden strategy" refers to an incumbent president not campaigning for reelection on the excuse that his duties as president are too demanding. If successful, it relieves the incumbent from defending his record on the hustings, where press and opponents will critically scrutinize his claims. It also creates the appearance that as president he is above the partisan politics that accompany campaigning. Finally, it forces the opponents to chase about trying to create issues, which does not appear presidential. In the 1976 campaign Gerald Ford attempted to use this strategy, until Ronald Reagan scored impressive primary victories. In 1980, Jimmy Carter was more successful. Senator Kennedy kept harping on the fact that Carter would not debate the issues and was hiding in the Rose Garden. Obviously, Kennedy believed he could not get his issues to solidify unless he successfully forced Carter into publicly campaigning. Equally obviously, from a political standpoint Carter had no incentive to leave the Rose Garden so long as he was winning primaries and caucuses.

63. *Time*, 7 January 1980, 18.

64. Broder et al., *Pursuit*, 107; Jordan, *Crisis*, 99.

65. Broder et al., *Pursuit*, 108.

66. Drew, *Portrait*, 37.

67. Drew, *Portrait*, 42.

68. *Time*, 18 February 1980, 24; *Time*, 17 March 1980, 14.

69. See, for example, "Interview with the President: Question-and-Answer Session with Reporters from Westinghouse Broadcasting Company, Inc. April 18, 1980," *WCPD* 16 (1980): 733; and "Interview with the President: Question-and-Answer Session with Reporters from Pennsylvania. April 19, 1980," *WCPD* 16 (1980): 744–45.

70. Contrary to custom, when Carter activated the switch for the lights on the national Christmas tree, only the star at the top was illuminated as a symbol of hope for the hostages' swift and safe return.

71. "Question-and-Answer Session with Reporters from Westinghouse," 733.

72. "News Conference of November 28," 2.

73. Germond and Witcover, *Blue Smoke,* 144–45.

74. One of the less fortunate flaps in the primaries occurred when Vice-president Mondale suggested that Kennedy's remarks on Iran were geared more to serve his own purposes than the welfare of the nation. The implied questioning of Kennedy's patriotism infuriated the senator and is indicative of the exclusiveness with which Carter viewed his right to speak on the hostage question. See Germond and Witcover, *Blue Smoke,* 142–43.

75. New York *Times,* 29 January 1980, sec. A, p. 12.

76. New York *Times,* 13 January 1980, sec. A, p. 18.

77. New York *Times,* 14 January 1980, sec. A, p. 16.

78. Drew, *Portrait,* 135.

79. "News Conference of April 17," *DOSB* 80 (May 1980): 8–11.

80. Germond and Witcover, *Blue Smoke,* 14. The authors add: "Strauss was convinced that Brzezinski was a political albatross, and he had repeated arguments with Carter about permitting the national security adviser to appear on network interview shows. Finally Strauss persuaded Caddell to test Brzezinski's public standing in a poll. Caddell dragged his feet until Strauss threatened to cut off campaign payments to him. Finally he made the test and reported that Brzezinski, according to Strauss, 'set new records in five states, and his best negative was 68 percent negative.' Strauss dutifully—and gleefully—reported the results to Carter, with Caddell present to back him up."

81. Germond and Witcover, *Blue Smoke,* 86.

82. "1980 Democratic Presidential Nomination: The President's Remarks Concerning His Candidacy and Campaign Plans. December 2, 1979," *WCPD* 15 (1979): 2194; Germond and Witcover, *Blue Smoke,* 89.

83. Broder et al., *Pursuit,* 61.

84. Broder et al., *Pursuit,* 57–58.

85. Martin Schram in Broder et al., *Pursuit,* 113.

86. Jordan's role in the negotiations with Iran is discussed in detail in Salinger, *Hostage;* and in his own book, *Crisis.*

87. Salinger, *Hostage,* 114.

88. Salinger, *Hostage,* 114.

89. *Newsweek,* 21 April 1980, 34.

90. Germond and Witcover, *Blue Smoke,* 160. Powell's version (*Other Side,* 228) has him saying to Secretary of Defense Brown, "Mr. Secretary, the President is going to go with this thing, I can sense it. If we can bring our people out of there, it will do more good for this country than anything that has happened in twenty years." Brown replies, "Yes, and if we fail, that will be the end of the Carter presidency."

91. Salinger, *Hostage,* 237–38.

92. See Zbigniew Brzezinski, "The Failed Mission: The Inside Account of the Attempt to Free the Hostages in Iran," New York *Times Magazine,* 24 April 1980, pp. 28ff., for an account of how the President arrived at his decision to attempt the rescue. A more comprehensive analysis, based on a collation of all available data, may be found in Paul B. Ryan, *The Iranian Rescue Mission: Why It Failed.* (Annapolis: Naval Institute Pr., 1985). Ryan has this to say in review of the planning process: "In sum, the actors included a president anxious to avoid 'wanton killings'; a national security advisor pushing for rescue; a cautious secretary of state who opposed the mission; a defense secretary whose role remains vague; senior military officers under pressure to organize a complicated operation on an ad hoc basis in the shortest possible time; and a commando officer whose recommendation for more helicopters was denied, a decision that augured ill for the mission" (61–62).

93. Drew, *Portrait,* 180.

94. Jody Powell expressed the precise source of this danger when he explained: "One of the reasons that [attacks on] the Rose Garden strategy . . . had not cut very much was that they weren't particularly credible. . . . I think most people judged up to that point that the President had a considerable amount of logic on his side, but in fact it wouldn't be credible anymore because [after the aborted rescue attempt] it wasn't true anymore." Cited in Germond and Witcover, *Blue Smoke,* 162.

95. *Time,* 12 May 1980, 31. My point is not that a genuinely public opinion formed against Carter but rather that popular mood and sentiment, as measured by the opinion polls, seemed to be swinging against him. Indeed, my argument throughout this analysis of campaign tactics has been that Carter misconceived the public as assembled through technological increments

measured by opinion surveys. He actually thwarted the formation of a truly *public* opinion by successfully restraining open debate of the salient issues implicit in the hostages' detention.

96. Germond and Witcover, *Blue Smoke*, 162–63.

97. "White House Briefing for Civic and Community Leaders: Remarks and a Question-and-Answer Session. April 10, 1980," *WCPD* 16 (1980): 804.

98. See, for example Jordan, *Crisis*, 284–88.

99. *Time*, 12 May 1980, 31.

100. *New Yorker*, 2 June 1980, 29.

101. *New Yorker*, 2 June 1980, 29.

102. Germond and Witcover, *Blue Smoke*, 1–22.

103. Germond and Witcover, *Blue Smoke*, 1–22.

104. See Edward W. Said, "Inside Islam," *Harpers*, January 1981, 25–32.

105. For a detailed discussion of an audience as a source of opportunity for establishing virtuosity, see Arendt, *Between Past and Future*, 148ff.

106. The American susceptibility to a rhetoric of "heroes" is suggested by Blaine Harden, "The Impresario of Heroism," *Washington Post*, 7 February 1982, sec. B, p. 1.

107. The president's success in defining the hostages as heroes, while failing to successfully present himself as a fit leader, is a permutation on the theme of a leader's relationship to the people.

108. For an insightful discussion of paternalism as a metaphor in social life see Richard Sennett, *Authority* (New York: Knopf, 1980), 50–83. This fourth conclusion is influenced extensively by Sennett's analysis.

TEN

The Rhetoric of Denial and Alternity

RICHARD B. GREGG

"TIME," EDWIN BLACK pointed out, "is always a brooding presence in our elections. . . . Our political experience is seasonal and cyclical. The rhythm of our public lives, a ponderous, biennial beat, and the presidential campaign is its systolic phase." Elizabeth Drew talks about the factor of time in a slightly different way. "A Presidential election year is not the frozen past but the historical hinge between what has gone before and what follows." Rightly or wrongly, Americans have a tendency to view an election year as a kind of historical marker, consigning the recent past to history and casting an ambience of the present over the ambiguous future. Thomas Cronin further accentuates the "periodic" nature of thought about the presidency by noting that "for convenience, if not always accurately, textbooks give eras or major events such labels as 'the Wilson years,' 'the Roosevelt revolution,' 'the Eisenhower period,' and 'the Kennedy Camelot years.' "[1] Our demarcating of historical "eras" is always arbitrary; one of the ways we demarcate is by using the boundaries of presidential terms of office. Therefore, it is easy to think of the year of a presidential campaign as a year of impending change, or to take notice of the perception that the major candidates appear to be so close in their views that no change is in the offing.

Certain presidential election years are determined to be landmark years, that is, years in which the landscape seems to register a significant enough measurement of change on the political Richter

385

scale to warrant lavish commentary. The presidential election of
1980 was such a year. During the campaign and immediately following the election, there was much speculation about what the election
of Ronald Reagan meant about the changing nature of public attitude, ideological alliance, and value orientation. There was the
usual commentary regarding the presidential candidates of that election in light of the public's judgments of the past and hopes for the
future.

In a sardonic tone, Lewis Lapham provided such a commentary:

> Mr. Reagan presented himself as the candidate bringing hope, faith, freedom,
> and prosperity to an electorate sorely in need of good news. As opposed to President
> Jimmy Carter, who spoke so mournfully about the passing of the American dream,
> Mr. Reagan held out the promise of a bright future. Maybe it was a fatuous promise
> and an illusory future, no more substantial than the idiot blessing of a California
> parking lot attendant reminding his patrons to "Have a Nice Day," but at least Mr.
> Reagan gave people an excuse to believe that the next ten years might be better
> than the last ten years.[2]

Lapham continues his description of the public's futuristic view of
the candidates with the following contrast: "The Democratic party
had nothing to say about even a spurious future. Mr. Carter spoke
of perils beyond measure, of poisoned seas and dwindling stores of
money and light, of blacks and Jews tearing at each other in second-
class restaurants, of Russians armed with invincible weapons. He
cast his politics as a medical report instead of a lullaby, and the
voters turned away from him as if from the specter of death."[3] The
election victory of Ronald Reagan was seen by many to be the
capstone of a decade of drift toward conservatism.

I

At the end of the decade of the 1960s, Gary Wills looked at the
political and social world around him and declared that America's
liberal ideology, which held sway since the turn of the century, was
moribund:

> Nixon's victory was the nation's concession of defeat, an admission that we have
> no politics left but the old individualism, a web of myths that have lost their magic.
> We cannot convincingly proclaim that where we stand is a "vital center." Our
> "mainstream" is a sludge. The "consensus" is no longer a matter of compromise but
> surrender. Our archetypal "self-made man" is not only self-effacing but almost self-
> obliterating.[4]

The tenets of traditional liberalism, the belief in individualism, discipline, self-regulation, achievement, and the competitive nature of the various "marketplaces" all constituted dead myths that President Nixon, by trying to restore them to life, "reduced to absurdity."[5] The decade of the 1960s was a turbulent one. Starting with the high hopes of the Kennedy administration, which culminated in the tragedy of assassination, it included racial and social unrest of national proportion and a war that heightened cynicism. It drove one president from office, and it ended with the election of another president who would bring himself down in odious, paranoid scandal. The mood of the early 1970s was far different from that of the early 1960s. As Godfrey Hodgson put it, "the United States had traveled in just ten years from the vigorous assurance of mid-Victorian England to something like the angry confusion and despair of Weimar Germany."[6]

Some saw conditions more profound than just the election of Reagan to account for an evolving future of different shape than the past. For example, in his *Changing of the Guard,* David Broder argued on behalf of pending change. He pointed out that in the 1980s national leadership would pass from the old to a new generation of men and women. The new leaders he described would not carry the scars of the Great Depression, nor an identification with the great war against totalitarian powers. The wars they were directly affected by ended without victory. The two-party political system, the nuclear family, and a good many other familiar institutions were showing signs of obsolescence. They were witness to the beginning of the space age and the ending of what has been termed the "American Century." "The voters of today," said Broder, "in increasing numbers, question the relevance of yesterday's heroes."[7] There would seem, then, to be fertile ground for the development of new perspectives.

The essay that follows is not meant to be a critical examination of the campaign rhetoric of 1980. Rather, I intend to select and examine several typical samples of rhetoric from the campaign to see whether they refer to possibilities for change or the need to change in any fundamental way. Then I shall peruse a broader horizon and identify and examine several contemporary outcroppings of rhetoric from our time that may portend significant conceptual change. My primary purpose is not to examine the two sets of samples for their own sake, but to reach beyond them to uncover the ideology that might be giving them life.

I mean by "ideology" what Black, who in turn borrowed from Marx, meant: "the network of interconnected convictions that func-

tion in a man epistemically and that shape his identity by determining how he views the world."[8] An ideology, a world view, is a
rhetorical phenomenon, selective in outlook, partisan in its valua-
tions, rejective of other possible world views. Because of the inter-
connectedness of beliefs that comprise it, an ideology can be long-
lived and slow to change. But over time, ideologies can be rendered
inefficacious by events and accompanying suasory interpretations. I
shall contend that an examination of the rhetorical samples reveals
differing world views in conflict, and therefore the possibility for
conceptual change is present. I shall further contend that the world
views have their essences captured by two conflicting metaphorical
patterns reflecting vastly different rhetorical-perceptual valences.
Should one metaphorical pattern come to prevail over the other,
the result would be consequential, for as Murray Edelman says:
"Thought is metaphorical and metaphor pervades language, for the
unknown, the new, the unclear, and the remote are apprehended
by one's perceptions of identities with the familiar. Metaphor, therefore, defines the pattern of perception to which people respond."[9]

The candidate who most openly and directly represented the
liberal position in 1980 was Massachusetts Senator Edward Kennedy.[10] At the outset of the campaign, Kennedy led President Carter
by a healthy margin, but he swiftly fell to a distant and doomed
second place in the polls to Carter. His televised interview with
Roger Mudd in November 1979 was extremely damaging. In that
interview, Kennedy's answers allowed the ghosts of Chappaquidick
to be resurrected, and he sounded uncertain, unable to articulate
his positions on issues or the reasons why he chose to run for the
presidency. In the beginning of the formal campaign, he failed to
chart a clear course for his candidacy and on most occasions his
speeches seemed either too harsh or too wooden. He misspoke on
occasion, and the press highlighted those mistakes, underlining the
perception that this Kennedy did not have the style to recover
Camelot. There were occasions, of course, when Kennedy's rhetorical performance was tremendously effective. But the public learned
little of them from the press. One outstanding exception came on
the second night of the Democratic convention, when Kennedy
addressed the delegates and the nation to announce that his candidacy was over and to make a final plea for ideas he felt were
important. His speech was the most exciting moment of the convention. Drew describes the moment:

> Kennedy's speech, while it is well written, contains more than a little soaring
> rhetoric, melodrama, and sentimentality, and it works. He has created and defined
> this moment. He is ringing emotional chimes that the audience seems to want to

hear. It is like listening to a great aria for its own sake, even though one knows
what is to happen next. Kennedy has absolutely taken over this hall. Perhaps if he
were still a candidate the audience would not be so receptive, but we shall never
know. It is clear that this will be one of the memorable moments of any Convention.[11]

He did not address the convention, he announced, to argue for
his candidacy, but rather to urge his listeners to affirm a cause. He
made the cause clear in a general way at the outset of the speech; he
wanted to renew the Democratic party's commitment to "economic
justice" and to "a fair and lasting prosperity that can put America
back to work."

The serious issue before us tonight is the cause for which the Democratic Party
has stood in its finest hours, the cause that keeps our party young and makes it, in
the second century of its age, the largest political party in this republic and the
longest lasting political party on this planet.

Our cause has been, since the days of Thomas Jefferson, the cause of the common
man and the common woman. Our commitment has been, since the days of
Andrew Jackson, to all those he called "the humble members of society—the
farmers, mechanics and laborers." On this foundation we have defined our values,
refined our policies and refreshed our faith.[12]

He then turned more specifically to economic policy, though he
termed what he was talking about a "moral issue." His concern
was with unemployment, high interest rates, and other economic
conditions that cause "human misery." He urged his listeners to
pledge that employment would be the first priority of an economic
policy, that all who were presently employed should have a guarantee
of security and that jobs would be created for all those who were
unemployed. "These are not simplistic pledges. Simply put, they are
the heart of our tradition; they have been the soul of our party across
generations. It is the glory and the greatness of our tradition to speak
for those who have no voice, to remember those who are forgotten,
to respond to the frustrations and fulfill the aspirations of all Americans seeking a better life in a better land." Kennedy does refer to
changing conditions that come with changing times, but his greater
stress falls upon the maintenance of tradition:

The commitment I seek is not to outworn views, but to old values that will never
wear out. Programs may sometimes become obsolete, but the ideal of fairness always
endures. Circumstances may change, but the work of compassion must continue.
It is surely correct that we cannot solve problems by throwing money at them, but
it is also correct that we dare not throw out national problems onto a scrap heap
of inattention and indifference. The poor may be out of political fashion, but they
are not without human needs. The middle class may be angry, but they have not
lost the dream that all Americans can advance together.

The demand of our people in 1980 is not for smaller government or bigger government but for better government. Some say that government is always bad and that spending for basic social programs is the root of our economic evils. But we reply, the present inflation and recession costs our economy $200 billion a year. We reply, inflation and unemployment are the biggest spenders of all.

The task of leadership in 1980 is not to parade scapegoats or to seek refuge in reaction but to match our power to the possibilities of progress.

As Democrats, we recognize that each generation of Americans has a rendezvous with a different reality. The answers of one generation become the questions of the next generation, but there is a guiding star in the American firmament. It is as old as the revolutionary belief that all people are created equal, and as clear as the contemporary condition of Liberty City and the South Bronx. Again and again, Democratic leaders have followed that star, and they have given new meaning to the old values of liberty and justice for all.

For those individuals weary of constant government intervention in the attempt to mitigate social problems and inequities, some of Kennedy's phrasing would have negative rhetorical connotations. Historically, the proximate images that could be evoked by Kennedy's reference to the "finest hours" of the tradition of the democratic party might call to mind the years of Lyndon Johnson's war on poverty, when federal government launched a plenitude of social programs, many of which later came to be judged not only inadequate, but inept and wasteful. Longer range images might recall the growth of governmental action and spending in Franklin Roosevelt's New Deal, the forerunner of the Johnson years. Other phrases and ideas are consistent with such images: "humble members of society," "job security," "work of compassion," and the notion that government leadership ought to ensure that all Americans could advance together. Kennedy explicitly decries the notion that government is bad and charges those who say the nation's economic woes are caused by spending for social programs with scapegoating. The traditional liberal ideology that permeates Kennedy's speech overrides his mention of obsolete programs or his acknowledgment that each generation has a rendezvous with a different reality.

Kennedy urged that there be no scapegoating at the very time many were looking for scapegoats and finding them in big government, in groups hindering industrial development by advocating constraining ecological standards, or in other groups undermining conventional morality by supporting liberal abortion laws. Kennedy asked for common sacrifice at a time when many felt they had sacrificed too long already. In his moving conclusion, in which he referred to his dead brothers, the liberal dream was evoked: "For all those whose cares have been our concern, the work goes on, the cause endures, the hope still lives and the dream shall never die."

For those who still retained faith in traditional liberalism, Kennedy's speech provided an emotional peak. But at a time when the majority of people seemed to be responding to more conservative impulses, his speech portrayed him, as Jeff Greenfield put it, as "an unregenerate liberal, a pro-poor, pro-black, pro-government-spending politician running in a time when the portents were not favorable to such a candidacy."[13] What Kennedy did achieve in practical political terms was to end his campaign by strongly refurbishing his own image as a gallant loser and to bring back to the Democratic party large numbers of liberals who had earlier flirted with the candidacy of John Anderson. Ideologically, he suggested nothing new, even though he briefly acknowledged the existence of new realities. If this generation of Americans faced a rendezvous with a new reality, then one would think there would be some kind of call for reconceiving and redefining the nation's goals in light of international and national conditions, of groups and classes of people in light of the demands and constraints of the times, and ultimately of individuals themselves in light of change and in relationship to their institutions and to each other. But Kennedy illustrated the major problem of the liberals generally at this time, namely the inability to break out of an old ideological mode to begin to construct a new and more timely one. Walter Mondale had the same problem in the presidential election of 1984, failing to articulate a vision of the future that appealed to the electorate and appearing to be the captive of such traditional liberal constituencies as organized labor, minorities, and the poor.

Ronald Reagan won the 1980 presidential election, and to many he symbolized a significant change in attitude on the part of the American people, away from the conventional liberal point of view. Large elements of the traditional Democratic party coalition voted for Reagan. As Greenfield put it, "In the end, what appears to have decided the election was a series of fundamental changes in the beliefs of millions of Americans."[14] It is too early to tell whether that observation is accurate. If in fact the ideological flag was firmly pointed in the Reagan direction, what might we learn about that direction by examining a small, but prominent, portion of Reagan's public rhetoric?

One can quickly get the sense of Reagan's proposed change by examining his acceptance speech before the Republican National Convention. Early in the speech, Reagan asserts—as many other nominees in many other historical eras have—that for the first time Americans face grave threats to their very existence. He was referring to a disintegrating economy, weakened defense capability, and "an energy policy based on the sharing of scarcity."

The major issue of this campaign is the direct political, personal and moral responsibility of Democratic Party Leadership—in the White House and in Congress—for this unprecedented calamity which has befallen us.

They tell us they have done the most that humanly could be done. They say that the United States has had its day in the sun: that our nation has passed its zenith.

They expect you to tell your children that the American people no longer have the will to cope with their problems; that the future will be one of sacrifice and few opportunities.

My fellow citizens, I utterly reject that view.[15]

Reagan next reflected on the virtues of the Founding Fathers and Abraham Lincoln's call to the American people to renew their dedication to a government of, for, and by the people. He urged the American people to restore the ideal of progress that marks the recent American past. Such language does not create a context in which one might perceive new ways of viewing things or doing things in the future.

The same spirit continues in Reagan's inaugural address, though the relationship of the people to the desired effort Reagan extolls becomes more clearly etched. The usual amenities are observed along with the usual recitation of ills and challenges the nation faces. Then, Reagan moves to the heart of his message:

If we look to the answer as to why for so many years we achieved so much, prospered as no other people on earth, it was because here in this land we unleashed the energy and individual genius of man to a greater extent than has ever been done before.

Freedom and the dignity of the individual have been more available and assured here than in any other place on earth. The price for this freedom at times has been high, but we have never been unwilling to pay that price.

It is no coincidence that our present troubles parallel and are proportionate to the intervention and intrusion in our lives that result from unnecessary and excessive growth of Government.

It is time for us to realize that we are too great a nation to limit ourselves to small dreams. We're not, as some would have us believe, doomed to an inevitable decline. I do not believe in a fate that will fall on us no matter what we do. I do believe in a fate that will fall on us if we do nothing.

So with all the creative energy at our command let us begin an era of national renewal. Let us renew our determination, our courage and our strength. And let us renew our faith and our hope. We have every right to dream heroic dreams.

Those who say that we're in a time when there are no heroes—they just don't know where to look. You can see heroes every day going in and out of factory gates. Others, a handful in number, produce enough food to feed all of us and then the world beyond.

You meet heroes across a counter—and they're on both sides of that counter. They are entrepreneurs with faith in themselves and faith in an idea who create new jobs, new wealth and opportunity.

There are individuals and families whose taxes support the Government and whose voluntary gifts support church, charity, culture, art and education. Their patriotism is quiet but deep. Their values sustain our national life.

Now, I have used the words "they" and "their" in speaking of those heroes. I could say "you" and "your" because I am addressing the heroes of whom I speak— you, the citizens of this blessed land.

Here is the heart of Reagan's message. It is an unabashed accolade to individual opportunity, individual challenge, individual achievement, individual commitment, and individual courage. The values heralded in Reagan's accolade are deeply embedded in American thought. Reagan rejects the thinking that the nation had achieved the height of its power and was on the way down. Rather, he would return to the "American compact" and "long standing American spirit." His rhetoric hearkens back to rugged individualism, an ideal that became enthroned early in the American experience and made mythic heroes of pioneers and frontiersmen, loners like Daniel Boone who kept moving beyond civilization, cutting trails through the wilderness as they went.

Throughout the American experience, the ideal of individualism and all that goes with it—competition, courage, diligence, self-improvement, efficiency, productivity, success—has been carried along through transforming contexts. While the contexts have changed, the ideal and its values have remained much the same. Ronald Reagan evokes the value cluster again and again in his rhetoric. In Reagan's rhetoric, there is not even much hint of changing context. There are still frontiers to be won, natural resources to be exploited, individual opportunities to be taken advantage of, the role of a chosen people to be played out. Reagan pledged that he would reduce the power and influence of the federal government, encourage the production of new energy sources, provide a phased 30 percent income tax reduction, improve business depreciation taxes, restore the national economy, stimulate jobs, and improve the nation's military capabilities while working for continued world peace.

He builds toward his conclusion:

Tonight let us dedicate ourselves to renewing the American compact. I ask you not simply to "trust me," but to trust your values—our values—and to hold me responsible for living up to them.

I ask you to trust that American spirit which knows no ethnic, religious, social, political, regional or economic boundaries; the spirit that burned with zeal in the hearts of millions of immigrants from every corner of the earth who came here in search of freedom.

Some say that spirit no longer exists. But I have seen it—I have felt it—all across the land; in the big cities, the small towns and in rural America. The

American spirit is still there, ready to blaze into life if you and I are willing to do what has to be done.

The time had come, said Reagan, for Americans to recapture their destiny.

It was Jimmy Carter who best expressed the idea that ideological reconceptualizations were necessary in the decade of the 1980s and beyond. Unfortunately, the full political context surrounding his statements pointing to the need for change did not encourage people to hear them for their own sake. Carter was carrying too many political burdens. He was seen by many to be a weak and vacillating president, unable to control errant members of his administration. He was never able to galvanize public support for his energy program, even though the public could see evidence of trouble all around it in the form of shortages and high fuel prices. Carter had to take the brunt of the discontent that arose because of inflation, unemployment, and a sagging economy, though these problems transcended his presidency.[16] In July 1979, a time when the American people seemed ready to respond to confidently presented and clearly articulated objectives and policies, Carter went on national television in a major speech in which he whined about what the press termed a "national malaise." During the course of the 1980 campaign, a certain nastiness crept into his attacks on Reagan that evoked negative response. A constant backdrop throughout the campaign, of course, was the continuing crisis in Iran and concern for the plight of the American hostages being held there. Carter's attempts to use the Iranian situation to his advantage, while helping him early in the campaign against Kennedy, ultimately boxed him in and proved to be severely damaging. All of these factors colored the public's perceptions of Jimmy Carter and the meanings people read into his statements. For instance, several times during the campaign he argued that he would be a better president in his second term because he had learned how to perform better during his first term. On the face of it, this is a reasonable assertion; those in a position to know generally agree that no one can be adequately equipped to assume the presidency before actually doing so and must necessarily learn how the job is done as they go along. But given the context in which Carter spoke, a context he himself contributed to, many people probably took the statement as an admission of past mistakes and doubted that he could improve.

In his acceptance speech before the Democratic convention, a speech that was anticlimactic following Ted Kennedy's performance the night before, Carter struck the general themes that he hoped would carry him to victory. He wanted to draw a sharp contrast between himself and Ronald Reagan and to emphasize that Reagan was a throwback to a simple world that no longer existed:

> This election is a stark choice between two men, two parties, two sharply different pictures of America and the world. But it is more than just that.
>
> It is a choice between two futures. The year 2000 is less than 20 years away—just four Presidential elections after this one. Children born this year will come of age in the 21st century.
>
> The time to shape the world of the year 2000 is now. The decisions of the next few years will steer our course—perhaps an irreversible course—and the most important of all choices will be made by the American people at the polls less than three months from tonight.[17]

If Reagan were elected, said Carter, the future would be one of despair for millions of people who would have to struggle alone to achieve equal opportunities and a good life. The "merchants of oil" would command this country's energy future, the economy would be misshapen by an inequitable tax program favoring the rich, programs benefiting the poor would be slashed, and everyone would be victimized by high inflation. Chances for war would be heightened through intensification of the nuclear arms race.

On the other hand, if Carter and the Democrats were reelected the people of the nation would experience justice through full employment, the opportunity to receive health care and education, and equal opportunities for all. They would be the benefactors of international peace guaranteed by America's military and moral strength. A renewed Carter administration would promise security and equal rights for all.

The Democrats, asserted Carter, would squarely face the realities of the present in building for the future whereas Reagan and the Republicans would refuse to see the world as it really was, offering instead a make-believe world that could never exist. In the Reagan-Republican vision,

> all the complex global changes since World War II have never happened. In their fantasy America, all their problems have simple solutions. Simple—and wrong.
>
> It is a make-believe world of good guys and bad guys, where some politicians shout first and ask questions later.
>
> No hard choices. No sacrifice. No tough decisions. It sounds too good to be true—and it is.
>
> The path of fantasy leads to irresponsibility. The path of reality leads to hope and peace. The two paths could not be more different. Nor could the futures to which they lead.

While it might seem that Carter was opening the door for a thorough discussion of the realities of the 1980s and 1990s, of the opportunities that would be possible, the constraints that would

force change, and the kinds of intellectual and emotional adjustments that would have to be made to accommodate to change, he
backed away from the threshold quickly. Rather than talking about
the implications of dwindling world resources, he proclaimed that
America was on the road to solving its energy problem. Instead of
admitting that the economic concerns of the world were rapidly
becoming interlocking and interdependent, he implied that
America could become independent of foreign interests. With conventional ideas of progress being questioned all around him, Carter
emphasized that the 1980s would be a time of growth in America
and that we would maintain our position as an economic superpower.
But the mood of the nation was one of uncertainty of Carter's ability
to lead in any sure and confident way, and Carter did little in this
speech or in the campaign to alter that mood.

The nationally televised debate on 28 October between Carter
and Reagan received the usual treatment from the press; more
attention was paid to candidate image and campaign tactics than to
the substance of the debate itself. Certainly images were in the
forefront of the candidates' concerns, with Carter eager to portray
Reagan as a dangerous threat to world peace and Reagan equally
intent upon erasing that image of himself. The American people
had an important choice to make, Carter said, because he favored
SALT II with the Soviet Union whereas Reagan opposed it and
believed the United States should increase its weapons production.
But whatever advantage Carter enjoyed on this issue and whatever
thought he might have provoked was undermined when he revealed
that he had consulted with his daughter, Amy, about what she felt
was the most important issue of the campaign, and she told him it
was the control of nuclear arms. The effect of his comment was to
turn attention away from important concerns on the issue to himself
as a butt for humor. His opportunity was aborted. Carter only
provided another incident that supported the conclusions already
arrived at by the majority of Americans that he was incompetent to
lead.

Two rhetorical events bracketed the presidential campaign, however, in which Carter cogently addressed the changing demands of
the future. The first occurred on 20 October 1979, at Columbia
Point, Dorchester, Massachusetts, where the president spoke at the
dedication of the John F. Kennedy Library. Early in his remarks,
in a manner befitting the occasion, Carter eulogized Kennedy's
accomplishments:

President Kennedy understood the past and respected its shaping of the future.
Yet he was very much a man of his own time. The first President born in this

century, he embodied the ideals of a generation as few public figures have ever done in the history of the earth. He summoned our nation out of complacency and he set it on a path of excitement and hope. . . .

President Kennedy took office understanding that the texture of social and economic life of our nation and our people was changing and that our nation and our people would have to change with it. "Change is the law of life," he once said. "And those who look only to the past or the present are certain to miss the future." He had a vision of how America could meet and master the forces of change that he saw around him.[18]

Carter recalled Kennedy's assassination, and the social discord, the Vietnam War, the Watergate scandal, and other events the American people had lived through in the ensuing years. Then he affirmed that the nation had survived and was ready to face the challenge of the 1980s with renewed confidence and spirit.

These challenges, of course, are not the same ones that confronted us a generation ago. The carved desk in the Oval Office which I use is the same as when John F. Kennedy sat behind it, but the problems that land on that desk are quite different.

President Kennedy was right: change is the law of life. The world of 1980 is as different from what it was in 1960 as the world of 1960 was from that of 1940. Our means of improving the world must also be different. . . .

We have a keener appreciation of limits now: the limits of government; limits on the use of military power abroad; the limits on manipulating without harm to ourselves a delicate and balanced natural environment.

We are struggling with a profound transition from a time of abundance to a time of growing scarcity and energy. We are only beginning to learn the new habits and to utilize the new technologies that will carry us to a future age of clean and renewable energy.

In these remarks Carter clearly established some of the guidelines for a public discussion that could range from the impact of new technologies on the one hand, to the need to redefine human goals and aspirations on the other. Underlying such a discussion would lie the need to reconceptualize our very nature as humans, to see ourselves in new ways with regard to the world around us. In his dedication speech Carter specified some of the contemporary conditions bearing on the need for such redefinition, conditions that could constrain the new definitions that might be formulated. Unfortunately, these concerns would quickly be removed from the center of the political stage by the presidential campaign about to begin. Even in the precampaign context of the library dedication, many interpreted Carter's statements as primarily political in nature, because they seemed to emphasize that the changing times demanded a different approach from the kind of liberalism symbolized by John Kennedy and represented by Ted Kennedy.

Following the election and his defeat Carter returned to the themes of change. Whatever his motives on 15 January 1981, the occasion of his farewell address to the nation, Carter had the opportunity to express his views in a genuine and forthright manner. He chose not to review the accomplishments of his administration in a way that would invite a positive verdict from history as some past presidents had done. Instead, he talked almost exclusively about the future, as if he felt the need to reaffirm an agenda which he feared the incoming administration would ignore. He wanted, he said, to step aside from his role as national leader, and address the citizens of the nation as a fellow citizen:

> It has now been 35 years since the first atomic bomb fell on Hiroshima. The great majority of the world's people cannot remember a time when the nuclear shadow did not hang over the earth. Our minds have adjusted to it, as after a time our eyes adjust to the dark. Yet the risk of a nuclear conflagration has not lessened. It has not happened yet, but that can give us little comfort—for it only has to happen once.
>
> The danger is becoming greater. As the arsenals of the super-powers grow in size and sophistication and as other governments acquire these weapons, it may only be a matter of time before madness, desperation, greed or miscalculation lets loose this terrible force.
>
> In an all-out nuclear war, more destructive power than in all of World War II would be unleashed every second for the long afternoon it would take for all the missiles and bombs to fall. A World War II every second—more people killed in the first few hours than all the wars of history put together. The survivors, if any, would live in despair amid the poisoned ruins of a civilization that had committed suicide.[19]

Carter attempts here to depict in graphic fashion an event very difficult to portray accurately, both because it has never happened and because few people seem able, for very long, to contemplate the horrors of nuclear war with any sense of reality or personal involvement. A few paragraphs later, Carter returns to graphic depiction with a much more positive, contrary image:

> Nuclear weapons are an expression of one side of our human character. But there is another side. The same rocket technology that delivers nuclear warheads has also taken us peacefully into space. From that perspective, we see our earth as it really is—a small and fragile and beautiful blue globe, the only home we have. We see no barriers of race or religion or country. We see the essential unity of our species and our planet; and with faith and common sense that bright vision will ultimately prevail.

Carter's next paragraph, though it comes in the middle portion of his speech, can be seen as a summary of the major thrust of the entire speech:

> The shadows that fall across the future are cast not only by the kinds of weapons we have built but by the kind of world we will either nourish or neglect. There are

real and growing dangers to our simple and most precious possession: the air we breathe, the water we drink and the land which sustains us. The rapid depletion of irreplaceable minerals, the erosion of topsoil, the destruction of beauty, the blight of pollution, the demand of increasing billions of people all combine to create problems which are easy to observe and predict but difficult to resolve. If we do not act, the world of the year 2000 will be much less able to sustain life than it is now.

In the portions of the speech included here, Carter is talking about extremely important matters. The preservation of the environment and need to avoid nuclear war are items easily placed at the top of a survival list. Finding a means of achieving the goals is a much more difficult matter to cope with. But the key to there ever being public consideration and discussion of either matter depends upon something Carter alluded to in his Kennedy Library dedication speech, namely, "keener appreciation" that certain institutions are incapable of solving problems and, more fundamentally, that there must come a new appreciation of the limits to human capability, control, and achievement. The kind of perception Carter is talking about is a view of reality and human nature that has not found a comfortable niche in American thought. We have always been able to find "new frontiers" in this land of progress. Hard work has long been lauded as the key to nearly any kind of success one might want to achieve. And success has been plentiful to observe. There have been successes in nearly every walk of life: in industrial development, in agricultural production, in war, in the standard of living, in science, in space, and the list could go on. It has been only in the past two decades—in fact, one could almost pick 1963 as the year— when conventional wisdom started being called into question. The questioning sprang from a number of different areas of concern and occurred in various communication modes. Television producer Fred Freed observed, for instance, that "one of the things that happened was that from 1960 to 1963 the news that people got from TV was essentially optimistic. From 1963 on, it wasn't."[20] Some forms of progress were now coming to be seen as harmful. Wars no longer seemed winnable. Foreign affairs became unpredictable and beyond our sure control. The economy appeared to be unmanageable. We seemed suddenly to be running out of those raw materials that not only undergirded productivity but were essential to sustaining the quality of life we had become accustomed to.

We Americans have proven to be adept at constructing rhetorical diversions that enable us to avoid unpleasantness. For instance, throughout our history, the romance of the American West, of the frontier, has been prominent in our mythology. The romance is

easily understood. In the beginning, our vast, uncharted land seemed
to offer unlimited opportunities for resources of all kinds, for growth,
and the promise of a new start and new wealth for those with the
diligence and courage to move West. For years, American oratory
and literature proclaimed it America's destiny to build a great nation
from ocean to ocean. Indeed, that destiny went beyond the shores
of the continent to affect the peoples of other cultures as well.[21]
Some of the promise was real, of course. There were vast resources
to be tapped and possibilities for building a new life. It is natural
that the promise of the West and the qualities of those individuals
who took advantage of them would become magnified and distorted
in American minds.

Over the years the country changed. The West filled and the
frontier vanished. Industrialization after the Civil War spelled an
end to the agrarian nature of American life and the beginning of
problems associated with urbanization, mass production and
crowded living conditions. As Henry Nash Smith pointed out, the
frontier myth was powerless to accommodate the issues that arose
in an increasingly technologized society. However, the myth was
not modified to reflect the times more accurately, but was stubbornly
maintained, even intensified.[22] The frontier myth encouraged
Americans to ignore the problems created by industrialization; indeed, the nation's attention was directed from reality for the entire
half-century during which we became the most highly developed
technological nation in the world. By fastening on the diversion
rather than the reality, we Americans exhibited the normal human
tendency to turn away from those phenomena that make us uncomfortable and to identify with a symbolic "reality" more to our liking.

I believe that many Americans were engaged in denial behavior
in 1980 when they identified, no matter how vaguely, with Ronald
Reagan and his ideological position. If we operate on the principle
that when we identify with a certain set of interests and ideas, we
at the same time, either explicitly and implicitly, identify against
interests and ideas that are in some measure obverse, then we can
see what many are turning away from by examining the major themes
of Reagan's campaign. Those themes add up to a celebration of
individualism. The call for a reduction of governmental activity, for
less regulation, for a reduction in the federal funding of many
programs, for a new sense of volunteerism, for a new spirit of
individual self-reliance, for a marketplace more reliant on individual
initiative and achievement, is a denial that we are living in a time
when such individualism is fast becoming obsolete. Yet the evidence
is all around us. We are clearly faced with the ultimate depletion of

certain natural resources. Even the smallest of wars between small countries has the potential to involve the superpowers, and in this age almost inevitably does. We Americans, so used to having our corporations extend our interests by investing in foreign concerns, now find foreign investments nestling snugly on American soil at a rate never before experienced. Domestic problems and activities such as the dumping of chemical wastes, the construction of nuclear facilities, and the occurrence of unemployment can no longer be just local problems, but affect entire regions of the nation. Television, of course, brings events from around the world to local attention. There has been a growing sense of unease over the fact that we, individually, are losing control of our own lives and fortunes to larger, distanced, impersonal forces. Ineffective as it may be, it is also understandable that many would want, rhetorically and symbolically, to hurl the banners of individualism against the forces undermining it.

But it is possible that we are on the verge of a fundamental change; there are portents of change in the air, among them the conditions mentioned earlier. There are also rhetorical currents running, some of them strongly, that are urging changes in our perceptions and therefore our attitudes and behaviors. Several of these currents are, in fact, exhorting us to move in the direction of the most radical change of all, namely, to modify our perception of ourselves, of what the potentialities and limits of humanness are, of our relationship to other humans, and our place in the total environment in which we live.

In the remainder of this essay, I wish to examine several of these rhetorical currents. I must examine them selectively rather than exhaustively. But the rhetorical messages I examine have political implications that could exert force for some time to come.

II

On or around 22 April 1970, in communities all across the country, Americans gathered to observe what was called "Earth Day." The event was both a celebration and a time for issuing warnings that we were ruining our natural environment through careless disposal of wastes, wanton use of chemicals, various types of pollution and dangerous industrial practices. Among those speaking at fifty-six various locations were Walter Mondale, Gaylord Nelson, Kurt Vonnegut, Jr., Eric Sevareid, George Wald, Rennie Davis, Kenneth

Boulding, I. F. Stone, and Margaret Mead. Among the subjects discussed were chemical defoliation in Vietnam, alternate energy sources, the noise factor of supersonic airplanes, the fouling of waters with sewage, urban blight, oil spills, and the need for legal and political action. The day was planned and coordinated by Environmental Action, a national organization working with a great many local groups. The local groups were on 2,000 university and college campuses, in 10,000 high schools and 2,000 communities; it was estimated that nearly 20 million people participated. In a foreword to a paperback book that contains portions of more than fifty messages delivered on Earth Day, Environmental Action announced that "on April 22, a generation dedicated itself to reclaiming the planet. A new kind of movement was born—a bizarre alliance that spans the ideological spectrum from campus militants to middle Americans. Its aim: to reverse our rush toward extinction. If the environmental movement succeeds it will profoundly change corporations, government and the way each of us lives."[23] The statement contains hyperbole, of course. Nonetheless, it is the case that millions more Americans are concerned about environmental issues than ever before.

There are a number of sources of impetus for the current concern, but one of the major ones must be Rachel Carson's *Silent Spring*, published in 1962. Carson was a mild-mannered person who possessed extensive scientific knowledge and a great love for nature. For years she was employed by the United States Fish and Wildlife Service as a writer and later editor of its publications. While employed there she began to write about the ecology and life of the ocean. In 1941 her first book, *Under the Sea Wind*, was published and received very positive critical acclaim, but the war that started for the United States just one week after the publication date diverted public attention. In 1951, she published *The Sea around Us* and became an immediate literary celebrity. The book was offered by the Book-of-the-Month Club, condensed in *Reader's Digest*, and translated into thirty-three languages. For eighty-six weeks it was on the best-seller list. To honor her achievement, she was awarded the 1951 National Book Award for nonfiction. In 1952 *Under the Sea Wind* was reissued, and it too became an instant success. In 1955 a book about life found along America's eastern shoreline entitled *The Edge of the Sea* was published.

During the war years, Carson became concerned about the growing use of chemicals, particularly DDT, which was being used to bring typhus epidemics among civilians and soldiers in Italy under control. Following the war, scientists began turning up disturbing evidence regarding the effects of DDT on the life cycle of various kinds of wildlife. In 1958, Carson turned her attention from the beauty of nature and began to research the horrible possibility of the destruction of such beauty. She started to amass data for a book she hoped to have finished by spring of 1958. Frank Graham describes Carson's conception of what *Silent Spring* would have to be:

It was clear now in Rachel Carson's mind what her book would be. Using science as its base, it must nonetheless transcend those limited confines of the average scientist's mind which had pulled the world into its current morass. It must not degenerate into vaguely mystical ideas, or smack of the emotional arguments of fringe groups which she always tried to keep at arm's length. Science must be the foundation for her work, as it always had been in the past, but it must be given another dimension by the sympathy and compassion without which the finest scientists in the world are dehumanized. She knew that her book must persuade as well as inform; it must synthesize scientific fact with the most profound sort of propaganda.[24]

As others learned of her work, Carson was encouraged by scientists and wildlife specialists from all over the world who urged her on and shared information with her. She also discovered that powerful interests, including the United States Department of Agriculture and the Department of the Interior, would fight her by denigrating her work. Even before the book was published in whole, portions of it appeared in *The New Yorker* in the summer of 1962, and chemical firms instructed their scientists to comb the articles for weaknesses. Velsical Chemical Corporation of Chicago sent the publisher, Houghton Mifflin, a letter suggesting that they reconsider publication because of alleged inaccuracies. Houghton Mifflin received a review of the disputed material from an independent toxicologist who confirmed Carson's accuracy and proceeded with publication of the book in September 1962. Offered through the Book-of-the-Month Club, advance sales had reached 40,000 in September; by December, sales were over 100,000.

I do not have space here to detail the uproar that followed the book's publication. I can only point out that there were many positive consequences amidst the negative attacks. By the end of 1962, forty bills had been introduced in state legislatures to regulate the use of pesticides. The Senate opened an investigation of all federal programs related to problems of environmental hazards. President John Kennedy's Science Advisory Committee studied pesticide use for eight months and issued a report that supported Carson's position. It is now generally agreed that Carson's argument brought issues of pollution out of the darkness and into the public's eye.[25]

Carson's descriptions of wildlife and natural conditions are exqui-

sitely and intimately drawn, so that a reader experiences the feeling
of being in the presence of her subject. At the same time there is
a firmness about her style, a kind of quiet power that etches scenes
and actions sharply in a reader's mind. It is this same style, used so
often to depict scenes of life and beauty, that Carson, in *Silent
Spring,* turns to scenes of death and destruction with equally telling
effect.

She states the general problems succinctly:

> Along with the possibility of the extinction of mankind by nuclear war, the
> central problem of our age has therefore become the contamination of man's total
> environment with such substances of incredible potential for harm—substances
> that accumulate in the tissues of plants and animals and even penetrate the germ
> cells to shatter or alter the materials of heredity upon which the shape of the future
> depends.
>
> Some would-be architects of our future look toward a time when it will be
> possible to alter the human germ plasm by design. But we may easily be doing so now
> by inadvertence, for many chemicals, like radiation, bring about gene mutation. It
> is ironic to think that man might determine his own future by something so
> seemingly trivial as the choice of an insect spray.
>
> All this has been risked—for what? Future historians may well be amazed by our
> distorted sense of proportion. How could intelligent beings seek to control a few
> unwanted species by a method that contaminated the entire environment and
> brought the threat of disease and death even to their own kind?[26]

Carson provides example after example of poisonous spraying
programs that resulted in the death of many kinds of insects and
animals. For instance, she turns her attention to Michigan, where,
in 1954, spraying for Dutch elm disease began. The next year, East
Lansing joined the program, adding it to attempts already underway
to control gypsy moths and mosquitoes.

> During 1954, the year of the first light spraying, all seemed well. The following
> spring the migrating robins began to return to the campus as usual. Like the
> bluebells in Tomlinson's haunting essay "The Lost Wood," they were "expecting
> no evil" as they reoccupied their familiar territories. But soon it became evident
> that something was wrong. Dead and dying robins began to appear on the campus.
> Few birds were seen in their normal foraging activities or assembling in their usual
> roosts. Few nests were built; few young appeared. The pattern was repeated with
> monotonous regularity in the succeeding springs. The sprayed area had become a
> lethal trap in which each wave of migrating robins would be eliminated in about
> a week. Then new arrivals would come in, only to add to the numbers of doomed
> birds seen on the campus in the agonized tremors that precede death.[27]

In a style that remains lucid and trenchant, Carson describes the
cycle of events that was causing the widespread death. Elm trees
were being sprayed with large doses of DDT, and all life on the tree
was poisoned. "The poison forms a tenacious film over the leaves

and bark. Rains do not wash it away. In autumn the leaves fall to the ground, accumulate in sodden layers, and begin the slow process of becoming one with the soil. In this they are aided by the toil of the earthworms who feed in the leaf litter, for elm leaves are among their favorite foods."[28]

The problem, however, is not caused by insects or wildlife. Throughout the book, Carson keeps the villain of this tragic drama clearly in view. It is always a purposeful human act that begins a cycle of death threatening all wildlife and insect life. Indeed, domestic pets may be included in the kill, and human life itself is endangered:

> These insecticides are not selective poisons; they do not single out the one species of which we desire to be rid. Each of them is used for the simple reason that it is a deadly poison. It therefore poisons all life with which it comes in contact: the cat beloved of some family, the farmer's cattle, the rabbit in the field, and the horned lark out of the sky. These creatures are innocent of any harm to man. Indeed, by their very existence they and their fellows make his life more pleasant. Yet he rewards them with a death that is not only sudden but horrible.[29]

Thus, while much of the book focuses on matters of nature, it is really the nature of humanity that is in question. Carson has succeeded in drawing the consequences of human action in a way that holds up a mirror to humanity so that it must question its own motives and perceive its own guilt. For Carson makes it clear that the problem of environmental pollution is fundamentally a moral one. Humans, in the mistaken belief that they can control their destiny, and in their desire to do so, wittingly or unwittingly destroy the natural environment that sustains all of life. Her condemnation brings us to the basic rhetorical issue that may result in dramatic change:

> The "control of nature" is a phrase conceived in arrogance, born of the Neanderthal age of biology and philosophy, when it was supposed that nature exists for the convenience of man. The concepts and practices of applied entomology for the most part date from the Stone Age of science. It is our alarming misfortune that so primitive a science has armed itself with the most modern and terrible weapons, and that in turning them against the insects it has also turned them against the earth.[30]

The greatest hazard of all, of course, would be a nuclear war, likely to lead to total nuclear holocaust. At the time of this writing, there appears to be a growing concern on the part of various sectors of the public about the threat of nuclear war, the consequences of such a war, and what steps might be taken to prevent one. The concrete proposals that many groups and individuals support run the gamut from an immediate freeze on the further development and testing of nuclear weapons to the pragmatic position that the cost of weapons systems is exorbitant. At the core of the antinuclear protest is the growing awareness of the terrible human price that would be paid should a nuclear conflagration occur.

An examination of the growing membership of the nuclear protest movement, and of the actions taken under its aegis, indicates that there is a substantial American audience for antinuclear rhetoric. The movement has become so large and noticeable that the Reagan administration has been forced to try to identify with it in some measure.

At the same time that Reagan was elected in 1980, three state senate districts in western Massachusetts voted, by large margins, in favor of a nonbinding resolution instructing state senators to urge the president of the United States to propose to the Soviet Union a freeze on the further development, testing, and deployment of nuclear weapons. The vote was the result of an organized campaign. In the months following, the movement became national and was supported by a variety of organizations. In 1982, efforts to freeze the nuclear arms race were underway in 297 House of Representative districts in 43 states around the nation. In 309 town meetings held in New England, 33 city councils around the country, 10 county councils, 7 state legislatures, and 1 house in the legislatures of 4 other states, resolutions urging a nuclear freeze have been passed. At that time, there were 24 cosponsors in the United States Senate for such a resolution and 166 in the House of Representatives.

The growth of one antinuclear organization provides some gauge of the increasing strength of the movement. The group called Physicians for Social Responsibility (PSR) was formed over a decade ago and was committed to educating the public about the effects of nuclear war. When it started, the organization had 3,000 members. Currently, it has 20,000 members. Lawyers, nurses, businessmen, and educators are forming groups patterned after PSR.

The proposal to freeze nuclear arms has proved to be galvanizing. In addition to the organizations mentioned above, a national movement called Ground Zero is devoted to raising the national consciousness about the dangers of nuclear war. A number of religious groups, peace organizations, and labor groups support the general movement. And in Orange County, California, a traditionally conservative area that gave Reagan 75 percent of its vote, more than 120,000 individuals signed a statewide petition on behalf of a nuclear freeze.[31]

At the time Rachel Carson wrote *Silent Spring*, there was no national climate of opinion that favored the banning of dangerous pesticides. A primary purpose for her writing the book was to create just such a climate, and that she did so is a rhetorical accomplishment of great magnitude. Two decades later, with a growing climate of opinion opposing nuclear armaments already underway, another book was published that may also have major rhetorical success. I refer to Jonathan Schell's *The Fate of the Earth*. The Book-of-Month Club considered its message to be so important that it offered it as an alternate selection for the very low price of two dollars.

Schell's book is a powerful discussion of the immediate possibility of the extinction of the human race in a nuclear holocaust. His description of what would happen to humanity and the ecosphere in such an event is graphic. His discussion of our moral obligation to preserve the world for future generations is compelling. His call for action is urgent.

It is interesting to compare Schell's book, which is trying to end the nuclear age, with a book that appeared at the beginning of it. In 1946, John Hersey's *Hiroshima* was published. The world first learned of the existence of the bomb when the initial one was dropped on Hiroshima, Japan, by the American air force on 6 August 1945. The world still had years to go before the power of nuclear energy would be understood. In the months that followed Hiroshima, the immediate local impact of the bomb would come to be comprehended. It would take much longer before the full implications of the threat of nuclear warfare would be appreciated.

Hersey did not have available to him the knowledge that Schell possessed. He chose not to undertake a scientific or military account of the Hiroshima catastrophe, but rather to present a personal description based on the experiences of six individuals who survived the blast. At the beginning of his book, he introduces the six in an informal, low-key narrative and deftly imparts a sense of the knowledge void that existed at the time of his writing:

> A hundred thousand people were killed by the atomic bomb, and these six were among the survivors. They still wonder why they lived when so many others died. Each of them counts many small items of chance of volition—a step taken in time, a decision to go indoors, catching one streetcar instead of the next—that spared him. And now each knows that in the act of survival he lived a dozen lives, and saw more death than he ever thought he would see. At the time, none of them knew anything.[32]

In a style that remains informal and low key, a style that gently invites us to identify with the participants and that understandably better captures the characteristics of the old era ending on that day than a new one being born, Hersey carries us into the event:

Miss Sasaki went back to her office and sat down at her desk.

She was quite far from the windows, which were off to her left, and behind her were a couple of tall bookcases containing all the books of the factory library, which the personnel department had organized. She settled herself at her desk, put some things in a drawer and shifted papers. She thought that before she began to make entries in her lists of new employees, discharges and departures for the Army, she would chat for a moment with the girl at her right. Just as she turned her head away from the window, the room was filled with a blinding light. She was paralyzed by fear, fixed still in her chair for a long moment (the plant was 1,600 yards from the center).

Everything fell, and Miss Sasaki lost consciousness. The ceiling dropped suddenly and the wooden floors above collapsed in splinters and the people up there came down and the roof above them gave way; but principally and first of all, the bookcases right behind her swooped forward and the contents threw her down, with her left leg twisted and breaking beneath her. There, in the tin factory, in the first moment of the atomic age, a human being was crushed by books.[33]

As carnage spread over the next few days, the living victims of the bombs—those who had the time to do so, that is— speculated about the nature of the weapon. They wondered if gasoline had been sprinkled from airplanes, or if a cluster of incendiary bombs had been dropped, or if parachutists had dropped to create the destruction, or if perhaps some kind of combustible gas had been used:

But, even if they had known the truth, most of them were too busy or too weary or too badly hurt to care that they were the objects of the first great experiment in the use of atomic power, which (as the voices on the short wave shouted) no country except the United States, with its industrial know-how, its willingness to throw two billion gold dollars into an important wartime gamble, could possibly have developed.[34]

The above passage is as close as Hersey comes to condemning the use of the bomb, except, of course, that the whole accounting is a condemnation of the use of nuclear weapons. Despite the low-key, personal quality of Hersey's narrative style, or perhaps because of it, the reader does not find it easy to become fully and intimately identified with the victims. One remains distanced from them and distanced from the event. That fault is not Hersey's alone. The fault lies partly in our difficulty, even after this many years, to grasp the magnitude of the disaster, and partly in our unwillingness to grasp it fully, our desire to deny the potentiality of nuclear technology and, in effect, the possibility of our own death. Hersey does not ever mention the possibility of the ultimate death, the nuclear extinction of the species. He does not raise questions about the state of human nature, or of power, or of nuclear impact on the ecosphere. In 1946 these matters were not salient as they are now. In Hersey's book we are left with the event only, and with some of the people affected by it. At the very end of this book, we are left with the innocence of the children of Hiroshima who, months after the event, talked of it as an exhilarating adventure, talked freely and gaily about it as a kind of lark. In so doing, but in doing it within the context of wondering what the long-range impact on the children might be, Hersey underscored the innocence of the vast majority of people at the time.

Jonathan Schell talks of innocent children in his book, too, but it is the children of unborn generations yet to come. He does so in order to directly raise the question of our moral obligation to preserve the earth for generations of humans not yet thought of.

Schell undertakes the difficult task of leading his readers to think about what many would like to believe is unthinkable: that is, to consider directly the very real possibility of a nuclear holocaust, the extinction of humanity, and the destruction of the environment and the ecosphere we know as the earth. Schell's accounting of what a nuclear holocaust would mean is not personal in the same way Hersey's is, but it is difficult to see how one could read it without feeling personally affected and involved.

At the beginning of his book, Schell acknowledges his problem, indeed the problem facing all of us: "Usually, people wait for things to occur before trying to describe them. . . . But since we cannot afford under any circumstances to let a holocaust occur, we are forced in this one case to become the historians of the future—to chronicle and commit to memory an event that we have never experienced and must never experience."[35]

Schell then proceeds with the description. It is devastating. He draws upon all kinds of scientific knowledge gathered by many highly credible sources, and the cumulative results indicate wave after wave of destruction until there is no more. Schell puts his general conclusion early in the book.

Nuclear weapons are unique in that they attack the support systems of life at every level. And these systems, of course, are not isolated from each other but are parts of a single whole: ecological collapse, if it goes far enough, will bring about individual deaths. Furthermore, the destructive consequences of a nuclear attack are immeasurably compounded by the likelihood that all or most of the bombs will be detonated within the space of a few hours, in a single huge concussion. Normally, a locality devastated by a catastrophe, whether natural or man-made, will sooner or later receive help from untouched outside areas, as Hiroshima and Nagasaki did after they were bombed; but a nuclear holocaust would devastate the "outside" areas as well, leaving the victims to fend for themselves in a shattered society and natural environment. And what is true for each city is true for the earth as a whole: a devastated earth can hardly expect "outside" help.[36]

The conclusion that there would be total destruction in a holocaust, that everyone and everything would likely be dead, appears
as a constant refrain throughout Schell's book. Time and time again
it drops into the discussion, almost as a kind of aside, as an "oh, by
the way" or "but of course" remark. The effect, however, is just the
opposite. The idea becomes more and more pronounced with each
appearance:

> The other obstacle to our understanding is that when we strain to picture what
> the scene would be like after a holocaust we tend to forget that for most people,
> and perhaps for all, it wouldn't be like anything, because they would be dead. To
> depict the scene as it would appear to the living is to that extent a falsification,
> and the greater the number killed, the greater the falsification. The right vantage
> point from which to view a holocaust is that of a corpse, but from that vantage
> point, of course, there is nothing to report. [37]

Schell discusses the kinds of efforts that might be made by various
civil defense groups to evacuate populations in the event of a nuclear
attack, then says:

> Obviously, none of this could come about. In the first place, in a full scale attack
> there would in all likelihood be no surviving communities, and, in the second
> place, everyone who sealed himself off from the outside environment for as long
> as several months would soon die of radiation sickness. Hence, in the months after
> a holocaust there would be no activity of any sort, as, in a reversal of the normal
> state of things, the dead would lie on the surface, and the living, if any, would be
> buried underground. [38]

A bit later, Schell remarks that it is often assumed that a full-
scale holocaust would be restricted to the northern hemisphere,
destroying Europe, China, Japan, the United States and the Soviet
Union. But he points out that at present, American and Soviet
leaders perceive that their rivalry has worldwide significance, and
therefore they might extend their attacks to other "lesser nations"
on the grounds that sheer survival would mean power. What the
superpowers would do is but one among many uncertainties that
enters any calculation of what the effects of a nuclear war might be.

> As I have already mentioned, there are uncertainties inherent in any attempt to
> predict the consequences of a nuclear holocaust; but when we try to estimate those
> consequences for the targeted countries it turns out that the readily calculable local
> primary effects of the bombs are so overwhelming that we can never arrive at
> uncertainties. Obviously, there can be no tangled interplay of destructive influences
> in society, if there is no society, and the local primary effects are more than enough
> to remove society from the picture. This is why those observers who speak of
> "recovery" after a holocaust or of "winning" a nuclear "war" are dreaming. They
> are living in a past that has been swept away by nuclear arms. [39]

Schell establishes his point in an unassailable fashion. Referring to data gathered by authoritative scientists and scientific groups, he concludes that a nuclear war would result in additive layers of totally destructive effect. Then, having dealt with the practical fact of the matter, he raises the moral issue of human responsibility for other humans, both to those humans in our own time and to those of other generations to come. Along with the more broadly moral issues, he brings in specific Christian viewpoints and concerns, a necessity if one wants to try to reach those fundamen- talist forces which, at the beginning of the decade of the 1980s, seemed to strongly support a general buildup of American arms. He challenges the military position that holds that we must have superior forces for winning a war on the grounds that there could be no meaningful outcome of a nuclear war. In short, he engages in as general a dialogue as he can, in a style that is direct, forceful without being fanatic, and clear enough that any layman can recognize that ultimately, it is his or her survival as a being of any kind that is at stake.

What then does Schell propose as a solution? He does not rest for long on practical steps. He calls for a total reconceptualization of human nature that would lead to a realization that we are a part of the earth as is every bird or beast, every blade of grass, strand of seaweed, pebble of sand, or puff of wind. We are no less, but we are no more, except that we have the power to destroy it all. The earth, he says, is a single system, a single organism, a realization that has only in our time undergone a change from a poetic metaphor to a fact of scientific investigation.[40]

In weighing the fate of the earth and, with it, our own fate, we stand before a mystery, and in tampering with the earth we are tampering with a mystery. We are in deep ignorance. Our ignorance should dispose us to wonder, our wonder should make us humble, our humility should inspire us to reverence and caution, and our reverence and caution should lead us to act without delay to withdraw the threat we now pose to the earth and to ourselves.[41]

Schell brings together the concerns of those who want to stop the selfish and wanton despoiling of the land, the pollution of the streams, the ruining of the air, the killing of wildlife, with those who wish to stop the proliferation of nuclear weapons so that human- ity might have a future. "The peril of human extinction, which exists not because every single person in the world would be killed by the immediate explosive and radioactive effects of a holocaust— something that is exceedingly unlikely, even at present levels of armament—but because a holocaust might render the biosphere unfit for human survival, is, in a word, an ecological peril."[42] Schell joins with Rachel Carson in raising the ultimate question facing humanity—shall we choose to live, or shall we choose to die?

The implications of the answer both Carson and Schell want us to reach are immense. They go far beyond what any of the major, aspiring candidates for the presidency in 1980 envisioned. They require us to reach the judgment that we are not in control of our destiny alone, but that our survival is intertwined with all of the other phenomena of life and all of the other environments of life around us, of which we are but a part. They require us to determine that many of the actions we have taken to fulfill the ideal of unlimited progress have soared to the point of dangerous extravagance, that there is no such thing as unlimited progress, and that the notion of progress itself has led us to a deadly celebration of our potentialities as humans. The opportunities of the frontier, that were never really there in the way envisaged by Americans, must now be recognized for the myths they always were. The freedom "to be" is meaningful only within the content of being with all that is around us. For without the rest of it, we would not be at all. There is no "race of life." In our age, and from now on, there is only life or no life. As Schell puts it, "The species' obligation to survive lays on each individual a new obligation to set aside his personal interest in favor of the general interest."[43]

One primary constituent of our redefinition, according to Schell, will be our realization that our worship of what we have referred to as the human trait of "reason," the ability to render all problems discursive, to avoid ambiguity, to fight paradox, to strive to fulfill our visions of superiority as a species, to "control" all that there is—all of this must now be seen to have become perverted.

It is as though Freud perceived that the balance between man's "lower," animal, and instinctual nature, which had historically been so much feared and despised by religious men and philosophers as a disruptive force in man's spiritual development, and his "higher" rational nature had tipped in favor of the latter—so that now the greater danger to man came not from rampant, uncontrolled instinct breaking down the restraining bonds of reason and self-control but from rampant reason oppressing and destroying instinct and nature. And rampant reason, man found, was, if anything, more to be feared than rampant instinct. Bestiality had been the cause of many horrors, but it had never threatened the species with extinction; some instinct for self-preservation was still at work. Only "selfless" reason could ever entertain the thought of self-extinction. Freud's merciful, solicitous attitude toward the animal in our nature foreshadowed the solicitude that we now need to show toward the animals and plants in our earthly environment. Now reason must sit at the knee of instinct and learn reverence for the miraculous instinctual capacity for creation.[44]

The willingness to admit that there are limits to our ability to reason, that we cannot control our environment but must exist within it, that our individual freedoms are not limited by the abstraction of the "other fellow's nose," but by life itself, is about as fundamental as any recognition can be, given the incremental building of symbolic meaning upon symbolic meaning that has occurred since we humans became conscious of ourselves.

III

The oratory of the 1984 presidential campaign was little, if any, improvement over the political discussion that occurred four years earlier. President Reagan still hearkened to the past much more than he guided to the future, and it seems a portion of the American public felt more comfortable looking back over their shoulders with him. As Drew puts it: "Reagan's is a melodramatic, heroic prose that other politicians would blush to use, but he gets away with it, because in his case it is authentic. He is a throwback out of the fifties, a time when problems seemed simpler and America's military might was unchallenged. He invokes God and the flag again and again, and he aligns himself foursquare with the family."[45]

The Democratic contenders, on the other hand, did not fare well with regard either to projecting a vision of the future or to inspiring public support for their projected image of leadership. In a political commentary on the 1984 Democratic primary season, Mary Mc-Grory notes that some voters liked Mondale for reasons they seemed uncertain of, but many complained that he was "old hat"; with all of his talk about new directions, Hart seemed unable to articulate his program in any way that was memorable; Jackson appealed to many because he was a viable black candidate, though the majority did not want or expect him to win the nomination. Even though the Democratic candidates engaged in more joint debates than ever before, well developed, in-depth positions did not emerge.[46] Henry Fairlie concluded, "Our politics is starved not only of eloquence but of argument as well." P. J. O'Rourke opined that the American audience seemed willing to do almost anything for its politicians except listen to their speeches, and he found good reason for its refusal: "The speeches stink."[47]

Perhaps in this age of electronic media, with its emphasis on the dramatic and colorful and its superficial analysis of public events, it is too much to expect coherent visions of the future to come from our political leaders. "If anyone doubts that oratory has all but been silenced in politics, he need read only the annual volumes of *Public Papers of the Presidents*: six for Richard Nixon, a stout two for Gerald Ford, and a whopping nine (all of them very fat) for Jimmy Carter. One's blood will not be stirred, one's mind will not be pricked or elevated, by a single speech in any of them."[48] Perhaps we can only expect that politicians, thinking primarily of their political futures, will try to avoid the obligations and commitments that come with thoroughly articulated viewpoints and will cling to conservative positions, believing them to be safest. It may be more reasonable to assume that the most forward, innovative conceptualizations for the future will come from persons not directly concerned with the practical business of getting elected.

The public discussion that has grown in recent years pertinent to the greatest ecological danger of our age, the threat of nuclear war, substantiates the assumption. Literature treating of nuclear matters is burgeoning, and this would not be the case if there were no audience for it. In his review of one new book on the subject, *Atlantic* editor James Fallows remarks, "The nuclear-policy books of the last few years have, as a class, been impressive; if there is a bright side to the nuclear arms race, it is the efflorescence of historical, technical and political writing it has provoked."[49]

In her dissertation, Martha Cooper traces the growth of public discussion of the nuclear issue. She finds that what discussion there was prior to 1939 occurred in science-fiction novels. During the war years, the government imposed a system of secrecy and classification that shut down public discussion nearly completely. Then, an explosion of public discourse came following President Truman's announcement in 1945 that the atom bomb had been dropped on Hiroshima. The majority of the American public, however, did not seem overly concerned during this period.

During the 1950s and 1960s, the number of specialized groups attempting to broaden public debate, like the National Committee for a Sane Nuclear Policy, grew; the public exhibited a bit more interest, but for the most part remained passive. Works of fiction such as *On the Beach* and *Fail-Safe* and the movie *Dr. Strangelove* enjoyed much wider audiences than did technical discussion.

A dramatic shift occurred in 1981–82, when the American public began generating discourse and attending to it. The popular weekly news magazines, *Time* and *Newsweek*, each made the nuclear issue a cover story. In March 1982, 161 Vermont town meetings endorsed resolutions calling for a mutual freeze on the production and deployment of nuclear weapons. In April, the National Council of Churches and the United States Bishops of the Catholic Church called for worldwide nuclear disarmament. A large variety of politically active groups favoring some kind of freeze on nuclear weaponry were formed during these two years.[50] Washington *Post* reporter Myra MacPherson indicates that the Vietnam generation produced potential leaders who could help structure an environment promoting change:

Unlike the '50s generation and the young of today, the Vietnam Generation was made to feel it had to believe in something, that it had to take a stand. There are quiet legacies of this portion of the '60s that thrive to this day.

The movement has become institutionalized in the country in ways that many anti-war people who have gone about their lives do not even understand. A network of independent thinkers are still active. You find them in everything from the nuclear-freeze movement to the environmentalist movement.[51]

It may be, then, that we are in a time of conceptual transformation, aided and abetted by various sorts of rhetorical messages. There are, currently, several conceptual-metaphorical patterns of reality underpinning public discussion. One pattern understands the human to be master of nature, user of the natural environment for human ends, involved in the business of accumulating goods, power, and status, engaged in the further production of phenomena for the sake of progress. A conflicting conceptual pattern sees the human as a part of the natural environment, needing to accept the limits imposed by nature, needing to achieve harmony with natural phenomena, more concerned with conservation and preservation than with producing and developing.

There is yet a third metaphorical pattern, articulated by Lewis Thomas, that might vie for contention. It postulates that humans are both the users of nature and in turn are used by nature. In what we refer to as the natural world, by which we mean the other-than-human world, various phenomena use each other in a symbiotic way to good effect. The clam, for example, enslaves green cells from plants, living off their photosynthesis. The plant cells, on the other hand, have captured the small lenses in the tissue of the clam that focus sunlight for their benefit. Because humans are a part of nature, and not apart from it, suggests Thomas, perhaps our true situation is like that of the rest of nature. Perhaps it is necessary for us to carry energy, create new arrangements, store up information, and carry seeds around the solar system, for the benefit of all of nature:

I would prefer this useful role, if I had any say, to the essentially unearthly creature we seem otherwise on the way to becoming. It would mean making some quite fundamental changes in our attitudes toward each other, if we were really to think of ourselves as indispensable elements of nature. We would surely become the environment to worry about the most. We would discover, in ourselves, the sources of wonderment and delight that we have discerned in all other manifestations of nature. Who knows, we might even acknowledge the fragility and vulnerability that always accompany high specialization in biology, and movements might start up for the protection of ourselves as a valuable, endangered species. We couldn't lose.[52]

It is difficult to predict the outcome of this conceptual- rhetorical conflict. But one thing is certain. If either of the latter two conceptual patterns should come to dominate, even though the transformation will have occurred in an evolutionary manner, the changes of attitudes and behaviors would be revolutionary.

Notes

1. Edwin Black, "Electing Time," *Quarterly Journal of Speech* 59 (April 1973): 125; Elizabeth Drew, *Portrait of an Election* (New York: Simon and Schuster, 1981), 11; Thomas E. Cronin, *The State of the Presidency,* 2d ed. (Boston: Little, Brown, 1980), 79.

2. Lewis H. Lapham, "Reagan's Academy Award," *Harpers,* January 1981, 8.

3. Lapham, "Reagan's Academy Award," 8.

4. Gary Wills, *Nixon Agonistes* (New York: New American Library, 1970), 536.

5. Wills, Nixon, 546.

6. Godfrey Hodgson, *America in Our Time* (New York: Random, 1976), 13.

7. David S. Broder, *Changing of the Guard* (New York: Simon and Schuster, 1980), 11–15.

8. Edwin Black, "The Second Persona," *Quarterly Journal of Speech* 56 (April 1970): 112.

9. Murray Edelman, *Politics as Symbolic Action* (Chicago: Markham, 1971), 67.

10. I do not include the campaign of John Anderson in this survey, because, as Jeff Greenfield points out, Anderson never effectively articulated a systematic set of ideas, and after the one occasion when he had the best opportunity to outline his philosophy and program to the most people—the nationally televised debate with Ronald Reagan on 12 September 1980—his public support fell away quickly because he was perceived to be a liberal; *The Real Campaign* (New York: Summit, 1982), 95–109, 194–210. Drew comments that after Anderson formally launched his campaign, he became "largely indistinguishable from any other politician seeking the Presidency, and what had become known as the Anderson 'difference' was gone"; Drew, *Portrait,* 280.

11. Drew, *Portrait,* 250, 251.

12. Speech transcript taken from tape recorded by the author, 11 August 1980.

13. Greenfield, *Campaign,* 70.

14. Greenfield, *Campaign,* 303.

15. Speech transcript taken from tape recorded by the author, 18 July 1980.

16. For a summary of the events that hounded the Carter administration, see Clark R. Mollenhoff, *The President Who Failed* (New York: Macmillan, 1980).

17. Speech transcript taken from tape recorded by the author, 13 August 1980.

18. Boston *Globe,* 21 October 1979.

19. New York *Times,* 15 January 1981.

20. Freed's observation may be found in Hodgson, *America,* 146.

21. See Albert K. Weinberg, *Manifest Destiny* (Chicago: Quadrangle, 1963).

22. Henry Nash Smith, *Virgin Land: The American West as Symbol and Myth* (Cambridge: Harvard Univ. Pr., 1950).

23. *Earth Day—The Beginning,* compiled and edited by the National Staff of Environmental Action (New York: Bantam, 1970), n.p.

24. Reprinted in Frank Graham, Jr., *Since Silent Spring* (Boston: Houghton Mifflin, 1970), 22.

25. A full discussion of reactions and events that followed the publication of *Silent Spring* can be found in Graham, *Since Silent Spring.*

26. Rachel Carson, *Silent Spring* (Boston: Houghton Mifflin, 1962), 8.

27. Carson, *Silent Spring,* 106.

28. Carson, *Silent Spring,* 107.

29. Carson, *Silent Spring,* 99.

30. Carson, *Silent Spring,* 297.

31. All of the data were drawn from Robert G. Kaiser, "Movement against Nuclear Arms Is Mushrooming," and Jay Matthews, "Reagan Territory Warms to Nuclear Freeze Idea," both of which appeared in Washington *Post,* Sunday, 11 April 1982, sec. A., pp. 1, 4.

32. John Hersey, *Hiroshima* (New York: Modern Library/Random, 1946), 4.

33. Hersey, *Hiroshima,* 23.

34. Hersey, *Hiroshima,* 66.

35. Jonathan Schell, *The Fate of the Earth* (New York: Knopf, 1982), 21.

36. Schell, *Fate,* 23.

37. Schell, *Fate,* 26.

38. Schell, *Fate,* 60.

39. Schell, *Fate,* 73.

40. Schell, *Fate,* 93.

41. Schell, *Fate,* 95.

42. Schell, *Fate,* 111.

43. Schell, *Fate,* 136.

44. Schell, *Fate,* 156.

45. Elizabeth Drew, "A Political Journal," *New Yorker* 20 February 1984, 131.

46. Mary McGrory, "A Hot Non-Political Story," Washington *Post,* 2 December, 1984, sec. R, p. 5.

47. Henry Fairlie, "The Decline of Oratory," *New Republic,* 28 May 1984, 15; P. J. O'Rourke, "Oh Shut Up," *New Republic,* 28 May 1984, 20.

48. Fairlie, "Decline," 15.

49. James Fallows, review of *Weapons and Hope* in Washington *Post Book World,* 22 April 1984, 1.

50. Martha Cooper, "The Implications of Foucaults' Archaeological Theory of Discourse for Contemporary Rhetorical Theory and Criticism" (Ph.D. diss., Pennsylvania State University), 1984.

51. Myra MacPherson, "What Did It Cost, Our Vietnam War?" Washington *Post,* 27 May 1984, sec. C, p. 4.

52. Lewis Thomas, *The Lives of a Cell* (New York: Bantam, 1975), 125.

Eugene E. White:
A Bibliography

Notes on Contributors

Eugene E. White
A Bibliography

1945   "Anti-Racial Agitation as a Campaign Device." *Southern Speech Journal* 10: 49–56.
"The Great Awakener: George Whitefield." *Southern Speech Journal* 11: 6–15.
"James Kimble Vardaman in the Mississipi Gubernatorial Campaign of 1903." *Journal of Mississippi History* 7: 91–110.

1948   "The Preaching of George Whitefield During the Great Awakening in America." *Speech Monographs* 15: 33–43.

1950   "Whitefield's Use of Proofs during the Great Awakening in America." *Western Speech* 14, no. 1: 3–6.
"George Whitefield's Preaching in Massachusetts and Georgia: A Case Study in Persuasion." *Southern Speech Journal* 15: 249–62.

1951   "Decline of the Great Awakening in New England: 1741 to 1746." *New England Quarterly* 24, no. 1: 35–52.
Contemporary Public Address as a Teaching Aid. Coral Gables: Univ. of Miami Pr.

1952   "A New Emphasis in Teaching Public Speaking." *The Speech Teacher* 1: 265–70. With Clair R. Henderlider.

1953   "Assembly Line Techniques: Teaching the Large Class in Speech Fundamentals." *The Speech Teacher* 2: 247–56.
"George Whitefield and the Paper War in New England." *Quarterly Journal of Speech* 39: 61–68.

1954   "The Protasis of the Great Awakening in New England." *Speech Monographs* 21: 10–20.
"What Harry Truman Told Us about His Speaking." *Quarterly Journal of Speech* 40: 37–42. With Clair R. Henderlider.
"What Norman Vincent Peale Told Us about His Speaking." *Quarterly Journal of Speech* 40: 407–16. With Clair R. Henderlider.
"Three Interpretations of the First Course in Speech." *Southern Speech Journal,* 20: 163–70.
Practical Public Speaking. New York: Macmillan. With Clair R. Henderlider.

1960   *Practical Speech Fundamentals.* New York: Macmillan.

1962   "Solomon Stoddard's Theories of Persuasion." *Speech Monographs* 29: 235–59.

1963   "Cotton Mather's Manuductio ad Ministerium." *Quarterly Journal of Speech* 49: 308–19.

1964   *Practical Public Speaking.* 2d ed. New York: Macmillan.

1966   *Speech Preparation Sourcebook.* Boston: Allyn and Bacon. With Robert T. Oliver and Carroll C. Arnold.
Selected Speeches from American History. Boston: Allyn and Bacon. Edited with Robert T. Oliver.

1967   "Using Speech Models: Supplementing Theory and Practice." *The Speech Teacher* 16: 24–27.
"Master Holdsworth and 'A Knowledge Very Useful and Necessary.' " *Quarterly Journal of Speech* 53: 1–16. [Awarded the James A. Winans Memorial Award for Distinguished Scholarship in Rhetoric and Public Address.]
"A Rationale for Grades." *The Speech Teacher* 16: 247–52.

1968   "Presidential Rhetoric: The State of the Union Address." *Quarterly Journal of Speech* 54: 71–76.

1970   "Puritan Preaching and the Authority of God." In *Preaching in American History,* 36–73. Edited by DeWitte Holland. Nashville: Abingdon Press. [Awarded the Speech Communication Association Golden Anniversary Award.]

1971   Sermons by John Cotton and Peter Bulkeley. Edited, with headnotes. In *Sermons in American History,* 25–51. Edited by DeWitte Holland. Nashville: Abingdon Press.

1972   *Puritan Rhetoric: The Issue of Emotion in Religion.* Carbondale: Southern Illinois Univ. Pr.

1973   "Changed Continuity." *Developments in Speech 1928–1973.* Baton Rouge: Louisiana State University.

1974 "Prospectus for the Future: Changing Continuity." *The Speech Teacher* 23: 139–43.

1978 *Practical Public Speaking.* 3d ed. New York: Macmillan.

1980 *Rhetoric in Transition: Studies in the Nature and Uses of Rhetoric.* Editor. University Park: The Pennsylvania State Univ. Pr. "Rhetoric as Historical Configuration." In *Rhetoric in Transition,* 7–20.

Notes on Contributors

James R. Andrews is Professor and Chairman of the Department of Speech Communication at Indiana University. He is author of *A Choice of Worlds: The Practice and Criticism of Public Address*, *Essentials of Public Communication*, *The Practice of Rhetorical Criticism*, and *Public Speaking: Principles into Practice* and coauthor of *The American Ideology: The Rhetoric of the Continuing American Revolution*, which won the Winans-Wichelns Award of the Speech Communication Association. He has published articles in *QJS*, *CM*, *CSSJ*, *WJC*, *CQ*, and *Quaker History*, and has contributed studies to *The History of Public Speaking in Pennsylvania* and *Rhetoric in Transition: Studies in the Nature and Uses of Rhetoric*. He twice won the American Forensic Association's award for outstanding research. Professor Andrews served as editor of *The Central States Speech Journal* and was a member of the editorial boards of *The Quarterly Journal of Speech* and *Communication Monographs*. He has been a member of the Executive Committee of the Central States Speech Association and Chair of the Public Address Division of the Speech Communication Association.

Carroll C. Arnold is Professor Emeritus, Speech Communication, The Pennsylvania State University. Arnold is Editor for Rhetoric and Communication for the University of South Carolina Press and a past editor of *Communication Monographs*. He is author or coauthor of eight books, the most recent of which is *Handbook of Rhetorical and Communication Theory* (1984), coedited with John Waite Bowers. He is author of approximately thirty-five scholarly articles and chapters on rhetorical theory and criticism and received the Distinguished Teacher (1976) and Emeritus Distinction (1984) awards from the Penn State College of Liberal Arts Alumni Society.

THOMAS W. BENSON is Professor of Speech Communication at The Pennsylvania State University. He is coeditor of *Readings in Classical Rhetoric* (with Michael Prosser), *Readings in Medieval Rhetoric* (with Joseph Miller and Michael Prosser), and *Rhetorical Dimensions in Media* (with Martin J. Medhurst); coauthor of *Nonverbal Communication* (with Kenneth Frandsen), *Reality Fictions: The Films of Frederick Wiseman* (with Carolyn Anderson), and *Documentary Dilemmas: Frederick Wiseman's "Titicut Follies"* (with Carolyn Anderson); and editor of *Speech Communication in the Twentieth Century*. He has served as editor of *Communication Quarterly* and *The Quarterly Journal of Speech* and is the recipient of the ECA Scholar and the Meritorious Service awards of the Eastern Communication Association and the Robert J. Kibler Award of the Speech Communication Association.

RICHARD B. GREGG is Professor of Speech Communication at The Pennsylvania State University. He has written articles and book chapters on rhetorical criticism, rhetorical theory, and American political rhetoric. He is coauthor of *Speech Behavior and Human Interaction* and author of *Symbolic Inducement and Knowing: A Study in the Foundations of Rhetoric*, which won the Winans-Wichelns Award of the Speech Communication Association.

GERARD A. HAUSER is Professor of Speech Communication at The Pennsylvania State University. He is a specialist in rhetorical theory and criticism. His research has dealt with political persuasion and the history and philosophical foundations of rhetorical theories of ancient Greece, the Scottish Enlightenment, and the present day. He is recipient of his college's Distinguished Teaching Award. He is the author of *An Introduction to Rhetorical Theory*, has served on the editorial boards of *Communication Monographs*, *Communication Quarterly*, and *The Rhetoric Society Quarterly*, and is associate editor of *Philosophy and Rhetoric*.

STEPHEN E. LUCAS is Professor of Communication Arts at the University of Wisconsin, Madison. He is the author of *Portents of*

Rebellion: Rhetoric and Revolution in Philadelphia, 1765-76, which was awarded the SCA Golden Anniversary Award for 1977, and *The Art of Public Speaking.*

MARTIN J. MEDHURST is Associate Professor of Speech Communication and Theatre Arts at Texas A&M University. He is coeditor, with Thomas W. Benson, of *Rhetorical Dimensions in Media* and has authored essays appearing in such journals as *Communication Monographs, Quarterly Journal of Speech, Studies in Visual Communication,* and the *Journal of Church and State.* In 1982 Medhurst was the recipient of the Speech Communication Association's Golden Anniversary Prize Fund Award for his essay "Political Cartoons as Rhetorical Form: A Taxonomy of Graphic Discourse" (with Michael A. DeSousa). Medhurst has served as associate editor of the *Western Journal of Speech Communication* and book review editor of *The Quarterly Journal of Speech.*

STEPHEN T. OLSEN is a marketing representative with the IBM Corporation. His chapter in this book is based on research originally done for his doctoral dissertation, directed by Eugene E. White.

LEWIS PERRY is Andrew Jackson Professor of History at Vanderbilt University and the author of *Intellectual Life in America: A History.*

LAWRENCE W. ROSENFIELD is Professor of Communication Arts at Queens College, CUNY. He is author of *Aristotle and Information Theory* (1971) and coauthor of *The Communicative Experience* (1976) and the monograph "The Functions of Human Communication in Pleasing" in *Handbook of Rhetorical and Communication Theory* (1984). He has authored several dozen book chapters, articles, and reviews in such journals as *Speech Monographs, Quarterly Journal of Speech, Philosophy and Rhetoric, Communication Education, Theoria,* and *Contemporary Psychology.* He has served as consulting editor for *Communication Quarterly, Philosophy and Rhetoric, Southern Speech Communication Journal,* and *Quarterly Journal of Speech.* In 1985 he lectured on art and rhetoric in the School of Communication, University of São Paulo, Brazil.